PENGUIN CL

LONDON LABOUR AND THE LONDON POOR

HENRY MAYHEW, journalist and social investigator, humorist, dramatist, novelist, author of works of travel and popular instruction, was born in 1812 and died in 1887. The son of a London solicitor, he was educated at Westminster School, from which he eventually ran away. Mayhew then went to sea and travelled to India before entering his father's office, which, however, he soon quitted to embark on a long and prolific but often penurious literary career. He started (with an old schoolfriend) *Figaro in London*, a pungent illustrated weekly, in 1831, wrote a very successful farce, *The Wandering Minstrel* (1834), and was one of the group which founded *Punch* in 1841; but in 1845 he severed his connection with the journal, which became increasingly conformist. The voluminous survey known as *London Labour and the London Poor* began publication in 1849 in the *Morning Chronicle*, and in 1851–2 bound volumes of the collected, uncompleted work were issued. Further publication was interrupted by litigation and not resumed until he found a new publisher in 1861, although in 1856 Mayhew embarked on another ambitious series of studies entitled *The Great World of London*, part of which appeared in 1862 as *The Criminal Prisons of London*. Mayhew's other noteworthy book is the readable *German Life and Manners* (1864). His work is distinguished by vivid reportage, unsentimental sympathy, humour and an eye for detail. During his life Mayhew was an outspoken advocate of social reform and a trenchant critic of *laissez-faire* doctrine, but even before his death his work had sunk into the obscurity in which it remained until interest in it revived during the 1940s.

VICTOR NEUBURG was born in Sussex in 1924 and educated at Varndean and at the universities of London and Leicester. At one time a soldier and schoolmaster, he is a former Senior Lecturer at the School of Librarianship, Polytechnic of North London (now the University of North London). He has been a visiting professor at State College, Buffalo, Dalhousie University, Nova Scotia, and Ruhr University, Bochum. In the summer of 1984 he was Simon Foster Haven Fellow of the American Antiquarian Society. His publications include *Popular Education in Eighteenth Century England* (1971), *Popular Literature* (Penguin, 1977), *The Batsford Companion to Popular Literature* (1982) and *A Guide to the Western Front* (Penguin, 1988).

Victor Neuberg is married, with a wife inured to his enthusiasm for book collecting, and has a daughter married to a doctor, and two granddaughters. Henry Mayhew has been an enthusiasm of his for many years.

ONE OF THE FEW REMAINING CLIMBING SWEEPS.

HENRY MAYHEW

LONDON LABOUR
AND
THE LONDON POOR

SELECTIONS MADE AND INTRODUCED BY
VICTOR NEUBURG

PENGUIN BOOKS

PENGUIN BOOKS

Published by the Penguin Group
Penguin Books Ltd, 80 Strand, London WC2R 0RL, England
Penguin Putnam Inc., 375 Hudson Street, New York, New York 10014, USA
Penguin Books Australia Ltd, 250 Camberwell Road, Camberwell, Victoria 3124, Australia
Penguin Books Canada Ltd, 10 Alcorn Avenue, Toronto, Ontario, Canada M4V 3B2
Penguin Books India (P) Ltd, 11 Community Centre, Panchsheel Park, New Delhi – 110 017, India
Penguin Books (NZ) Ltd, Cnr Rosedale and Airborne Roads, Albany, Auckland, New Zealand
Penguin Books (South Africa) (Pty) Ltd, 24 Sturdee Avenue, Rosebank 2196, South Africa

Penguin Books Ltd, Registered Offices: 80 Strand, London WC2R 0RL, England

www.penguin.com

This selection first published 1985

034

Selection and editorial material copyright © Victor Neuburg, 1985
All rights reserved

Printed and bound in Great Britain by Clays Ltd, Elcograf S.p.A.
Filmset in 9/11½ Monophoto Photina

ISBN-13: 978–0–140–43241–1

www.greenpenguin.co.uk

For Alison, Anne, Barbara, Caroline, Katherine, Stella,
– the ladies in my life.
And, of course, for Brian – best of friends –
who shares some of them with me.

CONTENTS

ACKNOWLEDGEMENTS

As ever I am more grateful than I can say to Barbara Gilbert, who has done her best to keep me on the path of stylistic virtue, and also typed an untidy manuscript impeccably. Gratitude as well to my wife Anne, long-suffering as ever in the face of a rising tide of books and papers. To Frank Cass and Michael Zaidner my thanks for their interest and the speedy unearthing of an indispensable book which they presented to me. And, to Annie Pike of Penguin Books, a special thankyou for invaluable help.

HENRY MAYHEW.

HENRY MAYHEW: A CHRONOLOGY

1812   Born 25 November, fourth surviving son of Joshua Dorset Joseph Mayhew, a successful solicitor, and Mary Ann (née Fenn).

1827   Runs away from Westminster School and is sent to India as a midshipman.

1831–9 Involved in various theatrical and journalistic projects.

1834   His play *The Wandering Minstrel* is produced.

1835   Becomes Editor of *Figaro in London* (magazine founded in 1831). This post relinquished in 1839. Probably meets Douglas Jerrold (1803–57, man of letters) and W. M. Thackeray in Paris.

1841   First number of *Punch*, 17 July. Mayhew is its Editor until 1842 and maintains contact with the magazine until 1845.

1844   Marries Jane Jerrold.

1846   Declared bankrupt.

1847   Bankruptcy suit.

1851–2 First edition of *London Labour and the London Poor*, published serially. Lawsuit with the printer, George Woodfall.

1854   Mayhew in Germany.

1858   Father dies.

1859   Editor of *Morning News* for the month of January – after which it ceases publication.

1861–2 Enlarged edition of *London Labour and the London Poor* published in four volumes. Mayhew in Germany again in 1861.

1865   Second printing of the four-volume edition.

1880   Wife Jane Jerrold Mayhew dies on 26 February.

1887   Mayhew dies of bronchitis on 25 July.

INTRODUCTION

I

It is strange that more is not known about the life of Henry Mayhew. He was a journalist, occasionally a minor dramatist, and a man of letters rubbing shoulders on friendly and even intimate terms with some of the best-known writers of his day; he married the daughter of Douglas Jerrold, a prolific and popular writer;[1] for a time he was Editor of the newly founded magazine *Punch*;[2] and yet Mayhew eludes the biographer. No cache of surviving letters is known and there was no contemporary biography, nor did he essay an autobiography. In the memoirs and biographies of his contemporaries he is of course mentioned, but the picture of him that has come down to posterity remains essentially shadowy.

The one indispensable guide to his life and work is Anne Humpherys's *Travels into the Poor Man's Country* (1977). It contains pretty well all the known facts about Mayhew – and there are not many of them! His father was a self-made successful lawyer, Joshua Dorset Joseph Mayhew, and his mother's maiden name was Mary Ann Fenn. Henry, one of seventeen children, was sent to Westminster School in 1822, and while there showed himself to be brilliant but indolent, always full of new projects and ideas but temperamentally unable or unwilling to bring them to fruition. Having refused to be flogged by the Headmaster, Dr Goodenough, for some misdemeanour he ran away from school. Then he was sent to India, where his brother Alfred was in the government service, and upon his return tried a career in law. In this he was remarkably unsuccessful, and, as a result of his forgetting to submit a vital document to court, Mayhew senior narrowly escaped being committed to prison for contempt.

After this Henry left home and drifted into journalism[3] and playwriting. His first play, *The Wandering Minstrel*, was performed in 1834, and *But*

1. See *The Life and Remains of Douglas Jerrold* by his son Blanchard Jerrold (W. Kent, 1849).
2. See Jerrold, op. cit., pp. 191–224; M. H. Spielmann, *The History of 'Punch'* (Cassell, 1895); A. A. Adrian, *Mark Lemon, First Editor of 'Punch'* (OUP, 1966).
3. The journalistic world of nineteenth-century London remains largely unexplored. For signposts see Jerrold, op. cit., and Spielmann, op. cit.; C. and M. Cowden Clarke, *Recollections of Writers* (1878); H. S. Edwards, *Personal Recollections* (1900); G. Hodder, *Memories of My Time* (1870); C. Mackay, *Forty Years' Recollections* (1877), and *Through the Long Day* (1887); G. A. Sala, *Life and Adventures* (1895); H. R. Vizetelly, *Glances Back Through Seventy Years* (1893); E. Yates, *Recollections and Experiences* (1885).

However and *A Troublesome Lodger* were staged in 1838 and 1839. It was in this latter year that the magazine *Figaro in London*, which Mayhew had helped to found in 1831 and which he had edited since 1835, came to an end. By this time he was well launched into a journalistic career, and some years later he was concerned with the founding of *Punch*, Number 1 of which was published on 17 July 1841. Three years later Mayhew married Jane, daughter of his friend and colleague Douglas Jerrold – with whom he was later to quarrel.[4] M. H. Spielmann[5] quotes an old but unnamed friend of Mayhew at about this time, who described him as 'lovable, jolly, charming, bright, coaxing and unprincipled. He rarely wrote himself, but would dictate, as he walked to and fro, to his wife, whom he would also leave to confront his creditors.'

It seems, then, characteristic of this man that when he gave up the editorship of *Punch* in 1842, the publishers Bradbury and Evans made a place for him as 'suggestor in chief'. However, he was never really happy with the reorganization that had put Mark Lemon in the Editor's chair, and he finally severed his connection with *Punch* in 1845.

Mayhew was clearly a man of considerable ability and full of ideas, but it is difficult to escape the conclusion that his temperament was unstable. His bankruptcy in 1846 suggests strongly that he had no head for business, and, as we have seen, he relied upon his wife to face his creditors. The bankruptcy was the direct result of Mayhew's attempt to capitalize upon the railway mania which was then sweeping the country. He began a newspaper called the *Iron Times*, to be published daily and to include gossip, chit-chat and serious news about railways. To launch the project he joined forces with Thomas Lyttleton Holt, former part-proprietor of *Figaro in London* and an active publisher. The venture proved unsuccessful: the *Iron Times* failed in the middle of 1846 and Mayhew went bankrupt.

So far as Jane was concerned the bankruptcy was a disaster. Mayhew had bought and lavishly furnished a house in Parson's Green called 'The Shrubbery'. He had accumulated debts of about £2,000, while his salary at the time of the crash was only around £300 per annum. Because of a change in the law he did not go to prison, though he was roughly handled in court by the Bankruptcy Commissioner, who censured him in brutal terms for his improvidence and irresponsibility in financial matters.

Through sheer energy and even ebullience, Mayhew bounced back into

4. The estrangement following the quarrel was so serious that when Blanchard Jerrold wrote the life of his father he did not mention Henry Mayhew in the Preface, though the latter's brother Horace was singled out as one who had been of help during its writing.
5. op. cit., p. 268.

active life apparently unencumbered by the bankruptcy. It is, though, worth reminding ourselves that the house in Parson's Green represented his first and last attempt at maintaining so respectable an establishment; and for Jane the catastrophe of the bankruptcy was such that she went to stay with her father in the Channel Islands, where she became so ill that her father later said she had 'made a "runaway knock at death's door!"'[6] At some point – it is impossible to say when – she returned to her husband, and eventually two children were born, Amy and Athol. The marriage cannot, however, have been easy, and Jane's life was made unhappier by a long-standing quarrel between her husband and her father. While few details are known, there seem to have been several separations, though none was permanent until some time in the late 1860s. Victorian census figures are not always reliable, but it does appear that she was not counted as a member of her husband's household in 1851, and during the 1860s he spent long periods in Germany without her. When she died at the age of fifty-three in 1880 her husband was not at her bedside.

Following the bankruptcy novels by Henry and Augustus Mayhew appeared, including *The Greatest Plague of Life* (1847) and *Whom to Marry* (1848), both of them illustrated by George Cruikshank. Designed for the popular end of the market, both books dealt with themes of interest to middle-class readers, the first being about the servant problem and the second recording the adventures of a young woman looking for a good husband. They found plenty of readers and were reissued in cheap editions. Two further novels, also written in collaboration with Augustus, indicate an advance in Mayhew's fiction. Both *The Good Genius That Turned Everything into Gold* (1847) and *The Magic of Kindness* (1849) show a more incisive style than that of the earlier works and are to some extent concerned with moral and social themes. In these later novels of the 1840s Mayhew was laying the foundations of the great work by which he would be remembered when all his other books were largely forgotten, *London Labour and the London Poor*.

The publication of this in 1851–2 did much to enhance Mayhew's reputation – though characteristically enough it was marred by an unseemly wrangle with George Woodfall, who printed the work. According to the contract he was to receive his money after Mayhew and John Howden, the publisher, had received their salaries and after necessary expenses connected with the serial publication had been paid. Something went wrong, and in March 1851 Woodfall filed a suit in Chancery

6. A. Humpherys, *Travels into the Poor Man's Country* (University of Georgia Press, 1977; Caliban Books, 1980), p. 9.

demanding that Mayhew and Howden should be prevented from selling further copies because the contract had been broken. The case proved to be a complicated one, although the sums involved were small – in one instance there was the matter of an unauthorized increase of £1 per week in Howden's salary. Woodfall had in fact attempted to reach a settlement before going to court, but Mayhew either neglected the matter or refused to cooperate. As a result, when the case was concluded in 1852 *London Labour and the London Poor* ceased publication. The first edition in book form with that year's date consisted of the two volumes so far completed.

Why did Mayhew behave in this way? Perhaps he was tired of the whole undertaking and wanted to end it, or perhaps it was an example of his instability and unwillingness to see a long-term project through to its end. Whatever the reason, a promising enterprise had been killed off, and little is known of Mayhew's activities between 1852 and 1854.

In 1856, however, his thoughts returned to the idea, and there were plans for David Bogue, a publisher with premises at 86 Fleet Street, to reissue and continue *London Labour and the London Poor*. They came to nothing when Bogue died in November of the same year, and Mayhew seems not to have persisted in the search for a new publisher and to have turned his mind to other things. In 1857 he began writing another novel, *Paved with Gold*, in collaboration with his brother Augustus, but he dropped out after the first five numbers and when the novel was eventually published in 1858 with illustrations by H. K. Browne ('Phiz'), the title page said 'by Augustus Mayhew'. It is a good novel, and demonstrates vividly the extraordinary fascination which the London streets held for the brothers Mayhew.

Henry, in the meantime, drifted from project to project. Nothing really seemed to interest him. He edited *Morning News* for the month of January 1859, after which the paper ceased publication; and his book *Young Benjamin Franklin* came out in 1861. However, at about this time – though nothing seems to be known about the circumstances surrounding the decision – the publishing firm of Griffin Bohn undertook to complete and issue *London Labour and the London Poor* in four volumes.[7] Three of these appeared in 1861 and the final volume came out in 1862. In this year also *The Criminal Prisons of London*, by Henry Mayhew and John Binny, was published. In 1865 the four volumes of *London Labour* were reprinted under the imprint of Charles Griffin.

7. It is worth noting in this connection that in the mid-1840s Henry Bohn had taken over David Bogue's copyrights. See F. A. Mumby, *Publishing and Bookselling* (Jonathan Cape, 1949), p. 263.

Mayhew's best work was done, and the last decades of his life were marked by a steady decline. He made abortive efforts to keep going. During the mid 1860s he pondered starting a rival to *Punch*, but such plans as there were came to nothing. At about this time, too, he brought out a series of monthly parts called *The Shops and Companies of London*, designed as a tribute to British industry. He was for a brief period Editor of a magazine called *Only Once a Year*; and he went to Germany again – in 1870 he was in Metz, where, with his son Athol, he acted as a foreign correspondent. Pretty well his last literary effort seems to have been made in 1874 when he and his son wrote a play called *Mont Blanc*, which turned out a failure. Mayhew's name appeared on the title page of a book called *London Characters* in 1874, but his involvement in it is problematic.[8]

After this, there was nothing. Mayhew died of bronchitis on 25 July 1887, and an obituary in the *Illustrated London News* commented, by the by, upon the Mayhew brothers:

But all of them being dead except Henry, who in his later years moved in rather a small circle, it was but natural that the world should regard the literary Mayhews as extinct. If the author of *London Labour and the London Poor* had died earlier, many people would have been present at his funeral in Kensal-Green Cemetery on Saturday last. As it was, those for whose causes he had so valiantly contended seem to have forgotten him.[9]

A sad comment, this, and all the sadder for being essentially true.

II

In their sheer bulk the four volumes of *London Labour and the London Poor* are both impressive and daunting. Printed virtually throughout in double column, averaging about five hundred pages per volume, they represent a tremendous achievement; and it is neither a denigration nor a devaluation of Mayhew's work to ponder its nature, more particularly since, as we have seen, his own approach to it, as indeed to all his work, was somewhat dilatory. Clearly, however, the great study of London (including of course *The Criminal Prisons of London*, published in 1862) compelled his mind and created its own momentum to enable him to bring it to a satisfactory conclusion.

This work represents Mayhew's journalism at its best. He provides us

8. See Bibliography, under heading 'Mayhewiana'.

9. J. L. Bradley (ed.), *Henry Mayhew: Selections from London Labour and the London Poor* (OUP, 1965), Introduction, p. xxxii.

with a stunning and detailed panorama of what life in the streets of London during the early Victorian period was like for a wide range of hucksters, pedlars, poor, destitute and unprivileged people; but unlike Frederick Engels, who had been exploring the slums of Manchester some years before him and who was primarily interested in the physical environment of poverty, Mayhew's focus was upon people. It is this which gives his writing its immediacy and its vividness.

Then, too, Mayhew was unencumbered by political theory and conscious ideology. His aim was to study the London poor, occupation by occupation, trade by trade, and he also explored the worlds of those who had neither trade nor occupation. What he did bring to this monumental survey was a deep sense of compassion for those he talked to, a reluctance to moralize and a mistrust for the kind of evangelical philanthropy which he described in these words:

> There is but one way of benefiting the poor, viz. by developing their powers of self-reliance, and certainly not in treating them like children. Philanthropists always seek to do too much, and in this is to be found the main cause of their repeated failures. The poor are expected to become angels in an instant, and the consequence is, they are merely made hypocrites. Moreover, no men of any independence of character will submit to be washed, and dressed, and fed like schoolboys; hence none but the worst classes come to be experimented upon. It would seem, too, that this overweening disposition to play the part of pedagogues (I use the word in its literal sense) to the poor, proceeds rather from a love of power than from a sincere regard for the people. Let the rich become the advisers and assistants of the poor, giving them the benefit of their superior education and means − but leaving the people to act for themselves − and they will do a great good, developing in them a higher standard of comfort and moral excellence, and so, by improving their tastes, inducing a necessary change in their habits.[10]

Sentiments like this − and in the great tide of evangelistic philanthropy they were comparatively unusual − probably dated from his days with *Punch*. They hardly add up, though, to a coherent political attitude, and his political ideas remain, as E. P. Thompson has pointed out, an enigma.[11] He did seem to become increasingly well informed about orthodox political economy; but whether he was a radical or not is uncertain. He was clear enough about his intentions:

> I shall consider the whole of the metropolitan poor under three separate phases, according as they *will* work, they *can't* work, and they *won't* work. Of those that

10. *London Labour and the London Poor*, Vol. 2, p. 298.

11. 'The Political Education of Henry Mayhew', *Victorian Studies*, Vol. XI, no. 1 (1967), p. 51.

will work, and yet are unable to obtain sufficient for their bodily necessities, I shall devote my attention first to such as receive no relief from the parish; and under this head will be included the poorly-paid – the unfortunate – and the improvident. While treating of the poorly-paid, I shall endeavour to lay before the reader a catalogue of such occupations in London as yield a bare subsistence to the parties engaged in them ... After this it is my intention to visit the dwellings of the unrelieved poor ... to discover, not only on how little they subsist, but how large a rate of profit they have to pay for the little upon which they do subsist – to ascertain what weekly rent they are charged for their waterless, drainless, floorless, and almost roofless tenements; to calculate the interest that the petty capitalist reaps from their necessities.[12]

Mayhew goes on to assert, '... however alive I may be to the wrongs of the poor, I shall not be misled by a morbid sympathy to see them only as suffering from the selfishness of others.'[13] And he taxes the poor with a want of temperance, energy, cleanliness, morality, knowledge ...

What Mayhew achieved was the fullest and most vivid picture of the experiences of labouring people in the world's greatest city in the nineteenth century. In his pages many of them speak for themselves, and we hear of their hopes, fears, customs, grievances, habits, in their own words. No other social investigator came near to him: in its scope and execution his work has no peer.

How did he do it? The book grew out of a series of articles that Mayhew wrote for the *Morning Chronicle*. The first of these, 'A Visit to the Cholera Districts of Bermondsey', was published in its columns on Monday 24 September 1849, and was to culminate in the four volumes of *London Labour and the London Poor* more than a dozen years later. Following the initial article, Mayhew persuaded the Editor of the paper that a series of articles on the social problems of the time would be worth undertaking. The idea was taken up and three journalists were assigned to the task: Charles Mackay (1814–89) was to cover the northern industrial centres; Shirley Brooks (1816–74) was to write from the Continent; and Mayhew was to cover London. An editorial in the *Chronicle* of 18 October 1849 defined the series and looked forward to 'a full and detailed description of the moral, intellectual, material, and physical condition of the industrial poor'.

Between 19 October 1849 and 31 October 1850 Mayhew's contribution consisted of seventy-six letters averaging 3,500 words each. They

12. Quoted in E. P. Thompson and E. Yeo, *The Unknown Mayhew* (Merlin Press, 1971; Penguin, 1973), pp. 102–3.
13. ibid.

dealt with poverty, exploitation and the precarious lives led by the London poor. Publication of these letters was interrupted by a dispute between Mayhew and the Editor. The latter had objected to an account of a successful West End tailoring establishment which, said Mayhew, was using sweated labour; and Mayhew believed that his freedom to write as he wished was being interfered with. The upshot was that Mayhew made no further contributions to the *Chronicle*, but he continued to write his letters and they were issued in twopenny parts until March 1852, when the quarrel with his printer, George Woodfall, to which I have already referred, meant that publication ceased. Meanwhile a two-volume edition of *London Labour and the London Poor* consisting of bound-up parts had been published, but it was not until more than ten years later that the complete four-volume edition appeared.

Because none of Mayhew's notebooks appears to have survived, we know little or nothing about his methods of work. A rather unsympathetic observer described him at work during the *Chronicle* days:

> He was in his glory at that time. He was largely paid, and, greatest joy of all, had an array of assistant writers, stenographers, and hansom cabmen constantly at his call. London labourers ... were brought to the *Chronicle* office, where they told their tales to Mayhew, who redictated them, with an added colour of his own, to the shorthand writer ... Augustus helped him in his vivid descriptions and an authority on political economy controlled his gay statistics.[14]

Despite the cattiness of this description, some fragments of reality seem to lurk beneath these half-truths. So far as the assistant writers are concerned, it must be remembered that Mayhew was producing material for a deadline and needed all the help he could get. We can accept that he must have 'led' his interviewees, and the writing-up of the final version was of course his own – and there is no doubt where his sympathies lay. Where did the interviews take place? Some, almost certainly, in his office; but many would surely have been conducted on the streets. The sheer number of people involved would support this conclusion, and there is the practical consideration that many of them, in a working situation, would have been too dirty to bring into an office. One can imagine their feeling miserably out of place there, and less than likely to give the detailed accounts which, as Mayhew reports them, so often have the ring of truth. One of the most compelling series of portraits drawn by Mayhew relates to dustmen and the disposal of refuse. The cogency of this section certainly did not derive from interviews at second or third hand conducted in a clean

14. H. S. Edwards, *Personal Recollections* (1900), p. 60.

office. Readers of Charles Dickens's *Our Mutual Friend* will recall Boffin and the dust yard ... Mayhew provides an authentic context for a setting in the novel which might otherwise be regarded as fancifully grotesque.

As for the reference to statistics, it is clear that Mayhew regarded them as an important and intrinsic part of his work, although for the modern reader they are perhaps the least valuable part of the survey. What makes it live is the record of human experience. From that above all 'Mayhew's London' draws its enduring vitality.

In the lack of sentimentality of his approach Mayhew was very much a pioneer;[15] but the streets of London had proved overwhelmingly fascinating to serious observers before he put pen to paper. In 1838 James Grant had published *Sketches in London*, which in its faithful descriptions and lack of condescension anticipated Mayhew. Another who did the same was a doctor, Hector Gavin, whose book *Sanitary Ramblings: Being Sketches and Illustrations of Bethnal Green* appeared in 1848. The wealth of statistical tables equally foreshadows Mayhew's use of figures to illuminate his text. *The Rookeries of London: Past, Present and Prospective* by Thomas Beames, published in 1850 and reprinted in 1852, indicates a widening interest in the themes discussed in the *Morning Chronicle* articles.

While it would be pointless, and untrue, to claim that Mayhew founded a school of writers, he did influence several who followed him. Notable amongst these was George Augustus Sala (1828–96), whose *Twice Round the Clock* (1862) presents a perceptive, if hurried, view of twenty-four hours in the life of the capital. Despite a facsimile reprint it remains – undeservedly I think – a largely forgotten book. It has very real merits, especially in that it looks at London without sentimentality and, like Mayhew's work, is journalism of a very high order.[16] The same is true of James Hain Friswell (1825–78), author of *Houses with Their Fronts Off* (1854), a series of prose sketches of people in London and the houses they lived in. It was a minor best-seller. Round about this time, too, Charles Manby Smith (1804–80) published his *Curiosities of London Life* (1853),

15. Compare, for example, Mayhew's descriptions of a coffee-stall keeper (p. 84 ff.) with the character of Daniel Standing in Hesba Stretton's best-selling novel *Jessica's First Prayer* (1867). On the other hand, in Augustus Mayhew's *Paved with Gold* (1858) the watercress market (Book 2, ch. 2, *passim*) is described with total realism. Clearly the author had been influenced by his brother Henry.

16. One can never be precise about literary influences. However, Sala did possess a set of Mayhew. He owned the first three volumes of *London Labour and the London Poor* in the 1865 edition and a first edition of Vol. 4. All the volumes, with Sala's signature in one of them, are in my possession.

which is a book of entertaining low-life reporting. He followed this in 1857 with a similar volume, *The Little World of London*.

Later in the century there was another wave of books about London streets and the London poor. Amongst the writers were James Greenwood (1852–1929)[17] and George R. Sims (1847–1922), who wrote about themes which were directly derived from Mayhew. The same can be said of Charles Booth (1840–1916), whose *Life and Labour of the People in London* stretched from one volume in 1889 to seventeen which were published between 1902 and 1903.[18]

The last book directly within the nineteenth-century Mayhew tradition that I have been able to trace is *A Vicarious Vagabond* (1910) by Denis Crane, a pseudonym of Walter Thomas Cranfield. His investigations were, in his own words, undertaken 'with the idea of bridging the gulf, so far as I myself was concerned, between a theoretical and an experimental knowledge of how the poor live...'[19] With this end in view he disguised himself and went out on to the streets of London. A conversation which he records with 'Ginger', outside porter of a City hotel, has echoes of Henry Mayhew, for it appears authentic and shows a natural acceptance of what he found:

He and I met in the following circumstances. We were standing together at the kerb, I hoarse with hawking my wares, he weary of fruitless waiting. He explained, with a touch of bitterness, that his line of business had declined of late owing to the popularity of the telephone, which had abolished the necessity for sending messages by hand. Furthermore, this particular hotel had lost its wealthier patrons.

'I haven't earned a pennypiece today,' he said; 'nor did I yesterday.'

'Then how do you live?'

'Borrow,' with a shrug of the shoulders. 'Sometimes I don't take anything for three days. Then it takes all I get to pay off my debts. It's only when I have a bit of luck that I really get straight, for I've got three kids.'

There was a note of tenderness in the tone.

'Ah,' quoth I, thinking of my own babies. 'So have I.'

'Two girls and a boy are mine. The youngster's seven this week.'

'And my boy's six – to-morrow.'

---

17. His *The Seven Curses of London* (1869) is now available as a paperback.

18. It will be quite apparent that I have done scant justice to a whole group of nineteenth-century authors who wrote non-fiction about the poor of London. Those mentioned are all of some importance. So far as I am aware, no survey of their work exists. With regard to fiction, there are two admirable studies: P. J. Keating, *The Working Classes in Victorian Fiction* (Routledge, 1971), and Sheila M. Smith, *The Other Nation: The Poor in the English Novels of the 1840s and 1850s* (OUP, 1980). Both have references to Mayhew.

19. op. cit., p. viii.

This touch of nature drew us closer, and I inquired what were his average earnings.

'About two bob a day; but they used to be more.'

Twelve shillings a week, with a wife and three children! Rent, though he lived in a cellar, could not be less than three or four shillings. And there were coals and boots, not to mention food.[20]

That the Mayhew tradition lives on is apparent in the work of the best-selling American writer Studs Terkel, whose *Hard Times* (1970) and *Working* (1972), within the context of twentieth-century America, catch the authentic Mayhew tone. 'Terkel has caught the sound of the people,' said the *Baltimore Sun* in a review quoted by Avon Books on the cover of a paperback edition. Mayhew had done precisely the same thing for the poor of London about one hundred and fifty years earlier.

After Mayhew's death *London Labour and the London Poor* became a very neglected book. The Second World War, however, was followed by a renewed interest in matters Victorian, and it came into its own again. Several volumes of selections were published, and eventually it was re-printed in its entirety.[21] Poverty is still a fact of life throughout much of the world. It remains a pressing issue – and at least one British politician has talked of a return to Victorian values. How should we assess the relevance now of Mayhew's work?

Current discussion of poverty amongst historians and social scientists may often obscure the reality that he described in nineteenth-century London. A recent contribution to the subject does just this. In *The Idea of Poverty: England in the Early Industrial Age* (Faber, 1984) the author, Gertrude Himmelfarb, discusses in the first of two projected volumes the problem of poverty as it was defined between 1780 and the 1840s. My own feeling is that Mayhew saw what he described at first hand – it was a reality of daily life – and for this reason his evidence, however critically we examine and evaluate it, remains inevitably more compelling than extended theoretical discussions of the word 'poverty'. In a sense, the detachment from reality implicit in the debate about terms allows a comforting neutrality to both participants and spectators. Mayhew, on the other hand, still has the power to disturb us, and this, I believe, is a major reason for the continuing vitality, popularity and even relevance of his work.

20. op. cit., pp. 30–31.
21. See Bibliography for some of the most important reprints.

xxiii

BIBLIOGRAPHY

Works by Mayhew

London Labour and the London Poor: 1852 edn, 2 vols.; 1861–2 edn, 4 vols.; new impression of 1865, 4 vols. The two latter editions are identical as regards text. Priority of issue, however, can be established by the imprint. The earlier one was published by Griffin, Bohn & Co., Stationers' Hall Court. Bohn went out of business in 1864, and the later imprint is Charles Griffin & Co., Stationers' Hall Court.

The Criminal Prisons of London (1862). Mayhew's co-author was John Binny. Although I have not used material from this volume, it should be considered with the four volumes of the previous title as completing Mayhew's survey of the metropolis. Both titles – five volumes in all – were reprinted by Frank Cass in 1967–8.

There have been several volumes, issued by various publishers, of selections from Mayhew. The best of them is *Henry Mayhew: Selections from London Labour and the London Poor*, chosen with an introduction by John L. Bradley (OUP, 1965). The 40-page introduction is excellent.

The Morning Chronicle

So far as the *Morning Chronicle* letters are concerned, three volumes of selections have been published:

E. P. Thompson and Eileen Yeo (eds.), *The Unknown Mayhew* (Merlin Press, 1971; Penguin, 1973). The editors contribute an 85-page introduction divided into two roughly equal sections, 'Mayhew and the *Morning Chronicle*' by E. P. Thompson, and 'Mayhew as a Social Investigator' by Eileen Yeo. Both are essential reading for an understanding of Mayhew's work.

Anne Humpherys (ed.), *Voices of the Poor* (Frank Cass, 1971). There is some overlap between the contents of this title and those of the preceding one. Both, however, are worth looking at. Anne Humpherys's introduction is brief but illuminating. The volume also contains a contemporary picture of Henry Mayhew playing the part of Knowell in Charles Dickens's amateur production of *Every Man in his Humour*.

P. E. Razzell and R. W. Wainwright (eds.), *The Victorian Working Class* (Frank Cass, 1973). The importance of this book lies in the fact that for the first time letters (not by Henry Mayhew) about the condition of the poor in various parts of England are reprinted from the *Morning Chronicle*. Although letters about London are included, those from other areas predominate.

All the letters to the *Morning Chronicle* by correspondents from outside London are currently being published by Frank Cass in eight volumes. The editor is Jules Ginswick. The following have already appeared: Vol. 1, Lancashire, Cheshire and Yorkshire; Vol. 2, Northumberland and Durham; Vol. 3, The Midlands. The remaining five volumes are scheduled for publication as follows: Vol. 4, Liverpool and Birkenhead; Vol. 5, Birmingham; Vol. 6, Midlands, Northern Counties; Vol. 7, South-western Counties; Vol. 8, Eastern Counties, South-eastern Counties.

There is also a six-volume paperback edition of *The Morning Chronicle Survey of Labour and the Poor: The Metropolitan Districts*, with an introduction by Peter Razzell (Caliban Books, 1983).

Biography

The standard biography of Henry Mayhew is Anne Humpherys, *Travels into the Poor Man's Country* (University of Georgia Press, 1977; Caliban Books, 1980). It contains a very full bibliography of books and articles by and about Mayhew.

For Mayhew's connection with *Punch* see A. A. Adrian, *Mark Lemon, First Editor of 'Punch'* (OUP, 1966).

Dickens and Mayhew

The picture of Mayhew as an actor in one of Dickens's amateur productions may suggest a closer relationship between the two men than has hitherto been suspected. Certainly Dickens was influenced by Mayhew's work. See F. R. and Q. D. Leavis, *Dickens the Novelist* (Chatto & Windus, 1970; Penguin, 1977). See also H. S. Nelson, 'Dickens' "Our Mutual Friend" and Henry Mayhew's "London Labour and the London Poor"', in *Nineteenth-Century Fiction*, XX (1965), pp. 207–22.

BIBLIOGRAPHY
About Mayhew

There is an admirable listing of articles in Anne Humpherys's biography. One of them, however, seems indispensable, being the first, so far as I know, to submit Mayhew's work to the scrutiny of a socio-economic historian: E. P. Thompson, 'The Political Education of Henry Mayhew', *Victorian Studies*, Vol. XI, no. 1 (1967), pp. 41–62.

Working People: Their Life and Experience

In the course of his work Mayhew reproduces the life stories of many of the people he met. They are prime examples of working-class auto-biography, and since historians have only recently turned their attention to this theme, the following book may be useful in assessing the validity and value of such material:

David Vincent, *Bread, Knowledge and Freedom: A Study of Nineteenth Century Working Class Autobiography* (Europa, 1981; Methuen, 1982).

Two recent books emphasize the importance of Mayhew as a social investigator:

James Bennett, *Oral History and Delinquency: The Rhetoric of Criminology* (Chicago University Press, 1981). Chapters 1 and 2 deal with Mayhew's investigations.

Raymond A. Kent, *A History of British Empirical Sociology* (Gower Publishing Company, 1981).

Mayhew's London

Three books are of especial value in tracing locations in Mayhew's work:

Anon., *The Pictorial Handbook of London* (H. G. Bohn, 1858). Now some-what scarce, but a definitive view, with a folding map of the London that Mayhew knew so well.

Peter Cunningham, *Hand-Book of London Past and Present*, 2nd edn (1850; reprinted by EP Publishing, 1978).

H. A. Harben, *A Dictionary of London* (Herbert Jenkins, 1918).

'Mayhewiana'

Two books are worth recording of Mayhew's association with them.

Anon., *London Characters* (Chatto & Windus, 1870). In 1874 there appeared a second edition, whose title page announced: 'By Henry Mayhew and Other Writers'. This edition was bigger than the first and contained new material by Mayhew. A third, identical edition appeared in 1881. Since Henry Mayhew was a well-known journalist, it seems unlikely that his name would have been omitted from the first edition if he had contributed to it. What probably happened was that the publishers used his name and incorporated material by him to promote sales of the book.

Augustus Mayhew, *Paved with Gold, or The Romance and Reality of the London Streets* (Chapman & Hall, 1858; reprinted by Frank Cass, 1971). Henry Mayhew was involved in the writing of the first few chapters of this novel. Illustrated by Hablot K. Browne ('Phiz'), it is an interesting work, with some of its best episodes set in the kind of milieu that Mayhew described in *London Labour and the London Poor*. Parts of it convey a strong sense of the reality of street life, which perhaps demonstrates the closeness of collaboration and discussion between the brothers Mayhew.

MAYHEW'S COLLABORATORS

Vol. IV of *London Labour and the London Poor* was partly written by Henry Mayhew. The following writers also had a share in this volume:

THE REV. WILLIAM TUCKNISS, B.A. (1833–64): Graduate of Magdalen College, Oxford (B.A. 1858); Chaplain to the Society for the Rescue of Young Women and Children.

BRACEBRIDGE HEMYNG (1841–1901): Barrister and author of popular novels; the creator of Jack Harkaway, whose adventures were first published in 1871. He spent some time in America.

JOHN BINNY: I have been able to discover nothing about Binny.

ANDREW HALLIDAY (1830–77): Writer of popular fiction; contributor to *Cornhill Magazine* and *All the Year Round*.

In the Preface to the first volume of bound parts of *London Labour and the London Poor* Henry Mayhew acknowledges the help of two collaborators. One is RICHARD KNIGHT ('late of the City Mission') and the other HENRY WOOD ('who may be considered as one of its authors').

NOTE ON THE TEXT

Mayhew's text presents no difficulties. I have used the 1865 four-volume impression published by Charles Griffin & Co., Stationers' Hall Court, from which illustrations used here are also taken. The extracts are grouped according to volume, and the page reference to the 1865 edition is given for each. A few new headings have been introduced and a few of Mayhew's headings re-positioned in order to lend coherence to the selections presented here.

Money

I have not attempted to 'translate' the old-style cash values in Mayhew's text. The following is a guide to their conversion into modern terms.

£1	Then, as now, the standard unit of coinage; known also as a sovereign or a quid
20 shillings	Made £1 (now 100 pence)
10 shillings	Half a quid (now 50 pence)
1 shilling	Known also as a bob (now 5 pence); abbreviated to 1s. This was made up of: 12 pence abbreviated to 12d.; *or* 24 half-pence; *or* 48 farthings (no modern equivalents for these old pence, half-pence or farthings)

£1 and 1 shilling (£1 1s.) made 1 guinea.
10 shillings and 6 pence (10s. 6d.) made half a guinea.

The following coins were also in use:

Crown	5 shillings (now 25 pence)
Half crown	2 shillings and 6 pence (now 12½ pence)
Florin	2 shillings (now the standard 10 penny piece)
Sixpence	6d.
Threepenny bit	3d.

He went along the Strand, over the crossing under the statue of Charles on horseback, and up Pall Mall East till he came to the opening into the park under the Duke of York's column. The London night world was alive as he made his way. From the Opera Colonnade shrill voices shrieked at him as he passed, and drunken men coming down from the night supper-houses in the Haymarket saluted him with affectionate cordiality. The hoarse waterman from the cabstand, whose voice had perished in the night air, croaked out at him the offer of a vehicle; and one of the night beggar-women who cling like burrs to those who roam the street at these unhallowed hours still stuck to him, as she had done ever since he had entered the Strand.

Anthony Trollope, *The Three Clerks* (1858)

Three o'clock, and half-past three, and they had passed over London Bridge. They had heard the rush of the tide against obstacles; and looked down, awed, through the dark vapour on the river; had seen little spots of lighted water where the bridge lamps were reflected, shining like demon eyes, with a terrible fascination in them for guilt and misery. They had shrunk past homeless people, lying coiled up in nooks. They had run from drunkards. They had started from slinking men, whistling and signing to one another at bye corners, or running away at full speed. Though everywhere the leader and the guide Little Dorrit, happy for once in her youthful appearance, feigned to cling to and rely upon Maggy. And more than once some voice, from among a knot of brawling or prowling figures in their path, had called out to the rest to 'let the woman and the child go by!'

Charles Dickens, *Little Dorrit* (1857)

LONDON LABOUR AND THE LONDON POOR

VOLUME ONE

OF THE LONDON STREET-FOLK

[pp. 5–6] Those who obtain their living in the streets of the metropolis are a very large and varied class; indeed, the means resorted to in order 'to pick up a crust', as the people call it, in the public thoroughfares (and such in many instances it *literally* is,) are so multifarious that the mind is long baffled in its attempts to reduce them to scientific order or classification.

It would appear, however, that the street-people may be all arranged under six distinct genera or kinds.

These are severally:

I. Street-sellers
II. Street-buyers
III. Street-finders
IV. Street-performers, artists, and showmen
V. Street-artizans, or working pedlars
VI. Street-labourers

The first of these divisions – the STREET-SELLERS – includes many varieties; viz. –

1. *The street-sellers of fish, &c.* – 'wet', 'dry', and shell-fish – and poultry, game, and cheese.

2. *The street-sellers of vegetables*, fruit (both 'green' and 'dry'), flowers, trees, shrubs, seeds, and roots, and 'green stuff' (as watercresses, chickweed and grun'sel, and turf).

3. *The street-sellers of eatables and drinkables,* – including the vendors of fried fish, hot eels, pickled whelks, sheep's trotters, ham sandwiches, peas'-soup, hot green peas, penny pies, plum 'duff', meat-puddings, baked potatoes, spice-cakes, muffins and crumpets, Chelsea buns, sweetmeats, brandy-balls, cough drops, and cat and dog's meat – such constituting the principal eatables sold in the street; while under the head of street-drinkables may be specified tea and coffee, ginger-beer, lemonade, hot wine, new milk from the cow, asses milk, curds and whey, and occasionally water.

4. *The street-sellers of stationery, literature, and the fine arts* – among whom are comprised the flying stationers, or standing and running

patterers; the long-song-sellers; the wall-song-sellers (or 'pinners-up', as they are technically termed); the ballad sellers; the vendors of playbills, second editions of newspapers, back numbers of periodicals and old books, almanacks, pocket books, memorandum books, note paper, sealing-wax, pens, pencils, stenographic cards, valentines, engravings, manuscript music, images, and gelatine poetry cards.

5. *The street-sellers of manufactured articles*, which class comprises a large number of individuals, as (*a*) the vendors of chemical articles of manufacture – viz., blacking, lucifers, corn-salves, grease-removing compositions, plating-balls, poison for rats, crackers, detonating-balls, and cigar-lights. (*b*) The vendors of metal articles of manufacture – razors and pen-knives, tea-trays, dog-collars, and key-rings, hardware, bird-cages, small coins, medals, jewellery, tin-ware, tools, card-counters, red-herring-toasters, trivets, gridirons, and Dutch ovens. (*c*) The vendors of china and stone articles of manufacture – as cups and saucers, jugs, vases, chimney ornaments, and stone fruit. (*d*) The vendors of linen, cotton, and silken articles of manufacture – as sheeting, table-covers, cotton, tapes and thread, boot and stay-laces, haberdashery, pretended smuggled goods, shirt-buttons, etc., etc.; and (*e*) the vendors of miscellaneous articles of manufacture – as cigars, pipes, and snuff-boxes, spectacles, combs, 'lots', rhubarb, sponges, wash-leather, paper-hangings, dolls, Bristol toys, sawdust, and pin-cushions.

6. *The street-sellers of second-hand articles* – of whom there are again four separate classes; as (*a*) those who sell old metal articles – viz. old knives and forks, keys, tin-ware, tools, and marine stores generally; (*b*) those who sell old linen articles – as old sheeting for towels; (*c*) those who sell old glass and crockery – including bottles, old pans and pitchers, old looking glasses, &c.; and (*d*) those who sell old miscellaneous articles – as old shoes, old clothes, old saucepan lids, &c., &c.

7. *The street-sellers of live animals* – including the dealers in dogs, squirrels, birds, gold and silver fish, and tortoises.

8. *The street-sellers of mineral productions and curiosities* – as red and white sand, silver sand, coals, coke, salt, spar ornaments, and shells.

These, so far as my experience goes, exhaust the whole class of street-sellers, and they appear to constitute nearly three-fourths of the entire number of individuals obtaining a subsistence in the streets of London.

The next class are the STREET-BUYERS, under which denomination come the purchasers of hare-skins, old clothes, old umbrellas, bottles, glass, broken metal, rags, waste paper, and dripping.

After these we have the STREET-FINDERS, or those who, as I said before, literally 'pick up' their living in the public thoroughfares. They are the 'pure' pickers, or those who live by gathering dogs'-dung; the cigar-end finders, or 'hard-ups', as they are called, who collect the refuse pieces of smoked cigars from the gutters, and having dried them, sell them as tobacco to the very poor; the dredgermen or coal-finders; the mud-larks, the bone-grubbers; and the sewer-hunters.

Under the fourth division, or that of the STREET-PERFORMERS, ARTISTS, AND SHOWMEN, are likewise many distinct callings.

1. *The street-performers*, who admit of being classified into (*a*) mountebanks – or those who enact puppet-shows, as Punch and Judy, the fantoccini, and the Chinese shades. (*b*) The street-performers of feats of strength and dexterity – as 'acrobats' or posturers, 'equilibrists' or balancers, stiff and bending tumblers, jugglers, conjurors, sword-swallowers, 'salamanders' or fire-eaters, swordsmen, etc. (*c*) The street-performers with trained animals – as dancing dogs, performing monkeys, trained birds and mice, cats and hares, sapient pigs, dancing bears, and tame camels. (*d*) The street-actors – as clowns, 'Billy Barlows', 'Jim Crows', and others.

2. *The street showmen*, including shows of (*a*) extraordinary persons – as giants, dwarfs, Albinoes, spotted boys, and pig-faced ladies. (*b*) Extraordinary animals – as alligators, calves, horses and pigs with six legs or two heads, industrious fleas, and happy families. (*c*) Philosophic instruments – as the microscope, telescope, thaumascope. (*d*) Measuring-machines – as weighing, lifting, measuring, and striking machines; and (*e*) miscellaneous shows – such as peep-shows, glass ships, mechanical figures, wax-work shows, pugilistic shows, and fortune-telling apparatus.

3. *The street-artists* – as black profile-cutters, blind paper-cutters, 'screevers' or draughtsmen in coloured chalks on the pavement, writers without hands, and readers without eyes.

4. *The street dancers* – as street Scotch girls, sailors, slack and tight rope dancers, dancers on stilts, and comic dancers.

5. *The street musicians* – as the street bands (English and German), players of the guitar, harp, bagpipes, hurdy-gurdy, dulcimer, musical bells, cornet, tom-tom, &c.

6. *The street singers*, as the singers of glees, ballads, comic songs, nigger melodies, psalms, serenades, reciters, and improvisatori.

7. *The proprietors of street games*, as swings, highflyers, roundabouts, puff-and-darts, rifle shooting, down the dolly, spin-'em-rounds, prick the garter, thimble-rig, etc.

Then comes the Fifth Division of the Street-folk, viz., the STREET-ARTIZANS, or WORKING PEDLARS;

These may be severally arranged into three distinct groups – (1) Those who *make* things in the streets; (2) Those who *mend* things in the streets; and (3) Those who *make* things *at home* and *sell* them in the *streets*.

1. Of *those who make things in the streets* there are the following varieties: (*a*) the metal workers – such as toasting-fork makers, pin makers, engravers, tobacco-stopper makers. (*b*) The textile-workers–stocking-weavers, cabbage-net makers, night-cap knitters, doll-dress knitters. (*c*) The miscellaneous workers, – the wooden spoon makers, the leather brace and garter makers, the printers, and the glass-blowers.

2. *Those who mend things in the streets*, consist of broken china and glass menders, clock menders, umbrella menders, kettle menders, chair menders, grease removers, hat cleaners, razor and knife grinders, glaziers, traveling bell hangers, and knife cleaners.

3. *Those who make things at home and sell them in the streets*, are (*a*) the wood workers – as the makers of clothes-pegs, clothes-props, skewers, needle-cases, foot-stools and clothes-horses, chairs and tables, tea-caddies, writing-desks, drawers, work-boxes, dressing-cases, pails and tubs. (*b*) The trunk, hat, and bonnet-box makers, and the cane and rush basket makers. (*c*) The toy makers – such as Chinese roarers, children's windmills, flying birds and fishes, feathered cocks, black velvet cats and sweeps, paper houses, cardboard carriages, little copper pans and kettles, tiny tin fire-places, children's watches, Dutch dolls, buy-a-brooms, and gutta-percha heads. (*d*) The apparel makers – viz., the makers of women's caps, boys' and men's cloth caps, night-caps, straw bonnets, children's dresses, watch-pockets, bonnet shapes, silk bonnets, and gaiters. (*e*) The metal workers, – as the makers of fire-guards, bird-cages, the wire workers. (*f*) The miscellaneous workers – or makers of ornaments for stoves, chimney ornaments, artificial flowers in pots and in nosegays, plaster-of-Paris night-shades, brooms, brushes, mats, rugs, hearthstones, firewood, rush matting, and hassocks.

Of the last division, or STREET-LABOURERS, there are four classes:

1. *The cleansers* – such as scavengers, nightmen, flushermen, chimney-sweeps, dustmen, crossing-sweepers, 'street-orderlies', labourers to sweeping-machines and to watering-carts.

2. *The lighters and waterers* – or the turn-cocks and the lamplighters.

3. *The street-advertisers* – viz., the bill-stickers, bill-deliverers, boardmen, men to advertising vans, and wall and pavement stencillers.

4. *The street-servants* – as horse holders, linkmen, coach-hirers, street-porters, shoe-blacks.

OF THE VARIETIES OF STREET-FOLK IN GENERAL,
AND COSTERMONGERS IN PARTICULAR

[pp. 8–9] Among the street-folk there are many distinct characters of people – people differing as widely from each in tastes, habits, thoughts and creed, as one nation from another. Of these the costermongers form by far the largest and certainly the mostly broadly marked class. They appear to be a distinct race – perhaps, originally, of Irish extraction – seldom associating with any other of the street-folks, and being all known to each other. The 'patterers', or the men who cry the last dying-speeches, &c. in the street, and those who help off their wares by long harangues in the public thoroughfares, are again a separate class. These, to use their own term, are 'the aristocracy of the street-sellers', despising the costers for their ignorance, and boasting that they live by their intellect. The public, they say, do not expect to receive from them an equivalent for their money – they pay to hear them talk. Compared with the costermongers, the patterers are generally an educated class, and among them are some classical scholars, one clergyman, and many sons of gentlemen. They appear to be the counterparts of the old mountebanks or street-doctors. As a body they seem far less improvable than the costers, being more 'knowing' and less impulsive. The street-performers differ again from those; these appear to possess many of the characteristics of the lower class of actors, viz., a strong desire to excite admiration, a love of the tap-room, though more for the society and display than for the drink connected with it, a great fondness for finery and predilection for the performance of dexterous or dangerous feats. Then there are the street mechanics, or artizans – quiet, melancholy, struggling men, who, unable to find any regular employment at their own trade, have made up a few things, and taken to hawk them in the streets, as the last shift of independence. Another distinct class of street-folk are the blind people (mostly musicians in a rude way), who, after the loss of their eyesight, have sought to keep themselves from the workhouse by some little excuse for alms-seeking. These, so far as my experience goes, appear to be a far more deserving class than is usually supposed – their affliction, in most cases, seems to have chastened them and to have given a peculiar religious cast to their thoughts.

Such are the several varieties of street-folk, intellectually considered – looked at in a national point of view, they likewise include many distinct people. Among them are to be found the Irish fruit-sellers; the Jew clothesmen; the Italian organ boys, French singing women, the German brass bands, the Dutch buy-a-broom girls, the Highland bagpipe players, and the Indian crossing-sweepers – all of whom I here shall treat of in due order.

The costermongering class or order has also its many varieties. These appear to be in the following proportions: One-half of the entire class are costermongers proper, that is to say, the calling with them is hereditary, and perhaps has been so for many generations; while the other half is composed of three-eighths Irish, and one-eighth mechanics, tradesmen, and Jews.

Under the term 'costermonger' is here included only such 'street-sellers' as deal in fish, fruit, and vegetables, purchasing their goods at the wholesale 'green' and fish markets. Of these some carry on their business at the same stationary stall or 'standing' in the street, while others go on 'rounds'. The itinerant costermongers, as contradistinguished from the stationary street-fishmongers and greengrocers, have in many instances regular rounds, which they go daily, and which extend from two to ten miles. The longest are those which embrace a suburban part; the shortest are through streets thickly peopled by the poor, where duly to 'work' a single street consumes, in some instances, an hour. There are also 'chance' rounds. Men 'working' these carry their wares to any part in which they hope to find customers. The costermongers, moreover, diversify their labours by occasionally going on a country round, travelling on these excursions, in all directions, from thirty to ninety and even a hundred miles from the metropolis. Some, again, confine their callings chiefly to the neighbouring races and fairs.

Of all the characteristics attending these diversities of traders, I shall treat severally. I may here premise, that the regular or 'thorough-bred costermongers', repudiate the numerous persons who sell only nuts or oranges in the streets, whether at a fixed stall, or any given locality, or who hawk them through the thoroughfares or parks. They repudiate also a number of Jews, who confine their street-trading to the sale of 'coker-nuts' on Sundays, vended from large barrows. Nor do they rank with themselves the individuals who sell tea and coffee in the streets, or such condiments as peas-soup, sweetmeats, spice-cakes, and the like; those articles not being purchased at the markets. I often heard all such classes called 'the illegitimates'.

Of Costermongering Mechanics

[p. 9] 'From the numbers of mechanics,' said one smart costermonger to me, 'that I know of in my own district, I should say there's now more than 1,000 costers in London that were once mechanics or labourers. They are driven to it as a last resource, when they can't get work at their trade. They don't do well, at least four out of five, or three out of four don't. They're not up to the dodges of the business. They go to market with fear, and don't know how to venture a bargain if one offers. They're inferior salesmen too, and if they have fish left that won't keep, it's a dead loss to them, for they aren't up to the trick of selling it cheap at a distance where the coster ain't known; or of quitting it to another, for candle-light sale, cheap, to the Irish or to the "lushingtons", that haven't a proper taste for fish. Some of these poor fellows lose every penny. They're mostly middle-aged when they begin costering. They'll generally commence with oranges or herrings. We pity them. We say, "Poor fellows! they'll find it out by-and-bye." It's awful to see some poor women, too, trying to pick up a living in the streets by selling nuts or oranges. It's awful to see them, for they can't set about it right; besides that, there's too many before they start. They don't find a living, *it's only another way of starving*.'

Of the Costermongers 'Economically' Considered

[pp. 10–11]   Political economy teaches us that, between the two great classes of producers and consumers, stand the distributors – or dealers – saving time, trouble, and inconvenience to, the one in disposing of, and to the other in purchasing, their commodities.

But the distributor was not always a part and parcel of the economical arrangements of the State. In olden times, the producer and consumer were brought into immediate contact, at markets and fairs, holden at certain intervals. The inconvenience of this mode of operation, however, was soon felt; and the pedlar, or wandering distributor, sprang up as a means of carrying the commodities to those who were unable to attend the public markets at the appointed times. Still the pedlar or wandering distributor was not without *his* disadvantages. He only came at certain periods, and commodities were occasionally required in the interim. Hence the shopkeeper, or stationary distributor, was called into existence, so that the consumer might obtain any commodity of the producer at any time he pleased. Hence we see that the pedlar is the primitive tradesman, and that the one is contradistinguished from the other by the fact, that the pedlar carries the goods to the consumer, whereas, in the case of the shopkeeper, the consumer goes after the goods. In country districts, remote from towns and villages, the pedlar is not yet wholly superseded; 'but a dealer who has a fixed abode, and fixed customers, is so much more to be depended on,' says Mr Stewart Mill, 'that consumers prefer resorting to him if he is conveniently accessible, and dealers, therefore, find their advantage in establishing themselves in every locality where there are sufficient customers near at hand to afford them a remuneration.' Hence the pedlar is now chiefly confined to the poorer districts, and is consequently distinguished from the stationary tradesman by the character and means of his customers, as well as by the amount of capital and extent of his dealings. The shopkeeper supplies principally the noblemen and gentry with the necessaries and luxuries of life, but the pedlar or hawker is the purveyor in general to the poor. He brings the greengrocery, the fruit, the fish, the water-cresses, the shrimps, the pies and puddings, the sweetmeats, the pine-apples, the stationery, the linendrapery, and the jewellery, such as it is, to the very door of the working classes; indeed, the poor man's food and clothing are mainly supplied to him in this manner. Hence the class of travelling tradesmen are important, not only as forming a large portion of the poor themselves, but as being the persons through whom the working people obtain a considerable part of their provisions and raiment.

But the itinerant tradesman or street-seller is still further distinguished from the regular fixed dealer – the *stall*keeper from the *shop*keeper – the *street*-wareman from the ware*house*man, by the arts they respectively employ to attract custom. The street-seller cries his goods aloud at the head of his barrow; the enterprising tradesman distributes bills at the door of his shop. The one appeals to the ear, the other to the eye. The cutting costermonger has a drum and two boys to excite attention to his stock; the spirited shopkeeper has a column of advertisements in the morning newspapers. They are but different means of attaining the same end.

The London Street Markets on a Saturday Night

[pp. 11–12] The street-sellers are to be seen in the greatest numbers at the London street markets on a Saturday night. Here, and in the shops immediately adjoining, the working-classes generally purchase their Sunday's dinner; and after pay-time on Saturday night, or early on Sunday morning, the crowd in the New-cut, and the Brill in particular, is almost impassable. Indeed, the scene in these parts has more of the character of a fair than a market. There are hundreds of stalls, and every stall has its one or two lights; either it is illuminated by the intense white light of the new self-generating gas-lamp, or else it is brightened up by the red smoky flame of the old-fashioned grease lamp. One man shows off his yellow haddock with a candle stuck in a bundle of firewood; his neighbour makes a candlestick of a huge turnip, and the tallow gutters over its sides; whilst the boy shouting 'Eight a penny, stunning pears!' has rolled his dip in a thick coat of brown paper, that flares away with the candle. Some stalls are crimson with the fire shining through the holes beneath the baked chestnut stove; others have handsome octohedral lamps, while a few have a candle shining through a sieve: these, with the sparkling ground-glass globes of the tea-dealers' shops, and the butchers' gaslights streaming and fluttering in the wind, like flags of flame, pour forth such a flood of light, that at a distance the atmosphere immediately above the spot is as lurid as if the street were on fire.

The pavement and the road are crowded with purchasers and street-sellers. The housewife in her thick shawl, with the market-basket on her arm, walks slowly on, stopping now to look at the stall of caps, and now to cheapen a bunch of greens. Little boys, holding three or four onions in their hand, creep between the people, wriggling their way through every interstice, and asking for custom in whining tones, as if seeking charity. Then the tumult of the thousand different cries of the eager dealers, all shouting at the top of their voices, at one and the same time, is almost bewildering. 'So-old again,' roars one. 'Chestnuts all 'ot, a penny a score,' bawls another. 'An 'aypenny a skin, blacking,' squeaks a boy. 'Buy, buy, buy, buy, buy – bu-u-uy!' cries the butcher. 'Half-quire of paper for a penny,' bellows the street stationer. 'An 'aypenny a lot ing-uns.' 'Two-pence a pound grapes.' 'Three a penny Yarmouth bloaters.' 'Who'll buy a bonnet for fourpence?' 'Pick 'em out cheap here! three pair for a halfpenny, bootlaces.' 'Now's your time! beautiful whelks, a penny a lot.' 'Here's ha'p'orths,' shouts the perambulating confectioner. 'Come and look at 'em! here's toasters!' bellows one with a Yarmouth bloater stuck on a toasting-fork. 'Penny a lot, fine russets,' calls the apple woman: and so the Babel goes on.

One man stands with his red-edged mats hanging over his back and chest, like a herald's coat; and the girl with her basket of walnuts lifts her brown-stained fingers to her mouth, as she screams, 'Fine warnuts! sixteen a penny, fine war-r-nuts.' A bootmaker, to 'ensure custom', has illuminated his shop-front with a line of gas, and in its full glare stands a blind beggar, his eyes turned up so as to show only 'the whites', and mumbling some begging rhymes, that are drowned in the shrill notes of the bamboo-flute-player next to him. The boy's sharp cry, the woman's cracked voice, the gruff, hoarse shout of the man, are all mingled together. Sometimes an Irishman is heard with his 'fine ating apples'; or else the jingling music of an unseen organ breaks out, as the trio of street singers rest between the verses.

Then the sights, as you elbow your way through the crowd, are equally multifarious. Here is a stall glittering with new tin saucepans; there another, bright with its blue and yellow crockery, and sparkling with white glass. Now you come to a row of old shoes arranged along the pavement; now to a stand of gaudy tea-trays; then to a shop with red handkerchiefs and blue checked shirts, fluttering backwards and forwards, and a counter built up outside on the kerb, behind which are boys beseeching custom. At the door of a tea-shop, with its hundred white globes of light, stands a man delivering bills, thanking the public for past favours, and 'defying competition'. Here, alongside the road, are some half-dozen headless tailors' dummies, dressed in Chesterfields and fustian jackets, each labelled, 'Look at the prices,' or 'Observe the quality.' After this is a butcher's shop, crimson and white with meat piled up to the first-floor, in front of which the butcher himself, in his blue coat, walks up and down, sharpening his knife on the steel that hangs to his waist. A little further on stands the clean family, begging; the father with his head down as if in shame, and a box of lucifers held forth in his hand – the boys in newly-washed pinafores, and the tidily got-up mother with a child at her breast. This stall is green and white with bunches of turnips – that red with apples, the next yellow with onions, and another purple with pickling cabbages. One minute you pass a man with an umbrella turned inside up and full of prints; the next, you hear one with a peepshow of Mazeppa, and Paul Jones the pirate, describing the pictures to the boys looking in at the little round windows. Then is heard the sharp snap of the percussion-cap from the crowd of lads firing at the target for nuts; and the moment afterwards, you see a black man half-clad in white, and shivering in the cold with tracts in his hand, or else you hear the sounds of music from 'Frazier's Circus', on the other side of the road, and the man outside the door of the penny concert, beseeching you to 'Be in time – be in time!' as Mr Somebody is just about to sing his favourite song of the 'Knife Grinder'. Such, indeed, is the riot, the struggle, and the scramble for a living, that the confusion and uproar of the New-cut on Saturday night have a bewildering and saddening effect upon the thoughtful mind.

Each salesman tries his utmost to sell his wares, tempting the passer-by with his bargains. The boy with his stock of herbs offers 'a double 'andful of fine parsley for a penny'; the man with the donkey-cart filled with turnips has three lads to shout for him to their utmost, with their 'Ho! ho! hi-i-i! What do you think of this here? A penny a bunch – hurrah for free trade! *Here's* your turnips!' Until it is seen and heard, we have no sense of the scramble that is going on throughout London for a living. The same scene takes place at the Brill – the same in Leather-lane – the same in Tottenham-court-road – the same in Whitecross-street; go to whatever corner of the metropolis you please, either on a Saturday night or a Sunday morning, and there is the same shouting and the same struggling to get the penny profit out of the poor man's Sunday dinner.

Since the above description was written, the New Cut has lost much of its noisy and brilliant glory. In consequence of a New Police regulation, 'stands' or 'pitches' have been forbidden, and each coster, on a market night, is now obliged, under pain of the lock-up house, to carry his tray, or keep moving with his barrow. The gay stalls have been replaced by deal boards, some sodden with wet fish, others stained purple with black-berries, or brown with walnut-peel; and the bright lamps are almost totally superseded by the dim, guttering candle. Even if the pole under the tray or 'shallow' is seen resting on the ground, the policeman on duty is obliged to interfere.

The mob of purchasers has diminished one-half; and instead of the road being filled with customers and trucks, the pavement and kerbstones are scarcely crowded.

The Sunday Morning Markets

[pp. 12–13]   Nearly every poor man's market does its Sunday trade. For a few hours on the Sabbath morning, the noise, bustle, and scramble of the Saturday night are repeated, and but for this opportunity many a poor family would pass a dinnerless Sunday. The system of paying the mechanic late on the Saturday night – and more particularly of paying a man his wages in a public-house – when he is tired with his day's work lures him to the tavern, and there the hours fly quickly enough beside the warm tap-room fire, so that by the time the wife comes for her husband's wages, she finds a large portion of them gone in drink, and the streets half cleared, so that the Sunday market is the only chance of getting the Sunday's dinner.

Of all these Sunday-morning markets, the Brill, perhaps, furnishes the busiest scene; so that it may be taken as a type of the whole.

The streets in the neighbourhood are quiet and empty. The shops are closed with their different-coloured shutters, and the people round about are dressed in the shiney cloth of the holiday suit. There are no 'cabs', and but few omnibuses to disturb the rest, and men walk in the road as safely as on the footpath.

As you enter the Brill the market sounds are scarcely heard. But at each step the low hum grows gradually into the noisy shouting, until at last the different cries become distinct, and the hubbub, din, and confusion of a thousand voices bellowing at once again fill the air. The road and footpath are crowded, as on the over-night; the men are standing in groups, smoking and talking; whilst the women run to and fro, some with the white round turnips showing out of their filled aprons, others with cabbages under their arms, and a piece of red meat dangling from their hands. Only a few of the shops are closed, but the butcher's and the coal-shed are filled with customers, and from the door of the shut-up baker's, the women come streaming forth with bags of flour in their hands, while men sally from the halfpenny barber's smoothing their clean-shaven chins. Walnuts, blacking, apples, onions, braces, combs, turnips, herrings, pens, and corn-plaster, are all bellowed out at the same time. Labourers and mechanics, still unshorn and undressed, hang about with their hands in their pockets, some with their pet terriers under their arms. The pavement is green with the refuse leaves of vegetables, and round a cabbage-barrow the women stand turning over the bunches, as the man shouts, 'Where you like, only a penny.' Boys are running home with the breakfast herring held in a piece of paper, and the side-pocket of the apple-man's stuff coat hangs down with the weight of the halfpence stored within it. Presently the tolling of the neighbouring church bells breaks forth. Then the bustle doubles itself, the cries grow louder, the confusion greater. Women run about and push their way through the throng, scolding the saunterers, for in half an hour the market will close. In a little time the butcher puts up his shutters, and leaves the door still open; the policemen in their clean gloves come round and drive the street-sellers before them, and as the clock strikes eleven the market finishes, and the Sunday's rest begins.

The following is a list of the street-markets, and the number of costers usually attending:

MARKETS ON THE SURREY SIDE

New-cut, Lambeth	300	Bermondsey	107
Lambeth-walk	104	Union-street, Borough	29
Walworth-road	22	Great Suffolk-street	46
Camberwell	15	Blackfriars-road	58
Newington	45		
Kent-street, Borough	38		764

MARKETS ON THE MIDDLESEX SIDE

Brill and Chapel-street,		Leather-lane	150
Somers' Town	300	St John's-street	47
Camden Town	50	Old-street (St Luke's)	46
Hampstead-road and		Whitecross-street, Cripplegate	150
Tottenham-court-road	333	Islington	79
St George's Market, Oxford-		City-road	49
street	177	Shoreditch	100
Marylebone	37	Bethnal-green	100
Edgeware-road	78	Whitechapel	258
Crawford-street	145	Mile End	105
Knightsbridge	46	Commercial-road (East)	114
Pimlico	32	Limehouse	88
Tothill-street and Broadway,		Ratcliffe Highway	122
Westminster	119	Rosemary-lane	119
Drury-lane	22		—
Clare-street	139		3147
Exmouth-street and Aylesbury-			—
street, Clerkenwell	142		

We find, from the foregoing list of markets, held in the various thorough-fares of the metropolis, that there are 10 on the Surrey side and 27 on the Middlesex side of the Thames. The total number of hucksters attending these markets is 3,911, giving an average of 105 to each market.

Habits and Amusements of Costermongers

[pp. 13–16] I find it impossible to separate these two headings; for the habits of the costermonger are not domestic. His busy life is past in the markets or the streets, and as his leisure is devoted to the beer-shop, the dancing-room, or the theatre, we must look for his habits to his demeanour at those places. Home has few attractions to a man whose life is a street-life. Even those who are influenced by family ties and affections, prefer to 'home' – indeed that word is rarely mentioned among them – the conversation, warmth, and merriment of the beer-shop, where they can take their ease among their 'mates'. Excitement or amusement are indispensable to uneducated men. Of beer-shops resorted to by costermongers, and principally supported by them, it is computed that there are 400 in London.

Those who meet first in the beer-shop talk over the state of trade and of the markets, while the later comers enter at once into what may be styled the serious business of the evening – amusement.

Business topics are discussed in a most peculiar style. One man takes the pipe from his mouth and says, 'Bill made a doogheno hit this morning.' 'Jem,' says another, to a man just entering, 'you'll stand a top o' reeb?' 'On,' answers Jem, 'I've had a trosseno tol, and have been doing dab.' For an explanation of what may be obscure in this dialogue, I must refer my readers to my remarks concerning the language of the class. If any strangers are present, the conversation is still further clothed in slang, so as to be unintelligible even to the partially initiated. The evident puzzlement of any listener is of course gratifying to the costermonger's vanity, for he feels that he possesses a knowledge peculiarly his own.

Among the in-door amusements of the costermonger is card-playing, at which many of them are adepts. The usual games are all-fours, all-fives, cribbage, and put. Whist is known to a few, but is never played, being considered dull and slow. Of short whist they have not heard; 'but,' said one, whom I questioned on the subject, 'if it's come into fashion, it'll soon be among us.' The play is usually for beer, but the game is rendered exciting by bets both among the players and the lookers-on. 'I'll back Jem for a yanepatine,' says one. 'Jack for a gen,' cries another. A penny is the lowest sum laid, and five shillings generally the highest, but a shilling is not often exceeded. 'We play fair among ourselves,' said a costermonger to me – 'aye, fairer than the aristocrats – but we'll take in anybody else.' Where it is known that the landlord will not supply cards, 'a sporting coster' carries a pack or two with him. The cards played with have rarely been stamped; they are generally dirty, and sometimes almost illegible, from long handling and spilled beer. Some men will sit patiently for hours at these games, and they watch the dealing round of the dingy cards intently, and without the attempt – common among politer gamesters – to appear indifferent, though they bear their losses well. In a full room of card-players, the groups are all shrouded in tobacco-smoke, and from them are heard constant sounds – according to the games they are engaged in – of 'I'm low, and Ped's high.' 'Tip and me's game.' 'Fifteen four and a flush of five.' I may remark it is curious that costermongers, who can neither read nor write, and who have no knowledge of the multiplication table, are skilful in all the intricacies and calculations of cribbage. There is not much quarrelling over the cards, unless strangers play with them, and then the costermongers all take part one with another, fairly or unfairly.

It has been said that there is a close resemblance between many of the characteristics of a very high class, socially, and a very low class. Those who remember the disclosures on a trial a few years back, as to how men of rank and wealth passed their leisure in card-playing – many of their lives being one continued leisure – can judge how far the analogy holds when the card-passion of the costermongers is described.

'Shove-halfpenny' is another game played by them; so is 'Three up'. Three halfpennies are thrown up, and when they fall all 'heads' or all 'tails', it is a mark; and the man who gets the greatest number of marks out of a given amount – three, or five, or more – wins. 'Three-up' is played fairly among the costermongers; but is most frequently resorted to when strangers are present to 'make a pitch', – which is, in plain words, to cheat any stranger who is rash enough to bet upon them. 'This is the way, sir,' said an adept to me; 'bless you, I can make them fall as I please. If I'm playing with Jo, and a stranger bets with Jo, why, of course, I make Jo win.' This adept illustrated his skill to me by throwing up three halfpennies, and, five times out of six, they fell upon the floor, whether he threw them nearly to the ceiling or merely to his shoulder, all heads or all tails. The halfpence were the proper current coins – indeed, they were my own; and the result is gained by a peculiar position of the coins on the fingers, and a peculiar jerk in the throwing. There was an amusing manifestation of the pride of art in the way in which my obliging informant displayed his skill.

'Skittles' is another favourite amusement, and the costermongers class themselves among the best players in London. The game is always for beer, but betting goes on.

A fondness for 'sparring' and 'boxing' lingers among the rude members of some classes of the working men, such as the tanners. With the great majority of the costermongers this fondness is still as dominant as it was among the 'higher classes', when boxers were the pets of princes and nobles. The sparring among the costers is not for money, but for beer and 'a lark' – a convenient word covering much mischief. Two out of every ten landlords, whose houses are patronised by these lovers of 'the art of self-defence', supply gloves. Some charge 2d. a night for their use; others only 1d. The sparring seldom continues long, sometimes not above a quarter of an hour; for the costermongers, though excited for a while, weary of sports in which they cannot personally participate, and in the beer-shops only two spar at a time, though fifty or sixty may be present. The shortness of the duration of this pastime may be one reason why it seldom leads to quarrelling. The stake is usually a 'top of reeb', and the winner is the man who gives the first 'noser'; a *bloody* nose however is required to show that the blow was veritably a noser. The costermongers boast of their skill in pugilism as well as at skittles. 'We are all handy with our fists,' said one man, 'and are matches, aye, and more than matches, for anybody but reg'lar boxers. We've stuck to the ring, too, and gone reg'lar to the fights, more than any other men.'

'Twopenny-hops' are much resorted to by the costermongers, men and women, boys and girls. At these dances decorum is sometimes, but not often, violated. 'The women,' I was told by one man, 'doesn't show their necks as I've seen the ladies do in them there pictures of high life in the shop-winders, or on the stage. Their Sunday gowns, which is their dancing gowns, ain't made that way.' At these 'hops' the clog-hornpipe is often danced, and sometimes a collection is made to ensure the per-formance of a first-rate professor of that dance; sometimes, and more frequently, it is volunteered gratuitously. The other dances are jigs, 'flash jigs' – hornpipes in fetters – a dance rendered popular by the success of the acted 'Jack Sheppard' – polkas, and country-dances, the last-mentioned being generally demanded by the women. Waltzes are as yet unknown to them. Sometimes they do the 'pipe-dance'. For this a number of tobacco-pipes, about a dozen, are laid close together on the floor, and the dancer places the toe of his boot between the different pipes, keeping time with the music. Two of the pipes are arranged as a cross, and the toe has to be inserted between each of the angles, without breaking them. The numbers present at these 'hops' vary from 30 to 100 of both sexes, their ages being from 14 to 45, and the female sex being slightly predominant as to the proportion of those in attendance. At these 'hops' there is nothing of the leisurely style of dancing – half a glide and half a skip – but vigorous, laborious capering. The hours are from half-past eight to twelve, some-times to one or two in the morning, and never later than two, as the costermongers are early risers. There is sometimes a good deal of drinking; some of the young girls being often pressed to drink, and frequently yielding to the temptation. From 1*l*. to 7*l*. is spent in drink at a hop; the youngest men or lads present spend the most, especially in that act of costermonger politeness – 'treating the gals'. The music is always a fiddle, sometimes with the addition of a harp and a cornopean. The band is provided by the costermongers, to whom the assembly is confined; but during the present and the last year, when the costers' earnings have been less than the average, the landlord has provided the harp, whenever that instrument has added to the charms of the fiddle. Of one use to which these 'hops' are put I have given an account, under the head of 'Marriage'.

The other amusements of this class of the community are the theatre and the penny concert, and their visits are almost entirely confined to the galleries of the theatres on the Surrey-side – the Surrey, the Victoria, the Bower Saloon, and (but less frequently) Astley's. Three times a week is an average attendance at theatres and dances by the more prosperous costermongers. The most intelligent man I met with among them gave me the following account. He classes himself with the many, but his tastes are really those of an educated man: 'Love and murder suits us best, sir; but within these few years I think there's a great deal more liking for deep tragedies among us. They set men a thinking; but then we all consider them too long. Of *Hamlet* we can make neither end nor side; and nine out of ten of us – ay, far more than that – would like it to be confined to the ghost scenes, and the funeral, and the killing off at the last. *Macbeth* would be better liked, if it was only the witches and the fighting. The high words in a tragedy we call jaw-breakers, and say we can't tumble to that barrikin. We always stay to the last, because we've paid for it all, or very few costers would see a tragedy out if any money was returned to those leaving after two or three acts. We are fond of music. Nigger music was very much liked among us, but it's stale now. Flash songs are liked, and sailors' songs, and patriotic songs. Most costers – indeed, I can't call to mind an exception – listen very quietly to songs that they don't in the least understand. We have among us translations of the patriotic French songs. "Mourir pour la patrie" is very popular, and so is the "Marseillaise". A song to take hold of us must have a good chorus.' 'They like something, sir, that is worth hearing,' said one of my informants, 'such as the "Soldier's Dream", "The Dream of Napoleon", or "I 'ad a dream – an 'appy dream".'

The songs in ridicule of Marshal Haynau, and in laudation of Barclay and Perkin's draymen, were and are very popular among the costers; but none are more popular than Paul Jones – 'A noble commander, Paul Jones was his name'. Among them the chorus of 'Britons never shall be slaves', is often rendered 'Britons always shall be slaves'. The most popular of all songs with the class, however, is 'Duck-legged Dick'; of which I give the first verse.

> Duck-legged Dick had a donkey,
>   And his lush loved much for to swill,
> One day he got rather lumpy,
>   And got sent seven days to the mill.
> His donkey was taken to the green-yard,
>   A fate which he never deserved.
> Oh! it was such a regular mean yard,
>   That alas! the poor moke got starved.

Oh! bad luck can't be prevented,
   Fortune she smiles or she frowns,
He's best off that's contented,
   To mix, sirs, the ups and the downs.

Their sports are enjoyed the more, if they are dangerous and require both courage and dexterity to succeed in them. They prefer, if crossing a bridge, to climb over the parapet, and walk along on the stone coping. When a house is building, rows of coster lads will climb up the long ladders, leaning against the unslated roof, and then slide down again, each one resting on the other's shoulders. A peep show with a battle scene is sure of its coster audience, and a favourite pastime is fighting with cheap theatrical swords. They are, however, true to each other, and should a coster, who is the hero of his court, fall ill and go to a hospital, the whole of the inhabitants of his quarter will visit him on the Sunday, and take him presents of various articles so that 'he may live well'.

Among the men, rat-killing is a favourite sport. They will enter an old stable, fasten the door and then turn out the rats. Or they will find out some unfrequented yard, and at night time build up a pit with apple-case boards, and lighting up their lamps, enjoy the sport. Nearly every coster is fond of dogs. Some fancy them greatly, and are proud of making them fight. If when out working, they see a handsome stray, whether he is a 'toy' or 'sporting' dog, they whip him up – many of the class not being *very* particular whether the animals are stray or not.

Their dog fights are both cruel and frequent. It is not uncommon to see a lad walking with the trembling legs of a dog shivering under a bloody handkerchief, that covers the bitten and wounded body of an animal that has been figuring at some 'match'. These fights take place on the sly – the tap-room or back-yard of a beer-shop, being generally chosen for the purpose. A few men are let into the secret, and they attend to bet upon the winner, the police being carefully kept from the spot.

Pigeons are 'fancied' to a large extent, and are kept in lath cages on the roofs of the houses. The lads look upon a visit to the Redhouse, Battersea, where the pigeon-shooting takes place, as a great treat. They stand without the hoarding that encloses the ground, and watch for the wounded pigeons to fall, when a violent scramble takes place among them, each bird being valued at 3*d*. or 4*d*. So popular has this sport become, that some boys take dogs with them trained to retrieve the birds, and two Lambeth costers attend regularly after their morning's work with their guns, to shoot those that escape the 'shots' within.

A good pugilist is looked up to with great admiration by the costers, and fighting is considered to be a necessary part of a boy's education. Among them cowardice in any shape is despised as being degrading and loathsome, indeed the man who would avoid a fight, is scouted by the whole of the court he lives in. Hence it is important for a lad and even a girl to know how to 'work their fists well' – as expert boxing is called among them. If a coster man or woman is struck they are obliged to fight. When a quarrel takes place between two boys, a ring is formed, and the men urge them on to have it out, for they hold that it is a wrong thing to stop a battle, as it causes bad blood for life; whereas, if the lads fight it out they shake hands and forget all about it. Everybody practises fighting, and the man who has the largest and hardest muscle is spoken of in terms of the highest commendation. It is often said in admiration of such a man that 'he could muzzle half a dozen bobbies before breakfast.'

To serve out a policeman is the bravest act by which a costermonger can distinguish himself. Some lads have been imprisoned upwards of a dozen times for this offence; and are consequently looked upon by their companions as martyrs. When they leave prison for such an act, a subscription is often got up for their benefit. In their continual warfare with the force, they resemble many savage nations, from the cunning and treachery they use. The lads endeavour to take the unsuspecting 'crusher' by surprise, and often crouch at the entrance of a court until a policeman passes, when a stone or a brick is hurled at him, and the youngster immediately disappears. Their love of revenge too, is extreme – their hatred being in no way mitigated by time; they will wait for months, following a policeman who has offended or wronged them, anxiously looking out for an opportunity of paying back the injury. One boy, I was told, vowed vengeance against a member of the force, and for six months never allowed the man to escape his notice. At length, one night, he saw the policeman in a row outside a public-house, and running into the crowd kicked him savagely, shouting at the same time: 'Now, you b—, I've got you at last.' When the boy heard that his persecutor was injured for life, his joy was very great, and he declared the twelvemonth's imprisonment he was sentenced to for the offence to be 'dirt cheap'. The whole of the court where the lad resided, sympathized with the boy, and vowed to a man, that had he escaped, they would have subscribed a pad or two of dry herrings, to send him into the country until the affair had blown over, for he had shown himself a 'plucky one'.

It is called 'plucky' to bear pain without complaining. To flinch from expected suffering is scorned, and he who does so is sneered at and told to wear a gown, as being more fit to be a woman. To show a disregard for pain, a lad, when without money, will say to his pal, 'Give us a penny, and you may have a punch at my nose.' They also delight in tattooing their chests and arms with anchors, and figures of different kinds. During the whole of this painful operation, the boy will not flinch, but laugh and joke with his admiring companions, as if perfectly at ease.

Of the Education of Costermongers' Children

[p. 26] I have used the heading of 'Education', but perhaps to say 'non-education', would be more suitable. Very few indeed of the costermongers' children are sent even to the Ragged Schools; and if they are, from all I could learn, it is done more that the mother may be saved the trouble of tending them at home, than from any desire that the children shall acquire useful knowledge. Both boys and girls are sent out by their parents in the evening to sell nuts, oranges, &c., at the doors of the theatres, or in any public place, or 'round the houses' (a stated circuit from their place of abode). This trade they pursue eagerly for the sake of 'bunts', though some carry home the money they take, very honestly. The costermongers are kind to their children, 'perhaps in a rough way, and the women make regular pets of them very often.' One experienced man told me, that he had seen a poor costermonger's wife – one of the few who could read – instructing her children in reading; but such instances were very rare. The education of these children is such only as the streets afford; and the streets teach them, for the most part – and in greater or lesser degrees, – acuteness – a precocious acuteness – in all that concerns their immediate wants, business, or gratifications; a patient endurance of cold and hunger; a desire to obtain money without working for it; a craving for the excitement of gambling; an inordinate love of amusement; and an irrepressible repugnance to any settled in-door industry.

The Literature of Costermongers

[pp. 27–8] We have now had an inkling of the London costermonger's notions upon politics and religion. We have seen the brutified state in which he is allowed by society to remain, though possessing the same faculties and susceptibilities as ourselves – the same power to perceive and admire the forms of truth, beauty, and goodness, as even the very highest in the state. We have witnessed how, instinct with all the elements of manhood and beasthood, the qualities of the beast are principally developed in him, while those of the man are stunted in their growth. It now remains for us to look into some other matters concerning this curious class of people, and, first, of their literature:

It may appear anomalous to speak of the literature of an uneducated body, but even the costermongers have their tastes for books. They are very fond of hearing any one read aloud to them, and listen very attentively. One man often reads the Sunday paper of the beer-shop to them, and on a fine summer's evening a costermonger, or any neighbour who has the advantage of being 'a schollard', reads aloud to them in the courts they inhabit. What they love best to listen to – and, indeed, what they are most eager for – are Reynolds's periodicals, especially the 'Mysteries of the Court'. 'They've got tired of Lloyd's blood-stained stories,' said one man, who was in the habit of reading to them, 'and I'm satisfied that, of all London, Reynolds is the most popular man among them. They stuck to him in Trafalgar-square, and would again. They all say he's "a trump", and Feargus O'Connor's another trump with them.'

One intelligent man considered that the spirit of curiosity manifested by costermongers, as regards the information or excitement derived from hearing stories read, augured well for the improvability of the class.

Another intelligent costermonger, who had recently read some of the cheap periodicals to ten or twelve men, women, and boys, all costermongers, gave me an account of the comments made by his auditors. They had assembled, after their day's work or their rounds, for the purpose of hearing my informant read the last number of some of the penny publications.

'The costermongers,' said my informant, 'are very fond of illustrations. I have known a man, what couldn't read, buy a periodical what had an illustration, a little out of the common way perhaps, just that he might learn from some one, who *could* read, what it was all about. They have all heard of Cruikshank, and they think everything funny is by him – funny scenes in a play and all. His "Bottle" was very much admired. I heard one man say it was very prime, and showed what "lush" did, but I saw the same man,' added my informant, 'drunk three hours afterwards. Look you here, sir,' he continued, turning over a periodical, for he had the number with him, 'here's a portrait of "Catherine of Russia". "Tell us about her," said one man to me last night; read it; what was she?" When I had read it,' my informant continued, 'another man, to whom I showed it, said, "Don't the cove as did that know a deal?" for they fancy – at least, a many do – that one man writes a whole periodical, or a whole newspaper. Now here,' proceeded my friend, 'you see's an engraving of a man hung up, burning over a fire, and some costers would go mad if they couldn't learn what he'd been doing, who he was, and all about him. "But about the picture?" they would say, and this is a very common question put by them whenever they see an engraving.

'Here's one of the passages that took their fancy wonderfully,' my informant observed:

"With glowing cheeks, flashing eyes, and palpitating bosom, Venetia Trelawney rushed back into the refreshment-room, where she threw herself into one of the arm-chairs already noticed. But scarcely had she thus sunk down upon the flocculent cushion, when a sharp click, as of some mechanism giving way, met her ears; and at the same instant her wrists were caught in manacles which sprang out of the arms of the treacherous chair, while two steel bands started from the richly carved back and grasped her shoulders. A shriek burst from her lips – she struggled violently, but all to no purpose: for she was a captive – and powerless!

"We should observe that the manacles and the steel bands which had thus fastened upon her, were covered with velvet, so that they inflicted no positive injury upon her, nor even produced the slightest abrasion of her fair and polished skin."

Here all my audience,' said the man to me, 'broke out with – "Aye! that's the way the harristocrats hooks it. There's nothing o' that sort among us; the rich has all the barrikin to themselves." "Yes, that's the b— way the taxes goes in," shouted a woman.

'Anything about the police sets them a talking at once. This did when I read it:

"The Ebenezers still continued their fierce struggle, and, from the noise they made, seemed as if they were tearing each other to pieces, to the wild roar of a chorus of profane swearing. The alarm, as Bloomfield had predicted, was soon raised, and some two or three policemen, with their bull's-eyes, and still more effective truncheons, speedily restored order."

"The blessed crushers is everywhere," shouted one. "I wish I'd been there to have had a shy at the eslops," said another. And then a man sung out: "O, don't I like the Bobbys?"

'If there's any foreign languages which can't be explained, I've seen the costers,' my informant went on, 'annoyed at it – quite annoyed. Another time I read part of one of Lloyd's numbers to them – but they like something spicier. One article in them – here it is – finishes in this way:

"The social habits and costumes of the Magyar *noblesse* have almost all the characteristics of the corresponding class in Ireland. This word *noblesse* is one of wide significance in Hungary; and one may with great truth say of this strange nation, that *'qui n'est point noble n'est rien.'*"

26

"I can't tumble to that barrikin," said a young fellow; "it's a jaw-breaker. But if this here – what d' ye call it, you talk about – was like the Irish, why they was a rum lot." "Noblesse," said a man that's considered a clever fellow, from having once learned his letters, though he can't read or write. "Noblesse! Blessed if I know what he's up to." Here was a regular laugh.'

From other quarters I learned that some of the costermongers who were able to read, or loved to listen to reading, purchased their literature in a very commercial spirit, frequently buying the periodical which is the largest in size, because when 'they've got the reading out of it,' as they say, 'it's worth a halfpenny for the barrow.'

Tracts they will rarely listen to, but if any persevering man *will* read tracts, and state that he does it for their benefit and improvement, they listen without rudeness, though often with evident unwillingness. 'Sermons or tracts,' said one of their body to me, 'give them the 'orrors.' Costermongers purchase, and not unfrequently, the first number of a penny periodical, 'to see what it's like.'

The tales of robbery and bloodshed, of heroic, eloquent, and gentlemanly highwaymen, or of gipsies turning out to be nobles, now interest the costermongers but little, although they found great delight in such stories a few years back. Works relating to Courts, potentates, or 'harristocrats', are the most relished by these rude people.

Of the Donkeys of the Costermongers

[p. 31] The costermongers almost universally treat their donkeys with kindness. Many a costermonger will resent the ill-treatment of a donkey, as he would a personal indignity. These animals are often not only favourites, but pets, having their share of the costermonger's dinner when bread forms a portion of it, or pudding, or anything suited to the palate of the brute. Those well-used, manifest fondness for their masters, and are easily manageable; it is, however, difficult to get an ass, whose master goes regular rounds, away from its stable for any second labour during the day, unless it has fed and slept in the interval. The usual fare of a donkey is a peck of chaff, which costs 1*d*., a quart of oats and a quart of beans, each averaging 1½*d*., and sometimes a pennyworth of hay, being an expenditure of 4*d*. or 5*d*. a day; but some give double this quantity in a prosperous time. Only one meal a day is given. Many costermongers told me, that their donkeys lived well when they themselves lived well.

'It's all nonsense to call donkeys stupid,' said one costermonger to me;

'them's stupid that calls them so; they're sensible. Not long since I worked Guildford with my donkey-cart and a boy. Jack (the donkey) was slow and heavy in coming back, until we got in sight of the lights at Vauxhall-gate, and then he trotted on like one o'clock, he did indeed! just as if he smelt it was London besides seeing it, and knew he was at home. He had a famous appetite in the country, and the fresh grass did him good. I gave a country lad 2*d.* to mind him in a green lane there. I wanted my own boy to do so, but he said, "I'll see you further first." A London boy hates being by himself in a lone country part. He's afraid of being burked; he is indeed. One can't quarrel with a lad when he's away with one in the country; he's very useful. I feed my donkey well. I sometimes give him a carrot for a luxury, but carrots are dear now. He's fond of mashed potatoes, and has many a good mash when I can buy them at 4lb. a penny.'

'There was a friend of mine,' said another man, 'had great trouble about his donkey a few months back. I saw part of it, and knew all about it. He was doing a little work on a Sunday morning at Wandsworth, and the poor thing fell down dead. He was very fond of his donkey and kind to it, and the donkey was very fond of him. He thought he wouldn't leave the poor creature he'd had a good while, and had been out with in all weathers, by the road side; so he dropped all notion of doing business, and with help got the poor dead thing into his cart; its head lolloping over the end of the cart, and its poor eyes staring at nothing. He thought he'd drag it home and bury it somewheres. It wasn't for the value he dragged it, for what's a dead donkey worth? There was a few persons about him, and they was all quiet and seemed sorry for the poor fellow and for his donkey; but the church-bells struck up, and up came a "crusher", and took the man up, and next day he was fined 10s., I can't exactly say for what. He never saw no more of the animal, and lost his stock as well as his donkey.'

Of the Costermongers' Capital

[pp. 31–6] The costermongers, though living by buying and selling, are seldom or never capitalists. It is estimated that not more than one-fourth of the entire body trade upon their own property. Some borrow their stock money, others borrow the stock itself, others again borrow the donkey-carts, barrows, or baskets, in which their stock is carried round, whilst others borrow even the weights and measures by which it is meted out.

The reader, however uninformed he may be as to the price the poor usually have to pay for any loans they may require, doubtlessly need not be told that the remuneration exacted for the use of the above-named commodities is not merely confined to the legal 5*l.* per centum per annum; still many of even the most 'knowing' will hardly be able to credit the fact that the ordinary rate of interest in the costermongers' money-market amounts to 20 per cent. per week, or no less than 1,040*l.* a year, for every 100*l.* advanced.

But the iniquity of this usury in the present instance is felt, not so much by the costermongers themselves, as by the poor people whom they serve; for, of course, the enormous rate of interest must be paid out of the profits on the goods they sell, and consequently added to the price, so that coupling this overcharge with the customary short allowance – in either weight or measure, as the case may be – we can readily perceive how cruelly the poor are defrauded, and how they not only get often too little for what they do, but have as often to pay too much for what they buy.

Premising thus much, I shall now proceed to describe the terms upon which the barrow, the cart, the basket, the weights, the measures, the stock-money, or the stock, is usually advanced to the needy costermongers by their more thrifty brethren.

The hire of a barrow is 3*d.* a day, or 1*s.* a week, for the six winter months; and 4*d.* a day, or 1*s.* 6*d.* a week, for the six summer months. Some are to be had rather lower in the summer, but never for less than 4*d.* – sometimes for not less than 6*d.* on a Saturday, when not unfrequently every barrow in London is hired. No security and no deposit is required, but the lender satisfies himself that the borrower is really what he represents himself to be. I am informed that 5,000 hired barrows are now in the hands of the London costermongers, at an average rental of 3*l.* 5*s.* each, or 16,250*l.* a year. One man lets out 120 yearly, at a return (dropping the 5*s.*) of 360*l.*; while the cost of a good barrow, new, is 2*l.* 12*s.*, and in the autumn and winter they may be bought new, or 'as good as new', at 30*s.* each; so that reckoning each to cost this barrow-letter 2*l.* – he receives 360*l.* rent or interest – exactly 150 per cent. per annum for property which originally cost but 240*l.*, and property which is still as good for the ensuing year's business as for the past. One man has rented a barrow for eight years, during which period he has paid 26*l.* for what in the first instance did not cost more than twice as many shillings, and which he must return if he discontinues its use. 'I know men well to do,' said an intelligent costermonger, 'who have paid 1*s.* and 1*s.* 6*d.* a week for a barrow for three, four, and five years; and they can't be made to understand that it's rather high rent for what might cost 40*s.* at first. They can't see they are losers. One barrow-lender sends his son out, mostly on a Sunday, collecting his rents (for barrows), but he's not a hard man.'

Some of the lenders complain that their customers pay them irregularly
and cheat them often, and that in consequence they must charge high;
while the 'borrowers' declare that it is very seldom indeed that a man
'shirks' the rent for his barrow, generally believing that he has made an
advantageous bargain, and feeling the want of his vehicle, if he lose it
temporarily. Let the lenders, however, be deceived by many, still, it is
evident, that the rent charged for barrows is most exorbitant, by the fact,
that all who take to the business become men of considerable property in
a few years.

Donkey-carts are rarely hired. 'If there's 2,000 donkey and pony-carts
in London, more or less, not 200 of them's borrowed; but of barrows five
to two is borrowed.' A donkey-cart costs from 2l. to 10l.; 3l. 10s. being
an average price. The hire is 2s. or 2s. 6d. a week. The harness costs 2l.
10s. new, but is bought, nineteen times out of twenty, second-hand, at
from 2s. 6d. to 20s. The donkeys themselves are not let out on hire, though
a costermonger may let out his donkey to another in the trade when he
does not require its services; the usual sum paid for the hire of a donkey
is 2s. 6d. or 3s. per week. The cost price of a pony varies from 5l. to 13l.;
that of a donkey from 1l. to 3l. There may be six donkeys, or more, in
costermonger use, to one pony. Some traffic almost weekly in these
animals, liking the excitement of such business.

The repairs to barrows, carts, and harness are almost always effected
by the costermongers themselves.

'Shallows' (baskets) which cost 1s. and 1s. 6d., are let out at 1d. a day;
but not five in 100 of those in use are borrowed, as their low price places
them at the costermonger's command. A pewter quart-pot, for measuring
onions, &c., is let out at 2d. a day, its cost being 2s. Scales are 2d., and
a set of weights 1d. a day.

Another common mode of usury is in the lending of stock-money. This
is lent by the costermongers who have saved the means for such use of
their funds, and by beer-shop keepers. The money-lending costermongers
are the most methodical in their usury – 1,040l. per cent. per annum, as
was before stated, being the rate of interest usually charged. It is seldom
that a lower sum than 10s. is borrowed, and never a higher sum than 2l.
When a stranger applies for a loan, the money-lender satisfies himself as
I have described of the barrow-lender. He charges 2d. a day for a loan of
2s. 6d.; 3d. a day for 5s.; 6d. a day for 10s.; and 1s. a day for 1l. If the
daily payments are rendered regularly, at a month's end the terms are
reduced to 6d. a week for 5s.; 1s. for 10s.; and 2s. for 1l. 'That's reckoned
an extraordinary small interest,' was said to me, 'only 4d. a day for a

pound.' The average may be 3s. a week for the loan of 20s.; it being only
to a few that a larger sum than 20s. is lent. 'I paid 2s. a week for 1l. for
a whole year,' said one man, 'or 5l. 4s. for the use of a pound, and then
I was liable to repay the 1l.' The principal, however, is seldom repaid; nor
does the lender seem to expect it, though he will occasionally demand it.
One money-lender is considered to have a floating capital of 150l. invested
in loans to costermongers. If he receives 2s. per week per 1l. for but
twenty-six weeks in the year (and he often receives it for the fifty-two
weeks) – his 150l. brings him in 390l. a year.

Sometimes a loan is effected only for a day, generally a Saturday, as
much as 2s. 6d. being sometimes given for the use of 5s.; the 5s. being of
course repaid in the evening.

The money-lenders are subject to at least twice the extent of loss to
which the barrow-lender is exposed, as it is far oftener that money is
squandered (on which of course no interest can be paid) than that a
barrow is disposed of.

The money-lenders, (from the following statement, made to me by one
who was in the habit of borrowing,) pursue their business in a not very
dissimilar manner to that imputed to those who advance larger sums: 'If
I want to borrow in a hurry,' said my informant, 'as I may hear of a good
bargain, I run to my neighbour L—'s, and he first says he hasn't 20s. to
lend, and his wife's by, and she hasn't 2s. in her pocket, so I can't be
accommodated. Then he said if I must have the money he'll have to pawn
his watch, – or to borrow it of Mr —, (an innkeeper) who would
charge a deal of interest, for he wasn't paid all he lent two months
back, and 1s. would be expected to be spent in drink – though L— don't
drink – or he must try if his sister would trust him, but she was sick and
wanted all her money – or perhaps his barrow-merchant would lend him
10s., if he'd undertake to return 15s. at night; and it ends by my thinking
I've done pretty well if I can get 1l. for 5s. interest, for a day's use of
it.'

The beer-shop keepers lend on far easier terms, perhaps at half the
interest exacted by the others, and without any regular system of charges;
but they look sharp after the repayment, and expect a considerable outlay
in beer, and will only lend to good customers; they however have even
lent money without interest.

'In the depth of last winter,' said a man of good character to me, 'I
borrowed 5s. The beer-shop keeper wouldn't lend; he'll rather lend to men
doing well and drinking. But I borrowed it at 6d. a day interest, and that
6d. a day I paid exactly four weeks, Sundays and all; and that was 15s.

in thirty days for the use of 5s. I was half starving all the time, and then I had a slice of luck, and paid the 5s. back slap, and got out of it.'

Many shopkeepers lend money to the stall-keepers, whom they know from standing near their premises, and that without interest. They generally lend, however, to the women, as they think the men want to get drunk with it. 'Indeed, if it wasn't for the women,' said a costermonger to me, 'half of us might go to the Union.'

Another mode of usurious lending or trading is, as I said before, to provide the costermonger – not with the stock-money – but with the stock itself. This mode also is highly profitable to the usurer, who is usually a costermonger, but sometimes a greengrocer. A stock of fruit, fish, or vegetables, with a barrow for its conveyance, is entrusted to a street-seller, the usual way being to 'let him have a sovereign's worth.' The value of this, however, at the market cost, rarely exceeds 14s., still the man entrusted with it must carry 20s. to his creditor, or he will hardly be trusted a second time. The man who trades with the stock is not required to pay the 20s. on the first day of the transaction, as he may not have realised so much, but he must pay some of it, generally 10s., and must pay the remainder the next day or the money-lender will decline any subsequent dealings.

It may be thought, as no security is given, and as the costermongering barrow, stock, or money-lender never goes to law for the recovery of any debt or goods, that the per centage is not so very exorbitant after all. But I ascertained that not once in twenty times was the money-lender exposed to any loss by the non-payment of his usurious interest, while his profits are enormous. The borrower knows that if he fails in his payment, the lender will acquaint the other members of his fraternity, so that no future loan will be attainable, and the costermonger's business may be at an end. One borrower told me that the re-payment of his loan of 2l., borrowed two years ago at 4s. a week, had this autumn been reduced to 2s. 6d. a week: 'He's a decent man I pay now,' he said; 'he has twice forgiven me a month at a time when the weather was very bad and the times as bad as the weather. Before I borrowed of him I had dealings with —. He *was* a scurf. If I missed a week, and told him I would make it up next week, "That won't do," he'd say, "I'll turn you up. I'll take d—d good care to stop you. *I'll* have you to rights." If I hadn't satisfied him, as I did at last, I could never have got credit again; never.' I am informed that most of the moneylenders, if a man paid for a year or so, will now 'drop it for a month or so in a very hard-up time, and go on again.' There is no I.O.U. or any memorandum given to the usurer. 'There's never a slip of paper about it, sir,' I was told.

I may add that a very intelligent man from whom I derived information, said to me concerning costermongers never going to law to recover money owing to them, nor indeed for any purpose: 'If any one steals anything from me – and that, as far as I know, never happened but once in ten years – and I catch him, I take it out of him on the spot. I give him a jolly good hiding and there's an end of it. I know very well, sir, that costers are ignorant men, but in my opinion' (laughing) 'our never going to law shows that in *that* point we are in advance of the aristocrats. I never heard of a coster in a law court, unless he was in trouble (charged with some offence) – for assaulting a crusher, or anybody he had quarrelled with, or something of that kind.'

The barrow-lender, when not regularly paid, sends some one, or goes himself, and carries away the barrow.

My personal experience with this peculiar class justifies me in saying that they are far less dishonest than they are usually believed to be, and much more honest than their wandering habits, their want of education and 'principle' would lead even the most charitable to suppose. Since I have exhibited an interest in the sufferings and privations of these neglected people, I have, as the reader may readily imagine, had many applications for assistance, and without vanity, I believe I may say, that as far as my limited resources would permit, I have striven to extricate the street-sellers from the grasp of the usurer. Some of whom I have *lent* small sums (for gifts only degrade struggling honest men into the apathy of beggars) have taken the money with many a protestation that they would repay it in certain weekly instalments, which they themselves proposed, but still have never made their appearance before me a second time – it may be from dishonesty and it may be from inability and shame – others, however, and they are not a few, have religiously kept faith with me, calling punctually to pay back a sixpence or a shilling as the precariousness of their calling would permit, and doing this, though they knew that I adjured all claims upon them but through their honour, and was, indeed, in most cases, ignorant where to find them, even if my inclination led me to seek or enforce a return of the loan. One case of this kind shows so high a sense of honour among a class, generally considered to rank among the most dishonourable, that, even at the risk of being thought egotistical, I will mention it here: 'Two young men, street-sellers, called upon me and begged hard for the loan of a little stock-money. They made needle-cases and hawked them from door to door at the east end of the town, and had not the means of buying the wood. I agreed to let them have ten shillings between them; this they promised to repay at a shilling a week. They were utter strangers to me; nevertheless, at the end of the first week one shilling of the sum was duly returned. The second week, however, brought no shilling, nor did the third, nor the fourth, by which time I got to look upon the money as lost; but at the end of the fifth week one of the men called with his sixpence, and told me how he should have been with me before but his mate had promised each week to meet him with his sixpence, and each week disappointed him; so he had come on alone. I thanked him, and the next week he came again; so he did the next, and the next after that. On the latter occasion he told me that in five more weeks he should have paid off his half of the amount advanced, and that then, as he had come with the other man, he would begin paying off *his* share as well!'

Those who are unacquainted with the character of the people may feel inclined to doubt the trustworthiness of the class, but it is an extraordinary fact that but few of the costermongers fail to repay the money advanced to them, even at the present ruinous rate of interest. The poor, it is my belief, have not yet been sufficiently tried in this respect; – pawnbrokers, loan-offices, tally-shops, dolly-shops, are the only parties who will trust them – but, as a startling proof of the good faith of the humbler classes generally, it may be stated that Mrs Chisholm (the lady who has exerted herself so benevolently in the cause of emigration) has lent out, at different times, as much as 160,000*l.* that has been entrusted to her for the use of the 'lower orders', and that the whole of this large amount has been returned – *with the exception of* 12*l.*!

I myself have often given a sovereign to professed thieves to get 'changed', and never knew one to make off with the money. Depend upon it, if we would really improve, we must begin by elevating instead of degrading.

The Life of a Coster-lad

[pp. 41–2]   One lad that I spoke to gave me as much of his history as he could remember. He was a tall stout boy, about sixteen years old, with a face utterly vacant. His two heavy lead-coloured eyes stared unmeaningly at me, and, beyond a constant anxiety to keep his front lock curled on his cheek, he did not exhibit the slightest trace of feeling. He sank into his seat heavily and of a heap, and when once settled down he remained motionless, with his mouth open and his hands on his knees – almost as if paralyzed. He was dressed in all the slang beauty of his class, with a bright red handkerchief and unexceptionable boots.

'My father' he told me in a thick unimpassioned voice, 'was a waggoner, and worked the country roads. There was two on us at home with mother, and we used to play along with the boys of our court, in Golding-lane, at buttons and marbles. I recollects nothing more than this – only the big boys used to cheat like bricks and thump us if we grumbled – that's all I recollects of my infancy, as you calls it. Father I've heard tell died when I was three and brother only a year old. It was worse luck for us! – Mother was so easy with us. I once went to school for a couple of weeks, but the cove used to fetch me a wipe over the knuckles with his stick, and as I wasn't going to stand that there, why you see I ain't no great schollard. We did as we liked with mother, she was so precious easy, and I never learned anything but playing buttons and making leaden "bonces", that's all,' (here the youth laughed slightly). 'Mother used to be up and out very early washing in families – anything for a living. She was a good mother to us. We was left at home with the key of the room and some bread and butter for dinner. Afore she got into work – and it was a goodish long time – we was shocking hard up, and she pawned nigh everything. Sometimes, when we hadn't no grub at all, the other lads, perhaps, would give us some of their bread and butter, but often our stomachs used to ache with the hunger, and we would cry when we was werry far gone. She used to be at work from six in the morning till ten o'clock at night, which was a long time for a child's belly to hold out again, and when it was dark we would go and lie down on the bed and try and sleep until she came home with the food. I was eight year old then.

'A man as know'd mother, said to her, "Your boy's got nothing to do, let him come along with me and yarn a few ha'pence," and so I became a coster. He gave me 4d. a morning and my breakfast. I worked with him about three year, until I learnt the markets, and then I and brother got baskets of our own, and used to keep mother. One day with another, the two of us together could make 2s. 6d. by selling greens of a morning, and going round to the publics with nuts of an evening, till about ten o'clock at night. Mother used to have a bit of fried meat or a stew ready for us when we got home, and by using up the stock as we couldn't sell, we used to manage pretty tidy. When I was fourteen I took up with a girl. She lived in the same house as we did, and I used to walk out of a night with her and give her half-pints of beer at the publics. She were about thirteen, and used to dress werry nice, though she weren't above middling pretty. Now I'm working for another man as gives me a shilling a week, victuals, washing, and lodging, just as if I was one of the family.

'On a Sunday I goes out selling, and all I yarns I keeps. As for going to church, why, I can't afford it, – besides, to tell the truth, I don't like it well enough. Plays, too, ain't in my line much; I'd sooner go to a dance – it's more livelier. The "penny gaffs" is rather more in my style; the songs are out and out, and makes our gals laugh. The smuttier the better, I thinks; bless you! the gals likes it as much as we do. If we lads ever has a quarrel, why, we fights for it. If I was to let a cove off once, he'd do it again; but I never give a lad a chance, so long as I can get anigh him. I never heard about Christianity, but if a cove was to fetch me a lick of the head, I'd give it him again, whether he was a big 'un or a little 'un. I'd precious soon see a henemy of mine shot afore I'd forgive him, – where's the use? Do I understand what behaving to your neighbour is? – In coorse I do. If a feller as lives next me wanted a basket of mine as I wasn't using, why, he might have it; if I was working it though, I'd see him further! I can understand that all as lives in a court is neighbours; but as for policemen, they're nothing to me, and I should like to pay 'em all off well. No; I never heerd about this here creation you speaks about. In coorse God Almighty made the world, and the poor bricklayers' labourers built the houses afterwards – that's *my* opinion; but I can't say, for I've never been in no schools, only always hard at work, and knows nothing about it. I have heerd a little about our Saviour, – they seem to say he were a goodish kind of a man; but if he says as how a cove's to forgive a feller as hits you, I should say he know'd nothing about it. In coorse the gals the lads goes and lives with thinks our walloping 'em wery cruel of us, but we don't. Why don't we? – why, because we don't. Before father died, I used sometimes to say my prayers, but after that mother was too busy getting a living to mind about my praying. Yes, I knows! – in the Lord's prayer they says, "Forgive us our trespasses, as we forgives them as trespasses agin us." It's a very good thing, in coorse, but no costers can't do it.'

Of the 'Penny Gaff'

[pp. 42–4] In many of the thoroughfares of London there are shops which have been turned into a kind of temporary theatre (admission one penny), where dancing and singing take place every night. Rude pictures of the performers are arranged outside, to give the front a gaudy and attractive look, and at night-time coloured lamps and transparencies are displayed to draw an audience. These places are called by the costers 'Penny Gaffs'; and on a Monday night as many as six performances will take place, each one having its two hundred visitors.

It is impossible to contemplate the ignorance and immorality of so numerous a class as that of the costermongers, without wishing to discover the cause of their degradation. Let any one curious on this point visit one of these penny shows, and he will wonder that *any* trace of virtue and honesty should remain among the people. Here the stage, instead of being the means for illustrating a moral precept, is turned into a platform to teach the cruelest debauchery. The audience is usually composed of children so young, that these dens become the school-rooms where the guiding morals of a life are picked up; and so precocious are the little things, that the girl of nine will, from constant attendance at such places, have learnt to understand the filthiest sayings, and laugh at them as loudly as the grown-up lads around her. What notions can the young female form of marriage and chastity, when the penny theatre rings with applause at the performance of a scene whose sole point turns upon the pantomimic imitation of the unrestrained indulgence of the most corrupt appetites of our nature? How can the lad learn to check his hot passions and think honesty and virtue admirable, when the shouts around him impart a glory to a descriptive song so painfully corrupt, that it can only have been made tolerable by the most habitual excess? The men who preside over these infamous places know too well the failings of their audiences. They know that these poor children require no nicely-turned joke to make the evening pass merrily, and that the filth they utter needs no double meaning to veil its obscenity. The show that will provide the most unrestrained de-bauchery will have the most crowded benches; and to gain this point, things are acted and spoken that it is criminal even to allude to.

Not wishing to believe in the description which some of the more intelligent of the costermongers had given of these places, it was thought better to visit one of them, so that all exaggeration might be avoided. One of the least offensive of the exhibitions was fixed upon.

The 'penny gaff' chosen was situated in a broad street near Smithfield; and for a great distance off, the jingling sound of music was heard, and the gas-light streamed out into the thick night air as from a dark lantern, glittering on the windows of the houses opposite, and lighting up the faces of the mob in the road, as on an illumination night. The front of a large shop had been entirely removed, and the entrance was decorated with paintings of the 'comic singers', in their most 'humourous' attitudes. On a table against the wall was perched the band, playing what the costers call 'dancing tunes' with great effect, for the hole at the money-taker's box was blocked up with hands tendering the penny. The crowd without was so numerous, that a policeman was in attendance to preserve order, and push the boys off the pavement – the music having the effect of drawing them insensibly towards the festooned green-baize curtain.

The shop itself had been turned into a waiting-room, and was crowded even to the top of the stairs leading to the gallery on the first floor. The ceiling of this 'lobby' was painted blue, and spotted with whitewash clouds, to represent the heavens; the boards of the trap-door, and the laths that showed through the holes in the plaster, being all of the same colour. A notice was here posted, over the canvass door leading into the theatre, to the effect that 'LADIES AND GENTLEMEN TO THE FRONT PLACES MUST PAY TWOPENCE.'

The visitors, with a few exceptions, were all boys and girls, whose ages seemed to vary from eight to twenty years. Some of the girls – though their figures showed them to be mere children – were dressed in showy cotton-velvet polkas, and wore dowdy feathers in their crushed bonnets. They stood laughing and joking with the lads, in an unconcerned, impudent manner, that was almost appalling. Some of them, when tired of waiting, chose their partners, and commenced dancing grotesquely, to the admiration of the lookers-on, who expressed their approbation in obscene terms, that, far from disgusting the poor little women, were received as compliments, and acknowledged with smiles and coarse repartees. The boys clustered together, smoking their pipes, and laughing at each other's anecdotes, or else jingling halfpence in time with the tune, while they whistled an accompaniment to it. Presently one of the performers, with a gilt crown on his well greased locks, descended from the staircase, his fleshings covered by a dingy dressing-gown, and mixed with the mob, shaking hands with old acquaintances. The 'comic singer', too, made his appearance among the throng – the huge bow to his cravat, which nearly covered his waistcoat, and the red end to his nose, exciting neither merriment nor surprise.

To discover the kind of entertainment, a lad near me and my companion was asked 'if there was any flash dancing'. With a knowing wink the boy answered, 'Lots! show their legs and all, prime!' and immediately the boy followed up his information by a request for a 'yennep' to get a 'tib of occabot'. After waiting in the lobby some considerable time, the performance inside was concluded, and the audience came pouring out through the canvass door. As they had to pass singly, I noticed them particularly. Above three-fourths of them were women and girls, the rest consisting chiefly of mere boys – for out of about two hundred persons I counted only eighteen men. Forward they came, bringing an overpowering stench with them, laughing and yelling as they pushed their way through the waiting-room. One woman carrying a sickly child with a bulging forehead, was reeling drunk, the saliva running down her mouth as she stared about her with a heavy fixed eye. Two boys were pushing her from side to side, while the poor infant slept, breathing heavily, as if stupified, through the din. Lads jumping on girls' shoulders, and girls laughing hysterically from being tickled by the youths behind them, every one shouting and jumping, presented a mad scene of frightful enjoyment.

When these had left, a rush for places by those in waiting began, that set at defiance the blows and strugglings of a lady in spangles who endeavoured to preserve order and take the checks. As time was a great object with the proprietor, the entertainment within began directly the first seat was taken, so that the lads without, rendered furious by the rattling of the piano within, made the canvass partition bulge in and out, with the strugglings of those seeking admission, like a sail in a flagging wind.

To form the theatre, the first floor had been removed; the whitewashed beams however still stretched from wall to wall. The lower room had evidently been the warehouse, while the upper apartment had been the sitting-room, for the paper was still on the walls. A gallery, with a canvass front, had been hurriedly built up, and it was so fragile that the boards bent under the weight of those above. The bricks in the warehouse were smeared over with red paint, and had a few black curtains daubed upon them. The coster-youths require no very great scenic embellishment, and indeed the stage – which was about eight feet square – could admit of none. Two jets of gas, like those outside a butcher's shop, were placed on each side of the proscenium, and proved very handy for the gentlemen whose pipes required lighting. The band inside the 'theatre' could not compare with the band without. An old grand piano, whose canvass-covered top extended the entire length of the stage, sent forth its wiry notes under the be-ringed fingers of a 'professor Wilkinsini', while another professional, with his head resting on his violin, played vigorously, as he stared unconcernedly at the noisy audience.

Singing and dancing formed the whole of the hours' performance, and, of the two, the singing was preferred. A young girl, of about fourteen years of age, danced with more energy than grace, and seemed to be well-known to the spectators, who cheered her on by her Christian name. When the dance was concluded, the proprietor of the establishment threw down a penny from the gallery, in the hopes that others might be moved to similar acts of generosity; but no one followed up the offering, so the young lady hunted after the money and departed. The 'comic singer', in a battered hat and the huge bow to his cravat, was received with deafening shouts.

Several songs were named by the costers, but the 'funny gentleman' merely requested them 'to hold their jaw', and putting on a 'knowing' look, sang a song, the whole point of which consisted in the mere utterance of some filthy word at the end of each stanza. Nothing, however, could have been more successful. The lads stamped their feet with delight; the girls screamed with enjoyment. Once or twice a young shrill laugh would anticipate the fun – as if the words were well known – or the boys would forestall the point by shouting it out before the proper time. When the song was ended the house was in a delirium of applause. The canvass front to the gallery was beaten with sticks, drum-like, and sent down showers of white powder on the heads in the pit. Another song followed, and the actor knowing on what his success depended, lost no opportunity of increasing his laurels. The most obscene thoughts, the most disgusting scenes were coolly described, making a poor child near me wipe away the tears that rolled down her eyes with the enjoyment of the poison. There were three or four of these songs sung in the course of the evening, each one being encored, and then changed. One written about 'Pine-apple rock', was the grand treat of the night, and offered greater scope to the rhyming powers of the author than any of the others. In this, not a single chance had been missed; ingenuity had been exerted to its utmost lest an obscene thought should be passed by, and it was absolutely awful to behold the relish with which the young ones jumped to the hideous meaning of the verses.

There was one scene yet to come, that was perfect in its wickedness. A ballet began between a man dressed up as a woman, and a country clown. The most disgusting attitudes were struck, the most immoral acts represented, without one dissenting voice. If there had been any feat of agility, any grimacing, or, in fact, anything with which the laughter of the uneducated classes is usually associated, the applause might have been accounted for; but here were two ruffians degrading themselves each time they stirred a limb, and forcing into the brains of the childish audience before them thoughts that must embitter a lifetime, and descend from father to child like some bodily infirmity.

When I had left, I spoke to a better class costermonger on this saddening subject. 'Well, sir, it is frightful,' he said, 'but the boys will have their amusements. If their amusements is bad they don't care; they only wants to laugh, and this here kind of work does it. Give 'em better singing and better dancing, and they'd go, if the price was as cheap as this is. I've seen, when a decent concert was given at a penny, as many as four thousand costers present, behaving themselves as quietly and decently as possible.

Their wives and children was with 'em, and no audience was better conducted. It's all stuff talking about them preferring this sort of thing. Give 'em good things at the same price, and I *know* they will like the good, better than the bad.'

My own experience with this neglected class goes to prove, that if we would really lift them out of the moral mire in which they are wallowing, the first step must be to provide them with *wholesome* amusements. The misfortune, however, is, that when we seek to elevate the character of the people, we give them such mere dry abstract truths and dogmas to digest, that the uneducated mind turns with abhorrence from them. We forget how we ourselves were originally won by our *emotions* to the consideration of such subjects. We do not remember how our own tastes have been formed, nor do we, in our zeal, stay to reflect how the tastes of a people generally are created; and, consequently, we cannot perceive that a habit of enjoying any matter whatsoever can only be induced in the mind by linking with it some aesthetic affection. The heart is the mainspring of the intellect, and the feelings the real educers and educators of the thoughts. As games with the young destroy the fatigue of muscular exercise, so do the sympathies stir the mind to action without any sense of effort. It is because 'serious' people generally object to enlist the emotions in the education of the poor, and look upon the delight which arises in the mind from the mere perception of the beauty of sound, motion, form, and colour – or from the apt association of harmonious or incongruous ideas – or from the sympathetic operation of the affections; it is because, I say, the zealous portion of society look upon these matters as *'vanity'*, that the amusements of the working-classes are left to venal traders to provide. Hence, in the low-priced entertainments which necessarily appeal to the poorer, and, therefore, to the least educated of the people, the proprietors, instead of trying to develop in them the purer sources of delight, seek only to gratify their audience in the coarsest manner, by appealing to their most brutal appetites. And thus the emotions, which the great Architect of the human mind gave us as the means of quickening our imaginations and refining our sentiments, are made the instruments of crushing every operation of the intellect and debasing our natures. It is idle and unfeeling to believe that the great majority of a people whose days are passed in excessive toil, and whose homes are mostly of an uninviting character, will forego *all* amusements, and consent to pass their evenings by their *no* firesides, reading tracts or singing hymns. It is folly to fancy that the mind, spent with the irksomeness of compelled labour, and depressed, perhaps, with the struggle to live by that labour after all, will not, when the work is over, seek out some place where at least it can forget its troubles or fatigues in the temporary pleasure begotten by some mental or physical stimulant. It is because we exact too much of the poor – because we, as it were, strive to make true knowledge and true beauty as forbidding as possible to the uneducated and unrefined, that they fly to their penny gaffs, their twopenny-hops, their beer-shops, and their gambling grounds for pleasures which we deny them, and which we, in our arrogance, believe it is possible for them to do without.

The experiment so successfully tried at Liverpool of furnishing music of an enlivening and yet elevating character at the same price as the concerts of the lowest grade, shows that the people may be won to delight in beauty instead of beastiality, and teaches us again that it is *our* fault to allow them to be as they are and not theirs to remain so. All men are compound animals, with many inlets of pleasure to their brains, and if one avenue be closed against them, why it but forces them to seek delight through another. So far from the perception of beauty inducing habits of gross enjoyment as 'serious' people generally imagine, a moment's reflection will tell us that these very habits are only the necessary consequences of the non-development of the aesthetic faculty; for the two assuredly cannot co-exist. To cultivate the sense of the beautiful is necessarily to inculcate a detestation of the sensual. Moreover, it is impossible for the mind to be accustomed to the contemplation of what is admirable without continually mounting to higher and higher forms of it – from the beauty of nature to that of thought – from thought to feeling, from feeling to action, and lastly to the fountain of all goodness – the great munificent Creator of the sea, the mountains, and the flowers – the stars, the sunshine, and the rainbow – the fancy, the reason, the love and the heroism of man and womankind – the instincts of the beasts – the glory of the angels – and the mercy of Christ.

Of the Coster-girls

[pp. 45–7] The costermongers, taken as a body, entertain the most imperfect idea of the sanctity of marriage. To their undeveloped minds it merely consists in the fact of a man and woman living together, and sharing the gains they may each earn by selling in the street. The father and mother of the girl look upon it as a convenient means of shifting the support of their child over to another's exertions; and so thoroughly do they believe this to be the end and aim of matrimony, that the expense of a church ceremony is considered as a useless waste of money, and the new pair are received by their companions as cordially as if every form of law and religion had been complied with.

The notions of morality among these people agree strangely, as I have said, with those of many savage tribes – indeed, it would be curious if it were otherwise. They are a part of the Nomades of England, neither knowing nor caring for the enjoyments of home. The hearth, which is so sacred a symbol to all civilized races as being the spot where the virtues of each succeeding generation are taught and encouraged, has no charms to them. The tap-room is the father's chief abiding place; whilst to the mother the house is only a better kind of *tent*. She is away at the stall, or hawking her goods from morning till night, while the children are left to play away the day in the court or alley, and pick their morals out of the gutter. So long as the limbs gain strength the parent cares for nothing else. As the younger ones grow up, their only notions of wrong are formed by what the policeman will permit them to do. If we, who have known from babyhood the kindly influences of a home, require, before we are thrust out into the world to get a living for ourselves, that our perceptions of good and evil should be quickened and brightened (the same as our perceptions of truth and falsity) by the experience and counsel of those who are wiser and better than ourselves, – if, indeed, it needed a special creation and example to teach the best and strongest of us the law of right, how bitterly must the children of the street-folk require tuition, training, and advice, when from their very cradles (if, indeed, they ever know such luxuries) they are doomed to witness in their parents, whom they naturally believe to be their superiors, habits of life in which passion is the sole rule of action, and where every appetite of our animal nature is indulged in without the least restraint.

I say thus much because I am anxious to make others feel, as I do myself, that *we* are the culpable parties in these matters. That they poor things should do as they do is but human nature – but that *we* should allow them to remain thus destitute of every blessing vouchsafed to ourselves – that we should willingly share what we enjoy with our brethren at the Antipodes, and yet leave those who are nearer and who, therefore, should be dearer to us, to want even the commonest moral necessaries is a paradox that gives to the zeal of our Christianity a strong savour of the chicanery of Cant.

The costermongers strongly resemble the North American Indians in their conduct to their wives. They can understand that it is the duty of the woman to contribute to the happiness of the man, but cannot feel that there is a reciprocal duty from the man to the woman. The wife is considered as an inexpensive servant, and the disobedience of a wish is punished with blows. She must work early and late, and to the husband must be given the proceeds of her labour. Often when the man is in one of his drunken fits – which sometimes last two or three days continuously – she must by her sole exertions find food for herself and him too. To live in peace with him, there must be no murmuring, no tiring under work, no fancied cause for jealousy – for if there be, she is either beaten into submission or cast adrift to begin life again – as another's leavings.

The story of one coster-girl's life may be taken as a type of the many. When quite young she is placed out to nurse with some neighbour, the mother – if a fond one – visiting the child at certain periods of the day, for the purpose of feeding it, or sometimes, knowing the round she has to make, having the infant brought to her at certain places, to be 'suckled'. As soon as it is old enough to go alone, the court is its play-ground, the gutter its school-room, and under the care of an elder sister the little one passes the day, among children whose mothers like her own are too busy out in the streets helping to get the food, to be able to mind the family at home. When the girl is strong enough, she in her turn is made to assist the mother by keeping guard over the younger children, or, if there be none, she is lent out to carry about a baby, and so made to add to the family income by gaining her sixpence weekly. Her time is from the earliest years fully occupied; indeed, her parents cannot afford to keep her without doing and getting *something*. Very few of the children receive the least education. 'The parents,' I am told, 'never give their minds to learning, for they say, "What's the use of it? *that* won't yarn a gal a living."' Everything is sacrificed – as, indeed, under the circumstances it must be – in the struggle to live – aye! and to live *merely*. Mind, heart, soul, are all absorbed in the belly. The rudest form of animal life, physiologists tell us, is simply a locomotive stomach. Verily, it would appear as if our social state had a tendency to make the highest animal sink into the lowest.

At about seven years of age the girls first go into the streets to sell. A shallow-basket is given to them, with about two shillings for stock-money, and they hawk, according to the time of year, either oranges, apples, or violets; some begin their street education with the sale of water-cresses. The money earned by this means is strictly given to the parents. Sometimes – though rarely – a girl who has been unfortunate during the day will not dare to return home at night, and then she will sleep under some dry arch or about some market, until the morrow's gains shall ensure her a safe reception and shelter in her father's room.

The life of the coster-girls is as severe as that of the boys. Between four and five in the morning they have to leave home for the markets, and sell in the streets until about nine. Those that have more kindly parents, return then to breakfast, but many are obliged to earn the morning's meal for themselves. After breakfast, they generally remain in the streets until about ten o'clock at night; many having nothing during all that time but one meal of bread and butter and coffee, to enable them to support the fatigue of walking from street to street with the heavy basket on their heads. In the course of a day, some girls eat as much as a pound of bread, and very seldom get any meat, unless it be on a Sunday.

There are many poor families that, without the aid of these girls, would be forced into the workhouse. They are generally of an affectionate disposition, and some will perform acts of marvellous heroism to keep together the little home. It is not at all unusual for mere children of fifteen to walk their eight or ten miles a day, carrying a basket of nearly two hundred weight on their heads. A journey to Woolwich and back, or to the towns near London, is often undertaken to earn the 1s. 6d. their parents are anxiously waiting for at home.

Very few of these girls are married to the men they afterwards live with. Their courtship is usually a very short one; for, as one told me, 'the life is such a hard one, that a girl is ready to get rid of a *little* of the labour at any price.' The coster-lads see the girls at market, and if one of them be pretty, and a boy take a fancy to her, he will make her bargains for her, and carry her basket home. Sometimes a coster working his rounds will feel a liking for a wench selling her goods in the street, and will leave his barrow to go and talk with her. A girl seldom takes up with a lad before she is sixteen, though some of them, when barely fifteen or even fourteen, will pair off. They court for a time, going to raffles and 'gaffs' together, and then the affair is arranged. The girl tells her parents 'she's going to keep company with so-and-so', packs up what things she has, and goes at once, without a word of remonstrance from either father or mother. A furnished room, at about 4s. a week, is taken, and the young couple begin life. The lad goes out as usual with his barrow, and the girl goes out with her basket, often working harder for her lover than she had done for her parents. They go to market together, and at about nine o'clock her day's selling begins. Very often she will take out with her in the morning what food she requires during the day, and never return home until eleven o'clock at night.

The men generally behave very cruelly to the girls they live with. They are as faithful to them as if they were married, but they are jealous in the extreme. To see a man talking to their girl is sufficient to ensure the poor thing a beating. They sometimes ill-treat them horribly – most unmercifully indeed – nevertheless the girls say they cannot help loving them still, and continue working for them, as if they experienced only kindness at their hands. Some of the men are gentler and more considerate in their treatment of them, but by far the larger portion are harsh and merciless. Often when the Saturday night's earnings of the two have been large, the man will take the entire money, and as soon as the Sunday's dinner is over, commence drinking hard, and continue drunk for two or three days together, until the funds are entirely exhausted. The women never gamble; they say, 'it gives them no excitement.' They prefer, if they have a spare moment in the evening, sitting near the fire making up and patching their clothes. 'Ah, sir,' said a girl to me, 'a neat gown does a deal with a man; he always likes a girl best when everybody else likes her too.' On a Sunday they clean their room for the week and go for a treat, if they can persuade their young man to take them out in the afternoon, either to Chalk Farm or Battersea Fields – 'where there's plenty of life'.

After a girl has once grown accustomed to a street-life, it is almost impossible to wean her from it. The muscular irritability begotten by continued wandering makes her unable to rest for any time in one place, and she soon, if put to any *settled* occupation, gets to crave for the severe exercise she formerly enjoyed. The least restraint will make her sigh after the perfect liberty of the coster's 'roving life'. As an instance of this I may relate a fact that has occurred within the last six months. A gentleman of high literary repute, struck with the heroic strugglings of a coster Irish girl to maintain her mother, took her to his house, with a view of teaching her the duties of a servant. At first the transition was a painful one to the poor thing. Having travelled barefoot through the streets since a mere child, the pressure of shoes was intolerable to her, and in the evening or whenever a few minutes' rest could be obtained, the boots were taken off, for with them on she could enjoy no ease. The perfect change of life, and the novelty of being in a new place, reconciled her for some time to the loss of her liberty. But no sooner did she hear from her friends, that sprats were again in the market, than, as if there were some magical influence in the fish, she at once requested to be freed from the confinement, and permitted to return to her old calling.

Such is the history of the lower class of girls, though this lower class, I regret to say, constitutes by far the greater portion of the whole. Still I would not for a moment have it inferred that *all* are bad. There are many young girls getting their living, or rather helping to get the living of others in the streets, whose goodness, considering the temptations and hardships besetting such an occupation, approximates to the marvellous. As a type of the more prudent class of coster-girls, I would cite the following narrative received from the lips of a young woman in answer to a series of questions.

The Life of a Coster-girl

[pp. 47–8] I wished to have obtained a statement from the girl whose portrait is here given, but she was afraid to give the slightest information about the habits of her companions, lest they should recognize her by the engraving and persecute her for the revelations she might make. After disappointing me some dozen times, I was forced to seek out some other coster girl.

The one I fixed upon was a fine-grown young woman of eighteen. She had a habit of curtseying to every question that was put to her. Her plaid shawl was tied over the breast, and her cotton-velvet bonnet was crushed in with carrying her basket. She seemed dreadfully puzzled where to put her hands, at one time tucking them under her shawl, warming them at the fire, or measuring the length of her apron, and when she answered a question she invariably addressed the fireplace. Her voice was husky from shouting apples.

'My mother has been in the streets selling all her lifetime. Her uncle learnt her the markets and she learnt me. When business grew bad she said to me, "Now you shall take care on the stall, and I'll go and work out charing." The way she learnt me the markets was to judge of the weight of the baskets of apples, and then said she, "Always bate 'em down, a'most a half." I always liked the street-life very well, that was if I was selling. I have mostly kept a stall myself, but I've known gals as walk about with apples, as have told me that the weight of the baskets is sich that the neck cricks, and when the load is took off, its just as if you'd a stiff neck, and the head feels as light as a feather. The gals begins working very early at our work; the parents makes them go out when a'most babies. There's a little gal, I'm sure she an't more than half-past seven, that stands selling water-cresses next my stall, and mother was saying, "Only look there, how that little one has to get her living afore she a'most knows what a penn'orth means."

'There's six on us in family, and father and mother makes eight. Father used to do odd jobs with the gas-pipes in the streets, and when work was slack we had very hard times of it. Mother always liked being with us at home, and used to manage to keep us employed out of mischief – she'd give us an old gown to make into pinafores for the children and such like! She's been very good to us, has mother, and so's father. She always liked to hear us read to her whilst she was washing or such like! and then we big ones had to learn the little ones. But when father's work got slack, if she had no employment charing, she'd say, "Now I'll go and buy a bushel of apples," and then she'd turn out and get a penny that way. I suppose by sitting at the stall from nine in the morning till the shops shuts up – say ten o'clock at night, I can earn about 1s. 6d. a day. It's all according to the apples – whether they're good or not – what we makes. If I'm unlucky, mother will say, "Well, I'll go out to-morrow and see what I can do;" and if I've done well, she'll say "Come you're a good hand at it; you've done famous." Yes, mother's very fair that way. Ah! there's many a gal I knows whose back has to suffer if she don't sell her stock well; but, thank God! I never get more than a blowing up. My parents is very fair to me.

'I dare say there ain't ten out of a hundred gals what's living with men, what's been married Church of England fashion. I know plenty myself, but I don't, indeed, think it right. It seems to me that the gals is fools to be 'ticed away, but, in coorse, they needn't go without they likes. This is why I don't think it's right. Perhaps a man will have a few words with his gal, and he'll say, "Oh! I ain't obligated to keep her!" and he'll turn her out: and then where's that poor gal to go! Now, there's a gal I knows as came to me no later than this here week, and she had a dreadful swole face and a awful black eye; and I says, "Who's done that?" and she says, says she, "Why, Jack" – just in that way; and then she says, says she, "I'm going to take a warrant out to-morrow." Well, he gets the warrant that same night, but she never appears again him, for fear of getting more beating. That don't seem to me to be like married people ought to be. Besides, if parties is married, they ought to bend to each other; and they won't, for sartain, if they're only living together. A man as is married is obligated to keep his wife if they quarrels or not; and he says to himself, says he, "Well, I may as well live happy, like." But if he can turn a poor gal off, as soon as he tires of her, he begins to have noises with her, and then gets quit of her altogether. Again, the men takes the money of the gals, and in coorse ought to treat 'em well – which they don't. This is another reason: when the gal is in the family way, the lads mostly sends them to the workhouse to lay in, and only goes sometimes to take them a bit of

THE COSTER-GIRL.

"Apples! An 'aypenny a lot, Apples!"

tea and shuggar; but, in coorse, married men wouldn't behave in such likes to their poor wives. After a quarrel, too, a lad goes and takes up with another young gal, and that isn't pleasant for the first one. The first step to ruin is them places of "penny gaffs", for they hears things there as oughtn't to be said to young gals. Besides, the lads is very insinivating, and after leaving them places will give a gal a drop of beer, and make her half tipsy, and then they makes their arrangements. I've often heerd the boys boasting of having ruined gals, for all the world as if they was the first noblemen in the land.

'It would be a good thing if these sort of doings on could be stopped. It's half the parents' fault; for if a gal can't get a living, they turns her out into the streets, and then what's to become of her? I'm sure the gals, if they was married, would be happier, because they couldn't be beat worse. And if they was married, they'd get a nice home about 'em; whereas, if they's only living together, they takes a furnished room. I'm sure, too, that it's a bad plan; for I've heerd the gals themselves say, "Ah! I wish I'd never seed Jack" (or Tom, or whatever it is); "I'm sure I'd never be half so bad but for him."

'Only last night father was talking about religion. We often talks about religion. Father has told me that God made the world, and I've heerd him talk about the first man and woman as was made and lived – it must be more than a hundred years ago – but I don't like to speak on what I don't know. Father, too, has told me about our Saviour what was nailed on a cross to suffer for such poor people as we is. Father has told us, too, about his giving a great many poor people a penny loaf and a bit of fish each, which proves him to have been a very kind gentleman. The Ten Commandments was made by him, I've heerd say, and he performed them too among other miracles. Yes! this is part of what our Saviour tells us. We are to forgive everybody, and do nobody no injury. I don't think I could forgive an enemy if she injured me very much; I'm sure I don't know why I couldn't, unless it is that I'm poor, and never learnt to do it. If a gal stole my shawl and didn't return it back or give me the value on it, I couldn't forgive her; but if she told me she lost it off her back, I shouldn't be so hard on her. We poor gals ain't very religious, but we are better than the men. We all of us thanks God for everything – even for a fine day; as for sprats, we always says they're God's blessing for the poor, and thinks it hard of the Lord Mayor not to let 'em come in afore the ninth of November, just because he wants to dine off them – which he always do. Yes, we knows for certain that they eats plenty of sprats at the Lord Mayor's "blanket". They say in the Bible that the world was made in six days: the beasts, the birds, the fish, and all – and sprats was among them in coorse. There was only one house at that time as was made, and that was the Ark for Adam and Eve and their family. It seems very wonderful indeed how all this world was done so quick. I should have thought that England alone would have took double the time; shouldn't you, sir? But then it says in the Bible, God Almighty's a just and true God, and in coorse time would be nothing to him. When a good person is dying, we says, "The Lord has called upon him, and he must go," but I can't think what it means, unless it is that an angel comes – like when we're a-dreaming – and tells the party he's wanted in heaven. I know where heaven is; it's above the clouds, and they're placed there to prevent us seeing into it. That's where all the good people go, but I'm afeerd,' – she continued solemnly – 'there's very few costers among the angels – 'specially those as deceives poor gals.

'No, I don't think this world could well go on for ever. There's a great deal of ground in it, certainly, and it seems very strong at present; but they say there's to be a flood on the earth, and earthquakes, and that will destroy it. The earthquake ought to have took place some time ago, as people tells me, but I never heerd any more about it. If we cheats in the streets, I know we shan't go to Heaven; but it's very hard upon us, for if we didn't cheat we couldn't live, profits is so bad. It's the same with the shops, and I suppose the young men there won't go to Heaven neither; but if people won't give the money, both costers and tradesmen must cheat, and that's very hard. Why, look at apples! customers want them for less than they cost us, and so we are forced to shove in bad ones as well as good ones; and if we're to suffer for that, it does seem to be dreadful cruel.'

Curious and extravagant as this statement may perhaps appear to the uninitiated, nevertheless it is here given as it was spoken; and it was spoken with an earnestness that proved the poor girl looked upon it as a subject, the solemnity of which forced her to be truthful.

Of Costermongers and Thieves

[p. 48] Concerning the connection of these two classes I had the following account from a costermonger: 'I've known the coster trade for twelve years, and never knew thieves go out a costering as a cloak; they may have done so, but I very much doubt it. Thieves go for an idle life, and costermongering don't suit them. Our chaps don't care a d—n who they associate with – if they're thieves they meet 'em all the same, or anything that way. But costers buy what they call "a gift" – may-be it's a watch or coat wot's been stolen – from any that has it to sell. A man will say: "If you've a few shillings, you may have a good thing of it. Why, this identical watch is only twenty shillings, and it's worth fifty"; so if the coster has money, he buys. Thieves will get 3d. where a mechanic or a coster will earn $\frac{1}{2}d$., and the most ignorant of our people has a queer sort of respect for thieves, because of the money they make. Poverty's as much despised among costers as among other people. People that's badly off among us are called "cursed". In bad weather it's common for costers to "curse themselves", as they call having no trade. "Well, I'm cursed," they say when they can make no money. It's a common thing among them to shout after any one they don't like, that's reduced, "Well, ain't you cursed?"' The costers, I am credibly informed, gamble a great deal with the wealthier class of thieves, and win of them the greater part of the money they get.

Of the Character of the Street-stalls

[p. 103] The stalls occupied by costermongers for the sale of fish, fruit, vegetables, &c., are chiefly constructed of a double cross-trestle or move-able frame, or else of two trestles, each with three legs, upon which is laid a long deal board, or tray. Some of the stalls consist merely of a few boards resting upon two baskets, or upon two herring-barrels. The fish-stalls are mostly covered with paper – generally old newspapers or periodicals – but some of the street-fishmongers, instead of using paper to display their fish upon, have introduced a thin marble slab, which gives the stall a cleaner, and, what they consider a high attribute, a 'respectable' appearance.

Most of the fruit-stalls are, in the winter time, fitted up with an apparatus for roasting apples and chestnuts; this generally consists of an old saucepan with a fire inside; and the woman who vends them, huddled up in her old faded shawl or cloak, often presents a picturesque appearance, in the early evening, or in a fog, with the gleam of the fire lighting up her half somnolent figure. Within the last two or three years, however, there has been so large a business carried on in roasted chest-nuts, that it has become a distinct street-trade, and the vendors have provided themselves with an iron apparatus, large enough to roast nearly half a bushel at a time. At the present time, however, the larger apparatus is less common in the streets, and more frequent in the shops, than in the previous winter.

There are, moreover, peculiar kinds of stalls – such as the hot eels and hot peas-soup stalls, having tin oval pots, with a small chafing-dish containing a charcoal fire underneath each, to keep the eels or soup hot. The early breakfast stall has two capacious tin cans filled with tea or coffee, kept hot by the means before described, and some are lighted up by two or three large oil-lamps; the majority of these stalls, in the winter time, are sheltered from the wind by a screen made out of an old clothes horse covered with tarpaulin. The cough-drop stand, with its distilling apparatus, the tin worm curling nearly the whole length of the tray, has but lately been introduced. The nut-stall is fitted up with a target at the back of it. The ginger-beer stand may be seen in almost every street, with its French-polished mahogany frame and bright polished taps, and its foot-bath-shaped reservoir of water, to cleanse the glasses. The hot elder wine stand, with its bright brass urns, is equally popular.

The sellers of plum-pudding, 'cake, a penny a slice', sweetmeats, cough-drops, pin-cushions, jewellery, chimney ornaments, tea and tablespoons, make use of a table covered over, some with old newspapers, or a piece of oil-cloth, upon which are exposed their articles for sale.

Such is the usual character of the street-stalls. There are, however, 'stands' or 'cans' peculiar to certain branches of the street-trade. The most important of these, such as the baked-potatoe can, and the meat-pie stand, I have before described.

The other means adopted by the street-sellers for the exhibition of their various goods at certain 'pitches' or fixed localities are as follows. Straw bonnets, boys' caps, women's caps, and prints, are generally arranged for sale in large umbrellas, placed 'upside down'. Haberdashery, with rolls of ribbons, edgings, and lace, some street-sellers display on a stall; whilst others have a board at the edge of the pavement, and expose their wares upon it as tastefully as they can. Old shoes, patched up and well blacked, ready for the purchaser's feet, and tin ware, are often ranged upon the ground, or, where the stock is small, a stall or table is used.

Many stationary street-sellers use merely baskets, or trays, either supported in their hand, or on their arm, or else they are strapped round their loins, or suspended round their necks. These are mostly fruit-women, watercress, blacking, congreves, sheep's-trotters, and ham-sandwich sellers.

Many stationary street-sellers stand on or near the bridges; others near the steam-packet wharfs or the railway terminuses; a great number of them take their pitch at the entrance to a court, or at the corners of streets; and stall-keepers with oysters stand opposite the doors of public-houses.

It is customary for a street-seller who wants to 'pitch' in a new locality to solicit the leave of the housekeeper, opposite whose premises he desires to place his stall. Such leave obtained, no other course is necessary.

Of Fruit-stall Keepers

[pp. 103–4] I had the following statement from a woman who has 'kept a stall' in Marylebone, at the corner of a street, which she calls 'my corner', for 38 years. I was referred to her as a curious type of the class of stall-keepers, and on my visit, found her daughter at the 'pitch'. This daughter had all the eloquence which is attractive in a street-seller, and so, I found, had her mother when she joined us. They are profuse in blessings; and on a bystander observing, when he heard the name of these street-sellers, that a jockey of that name had won the Derby lately, the daughter exclaimed, 'To be sure he did; he's my own uncle's relation, and what a lot of money came into the family! Bless God for all things, and bless every body! Walnuts, sir, walnuts, a penny a dozen! Wouldn't give you a bad one for the world, which is a great thing for a poor 'oman for to offer to do.' The daughter was dressed in a drab great-coat, which covered her whole person. When I saw the mother, she carried a similar great-coat, as she was on her way to the stall; and she used it as ladies do with their muffs, burying her hands in it. The mother's dark-coloured old clothes seemed, to borrow a description from Sir Walter Scott, flung on with a pitchfork. These two women were at first very suspicious, and could not be made to understand my object in questioning them; but after a little while, the mother became not only communicative, but garrulous, conversing – with no small impatience at any interruption – of the doings of the people in her neighbourhood. I was accompanied by an intelligent costermonger, who assured me of his certitude that the old woman's statement was perfectly correct, and I found moreover from other inquiries that it was so.

'Well, sir,' she began, 'what is it you want of me? Do I owe you anything? There's half-pay officers about here for no good; what is it you want? Hold your tongue, you young fool,' (to her daughter, who was beginning to speak;) 'what do you know about it?' [On my satisfying her that I had no desire to injure her, she continued, to say after spitting, a common practice with her class, on a piece of money, 'for luck',] 'Certainly, sir, that's very proper and good. Aye, I've seen the world – the town world and the country. I don't know where I was born; never mind about that – it's nothing to nobody. I don't know nothing about my father and mother; but I know that afore I was eleven I went through the country with my missis. She was a smuggler. I didn't know then what smuggling was – bless you, sir, I didn't; I knew no more nor I know who made that lamp-post. I didn't know the taste of the stuff we smuggled for two years – didn't know it from small beer; I've known it well enough since, God knows. My missis made a deal of money that time at Deptford Dockyard. The men wasn't paid and let out till twelve of a night – I hardly mind what night it was, days was so alike then – and they was our customers till one, two, or three in the morning – Sunday morning, for anything I know. I don't know what my missis gained; something jolly, there's not a fear of it. She was kind enough to me. I don't know how long I was with missis. After that I was a hopping, and made my 15s. regular at it, and a haymaking; but I've had a pitch at my corner for thirty-eight year – aye! turned thirty-eight. It's no use asking me what I made at first – I can't tell; but I'm sure I made more than twice as much as my daughter and me makes now, the two of us. I wish people that thinks we're idle now were with me for a day. I'd teach them. I don't – that's the two of us don't – make 15s. a week now, nor the half of it, when all's paid. D—d if I do. The d—d boys take care of that.' [Here I had a statement of the boys' tradings, similar to what I have given.] 'There's "Canterbury" has lots of boys, and they bother me. I can tell, and always could, how it is with working men. When mechanics is in good work, their children has half-pennies to spend with me. If they're hard up, there's no halfpennies. The pennies go to a loaf or to buy a candle. I might have saved money once, but had a misfortunate family. My husband? O, never mind about him. D—n him. I've been a widow many years. My son – it's nothing how many children I have – is married; he had the care of an ingine. But he lost it from ill health. It was in a feather-house, and the flue got down his throat, and coughed him; and so he went into the country, 108 miles off, to his wife's mother. But his wife's mother got her living by wooding, and other ways, and couldn't help him or his wife; so he left, and he's with me now. He has a job sometimes with a greengrocer, at 6d. a day and a bit of grub; a little bit – very. I must shelter him. I couldn't turn him out. If a Turk I knew was in distress, and I had only half a loaf, I'd give him half of that, if he was ever such a Turk – I would, sir! Out of 6d. a day, my son – poor fellow, he's only twenty-seven! – wants a bit of 'baccy and a pint of beer. It 'ud be unnatural to oppose that, wouldn't it, sir? He frets about his wife, that's staying with her mother, 108 miles off; and about his little girl; but I tell him to wait, and he may have more little girls. God knows, they come when they're not wanted a bit. I joke and say all my old sweethearts is dying away. Old Jemmy went off sudden. He lent me money sometimes, but I always paid him. He had a public once, and had some money when he died. I saw him the day afore he died. He was in bed, but wasn't his own man quite; though he spoke sensible enough to me. He said, said he, "Won't you have half a quartern of rum, as we've often had it?" "Certainly, Jemmy," says I, "I came for that very thing." Poor fellow! his friends are quarrelling now about what he left. It's 56l. they say, and they'll go to law very likely, and lose every thing. There'll be no such quarrelling when I die, unless it is for the pawn-tickets. I get a meal now, and got a meal afore; but it was a better meal then, sir. Then look at my expenses. I was a customer once, I used to buy, and plenty such did, blue cloth aprons, opposite Drury-lane theatre: the very shop's there still, but I don't know what it is now; I can't call to mind. I gave 2s. 6d. a yard, from twenty to thirty years ago, for an apron, and it took two yards, and I paid 4d. for making it, and so an apron cost 5s. 4d. – that wasn't much thought of in those times. I used to be different off then. I never go to church; I used to go when I was a little child at Sevenoaks. I suppose I was born somewhere thereabouts. I've forgot what the inside of a church is like. There's no costermongers ever go to church, except the rogues of them, that wants to appear good. I buy my fruit at Covent-garden. Apples is now 4s. 6d. a bushel there. I may make twice that in selling them; but a bushel may last me two, three, or four days.'

As I have already, under the street-sale of fish, given an account of the oyster stall-keeper, as well as the stationary dealers in sprats, and the principal varieties of wet fish, there is no necessity for me to continue this part of my subject.

THE HOMES OF THE STREET-IRISH

[pp. 115–17] In almost all of the poorer districts of London are to be found 'nests of Irish' – as they are called – or courts inhabited solely by the Irish costermongers. These people form separate colonies, rarely visiting or mingling with the English costers. It is curious, on walking through one of these settlements, to notice the manner in which the Irish deal among themselves – street-seller buying of street-seller. Even in some of the smallest courts there may be seen stalls of vegetables, dried herrings, or salt cod, thriving, on the associative principle, by mutual support.

The parts of London that are the most thickly populated with Irish lie about Brook-street, Ratcliff-cross, down both sides of the Commercial-road, and in Rosemary-lane, though nearly all the 'coster-districts' have their Irish settlements – Cromer-street, Saffron-hill and King-street, Drury-lane, for instance, being thickly peopled with the Irish; but the places I have mentioned above are peculiarly distinguished, by being almost entirely populated by visitors from the sister isle.

The same system of immigration is pursued in London as in America. As soon as the first settler is thriving in his newly chosen country, a certain portion of his or her earnings are carefully hoarded up, until they are sufficient to pay for the removal of another member of the family to England; then one of the friends left 'at home' is sent for; and thus by degrees the entire family is got over, and once more united.

Perhaps there is no quarter of London where the habits and habitations of the Irish can be better seen and studied than in Rosemary-lane, and the little courts and alleys that spring from it on each side. Some of these courts have other courts branching off from them, so that the locality is a perfect labyrinth of 'blind alleys'; and when once in the heart of the maze it is difficult to find the path that leads to the main-road. As you walk down 'the lane', and peep through the narrow openings between the houses, the place seems like a huge peep-show, with dark holes of gateways to look through, while the court within appears bright with the daylight; and down it are seen rough-headed urchins running with their feet bare through the puddles, and bonnetless girls, huddled in shawls, lolling against the door-posts. Sometimes you see a long narrow alley, with the houses so close together that opposite neighbours are talking from their windows; while the ropes, stretched zig-zag from wall to wall, afford just room enough to dry a blanket or a couple of shirts, that swell out dropsically in the wind.

I visited one of the paved yards round which the Irish live, and found that it had been turned into a complete drying-ground, with shirts, gowns, and petticoats of evey description and colour. The buildings at the end were completely hidden by 'the things', and the air felt damp and chilly, and smelt of soap-suds. The gutter was filled with dirty gray water emptied from the wash-tubs, and on the top were the thick bubbles floating about under the breath of the boys 'playing at boats' with them.

It is the custom with the inhabitants of these courts and alleys to assemble at the entrance with their baskets, and chat and smoke away the morning. Every court entrance has its little group of girls and women, lolling listlessly against the sides, with their heads uncovered, and their luxuriant hair fuzzy as oakum. It is peculiar with the Irish women that – after having been accustomed to their hoods – they seldom wear bonnets, unless on a long journey. Nearly all of them, too, have a thick plaid shawl, which they keep on all the day through, with their hands covered under it. At the mouth of the only thoroughfare deserving of the name of street – for a cart could just go through it – were congregated about thirty men and women, who rented rooms in the houses on each side of the road. Six women, with baskets of dried herrings, were crouching in a line on the kerbstone with the fish before them; their legs were drawn up so closely to their bodies that the shawl covered the entire figure, and they looked very like the podgy 'tombolers' sold by the Italian boys. As all their wares were alike, it was puzzling work to imagine how, without the strongest opposition, they could each obtain a living. The men were dressed in long-tail coats, with one or two brass buttons. One old dame, with a face wrinkled like a dried plum, had her cloak placed over her head like a hood, and the grisly hair hung down in matted hanks about her face, her black eyes shining between the locks like those of a Skye terrier; beside her was another old woman smoking a pipe so short that her nose reached over the bowl.

After looking at the low foreheads and long bulging upper lips of some of the group, it was pleasant to gaze upon the pretty faces of the one or two girls that lolled against the wall. Their black hair, smoothed with grease, and shining almost as if 'japanned', and their large gray eyes with the thick dark fringe of lash, seemed out of place among the hard features of their companions. It was only by looking at the short petticoats and large feet you could assure yourself that they belonged to the same class.

In all the houses that I entered were traces of household care and neatness that I had little expected to have seen. The cupboard fastened in the corner of the room, and stocked with mugs and cups, the mantelpiece with its images, and the walls covered with showy-coloured prints of saints and martyrs, gave an air of comfort that strangely disagreed with the reports of the cabins in 'ould Ireland'. As the doors to the houses were nearly all of them kept open, I could, even whilst walking along, gain some notion of the furniture of the homes. In one house that I visited there was a family of five persons, living on the ground floor and occupying two rooms. The boards were strewn with red sand, and the front apartment had three beds in it, with the printed curtains drawn closely round. In a dark room, at the back, lived the family itself. It was fitted up as a parlour, and crowded to excess with chairs and tables, the very staircase having pictures fastened against the wooden partition. The fire, although it was midday, and a warm autumn morning, served as much for light as for heat, and round it crouched the mother, children, and visitors, bending over the flame as if in the severest winter time. In a room above this were a man and woman lately arrived in England. The woman sat huddled up in a corner smoking, with the husband standing over her in, what appeared at first, a menacing attitude; I was informed, however, that they were only planning for the future. This room was perfectly empty of furniture, and the once white-washed walls were black, excepting the little square patches which showed where the pictures of the former tenants had hung. In another room, I found a home so small and full of furniture, that it was almost a curiosity for domestic management. The bed, with its chintz curtains looped up, filled one end of the apartment, but the mattress of it served as a long bench for the visitors to sit on. The table was so large that it divided the room in two, and if there was one picture there must have been thirty – all of 'holy men', with yellow glories round their heads. The window-ledge was dressed out with crockery, and in a tumbler were placed the beads. The old dame herself was as curious as her room. Her shawl was fastened over her large frilled cap. She had a little 'button' of a nose, with the nostrils entering her face like bullet holes. She wore over her gown an old pilot coat, well-stained with fish slime, and her petticoats being short, she had very much the appearance of a Dutch fisherman or stage smuggler.

Her story was affecting – made more so, perhaps, by the emotional manner in which she related it. Nine years ago 'the father' of the district – 'the Blissed Lady guard him!' – had found her late at night, rolling in the gutter, and the boys pelting her with orange-peel and mud. She was drunk – 'the Lorrud pass by her' – and when she came to, she found herself in the chapel, lying before the sanctuary, 'under the shadow of the holy cross'. Watching over her was the 'good father', trying to bring back her consciousness. He spoke to her of her wickedness, and before she left she took the pledge of temperance. From that time she prospered, and the 1s. 6d. the 'father' gave her 'had God's blissin' in it', for she became the best dressed woman in the court, and in less than three years had 15l. in the savings' bank, 'the father – Heaven chirish him' – keeping her book for her, as he did for other poor people. She also joined 'the Association of the Blissed Lady', (and bought herself the dress of the order 'a beautiful grane vilvit, which she had now, and which same cost her 30s.'), and then she was secure against want in old age and sickness. But after nine years prudence and comfort, a brother of hers returned home from the army, with a pension of 1s. a day. He was wild, and persuaded her to break her pledge, and in a short time he got all her savings from her and spent every penny. She couldn't shake him off, 'for he was the only kin she had on airth', and 'she must love her own flish and bones'. Then began her misery. 'It plased God to visit her ould limbs with aches and throubles, and her hips swole with the cowld', so that she was at last forced into a hospital, and all that was left of her store was 'aten up by sufferin's'. This, she assured me, all came about by the 'good father's' leaving that parish for another one, but now he had returned to them again, and, with his help and God's blessing, she would yet prosper once more.

Whilst I was in the room, the father entered, and 'old Norah', half-laughed and wept at the same time. She stood wiping her eyes with the shawl, and groaning out blessings on 'his rivirince's hid', begging of him not 'to scould her for she was a wake woman'. The renegade brother was had in to receive a lecture from 'his rivirince'. A more sottish idiotic face it would be difficult to imagine. He stood with his hands hanging down like the paws of a dog begging, and his two small eyes stared in the face of the priest, as he censured him, without the least expression even of consciousness. Old Norah stood by, groaning like a bagpipe, and writhing while the father spoke to her 'own brother', as though every reproach were meant for her.

The one thing that struck me during my visit to this neighbourhood, was the apparent listlessness and lazy appearance of the people. The boys at play were the only beings who seemed to have any life in their actions. The women in their plaid shawls strolled along the pavements, stopping each friend for a chat, or joining some circle, and leaning against the wall as though utterly deficient in energy. The men smoked, with their hands in their pockets, listening to the old crones talking, and only now and then grunting out a reply when a question was directly put to them. And yet it is curious that these people, who here seemed as inactive as negroes, will perform the severest bodily labour, undertaking tasks that the English are almost unfitted for.

OF THE SELLERS OF TREES, SHRUBS, FLOWERS (CUT AND IN POTS) ROOTS, SEEDS, AND BRANCHES

The better class of flower-girls reside in Lisson-grove, in the streets off Drury-lane, in St Giles's, and in other parts inhabited by the very poor. Some of them live in lodging-houses, the stench and squalor of which are in remarkable contrast to the beauty and fragrance of the flowers they sometimes have to carry thither with them unsold.

Of Two Orphan Flower Girls

[pp. 141–2]   Of these girls the elder was fifteen and the younger eleven. Both were clad in old, but not torn, dark print frocks, hanging so closely, and yet so loosely, about them as to show the deficiency of under-clothing; they wore old broken black chip bonnets. The older sister (or rather half-sister) had a pair of old worn-out shoes on her feet, the younger was barefoot, but trotted along, in a gait at once quick and feeble – as if the soles of her little feet were impervious, like horn, to the roughness of the road. The elder girl had a modest expression of countenance, with no pretensions to prettiness except in having tolerably good eyes. Her complexion was somewhat muddy, and her features somewhat pinched. The younger child had a round, chubby, and even rosy face, and quite a healthful look. Her portrait is here given.

They lived in one of the streets near Drury-lane. They were inmates of a house, not let out as a lodging-house, in separate beds, but in rooms, and inhabited by street-sellers and street-labourers. The room they occupied was large, and one dim candle lighted it so insufficiently that it seemed to exaggerate the dimensions. The walls were bare and dis-coloured with damp. The furniture consisted of a crazy table and a few chairs, and in the centre of the room was an old four-post bedstead of the larger size. This bed was occupied nightly by the two sisters and their brother, a lad just turned thirteen. In a sort of recess in a corner of the room was the decency of an old curtain – or something equivalent, for I could hardly see in the dimness – and behind this was, I presume, the bed of the married couple. The three children paid 2s. a week for the room, the tenant an Irishman out of work paying 2s. 9d., but the furniture was his, and his wife aided the children in their trifle of washing, mended their clothes, where such a thing was possible, and such like. The husband was absent at the time of my visit, but the wife seemed of a better stamp, judging by her appearance, and by her refraining from any direct, or even indirect, way of begging, as well as from the 'Glory be to Gods!' 'the heavens be your honour's bed!' or 'it's the thruth I'm telling of you sir', that I so frequently meet with on similar visits.

The elder girl said, in an English accent, not at all garrulously, but merely in answer to my questions: 'I sell flowers, sir; we live almost on flowers when they are to be got. I sell, and so does my sister, all kinds, but it's very little use offering any that's not sweet. I think it's the sweetness as sells them. I sell primroses, when they're in, and violets, and wall-flowers, and stocks, and roses of different sorts, and pinks, and carnations,

THE WALLFLOWER GIRL.

and mixed flowers, and lilies of the valley, and green lavender, and mignonette (but that I do very seldom), and violets again at this time of the year, for we get them both in spring and winter.' [They are forced in hot-houses for winter sale, I may remark.] 'The best sale of all is, I think, moss-roses, young moss-roses. We do best of all on them. Primroses are good, for people say: "Well, here's spring again to a certainty." Gentlemen are our best customers. I've heard that they buy flowers to give to the ladies. Ladies have sometimes said: "A penny, my poor girl, here's three-halfpence for the bunch." Or they've given me the price of two bunches for one; so have gentlemen. I never had a rude word said to me by a gentleman in my life. No, sir, neither lady nor gentleman ever gave me 6d. for a bunch of flowers. I never had a sixpence given to me in my life – never. I never go among boys, I know nobody but my brother. My father was a tradesman in Mitchelstown, in the County Cork. I don't know what sort of a tradesman he was. I never saw him. He was a tradesman I've been told. I was born in London. Mother was a chairwoman, and lived very well. None of us ever saw a father.' [It was evident that they were illegitimate children, but the landlady had never seen the mother, and could give me no information.] 'We don't know anything about our fathers. We were all "mother's children". Mother died seven years ago last Guy Faux day. I've got myself, and my brother and sister a bit of bread ever since, and never had any help but from the neighbours. I never troubled the parish. O, yes, sir, the neighbours is all poor people, very poor, some of them. We've lived with her' (indicating her landlady by a gesture) 'these two years, and off and on before that. I can't say how long.' 'Well, I don't know exactly,' said the landlady, 'but I've had them with me almost all the time, for four years, as near as I can recollect; perhaps more. I've moved three times, and they always followed me.' In answer to my inquiries the landlady assured me that these two poor girls, were never out of doors all the time she had known them after six at night. 'We've always good health. We can all read.' [Here the three somewhat insisted upon proving to me their proficiency in reading, and having produced a Roman Catholic book, the 'Garden of Heaven', they read very well.] 'I put myself,' continued the girl, 'and I put my brother and sister to a Roman Catholic school – and to Ragged schools – but I could read before mother died. My brother can write, and I pray to God that he'll do well with it. I buy my flowers at Covent Garden; sometimes, but very seldom, at Farringdon. I pay 1s. for a dozen bunches, whatever flowers are in. Out of every two bunches I can make three, at 1d. a piece. Sometimes one or two over in the dozen, but not so often as I would like. We make the bunches up ourselves. We get the rush to tie them with for nothing. We put their own leaves round these violets (she produced a bunch). The paper for a dozen costs a penny; sometimes only a halfpenny. The two of us doesn't make less than 6d. a day, unless it's very ill luck. But religion teaches us that God will support us, and if we make less we say nothing. We do better on oranges in March or April, I think it is, than on flowers. Oranges keep better than flowers you see, sir. We make 1s. a day, and 9d. a day, on oranges, the two of us. I wish they was in all the year. I generally go St John's-wood way, and Hampstead and Highgate way with my flowers. I can get them nearly all the year, but oranges is better liked than flowers, I think. I always keep 1s. stock-money, if I can. If it's bad weather, so bad that we can't sell flowers at all, and so if we've had to spend our stock-money for a bit of bread, *she* (the landlady) lends us 1s., if she has one, or she borrows one of a neighbour, if she hasn't, or if the neighbours hasn't it, she borrows it at a dolly-shop' (the illegal pawnshop). 'There's 2d. a week to pay for 1s. at a dolly, and perhaps an old rug left for it; if it's very hard weather, the rug must be taken at night time, or we are starved with the cold. It sometimes has to be put into the dolly again next morning, and then there's 2d. to pay for it for the day. We've had a frock in for 6d., and that's a penny a week, and the same for a day. We never pawned anything; we have nothing they would take in at the pawnshop. We live on bread and tea, and sometimes a fresh herring of a night. Sometimes we don't eat a bit all day when we're out; sometimes we take a bit of bread with us, or buy a bit. My sister can't eat taturs; they sicken her. I don't know what emigrating means.' [I informed her and she continued]: 'No, sir, I wouldn't like to emigrate and leave brother and sister. If they went with me I don't think I should like it, not among strangers. I think our living costs us 2s. a week for the two of us; the rest goes in rent. That's all we make.'

The brother earned from 1s. 6d. to 2s. a week, with an occasional meal, as a costermonger's boy. Neither of them ever missed mass on a Sunday.

Watercress Girl

[pp. 157–8] The little watercress girl who gave me the following statement, although only eight years of age, had entirely lost all childish ways, and was, indeed, in thoughts and manner, a woman. There was something cruelly pathetic in hearing this infant, so young that her features had scarcely formed themselves, talking of the bitterest struggles of life, with the calm earnestness of one who had endured them all. I did not know how to talk with her. At first I treated her as a child, speaking on childish subjects; so that I might, by being familiar with her, remove all shyness, and get her to narrate her life freely. I asked her about her toys and her games with her companions; but the look of amazement that answered me soon put an end to any attempt at fun on my part. I then talked to her about the parks, and whether she ever went to them. 'The parks!' she replied in wonder, 'where are they?' I explained to her, telling her that they were large open places with green grass and tall trees, where beautiful carriages drove about, and people walked for pleasure, and children played. Her eyes brightened up a little as I spoke; and she asked, half doubtingly, 'Would they let such as me go there – just to look?' All her knowledge seemed to begin and end with watercresses, and what they fetched. She knew no more of London than that part she had seen on her rounds, and believed that no quarter of the town was handsomer or pleasanter than it was at Farringdon-market or at Clerkenwell, where she lived. Her little face, pale and thin with privation, was wrinkled where the dimples ought to have been, and she would sigh frequently. When some hot dinner was offered to her, she would not touch it, because, if she eat too much, 'it made her sick,' she said; 'and she wasn't used to meat, only on a Sunday.'

The poor child, although the weather was severe, was dressed in a thin cotton gown, with a threadbare shawl wrapped round her shoulders. She wore no covering to her head, and the long rusty hair stood out in all directions. When she walked she shuffled along, for fear that the large carpet slippers that served her for shoes should slip off her feet.

'I go about the streets with water-creases, crying, "Four bunches a penny, water-creases." I am just eight years old – that's all, and I've a big sister, and a brother, and a sister younger than I am. On and off, I've been very near a twelvemonth in the streets. Before that, I had to take care of a baby for my aunt. No, it wasn't heavy – it was only two months old; but I minded it for ever such a time – till it could walk. It was a very nice baby, not a very pretty one; but, if I touched it under the chin, it would laugh. Before I had the baby, I used to help mother, who was in the fur trade; and, if there was any slits in the fur, I'd sew them up. My mother learned me to needle-work and to knit when I was about five. I used to go to school, too; but I wasn't there long. I've forgot all about it now, it's such a time ago; and mother took me away because the master whacked me, though the missus use'n't to never touch me. I didn't like him at all. What do you think? he hit me three times, ever so hard, across the face with his cane, and made me go dancing down stairs; and when mother saw the marks on my cheek, she went to blow him up, but she couldn't see him – he was afraid. That's why I left school.

'The creases is so bad now, that I haven't been out with 'em for three days. They're so cold, people won't buy 'em; for when I goes up to them, they say, "They'll freeze our bellies." Besides, in the market, they won't sell a ha'penny handful now – they're ris to a penny and tuppence. In summer there's lots, and 'most as cheap as dirt; but I have to be down at Farringdon-market between four and five, or else I can't get any creases, because everyone almost – especially the Irish – is selling them, and they're picked up so quick. Some of the saleswomen – we never calls 'em ladies – is very kind to us children, and some of them altogether spiteful. The good one will give you a bunch for nothing, when they're cheap; but the others, cruel ones, if you try to bate them a farden less than they ask you, will say, "Go along with you, you're no good." I used to go down to market along with another girl, as must be about fourteen, 'cos she does her back hair up. When we've bought a lot, we sits down on a door-step, and ties up the bunches. We never goes home to breakfast till we've sold out; but, if it's very late, then I buys a penn'orth of pudden, which is very nice with gravy. I don't know hardly one of the people, as goes to Farringdon, to talk to; they never speaks to me, so I don't speak to them. We children never play down there, 'cos we're thinking of our living. No; people never pities me in the street – excepting one gentleman, and he says, says he, "What do you do out so soon in the morning?" but he gave me nothink – he only walked away.

'It's very cold before winter comes on reg'lar – specially getting up of a morning. I gets up in the dark by the light of the lamp in the court. When the snow is on the ground, there's no creases. I bears the cold – you must; so I puts my hands under my shawl, though it hurts 'em to take hold of the creases, especially when we takes 'em to the pump to wash 'em. No; I never see any children crying – it's no use.

'Sometimes I make a great deal of money. One day I took 1s. 6d., and the creases cost 6d.; but it isn't often I get such luck as that. I oftener makes 3d. or 4d. than 1s.; and then I'm at work, crying, "Creases, four bunches a penny, creases!" from six in the morning to about ten. What do you mean by mechanics? – I don't know what they are. The shops buys most of me. Some of 'em says, "Oh! I ain't a-goin' to give a penny for these"; and they want 'em at the same price as I buys 'em at.

'I always give mother my money, she's so very good to me. She don't often beat me; but, when she do, she don't play with me. She's very poor, and goes out cleaning rooms sometimes, now she don't work at the fur.

I ain't got no father, he's a father-in-law. No; mother ain't married again
– he's a father-in-law. He grinds scissors, and he's very good to me. No; I
don't mean by that that he says kind things to me, for he never hardly
speaks. When I gets home, after selling creases, I stops at home. I puts the
room to rights: mother don't make me do it, I does it myself. I cleans the
chairs, though there's only two to clean. I takes a tub and scrubbing-brush
and flannel, and scrubs the floor – that's what I do three or four times a
week.

'I don't have no dinner. Mother gives me two slices of bread-and-butter
and a cup of tea for breakfast, and then I go till tea, and has the same.
We has meat of a Sunday, and, of course, I should like to have it every
day. Mother has just the same to eat as we has, but she takes more tea
– three cups, sometimes. No; I never has no sweet-stuff; I never buy none
– I don't like it. Sometimes we has a game of "honey-pots" with the girls
in the court, but not often. Me and Carry H— carries the little 'uns. We
plays, too, at "kiss-in-the-ring". I knows a good many games, but I don't
play at 'em, 'cos going out with creases tires me. On a Friday night, too,
I goes to a Jew's house till eleven o'clock on Saturday night. All I has to
do is to snuff the candles and poke the fire. You see they keep their Sabbath
then, and they won't touch anything; so they gives me my wittals and
$1\frac{1}{2}d.$, and I does it for 'em. I have a reg'lar good lot to eat. Supper of Friday
night, and tea after that, and fried fish of a Saturday morning, and meat
for dinner, and tea, and supper, and I like it very well.

'Oh, yes; I've got some toys at home. I've a fire-place, and a box of toys,
and a knife and fork, and two little chairs. The Jews gave 'em to me where
I go to on a Friday, and that's why I said they was very kind to me. I never
had no doll; but I misses little sister – she's only two years old. We don't
sleep in the same room; for father and mother sleeps with little sister in
the one pair, and me and brother and other sister sleeps in the top room.
I always goes to bed at seven, 'cos I has to be up so early.

'I am a capital hand at bargaining – but only at buying watercreases.
They can't take me in. If the woman tries to give me a small handful of
creases, I says, "I ain't a goin' to have that for a ha'porth," and I go to
the next basket, and so on, all round. I know the quantities very well. For
a penny I ought to have a full market hand, or as much as I could carry
in my arms at one time, without spilling. For $3d.$ I has a lap full, enough
to earn about a shilling; and for $6d.$ I gets as many as crams my basket.
I can't read or write, but I knows how many pennies goes to a shilling,
why, twelve, of course, but I don't know how many ha'pence there is,
though there's two to a penny. When I've bought $3d.$ of creases, I ties 'em

up into as many little bundles as I can. They must look biggish, or the people won't buy them, some puffs them out as much as they'll go. All my money I earns I puts in a club and draws it out to buy clothes with. It's better than spending it in sweet-stuff, for them as has a living to earn. Besides it's like a child to care for sugar-sticks, and not like one who's got a living and vittals to earn. I ain't a child, and I shan't be a woman till I'm twenty, but I'm past eight, I am. I don't know nothing about what I earns during the year, I only know how many pennies goes to a shilling, and two ha'pence goes to a penny, and four fardens goes to a penny. I knows, too, how many fardens goes to tuppence – eight. That's as much as I wants to know for the markets.'

OF THE STREET-SELLERS
OF EATABLES AND DRINKABLES

[p. 166] These dealers were, more numerous, even when the metropolitan population was but half its present extent. I heard several causes assigned for this – such as the higher rate of earnings of the labouring people at that time, as well as the smaller number of shopkeepers who deal in such cheap luxuries as penny pies, and the fewer places of cheap amusement, such as the 'penny gaffs'. These places, I was told, 'run away with the young people's pennies', which were, at one period, expended in the streets.

The class engaged in the manufacture, or in the sale, of these articles, are a more intelligent people than the generality of street-sellers. They have nearly all been mechanics who, from inability to procure employment at their several crafts – from dislike to an irksome and, perhaps, sedentary confinement – or from an overpowering desire 'to be their own masters', have sought a livelihood in the streets. The purchase and sale of fish, fruit, or vegetables require no great training or deftness; but to make the dainties, in which street-people are critical, and to sell them at the lowest possible price, certainly requires some previous discipline to produce the skill to combine and the taste to please.

I may here observe, that I found it common enough among these street-sellers to describe themselves and their fraternity not by their names or callings, but by the article in which they deal. This is sometimes ludicrous enough: 'Is the man you're asking about a pickled whelk, sir?' was said to me. In answer to another inquiry, I was told, 'Oh, yes, I know him – he's a sweet-stuff.' Such ellipses, or abbreviations, are common in all mechanical or commercial callings.

Men and women, and most especially boys, purchase their meals day after day in the streets. The coffee-stall supplies a warm breakfast; shell-fish of many kinds tempt to a luncheon; hot-eels or pea-soup, flanked by a potato 'all hot', serve for a dinner; and cakes and tarts, or nuts and oranges, with many varieties of pastry, confectionary, and fruit, woo to indulgence in a dessert; while for supper there is a sandwich, a meat pudding, or a 'trotter'.

The street provisions consist of cooked or prepared victuals, which may be divided into solids, pastry, confectionary, and drinkables.

Of the Street-sellers, and of the Preparation of Fried Fish

[pp. 173–5] Among the cooked food which has for many years formed a portion of the street trade is fried fish. The sellers are about 350, as a maximum and 250 as a minimum, 300 being an average number. The reason of the variation in number is, that on a Saturday night, and occasionally on other nights, especially on Mondays, stall-keepers sell fried fish, and not as an ordinary article of their trade. Some men, too, resort to the trade for a time, when they cannot be employed in any way more profitable or suitable to them. The dealers in this article are, for the most part, old men and boys, though there may be 30 or 40 women who sell it, but only 3 or 4 girls, and they are the daughters of the men in the business as the women are the wives. Among the fried-fish sellers there are not half a dozen Irish people, although fish is so especial a part of the diet of the poor Irish. The men in the calling have been, as regards the great majority, mechanics or servants; none, I was told, had been fishmongers, or their assistants.

The fish fried by street dealers is known as 'plaice dabs' and 'sole dabs', which are merely plaice and soles, 'dab' being a common word for any flat fish. The fish which supplies upwards of one half the quantity fried for the streets is plaice; the other fishes used are soles, haddocks, whitings, flounders, and herrings, but very sparingly indeed as regards herrings. Soles are used in as large a quantity as the other kinds mentioned altogether. On my inquiry as to the precise quantity of each description fried, the answer from the traders was uniform: 'I can't say, sir. I buy whatever's cheapest.' The fish is bought at Billingsgate, but some of the street dealers obtain another and even a cheaper commodity than at that great mart. This supply is known in the trade as 'friers', and consists of the overplus of a fishmonger's stock, of what he has not sold overnight, and does not care to offer for sale on the following morning, and therefore vends it to the costermongers, whose customers are chiefly among the poor. The friers are sometimes half, and sometimes more than half, of the wholesale price in Billingsgate. Many of the friers are good, but some, I was told, 'in any thing like muggy or close weather were very queer fish, very queer indeed', and they are consequently fried with a most liberal allowance of oil, 'which will conceal anything'.

The fish to be fried is first washed and gutted; the fins, head, and tail are then cut off, and the trunk is dipped in flour and water, so that in frying, oil being always used, the skin will not be scorched by the, perhaps, too violent action of the fire, but merely browned. Pale rape oil is generally used. The sellers, however, are often twitted with using lamp oil, even when it is dearer than that devoted to the purpose. The fish is cooked in ordinary frying-pans. One tradesman in Cripplegate, formerly a coster-monger, has on his premises a commodious oven which he had built for the frying, or rather baking, of fish. He supplies the small shopkeepers who deal in the article (although some prepare it themselves), and sells his fish retail also, but the street-sellers buy little of him, as they are nearly all 'their own cooks'. Some of the 'illegitimates', however, lay in their stock by purchase of the tradesman in question. The fish is cut into portions before it is fried, and the frying occupies about ten minutes. The quantity prepared together is from six to twenty portions, according to the size of the pans; four dozen portions, or 'pieces', as the street people call them, require a quart of oil.

The fried fish-sellers live in some out of the way alley, and not un-frequently in garrets; for among even the poorest class there are great objections to their being fellow-lodgers, on account of the odour from the frying. Even when the fish is fresh (as it most frequently is), and the oil pure, the odour is rank. In one place I visited, which was, moreover, admirable for cleanliness, it was very rank. The cooks, however, whether husbands or wives – for the women often attend to the pan – when they hear of this disagreeable rankness, answer that it may be so, many people say so; but for their parts they cannot smell it at all. The garments of the fried-fish sellers are more strongly impregnated with the smell of the fish than were those of any 'wet' or other fish-sellers whom I met with. Their residences are in some of the labyrinths of courts and alleys that run from Gray's-inn-lane to Leather-lane, and similar places between Fetter and Chancery-lanes. They are to be found, too, in the courts running from Cow-cross, Smithfield; and from Turnmill-street and Ray-street, Clerken-well; also, in the alleys about Bishopsgate-street and the Kingsland-road, and some in the half-ruinous buildings near the Southwark and Borough-roads. None, or very few, of those who are their own cooks, reside at a greater distance than three miles from Billingsgate. A gin-drinking neighbourhood, one coster said, suits best 'for people hasn't their smell so correct there'.

The sale is both on rounds and at stalls, the itinerants being twice as numerous as the stationary. The round is usually from public-house to public-house, in populous neighbourhoods. The itinerants generally confine themselves to the trade in fried fish, but the stall-keepers always sell other articles, generally fish of some kind, along with it. The sale in the public-houses is the greatest.

At the neighbouring races and fairs there is a great sale of fried fish. At last Epsom races, I was told, there were at least fifty purveyors of that dainty from London, half of them perhaps being costermongers, who speculated in it merely for the occasion, preparing it themselves. Three men joined in one speculation, expending 8*l*. in fish, and did well, selling at the usual profit of cent. per cent., but with the drawback of considerable expenses. Their customers at the races and fairs are the boys who hold horses or brush clothes, or who sell oranges or nuts, or push at roundabouts, and the costers who are there on business. At Epsom races there was plenty of bread, I was informed, to be picked up on the ground; it had been flung from the carriages after luncheon, and this, with a piece of fish, supplied a meal or 'a relish' to hundreds.

In the public-houses, a slice of bread, 16 or 32 being cut from a quartern loaf – as they are whole or half slices – is sold or offered with the fish for a penny. The cry of the seller is, 'fish and bread, a penny'. Sometimes for an extra-sized piece, with bread, 2*d*. is obtained, but very seldom, and sometimes two pieces are given for 1½*d*. At the stalls bread is rarely sold with the edible in question.

For the itinerant trade, a neatly painted wooden tray, slung by a leathern strap from the neck, is used: the tray is papered over generally with clean newspapers, and on the paper is spread the shapeless brown lumps of fish. Parsley is often strewn over them, and a salt-box is placed at the discretion of the customer. The trays contain from two to five dozen pieces. I understand that no one has a trade greatly in advance of his fellows. The whole body complain of their earnings being far less than was the case four or five years back.

The itinerant fried fish-sellers, when pursuing their avocation, wear generally a jacket of cloth or fustian buttoned round them, but the rest of their attire is hidden by the white sleeves and apron some wear, or by the black calico sleeves and dark woollen aprons worn by others.

The capital required to start properly in the business is: frying-pan 2s. (second-hand 9d.); tray 2s. 6d. (second-hand 8d.); salt-box 6d. (second-hand 1d.); and stock-money 5s. – in all 10s. A man has gone into the trade, however, with 1s., which he expended in fish and oil, borrowed a frying-pan, borrowed an old teaboard, and so started on his venture.

Of the Experience of a Fried Fish-seller,
and of the Class of Customers

[pp. 175–6] The man who gave me the following information was well-looking, and might be about 45 or 50. He was poorly dressed, but his old brown surtout fitted him close and well, was jauntily buttoned up to his black satin stock, worn, but of good quality; and, altogether, he had what is understood among a class as 'a *betterly* appearance about him'. His statement, as well as those of the other vendors of provisions, is curious in its details of public-house vagaries.

'I've been in the trade,' he said, 'seventeen years. Before that, I was a gentleman's servant, and I married a servant-maid, and we had a family, and, on that account, couldn't, either of us, get a situation, though we'd good characters. I was out of employ for seven or eight months, and things was beginning to go to the pawn for a living; but at last, when I gave up any hope of getting into a gentleman's service, I raised 10s., and determined to try something else. I was persuaded, by a friend who kept a beer-shop, to sell oysters at his door. I took his advice, and went to Billingsgate for the first time in my life, and bought a peck of oysters for 2s. 6d. I was dressed respectable then – nothing like the mess and dirt I'm in now' [I may observe, that there was no dirt about him]; 'and so the salesman laid it on, but I gave him all he asked. I know a deal better now. I'd never been used to open oysters, and I couldn't do it. I cut my fingers with the knife slipping all over them, and had to hire a man to open for me, or the blood from my cut fingers would have run upon the oysters. For all that, I cleared 2s. 6d. on that peck, and I soon got up to the trade, and did well; till, in two or three months, the season got over, and I was advised, by the same friend, to try fried fish. That suited me. I've lived in good families, where there was first-rate men-cooks, and I know what good cooking means. I bought a dozen plaice; I forget what I gave for them, but they were dearer then than now. For all that, I took between 11s. and 12s. the first night – it was Saturday – that I started; and I stuck to it, and took from 7s. to 10s. every night, with more, of course, on Saturday, and it was half of it profit then. I cleared a good mechanic's earnings at that time – 30s. a week and more. Soon after, I was told that, if agreeable, my wife could have a stall with fried fish, opposite a wine-vaults just opened, and she made nearly half as much as I did on my rounds. I served the public-houses, and soon got known. With some landlords I had the privilege of the parlour, and tap-room, and bar, when other tradesmen have been kept out. The landlords will say to me still: "*You* can go in, Fishy." Somehow, I got the name of "Fishy" then, and I've kept it ever since. There was hospitality in those days. I've gone into a room in a public-house, used by mechanics, and one of them has said: 'I'll stand fish round, gentlemen"; and I've supplied fifteen penn'orths. Perhaps he was a stranger, such a sort of customer, that wanted to be agreeable. Now, it's more likely I hear: "Jack, lend us a penny to buy a bit of fried"; and then Jack says: "You be d—d! here, lass, let's have another pint.' The insults and difficulties I've had in the public-house trade is dreadful. I once sold 16*d.* worth to three rough-looking fellows I'd never seen before, and they seemed hearty, and asked me to drink with them, so I took a pull; but they wouldn't pay me when I asked, and I waited a goodish bit before I did ask. I thought, at first, it was their fun, but I waited from four to seven, and I found it was no fun. I felt upset, and ran out and told the policeman, but he said it was only a debt, and he couldn't interfere. So I ran to the station, but the head man there said the same, and told me I should hand over the fish with one hand, and hold out the other hand for my money. So I went back to the public-house, and asked for my money – and there was some mechanics that knew me there then – but I got nothing but "—you's!" and one of 'em used most dreadful language. At last, one of the mechanics said: "Muzzle him, Fishy, if he won't pay." He was far bigger than me, him that was one in debt; but my spirit was up, and I let go at him and gave him a bloody nose, and the next hit I knocked him backwards, I'm sure I don't know how, on to a table, but I fell on him, and he clutched me by the coat-collar – I was respectable dressed then – and half smothered me. He tore the back of my coat, too, and I went home like Jim Crow. The potman and the others parted us, and they made the man give me 1*s.*, and the waiter paid me the other 4*d.*, and said he'd take his chance to get it – but he never got it. Another time I went into a bar, and there was a ball in the house, and one of the ball gents came down and gave my basket a kick without ever a word, and started the fish; and in a scuffle – he was a little fellow, but my master – I had this finger put out of joint – you can see that, sir, still – and was in the hospital a week from an injury to my leg; the tiblin bone was hurt, the doctors said' [the tibia.] 'I've had my tray kicked over for a lark in a public-house, and a scramble for my fish, and all gone, and no help and no money for me. The landlords always prevent such things, when they can, and interfere for a poor man; but then it's done sudden, and over in an instant. That sort of thing wasn't the worst. I once had some powdery stuff flung sudden over me at a parlour door. My fish fell off, for I jumped, because I felt blinded, and what became of them I don't know; but I aimed at once for home – it was very late – and had to feel my way almost like a blind man. I can't tell what I suffered. I found it was something black, for I kept rubbing my face with my apron, and could just tell it came away black. I let myself in with my latch, and my wife was in bed, and I told her to get up and look at my face and get some water, and she thought I was joking, as she was half asleep; but when she got up and got a light, and a glass, she screamed, and said I looked such a shiny image; and so I did, as well as I could see, for it was black lead – such as they use for grates – that was flung on me. I washed if off, but it wasn't easy, and my face was sore days after. I had a respectable coat on then, too, which was greatly spoiled, and no remedy at all. I don't know who did it to me. I heard some one say: "You're served out beautiful." It's men that calls themselves gentlemen that does such things. I know the style of them then – it was eight or ten years ago; they'd heard of Lord —, and his goings on. That way it's better now, but worse, far, in the way of getting a living. I dare say, if I had dressed in rough corderoys, I shouldn't have been larked at so much, because they might have thought I was a regular coster, and a fighter; but I don't like that sort of thing – I like to be decent and respectable, if I can.

'I've been in the "fried" trade ever since, except about three months that I tried the sandwiches. I didn't do so well in them, but it was a far easier trade; no carrying heavy weights all the way from Billingsgate: but I went back to the fried. Why now, sir, a good week with me – and I've only myself in the trade now' [he was a widower] 'is to earn 12s., a poor week is 9s.; and there's as many of one as of the other. I'm known to sell the best of fish, and to cook it in the best style. I think half of us, take it round and round for a year, may earn as much as I do, and the other half about half as much. I think so. I might have saved money, but for a family. I've only one at home with me now, and he really *is* a good lad. My customers are public-house people that want a relish or a sort of supper with their beer, not so much to drinkers. I sell to tradesmen, too; 4d. worth for tea or supper. Some of them send to my place, for I'm known. The Great Exhibition can't be any difference to me. I've a regular round. I used to sell a good deal to women of the town, but I don't now. They haven't the money, I believe. Where I took 10s. of them, eight or ten years ago, I now take only 6d. They may go for other sorts of relishes now; I can't say. The worst of my trade is, that people must have as big penn'orths when fish is dear as when it's cheap. I never sold a piece of fish to an Italian boy in my life, though they're Catholics. Indeed, I never saw an Italian boy spend a halfpenny in the streets on anything.'

A working-man told me that he often bought fried fish, and accounted it a good to men like himself. He was fond of fried fish to his supper; he couldn't buy half so cheap as the street-sellers, perhaps not a quarter; and, if he could, it would cost him 1d. for dripping to fry the fish in, and he got it ready, and well fried, and generally good, for 1d.

Subsequent inquiries satisfied me that my informant was correct as to his calculations of his fellows' earnings, judging from his own. The price of plaice at Billingsgate is from ½d. to 2d. each, according to size (the fried fish purveyors never calculate by the weight), ¾d. being a fair average. A plaice costing 1d. will now be fried into four pieces, each 1d.; but the addition of bread, cost of oil, &c., reduces the 'fried' peoples' profits to rather less than cent. per cent. Soles and the other fish are, moreover, 30 per cent. dearer than plaice. As 150 sellers make as much weekly as my informant, and the other 150 half that amount, we have an average yearly earning of 27l. 6s. in one case, and of 13l. 13s. in the other. Taking only 20l. a year as a medium earning, and adding 90 per cent for profit, the outlay on the fried fish supplied by London street-sellers is 11,400l.

Of the Street Trade in Baked Potatoes

[pp. 181-3] The baked potato trade, in the way it is at present carried on, has not been known more than fifteen years in the streets. Before that, potatoes were sometimes roasted as chestnuts are now, but only on a small scale. The trade is more profitable than that in fruit, but continues for but six months of the year.

The potatoes, for street-consumption, are bought of the greengrocers, at the rate of 5s. 6d. the cwt. They are usually a large-sized 'fruit', running about two or three to the pound. The kind generally bought is what are called the 'French Regent's'. French potatoes are greatly used now, as they are cheaper than the English. The potatoes are picked, and those of a large size, and with a rough skin, selected from the others because they are the mealiest. A waxy potato shrivels in the baking. There are usually from 280 to 300 potatoes in the cwt.; these are cleaned by the huckster, and, when dried, taken in baskets, about a quarter cwt. at a time, to the baker's, to be cooked. They are baked in large tins, and require an hour and a half to do them well. The charge for baking is 9*d*. the cwt., the baker usually finding the tins. They are taken home from the bakehouse in a basket, with a yard and a half of green baize in which they are covered up, and so protected from the cold. The huckster then places them in his can, which consists of a tin with a half-lid; it stands on four legs, and has a large handle to it, while an iron fire-pot is suspended immediately beneath the vessel which is used for holding the potatoes. Directly over the fire-pot is a boiler for hot water. This is concealed within the vessel, and serves to keep the potatoes always hot. Outside the vessel where the potatoes are kept is, at one end, a small compartment for butter and salt, and at the other end another compartment for fresh charcoal. Above the boiler, and beside the lid, is a small pipe for carrying off the steam. These potato-cans are sometimes brightly polished, sometimes painted red, and occasionally brass-mounted. Some of the handsomest are all brass, and some are highly ornamented with brass-mountings. Great pride is taken in the cans. The baked-potato man usually devotes half an hour to polishing them up, and they are mostly kept as bright as silver. The handsomest potato-can is now in Shoreditch. It cost ten guineas, and is of brass mounted with German silver. There are three lamps attached to it, with coloured glass, and of a style to accord with that of the machine; each lamp cost 5*s*. The expense of an ordinary can, tin and brass-mounted, is about 50*s*. They are mostly made by a tinman in the Ratcliffe-highway. The usual places for these cans to stand are the principal thoroughfares and street-markets. It is considered by one who has been many years at the business, that there are, taking those who have regular stands and those who are travelling with their cans on their arm, at least two hundred individuals engaged in the trade in London. There are three at the bottom of Farringdon-street, two in Smithfield, and three in Tottenham-court-road (the two places last named are said to be the best 'pitches' in all London), two in Leather-lane, one on Holborn-hill, one at King's-cross, three at the Brill, Somers-town, three in the New-cut, three in Covent-garden (this is considered to be on market-days the second-best pitch), two at the Elephant and Castle, one at Westminster-bridge, two at the top of Edgeware-road, one in St Martin's-lane, one in Newport-market, two at the upper end of Oxford-street, one in Clare-market, two in Regent-street, one in Newgate-market, two at the Angel, Islington, three at Shoreditch church, four about Rosemary-lane, two at Whitechapel, two near Spitalfields-market, and more than double the above number wandering about London. Some of the cans have names – as the 'Royal Union Jack' (engraved in a brass plate), the 'Royal George', the 'Prince of Wales', the 'Original Baked Potatoes', and the '*Old* Original Baked Potatoes'.

The business begins about the middle of August and continues to the latter end of April, or as soon as the potatoes get to any size, – until they are pronounced 'bad'. The season, upon an average, lasts about half the year, and depends much upon the weather. If it is cold and frosty, the trade is brisker than in wet weather; indeed then little is doing. The best hours for business are from half-past ten in the morning till two in the afternoon, and from five in the evening till eleven or twelve at night. The night trade is considered the best. In cold weather the potatoes are frequently bought to warm the hands. Indeed, an eminent divine classed them, in a public speech, among the best of modern improvements, it being a cheap luxury to the poor wayfarer, who was benumbed in the night by cold, and an excellent medium for diffusing warmth into the system, by being held in the gloved hand. Some buy them in the morning for lunch and some for dinner. A newsvendor, who had to take a hasty meal in his shop, told me he was 'always glad to hear the baked-potato cry, as it made a dinner of what was only a snack without it.' The best time at night, is about nine, when the potatoes are purchased for supper.

The customers consist of all classes. Many gentlefolks buy them in the street, and take them home for supper in their pockets; but the working classes are the greatest purchasers. Many boys and girls lay out a half-penny in a baked potato. Irishmen are particularly fond of them, but they are the worst customers, I am told, as they want the largest potatoes in the can. Women buy a great number of those sold. Some take them home, and some eat them in the street. Three baked potatoes are as much as will satisfy the stoutest appetite. One potato dealer in Smithfield is said to sell about 2½ cwt. of potatoes on a market-day; or, in other words, from 900 to 1,000 potatoes, and to take upwards of 2*l.* One informant told me that he himself had often sold 1½ cwt. of a day, and taken 1*l.* in halfpence. I am informed, that upon the average, taking the good stands with the bad ones throughout London, there are about 1 cwt. of potatoes sold by each baked-potato man – and there are 200 of these throughout the metropolis – making the total quantity of baked potatoes consumed every day 10 tons. The money spent upon these comes to within a few shillings of 125*l.* (calculating 300 potatoes to the cwt., and each of those potatoes to be sold at a halfpenny). Hence, there are 60 tons of baked potatoes eaten in London streets, and 750*l.* spent upon them every week during the season. Saturdays and Mondays are the best days for the sale of baked potatoes in those parts of London that are not near the markets; but in those in the vicinity of Clare, Newport, Covent-garden, Newgate, Smithfield, and other markets, the trade is briskest on the market-days. The baked-potato men are many of them broken-down tradesmen. Many are labourers who find a difficulty of obtaining employment in the winter time; some are coster-mongers; some have been artisans; indeed, there are some of all classes among them.

After the baked potato season is over, the generality of the hucksters take to selling strawberries, raspberries, or anything in season. Some go to labouring work. One of my informants, who had been a bricklayer's labourer, said that after the season he always looked out for work among the bricklayers, and this kept him employed until the baked potato season came round again.

'When I first took to it,' he said, 'I was very badly off. My master had no employment for me, and my brother was ill, and so was my wife's sister, and I had no way of keeping 'em, or myself either. The labouring men are mostly out of work in the winter time, so I spoke to a friend of mine, and he told me how he managed every winter, and advised me to do the same. I took to it, and have stuck to it ever since. The trade was much better then. I could buy a hundred-weight of potatoes for 1s. 9d. to 2s. 3d., and there were fewer to sell them. We generally use to a cwt. of potatoes three-quarters of a pound of butter – tenpenny salt butter is what we buy – a pennyworth of salt, a pennyworth of pepper, and five pennyworth of charcoal. This, with the baking, 9d., brings the expenses to just upon 7s. 6d. per cwt., and for this our receipts will be 12s. 6d., thus leaving about 5s. per cwt. profit.' Hence the average profits of the trade are about 30s. a week – 'and more to some,' said my informant. A man in Smithfield-market, I am credibly informed, clears at the least 3l. a week. On the Friday he has a fresh basket of hot potatoes brought to him from the baker's every quarter of an hour. Such is his custom that he has not even time to take money, and his wife stands by his side to do so.

Another potato-vendor who shifted his can, he said, 'from a public-house where the tap dined at twelve', to another half-a-mile off, where it 'dined at one, and so did the parlour', and afterwards to any place he deemed best, gave me the following account of his customers:

'Such a day as this, sir [Jan. 24], when the fog's like a cloud come down, people looks very shy at my taties, very; they've been more suspicious ever since the taty rot. I thought I should never have rekivered it; never, not the rot. I sell most to mechanics – I was a grocer's porter myself before I was a baked taty – for their dinners and they're on for good shops where I serves the taps and parlours, and pays me without grumbling, like gentlemen. Gentlemen does grumble though, for I've sold to them at private houses when they've held the door half open as they've called me – aye, and ladies too – and they've said, "Is *that* all for 2*d.*?" If it'd been a peck they'd have said the same, I know. Some customers is very pleasant with me, and says I'm a blessing. One always says he'll give me a ton of taties when his ship comes home, 'cause he can always have a hot murphy to his cold saveloy, when tin's short. He's a harness-maker, and the railways has injured him. There's Union-street and there's Pearl-row, and there's Market-street, now, – they're all off the Borough-road – if I go there at ten at night or so, I can sell 3*s.* worth, perhaps, 'cause they know me, and I have another baked taty to help there sometimes. They're women that's not reckoned the best in the world that buys there, but they pay me. I know why I got my name up. I had luck to have good fruit when the rot was about, and they got to know me. I only go twice or thrice a week, for it's two miles from my regular places. I've trusted them sometimes. They've said to me, as modest as could be, "Do give me credit, and 'pon my word you shall be paid; there's a dear!" I am paid mostly. Little shopkeepers is fair customers, but I do best for the taps and parlours. Perhaps I make 12*s.* or 15*s.* a week – I hardly know, for I've only myself and keep no 'count – for the season; money goes one can't tell how, and 'specially if you drinks a drop, as I do sometimes. Foggy weather drives me to it, I'm so worritted; that is, now and then, you'll mind, sir.'

There are, at present 300 vendors of hot baked potatoes getting their living in the streets of London, each of whom sell, upon an average, ½ cwt. of potatoes daily. The average takings of each vendor is 6*s.* a day; and the receipts of the whole number throughout the season (which lasts from the latter end of September till March inclusive), a period of 6 months, is 14,000*l.*

A capital is required to start in this trade as, follows: can, 2*l.*; knife, 3*d.*; stock-money, 8*s.*; charge for baking 100 potatoes, 1*s.*; charcoal, 4*d.*; butter, 2*d.*; salt, 1*d.* and pepper, 1*d.*; altogether, 2*l.* 9*s.* 11*d.* The can and knife is the only property described as fixed, stock-money, &c., being daily occurring, amounts to 75*l.* during the season.

Of the Street-sellers of Ham-sandwiches

[p. 185] The ham-sandwich-seller carries his sandwiches on a tray or flat basket, covered with a clean white cloth; he also wears a white apron, and white sleeves. His usual stand is at the doors of the theatres.

The trade was unknown until eleven years ago, when a man who had been unsuccessful in keeping a coffee-shop in Westminster, found it necessary to look out for some mode of living, and he hit upon the plan of vending sandwiches, precisely in the present style, at the theatre doors. The attempt was successful; the man soon took 10s. a night, half of which was profit. He 'attended' both the great theatres, and was 'doing well'; but at five or six weeks' end, competitors appeared in the field, and increased rapidly, and so his sale was affected, people being regardless of his urging ⁺hat he 'was the original ham-sandwich'. The capital required to start in the trade was small; a few pounds of ham, a proportion of loaves, and a little mustard was all that was required, and for this 10s. was ample. That sum, however, could not be commanded by many who were anxious to deal in sandwiches; and the man who commenced the trade supplied them at 6d. a dozen, the charge to the public being 1d. a-piece. Some of the men, however, murmured, because they thought that what they thus bought were not equal to those the wholesale sandwich-man offered for sale himself; and his wholesale trade fell off, until now, I am told, he has only two customers among street-sellers.

Ham sandwiches are made from any part of the bacon which may be sufficiently lean, such as 'the gammon', which now costs 4d. and 5d. the pound. It is sometimes, but very rarely, picked up at 3½d. When the trade was first started, 7d. a pound was paid for the ham, but the sandwiches are now much larger. To make three dozen a pound of meat is required, and four quartern loaves. The 'ham' may cost 5d., the bread 1s. 8d. or 1s. 10d., and the mustard 1d. The proceeds for this would be 3s., but the trade is very precarious: little can be done in wet weather. If unsold, the sandwiches spoil, for the bread gets dry, and the ham loses its fresh colour; so that those who depend upon this trade are wretchedly poor. A first-rate week is to clear 10s.; a good week is put at 7s.; and a bad week at 3s. 6d. On some nights they do not sell a dozen sandwiches. There are half penny sandwiches, but these are only half the size of those at a penny.

The persons carrying on this trade have been, for the most part, in some kind of service – errand-boys, pot-boys, foot-boys (or pages), or lads engaged about inns. Some few have been mechanics. Their average weekly earnings hardly exceed 5s., but some 'get odd jobs' at other things.

'There are now, sir, at the theatres this (the Strand) side the water, and at Ashley's, the Surrey, and the Vic., two dozen and nine sandwiches.' So said one of the trade, who counted up his brethren for me. This man calculated also that at the Standard, the saloons, the concert-rooms, and at Limehouse, Mile-end, Bethnal-green-road, and elsewhere, there might be more than as many again as those 'working' the theatres – or 70 in all. They are nearly all men, and no boys or girls are now in the trade. The number of these people, when the large theatres were open with the others, was about double what it is now.

The information collected shows that the expenditure in ham-sandwiches, supplied by street-sellers is 1,820*l*. yearly, and a consumption of 436,800 sandwiches.

To start in the ham-sandwich street-trade requires 2*s*. for a basket, 2*s*. for kettle to boil ham in, 6*d*. for knife and fork, 2*d*. for mustard-pot and spoon, 7*d*. for ½ cwt. of coals, 5*s*. for ham, 1*s*. 3*d*. for bread, 4*d*. for mustard, 9*d*. for basket, cloth, and apron, 4*d*. for over-sleeves – or a capital of 12*s*. 11*d*.

Of the Experience of a Ham Sandwich-seller

[pp. 185–6] A young man gave me the following account. His look and manners were subdued; and, though his dress was old and worn, it was clean and unpatched.

'I hardly remember my father, sir,' he said; 'but I believe, if he'd lived, I should have been better off. My mother couldn't keep my brother and me – he's older than me – when we grew to be twelve or thirteen, and we had to shift for ourselves. She works at the stays, and now makes only 3*s*. a week, and we can't help her. I was first in place as a sort of errand-boy, then I was a stationer's boy, and then a news agent's boy. I wasn't wanted any longer, but left with a good character. My brother had gone into the sandwich trade – I hardly knew what made him – and he advised me to be a ham sandwich-man, and so I started as one. At first, I made 10*s*., and 7*s*., and 8*s*. a week – that's seven years or so – but things are worse now, and I make 3*s*. 6*d*. some weeks, and 5*s*. others, and 6*s*. is an out-and-outer. My rent's 2*s*. a week, but I haven't my own things. I am so sick of this life, I'd do anything to get out of it; but I don't see a way. Perhaps I might have been more careful when I was in it; but, really, if you do make 10*s*. a week, you want shoes, or a shirt – so what is 10*s*. after all? I wish I had it now, though. I used to buy my sandwiches at 6*d*. a dozen, but I found that wouldn't do; and now I buy and boil the stuff, and make them myself. What *did* cost 6*d*., now costs me 4*d*. or 4½*d*. I work the theatres this side of the water, chiefly the 'Lympic and the 'Delphi. The best theatre I ever had was the Garding, when it had two galleries, and was dramatic – the operas there wasn't the least good to me. The Lyceum was good, when it was Mr Keeley's. I hardly know what sort my customers are, but they're those that go to theaytres: shopkeepers and clerks, I think.

Gentlemen don't often buy of me. They *have* bought, though. Oh, no, they never give a farthing over; they're more likely to want seven for 6*d*. The women of the town buy of me, when it gets late, for themselves and their fancy men. They're liberal enough when they've money. They sometimes treat a poor fellow in a public-house. In summer I'm often out 'till four in the morning, and then must lie in bed half next day. The 'Delphi was better than it is. I've taken 3*s*. at the first "turn out" (the leaving the theatre for a short time after the first piece), 'but the turn-outs at the Garding was better than that. A penny pie-shop has spoiled us at the 'Delphi and at Ashley's. I go out between eight and nine in the evening. People often want more in my sandwiches, though I'm starving on them. "Oh," they'll say, "you've been 'prenticed to Vauxhall, you have." "They're 1*s*. there," says I, "and no bigger. I haven't Vauxhall prices." I stand by the night-houses when it's late – not the fashionables. Their customers wouldn't look at me; but I've known women, that carried their heads very high, glad to get a sandwich afterwards. Six times I've been upset by drunken fellows, on purpose, I've no doubt, and lost all my stock. Once, a gent, kicked my basket into the dirt, and he was going off – for it was late – but some people by began to make remarks about using a poor fellow that way, so he paid for all, after he had them counted. I am *so* sick of this life, sir. I *do* dread the winter so. I've stood up to the ankles in snow till after midnight, and till I've wished I was snow myself, and could melt like it and have an end. I'd do anything to get away from this, but I can't. Passion Week's another dreadful time. It drives us to starve, just when we want to get up a little stock-money for Easter. I've been bilked by cabmen, who've taken a sandwich; but, instead of paying for it, have offered to fight me. There's no help. We're knocked about sadly by the police. Time's very heavy on my hands, sometimes, and that's where you feel it. I read a bit, if I can get anything to read, for I was at St Clement's school; or I walk out to look for a job. On summer-days I sell a trotter or two. But mine's a wretched life, and so is most ham sandwich-men. I've no enjoyment of my youth, and no comfort.

'Ah, sir! I live very poorly. A ha'porth or a penn'orth of cheap fish, which I cook myself, is one of my treats – either herrings or plaice – with a 'tatur, perhaps. Then there's a sort of meal, now and then, off the odds and ends of the ham, such as isn't quite viewy enough for the public, along with the odds and ends of the loaves. I can't boil a bit of greens with my ham, 'cause I'm afraid it might rather spoil the colour. I don't slice the ham till it's cold – it cuts easier, and is a better colour then, I think. I wash my aprons, and sleeves, and cloths myself, and iron them too. A man that sometimes makes only 3s. 6d. a week, and sometimes less, and must pay 2s. rent out of that, must look after every farthing. I've often walked eight miles to see if I could find ham a halfpenny a pound cheaper anywhere. If it was tainted, I know it would be flung in my face. If I was sick there's only the parish for me.'

Of the Street-sale of Drinkables

[p. 191] The street-sellers of the drinkables, who have now to be considered, belong to the same class as I have described in treating of the sale of street-provisions generally. The buyers are not precisely of the same class, for the street-eatables often supply a meal, but with the exception of the coffee-stalls, and occasionally of the rice-milk, the drinkables are more of a luxury than a meal. Thus the buyers are chiefly those who have 'a penny to spare', rather than those who have 'a penny to dine upon'. I have described the different classes of purchasers of each potable, and perhaps the accounts – as a picture of street-life – are even more curious than those I have given of the purchasers of the eatables – of (literally) the diners *out*.

Of Coffee-stall Keepers

[pp. 191–6] The vending of tea and coffee, in the streets, was little if at all known twenty years ago, saloop being then the beverage supplied from stalls to the late and early wayfarers. Nor was it until after 1842 that the stalls approached to anything like their present number, which is said to be upwards of 300 – the majority of the proprietors being women. Prior to 1824, coffee was in little demand, even among the smaller tradesmen or farmers, but in that year the duty having been reduced from 1s. to 6d. per lb., the consumption throughout the kingdom in the next seven years was nearly trebled, the increase being from 7,933,041 lbs., in 1824, to 22,745,627 lbs., in 1831. In 1842, the duty on coffee, was fixed at 4d., from British possessions, and from foreign countries at 6d.

But it was not owing solely to the reduced price of coffee, that the street-vendors of it increased in the year or two subsequent to 1842, at least 100 per cent. The great facilities then offered for a cheap adulteration, by mixing ground chicory with the ground coffee, was an enhancement of the profits, and a greater temptation to embark in the business, as a smaller amount of capital would suffice. Within these two or three years, this cheapness has been still further promoted, by the medium of adulteration, the chicory itself being, in its turn, adulterated by the admixture of baked carrots, and the like saccharine roots, which, of course, are not subjected to any duty, while foreign chicory is charged 6*d*. per lb. English chicory is not chargeable with duty, and is now cultivated, I am assured, to the yield of between 4,000 and 5,000 tons yearly, and this nearly all used in the adulteration of coffee. Nor is there greater culpability in this trade among street-vendors, than among 'respectable' shopkeepers; for I was assured, by a leading grocer, that he could not mention twenty shops in the city, of which he could say: 'You can go and buy a pound of ground coffee there, and it will not be adulterated.' The revelations recently made on this subject by the *Lancet* are a still more convincing proof of the *general* dishonesty of grocers.

The coffee-stall keepers generally stand at the corner of a street. In the fruit and meat markets there are usually two or three coffee-stalls, and one or two in the streets leading to them; in Covent-garden there are no less than four coffee-stalls. Indeed, the stalls abound in all the great thoroughfares, and the most in those not accounted 'fashionable' and great 'business' routes, but such as are frequented by working people, on their way to their day's labour. The best 'pitch' in London is supposed to be at the corner of Duke-street, Oxford-street. The proprietor of that stall is said to take full 30*s*. of a morning, in halfpence. One stall-keeper, I was informed, when 'upon the drink' thinks nothing of spending his 10*l*. or 15*l*. in a week. A party assured me that once, when a stall-keeper above mentioned was away 'on the spree', he took up his stand there, and got from 4*s*. to 5*s*. in the course of ten minutes, at the busy time of the morning.

The coffee-stall usually consists of a spring-barrow, with two, and occasionally four, wheels. Some are made up of tables, and some have a tressel and board. On the top of this are placed two or three, and sometimes four, large tin cans, holding upon an average five gallons each. Beneath each of these cans is a small iron fire-pot, perforated like a rushlight shade, and here charcoal is continually burning, so as to keep the coffee or tea hot, with which the cans are filled, hot throughout the early part of the morning. The board of the stall has mostly a compartment for bread and butter, cake, and ham sandwiches, and another for the coffee mugs. There is generally a small tub under each of the stalls, in which the mugs and saucers are washed. The 'grandest' stall in this line is the one beforementioned, as standing at the corner of Duke-street, Oxford-street (of which an engraving is here given). It is a large truck on four wheels, and painted a bright green. The cans are four in number, and of bright polished

THE LONDON COFFEE-STALL.

tin, mounted with brass-plates. There are compartments for bread and butter, sandwiches, and cake. It is lighted by three large oil lamps, with bright brass mountings, and covered in with an oil-cloth roof. The coffee-stalls, generally, are lighted by candle-lamps. Some coffee-stalls are covered over with tarpaulin, like a tent, and others screened from the sharp night or morning air by a clothes-horse covered with blankets, and drawn half round the stall.

Some of the stall-keepers make their appearance at twelve at night, and some not till three or four in the morning. Those that come out at midnight, are for the accommodation of the 'night-walkers' - 'fast gentlemen' and loose girls; and those that come out in the morning, are for the accommodation of the working men.

It is, I may add, piteous enough to see a few young and good-looking girls, some without the indelible mark of habitual depravity on their countenances, clustering together for warmth round a coffee-stall, to which a penny expenditure, or the charity of the proprietor, has admitted them. The thieves do not resort to the coffee-stalls, which are so immediately under the eye of the policeman.

The coffee-stall keepers usually sell coffee and tea, and some of them cocoa. They keep hot milk in one of the large cans, and coffee, tea, or cocoa in the others. They supply bread and butter, or currant cake, in slices – ham sandwiches, water-cresses, and boiled eggs. The price is 1d. per mug, or ½d. per half-mug, for coffee, tea, or cocoa; and ½d. a slice the bread and butter or cake. The ham sandwiches are 2d. (or 1d.) each, the boiled eggs 1d., and the water-cresses a halfpenny a bunch. The coffee, tea, cocoa, and sugar they generally purchase by the single pound, at a grocer's. Those who do an extensive trade purchase in larger quantities. The coffee is usually bought in the berry, and ground by themselves. All purchase chicory to mix with it. For the coffee they pay about 1s.; for the tea about 3s.; for the cocoa 6d. per lb.; and for the sugar 3½d. to 4d. For the chicory the price is 6d. (which is the amount of the duty alone on foreign chicory), and it is mixed with the coffee at the rate of 6 ozs. to the pound; many use as much as 9 and 12 ozs. The coffee is made of a dark colour by means of what are called 'finings', which consist of burnt sugar – such, as is used for browning soups. Coffee is the article mostly sold at the stalls; indeed, there is scarcely one stall in a hundred that is supplied with tea, and not more than a dozen in all London that furnish cocoa. The stall-keepers usually make the cake themselves. A 4 lb. cake generally consists of half a pound of currants, half a pound of sugar, six ounces of beef dripping, and a quartern of flour. The ham for sandwiches costs 5½d. or 6d. per lb.;

86

and when boiled produces in sandwiches about 2s. per lb. It is usually cut
up in slices little thicker than paper. The bread is usually 'second bread';
the butter, salt, at about 8d. the pound. Some borrow their barrows, and
pay 1s. a week for the hire of them. Many borrow the capital upon which
they trade, frequently of their landlord. Some get credit for their grocery
– some for their bread. If they borrow, they pay about 20 per cent. per week
for the loan. I was told of one man that makes a practice of lending money
to the coffee-stall-keepers and other hucksters, at the rate of at least 20
per cent. a week. If the party wishing to borrow a pound or two is
unknown to the money-lender, he requires security, and the interest to
be paid him weekly. This money-lender, I am informed, has been transported once for receiving stolen property, and would now purchase any
amount of plate that might be taken to him.

The class of persons usually belonging to the business have been either
cab-men, policemen, labourers, or artisans. Many have been bred to
dealing in the streets, and brought up to no other employment, but many
have taken to the business owing to the difficulty of obtaining work at their
own trade. The generality of them are opposed to one another. I asked one
in a small way of business what was the average amount of his profits,
and his answer was:

'I usually buy 10 ounces of coffee a night. That costs, when good, 1s.
0½d. With this I should make five gallons of coffee, such as I sell in the
street, which would require 3 quarts of milk, at 3d. per quart, and 1½ lb.
of sugar, at 3½d. per lb., there is some at 3d. This would come to 2s. 2¾d.;
and, allowing 1¼d. for a quarter of a peck of charcoal to keep the coffee
hot, it would give 2s. 4d. for the cost of five gallons of coffee. This I should
sell out at about 1½d. per pint; so that the five gallons would produce me
5s., or 2s. 8d. clear. I generally get rid of one quartern loaf and 6 oz. of
butter with this quantity of coffee, and for this I pay 5d. the loaf and 3d.
the butter, making 8d.; and these I make into twenty-eight slices at ½d. per
slice; so the whole brings me in 1s. 2d., or about 6d. clear. Added to this,
I sell a 4 lb. cake, which costs me 3½d. per lb. 1s. 2d. the entire cake; and
this in twenty-eight slices, at 1d. per slice, would yield 2s. 4d., or 1s. 2d.
clear; so that altogether my clear gains would be 4s. 4d. upon an expenditure of 2s. 2d. – say 200 per cent.'

This is said to be about the usual profit of the trade. Sometimes they give
credit. One person assured me he trusted as much as 9½d. that morning,
and out of that he was satisfied there was 4d., at least, he should never
see. Most of the stalls are stationary, but some are locomotive. Some cans
are carried about with yokes, like milk-cans, the mugs being kept in a

basket. The best district for the night-trade is the City, and the approaches
to the bridges. There are more men and women, I was told, walking along
Cheapside, Aldersgate street, Bishopsgate-street, and Fleet-street. In the
latter place a good trade is frequently done between twelve at night and
two in the morning. For the morning trade the best districts are the Strand,
Oxford-street, City-road, New-road (from one end to the other), the
markets, especially Covent Garden, Billingsgate, Newgate, and the
Borough. There are no coffee-stalls in Smithfield. The reason is that the
drovers, on arriving at the market, are generally tired and cold, and prefer
sitting down to their coffee in a warm shop rather than drink it in the open
street. The best days for coffee-stalls are market mornings, viz. Tuesday,
Thursday, and Saturday. On these days the receipts are generally half as
much again as those of the other mornings. The best time of the year for
the business is the summer. This is, I am told, because the workpeople and
costermongers have more money to spend. Some stall-keepers save
sufficient to take a shop, but these are only such as have a 'pitch' in the
best thoroughfares. One who did a little business informed me that he
usually cleared, including Sunday, 14s. – last week his gains were 15s.;
the week before that he could not remember. He is very frequently out all
night, and does not earn sixpence. This is on wet and cold nights, when
there are few people about. His is generally the night-trade. The average
weekly earnings of the trade, throughout the year, are said to be 1l. The
trade, I am assured by all, is overstocked. They are half too many, they
say. 'Two of us,' to use their own words, 'are eating one man's bread.'
'When coffee in the streets first came up, a man could go and earn,' I am
told, 'his 8s. a night at the very lowest; but now the same class of men
cannot earn more than 3s.' Some men may earn comparatively a large
sum, as much as 38s. or 2l., but the generality of the trade cannot make
more than 1l. per week, if so much. The following is the statement of one
of the class:

'I was a mason's labourer, a smith's labourer, a plasterer's labourer, or
a bricklayer's labourer. I was, indeed, a labouring man. I could not get
employment. I was for six months without any employment. I did not
know which way to support my wife and child (I have only one child).
Being so long out of employment, I saw no other means of getting a living
but out of the streets. I was almost starving before I took to it – that I
certainly was. I'm not ashamed of telling anybody that, because it's true,
and I sought for a livelihood wherever I could. Many said they wouldn't
do such a thing as keep a coffee-stall, but I said I'd do anything to get a
bit of bread honestly. Years ago, when I was a boy, I used to go out selling

88

water-cresses, and apples, oranges, and radishes, with a barrow, for my landlord; so I thought, when I was thrown out of employment, I would take to selling coffee in the streets. I went to a tinman, and paid him 10s. 6d. (the last of my savings, after I'd been four or five months out of work) for a can, I didn't care how I got my living so long as I could turn an honest penny. Well; I went on, and knocked about, and couldn't get a pitch anywhere; but at last I heard that an old man, who had been in the habit of standing for many years at the entrance of one of the markets, had fell ill; so, what did I do, but I goes and pops into his pitch, and there I've done better than ever I did afore. I get 20s. now where I got 10s. one time; and if I only had such a thing as 5l. or 10l., I might get a good living for life. I cannot do half as much as the man that was there before me. He used to make his coffee down there, and had a can for hot water as well; but I have but one can to keep coffee and all in; and I have to borrow my barrow, and pay 1s. a week for it. If I sell my can out, I can't do any more. The struggle to get a living is so great, that, what with one and another in the coffee-trade, it's only those as can get good "pitches" that can get a crust at it.'

As it appears that each coffee-stall keeper on an average, clears 1l. a week, and his takings may be said to be at least double that sum, the yearly street expenditure for tea, coffee, &c., amounts to 31,200l. The quantity of coffee sold annually in the streets, appears to be about 550,000 gallons.

To commence as a coffee-stall keeper in a moderate manner requires about 5l. capital. The truck costs 2l., and the other utensils and materials 3l. The expense of the cans is near upon 16s. each. The stock-money is a few shillings.

Of the Street Sale of Ginger-beer, Sherbet, Lemonade, &c.

[p. 196] The street-trade in ginger-beer – now a very considerable traffic – was not known to any extent until about thirty years ago. About that time (1822) a man, during a most sultry drought, sold extraordinary quantities of 'cool ginger-beer' and of 'soda-powders', near the Royal Exchange, clearing, for the three or four weeks the heat continued, 30s. a day, or 9l. weekly. Soda-water he sold 'in powders', the acid and the alkali being mixed in the water of the glass held by the customer, and drunk whilst effervescing. His prices were 2d. and 3d. a glass for ginger-beer; and 3d. and 4d. for soda-water, 'according to the quality'; though there was in reality no difference whatever in the quality – only in the price. From that time, the numbers pursuing this street vocation increased gradually; they have however fallen off of late years.

The street-sellers who 'brew their own beer' generally prepare half a gross (six dozen) at a time. For a 'good quality' or the 'penny bottle' trade, the following are the ingredients and the mode of preparation: 3 gallons of water; 1 lb. of ginger, 6d.; lemon-acid, 2d.; essence of cloves, 2d.; yeast, 2d.; and 1 lb. of raw sugar, 7d. This admixture, the yeast being the last ingredient introduced, stands 24 hours, and is then ready for bottling. If the beverage be required in 12 hours, double the quantity of yeast is used. The bottles are filled only 'to the ridge', but the liquid and the froth more than fill a full-sized half-pint glass. 'Only half froth,' I was told, 'is reckoned very fair, and it's just the same in the shops.' Thus, 72 bottles, each to be sold at 1d., cost – apart from any outlay in utensils, or any consideration of the value of labour – only 1s. 7d., and yield, at 1d. per bottle, 6s. For the cheaper beverage – called 'playhouse ginger-beer' in the trade – instead of sugar, molasses from the 'private distilleries' is made available. The 'private' distilleries are the illicit ones: '"Jiggers," we call them,' said one man; 'and I could pass 100 in 10 minutes' walk from where we're talking.' Molasses, costing 3d. at a jigger's, is sufficient for a half-gross of bottles of ginger-beer; and of the other ingredients only half the quantity is used, the cloves being altogether dispensed with, but the same amount of yeast is generally applied. This quality of 'beer' is sold at ½d. the glass.

About five years ago 'fountains' for the production of ginger-beer became common in the streets. The ginger-beer trade in the open air is only for a summer season, extending from four to seven months, according to the weather, the season last year having been over in about four months. There were then 200 fountains in the streets, all of which, excepting 20 or 30 of the best, were hired of the ginger-beer manufacturers, who drive a profitable trade in them. The average value of a street-fountain, with a handsome frame or stand, which is usually fixed on a wheeled and movable truck, so as one man's strength may be sufficient to propel it, is 7l.; and, for the rent of such a fountain, 6s. a week is paid when the season is brisk, and 4s. when it is slack; but last summer, I am told, 4s. 6d. was an average. The largest and handsomest ginger-beer fountain in London was – I speak of last summer – in use at the East-end, usually standing in Petticoat-lane, and is the property of a dancing-master. It is made of mahogany, and presents somewhat the form of an upright piano on wheels. It has two pumps, and the brass of the pump-handles and the glass receivers is always kept bright and clean, so that the whole glitters handsomely to the light. Two persons 'serve' at this fountain; and on a fine Sunday morning, from six to one, that being the best trading time, they take 7*l.* or 8*l.* in halfpennies – for 'the beer' is ½*d.* a glass – and 2*l.* each other day of the week. This machine, as it may be called, is drawn by two ponies, said to be worth 10*l.* a-piece; and the whole cost is pronounced – perhaps with a sufficient exaggeration – to have been 150*l.* There were, in the same neighbourhood, two more fountains on a similar style, but commoner, each drawn by only one pony instead of the aristocratic 'pair'.

The ingredients required to feed the 'ginger-beer' fountains are of a very cheap description. To supply 10 gallons, 2 quarts of lime-juice (as it is called, but it is, in reality, lemon-juice), costing 3*s.* 6*d.*, are placed in the recess, sometimes with the addition of a pound of sugar (4*d.*); while some, I am assured, put in a smaller quantity of juice, and add two-pennyworth of oil of vitriol, which 'brings out the sharpness of the lime-juice'. The rest is water.

Of the Street Sale of Peppermint-water

[p. 201] Perhaps the only thing which can be called a cordial or a liqueur sold in the streets (if we except elder wine), is peppermint-water, and of this the sale is very limited. For the first 15 or 20 years of the present century, I was told by one who spoke from a personal knowledge, 'a pepperminter' had two little taps to his keg, which had a division in the interior. From one tap was extracted 'peppermint-water'; from the other, 'strong peppermint-water'. The one was at that time 1*d.* a glass, the other from 2*d.* to 4*d.*, according to the size of the glass. With the 'strong' beverage was mixed smuggled spirit, but so strongly impregnated with the odour of the mint, that a passer-by could not detect the presence of the illicit compound. There are six persons selling peppermint-water in the winter, and only half that number in the summer. The trade is irregular, as some pursue it only of a night, and generally in the street markets; others sell at Billingsgate, and places of great traffic, when the traffic is being carried on. They are stationary for awhile, but keep shifting their ground. The vendors generally 'distilled their own mint', when the sale was greater, but within these six or eight years they have purchased it at a distilling chemist's, and have only prepared it for sale. Water is added to the distilled liquid bought of the chemist, to increase the quantity; but to enhance the heat of the draught – which is a draw to some buyers – black pepper (unground), or ginger, or, but rarely, capsicums, are steeped in the beverage. The peppermint-water is lauded by the vendors, when questioned concerning it, as an excellent stomachic; but nothing is said publicly of its virtues, the cry being merely, 'Pep-permint water, a half-penny a glass.'

The sellers will generally say that they distil the peppermint-water themselves, but this is not now commonly the case. The process, however, is simple enough. The peppermint used is gathered just as it is bursting into flower, and the leaves and buds are placed in a tub, with just water enough to cover them. This steeping continues 24 hours, and then a still is filled three-parts full, and the water is 'over' drawn very slowly.

The price at the chemist's is 1s. a quart for the common mint-water; the street price is ½d. a glass, containing something short of the eighth of a pint. What costs 1s., the street-seller disposes of for 2s., so realising the usual cent. per cent.

To take 2s. is now accounted 'a tidy day's work'; and calculating that four 'pepperminters' take that amount the year round, Sundays excepted, we find that nearly 125l. is spent annually in peppermint-water and 900 gallons of it consumed every year in the streets of London.

The capital required is, keg, 3s.6d., or jar, 2s. (for they are used indifferently); four glasses, 1s.; towel, 4d., and stock-money, 4s.; or, in all, about 8s. The 'water'-keg, or jar, is carried by the vendor, but sometimes it is rested on a large stool carried for the purpose. A distilling apparatus, such as the street-sellers used, was worth about 10s. The vendors are of the same class of street-sellers as the ginger-beer people.

Of Milk Selling in St James's Park

[pp. 201–2] The principal sale of milk from the cow is in St James's Park. The once fashionable drink known as syllabubs – the milk being drawn warm from the cow's udder, upon a portion of wine, sugar, spice, &c. – is now unknown. As the sellers of milk in the park are merely the servants of cow-keepers, and attend to the sale as a part of their business, no lengthened notice is required.

The milk-sellers obtain leave from the Home Secretary, to ply their trade in the park. There are eight stands in the summer, and as many cows, but in the winter there are only four cows. The milk-vendors sell upon an average, in the summer, from eighteen to twenty quarts per day; in the winter, not more than a third of that quantity. The interrupted milking of the cows, as practised in the Park, often causes them to give less milk, than they would in the ordinary way. The chief customers are infants, and adults, and others, of a delicate constitution, who have been recommended to take new milk. On a wet day scarcely any milk can be disposed of. Soldiers are occasional customers.

A somewhat sour-tempered old woman, speaking as if she had been crossed in love, but experienced in this trade, gave me the following account:

'It's not at all a lively sort of life, selling milk from the cows, though some thinks it's a gay time in the Park! I've often been dull enough, and could see nothing to interest one, sitting alongside a cow. People drink new milk for their health, and I've served a good many such. They're mostly young women, I think, that's delicate, and makes the most of it. There's twenty women, and more, to one man what drinks new milk. If they was set to some good hard work, it would do them more good than new milk, or ass's milk either, I think. Let them go on a milk-walk to cure them – that's what I say. Some children come pretty regularly with their nurses to drink new milk. Some bring their own china mugs to drink it out of; nothing less was good enough for them. I've seen the nurse-girls frightened to death about the mugs. I've heard one young child say to another: "I shall tell mama that Caroline spoke to a mechanic, who came and shook hands with her." The girl was as red as fire and said it was her brother. Oh, yes, there's a deal of brothers comes to look for their sisters in the Park. The greatest fools I've sold milk to is servant-gals out for the day. Some must have a day, or half a day, in the month. Their mistresses ought to keep them at home, I say, and not let them out to spend their money, and get into nobody knows what company for a holiday; mistresses is too easy that way. It's such gals as makes fools of themselves in liking a soldier to run after them. I've seen one of them – yes, some would call her pretty, and the prettiest is the silliest and easiest tricked out of money, that's my opinion, anyhow – I've seen one of them, and more than one, walk with a soldier, and they've stopped a minute, and she's taken something out of her glove and given it to him. Then they've come up to me, and he's said to her, "Mayn't I treat you with a little new milk, my dear?' and he's changed a shilling. Why, of course, the silly fool of a gal had given him that there shilling. I thought, when Annette Myers shot the soldier, it would be a warning, but nothing's a warning to some gals. *She* was one of those fools. It was a good deal talked about at the stand, but I think none of us know'd her. Indeed, we don't know our customers but by sight. Yes, there's now and then some oldish gentlemen – I suppose they're gentlemen, anyhow, they're idle men – lounging about the stand: but there's no nonsense there. They tell me, too, that there's not so much lounging about as there was; those that's known the trade longer than me thinks so. Them children's a great check on the nusses, and they can't be such fools as the servant-maids. I don't know how many of them I've served with milk along with soldiers: I never counted them. They're nothing to me. Very few elderly people drink new milk. It's mostly the young. I've been asked by strangers when the Duke of Wellington would pass to the Horse-Guards or to the House of Lords. He's pretty regular. I've had 6d. given me – but not above once or twice a year – to tell strangers where was the best place to see him from as he passed. I don't understand about this Great Exhibition, but, no doubt, more new milk will be sold when it's opened, and that's all I cares about.'

Of the Street Sale of Milk

[p. 202] During the summer months milk is sold in Smithfield, Billingsgate, and the other markets, and on Sundays in Battersea-fields, Clapham-common, Camberwell-green, Hampstead-heath, and similar places. About twenty men are engaged in this sale. They usually wear a smock frock, and have the cans and yoke used by the regular milk-sellers; they are not itinerant. The skim milk – for they sell none else – is purchased at the dairies at $1\frac{1}{2}d$. a quart, and even the skim milk is also further watered by the street-sellers. Their cry is 'Half-penny half-pint! Milk!' The tin measure however in which the milk-and-water is served is generally a 'slang', and contains but half of the quantity proclaimed. The purchasers are chiefly boys and children; rarely men, and never costermongers, I was told, 'for they reckon milk sickly'. These street-sellers – who have most of them been employed in the more regular milk-trade – clear about 1s. 6d. a day each, for three months; and as the profit is rather more than cent. per cent. it appears that about 4,000 gallons of milk are thus sold, and upwards of 260l. laid out upon these persons, yearly in its purchase.

A pair of cans with the yoke cost 15s., and 1l. is amply sufficient as capital to start in this trade, as the two measures used may be bought for 2s.; and 3s. can be devoted to the purchase of the liquid.

Of Street Piemen

[pp. 205–7] The itinerant trade in pies is one of the most ancient of the street callings of London. The meat pies are made of beef or mutton; the fish pies of eels; the fruit of apples, currants, gooseberries, plums, damsons, cherries, raspberries, or rhubarb, according to the season – and occasionally of mince-meat. A few years ago the street pie-trade was very profitable, but it has been almost destroyed by the 'pie-shops', and further, the few remaining street-dealers say 'the people now haven't the pennies to spare'. Summer fairs and races are the best places for the piemen. In London the best times are during any grand sight or holiday-making, such as a review in Hyde-park, the Lord Mayor's show, the opening of Parliament, Greenwich fair, &c. Nearly all the men of this class, whom I saw, were fond of speculating as to whether the Great Exhibition would be 'any good' to them, or not.

The London piemen, who may number about forty in winter, and twice that number in summer, are seldom stationary. They go along with their pie-cans on their arms, crying, 'Pies all 'ot! eel, beef, or mutton pies! Penny pies, all 'ot – all 'ot!' The 'can' has been before described. The pies are kept hot by means of a charcoal fire beneath, and there is a partition in the body of the can to separate the hot and cold pies. The 'can' has two tin drawers, one at the bottom, where the hot pies are kept, and above these are the cold pies. As fast as the hot dainties are sold, their place is supplied by the cold from the upper drawer.

A teetotal pieman in Billingsgate has a pony and 'shay cart'. His business is the most extensive in London. It is believed that he sells 20s. worth or 240 pies a day, but his brother tradesmen sell no such amount. 'I was out last night,' said one man to me, 'from four in the afternoon till half-past twelve. I went from Somers-town to the Horse Guards, and looked in at all the public-houses on my way, and I didn't take above 1s. 6d. I have been out sometimes from the beginning of the evening till long past midnight, and haven't taken more than 4d., and out of that I have to pay 1d. for charcoal.'

The pie-dealers usually make the pies themselves. The meat is bought in 'pieces', of the same part as the sausage-makers purchase – the 'stickings' – at about 3d. the pound. 'People, when I go into houses,' said one man, 'often begin crying, "Mee-yow," or "Bow-wow-wow!" at me; but there's nothing of that kind now. Meat, you see, is so cheap.' About five-dozen pies are generally made at a time. These require a quartern of flour at 5d. or 6d.; 2 lbs. of suet at 6d.; 1½ lb. meat at 3d., amounting in all to about 2s. To this must be added 3d. for baking; 1d. for the cost of keeping hot, and 2d. for pepper, salt, and eggs with which to season and wash them over. Hence the cost of the five dozen would be about 2s. 6d., and the profit the same. The usual quantity of meat in each pie is about half an ounce. There are not more than 20 *hot*-piemen now in London. There are some who carry pies about on a tray slung before them; these are mostly boys, and, including them, the number amounts to about sixty all the year round, as I have stated.

The penny pie-shops, the street men say, have done their trade a great deal of harm. These shops have now got mostly all the custom, as they make the pies much larger for the money than those sold in the streets. The pies in Tottenham-court-road are very highly seasoned. 'I bought one there the other day, and it nearly took the skin off my mouth; it was full of pepper,' said a street-pieman, with considerable bitterness, to me. The reason why so large a quantity of pepper is put in is, because persons can't tell the flavour of the meat with it. Piemen generally are not very particular about the flavour of the meat they buy, as they can season it up into anything. In the summer, a street pieman thinks he is doing a good business if he takes 5s. per day, and in the winter if he gets half that. On Saturday night, however, he generally takes 5s. in the winter, and about 8s. in the summer. At Greenwich fair he will take about 14s. At a review in Hyde-park, if it is a good one, he will sell about 10s. worth. The generality of the customers are the boys of London. The women seldom, if ever, buy pies in the streets. At the public-houses a few pies are sold, and the pieman makes a practice of 'looking in' to all the taverns on his way. Here his customers are found principally in the tap-room. 'Here's all 'ot!' the pieman cries, as he walks in; 'toss or buy! up and win 'em!' This is the only way that the pies can be got rid of. 'If it wasn't for tossing we shouldn't sell one.'

To 'toss the pieman' is a favourite pastime with costermongers' boys and all that class; some of them aspire to the repute of being gourmands, and are critical on the quality of the comestible. If the pieman win the toss, he receives 1d. without giving a pie; if he lose, he hands it over for nothing. The pieman himself never 'tosses', but always calls head or tail to his customer. At the week's end it comes to the same thing, they say, whether they toss or not: 'I've taken as much as 2s. 6d. at tossing, which I shouldn't have had if I hadn't done so. Very few people buy without tossing, and the boys in particular. Gentlemen "out on the spree" at the late public-houses will frequently toss when they don't want the pies, and when they win they will amuse themselves by throwing the pies at one another, or at me. Sometimes I have taken as much as half-a-crown, and the people of whom I had the money have never eaten a pie. The boys has the greatest love of gambling, and they seldom, if ever, buys without tossing.' One of the reasons why the street boys delight in tossing, is, that they can often obtain a pie by such means when they have only a halfpenny wherewith to gamble. If the lad wins he gets a penny pie for his halfpenny.

For street mince-meat pies the pieman usually makes 5lb. of mince-meat at a time, and for this he will put in 2 doz. of apples, 1lb. of sugar, 1lb. of currants, 2lb. of 'critlings' (critlings being the refuse left after boiling down the lard), a good bit of spice to give the critlings a flavour, and plenty of treacle to make the mince-meat look rich.

The 'gravy' which used to be given with the meat-pies was poured out of an oil-can, and consisted of a little salt and water browned. A hole was made with the little finger in the top of the meat pie, and the 'gravy' poured in until the crust rose. With this gravy a person in the line assured me that he has known pies four days old to go off very freely, and be pronounced excellent. The street piemen are mostly bakers, who are unable to obtain employment at their trade. 'I myself,' said one, 'was a bread and biscuit baker. I have been at the pie business now about two years and a half, and can't get a living at it. Last week my earnings were not more than 7s. all the week through, and I was out till three in the morning to get that.' The piemen seldom begin business till six o'clock, and some remain out all night. The best time for the sale of pies is generally from ten at night to one in the morning.

Calculating that there are only fifty street piemen plying their trade in London, the year through, and that their average earnings are 8s. a week, we find a street expenditure exceeding 3,000l., and a street consumption of pies amounting nearly to three quarters of a million yearly.

To start in the penny pie business of the streets requires 1l. for a 'can', 2s. 6d. for a 'turn-halfpenny' board to gamble with, 12s. for a gross of tin pie-dishes, 8d. for an apron, and about 6s. 6d. for stock money – allowing 1s. for flour, 1s. 3d. for meat, 2d. for apples, 4d. for eels, 2s. for pork flare or fat, 2d. for sugar, ¼d. for cloves, 1d. for pepper and salt, 1d. for an egg to wash the pies over with, 6d. for baking, and 1d. for charcoal to keep the pies hot in the streets. Hence the capital required would be about 2l. in all.

Of the Street-sellers of Plum 'Duff' or Dough

[pp. 207–8] Plum dough is one of the street-eatables – though perhaps it is rather a violence to class it with the street-pastry – which is usually made by the vendors. It is simply a boiled plum, or currant, pudding, of the plainest description. It is sometimes made in the rounded form of the plum-pudding; but more frequently in the 'roly-poly' style. Hot pudding used to be of much more extensive sale in the streets. One informant told me that twenty or thirty years ago, batter, or Yorkshire, pudding, 'with plums in it', was a popular street business. The 'plums', as in the orthodox plum-puddings, are raisins. The street-vendors of plum 'duff' are now very few, only six as an average, and generally women, or if a man be the salesman he is the woman's husband. The sale is for the most part an evening sale, and some vend the plum dough only on a Saturday night. A woman in Leather-lane, whose trade is a Saturday night trade, is accounted 'one of the best plum duffs' in London, as regards the quality of the comestible, but her trade is not considerable.

The vendors of plum dough are the street-sellers who live by vending other articles, and resort to plum dough, as well as to other things, 'as a help'. This dough is sold out of baskets in which it is kept hot by being covered with cloths, sometimes two and even three, thick; and the smoke issuing out of the basket, and the cry of the street-seller, 'Hot plum duff, hot plum', invite custom. A quartern of flour, 5*d*.; ½ lb. Valentia raisins, 2*d*.; dripping and suet in equal proportions, 2½*d*.; treacle, ½*d*.; and all-spice, ½*d*. – in all 10½*d*.; supply a roly-poly of twenty pennyworths. The treacle, however, is only introduced 'to make the dough look rich and spicy', and must be used sparingly.

The plum dough is sold in slices at ½*d*. or 1*d*. each, and the purchasers are almost exclusively boys and girls – boys being at least three-fourths of the revellers in this street luxury. I have ascertained – as far as the information of the street-sellers enables me to ascertain – that take the year through, six 'plum duffers' take 1*s*. a day each, for four winter months, including Sundays, when the trade is likewise prosecuted. Some will take from 4*s*. to 10*s*. (but rarely 10*s*.) on a Saturday night, and nothing on other nights, and some do a little in the summer. The vendors, who are all stationary, stand chiefly in the street-markets and reside near their stands, so that they can get relays of hot dough.

If we calculate then 42*s*. a week as the takings of six persons, for five months, so including the summer trade, we find that upwards of 200*l*. is expended in the street purchase of plum dough, nearly half of which is profit. The trade, however, is reckoned among those which will disappear altogether from the streets.

The capital required to start is: basket, 1*s*. 9*d*.; cloths, 6*d*.; pan for boiling, 2*s*.; knife, 2*d*.; stock-money, 2*s*.; in all about, 7*s*. 6*d*.

Of the Street-sellers of Cakes, Tarts, &c.

[p. 208]   These men and boys – for there are very few women or girls in the trade – constitute a somewhat numerous class. They are computed (including Jews) at 150 at the least, all regular hands, with an addition, perhaps, of 15 or 20, who seek to earn a few pence on a Sunday, but have some other, though poorly remunerative, employment on the week-days. The cake and tart-sellers in the streets have been, for the most part, mechanics or servants; a fifth of the body, however, have been brought up to this or to some other street-calling.

The cake-men carry their goods on a tray slung round their shoulders when they are offering their delicacies for sale, and on their heads when not engaged in the effort to do business. They are to be found in the vicinity of all public places. Their goods are generally arranged in pairs on the trays; in bad weather they are covered with a green cloth.

None of the street-vendors make the articles they sell; indeed, the diversity of those articles renders that impossible. Among the regular articles of this street-sale are 'Coventrys', or three-cornered puffs with jam inside; raspberry biscuits; cinnamon biscuits; 'chonkeys', or a kind of mince-meat baked in crust; Dutch butter-cakes; Jews' butter-cakes; 'bowlas', or round tarts made of sugar, apple, and bread; 'jumbles', or thin crisp cakes made of treacle, butter, and flour; and jams, or open tarts with a little preserve in the centre.

All these things are made for the street-sellers by about a dozen Jew pastry-cooks, the most of whom reside about Whitechapel. They confine themselves to the trade, and make every description. On a fine holiday morning their shops, or rather bake-houses, are filled with customers, as they supply the small shops as well as the street-sellers of London. Each article is made to be sold at a halfpenny, and the allowance by the wholesale pastry-cook is such as to enable his customers to realise a profit of 4d. in 1s.; thus he charges 4d. a dozen for the several articles. Within the last seven years there has been, I am assured, a great improvement in the composition of these cakes, &c. This is attributable to the Jews having introduced superior dainties, and, of course, rendered it necessary for the others to vie with them; the articles vended by these Jews (of whom there are from 20 to 40 in the streets) are still pronounced, by many connoisseurs in street-pastry, as the best. Some sell penny dainties also, but not to a twentieth part of the halfpenny trade. One of the wholesale pastry-cooks takes 40l. a week. These wholesale men, who sometimes credit the street-people, buy ten, fifteen, or twenty sacks of flour at a time whenever a cheap bargain offers. They purchase as largely in Irish butter, which they have bought at 3d. or 2½d. the pound. They buy also 'scrapings', or what remains in the butter-firkins when emptied by the butter-sellers in the shops. 'Good scrapings' are used for the best cakes; the jam they make themselves. To commence the wholesale business requires a capital of 600*l.* To commence the street-selling requires a capital of only 10*s.*; and this includes the cost of a tray, about 1*s.* 9*d.*; a cloth 1*s.*; and a leathern strap, with buckle, to go round the neck, 6*d.*; while the rest is for stock, with a shilling or two as a reserve. All the street-sellers insist upon the impossibility of any general baker making cakes as cheap as those they vend. 'It's impossible, sir,' said one man to me, 'it's a trade by itself; nobody else can touch it. They was miserable little things seven years ago.'

OF THE STREET-SELLERS OF STATIONERY, LITERATURE, AND THE FINE ARTS

[pp. 227–9] We now come to a class of street-folk wholly distinct from any before treated of. As yet we have been dealing principally with the uneducated portion of the street-people – men whom, for the most part, are allowed to remain in nearly the same primitive and brutish state as the savage – creatures with nothing but their appetites, instincts, and passions to move them, and made up of the same crude combination of virtue and vice – the same generosity combined with the same predatory tendencies as the Bedouins of the desert – the same love of revenge and disregard of pain, and often the same gratitude and susceptibility to kindness as the Red Indian – and, furthermore, the same insensitivity to female honour and abuse of female weakness, and the same utter ignorance of the Divine nature of the Godhead as marks either Bosjesman, Carib, or Thug.

The costers and many other of the street-sellers before described, however, are bad – not so much from their own perversity as from our selfishness. That they partake of the natural evil of human nature is not their fault but ours, – who would be like them if we had not been taught by others better than ourselves to control the bad and cherish the good principles of our hearts.

The street-sellers of stationery, literature, and the fine arts, however, differ from all before treated of in the *general*, though far from universal, education of the sect. They constitute principally the class of street-orators, known in these days as 'patterers', and formerly termed 'mountebanks', – people who, in the words of Strutt, strive to 'help off their wares by pompous speeches, in which little regard is paid either to truth or propriety.' To patter, is a slang term, meaning to speak. To indulge in this kind of oral puffery, of course, requires a certain exercise of the intellect, and it is the consciousness of their mental superiority which makes the patterers look down upon the costermongers as an inferior body, with whom they object either to be classed or to associate. The scorn of some of the 'patterers' for the mere costers is as profound as the contempt of the pickpocket for the pure beggar. Those who have not witnessed this pride of class among even the most degraded, can form no adequate idea of the arrogance with which the skilled man, no matter how base the art, looks upon the unskilled. 'We are the haristocracy of the streets,' was said to me by one of the street-folks, who told penny fortunes with a bottle. 'People don't pay us for what we gives 'em, but only to hear us talk. We live like yourself, sir, by the hexercise of our hinterllects – we by talking, and you by writing.'

But notwithstanding the self-esteem of the patterers, I am inclined to think that they are less impressionable and less susceptible of kindness than the costers whom they despise. Dr Conolly has told us that, even among the insane, the educated classes are the most difficult to move and govern through their affections. They are invariably suspicious, attributing unworthy motives to every benefit conferred, and consequently incapable of being touched by any sympathy on the part of those who may be affected by their distress. So far as my experience goes it is the same with the street-patterers. Any attempt to befriend them is almost sure to be met with distrust. Nor does their mode of life serve in any way to lessen their misgivings. Conscious how much their own livelihood depends upon assumption and trickery, they naturally consider that others have some 'dodge', as they call it, or some latent object in view when any good is sought to be done them. The impulsive costermonger, however, approximating more closely to the primitive man, moved solely by his feelings, is as easily humanized by any kindness as he is brutified by any injury.

The patterers, again, though certainly more intellectual, are scarcely less immoral than the costers. Their superior cleverness gives them the power of justifying and speciously glossing their evil practices, but serves in no way to restrain them; thus affording the social philosopher another melancholy instance of the evil of developing the intellect without the conscience – of teaching people to *know* what is morally beautiful and ugly, without teaching them at the same time to feel and delight in the one and abhor the other – or, in other words, of quickening the cunning and checking the emotions of the individual.

Among the patterers marriage is as little frequent as among the costermongers; with the exception of the older class, who 'were perhaps married before they took to the streets'. Hardly one of the patterers, however, has been bred to a street life; and this constitutes another line of demarcation between them and the costermongers.

The costers, we have seen, are mostly hereditary wanderers – having been as it were born to frequent the public thoroughfares; some few of the itinerant dealers in fish, fruit, and vegetables, have it is true been driven by want of employment to adopt street-selling as a means of living, but these are, so to speak, the aliens rather than the natives of the streets. The patterers, on the other hand, have for the most part neither been born and bred nor driven to a street life – but have rather *taken* to it from a natural love of what they call 'roving'. This propensity to lapse from a civilized into a nomad state – to pass from a settler into a wanderer – is a peculiar characteristic of the pattering tribe. The tendency however is by no means extraordinary; for ethnology teaches us, that whereas many abandon the habits of civilized life to adopt those of a nomadic state of existence, but very few of the wandering tribes give up vagabondising and betake themselves to settled occupations. The innate 'love of a roving life', which many of the street-people themselves speak of as the cause of their originally taking to the streets, appears to be accompanied by several peculiar characteristics; among the most marked of these are an indomitable 'self-will' or hatred of the least restraint or control – an innate aversion to every species of law or government, whether political, moral, or domestic – a stubborn, contradictory nature – an incapability of continuous labour, or remaining long in the same place occupied with the same object, or attending to the same subject – an unusual predilection for amusements, and especially for what partakes of the ludicrous – together with a great relish of all that is ingenious, and so finding extreme delight in tricks and frauds of every kind. There are two patterers now in the streets (brothers) – well-educated and respectably connected – who candidly confess they prefer that kind of life to any other, and would not leave it if they could.

Nor are the patterers less remarkable than the costermongers for their utter absence of all religious feeling. There is, however, this distinction between the two classes – that whereas the creedlessness of the one is but the consequence of brutish ignorance, that of the other is the result of natural perversity and educated scepticism – as the street-patterers include many men of respectable connections, and even classical attainments. Among them, may be found the son of a military officer, a clergyman, a man brought up to the profession of medicine, two Grecians of the Blue-coat School, clerks, shopmen, and a class who have been educated to no especial calling – some of the latter being the natural sons of gentlemen and noblemen – and who, when deprived of the support of their parents or friends, have taken to the streets for bread. Many of the younger and smarter men, I am assured, reside with women of the town, though they may not be dependent for their livelihood on the wages got by the infamy of these women. Not a few of the patterers, too, in their dress and appearance, present but little difference to that of the 'gent'. Some wear a moustache, while others indulge in a Henri-Quatre beard. The patterers are, moreover, as a body, not distinguished by that good and friendly feeling one to another which is remarkable among costermongers. If an absence of heartiness and good fellowship be characteristic of an aristocracy – as some political philosophers contend – then the patterers may indeed be said to be the aristocrats of the streets.

The patterers or oratorical street-sellers include among their class many itinerant traders, other than the wandering 'paper-workers' – as those vending the several articles of street-literature are generally denominated. The Cheap Jacks, or oratorical hucksters of hardware at fairs and other places, are among the most celebrated and humorous of this class. The commercial arts and jests of some of these people, display considerable cleverness. Many of their jokes, it is true, are traditional – and as purely a matter of parrotry as the witticisms of the 'funny gentlemen' on the stage, but their ready adaptation of accidental circumstances to the purposes of their business, betrays a modicum of wit far beyond that which falls to the share of ordinary 'low comedians'. The street-vendors of cough drops – infallible cures for the toothache and other ailments – also belong to the pattering class. These are, as was before stated, the remains of the obsolete mountebanks of England and the *saltinbanque* of France – a class of *al fresco* orators who derived their names from the *bench* – the street pulpit, rostrum, or platform – that they ascended, in order the better to deliver their harangues. The street jugglers, actors, and showmen, as well as the street-sellers of grease-removing compositions, corn-salve, razor-paste, plating-balls, waterproof blacking, rat poisons, sovereigns sold for wagers, and a multiplicity of similar street-trickeries – such as oratorical begging – are other ingenious and wordy members of the same chattering, jabbering, or 'pattering' fraternity. These will all be spoken of under the head of the different things they respectively sell or do. For the present we have only to deal with that portion of the 'pattering' body who are engaged in the street sale of literature – or the 'paper-workers' as they call themselves. The latter include the 'running patterers', or 'death-hunters'; being men (no women) engaged in vending last dying speeches and confessions – in hawking 'se-cond edi-tions' of newspapers – or else in 'working', that is to say, in getting rid of what are technically termed 'cocks'; which, in polite language, means accounts of fabulous duels between ladies of fashion – of apochryphal elopements, or fictitious love-letters of sporting noblemen and certain young milliners not a hundred miles from the spot – 'cooked' assassinations and sudden deaths of eminent individuals – pretended jealous affrays between Her Majesty and the Prince Consort (but these papers are now never worked) – or awful tragedies, including mendacious murders, impossible robberies, and delusive suicides.

The sellers of these choice articles, however, belong more particularly to that order or species of the pattering genus known as 'running patterers', or 'flying stationers', from the fact of their being continually on the move while describing the attractions of the 'papers' they have to sell. Contradistinguished from them, however, are the 'standing patterers', or those for whose less startling announcements a crowd is necessary, in order that the audience may have time to swallow the many marvels worked by their wares. The standing patterers require, therefore, what they term a 'pitch', that is to say a fixed locality, where they can hold forth to a gaping multitude for, at least, some few minutes continuously. They are mainly such street-sellers as deal in nostrums and the different kinds of street 'wonders'. Occasionally, however, the running patterer (who is especially literary) transmigrates into a standing one, betaking himself to 'board work', as it is termed in street technology, and stopping at the corners of thoroughfares with a large pictorial placard raised upon a pole, and glowing with a highly-coloured exaggeration of the interesting terrors of the pamphlet he has for sale. This is either 'The Life of Calcraft, the Hangman', 'The Diabolical Practices of Dr — on his Patients when in a state of Mesmerism', or 'The Secret Doings at the White House, Soho', and other similar attractively-repulsive details. Akin to this 'board work' is the practice of what is called 'strawing', or selling straws in the street, and giving away with them something that is either really or fictionally forbidden to be sold, – as indecent papers, political songs, and the like. This practice, however, is now seldom resorted to, while the sale of 'secret papers' is rarely carried on in public. It is true, there are three or four patterers who live chiefly by professing to dispose of 'sealed packets' of obscene drawings and cards for gentlemen; but this is generally a trick adopted to extort money from old debauchees, young libertines, and people of degraded or diseased tastes; for the packets, on being opened, seldom contain anything but an odd number of some defunct periodical.

There is, however, a large traffic in such secret papers carried on in what is called 'the public-house trade', that is to say, by itinerant 'paper-workers' (mostly women), who never make their appearance in the streets, but obtain a livelihood by 'busking', as it is technically termed, or, in other words, by offering their goods for sale only at the bars and in the tap-rooms and parlours of taverns. The excessive indulgence of one appetite is often accompanied by the disease of a second; the drunkard, of course, is super-eminently a sensualist, and is therefore easily taken by anything that tends to stimulate his exhausted desires: so sure is it that one form of bestiality is a necessary concomitant of another. There is another species of patterer, who, though usually included among the standing patterers, belongs rather to an intermediate class, viz., those who neither stand nor 'run', as they descant upon what they sell; but those walk at so slow a rate that, though never stationary, they can hardly be said to move. These are the reciters of dialogues, litanies, and the various street 'squibs' upon passing events; they also include the public pro-pounders of conundrums, and the 'hundred and fifty popular song' enumerators − such as are represented in the engraving here given. Closely connected with them are the 'chaunters', or those who do not cry, but (if one may so far stretch the English language) *sing* the contents of the 'papers' they vend.

These traffickers constitute the principal street-sellers of literature, or 'paper-workers', of the 'pattering' class. In addition to them there are many others vending 'papers' in the public thoroughfares, who are mere traders resorting to no other acts for the disposal of their goods than a simple cry or exposition of them; and many of these are but poor, humble, struggling, and inoffensive dealers. They do not puff or represent what they have to sell as what it is not − (allowing them a fair commercial latitude). They are not of the 'enterprising' class of street tradesmen. Among these are the street-sellers of stationery − such as note-paper, envelopes, pens, ink, pencils, sealing-wax, and wafers. Belonging to the same class, too, are the street-vendors of almanacs, pocket-books, memorandum and account-books. Then there are the sellers of odd numbers of periodicals and broadsheets, and those who vend either playing cards, conversation cards, stenographic cards, and (Epsom, Ascot, &c.) racing cards. Besides these, again, there are the vendors of illustrated cards, such as those embellished with engravings of the Crystal Palace, Views of the Houses of Parliament, as well as the gelatine poetry cards − all of whom, with the exception of the racing-card sellers (who belong generally to the pattering tribe), partake of the usual characteristics of the street-selling class.

After these may be enumerated the vendors of old engravings out of inverted umbrellas, and the hawkers of coloured pictures in frames. Then there are the old book-stalls and barrows, and 'the pinners-up', as they are termed, or sellers of old songs pinned against the wall, as well as the vendors of manuscript music. Moreover, appertaining to the same class, there are the vendors of playbills and 'books of the performance' outside the theatre; and lastly, the pretended sellers of tracts – such as the Lascars and others, who use this kind of street traffic as a cloak for the more profitable trade of begging. The street-sellers of images, although strictly comprised within those who vend fine art productions in the public thoroughfares will be treated of under the head of THE STREET ITALIANS, to which class they mostly belong.

Of the Sale of Newspapers, Books, &c
at the Railway Stations

[pp. 315–16]   Although the sale of newspapers at the railway termini, &c., cannot strictly be classed as a street-sale, it is so far an open-air traffic as to require some brief notice, and it has now become a trade of no small importance.

The privilege of selling to railway-passengers, within the precincts of the terminus, is disposed of by tender. At present the newsvendor on the North-Western Line, I am informed, pays to the company, for the right of sale at the Euston-square terminus, and the provincial stations, as large a sum as 1,700l. per annum. The amount usually given is of course in proportion to the number of stations, and the traffic of the railway.

The purchaser of this exclusive privilege sends his own servants to sell the newspapers and books, which he supplies to them in the quantity required. The men thus engaged are paid from 20s. to 30s. a week, and the boys receive from 6s. to 10s. 6d. weekly, but rarely 10s. 6d.

All the morning and evening papers are sold at the Station, but of the weekly press, those are sent for sale which in the manager's judgment are likely to sell, or which his agent informs him are 'asked for'. It is the same with the weekly unstamped publications. The reason seems obvious; if there be more than can be sold, a dead loss is incurred, for the surplusage, as regards newspapers, is only saleable as waste paper.

The books sold at railways are nearly all of the class best known as 'light reading', or what some account light reading. The price does not often exceed 1s.; and among the books offered for sale in these places are novels in one volume, published at 1s. – sometimes in two volumes, at 1s. each;

'monthly parts' of works issued in weekly numbers; shilling books of poetry; but rarely political or controversial pamphlets. One man, who understood this trade, told me that 'a few of the pamphlets about the Pope and Cardinal Wiseman sold at first; but in a month or six weeks, people began to say, "A shilling for that! I'm sick of the thing."'

The large sum given for the privilege of an exclusive sale, shows that the number of books and papers sold at railway stations must be very considerable. But it must be borne in mind, that the price, and consequently the profit on the daily newspapers, sold at the railways, is greater than elsewhere. None are charged less than 6*d.*, the regular price at the news-agent's shop being 5*d.*, so that as the cost price is 4*d.* the profit is double. Nor is it unusual for a passenger by an early train, who grows impatient for his paper, to cry out, 'A shilling for the *Times!*' This, however, is only the case, I am told, with those who start very early in the morning; for the daily papers are obtained for the railway stations from among the earliest impressions, and can be had at the accustomed price as early as six o'clock, although, if there be exciting news and a great demand, a larger amount may be given.

OF THE LOW LODGING-HOUSES OF LONDON

[pp. 269–72]   The patterers, as a class, usually frequent the low lodging-houses. I shall therefore now proceed to give some further information touching the abodes of these people – reminding the reader that I am treating of patterers in general, and not of any particular order, as the 'paper workers'.

In applying the epithet 'low' to these places, I do but adopt the word commonly applied, either in consequence of the small charge for lodging, or from the character of their frequenters. To some of these domiciles, however, as will be shown, the epithet, in an opprobrious sense, is unsuited.

An intelligent man, familiar for some years with some low lodging-house life, specified the quarters where those abodes are to be found, and divided them into the following districts, the correctness of which I caused to be ascertained.

Drury-lane District. Here the low lodging-houses are to be found principally in the Coalyard, Charles-street, King-street, Parker-street, Short's-gardens, Great and Little Wyld-streets, Wyld-court, Lincoln-court, Newton-street, Star-court.

Gray's-inn District. Fox-court, Charlotte-buildings, Spread Eagle-court,

Portpool-lane, Bell-court, Baldwin's-gardens, Pheasant-court, Union-buildings, Laystall-street, Cromer-street, Fulwood's-rents (High Holborn).

Chancery-lane. Church-passage, and the Liberty of the Rolls.

Bloomsbury. George-street, Church-lane, Queen-street, Seven-dials, Puckeridge-street (commonly called the Holy Land).

Saffron-hill and Clerkenwell. Peter-street, Cow-cross, Turnmill-street, Upper and Lower Whitecross-street, St Helen's-place, Playhouse-yard, Chequer-alley, Field-lane, Great Saffron-hill.

Westminster. Old and New Pye-streets, Ann-street, Orchard-street, Perkins's-rents, Rochester-row.

Lambeth. Lambeth-walk, New-cut.

Marylebone. York-court, East-street.

St Pancras. Brooke-street.

Paddington. Chapel-street, Union-court.

Shoreditch. Baker's-rents, Cooper's-gardens.

Islington. Angel-yard.

Whitechapel, Spitalfields, &c. George-yard, Thrawl-street, Flower and Dean-street, Wentworth-street, Keate-street, Rosemary-lane, Glasshouse-yard, St George-street, Lambeth-street, Whitechapel, High-street.

Borough. Mint-street, Old Kent-street, Long-lane, Bermondsey.

Stratford. High-street.

Limehouse. Hold (commonly called Hole).

Deptford. Mill-lane, Church-street, Gifford-street.

There are other localities (as in Mile-end, Ratcliffe-highway, Shadwell, Wapping, and Lisson-grove), where low lodging-houses are to be found; but the places I have specified may be considered the *districts* of these hotels for the poor. The worst places, both as regards filth and immorality, are in St Giles's and Wentworth-street, Whitechapel. The best are in Orchard-street, Westminster (the thieves having left it in consequence of the recent alterations and gone to New Pye-street), and in the Mint, Borough. In the last-mentioned district, indeed, some of the proprietors of the lodging-houses have provided considerable libraries for the use of the inmates. In the White Horse, Mint-street, for instance, there is a collection of 500 volumes, on all subjects, bought recently, and having been the contents of a circulating library, advertised for sale in the *Weekly Dispatch*.

Of lodging-houses for 'travellers' the largest is known as the Farm House, in the Mint: it stands away from any thoroughfare, and lying low is not seen until the visitor stands in the yard. Tradition rumour states that the house was at one time Queen Anne's, and was previously Cardinal Wolsey's. It was probably some official residence. In this lodging-house are forty rooms, 200 beds (single and double), and accommodation for 200 persons. It contains three kitchens, – of which the largest, at once kitchen and sitting-room, holds 400 people, for whose uses in cooking there are two large fire-places. The other two kitchens are used only on Sundays; when one is a preaching-room, in which missionaries from Surrey Chapel (the Rev. James Sherman's), or some minister or gentleman of the neighbourhood, officiates. The other is a reading-room, supplied with a few newspapers and other periodicals; and thus, I was told, the religious and irreligious need not clash. For the supply of these papers each person pays 1d. every Sunday morning; and as the sum so collected is more than is required for the expenses of the reading-room, the surplus is devoted to the help of the members in sickness, under the management of the proprietor of the lodging-house, who appears to possess the full confidence of his inmates. The larger kitchen is detached from the sleeping apartments, so that the lodgers are not annoyed with the odour of the cooking of fish and other food consumed by the poor; for in lodging-houses every sojourner is his own cook. The meal in most demand is tea, usually with a herring, or a piece of bacon.

The yard attached to the Farm House, in Mint-street, covers an acre and a half; in it is a washing-house, built recently, the yard itself being devoted to the drying of the clothes – washed by the customers of the establishment. At the entrance to this yard is a kind of porter's lodge, in which reside the porter and his wife who act as the 'deputies' of the lodging-house. This place has been commended in sanitary reports, for its cleanliness, good order, and care for decency, and for a proper division of the sexes. On Sundays there is no charge for lodging to known customers; but this is a general practice among the low lodging-houses of London.

In contrast to this house I could cite many instances, but I need do no more in this place than refer to the statements, which I shall proceed to give; some of these were collected in the course of a former inquiry, and are here given because the same state of things prevails now. I was told by a trustworthy man that not long ago he was compelled to sleep in one of the lowest (as regards cheapness) of the lodging-houses. All was dilapidation, filth, and noisomeness. In the morning he drew, for purposes of ablution, a basinfull of water from a pailfull kept in the room. In the water were floating alive, or apparently alive, bugs and lice, which my informant was convinced had fallen from the ceiling, shaken off by the tread of some one walking in the rickety apartments above!

'Ah, sir,' said another man with whom I conversed on the subject, 'if you had lived in the lodging-houses, you would say what a vast difference a penny made, – it's often all in all. It's 4*d*. in the Mint House you've been asking me about; you've sleep and comfort there, and I've seen people kneel down and say their prayers before they went to bed. Not so many, though. Two or three in a week at nights, perhaps. And it's wholesome and sweet enough there, and large separate beds; but in other places there's nothing to smell or feel but bugs. When daylight comes in the summer – and it's often either as hot as hell or as cold as icicles in those places; but in summer, as soon as it's light, if you turn down the coverlet, you'll see them a-going it like Cheapside when it's throngest.' The poor man seemed to shudder at the recollection.

One informant counted for me 180 of these low lodging-houses; and it is reasonable to say that there are, in London, at least 200 of them. The average number of beds in each was computed for me, by persons cognizant of such matters from long and often woeful experience, at 52 single or 24 double beds, where the house might be confined to single men or single women lodgers, or to married or pretendedly married couples, or to both classes. In either case, we may calculate the number that can be, and generally are, accommodated at 50 per house; for children usually sleep with their parents, and 50 may be the lowest computation. We have thus no fewer than 10,000 persons domiciled, more or less permanently, in the low lodging-houses of London – a number more than doubling the population of many a parliamentary borough.

The proprietors of these lodging-houses mostly have been, I am assured, vagrants, or, to use the civiller and commoner word, 'travellers' themselves, and therefore sojourners, on all necessary occasions, in such places. In four cases out of five I believe this to be the case. The proprietors have raised capital sufficient to start with, sometimes by gambling at races, sometimes by what I have often, and very vaguely, heard described as a 'run of luck'; and sometimes, I am assured, by the proceeds of direct robbery. A few of the proprietors may be classed as capitalists. One of them, who has a country house in Hampstead, has six lodging-houses in or about Thrawl-street, Whitechapel. He looks in at each house every Saturday, and calls his deputies – for he has a deputy in each house – to account; he often institutes a stringent check. He gives a poor fellow money to go and lodge in one of his houses, and report the number present. Sometimes the person so sent meets with the laconic repulse – 'Full'; and woe to the deputy if his return do not evince this fulness. Perhaps one in every fifteen of the low lodging-houses in town is also a beer-shop. Very commonly so in the country.

To 'start' a low lodging-house is not a very costly matter. Furniture which will not be saleable in the ordinary course of auction, or of any traffic, is bought by a lodging-house 'starter'. A man possessed of some money, who took an interest in a bricklayer, purchased for 20*l.*, when the Small Pox Hospital, by King's-cross, was pulled down, a sufficiency of furniture for *four* lodging-houses, in which he 'started' the man in question. None others would buy this furniture, from a dread of infection.

It was the same at Marlborough-house, Peckham, after the cholera had broken out there. The furniture was sold to a lodging-house keeper, at 9*d.* each article. 'Big and little, sir,' I was told; 'a penny pot and a bedstead – all the same; each 9*d.* Nobody else would buy.'

To about three-fourths of the low lodging-houses of London, are 'deputies'. These are the conductors or managers of the establishment, and are men or women (and not unfrequently a married, or proclaimed a married couple), and about in equal proportion. These deputies are paid from 7*s.* to 15*s.* a week each, according to the extent of their supervision; their lodging always, and sometimes their board, being at the cost of 'the master'. According to the character of the lodging-house, the deputies are civil and decent, or roguish and insolent. Their duty is not only that of general superintendence, but in some of the houses of a nocturnal inspection of the sleeping-rooms; the deputy's business generally keeping him up all night. At the better-conducted houses strangers are not admitted after twelve at night; in others, there is no limitation as to hours.

The rent of the low lodging-houses varies, I am informed, from 8*s.* to 20*s.* a week, the payment being for the most part weekly; the taxes and rates being of course additional. It is rarely that the landlord, or his agent, can be induced to expend any money in repairs, – the wear and tear of the floors, &c., from the congregating together of so many human beings being excessive: this expenditure in consequence falls upon the tenant.

Some of the lodging-houses present no appearance differing from that of ordinary houses; except, perhaps, that their exterior is dirtier. Some of the older houses have long flat windows on the ground-floor, in which there is rather more paper, or other substitutes, than glass. 'The windows there, sir,' remarked one man, 'are not to let the light in, but to keep the cold out.'

In the abodes in question there seems to have become tacitly established an arrangement as to what character of lodgers shall resort thither; the thieves, the prostitutes, and the better class of street-sellers or traders, usually resorting to the houses where they will meet the same class of persons. The patterers reside chiefly in Westminster and Whitechapel.

Some of the lodging-houses are of the worst class of low brothels, and some may even be described as brothels for children.

On many of the houses is a rude sign, 'Lodgings for Travellers, 3*d*. a night. Boiling water always ready,' or the same intimation may be painted on a window-shutter, where a shutter is in existence. A few of the better order of these housekeepers post up small bills, inviting the attention of 'travellers', by laudations of the cleanliness, good beds, abundant water, and 'gas all night', to be met with. The same parties also give address-cards to travellers, who can recommend one another.

The beds are of flock, and as regards the mere washing of the rug, sheet, and blanket, which constitute the bed-furniture, are in better order than they were a few years back; for the visitations of the cholera alarmed even the reckless class of vagrants, and those whose avocations relate to vagrants. In perhaps a tenth of the low lodging-houses of London, a family may have a room to themselves, with the use of the kitchen, at so much a week – generally 2*s*. 6*d*. for a couple without family, and 3*s*. 6*d*. where there are children. To let out 'beds' by the night is however the general rule.

The illustration presented this week is of a place in Fox-court, Gray's-inn-lane, long notorious as a 'thieves' house', but now far less frequented. On the visit, a few months back, of an informant (who declined staying there), a number of boys were lying on the floor gambling with marbles and halfpennies, and indulging in savage or unmeaning blasphemy. One of the lads jumped up, and murmuring something that it wouldn't do to be idle any longer, induced a woman to let him have a halfpenny for 'a stall'; that is, as a pretext with which to enter a shop for the purpose of stealing, the display of the coin forming an excuse for his entrance. On the same occasion a man walked into 'the kitchen', and coolly pulled from underneath the back of his smock-frock a large flat piece of bacon, for which he wanted a customer. It would be sold at a fourth of its value.

I am assured that the average takings of lodging-house keepers may be estimated at 17*s*. 6*d*. a night, not to say 20*s*.; but I adopt the lower calculation. This gives a weekly payment by the struggling poor, the knavish, and the outcast, of 1,000 guineas weekly, or 52,000 guineas in the year. Besides the rent and taxes, the principal expenditure of the lodging-house proprietors is for coals and gas. In some of the better houses, blacking, brushes, and razors are supplied, without charge, to the lodgers: also pen and ink, soap, and, almost always, a newspaper. For the meals of the frequenters salt is supplied gratuitously, and sometimes, but far less frequently, pepper also; never vinegar or mustard. Sometimes a halfpenny is charged for the use of a razor and the necessary shaving apparatus. In one house in Kent-street, the following distich adorns the mantel-piece:

> To save a journey up the town,
> A razor lent here for a *brown*:
> But if you think the price too high,
> I beg you won't the razor try.

In some places a charge of a halfpenny is made for hot water, but that is rarely the case. Strong drink is admitted at almost any hour in the majority of the houses, and the deputy is generally ready to bring it; but little is consumed in the houses, those addicted to the use or abuse of intoxicating liquors preferring the tap-room or the beer-shop.

Of the Filth, Dishonesty, and Immorality of Low Lodging-houses

[pp. 272–7] In my former and my present inquiries, I received many statements on this subject. Some details, given by coarse men and boys in the grossest language, are too gross to be more than alluded to, but the full truth must be manifested, if not detailed. It was remarked when my prior account appeared, that the records of gross profligacy on the part of some of the most licentious of the rich (such as the late Marquis of Hertford and other worthies of the same depraved habits) were equalled, or nearly equalled, by the account of the orgies of the lowest lodging-houses. Sin, in any rank of life, shows the same features.

And first, as to the want of cleanliness, comfort, and decency: 'Why, sir,' said one man, who had filled a commercial situation of no little importance, but had, through intemperance, been reduced to utter want. 'I myself have slept in the top room of a house not far from Drury-lane, and you could study the stars, if you were so minded, through the holes left by the slates having been blown off the roof. It was a fine summer's night, and the openings in the roof were then rather an advantage, for they admitted air, and the room wasn't so foul as it might have been without them. I never went there again, but you may judge what thoughts went through a man's mind – a man who had seen prosperous days – as he lay in a place like that, without being able to sleep, watching the sky.'

The same man told me (and I received abundant corroboration of his statement, besides that incidental mention of the subject occurs elsewhere), that he had scraped together a handful of bugs from the bed-clothes, and crushed them under a candlestick, and had done that many a time, when he could only resort to the lowest places. He had slept in rooms so crammed with sleepers – he believed there were 30 where 12 would have been a proper number – that their breaths in the dead of night and in the unventilated chamber, rose (I use his own words) 'in one foul, choking steam of stench'. This was the case most frequently a day or two prior to Greenwich Fair or Epsom Races, when the congregation of the wandering classes, who are the supporters of the low lodging-houses, was the thickest. It was not only that two or even three persons jammed themselves into a bed not too large for one full-sized man; but between the beds – and their partition one from another admitted little more than the passage of a lodger – were placed shakes-down, or temporary accommodation for nightly slumber. In the better lodging-houses the shake-downs are small palliasses or mattresses; in the worst, they are bundles of rags of any kind; but loose straw is used only in the country for shake-downs. One informant saw a traveller, who had arrived late, eye his shake-down in one of the worst houses with anything but a pleased expression of countenance; and a surly deputy, observing this, told the customer he had his choice, 'which', the deputy added, 'it's not all men as has, or I shouldn't have been waiting here on you. But you has your choice, I tell you; – sleep there on that shake-down, or turn out and be d—; that's fair.' At some of the busiest periods, numbers sleep on the kitchen floor, all huddled together, men and women (when indecencies are common enough), and without bedding or anything but their scanty clothes to soften the hardness of the stone or brick floor. A penny is saved to the lodger by this means. More than 200 have been accommodated in this way in a large house. The Irish, at harvest-time, very often resort to this mode of passing the night.

I heard from several parties, of the surprise, and even fear or horror, with which a decent mechanic – more especially if he were accompanied by his wife – regarded one of these foul dens, when destitution had driven him there for the first time in his life. Sometimes such a man was seen to leave the place abruptly, though perhaps he had pre-paid his last half-penny for the refreshment of a night's repose. Sometimes he was seized with sickness. I heard also from some educated persons who had 'seen better days', of the disgust with themselves and with the world, which they felt on first entering such places. 'And I have some reason to believe,' said one man, 'that a person, once well off, who has sunk into the very depths of poverty, often makes his first appearance in one of the worst of those places. Perhaps it is because he keeps away from them as long as he can, and then, in a sort of desperation fit, goes into the cheapest he meets with; or if he knows it's a vile place, he very likely says to himself – I did – "I may as well know the worst at once."'

Another man who had moved in good society, said, when asked about his resorting to a low lodging-house: 'When a man's lost caste in society, he may as well go the whole hog, bristles and all, and a low lodging-house is the entire pig.'

Notwithstanding many abominations, I am assured that the lodgers, in even the worst of these habitations, for the most part sleep soundly. But they have, in all probability, been out in the open air the whole of the day, and all of them may go to their couches, after having walked, perhaps, many miles, exceedingly fatigued, and some of them half-drunk. 'Why, in course, sir,' said a 'traveller', whom I spoke to on this subject, 'if you is in a country town or village, where there's only one lodging-house, perhaps, and that a bad one – an old hand can always suit his-self in London – you *must* get half-drunk, or your money for your bed is wasted. There's so much rest owing to you, after a hard day; and bugs and bad air'll prevent its being paid, if you don't lay in some stock of beer, or liquor of some sort, to sleep on. It's a duty you owes yourself; but, if you haven't the browns, why, then, of course, you can't pay it.' I have before remarked, and, indeed, have given instances, of the odd and sometimes original manner in which an intelligent patterer, for example, will express himself.

The information I obtained in the course of this inquiry into the condition of low lodging-houses, afforded a most ample corroboration of the truth of a remark I have more than once found it necessary to make before – that persons of the vagrant class will sacrifice almost anything for warmth, not to say heat. Otherwise, to sleep, or even sit, in some of the apartments of these establishments would be intolerable.

From the frequent state of weariness to which I have alluded, there is generally less conversation among the frequenters of the low lodging-houses than might be expected. Some are busy cooking, some (in the better houses) are reading, many are drowsy and nodding, and many are smoking. In perhaps a dozen places of the worst and filthiest class, indeed, smoking is permitted even in the sleeping-rooms; but it is far less common than it was even half-a-dozen years back, and becomes still less common yearly. Notwithstanding so dangerous a practice, fires are and have been very unfrequent in these places. There is always some one awake, which is one reason. The lack of conversation, I ought to add, and the weariness and drowsiness, are less observable in the lodging-houses patronised by thieves and women of abandoned character, whose lives are comparatively idle, and whose labour a mere nothing. In their houses, if the conversation be at all general, it is often of the most unclean character. At other times it is carried on in groups, with abundance of whispers, shrugs, and slang, by the members of the respective schools of thieves or lurkers.

I have now to speak of the habitual violation of all the injunctions of law, of all the obligations of morality, and of all the restraints of decency, seen continually in the vilest of the lodging-houses. I need but cite a few facts, for to detail minutely might be to disgust. In some of these lodging-houses, the proprietor – or, I am told, it might be more correct to say, the proprietress, as there are more women than men engaged in the nefarious traffic carried on in these houses – are 'fences', or receivers of stolen goods in a small way. *Their* 'fencing', unless as the very exception, does not extend to any plate, or jewellery, or articles of value, but is chiefly confined to provisions, and most of all to those which are of ready sale to the lodgers.

Of very ready sale are 'fish got from the gate' (stolen from Billingsgate); 'sawney' (thieved bacon), and 'flesh found in Leadenhall' (butcher's-meat stolen from that market). I was told by one of the most respectable tradesmen in Leadenhall-market, that it was infested – but not now to so great an extent as it was – with lads and young men, known there as 'finders'. They carry bags round their necks, and pick up bones, or offal, or pieces of string, or bits of papers, or 'anything, sir, please, that a poor lad, that has neither father nor mother, and is werry hungry, can make a ha'penny by to get him a bit of bread, please, sir.' This is often but a cover for stealing pieces of meat, and the finders, with their proximate market for disposal of their meat in the lowest lodging-houses in Whitechapel, go boldly about their work, for the butchers, if the 'finder' be detected, 'won't', I was told by a sharp youth who then was at a low lodging-house in Keate-street, 'go bothering theirselves to a beak, but gives you a scruff of the neck and a kick and lets you go. But some of them kicks werry hard.' The tone and manner of this boy – and it is a common case enough with the 'prigs' – showed that he regarded hard kicking merely as one of the in-conveniences to which his business-pursuits were unavoidably subjected; just as a struggling housekeeper might complain of the unwelcome calls of the tax-gatherers. These depredations are more frequent in Leadenhall-market than in any of the others, on account of its vicinity to Whitechapel. Even the Whitechapel meat-market is less the scene of prey, for it is a series of shops, while Leadenhall presents many stalls, and the finders seem loath to enter shops without some plausible pretext.

Groceries, tea especially, stolen from the docks, warehouses, or shops, are things in excellent demand among the customers of a lodging-house fence. Tea, known or believed to have been stolen 'genuine' from any dock, is bought and sold very readily; 1s. 6d., however, is a not unfrequent price for what is known as 5s. tea. Sugar, spices, and other descriptions of stolen grocery, are in much smaller request.

Wearing-apparel is rarely bought by the fences I am treating of; but the stealers of it can and do offer their wares to the lodgers, who will often, before buying, depreciate the garment, and say 'It's never been nothing better nor a Moses.'

'Hens and chickens' are a favourite theft, and 'go at once to the pot', but in no culinary sense. The hens and chickens of the roguish low lodging-houses are the publicans' pewter measures; the bigger vessels are 'hens'; the smaller are 'chickens'. Facilities are provided for the melting of these stolen vessels, and the metal is sold by the thief – very rarely if ever, by the lodging-house keeper, who prefers dealing with the known customers of the establishment – to marine-store buyers.

A man who at one time was a frequenter of a thieves' lodging-house, related to me a conversation which he chanced to overhear – he himself being then in what his class would consider a much superior line of business – between a sharp lad, apparently of twelve or thirteen years of age, and a lodging-house (female) fence. But it occurred some three or four years back. The lad had 'found' a piece of Christmas beef, which he offered for sale to his landlady, averring that it weighed 6 lbs. The fence said and swore that it wouldn't weigh 3 lbs., but she would give him 5d. for it. It probably weighed above 4 lbs. 'Fip-pence!' exclaimed the lad, indignantly; 'you haven't no fairness. Vy, it's sixpun' and Christmas time. Fip-pence! A tanner and a flag (a sixpence and a four-penny piece) is the werry lowest terms.' There was then a rapid and interrupted colloquy, in which the most frequent words were 'Go to blazes!' with retorts of 'You go to blazes!' and after strong and oathful imputations of dishonest endeavours on the part of each contracting party, to over-reach the other, the meat was sold to the woman for 6d.

Some of the 'fences' board, lodge, and clothe, two or three boys or girls, and send them out regularly to thieve, the fence usually taking all the proceeds, and if it be the young thief has been successful, he is rewarded with a trifle of pocket-money, and is allowed plenty of beer and tobacco.

One man, who keeps three low lodging-houses (one of which is a beer-shop), not long ago received from a lodger a valuable great-coat, which the man said he had taken from a gig. The fence (who was in a larger way of business than others of his class, and is reputed rich,) gave 10s. for the garment, asking at the same time, 'Who was minding the gig?' 'A charity kid,' was the answer. 'Give him a deuce' (2d.), 'and stall him off' (send him an errand), said the fence, 'and bring the horse and gig, and I'll buy it.' It was done, and the property was traced in two hours, but only as regarded the gig, which had already had a new pair of wheels attached to it, and was so metamorphosed, that the owner, a medical gentleman, though he had no moral doubt on the subject, could not swear to his own vehicle. The thief received only 4*l.* for gig and horse; the horse was never traced.

The licentiousness of the frequenters, and more especially of the juvenile frequenters, of low lodging-houses, must be even more briefly alluded to. In some of these establishments, men and women, boys and girls, – but perhaps in no case, or in very rare cases, unless they are themselves consenting parties, herd together promiscuously. The information which I have given from a reverend informant indicates the nature of the proceedings, when the sexes are herded indiscriminately, and it is impossible to present to the reader, in full particularity, the records of the vice practised.

Boys have boastfully carried on loud conversations, and from distant parts of the room, of their triumphs over the virtue of girls, and girls have laughed at and encouraged the recital. Three, four, five, six, and even more boys and girls have been packed, head and feet, into one small bed; some of them perhaps never met before. On such occasions any clothing seems often enough to be regarded as merely an incumbrance. Sometimes there are loud quarrels and revilings from the jealousy of boys and girls, and more especially of girls whose 'chaps' have deserted or been inveigled from them. At others, there is an amicable interchange of partners, and next day a resumption of their former companionship. One girl, then fifteen or sixteen, who had been leading this vicious kind of life for nearly three years, and had been repeatedly in prison, and twice in hospitals – and who expressed a strong desire to 'get out of the life' by emigration – said: 'Whatever that's bad and wicked, that any one can fancy could be done in such places among boys and girls that's never been taught, or won't be taught, better, *is* done, and night after night.' In these haunts of low iniquity, or rather in the room into which the children are put, there are seldom persons above twenty. The younger lodgers in such places live by thieving and pocket-picking, or by prostitution. The charge for a night's lodging is generally 2*d.*, but smaller children have often been admitted for 1*d.* If a boy or girl resort to one of these dens at night without the means of defraying the charge for accommodation, the 'mot of the ken' (mistress of the house) will pack them off, telling them plainly that it will be no use their returning until they have stolen something worth 2*d*. If a boy or girl do not return in the evening, and have not been heard to express their intention of going elsewhere, the first conclusion arrived at by their mates is that they have 'got into trouble' (prison).

The indiscriminate admixture of the sexes among adults, in many of these places, is another evil. Even in some houses considered of the better sort, men and women, husbands and wives, old and young, strangers and acquaintances, sleep in the same apartment, and if they choose, in the same bed. Any remonstrance at some act of gross depravity, or impropriety on the part of a woman not so utterly hardened as the others, is met with abuse and derision. One man who described these scenes to me, and had long witnessed them, said that almost the only women who ever hid their faces or manifested dislike of the proceedings they could not but notice (as far as he saw), were poor Irishwomen, generally those who live by begging: 'But for all that,' the man added, 'an Irishman or Irishwoman of that sort will sleep anywhere, in any mess, to save a halfpenny, though they may have often a few shillings, or a good many, hidden about them.'

There is no provision for purposes of decency in some of the places I have been describing, into which the sexes are herded indiscriminately; but to this matter I can only allude. A policeman, whose duty sometimes called him to enter one of those houses at night, told me that he never entered it without feeling sick.

There are now fewer of such filthy receptacles than there were. Some have been pulled down – especially for the building of Commercial-street, in Whitechapel, and of New Oxford-street – and some have fallen into fresh and improved management. Of those of the worst class, however, there may now be at least thirty in London; while the low lodgings of all descriptions, good or bad, are more frequented than they were a few years back. A few new lodging-houses, perhaps half a dozen, have been recently opened, in expectations of a great influx of 'travellers' and vagrants at the opening of the Great Exhibition.

Of the Children in Low Lodging-houses

[pp. 277–8]   The informant whose account of patterers and of vagrant life in its other manifestations I have already given, has written from personal knowledge and observation the following account of the children in low lodging-houses:

'Of the mass of the indigent and outcast,' he says, 'of whom the busy world know nothing, except from an occasional paragraph in the newspaper, the rising generation, though most important, is perhaps least considered. Every Londoner must have seen numbers of ragged, sickly, and ill-fed children, squatting at the entrances of miserable courts, streets, and alleys, engaged in no occupation that is either creditable to themselves or useful to the community. These are, in many cases, those whose sole homes are in the low lodging-houses; and I will now exhibit a few features of the "juvenile performers" among the "London Poor".

'In many cases these poor children have lost *one* of their parents; in some, they are without either father or mother; but even when both parents are alive, the case is little mended, for if the parents be of the vagrant or dishonest class, their children are often neglected, and left to provide for the cost of their food and lodging as they best may. The following extract from the chaplain's report of one of our provincial jails, gives a melancholy insight into the training of many of the families. It is not, I know, without exception; but, much as we could wish it to be otherwise, it is so general an occurrence, varied into its different forms, that it may be safely accounted as the rule of action.

'"J. G. was born of poor parents. At five years old his father succeeded to a legacy of 500*l*. He was quiet, indolent, fond of drink, a good scholar, and had twelve children. He never sent any of them to school! 'Telling lies,' said the child, 'I learned from my mother; she did things unknown to father, and gave me a penny not to tell him!' The father (on leaving home) left, by request of the mother, some money to pay a man; she slipped up stairs, and told the children to say she was out.

'"From ten to twelve years of age I used to go to the ale-house. I stole the money from my father, and got very drunk. My father never punished me for all this, as he ought to have done. In course of time I was apprenticed to a tanner; he ordered me to chapel, instead of which I used to play in the fields. When out of my time I got married, and still carried on the same way, starving my wife and children. I used to take my little boy, when only five years old, to the public-house, and make him drunk with whatever I drank myself. A younger one could act well a drunken man on the floor. My wife was a sober steady woman; but, through coming to fetch me home she learned to drink too. One of our children used to say, 'Mam, you are drunk, like daddy.'"

'It may be argued that this awful "family portrait" is not the average character, but I have witnessed too many similar scenes to doubt the *general* application of the sad rule.

'Of those children of the poor, as has been before observed, the most have either no parents, or have been deserted by them, and have no regular means of living, nor moral superintendance on the part of relatives or neighbours; consequently, they grow up in habits of idleness, ignorance, vagrancy, or crime. In some cases they are countenanced and employed. Here and there may be seen a little urchin holding a few onions in a saucer, or a diminutive sickly girl standing with a few laces or a box or two of lucifers. But even *these* go with the persons who have "set them up" daily to the public-house (and to the lodging-house at night); and after they have satisfied the cravings of hunger, frequently expend their remaining halfpence (if any) in gingerbread, and as frequently in gin. I have overheard a proposal for "half-a-quartern and a two-out" (glass) between a couple of shoeless boys under nine years old. One little fellow of eleven, on being remonstrated with, said that it was the only pleasure in life that he had, and he weren't a-going to give that up. Both sexes of this juvenile class frequent, when they can raise the means, the very cheap and "flash" places of amusement, where the precocious delinquent acquires the most abandoned tastes, and are often allured by elder accomplices to commit petty frauds and thefts.

'Efforts have been made to redeem these young recruits in crime from their sad career, with its inevitable results. In some cases, I rejoice to believe that success has crowned the endeavour. There is that, however, in the cunning hardihood of the majority of these immature delinquents, which presents almost insuperable barriers to benevolence, and of this I will adduce an instance.

'A gentleman, living at Islington, who attends one of the city churches, is in the habit of crossing the piece of waste ground close to Saffron-hill. Here he often saw (close to the ragged school) a herd of boys, and as nearly as he could judge always the *same* boys. One of them always bowed to him as he passed. He thought – and thought right – that they were gambling, and after, on one occasion, talking to them very seriously, he gave each of them twopence and pursued his way. However, he found himself followed by the boy before alluded to, accompanied by a younger lad, who turned out to be his brother. Both in one breath begged to know if "his honour" could please give them any sort of a job. The gentleman gave them his card, inquired their place of residence (a low lodging-house) and the next morning, at nine o'clock, both youths were at his door. He gave them a substantial breakfast, and then took them into an out-house where was a truss of straw, and having himself taken off the band, he desired them to convey the whole, *one straw at a time*, across the garden and deposit it in another out-house. The work was easy and the terms liberal, as each boy was to get dinner and tea, and one shilling per day as long as his services should be required. Their employer had to go to town, and left orders with one of his domestics to see that the youths wanted nothing, and to watch their proceedings; their occupation was certainly not laborious, but then it was *work*, and although that was the first of their requests, it was also the last of their wishes.

'Taking advantage of an adjoining closet, the servant perceived that the weight even of a straw had been too much for these hopeful boys. They were both seated on the truss, and glibly recounting some exploits of their own, and how they had been imposed upon by others. The eldest – about fourteen – was vowing vengeance upon "Taylor Tom" for attempting to "walk the barber" (seduce his "gal"); while the younger – who had scarcely seen eleven summers – averred that it was "wery good of the swell to give them summut to eat," but "precious bad to be shut up in that crib all day without a bit o' backer"). Before the return of their patron they had transported all the straw to its appointed designation; as it was very discernible, however, that this had been effected by a wholesale process, the boys were admonished, paid, and dismissed. They are now performing more ponderous work in one of the penal settlements. Whether the test adopted by the gentleman in question was the best that might have been resorted to, I need not now inquire.

'It would be grateful to my feelings if in these disclosures I could omit the misdemeanors of the other sex of juveniles; but I am obliged to own, on the evidence of personal observation, that there are girls of ages varying from eleven to fifteen who pass the day with a "fakement" before them ("Pity a poor orphan"), and as soon as evening sets in, loiter at shop-windows and ogle gentlemen in public walks, making requests which might be expected only from long-hardened prostitution. Their nights are generally passed in a low lodging-house. They frequently introduce themselves with "Please, sir, can you tell me what time it is?" If they get a kindly answer, some other casual observations prepare the way for hints which are as unmistakeable as they are unprincipled.

Of the Life of a Cheap-John

[pp. 372–4] The following narrative, relative to this curious class, who, in many respects, partake of the characteristics which I have pointed out as proper to the mountebank of old, was taken from one of the fraternity. It may be cited as an example of those who are bred to the streets: 'My father and mother,' said he, 'both followed a travelling occupation, and were engaged in vending different things, from the old brimstone matches up to clothes lines, clothes props, and clothes pegs. They never got beyond these, – the other articles were thread, tapes, nutmeg graters, shoe-ties, stay-laces, and needles. My father, my mother used to tell me, was a great scholard, and had not always been a travelling vagrant. My mother had never known any other life. I, however, did not reap any benefit from my father's scholarship. At a very early age, five or six perhaps, I recollect myself a poor little neglected wretch, sent out each day with a roll of matches, with strict injunctions not to come home without selling them, and to bring home a certain sum of money, upon pain of receiving a sound thrashing, which threat was mostly put into execution whenever I failed to perform the task imposed upon me. My father seldom worked, that is, seldom hawked, but my mother, poor thing, had to travel and work very hard to support four of us – my father, myself, and a sister, who is since dead. I was but little assistance, and sometimes when I did not bring home the sum required, she would make it up, and tell my father I had been a good boy. My father was an inveterate drinker, and a very violent temper. My mother, I am sorry to say, used to drink too, but I believe that ill-usage drove her to it. They led a dreadful life; I scarcely felt any attachment for them; home we had none, one place was as good as another to us. I left my parents when scarcely eight years old. I had received a thrashing the day before for being a defaulter in my sale, and I determined the following morning to decamp; and accordingly, with my nine-pennyworth of matches (the quantity generally allotted me), I set out to begin the world upon my own account. Although this occurred 25 years ago, I have never met my parents since. My father, I heard, died a few years after my leaving, but my mother I know not whether she be living or dead. I left my parents at Dover, and journeyed on to London. I knew there were lodging-houses for travellers in every town, some of them I had stopped at with my father and mother. I told the people of these houses that my parents would arrive the following day, and paid my 2d. for the share of a third, fourth, fifth, or even sixth part of a bed, according to the number of children who inhabited the lodging-house upon that particular night. My matches I could always sell if I tried, but I used to play my time away, and many times night has arrived before I thought of effecting sales sufficient to pay my expenses at the beggar's hotel. Broken victuals I got in abundance, indeed more than sufficient for my own consumption. The money I received for the matches, after paying my lodging, and purchasing a pennyworth of brimstone to make more (the wood I begged at the carpenters), I gambled away at cards. Yes, young as I was, I understood Blind Hookey. I invariably lost; of course I was cheated.

'I remained in a lodging house in Mill-lane, Deptford, for two years, discontinued the match-selling, and, having a tidy voice, took to hawking songs through the public-houses. The sailors used to ask me to sing, and there were few days that I did not accumulate 2s. 6d., and from that to 4s., especially when I chose to be industrious; but my love of pitch and toss and blind hookey always kept me poor. I often got into debt with my landlady, and had no difficulty in doing so, for I always felt a pride in paying. From selling the printed songs, I imbibed a wish to learn to read, and, with the assistance of an old soldier, I soon acquired sufficient knowledge to make out the names of each song, and shortly afterwards I could study a song and learn the words without any one helping me. I stopped in Deptford until I was something more than twelve years old. I had then laid the songs aside, and taken to hawking small wares, tapes, thread, &c.; and in the winter season I was a buyer of rabbit and hare skins. I kept at this for about three years, sometimes entirely without a stock. I had run it out, perhaps gambled it away; and at such times I suffered great privations. I never could beg. I have often tried, but never could. I have approached a house with a begging intention, knocked at the door, and when it has been opened I have requested a drink of water. When I was about 16 I joined in partnership with a man who used to make phosphorus boxes. I sold them for him. A piece of phosphorus was stuck in a tin tube, the match was dipped into the phosphorus, and it would ignite by friction. I was hawking these boxes in Norwich, when the constable considered they were dreadful affairs, and calculated to encourage and assist thieves and burglars. He took me before the magistrate, at the beak's own private house, and he being equally horrified, I was sent to prison for a month. I have often thought since that the proceeding was illegal. What would be said now if a man was to be sent to jail for selling lucifer matches? In Norwich prison I associated with the rest, and if I had been inclined to turn thief I had plenty of opportunities and offers of gratuitous instruction. The separate or silent system was not in vogue then. I worked on the treadmill. Dinner was allowed to be sent in on the Sunday by the prisoner's friends. My dinner was sent in on the first Sunday by the man I sold the boxes for, as it was on the second, third, and fourth; but I had lost it before I received it. I had always gambled it away, for there were plenty of opportunities of doing so in the prisons then. On leaving the jail I received 1s.; with this I purchased some songs and travelled to Yarmouth. I could do best among sailors. After a few weeks I had accumulated about 8s., and with that sum I purchased some hardware at the swag-shop, commenced hawking, and cut the vocal department altogether; still I gambled and kept myself in poverty. In the course of time, however, I had amassed a basket of goods, worth, perhaps, 3*l*. I gambled and lost them all in one night. I was so downcast and unhappy from this circumstance, that it caused me to reflect seriously, and I made an oath that I never would gamble again. I have kept it, and have reason to bless the day that I made so good a resolution. After losing my basket of goods, the winner gave me articles amounting to a few shillings, and I began the world once more. Shortly afterwards I commenced rag gatherer, and changed my goods for old rags, of course not refusing cash in payment. My next step was to have some bills printed, whereon I requested all thrifty wives to look out their old rags or old metal, or old bones, &c.; stating at the bottom that the bill would be called for, and that a good price in ready money would be given for all useless lumber, &c. Some months at this business realized me a pretty sum of money. I was in possession of nearly 5*l*. Then I discontinued the rag-gathering; not that the trade was declining, but I did not like it – I was ambitious. I purchased a neat box, and started to sell a little Birmingham jewellery. I was now respectably dressed, was getting a living, and had entirely left off stopping at common lodging-houses; but I confined my visits to small villages – I was afraid of the law; and as I was pursuing my calling near Wakefield, a constable inquired for my hawker's licence. I had none to produce. He took me into custody, and introduced me to a magistrate, who committed me to prison for a month, and took away my box of goods. I endured the month's imprisonment upon the silent system; they cut my hair short; and at the expiration of the term I was thrust out upon the world heart-broken, without a shilling, to beg, to steal, or to starve.

'I proceeded to Leeds, the fair was on at this time. I got engaged to assist a person, from whom I had been accustomed occasionally to purchase goods. He was a "Cheap-John". In the course of the day he suggested that I should have a try at the hand-selling. I mounted the platform, and succeeded beyond my own expectations or that of my master. He offered me a regular engagement, which I accepted. At times I would help him sell, and at other times I hawked with his licence. I had regular wages, besides all I could get above a certain price that he placed upon each of the goods. I remained with this person some fifteen months, at the end of which period I commenced for myself, having saved nearly 25*l*. I began at once the hand-selling, and purchased a hawker's licence, which enabled me to sell without danger. Then I always called at the constable's house, and gave a louder knock at his door than any other person's, proud of my authority, and assured of my safety. At first I borrowed an empty cart, in which I stood and sold my wares. I could chaff as well as the best, and was as good a salesman as most of them. After that I purchased a second-hand cart from a person who had lately started a waggon. I progressed and improved in circumstances, and at last bought a very handsome waggon for myself. I have now a nice caravan, and good stock of goods, worth at least 500*l*. Money I have but little. I always invest it in goods. I am married, and have got a family. I always travel in the summer, but remain at home during the winter. My wife never travels. She remains behind, and manages a little swag-shop, which always turns in at least the family expenses.'

Of the Street-sellers of 'Small-ware', or Tape, Cotton, &c.

[pp. 427–8] The street-sellers of tape and cotton are usually elderly females; and during my former inquiry I was directed to one who had been getting her living in the street by such means for nine years. I was given to understand that the poor woman was in deep distress, and that she had long been supporting a sick husband by her little trade, but I was wholly unprepared for a scene of such startling misery, sublimed by untiring affection and pious resignation, as I there discovered.

I wish the reader to understand that I do not cite this case as a type of the sufferings of this particular class, but rather as an illustration of the afflictions which frequently befall those who are solely dependent on their labour, or their little trade, for their subsistence, and who, from the smallness of their earnings, are unable to lay by even the least trifle as a fund against any physical calamity.

The poor creatures lived in one of the close alleys at the east end of London. On inquiring at the house to which I had been directed, I was told I should find them in 'the two-pair back'. I mounted the stairs, and on opening the door of the apartment I was terrified with the misery before me. There, on a wretched bed, lay an aged man in almost the last extremity of life. At first I thought the poor old creature was really dead, but a tremble of the eyelids as I closed the door, as noiselessly as I could, told me that he breathed. His face was as yellow as clay, and it had more the cold damp look of a corpse than that of a living man. His cheeks were hollowed in with evident want, his temples sunk, and his nostrils pinched close. On the edge of the bed sat his heroic wife, giving him drink with a spoon from a tea-cup. In one corner of the room stood the basket of tapes, cottons, combs, braces, nutmeg-graters, and shaving-glasses, with which she strove to keep her old dying husband from the workhouse. I asked her how long her good man had been ill, and she told me he had been confined to his bed five weeks last Wednesday, and that it was ten weeks since he had eaten the size of a nut in solid food. Nothing but a little beef-tea had passed his lips for months. 'We have lived like children together,' said the old woman, as her eyes flooded with tears, 'and never had no dispute. He hated drink, and there was no cause for us to quarrel. One of my legs, you see, is shorter than the other,' said she, rising from the bed-side, and showing me that her right foot was several inches from the ground as she stood. 'My hip is out. I used to go out washing, and walking in my pattens I fell down. My hip is out of the socket three-quarters of an inch, and the sinews is drawn up. I am obliged to walk with a stick.' Here the man groaned and coughed so that I feared the exertion must end his life. 'Ah, the heart of a stone would pity that poor fellow,' said the good wife.

'After I put my hip out, I couldn't get my living as I'd been used to do. I couldn't stand a day if I had five hundred pounds for it. I must sit down. So I got a little stall, and sat at the end of the alley here with a few laces and tapes and things. I've done so for this nine year past, and seen many a landlord come in and go out of the house that I sat at. My husband used to sell small articles in the streets – black lead and furniture paste, and blacking. We got a sort of a living by this, the two of us together. It's very seldom though we had a bit of meat. We had 1s. 9d. rent to pay – Come, my poor fellow, will you have another little drop to wet your mouth?' said the woman, breaking off. 'Come, my dearest, let me give you this,' she added, as the man let his jaw fall, and she poured some warm sugar and water flavoured with cinnamon – all she had to give him – into his mouth. 'He's been an ailing man this many a year. He used to go of errands and buy my little things for me, on account of my being lame. We assisted one another, you see. He wasn't able to work for his living, and I wasn't able to go about, so he used to go about and buy for me what I sold. I am sure he never earned above 1s. 6d. in the week. He used to attend me, and many a time I've sat for ten and fourteen hours in the cold and wet and didn't take a sixpence. Some days I'd make a shilling, and some days less; but whatever I got I used to have to put a good part into the basket to keep my little stock.' [A knock here came to the door; it was for a halfpenny-worth of darning cotton.] 'You know a shilling goes further with a poor couple that's sober than two shillings does with a drunkard. We lived poor, you see, never had nothing but tea, or we couldn't have done anyhow. If I'd take 18d. in the day I'd think I was grandly off, and then if there was 6d. profit got out of that it would be almost as much as it would. You see these cotton braces here' (said the old woman, going to her tray). 'Well,

I gives 2s. 9d. a dozen for them here, and I sells 'em for 4½d., and sometimes 4d. a pair. Now, this piece of tape would cost me seven farthings in the shop, and I sells it at six yards a penny. It has the *name* of being eighteen yards. The profit out of it is five farthings. It's beyond the power of man to wonder how there's a bit of bread got out of such a small way. And the times is so bad, too! I think I could say I get 8d. a day profit if I have any sort of custom, but I don't exceed that at the best of times. I've often sat at the end of the alley and taken only 6d., and that's not much more than 2d. clear – it an't 3d. I'm sure. I think I could safely state that for the last nine year me and my husband has earned together 5s. a week, and out of that the two of us had to live and pay rent – 1s. 9d. a week. Clothes I could buy none, for the best garment is on me; but I thank the Lord still. I've paid my rent all but three weeks, and that isn't due till to-morrow. We have often reckoned it up here at the fire. Some weeks we have got 5s. 3d., and some weeks less, so that I judge we have had about 3s. to 3s. 6d. a week to live upon the two of us, for this nine year past. Half-a-hundred of coals would fit me the week in the depths of winter. My husband had the kettle always boiling for me against I came in. He used to sit here reading his book – he never was fit for work at the best – while I used to be out minding the basket. He was so sober and quiet too. His neighbours will tell that of him. Within the last ten weeks he's been very ill indeed, but still I could be out with the basket. Since then he's never earnt me a penny – poor old soul, he wasn't able! All that time I still attended to my basket. He wasn't so ill then but what he could do a little here in the room for hisself; but he wanted little, God knows, for he couldn't eat. After he fell ill, I had to go all my errands myself. I had no one to help me, for I'd nothing to pay them, and I'd have to walk from here down to Sun-street with my stick, till my bad leg pained me so that I could hardly stand. You see the hip being put out has drawn all the sinews up into my groin, and it leaves me incapable of walking or standing constantly; but I thank God that I've got the use of it anyhow. Our lot's hard enough, goodness knows, but we are content. We never complain, but bless the Lord for the little he pleases to give us. When I was away on my errands, in course I couldn't be minding the basket; so I lost a good bit of money that way. Well, five weeks on Wednesday he has been totally confined to his bed, excepting when I lifted him up to make it some nights; but he can't bear *that* now. Still the first fortnight he was bad, I did manage to leave him, and earn a few pence; but, latterly, for this last three weeks, I haven't been able to go out at all, to do anything.'

'She's been stopping by me, minding me here night and day all that time,' mumbled the old man, who now for the first time opened his gray glassy eyes and turned towards me, to bear, as it were, a last tribute to his wife's incessant affection. 'She has been most kind to me. Her tenderness and care has been such that man never knew from woman before, ever since I lay upon this sick bed. We've been married five-and-twenty years. We have always lived happily – very happily, indeed – together. Until sickness and weakness overcome me I always strove to help myself a bit, as well as I could; but since then she has done all in her power for me – worked for me – ay, she has worked for me, surely – and watched over me. My creed through life has been repentance towards God, faith in Jesus Christ, and love to all my brethren. I've made up my mind that I must soon change this tabernacle, and my last wish is that the good people of this world will increase her little stock for her. She cannot get her living out of the little stock she has, and since I lay here it's so lessened, that neither she nor no one else can live upon it. If the kind hearts would give her but a little stock more, it would keep her old age from want, as she has kept mine. Indeed, indeed, she does deserve it. But the Lord, I know, will reward her for all she has done to me.' Here the old man's eyelids dropped exhausted.

'I've had a shilling and a loaf twice from the parish,' continued the woman. 'The overseer came to see if my old man was fit to be removed to the workhouse. The doctor gave me a certificate that he was not, and then the relieving officer gave me a shilling and a loaf of bread, and out of that shilling I bought the poor old fellow a sup of port wine. I bought a quartern of wine, which was 4d., and I gave 5d. for a bit of tea and sugar, and I gave 2d. for coals; a halfpenny rushlight I bought, and a short candle, that made a penny – and that's the way I laid out the shilling. If God takes him, I know he'll sleep in heaven. I know the life he's spent, and am not afraid; but no one else shall take him from me – nothing shall part us but death in this world. Poor old soul, he can't be long with me. He's a perfect skeleton. His bones are starting through his skin.'

I asked what could be done for her, and the old man thrust forth his skinny arm, and laying hold of the bed-post, he raised himself slightly in his bed, as he murmured, 'If she could be got into a little parlour, and away from sitting in the streets, it would be the saving of her.' And, so saying, he fell back overcome with the exertion, and breathed heavily.

The woman sat down beside me, and went on. 'What shocked him most was that I was obligated in his old age to go and ask for relief at the parish. You see, he was always a spiritful man, and it hurted him sorely that he should come to this at last, and for the first time in his lifetime. The only parish money that ever we had was this, and it *does* hurt him every day to think that he must be buried by the parish after all. He was always proud, you see.'

I told the kind-hearted old dame that some benevolent people had placed certain funds at my disposal for the relief of such distress as hers and I assured her that neither she nor her husband should want for anything that might ease their sufferings.

The day after the above was written, the poor old man died. He was buried out of the funds sent to the 'Morning Chronicle', and his wife received some few pounds to increase her stock; but in a few months the poor old woman went mad, and is now, I believe, the inmate of one of the pauper lunatic asylums.

Of the Packmen, or Hawkers of Soft Wares

[pp. 419–21]   The packman, as he is termed, derives his name from carrying his merchandise or pack upon his back. These itinerant distributors are far less numerous than they were twenty or twenty-five years since. A few years since, they were mostly Irishmen, and their principal merchandise, Irish linens – a fabric not so generally worn now as it was formerly.

The packmen are sometimes called Manchestermen. These are the men whom I have described as the sellers of shirtings, sheetings, &c. One man, who was lately an assistant in the trade, could reckon twenty men who were possessed of good stocks, good connections, and who had saved money. They traded in an honourable manner, were well known, and much respected. The majority of them were natives of the north of Ireland, and two had been linen manufacturers. It is common, indeed, for all the Irishmen in this trade to represent themselves as having been connected with the linen manufacture in Belfast.

This trade is now becoming almost entirely a country trade. There are at present, I am told, only five pursuing it in London, none of them having a very extensive connection, so that only a brief notice is necessary. Their sale is of both cottons and linens for shirts. They carry them in rolls of 36 yards, or in smaller rolls, each of a dozen yards, and purchase them at the haberdashery swag-shops, at from 9*d*. to 18*d*. a yard. I now speak of good articles. Their profits are not very large – as for the dozen yards, which cost them 9*s*., they often have a difficulty in getting 12*s*. – while in street-sale, or in hawking from house to house, there is great delay. A well-furnished pack weighs about one cwt., and so necessitates frequent stoppages. Cotton, for sheetings, is sold in the same manner, costing the vendors from 6*d*. to 1*s*. 3*d*. a yard.

Of the tricks of the trade, and of the tally system of one of these chapmen, I had the following account from a man who had been, both as principal and assistant, a travelling packman, but was best acquainted with the trade in and about London.

'My master,' he said, 'was an Irishman, and told everybody he had been a manager of a linen factory in Belfast. I believe he was brought up to be a shoemaker, and was never in the north of Ireland. Anyhow, he was very shy of talking about Irish factories to Irish gentlemen. I heard one say of him, "Don't tell me, you have the Cork brogue." I know he'd got some knowledge of linen weaving at Dundee, and could talk about it very clever; indeed he was a clever fellow. Sometimes, to hear him talk, you'd think he was quite a religious man, and at others that he was a big blackguard. It wasn't drink that made the difference, for he was no drinker. It's a great thing on a round to get a man or woman into a cheerful talk, and put in a joke or two; and that he could do, to rights. I had 12*s*. a week, standing wages, from him, and bits of commissions on sales that brought me from 3*s*. to 5*s*. more. He was a buyer of damaged goods, and we used to "doctor" them. In some there was perhaps damages by two or three threads being out all the way, so the manufacturers wouldn't send them to their regular customers. My master pretended it was a secret where he got them, but, lord, I knew; it was at a swag-shop. We used to cut up these in twelves (twelve yards), sometimes less if they was very bad, and take a Congreve, and just scorch them here and there, where the flaws was worst, and plaster over other flaws with a little flour and dust, to look like a stain from street water from the fire-engine. Then they were from the stock of Mr Anybody, the great draper, that had his premises burnt down – in Manchester or Glasgow, or London – if there'd been a good fire at a draper's – or anywhere; we wasn't particular. They was fine or strong shirtings, he'd say – and so they was, the sound parts of them – and he'd sell as cheap as common calico. I've heard him say, "Why, marm, sure marm, with your eyes and scissors and needle, them burns – ah! fire's a dreadful judgment on a man – isn't the least morsel of matter in life. The stains is cured in a wash-tub in no time. It's only *touched* by the fire, and you can humour it, I know, in cutting out as a shirt ought to be cut; it should be as carefully done as a coat." Then we had an Irish linen, an imitation, you know, a kind of "Union", which we call double twist. It is made, I believe, in Manchester, and is a mixture of linen and cotton. Some of it's so good that it takes a judge to tell the difference between it and real

Irish. He got some beautiful stuff at one time, and once sold to a fine-dressed young woman in Brompton, a dozen yards, at 2s. 6d. a yard, and the dozen only cost him 14s. Then we did something on tally, but he was dropping that trade. The shopkeepers undersold him. "If you get 60l. out of 100l., in tally scores," he often said, "it's good money, and a fair living profit; but he got far more than that. What was worth 8s. was 18s. on tally, pay 1s. a week. He did most that way with the masters of coffee-shops and the landlords of little public-houses. Sometimes, if they couldn't pay, we'd have dinner, and that went to account, and he'd quarrel with me after it for what was my share. There's not much of this sort of trade now, sir. I believe my old master got his money together and emigrated.'

'Do you want any ginuine Irish linin, ma'am?' uttered in unmistakable brogue, seemed to authenticate the fact, that the inquirer (being an Irishman) in all likelihood possessed the legitimate article; but as to their obtaining their goods from Coleraine and other places in the Emerald Isle, famed for the manufacture of linen, it was and is as pure fiction as the Travels of Baron Munchausen.

The majority of these packmen have discontinued dealing in linens exclusively, and have added silks, ladies' dresses, shawls and various articles connected with the drapery business. The country, and small towns and villages, remote from the neighbourhood of large and showy shops, are the likeliest markets for the sale of their goods. In London the Irish packmen have been completely driven out by the Scotch tallymen, who indeed are the only class of packmen likely to succeed in London. If the persevering Scotch tallyman can but set foot in a decent-looking residence, and be permitted to display his tempting finery to the 'lady of the house', he generally manages to talk her into purchasing articles that perhaps she has no great occasion for, and which serve often to involve her in difficulties for a considerable period – causing her no little perplexity, and requiring much artifice to keep the tallyman's weekly visits a secret from her husband – to say nothing of paying an enormous price for the goods; for the many risks which the tallyman incurs, necessitates of course an exorbitant rate of profit.

'The number of packmen or hawkers of shawls, silks, &c., I think' (says one of their own body) 'must have decreased full one-half within the last few years. The itinerant haberdashery trade is far from the profitable business that it used to be, and not unfrequently do I travel a whole day without taking a shilling: still, perhaps, one day's good work will make up for half a dozen bad ones. All the packmen have hawkers' licences, as they have mostly too valuable a stock to incur the risk of losing it for want of such a privilege. Some of the fraternity' (says my informant) 'do not always deal "upon the square"; they profess to have just come from India or China, and to have invested all their capital in silks of a superior description manufactured in those countries, and to have got them on shore "unbeknown to the Custom-house authorities". This is told in confidence to the servant-man or woman who opens the door – "be so good as tell the lady as much," says the hawker, "for really I'm afraid to carry the goods much longer, and I have already sold enough to pay me well enough for my spec – go, there's a good girl, tell your missus I have splendid goods, and am willing almost to give them away, and if we makes a deal of it, why I don't mind giving you a handsome present for yourself."' This is a bait not to be resisted. Should the salesman succeed with the mistress, he carries out his promise to the maid by presenting her with a cap ribbon, or a cheap neckerchief.

The most primitive kind of packmen, or hawkers of soft-wares, who still form part of the distributing machinery of the country, traverse the highlands of Scotland. They have their regular rounds, and regular days of visiting their customers; their arrival is looked for with interest by the country people; and the inmates of the farm-house where they locate for the night consider themselves fortunate in having to entertain the packman; for he is their newsmonger, their story-teller, their friend, and their acquaintance, and is always made welcome. His wares consist of hose – linsey wolsey, for making petticoats – muslins for caps – ribbons – an assortment of needles, pins, and netting-pins – and all sorts of small wares. He always travels on foot. It is suspected that he likewise does a little in the 'jigger line', for many of these Highlanders have, or are supposed to have, their illicit distilleries; and the packmen are suspected of trafficking without excise interference. Glasgow, Dundee, Galashiels, and Harwick are the principal manufacturing towns where the packman replenishes his stock. 'My own opinion,' says an informant of considerable experience, 'is that these men seldom grow rich; but the prevailing idea in the country parts of Scotland is, that the pedlar has an unco lang stockin wi' an awfu' amount o goden guineas in it, and that his pocket buik is plumped out wi' a thick roll of bank notes. Indeed there are many instances upon record of poor packmen having been murdered – the assassins, doubtlessly, expecting a rich booty.' It scarcely ever costs the packman of Scotland anything for his bed and board. The Highlanders are a most hospitable people with acquaintances – although with strangers at first they are invariably shy and distant. In Ireland there is also the travelling pedlar, whose habits and style of doing business are nearly similar to that of the Scotchman. Some of the packmen of Scotland have risen to eminence and distinction. A quondam lord provost of Glasgow, a gentleman still living, and upon whom the honour of knighthood has been conferred, was, according to common report, in his earlier days a packman; and rumour also does the gentleman the credit to acknowledge that he is not ashamed to own it.

I am told by a London hawker of soft goods, or packman, that the number of his craft, hawking London and its vicinity, as far as he can judge, is about 120 (the census of 1841 makes the London hawkers, hucksters and pedlars amount to 2041). In the 120 are included the Irish linen hawkers. I am also informed that the fair trader's profits amount to about 20 per cent., while those of the not over-particular trader range from 80 to 200 per cent. In a fair way of business it is said the hawker's taking will amount, upon an average, to 7*l*. or 8*l*. per week; whereas the receipts of the 'duffer', or unfair hawker, will sometimes reach to 50*l*. per week. Many, however, travel days, and do not turn a penny.

Statement of a Packman

[pp. 421–2] Of the way of trading of a travelling-pedlar I had the following account from one of the body. He was well dressed, and a good but keen-looking man of about thirty-five, slim, and of rather short stature, with quick dark eyes and bushy whiskers, on which it was evident no small culture was bestowed. His manners were far from obtrusive or importunate – to those whom he sought to make customers – for I happened to witness a portion of his proceedings in that respect; but he had a quiet perseverance with him, which, along with perfect civility, and something like deference, might be the most efficient means of recommending himself to the maid-servants, among whom lay his chief customers. He showed a little of the pride of art in describing the management of his business, but he would not hear that he 'pattered': he talked to his customers, he declared, as any draper, who knew his business well, might talk to *his*.

When I saw him, his pack, which he carried slung over one shoulder, contained a few gown-pieces of printed cotton, nearly all with pink grounds; a few shawls of different sizes; and three rolls firmly packed, each with a card-label on which was neatly written, 'French Merino. Full duty paid. A.B. – L.F. – 18 – 33 – 1851–. French Chocolate.' There were also six neat paper packages, two marked 'worked collars', three, 'gauze handkerchiefs', and the other 'beautiful child's gros de naples'. The latter consisted of 4½ yards of black silk, sufficient for a child's dress. He carried with him, moreover, 5 umbrellas, one inclosed in a bright glazed cover, while from its mother-of-pearl handle hung a card addressed – 'The Lady's Maid, Victoria Lodge, 13s. 6d.'

'This is a very small stock,' he said, 'to what I generally carry, but I'm going on a country round to-morrow, and I want to get through it before I lay in a new one. I tell people that I want to sell off my goods cheap, as they're too good for country sale; and that's true, the better half of it.'

On my expressing some surprise that he should be leaving London at this particular time, he answered:

'I go into the country because I think all the hawkers will be making for town, and there'll be plenty of customers left in the country, and fewer to sell to them at their own places. That's my opinion.

'I sell to women of all sorts. Smart-dressing servant-maids, perhaps, are my best customers, especially if they live a good way from any grand ticketing shop. I sold one of my umbrellas to one of them just before you spoke to me. She was standing at the door, and I saw her give half a glance at the umbrellas, and so I offered them. She first agreed to buy a very nice one at 3s. 3d. (which should have been 4s.) but I persuaded her to take one at 3s. 9d. (which should have been 4s. 6d.). "Look here, ma'am," said I, "this umbrella is much bigger you see, and will carry double so when you're coming from church of a wet Sunday evening, a friend can have share of it, and very grateful he'll be, as he's sure to have his best hat on. There's been many a question put under an umbrella that way that's made a young lady blush, and take good care of her umbrella when she was married, and had a house of her own. I look sharp after the young and pretty ladies, Miss, and shall as long as I'm a bachelor." "O," says she, "such ridiculous nonsense. But I'll have the bigger umbrella, because it's often so windy about here, and then one must have a good cover if it rains as well."

'That's my way, sir. I don't mind telling that, because they do the same in the shops. I've heard them, but they can't put love and sweet-hearting so cleverly in a crowded shop as we can in a quiet house. It's that I go for, love and sweet-hearting; and I always speak to any smart servant as if I thought she was the mistress, or as if I wasn't sure whether she was the mistress or the lady's-maid; three times out of four she's house-maid or maid of all work. I call her "ma'am", and "young lady", and sometimes "miss". It's no use offering to sell until a maid has tidied herself in the afternoon – not a bit. I should made a capital draper's shopman, I know, only I could never bear the confinement. I never will hear such words as

"I don't want it", or, "nothing more to-day", no more than if I was behind a counter.

'The great difficulty I have is to get a chance of offering my goods. If I ring at a gate – for I always go a little way out of town – they can see who it is, and I may ring half an hour for nothing. If the door's opened it's often shut again directly, and I just hear "bother". I used to leave a few bills, and I do so still in some parts of the country, with a list of goods, and "this bill to be called for" printed at the bottom. But I haven't done that in town for a long time; it's no good. People seem to think it's giving double trouble. One of the prettiest girls I ever saw where I called one evening, pointed – just as I began to say, "I left a bill and" – to some paper round a candle in a stick, and shut the door laughing.

'In selling my gown-pieces I say they are such as will suit the complexion, and such like; and I always use my judgment in saying so. Why shouldn't I? It's the same to me what colour I sell. "It's a genteel thing, ma'am," I'll say to a servant-maid, "and such as common people won't admire. It's not staring enough for them. I'm sure it would become you, ma'am, and is very cheap; cheaper than you could buy at a shop; for all these things are made by the same manufacturers, and sold to the wholesale dealers at the same price, and a shopkeeper, you know, has his young men, and taxes, and rates, and gas, and fine windows to pay for, and I haven't, so it don't want much judgment to see that I must be able to sell cheaper than shopkeepers, and I think your own taste, ma'am, will satisfy you that these here are elegant patterns."

'That's the way I go on. No doubt there's others do the same, but I know and care little about them. I have my own way of doing business, and never trouble myself about other people's patter or nonsense.

'Now, that piece of silk I shall, most likely, sell to the landlady of a public-house, where I see there's children. I shall offer it after I've got a bit of dinner there, or when I've said I want a bit. It's no use offering it there, though, if it isn't cheap; they're too good judges. Innkeepers aren't bad customers, I think, taking it altogether, to such as me, if you can get to talk to them, as you sometimes can at their bars. They're generally wanting something, that's one step. I always tell them that they ought to buy of men, in my way, who live among them, and not of fine shop-keepers, who never came a-near their houses. I've sold them both cottons and linens, after such talk as that. I live at public-houses in the country. I sleep nowhere else.

'My trade in town is nothing to what it was ten or a dozen years back. I don't know the reason exactly. I think so many threepenny busses is one;

for they'll take any servant, when she's got an afternoon, to a thorough-fare full of ticket-shops, and bring her back, and her bundle of purchases too, for another 3d. I shall cut it altogether, I think, and stick to the country. Why, I've known the time when I should have met from half-a-dozen to a dozen people trading in my way in town, and for these three days, and dry days too, I haven't met one. My way of trading in the country is just the same as in town. I go from farm-house to farm-house, or call at gentlemen's grand seats – if a man's known to the servants there, it may be the best card he can play – and I call at every likely house in the towns or villages. I only go to a house and sell a mistress or maid the same sort of goods (a little cheaper, perhaps), and recommend them in the same way, as is done every day at many a fine city, and borough, and West-End shop. I never say they're part of a bankrupt's stock; a packfull would seem nothing for that. I never pretend that they're smuggled. Mine's a respectable trade, sir. There's been so much dodging that way, it's been a great stop to fair trading; and I like to go on the same round more than once. A person once taken-in by smuggled handkerchiefs, or anything, won't deal with a hawker again, even though there's no deception. But "duffing", and all that is going down fast, and I wish it was gone altogether. I do nothing in tally. I buy my goods; and I've bought all sorts, in wholesale houses, of course, and I'd rather lay out 10l. in Manchester than in London. O, as to what I make, I can't say it's enough to keep me (I've only myself), and escape the income-tax. Sometimes I make 10s. a week; sometimes 20s.; sometimes 30s.; and I have made 50s.; and one week, the best I ever did, I made as much as 74s. 6d. That's all I can say.'

Perhaps it may be sufficiently accurate to compute the average weekly earnings of a smart trader like my informant, at from 21s. to 25s. in London, and from 25s. to 30s. in the country.

OF THE WOMEN STREET-SELLERS

[pp. 511–17] As the volume is now fast drawing to a close, and a specific account has been furnished of almost every description of street-*seller* (with the exception of those who are the *makers* of the articles they vend), I purpose giving a more full and general history and classification than I have yet done of the feminine portion of the traders in the streets.

The women engaged in street-sale are of all ages and of nearly all classes. They are, however, chiefly of two countries, England and Ireland. There are (comparatively) a few Jewesses, and a very few Scotchwomen and Welchwomen who are street-traders; and they are so, as it were, accidentally, from their connection, by marriage or otherwise, with male street-sellers. Of foreigners there are German broom-women, and a few Italians with musical instruments.

The first broad and distinctive view of the female street-sellers, is regarding them *nationally*, that is to say, either English or Irish women – two classes separated by definite characteristics from each other.

The Irishwomen – to avoid burthening the reader with an excess of subdivisions – I shall speak of generally; that is to say, as one homogeneous class, referring those who require a more specific account to the description before given of the street-sellers.

The Englishwomen selling in the streets appear to admit of being arranged into four distinct groups, viz.:

1. The wives of street-sellers.

2. Mechanics' or labourers' wives, who go out street-selling (while their husbands are at work) as a means of helping out the family income.

3. Widows of former street-sellers.

4. Single women.

I do not know of any street-trade carried on *exclusively* by women. The sales in which they are principally concerned are in fish (including shrimps and oysters), fruit and vegetables (widows selling on their own account), fire-screens and ornaments, laces, millinery, artificial flowers (but not in any great majority over the male traders), cut flowers, boot and stay-laces and small wares, wash-leathers, towels, burnt linen, combs, bonnets, pin-cushions, tea and coffee, rice-milk, curds and whey, sheeps'-trotters, and dressed and undressed dolls.

What may be called the 'heavier' trades, those necessitating the carrying of heavy weights, or the pushing of heavily laden barrows, are in the hands of men; and so are, even more exclusively, what may be classed as the more skilled trades of the streets, viz. the sale of stationery, of books, of the most popular eatables and drinkables (the coffee-stalls excepted), and in every branch dependent upon the use of patter. In such callings as root-selling, crock-bartering, table-cover selling, mats, game, and poultry, the wife is the helpmate of her husband; if she trade separately in these things, it is because there is a full stock to dispose of, which requires the exertions of two persons, perhaps with some hired help just for the occasion.

The difference in the street-traffic, as carried on by Englishwomen and Irishwomen, is marked enough. The Irishwoman's avocations are the least skilled, and the least remunerative, but as regards mere toil, such as the carrying of a heavy burthen, are by far the most laborious. An Irishwoman, though not reared to the streets, will carry heavy baskets of oranges or apples, principally when those fruits are cheap, along the streets while her English co-trader (if not a costermonger) may be vending laces, millinery, artificial flowers, or other commodities of a 'light', and in some degree of street estimation a 'genteel' trade. Some of the less laborious callings, however, such as that in wash-leathers, are principally in the hands of young and middle-aged Irishwomen, while that in sheeps'-trotters, which does not entail heavy labour, are in the hands mostly of elderly Irishwomen. The sale of such things as lucifer-matches and watercresses, and any 'stock' of general use, and attainable for a few pence, is resorted to by the very poor of every class. The Irishwoman more readily unites begging with selling than the Englishwoman, and is far more fluent and even eloquent; perhaps she pays less regard to truth, but she unquestionably pays a greater regard to chastity. When the un-educated Irishwoman, however, has fallen into licentious ways, she is, as I once heard it expressed, the most 'savagely wicked' of any.

After these broad distinctions I proceed to details.

1. From the best information at my command it may be affirmed that about one-half of the women employed in the diverse trades of the streets, are the wives or concubines (permanently or temporarily) of the men who pursue a similar mode of livelihood – the male street-sellers. I may here observe that I was informed by an experienced police-officer – who judged from his personal observation, without any official or even systematic investigation – that the women of the town, who survived their youth or their middle age, did not resort to the sale of any commodity in the streets, but sought the shelter of the workhouse, or died, he could not tell where or under what circumstances. Of the verity of this statement I have no doubt, as a street-sale entails some degree of industry or of exertion, for which the life of those wretched women may have altogether unfitted them.

In the course of the narratives and statements I have given, it is shown that some wives pursue one (itinerant or stationary) calling, while the husband pursues another. The trades in which the husband and wife (and I may here remark that when I speak of 'wives', I include all, so regarded in street life, whether legally united or not) – the trades in which the woman is, more than in any others, literally the help-mate of the man, are the costermonger's (including the flower, or root, sellers) and the crockery-ware people. To the costermonger some help is often in-dispensable, and that of a wife is the cheapest and the most honest (to say nothing of the considerations connected with a home) which can be obtained. Among the more prosperous costermongers too, especially those who deal in fish, the wife attends to the stall while the husband goes 'a round', and thus a greater extent of business is transacted. In the root and crockery-trades the woman's assistance is necessary when barter takes place instead of sale, as the husband may be ignorant of the value of the old female attire which even 'high-hip ladies', as they were described to me, loved to exchange for a fuchsia or a geranium; for a glass cream-jug or a china ornament. Of the married women engaged in any street-trade, I believe nineteen-twentieths are the wives of men also pursuing some street avocation.

2. There are, however, large classes of female street-sellers who may be looked upon as exceptions, the wife selling in the streets while the husband is engaged in some manual labour, but they are only partially exceptions. In the sale of wash-leathers, for instance, are the wives of many Irish bricklayers' labourers; the woman may be constantly occupied in disposing of her wares in the streets or suburbs, and the man labouring at any building; but in case of the deprivation of work, such a man will at once become a street-seller, and in the winter many burly Irish labourers sell a few nuts or 'baked tatties', or a few pairs of braces, or some article which seems little suitable for the employment of men of thews and muscle. In the course of my present inquiry I have, in only very rare instances, met with a poor Irishman, who has not a reason always at his tongue's end to justify anything he was doing. Ask a bricklayer's labourer why, in his youth and strength, he is selling nuts, and he will at once reply; 'Sure thin, your honnur, isn't it better than doin' nothing? I must thry and make a pinny, til I'm in worruk again, and glory be to God, I hope that'll be soon.'

An experienced man, who knows all the street-folk trading in Whitechapel and its neighbourhood, and about Spitalfields, told me that he could count up 100 married women, in different branches of open-air commerce, and of them only two had husbands who worked regularly indoors. The husband of one woman works for a slop-tailor, the other is a bobbin turner; the tailor's wife sells water-cresses every morning and afternoon; the turner's wife is a 'small-ware woman'. The tailor, however, told my informant that his eyesight was failing him, that his earnings became less and less, that he was treated like dirt, and would go into some street-trade himself before long. When the man and his wife are both in the street-trade, it is the case in three instances out of four (excluding of course the costermongers, root-sellers, and crock-man's pursuits) that the couple carry on different callings.

In the full and specific accounts I gave of the largest body of street-sellers, viz., the costermongers, I showed that concubinage among persons of all ages was the rule, and marriage the exception. It was computed that, taking the mass of costermongers, only one couple in twenty, living together, were married, except in Clerkenwell, where the costers are very numerous, and where the respected incumbent at certain seasons marries poor persons gratuitously; there one couple in ten were really man and wife.

Of the other classes of women street-sellers, directly the reverse is the case; of those living as man and wife, one couple in twenty may be *unmarried*. An intelligent informant thought this average too high, and that it was more probably one in sixteen. But I incline to the opinion of one in twenty, considering how many of the street-traders have 'seen better days', and were married before they apprehended being driven to a street career. In this enumeration I include only street-*traders*. Among such people as ballad singers, concubinage, though its wrongfulness is far better understood than among ignorant costermongers, is practised even more fully; and there is often among such classes even worse than concubinage – a dependance, more or less, on the wages of a woman's prostitution, and often a savage punishment to the wretched woman, if those wages of sin are scant or wanting.

3. The widows in the street-trades are very generally the widows of street-sellers. I believe that very few of the widows of mechanics, when left unprovided for on their husbands' demise, resort to street traffic. If they have been needle-women before marriage, they again seek for employment at needle-work; if they have been servants, they become charwomen, or washerwomen, or again endeavour to obtain a livelihood in domestic service.

There are some to whom those resources are but starvation, or a step from starvation, or whom they fail entirely, and then they '*must* try the streets', as they will describe it. If they are young and reckless, they become prostitutes; if in more advanced years, or with good principles, they turn street-sellers; but this is only when destitution presses sharply.

4. The single women in the street-callings are generally the daughters of street-sellers, but their number is not a twentieth of the others, excepting they are the daughters of Irish parents. The costermongers' daughters either help their parents, with whom they reside, or carry on some similar trade, or they soon form connections with the other sex, and easily sever the parental tie, which very probably has been far too lax or far too severe. I made many inquiries, but I did not hear of any unmarried

young woman, not connected with street-folk by birth or rearing, such as a servant maid, – endeavouring to support herself when out of work or place by a street avocation. Such a person will starve on slop millinery or slop shirt-making; or will, as much or more from desperation than from viciousness, go upon the town. With the Irish girls the case is different: brought up to a street-life, used to whine and blarney, they grow up to womanhood in street-selling, and as they rarely form impure connections, and as no one may be induced to offer them marriage, their life is often one of street celibacy. A young Irishwoman, to whom I was referred in the course of my inquiry among fruit-sellers, had come to London in the hopes of meeting her brother, with whom she was to emigrate; but she could learn nothing of him, and, concluding that he was dead, became an apple-seller. She sat, when I saw her, on cold wintry days, at the corner of a street in the Commercial-road, seemingly as much dead as alive, and slept with an aunt, also a single woman, who was somewhat similarly circumstanced; and thus these two women lived on about 6d. a day each. Their joint bed was 1s. a week, and they contrived to subsist on what remained when this shilling was paid. The niece referred me, not without a sense of pride, to her priest, as to her observance of her religious duties, and declared that where she lodged there were none but women lodgers, and those chiefly her own countrywomen. I believe such cases are not uncommon. A few, who have had the education of ladies (as in the case of an envelope-seller whose statement I gave), are driven to street-trading, but it is as a desperate grasp at something to supply less bitter bread, however little of it, than is supplied in the workhouse. I have many a time heard poor women say: 'God knows, sir, I should live far better, and be better lodged and better cared for in the house (they seldom call it work-house), but I'd rather live on 2d. a day.' Into the question of out and in-door relief I need not now enter, but the prevalent feeling I have indicated is one highly honourable to the English poor. I have heard it stated that the utter repugnance to a workhouse existence was weaker than it used to be among the poor, but I have not met with anything to uphold such an opinion.

Such constitute the several classes of women street-sellers. I shall now proceed to speak of the habits and characters of this peculiar portion of the street-folk.

As regards the religion of the women in street-trades, it is not difficult to describe it. The Irishwomen are Roman Catholics. Perhaps I am justified in stating that they are *all* of that faith. The truth of this assertion is proved, moreover, to as full a demonstration as it very well can be proved without actual enumeration, by the fact that the great majority of the Irishwomen in the streets are from the Catholic provinces of Connaught, Leinster, and Munster; there are very few from Ulster, and not one-twentieth of the whole from any one of the other provinces. Perhaps, again, it is not extravagant to estimate that three-fourths of the women and girls from the sister island, now selling things in the streets, have been, when in their own country, connected through their husbands or parents with the cultivation of the land. It is not so easy to speak of what the remaining fourth were before they became immigrants. Some were the wives of mechanics, who, when their husbands failing to obtain work in London became street-traders, had adopted the same pursuits. I met with one intelligent man having a stall of very excellent fruit in Battle-bridge, who had been a brogue-maker. He had been in business on his own account in Tralee, but mended the indifferent profits of brogue-making by a little trade in 'dry goods'. This, he told me with a cautious glance around him and in a half whisper, though it was twenty-eight years since he left his country, meant smuggled tobacco. He found it advisable, on account of being 'wanted' by the revenue officers, to leave Tralee in great haste. He arrived in London, got employment as a bricklayer's labourer, and sent for his wife to join him. This she did, and from her first arrival, sold fruit in the streets. In two or three years the husband's work among the builders grew slack, and he then took to the streets. Another man, a shoemaker, who came from Dublin to obtain work in London, as he was considered 'a good hand', could not obtain it, but became a street-seller, and *his* wife, previously to himself, had resorted to a street-trade in fruit. He became a widower and married as 'his second', the daughter of an Irish carpenter who had been disappointed in emigrating from London, and whose whole family had become fruit-sellers. A third man, who had worked at his trade of a tailor in Cork, Waterford, Wicklow, and Dublin (he 'tramped' from Cork to Dublin) had come to London and been for many years a street-seller in different capacities. His wife and daughter now assist him, or trade independently, in selling 'roots'. 'Rayther,' this man said, 'than put up wid the wages and the *ter-ratement* (said very emphatically) o' thim slop masters at the Aist Ind, I'd sill myself as a slave. The sthraits doesn't degrade a man like thim thieves o' the worruld.' This man knew, personally, ten Irish mechanics who were street-sellers in London, as were their wives and families, including some five-and-twenty females.

I adduce these and the following details somewhat minutely, as they tend to show by what class of Irish immigrants the streets of the imperial metropolis are stocked with so large a body of open-air traders.

There is also another class of women who, I am informed on good authority, sometimes become street-sellers, though I met with no instance myself. The orphan children of poor Irish parents are, on the demise of their father and mother sometimes taken into a workhouse and placed out as domestic servants. So, as regards domestic servants, are the daughters of Irish labourers, by their friends or the charitable. As the wages of these young girls are small and sometimes nominal, the work generally hard, and in no few instances the food scanty and the treatment severe, domestic service becomes distasteful, and a street life 'on a few oranges and limmons' is preferred. There is, moreover, with some of this class another cause which almost compels the young Irish girl into the adoption of some street calling. A peevish mistress, whose numerous family renders a servant necessary, but whose means are small or precarious, becomes bitterly dissatisfied with the awkwardness or stupidity of her Irish hand-maiden; the girl's going, or 'teasing to go', every Sunday morning to mass is annoying, and the girl is often discharged, or discharges herself 'in a huff'. The mistress, perhaps, with the low tyranny dear to vulgar minds, refuses her servant a character, or, in giving one, suppresses any good qualities, and exaggerates the failings of impudence, laziness, lying, and dirtiness. Thus the girl cannot obtain another situation, and perforce perhaps she becomes a street-seller.

The readiness with which young Irish people thus adapt themselves to all the uncertainties and hardships of a street life is less to be wondered at when we consider that the Irish live together, or at any rate associate with one another, in this country, preserving their native tastes, habits, and modes of speech. Among their tastes and habits, a dislike to a street life does not exist as it does among English girls.

The poor Irish females in London are for the most part regular in their attendance at mass, and this constant association in their chapels is one of the links which keeps the street-Irish women so much distinct from the street-English. In the going to and returning from the Roman Catholic chapels, there is among these people – I was told by one of the most intelligent of them – a talk of family and secular matters, – of the present too high price of oranges to leave full 6d. a day at two a penny, and the probable time when cherries would be 'in' and cheap, 'plaze God to prosper them'. In these colloquies there is an absence of any interference by English street-sellers, and an unity of conversation and interest peculiarly Irish. It is thus that the tie of religion, working with the other causes, keeps the Irish in the London streets knitted to their own ways, and is likely to keep them so, and, perhaps, to add to their number.

It was necessary to write somewhat at length of so large a class of women who *are* professors of a religion, but of the others the details may be brief; for, as to the great majority, religion is almost a nonentity. For this absence of religious observances, the women street-sellers make many, and sometimes, I must confess, valiant excuses. They must work on a Sunday morning, they will say, or they can't eat; or else they tell you, they are so tired by knocking about all the week that they must rest on a Sunday; or else they have no clothes to go to church in, and ar'n't a-going there just to be looked down upon and put in any queer place as if they had a fever, and for ladies to hold their grand dresses away from them as they walked in to their grand pews. Then, again, some assert they are not used to sit still for so long a time, and so fall asleep. I have heard all these causes assigned as reasons for not attending church or chapel.

A few women street-sellers, however, *do* attend the Sunday service of the Church of England. One lace-seller told me that she did so because it obliged Mrs —, who was the best friend and customer she had, and who always looked from her pew in the gallery to see who were on the poor seats. A few others, perhaps about an equal number, attend dissenting places of worship of the various denominations – the Methodist chapels comprising more than a half. If I may venture upon a calculation founded on the result of my inquiries, and on the information of others who felt an interest in the matter, I should say that about five female street-sellers attended Protestant places of worship, in the ratio of a hundred attending the Roman Catholic chapels.

The localities in which the female street-sellers reside are those (generally) which I have often had occasion to specify as the abodes of the poor. They congregate principally, however, in the neighbourhood of some street-market. The many courts in Ray-street, Turnmill-street, Cow-cross, and other parts of Clerkenwell, are full of street-sellers, especially coster-mongers, some of those costermongers being also drovers. Their places of sale are in Clerkenwell-green, Aylesbury-street, and St John-street. Others reside in Vine-street (late Mutton-hill), Saffron-hill, Portpool Lane, Baldwin's-gardens, and the many streets or alleys stretching from Leather-lane to Gray's-inn-lane, with a few of the better sort in Cromer-street. Their chief mart is Leather-lane, now one of the most crowded markets in London. The many who use the Brill as their place of street-traffic, reside in Brill-row, in Ossulston-street, Wilstead-street, Chapel-street, and in the many small intersecting lanes and alleys connected with those streets, and in other parts of Somers-town. The saleswomen in the Cripplegate street-markets, such as Whitecross-street, Fore-street, Goldenlane, &c., reside in Play-house-yard, and in the thick congregation of courts and alleys, approximating to Aldersgate-street, Fore-street, Bunhill-row, Chiswell-street, Barbican, &c., &c. Advancing eastward, the female street-sellers in Shoreditch (including the divisions of the Bishopsgate-streets Within and Without, Norton Folgate, and Holywell-street) reside in and about Artillery-lane, Half-moon-street, and the many narrow 'clefts' (as they are called in one of Leigh Hunt's essays) stretching on the right hand as you proceed along Bishopsgate-street, from its junction with Cornhill; 'clefts' which, on my several visits, have appeared to me as among the foulest places in London. On the left-hand side, proceeding in the same direction, the street-sellers reside in Long-alley, and the many yards connected with that, perhaps narrowest, in proportion to its length, of any merely pedestrian thoroughfare in London. Mixed with the poor street-sellers about Long-alley, I may observe, are a mass of the tailors and shoemakers employed by the east-end slop-masters; they are principally Irish workmen, carrying on their crafts many in one room, to economise the rent, while some of their wives are street-sellers.

The street-sellers in Spitalfields and Bethnal-green are so mixed up as to their abodes with the wretchedly underpaid cabinet-makers who supply the 'slaughter-houses'; with slop-employed tailors and shoemakers (in the employ of a class, as respects shoemakers, known as 'garret-masters' or middle-men, between the workman and the wholesale warehouse-man), bobbin-turners, needle-women, slop-milliners, &c., that I might tediously enumerate almost every one of the many streets known, emphatically enough, as the 'poor streets'. These poor streets are very numerous, running eastward from Shoreditch to the Cambridge-road, and southward from the Bethnal-green-road to Whitechapel and the Mile End-road. The female street-sellers in Whitechapel live in Wentworth-street, Thrawl-street, Osborne-street, George-yard, and in several of their inter-minglements with courts and narrow streets. The Petticoat-lane street-dealers are generally Jews, and live in the poorer Jewish quarters, in Petticoat-lane and its courts, and in the streets running on thence to Houndsditch. Rosemary-lane has many street-sellers, but in the lane itself and its many yards and blind alleys they find their domiciles. Westward in the metropolis one of the largest street-markets is in Tottenham-court-road; and in the courts between Fitzroy-market and Tottenham-court-road are the rooms of the women vending their street goods. Those occupying the Hampstead-road with their stalls – which is but a continuation of the Tottenham-court-road market – live in the same quarters. In what is generally called the St George's-market, meaning the stalls at the western extremity of Oxford-street, the women who own those stalls reside in and about Thomas-street, Tom's-court, and the wretched places – the very existence of which is perhaps unknown to their aristocratic neighbourhood – about Grosvenor-square; some of them lamentably wretched places. It might be wearisome to carry on this enumeration further. It may suffice to observe, that in the populous parts of Southwark, Lambeth, and Newington, wherever there is a street-market, are small or old streets inhabited by the street-sellers, and at no great distance. From the Obelisk at the junction, or approximate junction, of the Westminster, Waterloo, Blackfriars, Borough, and London-roads, in pretty well every direction to the banks of the Thames, are a mass of private-looking streets – as far as the absence of shops constitutes the privacy of a street – old and half-ruinous, or modern and trim, in all of which perhaps may be found street-sellers, and in some of which are pickpockets, thieves, and prostitutes.

Of course it must be understood that these specified localities are the residence of the male, as well as the female street-sellers, both adults and children.

The proportion of female street-traders who reside in lodging-houses may be estimated at one-tenth of the entire number. This may appear a small proportion, but it must be remembered that the costermongering women do not reside in lodging-houses – so removing the largest class of street-folk from the calculation of the numbers thus accommodated – and that the Irish who pursue street callings with any regularity generally prefer living, if it be two or three families in a room, in a place of their own. The female street-folk sleeping in lodging-houses, and occasionally taking their meals there, are usually those who are itinerant; the women who have a settled trade, especially a 'pitch', reside in preference in some 'place of their own'. Of the number in lodging-houses one half may be regular inmates, some having a portion of a particular room to themselves; the others are casual sojourners, changing their night's shelter as convenience prompts.

Of the female street-sellers residing in houses of ill-fame there are not many; perhaps not many more than 100. I was told by a gentleman whose connection with parochial matters enabled him to form an opinion, that about Whitecross-street, and some similar streets near the Cornwall-road, and stretching away to the Blackfriars and Borough-roads – (the locality which of any in London is perhaps the most rank with prostitution and its attendant evils) – there might be 600 of those wretched women and of all ages, from 15 to upwards of 40; and that among them he believed there were barely a score who occupied themselves with street-sale. Of women, and more especially of girl, street-sellers, such as flower-girls, those pursuing immoral courses are far more numerous than 100, but they do not often reside in houses notoriously of ill-fame, but in their own rooms (and too often with their parents) and in low lodging-houses. For women who are street-sellers, without the practice of prostitution, to reside in a house of ill-fame, would be a reckless waste of money; as I am told that in so wretched a street as White-horse-street, the rent of a front kitchen is 4s. 6d. a week; of a back kitchen, 3s. 6d.; of a front parlour, 6s.; and of a back parlour, 4s. 6d.; all being meagrely furnished and very small. This is also accounted one of the cheapest of all such streets. The rent of a street-seller's unfurnished room is generally 1s. 6d. or even 1s. a week; a furnished room is 3s. or 2s. 6d.

The state of education among the female street-sellers is very defective. Perhaps it may be said that among the English costers not one female in twenty can read, and not one in forty can write. But they are fond of listening to any one who reads the newspaper or any exciting story. Among the street-selling Irish, also, education is very defective. As regards the adults, who have been of woman's estate before they left Ireland, a knowledge of reading and writing may be as rare as among the English costerwomen; but with those who have come to this country sufficiently young, or have been born here, education is far more diffused than among the often more prosperous English street children. This is owing to the establishment of late years of many Roman Catholic schools, at charges suited to the poor, or sometimes free, and of the Irish parents having availed themselves (probably on the recommendation of the priest) of such opportunities for the tuition of their daughters, which the English costers have neglected to do with equal chances. Of the other classes whom I have specified as street-sellers, I believe I may say that the education of the females is about the average of that of 'servants of all work' who have been brought up amidst struggles and poverty; they can read, but with little appreciation of what they read, and have therefore little taste for books, and often little leisure even if they have taste. As to writing, a woman told me that at one time, when she was 'in place', and kept weekly accounts, she had been complimented by her mistress on her neat hand, but that she and her husband (a man of indifferent character) had been street-sellers for seven or eight years, and during all that time she had only once had a pen in her hand; this was a few weeks back, in signing a petition – something about Sundays, she said – she wrote her name with great pain and difficulty, and feared that she had not even spelled it aright! I may here repeat that I found the uneducated always ready to attribute their want of success in life to their want of education; while the equally poor street-sellers, who were 'scholars', are as apt to say, 'It's been of no manner of use to me.' In all these matters I can but speak generally. The male street-sellers who have seen better days have of course been better educated, but the most intelligent of the street class are the patterers, and of them the females form no portion.

The diet of the class I am describing is, as regards its poorest members, tea and bread or bread and grease; a meal composed of nothing else is their fare twice or thrice a day. Sometimes there is the addition of a herring – or a plaice, when plaice are two a penny – but the consumption of cheap fish, with a few potatoes, is more common among the poor Irish than the poor English female street-sellers. 'Indeed, sir,' said an elderly woman, who sold cakes of blacking and small wares, 'I could make a meal on fish and potatoes, cheaper than on tea and bread and butter, though I don't take milk with my tea – I've got to like it better without milk than with it – but if you're a long time on your legs in the streets and get to your bit of a home for a cup of tea, you want a bit of rest over it, and if you have to cook fish it's such a trouble. O, no, indeed, this time of year there's no 'casion to light a fire for your tea – and tea 'livens you far more nor a herring – because there's always some neighbour to give a poor woman a jug of boiling water.' Married women, who may carry on a trade distinct from that of their husbands, live as well as their earnings and the means of the couple will permit; what they consider good living is a dinner daily off 'good block ornaments' (small pieces of meat, discoloured and dirty, but not tainted, usually set for sale on the butcher's block), tripe, cow-heel, beef-sausages, or soup from a cheap cook-shop, 'at 2*d*. a pint'. To this there is the usual accompaniment of beer, which, in all populous neighbour-hoods, is '3*d*. a pot (quart) in your own jugs'. From what I could learn, it seems to me that an inordinate or extravagant indulgence of the palate, under any circumstances, is far less common among the female than the male street-sellers.

During the summer and the fine months of spring and autumn, there are, I am assured, one-third of the London street-sellers – male and female – 'tramping' the country. At Maidstone Fair the other day, I was told by an intelligent itinerant dealer, there were 300 women, all of whose faces he believed he had seen at one time or other in London. The Irish, however, tramp very little into the country for purposes of trade, but they travel in great numbers from one place to another for purposes of mendicancy; or, if they have a desire to emigrate, they will tramp from

London to Liverpool, literally begging their way, no matter whether they have or have not any money. The female street-sellers are thus a fluctuating body.

The beggars among the women who profess to be street-traders are chiefly Irishwomen, some of whom, though otherwise well-conducted, sober and chaste, beg shamelessly and with any mendacious representation. It is remarkable enough, too, that of the Irishwomen who will thus beg, many if employed in any agricultural work, or in the rougher household labours, such as scouring or washing, will work exceedingly hard. To any feeling of self-respect or self-dependence, however, they seem dead; their great merit is their chastity, their great shame their lying and mendicancy.

The female street-sellers are again a fluctuating body, as in the summer and autumn months. A large proportion go off to work in market-gardens, in the gathering of peas, beans, and the several fruits; in weeding, in hay-making, in the corn-harvest (when they will endeavour to obtain leave to glean if they are unemployed more profitably), and afterwards in the hopping. The women, however, thus seeking change of employment, are the ruder street-sellers, those who merely buy oranges at 4d. to sell at 6d., and who do not meddle with any calling mixed up with the necessity of skill in selection, or address in recommending. Of this half-vagrant class, many are not street-sellers usually, but are half prostitutes and half thieves, not unfrequently drinking all their earnings, while of the habitual female street-sellers, I do not think that drunkenness is now a very prevalent vice. Their earnings are small, and if they become habituated to an indulgence in drink, their means are soon dissipated; in which case they are unable to obtain stock-money, and they cease to be street-sellers.

If I may venture upon an estimation, I should say that the women engaged in street sale – wives, widows, and single persons – number from 25,000 to 30,000, and that their average earnings run from 2s. 6d. to 4s. a week.

I shall now proceed to give the histories of individuals belonging to each of the above class of female street-sellers, with the view of illustrating what has been said respecting them generally.

Of a Single Woman, as a Street-seller

[pp. 517–18] I had some difficulty, for the reasons I have stated, in finding a single woman who, by her unaided industry, supported herself on the sale of street merchandise. There were plenty of single young women so engaged, but they lived, or lodged, with their parents or with one parent, or they had some support, however trifling, from some quarter or other. Among the street-sellers I could have obtained statements from many single women who depended on their daily sale for their daily bread, but I have already given instances of their street life. One Irishwoman, a spinster of about 50, for I had some conversation with her in the course of a former inquiry, had supported herself alone, by street sale, for many years. She sat, literally packed in a sort of hamper-basket, at the corner of Charles-street, Leather-lane. She seemed to fit herself cross-legged, like a Turk, or a tailor on his shop-board, into her hamper; her fruit stall was close by her, and there she seemed to doze away life day by day – for she usually appeared to be wrapped in slumber. If any one approached her stall, however, she seemed to awake, as it were, mechanically. I have missed this poor woman of late, and I believe she only packed herself up in the way described when the weather was cold.

A woman of about 26 or 27 – I may again remark that the regular street-sellers rarely know their age – made the following statement. She was spare and sickly looking, but said that her health was tolerably good.

'I used to mind my mother's stall,' she stated, 'when I was a girl, when mother wasn't well or had a little work at pea-shelling or such like. She sold sweet-stuff. No, she didn't make it, but bought it. I never cared for it, and when I was quite young I've sold sweet-stuffs as I never tasted. I never had a father. I can't read or write, but I like to hear people read. I go to Zion Chapel sometimes of a Sunday night, the singing's so nice. I don't know what religion you may call it of, but it's a Zion Chapel. Mother's been dead these – well I don't know how long, but it's a long time. I've lived by myself ever since, and kept myself, and I have half a room with another young woman who lives by making little boxes. I don't know what sort of boxes. Pill-boxes? Very likely, sir, but I can't say I ever saw any. She goes out to work on another box-maker's premises. She's no better off nor me. We pays 1s. 6d. a-week between us; it's my bed, and the other sticks is her'n. We 'gree well enough. I haven't sold sweet stuff for a great bit. I've sold small wares in the streets, and artificials (artificial flowers), and lace, and penny dolls, and penny boxes (of toys). No, I never hear anything improper from young men. Boys has sometimes said, when I've been selling sweets, "Don't look so hard at 'em, or they'll turn sour." I never minded such nonsense. I has very few amusements. I goes once or twice a month, or so, to the gallery at the Wick (Victoria Theatre), for I live near. It's beautiful there. O, it's really grand. I don't know what they call what's played, because I can't read the bills.

'I hear what they're called, but I forgets. I knows Miss Vincent and John Herbert when they come on. I likes them the best. I'm a going to leave the streets. I have an aunt a laundress, because she was mother's sister, and I always helped her and she taught me laundressing. I work for her three and sometimes four days a-week now, because she's lost her daughter Ann, and I'm known as a good ironer. Another laundress will employ me next week, so I'm dropping the streets, as I can do far better. I'm not likely to be married and I don't want to.'

Of a Mechanic's Wife, as a Street-seller

[pp. 518–21] A middle-aged woman, presenting what may be best understood as a decency of appearance, for there was nothing remarkable in her face or dress, gave me the following account of her experience as a street-seller, and of her feelings when she first became one:

'I went into service very young in the country,' she said, 'but mistress brought me up to London with her, where master had got a situation: the children was so fond of me. I saved a little money in that and other places as girls often does, and they seems not to save it so much for themselves as for others. Father got the first bit of money I saved, or he would have been seized for rent – he was only a working man (agricultural labourer) – and all the rest I scraped went before I'd been married a fortnight, for I got married when I was 24. O no, indeed, I don't mean that my money was wasted by my husband. It was every farthing laid out in the house, besides what he had, for we took a small house in a little street near the Commercial-road, and let out furnished rooms. We did very well at first with lodgings, but the lodgers were mates of vessels, or people about the river and the docks, and they were always coming and going, and the rooms was often empty, and some went away in debt. My husband is a smith, and was in middling work for a good while. Then he got a job to go with some horses to France, for he can groom a horse as well as shoe it, and he was a long time away, three or four months, for he was sent into another country when he got to France, but I don't understand the particulars of it. The rooms was empty and the last lodger went away without paying, and I had nothing to meet the quarter's rent, and the landlord, all of a sudden almost, put in the brokers, for he said my husband would never come back, and perhaps I should be selling the furniture and be off to join him, for he told me it was all a planned thing he knew. And so the furniture was sold for next to nothing, and 1l. 6s. was given to me after the sale; I suppose that was over when all was paid, but I'd been forced to part with some linen and things to live upon and pay the rates, that came very heavy. My husband came back to an empty house three days after, and he'd been unlucky, for he brought home only 4*l*. instead of 10*l*. at least, as he expected, but he'd been cheated by the man he went into the other country with. Yes, the man that cheated him was an Englishman, and my poor John was put to great trouble and expense, and was in a strange place without knowing a word of the language. But the foreigners was very kind to him, he said, and didn't laugh at him when he tried to make hisself understood, as I've seen people do here many a time. The landlord gave us 1*l*. to give up the house, as he had a good offer for it, and so we had to start again in the world like.

'Our money was almost all gone before John got regular work, tho' he had some odd jobs, and then he had for a good many months the care of a horse and cart for a tradesman in the City. Shortly after that he was laid up a week with a crushed leg, but his master wouldn't wait a week for him, so he hired another: "I have nothing to say against John," says he, when I told his master of the accident, "and I'm sorry, very sorry, but my business can't be hindered by waiting for people getting better of accidents." John got work at his own business next, but there was always some stopper. He was ill, or I was ill, and if there was 10*s*. in the house, then it went and wasn't enough. And so we went on for a good many years, I don't know how many. John kept working among horses and carts, or at his own business, but what with travelling abroad, I suppose, and such like, he got to like best to be in the streets, and he has his health best that way.' (The husband, it is evident, was afflicted with the restlessness of the tribe.) 'About seven years ago we were very badly off – no work, and no money, and neither of us well. Then I used to make a few women's plain night-caps and plain morning caps for servants, and sell them to a shopkeeper, but latterly I couldn't sell them at all, or get no more than the stuff cost me, without any profit for labour. So at last – and it was on a Friday evening of all unlucky times – my gold wedding-ring that cost 8*s*. 6*d*., and that I'd stuck to all along, had to be pawned for 4*s*. 6*d*. for rent and bread. That *was* a shocking time, sir. We've sat in the dark of an evening, for we could get neither coals nor a candle as we was a little in debt, and John said, it was a blessing after all perhaps that we hadn't no family, for he often, both joking and serious, wished for children, but it wasn't God's will you see that we should have any. One morning when I woke very early I found my husband just going out, and when I asked him what sent him out so soon, he says: "It's for nothing bad, so don't fret yourself, old gal." That day he walked all over London and called on all the masters as had employed him, or knowed him, and told them how he was situated, and said that if he could borrow 20s. up and down, he could do a little, he knew – the thought of it came into his mind all of a sudden – in going about with a horse and cart, that he could hire, and sell coals to poor people. He raised 8s. 6d., I think it was, and started with a quarter of a ton of coals, and then another quarter when the first was sold, and he carried it on for three or four weeks. But the hire of the horse and cart took all the profit, and the poor people wanted credit, besides people must cheat to thrive as sells coals in the street. All this time I could do nothing – though I tried for washing and charing, but I'm slow at washing – but starve at home, and be afraid every knock was the landlord. After that John was employed to carry a very heavy board over his shoulder, and so as to have it read on both sides. It was about an eating-house, and I went with him to give little bills about it to all we met, for it was as much as a man could do to carry the board. He had 1s. a day, and I had 6d. That was my first time in the streets and I felt so 'shamed to come to that. I thought if I met any people I knew in Essex, or any of my old mistresses, what would they think. Then we had all sorts of jokes to stand. We both looked pinched, and young gents used to say, "Do you dine there yourselves?" and the boys – O, of all the torments! – they've shouted out, "Excellent Dining-rooms" that was on the board, sir, "and two jolly speciments of the style of grub!" I could have knocked their saucy heads together. We was resting in the shade one day – and we were anxious to do our best, for 1s. 6d. a day was a great thing then – and an old gentleman came up and said he was glad to get out of the sun. He looked like a parson, but was a joky man, and he'd been having some wine, I think, he smelled of it so. He began to talk to us and ask us questions, such as you have, sir, and we told him how we was situated. "God bless you," says he, "for I think you're honest folks. People that lie don't talk like you; here's some loose silver I have," and he gave John 5s. 6d. and went away. We could hardly think it was real; it seemed such a lot of money just then, to be got clear all at once. I've never seen him since, and never saw him, as I knows of, before, but may God Almighty bless him wherever he is, for I think that 5s. 6d. put new life into us, and brought a blessing. A relation of John's came to London not long after and gave him a sovereign and sent him some old clothes, and very good ones, when he went back. Then John hired a barrow – it's his own now – and started as a costermonger. A neighbour of ourn told him how to do it, and he's done very well at it since.

'Well, you know, sir, I couldn't like to stay at home by myself doing of a nothing, and I couldn't get any charing; besides John says, "Why, can't *you* sell something?" So I made some plain women's caps, and as we lived in Anne's-place, Waterloo-road, then, I went into the New Cut with them on a Saturday night. But there was such crowding, and shoving, and shouting, that I was kept under and sold only one cap. I was very much nervoused before I went and thought again – it was very foolish, I know – "if I saw anybody from Essex", for country people seem to think all their friends in London are making fortunes! Before I went my landlady *would* treat me to a little drop of gin to give me spirits, and "for luck", but I think it made me more nervoused. I very seldom taste any. And John's very good that way. He takes his pint or two every now and then, but I know where he uses, and if it gets late I go for him and he comes home. The next time I went to sell in the Cut I got bold, for I knew I was doing nothing but what was honest; I've sold caps, and millinery, and laces, and artificial flowers, and such like ever since. We've saved a little money now, which is in the bank, thank God, but that's not done by costering, or by my trade. But my husband buys a poney every now and then, and grooms and fattens it up well, and makes it quite another thing, and so clears a pound or two; he once cleared 3*l.* 15*s.* on it. We don't go to church or chapel on a Sunday, we're so tired out after the week's work. But John reads a tract that a young lady leaves 'till he falls asleep over it.'

Of an Irishwoman, as a Street-seller

[pp. 521–3] I have before had occasion to remark the aptitude of the poor Irish in the streets of London not so much to lie, which may be too harsh a word when motives and idiosyncrasy are considered, but to exaggerate, and misrepresent, and colour in such a way that the truth becomes a mere incident in the narrative, instead of being the animating principle throughout. I speak here not as regards any direct question or answer on one specific point, but as regards a connected statement. Presuming that a poor Irishwoman, for instance, had saved up a few shillings, very likely for some laudable purpose, and had them hidden about her person, and was asked if she had a farthing in the world, she would reply with a look of most stolid innocence, 'Sorra a fardin, sir.' This of course is an unmitigated lie. Then ask her *why* she is so poor and what are her hopes for the future, and a very slender substratum of truth will suffice for the putting together of a very ingenious history, if she think the occasion requires it.

It is the same when these poor persons are questioned as to their former life. They have heard of societies to promote emigration, and if they fancy that any inquiries are made of them with a view to emigration, they will ingeniously shape their replies so as to promote or divert that object, according to their wishes. If they think the inquiries are for some charitable purpose, their tale of woe and starvation is heart-rending. The probability is that they may have suffered much, and long, and bravely, but they will still exaggerate. In one thing, however, I have found them understate the fact, and that I believe principally, or wholly, when they had been previously used to the most wretched of the Irish hovels. I mean as to their rooms. 'Where do you live,' may be asked. 'Will, thin, in Paraker-street [Parker-street], Derwry-lane.' 'Have you a decent room?' 'Shure, thin, and it is dacint for a poor woman.' On a visit, perhaps the room will be found smoky, filthy, half-ruinous, and wretched in every respect. I believe, however, that if these poor people could be made to comprehend the motives which caused their being questioned for the purposes of this work, the elucidation of the truth – motives which they cannot be made to understand – they would speak with a far greater regard to veracity. But they *will* suspect an ulterior object, involving some design on the part of the querist, and they will speak accordingly. To what causes, social or political, national, long-rooted, or otherwise, this spirit may be owing, it is not now my business to inquire.

At the outset of my inquiries amongst the poor Irish, whose civility and often native politeness, where there is a better degree of intelligence, makes it almost impossible to be angry with them even when you listen to a story of which you believe not one-sixth – at the outset of my inquiries, I say, I was told by an Irish gentleman that I was sure to hear the truth if I had authority to use the name of their priest. I readily obtained the consent of reverend gentlemen to use their names and for any purpose of inquiry, a courtesy which I thankfully acknowledged. I mention this more especially, that it may not be thought that there has been exaggeration in my foregoing or in the following statement, where the Irish are the narrators. I have little doubt of their truth.

It may be but proper to remark, in order that one class of poor people may not be unduly *depreciated*, while another class is, perhaps, unduly *appreciated*, that the poor Irishman is much more imaginative, is readier of wit and far readier of speech, than an Englishman of a corresponding grade; and were the untaught Englishman equally gifted in those respects, who will avouch that *his* regard for the truth would be much more severe?

Of the causes which induced a good-looking Irish woman to become a street-seller I had the following account, which I give in its curious details:

''Deed thin, sir, it's more than 20 long years since I came from Dublin to Liverpool wid my father and mother, and brother William that's dead and gone, rest his soul. He died when he was fourteen. They was masons in Ireland. Was both father and mother masons, sir? Well, then, in any quiet job mother helped father, for she was a strong woman. They came away sudden. They was in some thrubble, but I never knew what, for they wouldn't talk to me about it. We thravelled from Liverpool to London, for there was no worruk at Liverpool; and he got worruk on buildings in London, and had 18s. a week; and mother cleaned and worruked for a greengrocer, as they called him – he sold coals more than anything – where we lodged, and it wasn't much, she got, but she airned what is such a thrubble to poor people, the rint. We was well off, and I was sent to school; and we should have been better off, but father took too much to the dhrop, God save him. He fell onste and broke his leg; and though the hospital gintlemen, God bless them for good Christians, got him through it, he got little worruk when he came out again, and died in less than a year. Mother wasn't long afther him; and on her death-bed she said, so low I could hardly hear her, "Mary, my darlint, if you starruve, be vartuous. Rimimber poor Illen's funeral." When I was quite a child, sir, I went wid mother to a funeral – she was a relation – and it was of a young woman that died after her child had been borrun a fortnight, and she wasn't married; that was Illen. Her body was brought out of the lying-in hospital – I've often heard spake of it since – and was in the churchyard to be buried; and her brother, that hadn't seen her for a long time came and wanted to see her in her coffin, and they took the lid off, and then he currused her in her coffin afore him; she'd been so wicked. But he wasn't a good man hisself, and was in dhrink too; still nobody said anything, and he walked away. It made me ill to see Illen in her coffin, and hear him curruse, and I've remembered it ever since.

'I was thin fifteen, I believe, and hadn't any friends that had any tie to me. I was lone, sir. But the neebours said, "Poor thing, she's left on the shuckrawn" (homeless); and they helped me, and I got a place. Mistress was very kind at first, that's my first mistress was, and I had the care of a child of three years old; they had only one, because mistress was busy making waistcoats. Master was a hatter, and away all day, and they was well off. But some women called on mistress once, and they had a deal of talkin', and bladherin', and laughin', and I don't know how often I was sent out for quarters of gin. Then they all went out together; and mistress came home quite tipsy just afore master, and went upstairs, and had just time to get into bed; she told me to tell master she had one of her sick headaches and was forced to go to bed; she went on that way for three or four days, and master and she used to quarrel of a night, for I could hear them. One night he came home sooner than common, and he'd been drinking, or perhaps it might be thrubble, and he sent me to bed wid the child; and sometime in the night, I don't know what time, but I could only see from a gas-lamp that shined into the room, he came in, for there was no fastenin' inside the door, it was only like a closet, and be began to ask me about mistress. When he larned she'd been drinking wid other women, he used dreadful language, and pulled me out of bed, and struck me with a stick that he snatched up, he could see it in the gas-light, it was little Frank's horse, and swore at me for not telling him afore. He only struck me onste, but I screamed ever so often, I was so frightened. I dressed myself, and lay down in my clothes, and go up as soon as it was light – it was summer time – and thought I would go away and complain to some one. I would ask the neebours who to complain to. When I was going out there was master walking up and down the kitchen. He'd never been to bed, and he says, says he, "Mary, where are you going?" So I told him, and he begged my pardon, and said he was ashamed of what he'd done, but he was half mad; then he began to cry, and so I cried, and mistress came home just then, and when she saw us both crying together, *she* cried, and said she wasn't wanted, as we was man and wife already. Master just gave her a push and down she fell, and he ran out. She seemed so bad, and the child began to cry, that I couldn't lave thin; and master came home drunk that night, but he wasn't cross, for he'd made out that mistress had been drinking with some neebours, and had got to her mother's, and that she was so tipsy she fell asleep, they let her stay till morning, and then some woman set her home, but she'd been there all night. They made it up at last, but I wouldn't stay. They was very kind to me when I left, and paid me all that was owing, and gave me a good pair of shoes, too; for they was well off.

'I had a many places for seven years; after that, and when I was out of a place, I stayed wid a widder, and a very dacint woman, she was wid a daughter working for a bookbinder, and the old woman had a good pitch with fruit. Some of my places was very harrud, but shure, again, I met some as was very kind. I left one because they was always wanting me to go to a Methodist chapel, and was always running down my religion, and did all they could to hinder my ever going to mass. They would hardly pay me when I left, because I wouldn't listen to them, they said – the haythens! – when they would have saved my soul. *They* save my soul, indeed! The likes o' thim! Yes, indeed, thin, I had wicked offers sometimes, and from masters that should have known better. I kept no company wid young men. One mistress refused me a karackter, because I was so unhandy, she said; but she thought better of it. At last, I had a faver (fever), and wasn't expected for long (not expected to live); when I was getting well, everything went to keep me. What wasn't good enough for the pawn went to the dolly (dolly-shop, generally a rag and bottle shop, or a marine store). When I could get about, I was so shabby, and my clothes hung about me so, that the shops I went to said, "Very sorry, but can't recommend you anywhere"; and mistresses looked strange at me, and I didn't know what to do and was miserable. I'd been miserable sometimes in place, and had many a cry, and thought how "lone" I was, but I never was so miserable as this. At last, the old woman I stayed along wid – O, yes, she was an Irishwoman – advised me to sill fruit in the streets, and I began on strawberries, and borrowed 2s. 6d. to do it wid. I had my hilth better than ever thin; and after I'd sold fruit of all kinds for two years, I got married. My husband had a potato can thin. I knew him because he lived near, and I saw him go in and out, and go to mass. After that he got a porter's place and dropped his can, and he porters when he has a chance still, and has a little work in sewing sacks for the corn-merchants. Whin he's at home at his sacks, as he is now, he can mind the children – we have two – and I sells a few oranges to make a thrifle. Whin there's nothing ilse for him to do, he sills fruit in the sthreets, and thin I'm at home. We do middlin, God be praised.'

There is no doubt my informant was a modest, and, in her way, a worthy woman. But it may be doubted if any English girl, after seven years of domestic service, would have so readily adapted herself to a street calling. Had an English girl been living among, and used to the society of women who supported themselves by street labour, her repugnance to such a life might have been lessened; but even then, I doubt if she, who had the virtue to resist the offers told of by my Irish informant, could have made the attempt to live by selling fruit. I do not mean that she would rather have fallen into immoral courses than honestly live upon the sale of strawberries, but that she would have struggled on and striven to obtain any domestic labour in preference to a street occupation.

Of a Widow, a Street-seller

[pp. 523–4]   A woman, apparently about 50, strong-built and red-faced, speaking in a loud tone, and what people of her class account a *hearty* manner, gave me the following account. I can readily condense it, for in her street career there was nothing very novel. She was the daughter of a costermonger, and she married a costermonger before she was 20. On my hinting that sometimes the marriage ceremony was not considered indispensable, the good woman laughed and said, 'married, or as good, it's hall as one – but we was married.' The marriage was not one of unalloyed happiness, for the couple often wrangled and occasionally fought. This was told to me with some laughter, and with perfect good humour; for the widow seemed interested to have a listener. She did not, I feel confident, exaggerate the merits of the deceased, nor, perhaps, his failings. He was the best judge of fish in the streets, she said, and was the neatest hand in cutting it up, or showing it off; he was not 'a bad sort', and was very fond of his children. When sober and at work he was a quiet fellow, without a cross word for a whole morning, but when drunk, which was far too often (unless *very* drunk, and then he was silly), he went about tearing and swearing 'like one o'clock'. But if he saw his wife take but a glass or two, to do her good, he went on like a madman, and as if he never touched it himself. He never had nothing to say to other women – if he had she would have clawed their eyes out, and his'n too – he was as good that way as any nobleman could be, and he was a fine man to look at; and on a Sunday, when he dressed hisself, he was beautiful. He was never in a church in his life, and didn't trouble hisself about such things; they was no concern of his'n.

It may be thought that I have treated this matter too lightly, but the foregoing is really the substance, and certainly it is the tone, of the widow's talk, which she poured forth freely, without expressing wonder why any one, a perfect stranger, cared to listen to such a history. She needed but a few hints and leading questions to make her talk on. Nor is this an uncommon quality even among classes who would be shocked to be classed, in any respect, with the Widowed Street-Seller. Their own career, their own sayings and doings, hopes and disappointments, alone interest masses of people, and with the simplicity which not seldom pertains to selfishness, they will readily talk of all that interests themselves, as if it must necessarily interest others. On the whole, though the departed costermonger was greatly deplored by his widow and family, they did very well without him, and carry on the business to this day. He died four or five years back.

I have no doubt this widow is a shrewd sales woman enough. I have heard her cry 'mack'rel, live mack'rel, eight a shilling, mack'rel!' and at other times, 'Eight a bob, fine mack'rel, mack'rel, eight a bob, eight a bob!' On my inquiring as to the cause of this difference in her cries, the fish-seller laughed and said, 'I cries eight a bob when I sees people as I thinks is likely to like slang; to others I cries eight a shilling, which no doubt is the right way of talking.'

OF THE CHILDREN STREET-SELLERS OF LONDON

[pp. 524–37]   When we consider the spirit of emulation, of imitation, of bravado, of opposition, of just or idle resentment, among boys, according to their training, companionship, natural disposition, and, above all, home treatment, it seems most important to ascertain how these feelings and inclinations are fostered or stimulated by the examples of the free street-life of other lads to be seen on every side. There is no doubt that to a large class of boys, whose parents are not in poverty, the young street ruffian is a hero.

If this inquiry be important, as it unquestionably is, concerning boys, how much more important is it, when it includes the female children of the streets; when it relates to the sex who, in all relations of life, and in all grades of society, are really the guardians of a people's virtue.

The investigation is, again, rendered more interesting and more important, when it includes those children who have known no guidance from parent, master, or relative, but have been flung into the streets through neglect, through viciousness, or as outcasts from utter destitution. Mixed with the children who really *sell* in the streets, are the class who assume to sell that they may have the better chance to steal, or the greater facility to beg.

Before I classify what I consider to be the causes which have driven children to a street career, with all its hardening consequences, I may point out that culpability cannot be imputed to them at the commencement of their course of life. They have been either untaught, mistaught, maltreated, neglected, regularly trained to vice, or fairly turned into the streets to shift for themselves. The censure, then, is attributable to parents, or those who should fill the place of parents – the State, or society. The exceptions to this culpability as regards parents are to be found in the instances where a costermonger employs his children to aid him in his business occupation, which the parents, in their ignorance or prejudices, may account as good as any other, and the youths thus become unfit, perhaps, for any other than a scrambling street life. A second exception may be where the children in a poor family (as continually happens among the Irish in London) *must* sell in the streets, that they may eat in any place.

In the following details I shall consider all to be children who are under fifteen years of age. It is just beyond that age (or the age of puberty) that, as our prison statistics and other returns show, criminal dispositions are developed, 'self-will' becomes more imperious and headstrong, that destructive propensity, or taste, which we term the ruling passion or character of the individual is educed, and the density of the human being, especially when apart from the moulding and well-directed care of parents or friends, is influenced perhaps for life.

The Causes, then, which fill our streets with children who either manifest the keen and sometimes roguish propensity of a precocious trader, the daring and adroitness of the thief, or the loutish indifference of the mere dull vagabond, content if he can only eat and sleep, I consider to be these:

1. The conduct of parents, masters, and mistresses.
2. The companionship and associations formed in tender years.
3. The employment of children by costermongers and others who live by street traffic, and the training of costermongers' children to a street life.
4. Orphanhood, friendlessness, and utter destitution.
5. Vagrant dispositions and tastes on the part of children, which cause them to be runaways.

After this I shall treat of (*a*) the pursuits of the street-trading children; (*b*) their earnings; (*c*) the causes or influences which have induced children to adopt some especial branch of a street life; (*d*) their state of education; (*e*) their morals, religion, opinions, and conduct; (*f*) places and character of dwellings; (*g*) diet; (*h*) amusements; (*i*) clothing; (*j*) propensities.

Concerning cause 1, viz., 'The conduct of parents, masters, and mistresses', I should have more to say were I treating of the juvenile criminals, instead of sellers in the streets. The brute tyranny of parents, manifested in the wreaking of any annoyances or disappointments they may have endured, in the passionate beating and cursing of their children, for trifling or for no causes, is among the worst symptoms of a depraved nature. This conduct may be the most common among the poor, for among them are fewer conventional restraints; but it exists among and debases other classes. Some parents only exercise this tyranny in their fits of drunkenness, and make that their plea in mitigation; but their dispositions are then only the more undisguisedly developed, and they would be equally unjust or tyrannical when sober, but for some selfish fear which checks them. A boy perhaps endures this course of tyranny some time, and then finding it increase he feels its further endurance intolerable, and runs away. If he have no friends with whom he can hope to find a shelter, the streets only are open to him. He soon meets with comrades, some of whom perhaps had been circumstanced like himself, and, if not strongly disposed to idleness and vicious indulgencies, goes through a course of horse-holding, errand-running, parcel-carrying, and such like, and so becomes, if honestly or prudently inclined, a street-seller, beginning with fuzees, or nuts, or some unexpensive stock. The where to buy and the how to sell he will find plenty to teach him at the lodging-houses, where he *must* sleep when he can pay for a bed.

When I was collecting information concerning brace-selling I met with a youth of sixteen who about two years previously had run away from Birmingham, and made his way to London, with 2s. 6d. Although he earned something weekly, he was so pinched and beaten by a step-mother (his father was seldom at home except on Sunday) that his life was miserable. This went on for nearly a year, until the boy began to resist, and one Saturday evening, when beaten as usual, he struck in return, drawing blood from his step-mother's face. The father came home before the fray was well ended; listened to his wife's statement, and would not listen to the boy's, and in his turn chastised the lad mercilessly. In five minutes after the boy, with aching bones and a bitter spirit, left his father's house and made his way to London, where he was then vending cheap braces. This youth could neither read nor write, and seemed to possess no quickness or intelligence. The only thing of which he cared to talk was his step-mother's treatment of him; all else was a blank with him, in comparison; this was the one burning recollection.

I may here observe, that I heard of several instances of children having run away and adopted a street life in consequence of the violence of step-mothers far more than of step-fathers.

I cite the foregoing instance, as the boy's career was exactly that I have described; but the reader will remember, that in the many and curious narratives I have collected, how often the adult street-seller had begun such a life by being a runaway from domestic tyranny. Had this Birmingham boy been less honest, or perhaps less dull, it would have been far easier for him to have become a thief than a street-trader. To the gangs of young thieves, a new boy, who is not known to the police is often (as a smart young pickpocket, then known as the Cocksparrow, described it to me) 'a God-send'.

My readers will remember that in the collected statements of the street-folk, there are several accounts of runaways, but they were generally older than the age I have fixed, and it was necessary to give an account of one who comes within my classification of a child.

I did not hear of any girls who had run away from their homes having become street-sellers merely. They more generally fall into a course of prostitution, or sometimes may be ostensibly street-sellers as a means of accosting men, and, perhaps, for an attractive pretence to the depraved, that they are poor, innocent girls, struggling for an honest penny. If they resort to the low lodging-houses, where the sexes are lodged indiscriminately, their ruin seems inevitable.

2. That the 'companionship and associations fortified in tender years' lead many children to a street life is so evident, that I may be brief on the subject. There are few who are in the habit of noting what they may observe of poor children in the streets and quieter localities, who have not seen little boys playing at marbles, or gambling with halfpennies, farthings, or buttons, with other lads, and who have laid down their basket of nuts or oranges to take part in the play. The young street-seller has probably more halfpence at his command, or, at any rate, in his possession, than his non-dealing playmates; he is also in the undoubted possession of what appears a large store of things for which poor boys have generally a craving and a relish. Thus the little itinerant trader is envied and imitated.

This attraction to a street career is very strong, I have ascertained, among the neglected children of the poor, when the parents are absent at their work. On a Saturday morning, some little time since, I was in a flagged court near Drury-lane, a wretched place, which was full of children of all ages. The parents were nearly all, I believe, then at work, or 'on the look out for a job', as porters in Covent Garden-market, and the children played in the court until their return. In one corner was a group of four or five little boys gambling and squabbling for nuts, of which one of the number was a vendor. A sharp-looking lad was gazing enviously on, and I asked him to guide me to the room of a man whom I wished to see. He did so, and I gave him a penny. On my leaving the court I found this boy the most eager of the players, gambling with the penny I had given him. I had occasion to return there a few hours after, and the same lad was leaning against the wall, with his hands in his pockets, as if suffering from listlessness. He had had no luck with the nut covey, he told me, but he hoped before long to sell nuts himself. He did not know his age, but he appeared to be about eleven. Only last week I saw this same lad hawking a basket, very indifferently stocked with oranges. He had raised a shilling, he said, and the 'Early Bird' (the nick-name of a young street-seller) had put him up to the way to lay it out. On my asking if his father (a journeyman butcher) knew what he was doing, he replied that so long as he didn't bother his father he could do what he pleased, and the more he kept out of his (the father's) way the better he would be liked and treated.

The association of poor boys and girls with the children of the costermongers, and of the Irish fruit-sellers, who are employed in itinerant vending, is often productive of a strong degree of envy on the part of unemployed little ones, who look upon having the charge of a basket of fruit, to be carried in any direction, as a species of independence.

3. 'The employment of children by costermongers, and others who live by street traffic; and the training of costermongers' children to a street life, is the ordinary means of increase among the street-folk.'

The children of the costermongers become necessarily, as I have already intimated, street-dealers, and perhaps more innocently than in any other manner, by being required, as soon as their strength enables them, to assist their parents in their work, or sell trifles, single-handed, for the behoof of their parents. The child does but obey his father and the father does but rear the child to the calling by which his daily bread is won. This is the case particularly with the Irish, who often have large families, and bring them with them to London.

There are, moreover, a great number of boys, 'anybody's children', as I heard them called, who are tempted and trained to pursue an open-air traffic, through being engaged by costermongers or small tradesmen to sell upon commission, or, as it is termed, for 'bunse'. In the curious, and almost in every instance novel, information which I gave to the public concerning the largest body of the street-sellers, the costermongers, this word 'bunse' (probably a corruption of *bonus*, *bone* being the slang for good) first appeared in print. The mode is this: a certain quantity of saleable, and sometimes of not very saleable, commodities is given to a boy whom a costermonger knows and perhaps employs, and it is arranged that the young commission-agent is to get a particular sum for them, which must be paid to the costermonger; I will say 3s., that being somewhere about the maximum. For these articles the lad may ask and obtain any price he can, and whatever he obtains beyond the stipulated 3s. is his own profit or 'bunse'. The remuneration thus accruing to the boy-vendor of course varies very materially, according to the season of the year, the nature of the article, and the neighbourhood in which it is hawked. Much also depends upon whether the boy has a regular market for his commodities; whether he has certain parties to whom he is known and upon whom he can call to solicit custom; if he has, of course his facilities for disposing of his stock in trade are much greater than in the case of one who has only the chance of attracting attention and obtaining custom by mere crying and bawling 'Penny a piece, Col-ly-flowers', 'Five bunches a penny, Red-dish-es', and such like. The Irish boys call this 'having a back', an old Hibernian phrase formerly applied to a very different subject and purpose.

Another cause of the abundance of street-dealers among the boyish fraternity, whose parents are unable or unwilling to support them, is that some costers keep a lad as a regular assistant, whose duty it is to pull the barrow of his master about the streets, and assist him in 'crying' his wares. Sometimes the man and the boy call out together, sometimes separately and alternately, but mostly the boy alone has to do this part of the work, the coster's voice being generally rough and hoarse, while the shrill sound of that of the boy re-echoes throughout the street along which they slowly move, and is far more likely to strike the ear, and consequently to attract attention, than that of the man. This mode of 'practising the voice' is, however, perfectly ruinous to it, as in almost every case of this description we find the natural tone completely annihilated at a very early age, and a harsh, hoarse, guttural, disagreeable mode of speaking acquired. In addition to the costers there are others who thus employ boys in the streets: the hawkers of coal do so invariably, and the milkmen – especially those who drive cows or have a cart to carry the milk-pails in. Once in the streets and surrounded with street-associates, the boy soon becomes inured to this kind of life, and when he leaves his first master, will frequently start in some branch of costermongering for himself, without seeking to obtain another constant employment.

This mode of employing lads, and on the whole perhaps they are fairly enough used by the costermongers, and generally treated with great kindness by the costers' wives or concubines, is, I am inclined to think, the chief cause of the abundance and even increase of the street-sellers of fish, fruit, and vegetables.

4. To 'orphanhood, friendlessness, and utter destitution', the commerce of the streets owes a considerable portion of its merchants. A child finds himself or herself an orphan; the parents having been miserably poor, he or she lives in a place where street-folk abound; it seems the only road to a meal and a bed, and the orphan 'starts' with a few lucifer-matches, boot-laces, nuts, or onions. It is the same when a child, without being an orphan, is abandoned or neglected by the parents, and, perhaps without any injunctions either for or against such a course, is left to his or her own will to sell or steal in the streets.

5. The 'vagrant dispositions and tastes' of lads, and, it may be, now and then somewhat of a reckless spirit of adventure, which in our days has far fewer fields than it once had, is another cause why a street-life is

embraced. Lads have been known to run away from even comfortable homes through the mere spirit of restlessness; and sometimes they have done so, but not perhaps under the age of fifteen, for the unrestrained indulgence of licentious passions. As this class of runaways, however, do not ordinarily settle into regular street-sellers, but become pickpockets, or trade only with a view to cloak their designs of theft, I need not further allude to them under this head.

I now come to the second part of my subject, the *Pursuits*, &c., of the children in street avocations.

As I have shown in my account of the women street-sellers, there is no calling which this body of juveniles monopolize, none of which they are the *sole* possessors; but some are principally in their hands, and there are others, again, to which they rarely incline.

Among the wares sold by the boys and girls of the streets are:— money-bags, lucifer-match boxes, leather straps, belts, firewood (common, and also 'patent', that is, dipped into an inflammable composition), fly-papers, a variety of fruits, especially nuts, oranges, and apples; onions, radishes, water-cresses, cut flowers and lavender (mostly sold by girls), sweet-briar, India rubber, garters, and other little articles of the same material, including elastic rings to encircle rolls of paper-music, toys of the smaller kinds, cakes, steel pens and penholders with glass handles, exhibition medals and cards, gelatine cards, glass and other cheap seals, brass watch-guards, chains, and rings; small tin ware, nutmeg-graters, and other articles of a similar description, such as are easily portable; iron skewers, fuzees, shirt buttons, boot and stay-laces, pins (and more rarely needles), cotton bobbins, Christmasing (holly and other evergreens at Christmas-tide), May-flowers, coat-studs, top-pottery, blackberries, groundsel and chickweed, and clothes'-pegs.

There are also other things which children sell temporarily, or rather in the season. This year I saw lads selling wild birds'-nests with their eggs, such as hedge-sparrows, minnows in small glass globes, roots of the wild Early Orchis (Orchis mascula), and such like things found only out of town.

Independently of the vending of these articles, there are many other ways of earning a penny among the street boys: among them are found – tumblers, mud-larks, water-jacks, Ethiopians, ballad-singers, bagpipe boys, the variety of street musicians (especially Italian boys with organs), Billingsgate boys or young 'roughs', Covent Garden boys, porters, and shoeblacks (a class recently increased by the Ragged School Brigade). A great many lads are employed also in giving away the cards and placards of advertising and puffing tradesmen, and around the theatres are children of both sexes (along with a few old people) offering play-bills for sale, but this is an occupation less pursued than formerly, as some managers sell their own bills inside the house and do not allow any to pass from the hands of the printer into those of the former vendors. Again: amid the employments of this class may be mentioned – the going on errands and carrying parcels for persons accidentally met with; holding horses; sweeping crossings (but the best crossings are usually in the possession of adults); carrying trunks for any railway traveller to or from the terminus, and carrying them from an omnibus when the passenger is not put down at his exact destination. During the frosty days of the winter and early spring, some of these little fellows used to run along the foot-path – Baker-street was a favourite place for this display – and keep pace with the omnibuses, not merely by using their legs briskly, but by throwing themselves every now and then on their hands and progressing a few steps (so to speak) with their feet in the air. This was done to attract attention and obtain the preference if a job were in prospect; done, too, in hopes of a halfpenny being given the urchin for his agility. I looked at the hands of one of these little fellows and the fleshy parts of the palm were as hard as soling-leather, as hard, indeed, as the soles of the child's feet, for he was bare-footed. At the doors of the theatres, and of public places generally, boys are always in waiting to secure a cab from the stand, their best harvest being when the night has 'turned out wet' after a fine day. Boys wait for the same purpose, lounging all night, and until the place closes, about the night-houses, casinos, saloons, &c., and sometimes without receiving a penny. There are, again, the very many ways in which street boys employed to 'help' other people, when temporary help is needed, as when a cabman must finish the cleaning of his vehicle in a hurry, or when a porter finds himself over-weighted in his truck. Boys are, moreover, the common custodians of the donkeys on which young ladies take in-vigorating exercise in such places as Hampstead-heath and Blackheath. At pigeon-shooting matches they are in readiness to pick up the dead birds, and secure the poor fluttering things which are 'hard hit' by the adventurous sportsman, without having been killed. They have their share again in the picking of currants and gooseberries, the pottling of strawberries, in weeding, &c., &c., and though the younger children may be little employed in haymaking, or in the more important labours of the corn harvest, they have their shares, both with and without the company of their parents, in the 'hopping'. In fine there is no business carried on to any extent in the streets, or in the open air, but it will be found that boys have their portion. Thus they are brought into contact with all classes; another proof of what I have advanced touching the importance of this subject.

It will be perceived that, under this head, I have had to speak far more frequently of boys than of girls, for the boy is far more the child of the streets than is the girl. The female child can do little but *sell* (when a livelihood is to be gained without a recourse to immorality); the boy can not only sell, but *work*.

The many ramifications of child-life and of child-work in our teeming streets, which I have just enumerated, render it difficult to arrive at a very nice estimation of the *earnings of the street boys and girls.* The gains of this week are not necessarily the gains of the next; there is the influence of the weather; there may be a larger or a smaller number of hands 'taking a turn' at any particular calling this week than in its predecessor; and, above all, there is that concatenation of circumstances, which street-sellers include in one expressive word – 'luck'. I mean the opportunities to earn a few pence, which on some occasions present themselves freely, and at others do not occur at all. Such 'luck', however is more felt by the holders of horses, and the class of waiters upon opportunity (so to speak), than by those who depend upon trade.

I believe, however, both in consequence of what I have observed, and from the concurrent testimony of persons familiar with the child-life of London streets, that the earnings of the children, when they are healthful and active, are about the same in the several capacities they exercise. The waiter on opportunity, the lad 'on the look-out for a job', may wait and look out all day bootlessly, but in the evening some fortunate chance may realize him 'a whole tanner all in a lump'. In like manner, the water-cress girl may drudge on from early morning until 'cresses' are wanted for tea, and, with 'a connection', and a tolerably regular demand, earn no more than the boy's 6*d.*, and probably not so much.

One of the most profitable callings of the street-child is in the sale of Christmasing, but that is only for a very brief season; the most regular returns in the child's trade, are in the sale of such things as water-cresses, or any low-priced article of daily consumption, wherever the youthful vendor may be known.

I find it necessary to place the earnings of the street-child higher than those of the aged and infirm. The children are more active, more persevering, and perhaps more impudent. They are less deterred by the weather, and can endure more fatigue in walking long distances than old people. This, however, relates to the boys more especially, some of whom are very sturdy fellows.

The oranges which the street-children now vend at two a-penny, leave them a profit of 4*d*. in the shilling. To take 1*s*. 6*d*. with a profit of 6*d*. is a fair day's work; to take 1*s*. with a profit of 4*d*. is a poor day's work. The dozen bunches of cut-flowers which a girl will sell on an average day at 1*d*. a bunch, cost her 6*d*., that sum being also her profit. These things supply, I think, a fair criterion. The children's profits may be 6*d*. a day, and including Sunday trade, 3*s*. 6*d*. a week; but with the drawbacks of bad weather, they cannot be computed at more than 2*s*. 6*d*. a week the year through. The boys may earn 2*d*. or 3*d*. a week on an average more than the girls, except in such things (which I shall specify under the next head) as seem more particularly suited for female traffic.

Of the causes which influence children to follow this or that course of business when a street career has been their choice or their lot, I have little to say. It seems quite a matter of chance, even where a preference may exist. A runaway lad meets with a comrade who perhaps sells fuzees, and he accordingly begins on fuzees. One youth, of whom I have given an account (but he was not of child's estate), began his street career on fly-papers. When children are sent into the streets to sell on account of their parents, they, of course, vend just what their parents have supplied to them. If 'on their own hook', they usually commence their street career on what it is easiest to buy and easiest to sell; a few nuts or oranges bought in Duke's-place, lucifer-boxes, or small wares. As their experience increases they may become general street-sellers. The duller sort will continue to carry on the trades that any one with ordinary lungs and muscles can pursue. 'All a fellow wants to know to sell potatoes,' said a master street-seller to me, 'is to tell how many tanners make a bob, and how many yenaps a tanner.' [How many sixpences make a shilling, and how many pence a sixpence.] The smarter and bolder lads ripen into patterers, or street-performers, or fall into theft. For the class of adventurous runaways, the patterer's or, rather, the paper-working patterer's life, with its alter-nations of town and country, fairs and hangings, the bustle of race-grounds and the stillness of a village, has great attractions. To a pattering and chaunting career, moreover, there is the stimulus of that love of approbation and of admiration, as strong among the often penniless professionals of the streets as on the boards of the opera house.

Perhaps there is not a child of either sex, now a street-seller, who would not to-morrow, if they thought they could clear a penny or two a day more by it, quit their baskets of oranges and sell candle-ends, or old bones, or anything. In a street career, and most especially when united with a lodging-house existence, there is no daintiness of the senses and no exercise of the tastes. The question is not 'What do I like best to sell?' but 'What is likely to pay me best?' This cannot be wondered at; for if a child earn but 5d. a day on apples, and can make 6d. on onions, its income is increased by 20 per cent.

The trades which I have specified as in the hands of street-children are carried on by both sexes. I do not know that even the stock in trade which most taxes the strength is more a boy's than a girl's pursuit. A basket of oranges or of apples is among the heaviest of all the stocks hawked by children; and in those pursuits there are certainly as many, or rather more, girls than boys. Such articles as fly-papers, money-bags, tins, fuzees, and Christmasing, are chiefly the boys' sale; cut-flowers, lavender, water-cresses, and small wares, are more within the trading of the girls.

The callings with which children do not meddle are those which require 'patter'. Some of the boys very glibly announce their wares, and may be profuse now and then in commendations of their quality, cheapness, and superiority, but it requires a longer experience to patter according to the appreciation of a perhaps critical street audience. No child, for instance, ventures upon the sale of grease-removing compositions, corn-salve, or the 'Trial and Execution of Thomas Drory', with an 'Affecting Copy of Werses'.

A gentleman remarked to me that it was rather curious that boys' playthings, such as marbles and tops were not hawked by street juveniles, who might be very well able to recommend them. I do not remember to have seen any such things vended by children.

Education is, as far as I have been able to ascertain, more widely extended among street children than it was twelve or fifteen years ago. The difficulty in arriving at any conclusion on such a subject is owing to the inability to find any one who knew, or could even form a tolerably accurate judgment of what was the state of education among these juveniles even twelve years back.

Perhaps it may be sufficiently correct to say that among a given number of street children, where, a dozen years ago, you met twenty who could read you will now meet upwards of thirty. Of sixteen children, none apparently fifteen years of age, whom I questioned on the subject, nine admitted that they could not read; the other seven declared that they could, but three annexed to the avowal the qualifying words – 'a little'. Ten were boys and six were girls, and I spoke to them promiscuously as

I met them in the street. Two were Irish lads, who were 'working' oranges in company, and the bigger answered – 'Shure, thin, we *can* rade, your honour, sir.' I have little doubt that they could, but in all probability, had either of those urchins thought he would be a penny the better by it, he would have professed, to a perfect stranger, that he had a knowledge of algebra. 'Yis, sir, I do, thin,' would very likely be his response to any such inquiry; and when told he could not possibly know anything about it, he would answer, 'Arrah, thin, but I didn't understand your honour.'

To the Ragged Schools is, in all probability, owing this extension of the ability to read. It appears that the attendance of the street children at the Ragged School is most uncertain; as, indeed, must necessarily be the case where the whole time of the lad is devoted to obtaining a subsistence. From the best information I can collect, it appears that the average attendance of these boys at these schools does not exceed two hours per week, so that the amount of education thus acquired, if education it may be called, must necessarily be scanty in the extreme; and is frequently forgotten as soon as learned.

With many of these little traders a natural shrewdness compensates in some measure for the deficiency of education, and enables them to carry on their variety of trades with readiness and dexterity, and sometimes with exactness. One boy with whom I had a conversation, told me that he never made any mistake about the 'coppers', although, as I subsequently discovered, he had no notion at all of arithmetic beyond the capability of counting how many pieces of coin he had, and how much copper money was required to make a 'tanner' or a 'bob'. This boy vended coat-studs: he had also some metal collars for dogs, or as he said, 'for cats aither'. These articles he purchased at the same shop in Houndsditch, where 'there was a wonderful lot of other things to be had, on'y some on 'em cost more money.'

In speaking of money, the slang phrases are constantly used by the street lads; thus a sixpence is a 'tanner'; a shilling a 'bob', or a 'hog'; a crown is 'a bull'; a half-crown 'a half-bull', &c. Little, as a modern writer has remarked, do the persons using these phrases know of their remote and somewhat classical origin, which may, indeed, be traced to the period antecedent to that when monarchs monopolized the surface of coined money with their own images and superscriptions. They are identical with the very name of money among the early Romans, which was *pecunia*, from *pecus*, a flock. The collections of coin dealers amply show, that the figure of a hog was anciently placed on a small silver coin, and that that of a bull decorated larger ones of the same metal: these coins were frequently deeply crossed on the reverse: this was for the convenience of easily breaking them into two or more pieces, should the bargain for which they were employed require it, and the parties making it had no smaller change handy to complete the transaction. Thus we find that the 'half-bull' of the itinerant street-seller or 'traveller', so far from being a phrase of modern invention, as is generally supposed, is in point of fact referable to an era extremely remote. Numerous other instances might be given of the classical origin of many of the flash or slang words used by these people.

I now give the answers I received from two boys. The first, his mother told me, was the best scholar at his school when he was there, and before he had to help her in street sale. He was a pale, and not at all forward boy, of thirteen or fourteen, and did not appear much to admire being questioned. He had not been to a Ragged School, but to an 'academy' kept by an old man. He did not know what the weekly charge was, but when father was living (he died last autumn) the schoolmaster used to take it out in vegetables. Father was a costermonger; mother minded all about his schooling, and master often said she behaved to him like a lady. 'God,' this child told me, 'was our Heavenly Father, and the maker of all things; he knew everything and everybody; he knew people's thoughts and every sin they committed if no one else knew it. His was the kingdom and the power, and the glory, for ever and ever, Amen. Jesus Christ was our Lord and Saviour; he was the son of God, and was crucified for our sins. He was a God himself.' [The child understood next to nothing of the doctrine of the Trinity, and I did not press him.] 'The Scriptures, which were the Bible and testament, were the Word of God, and contained nothing but what was good and true. If a boy lied, or stole, or committed sins,' he said, 'he would be punished in the next world, which endured for ever and ever, Amen. It was only after death, when it was too late to repent, that people went to the next world. He attended chapel, sometimes.'

As to mundane matters, the boy told me that Victoria was Queen of Great Britain and Ireland. She was born May 24, 1819, and succeeded his late Majesty, King William IV., July 20, 1837. She was married to his Royal Highness Prince Albert, &c., &c. France was a different country to this: he had heard there was no king or queen there, but didn't understand about it. You couldn't go to France by land, no more than you could to Ireland. Didn't know anything of the old times in history; hadn't been told. Had heard of the battle of Waterloo; the English licked. Had heard of the battle of Trafalgar, and of Lord Nelson; didn't know much about him; but there was his pillar at Charing-cross, just by the candlesticks (fountains).

When I spoke of astronomy, the boy at once told me he knew nothing about it. He had heard that the earth went round the sun, but from what he'd noticed, shouldn't have thought it. He didn't think that the sun went round the earth, it seemed to go more sideways. Would like to read more, if he had time, but he had a few books, and there was hundreds not so well off as he was.

I am far from undervaluing, indeed I would not indulge in an approach to a scoff, at the extent of this boy's knowledge. Many a man who piques himself on the plenitude of his breeches' pocket, and who attributes his success in life to the fulness of his knowledge, knows no more of Nature, Man, and God, than this poor street child.

Another boy, perhaps a few months older, gave me his notions of men and things. He was a thick-limbed, red-cheeked fellow; answered very freely, and sometimes, when I could not help laughing at his replies, laughed loudly himself, as if he entered into the joke.

Yes, he had heer'd of God who made the world. Couldn't exactly recollec' when he'd heer'd on him, but he had, most sarten-ly. Didn't know when the world was made, or how anybody could do it. It must have taken a long time. It was afore his time, 'or yourn either, sir'. Knew there was a book called the Bible; didn't know what it was about; didn't mind to know; knew of such a book to a sartinty, because a young 'oman took one to pop (pawn) for an old 'oman what was on the spree – a bran new 'un – but the cove wouldn't have it, and the old 'oman said he might be d—d. Never heer'd tell on the deluge; of the world having been drownded; it couldn't, for there wasn't water enough to do it. He weren't a going to fret hisself for such things as that. Didn't know what happened to people after death, only that they was buried. Had seen a dead body laid out; was a little afeared at first; poor Dick looked so different, and when you touched his face, he was so cold! oh, so cold! Had heer'd on another world; wouldn't mind if he was there hisself, if he could do better, for things was often queer here. Had heered on it from a tailor – such a clever cove, a stunner – as went to 'Straliar (Australia), and heer'd him say he was going into another world. Had never heer'd of France, but had heer'd of Frenchmen; there wasn't half a quarter so many on 'em as of Italians, with their earrings like flash gals. Didn't dislike foreigners, for he never saw none. What was they? Had heer'd of Ireland. Didn't know where it was, but it couldn't be very far, or such lots wouldn't come from there to London. Should say they walked it, aye, every bit of the way, for he'd seen them come in, all covered with dust. Had heer'd of people going to sea, and had seen the ships in the river, but didn't know nothing about it, for he was very seldom that way. The sun was made of fire, or it wouldn't make you feel so warm. The stars was fire, too, or they wouldn't shine. They didn't make it warm, they was too small. Didn't know any use they was of. Didn't know how far they was off; a jolly lot higher than the gas lights some on 'em was. Was never in a church; had heer'd they worshipped God there; didn't know how it was done; had heer'd singing and playing inside when he'd passed; never was there, for he hadn't no togs to go in, and wouldn't be let in among such swells as he had seen coming out. Was a ignorant chap, for he'd never been to school, but was up to many a move, and didn't do bad. Mother said he would make his fortin yet.

Had heer'd of the Duke of Wellington; he was Old Nosey; didn't think he ever seed him, but had seed his statty. Hadn't heer'd of the battle of Waterloo, nor who it was atween; once lived in Webber-row, Waterloo-road. Thought he had heer'd speak of Buonaparte; didn't know what he was; thought he had heer'd of Shakespeare, but didn't know whether he was alive or dead, and didn't care. A man with something like that name kept a dolly and did stunning; but he was sich a hard cove that if *he* was dead it wouldn't matter. Had seen the Queen, but didn't recollec' her name just at the minute; oh! yes, Wictoria and Albert. Had no notion what the Queen had to do. Should think she hadn't such power [he had first to ask me what 'power' was] as the Lord Mayor, or as Mr Norton as was the Lambeth beak, and perhaps is still. Was never once before a beak and didn't want to. Hated the crushers; what business had they to interfere with him if he was only resting his basket in a street? Had been once to the Wick, and once to the Bower: liked tumbling better; he meant to have a little pleasure when the peas came in.

The knowledge and the ignorance of these two striplings represent that of street children generally. Those who may have run away from a good school, or a better sort of home as far as means constitute such betterness, of course form exceptions. So do the utterly stupid.

The morals, religion, and opinions of the street-trading children are the next topic. Their business morals have been indicated in the course of my former statements, and in the general tone of the remarks and conversation of street-sellers.

As traders their morals may be lax enough. They give short weight, and they give short measure; they prick the juice out of oranges; and brush up old figs to declare they're new. Their silk braces are cotton, their buck-leather braces are wash-leather, their sponge is often rotten, and their salves and cures quackeries.

Speak to any one of the quicker-witted street-sellers on the subject, and though he may be unable to deny that his brother traders are guilty of these short-comings, he will justify them all by the example of shop-keepers. One man, especially, with whom I have more than once conversed on the subject, broadly asserts that as a whole the streets are in all matters of business honester than the shops. 'It ain't *we*,' runs the purport of his remarks, 'as makes coffee out of sham chickory; it ain't *we* as makes cigars out of rhubarb leaves; *we* don't make duffers handker-chiefs, nor weave cotton things and call them silk. If we quacks a bit, does *we* make fortins by it as shopkeepers does with their ointments and pills! If we give slang weights, how many rich shopkeepers is fined for that there? And how many's never found out? And when one on 'em's fined, why he calculates how much he's into pocket, between what he's made by slanging, and what he's been fined, and on he goes again. *He* didn't know that there ever was short weight given in his shop: not *he*! No more do *we* at our stalls or barrows! Who 'dulterates the beer? Who makes old tea-leaves into new? Who grinds rice among pepper? And as for smuggling – but nobody thinks there's any harm in buying smuggled things. What *we* does is like that pencil you're writing with to a great tree, compared to what the rich people does. O, don't tell me, sir, a gentleman like you that sees so much of what's going on, must know *we're* better than the shopkeepers are.'

To remarks such as these I have nothing to answer. It would be idle to point out to such casuists, that the commission of one wrong can never justify another. The ignorant reverse the doctrine of right, and live, not by rule, but by example. I have unsparingly exposed the rogueries and trickeries of the street-people, and it is but fair that one of them should be heard in explanation, if not in justification. The trade ethics of the adult street-folk are also those of the juveniles, so on this subject I need dwell no longer.

What I have said of the religion of the women street-sellers applies with equal truth to the children. Their religious feelings are generally formed for them by their parents, especially their mothers. If the children have no such direction, then they have no religion. I did not question the street-seller before quoted on this subject of the want of the Christian spirit among his fraternity, old or young, or he would at once have asked me, in substance, to tell him in what class of society the real Christian spirit was to be found?

As to the opinions of the street-children I can say little. For the most part they have formed no opinions of anything beyond what affects their daily struggles for bread. Of politics such children can know nothing. If they are anything, they are Chartists in feeling, and are in general honest haters of the police and of most constituted authorities, whom they often confound with the police officer. As to their opinions of the claims of friendship, and of the duty of assisting one another, I believe these children feel and understand nothing about such matters. The hard struggles of their lives, and the little sympathy they meet with, make them selfish. There may be companionship among them, but no friendship, and this applies, I think, alike to boys and girls. The boy's opinion of the girl seems to be that she is made to help *him*, or to supply gratification to his passions.

There is yet a difficult inquiry, – as to the opinions which are formed by the young females reared to a street-life. I fear that those opinions are not, and cannot be powerfully swayed in favour of chastity, especially if the street-girl have the quickness to perceive that marriage is not much honoured among the most numerous body of street-folk. If she have not the quickness to understand this, then her ignorance is in itself most dangerous to her virtue. She may hear, too, expressions of an opinion that 'going to church to be wed' is only to put money into the clergyman's, or as these people say the 'parson's', pocket. Without the watchful care of the mother, the poor girl may form an illicit connection, with little or no knowledge that she is doing wrong; and perhaps a kind and indulgent mother may be herself but a concubine, feeling little respect for a ceremony she did not scruple to dispense with. To such opinions, however, the Irish furnish the exception.

The dwelling-places of the street-children are in the same localities as I specified regarding the women. Those who reside with their parents or employers sleep usually in the same room with them, and sometimes in the same bed. Nearly the whole of those, however, who support themselves by street-trade live, or rather sleep, in the lodging-houses. It is the same with those who live by street-vagrancy or begging, or by street-theft; and for this lazy or dishonest class of children the worst description of lodging-houses have the strongest attractions, as they meet continually with 'tramps' from the country, and keep up a constant current of scheming and excitement.

It seems somewhat curious that, considering the filth and noisomeness of some of these lodging-houses, the children who are inmates suffer only the average extent of sickness and mortality common to the districts crammed with the poor. Perhaps it may be accounted for by the circumstance of their being early risers, and their being in the open air all day, so that they are fatigued at the close of the day, and their sleep is deep and unbroken. I was assured by a well-educated man, who was compelled to resort to such places, that he has seen children sleep most profoundly in a lodging-house throughout a loud and long-continued disturbance. Many street-children who are either 'alone in the world', or afraid to return home after a bad day's sale, sleep in the markets or under the dry arches.

There are many other lads who, being unable to pay the 1*d.*, 2*d.*, or 3*d.* demanded, in pre-payment, by the lodging-house keepers, pass the night in the streets, wherever shelter may be attainable. The number of outcast boys and girls who sleep in and about the purlieus of Covent Garden-market each night, especially during the summer months, has been computed variously, and no doubt differs according to circumstances; but those with whom I have spoken upon the subject, and who of all others are most likely to know, consider the average to be upwards of 200.

The diet of the street-children is in some cases an alternation of surfeit and inanition, more especially that of the stripling who is 'on his own hook'. If money be unexpectedly attained, a boy will gorge himself with such dainties as he loves; if he earn no money, he will fast all day patiently enough, perhaps drinking profusely of water. A cake-seller told me that a little while before I saw him a lad of twelve or so had consumed a shilling's worth of cakes and pastry, as he had got a shilling by 'fiddling'; not, be it understood, by the exercise of any musical skill, for 'fiddling', among the initiated, means the holding of horses, or the performing of any odd jobs.

Of these cakes and pastry – the cakes being from two to twelve a penny, and the pastry, tarts, and 'Coventrys' (three-cornered tarts) two a penny – the street-urchins are very fond. To me they seemed to possess no recommendation either to the nose or the palate. The 'strong' flavour of these preparations is in all probability as grateful to the palate of an itinerant youth, as is the high *gout* of the grouse or the woodcock to the fashionable epicure. In this respect, as in others which I have pointed out, the 'extremes' of society 'meet'.

These remarks apply far more to the male than to the female children. Some of the street-boys will walk a considerable distance, when they are in funds, to buy pastry of the Jew-boys in the Minories, Houndsditch, and Whitechapel; those keen traders being reputed, and no doubt with truth, to supply the best cakes and pastry of any.

A more staple article of diet, which yet partakes of the character of a dainty, is in great demand by the class I treat of – pudding. A halfpenny or a penny-worth of baked plum, boiled plum (or plum dough), currant or plum batter (batter-pudding studded with raisins), is often a dinner. This pudding is almost always bought in the shops; indeed, in a street apparatus there could hardly be the necessary heat diffused over the surface required; and as I have told of a distance being travelled to buy pastry of the Jew-boys, so is it traversed to buy pudding at the best shops. The proprietor of one of those shops, upon whom I called to make inquiries, told me that he sold about 300 pennyworths of pudding in a day. Two-thirds of this quantity he sold to juveniles under fifteen years of age; but he hadn't noticed particularly, and so could only guess. This man, when he understood the object of my inquiry, insisted upon my tasting his 'batter', which really was very good, and tasted – I do not know how otherwise to describe it – honest. His profits were not large, he said, and judging from the size and quality of his oblong halfpenny and penny-worth's of batter pudding, I have no doubt he stated the fact. 'There's many a poor man and woman,' he said, 'aye, sir, and some that you would think from their appearance might go to an eating-house to dine, make a meal off my pudding, as well as the street little ones. The boys are often tiresome: "Master," they'll say, "can't you give us a plummier bit than this?" or, "Is it just up? I likes it 'ot, all 'ot."'

The 'baked tatur', from the street-dealer's can more frequently than from the shops, is another enjoyable portion of the street child's diet. Of the sale to the juvenile population of pickled whelks, stewed eels, oysters, boiled meat puddings, and other articles of street traffic, I have spoken under their respective heads.

The Irish children who live with their parents fare as the parents fare. If very poor, or if bent upon saving for some purpose, their diet is tea and bread and butter, or bread without butter. If not so *very* poor, still tea, &c., but sometimes with a little fish, and sometimes with a piece of meat on Sundays; but the Sunday's meat is more common among the poor English than the poor Irish street-traders; indeed the English street-sellers generally 'live better' than the Irish. The coster-boys often fare well and abundantly.

The children living in the lodging-houses, I am informed, generally, partake only of such meals as they can procure abroad. Sometimes of a night they may partake of the cheap beef or mutton, purveyed by some inmate who has been 'lifting flesh' (stealing meat) or 'sawney' (bacon). Vegetables, excepting the baked potato, they rarely taste. Of animal food, perhaps, they partake more of bacon, and relish it the most.

Drinking is not, from what I can learn, common among the street boys. The thieves are generally sober fellows, and of the others, when they are 'in luck', a half-pint of beer, to relish the bread and saveloy of the dinner, and a pennyworth of gin 'to keep the cold out', are often the extent of the potations. The exceptions are among the ignorant coster-lads, who when they have been prosperous in their 'bunse', drink, and ape the vices of men. The girls, I am told, are generally fonder of gin than the boys. Elderwine and gingerbeer are less popular among children than they used to be. Many of the lads smoke.

The amusements of the street-children are such as I have described in my account of the costermongers, but in a moderate degree, as those who partake with the greatest zest of such amusements as the Penny Gaff (penny theatre) and the Twopenny Hop (dance) are more advanced in years. Many of the Penny Gaffs, however, since I last wrote on the subject, have been suppressed, and the Twopenny Hops are not half so frequent as they were five or six years back. The Jew-boys of the streets play at draughts or dominoes in coffee-shops which they frequent; in one in the London-road at which I had occasion to call were eight of these urchins thus occupied; and they play for money or its equivalent, but these sedentary games obtain little among the other and more restless street-lads. I believe that not one-half of them 'know the cards', but they are fond of gambling at pitch and toss, for halfpennies or farthings.

The clothing of the street-children, however it may vary in texture, fashion, and colour, has one pervading characteristic – it is never made for the wearers. The exceptions to this rule seem to be those, when a child has run away and retains, through good fortune or natural acuteness, the superior attire he wore before he made the choice – if choice he had – of a street life; and where the pride of a mother whose costermonger husband is 'getting on', clothes little Jack or Bill in a new Sunday suit. Even then the suit is more likely to be bought ready-made than 'made to measure', nor is it worn in business hours until the gloss of novelty has departed.

The boys and girls wear every variety of clothing; it is often begged, but if bought is bought from the fusty stocks of old clothes in Petticoat and Rosemary-lanes. These rags are worn by the children as long as they will hold, or can be tied or pinned together, and when they drop off from continued wear, from dirt, and from the ravages of vermin, the child sets his wits to work to procure more. One mode of obtaining a fresh supply is far less available than it was three or four years back. This was for the lads to denude themselves of their rags, and tearing them up in the casual-ward of a workhouse, as it were compel the parish-officers to provide them with fresh apparel.

This mode may be successful in parts of the country still, but it is not so, or to a very limited extent, in town. The largest, and what was accounted by the vagrants the most liberal, of all the casual wards of the metropolitan workhouses, that of Marylebone, has been closed above two years. So numerous were the applicants for admission, and so popular among the vagrants was Marylebone workhouse, that a fever resulted, and attacked that large establishment. It was not uncommon for the Irish who trudged up from Liverpool, to be advised by some London vagrant whom they met, to go at once, when they reached the capital, to Marylebone workhouse, and that the Irishman might not forget a name that was new to him, his friendly adviser would write it down for him, and a troop of poor wretched Irish children, with parents as wretched, would go to Marylebone workhouse, and in their ignorance or simplicity, present the address which had been given to them, as if it were a regular order for admission! Boys have sometimes committed offences that they might get into prison, and as they contrived that their apparel should be unfit for purposes of decency, or perhaps their rags had become unfit to wear, they could not be sent naked into the streets again, and so had clothing given to them. A shirt will be worn by one of those wretched urchins, without washing, until it falls asunder, and many have no shirts. The girls are on the whole less ragged than the boys, the most disgusting parts of their persons or apparel – I speak here more of the vagrant or the mixed vagrant trading and selling girl (often a child prostitute) than of the regular street-seller – the worst particular of these girls' appearance, I repeat, is in their foul and matted hair, which looks as if it would defy sponge, comb, and brush to purify it, and in the broken and filthy boots and stockings, which they seem never to button or to garter.

The propensities of the street-children are the last division of my inquiry, and an ample field is presented, alike for wonder, disgust, pity, hope, and regret.

Perhaps the most remarkable characteristic of these wretched children is their extraordinary licentiousness. Nothing can well exceed the extreme animal fondness for the opposite sex which prevails amongst them; some rather singular circumstances connected with this subject have come to my knowledge, and from these facts it would appear that the age of puberty, or something closely resembling it, may be attained at a much less numerical amount of years than that at which most writers upon the human species have hitherto fixed it. Probably such circumstances as the promiscuous sleeping together of both sexes, the example of the older persons indulging in the grossest immorality in the presence of the young, and the use of obscene expressions, may tend to produce or force an unnatural precocity, a precocity sure to undermine health and shorten life. Jealousy is another characteristic of these children and perhaps less among the girls than the boys. Upon the most trivial offence in this respect, or on the suspicion of an offence, the 'gals' are sure to be beaten cruelly and savagely by their 'chaps'. This appears to be a very common case.

The details of filthiness and of all uncleanness which I gave in a recent number as things of course in certain lodging-houses, render it unnecessary to dwell longer upon the subject, and it is one from which I willingly turn to other matters.

In addition to the licentious, the vagabond propensities of this class are very striking. As soon as the warm weather commences, boys and girls, but more especially boys, leave the town in shoals, traversing the country in every direction; some furnished with trifling articles (such as I have already enumerated) to sell, and others to begging, lurking, or thieving. It is not the street-sellers who so much resort to the tramp, as those who are devoid of the commonest notions of honesty; a quality these young vagrants sometimes respect when in fear of a gaol, and the hard work with which such a place is identified in their minds – and to which, with the peculiar idiosyncrasy of a roving race, they have an insuperable objection.

I have met with boys and girls, however, to whom a gaol had no terrors, and to whom, when in prison, there was only one dread, and that a common one among the ignorant, whether with or without any sense of religion – superstition. 'I lay in prison of a night, sir,' said a boy who was generally among the briskest of his class, 'and think I shall see things.' The 'things' represent the vague fears which many, not naturally stupid, but untaught or ill-taught persons, entertain in the dark. A girl, a perfect termagant in the breaking of windows and such like offences, told me something of the same kind. She spoke well of the treatment she experienced in prison, and seemed to have a liking for the matron and officials; her conduct there was quiet and respectful. I believe she was not addicted to drink.

Many of the girls, as well as the boys, of course trade as they 'tramp'. They often sell, both in the country and in town, little necklaces, composed of red berries strung together upon thick thread, for dolls and children: but although I have asked several of them, I have never yet found one who collected the berries and made the necklaces themselves; neither have I met with a single instance in which the girl vendors knew the name of the berries thus used, nor indeed even that they *were* berries. The invariable reply to my questions upon this point has been that they 'are called necklaces'; that 'they are just as they sells 'em to us'; that they 'don't know whether they are made or whether they grow'; and in most cases, that they 'gets them in London, by Shoreditch'; although in one case a little brown-complexioned girl, with bright sparkling eyes, said that 'she got them from the gipsies'. At first I fancied, from this child's appearance, that she was rather superior in intellect to most of her class; but I soon found that she was not a whit above the others, unless, indeed, it were in the possession of the quality of cunning.

Some of the boys, on their country excursions, trade in dominoes. They carry a variety of boxes, each differing in size and varying accordingly in price: the lowest-priced boxes are mostly 6d. each (sometimes 4d., or even 3d.), the highest 1s. An informant told me that these boxes are charged to him at the rate of 20 to 25 per cent. less; but if, as is commonly the case, he could take a number at a time, he would have them at a smaller price still. They are very rudely made, and soon fall to pieces, unless handled with extreme care. Most of the boys who vend this article play at the game themselves, and some with skill; but in every case, I believe, there is a willingness to cheat, or take advantage, which is hardly disguised; one boy told me candidly that those who make the most money are considered to be the cleverest, whether by selling or cheating, or both, at the game; nor can it be said that this estimation of cleverness is peculiar to these children.

At this season of the year great numbers of the street-children attend the races in different parts of the country, more especially at those in the vicinity of a large town. The race-course of Wolverhampton, for instance, is usually thronged with them during the period of the sport. While taking these perigrinations they sometimes sleep in the low lodging-houses with which most of our provincial towns abound: frequently 'skipper it' in the open air, when the weather is fine and warm, and occasionally in barns or outhouses attached to farms and cottages. Sometimes they travel in couples – a boy and a girl, or two boys or two girls; but the latter is not so common a case as either of the former. It is rare that more than two may be met in company with each other, except, indeed, of a night, and then they usually herd together in numbers. The boys who carry dominoes sometimes, also, have a sheet of paper for sale, on which is rudely printed a representation of a draught-board and men – the latter of which are of two colours (black and white) and may be cut out with a pair of scissors; thus forming a ready means of playing a game so popular in rustic places. These sheets of paper are sold (if no more can be got for them) at a penny each. The boy who showed them to me said he gave a halfpenny a piece for them, or 6d. for fifteen. He said he always bought them in London, and that he did not know any other place to get them at, nor had 'ever heard any talk of their being bought nowhere else'.

The extraordinary lasciviousness of this class which I have already mentioned, appears to continue to mark their character during their vagabondizing career in the country as fully as in town; indeed, an informant, upon whom I think I may rely, says, that the nightly scenes of youthful or even childish profligacy in the low lodging-houses of the small provincial towns quite equal – even if they do not exceed – those which may be witnessed in the metropolis itself. Towards the approach of winter these children (like the vagrants of an older growth) advance towards London; some remain in the larger towns, such as Liverpool, Manchester, Birmingham, Sheffield, &c., but the greater proportion appear to return to the metropolis, where they resume the life they had previously led, anything but improved in education, morals, manners, or social position generally, by their summer's excursion.

The language spoken by this rambling class is peculiar in its construction: it consists of an odd medley of cockneyfied English, rude provincialisms, and a large proportion of the slang commonly used by gipsies and other 'travellers', in conveying their ideas to those whom they wish to purchase their commodities.

Among the propensities of the street-boys I do not think that pugnacity, or a fondness, or even a great readiness, for fighting, is a predominant element. Gambling and thieving may be rife among a class of these poor wretches; and it may not unfrequently happen that force is resorted to by one boy bigger than another to obtain the halfpence of which the smaller child is known to be possessed. Thus quarrels among them are very frequent, but they rarely lead to fighting. Even in the full swing and fury of their jealousy, it does not appear that these boys attack the object of their suspicions, but prefer the less hazardous course of chastising the delinquent or unjustly suspected girl. The girls in the low lodging-houses, I was told a little time since, by a woman who used to frequent them, sometimes, not often, scratched one another until the two had bloody faces; and they tried to bite one another now and then, but they seldom fought. What was this poor woman's notion of a fight between two girls, it may not be very easy to comprehend.

The number of children out daily in the streets of London, employed in the various occupations I have named, together with others which may possibly have been overlooked – including those who beg without offering any article for sale – those who will work as light porters, as errand boys and the like, for chance passengers, has been variously calculated;

probably nothing like exactitude can be hoped for, much less expected, in such a speculation, for when a government census has been so frequently found to fail in correctness of detail, it appears highly improbable that the number of those so uncertain in their places of resort and so migratory in their habits, can be ascertained with anything like a definite amount of certainty by a private individual. Taking the returns of accommodation afforded to these children in the casual wards of workhouses, refuges for the destitute and homeless poor; of the mendicity and other societies of a similar description, and those of our hospitals and gaols, – and these sources of information upon this subject can alone be confidently relied upon, – and then taking into the calculation the additional numbers, who pass the night in the variety of ways I have already enumerated, I think it will be found that the number of boys and girls selling in the streets of this city, and often dependent upon their own exertions for the commonest necessaries of life, may be estimated at some thousands, but nearer 10,000 than 20,000.

The consideration which I have devoted to this branch of my subject has been considerable, but still not, in my own opinion, commensurate to the importance of its nature. Steps ought most unquestionably to be taken to palliate the evils and miseries I have pointed out, even if a positive remedy be indeed impossible.

Each year sees an increase of the numbers of street-children to a very considerable extent, and the exact nature of their position may be thus briefly depicted: what little *information* they receive is obtained from the worst class – from cheats, vagabonds, and rogues; what little *amusement* they indulge in, springs from sources the most poisonous – the most fatal to happiness and welfare; what little they know of a *home* is necessarily associated with much that is vile and base; their very means of existence, uncertain and precarious as it is, is to a great extent identified with petty chicanery, which is quickly communicated by one to the other; while their physical sufferings from cold, hunger, exposure to the weather, and other causes of a similar nature, are constant, and at times extremely severe. Thus every means by which a proper intelligence may be conveyed to their minds is either closed or at the least tainted, while every duct by which a bad description of knowledge may be infused is sedulously cultivated and enlarged. Parental instruction; the comforts of a home, however humble – the great moral truths upon which society itself rests; – the influence of proper example; the power of education; the effect of useful amusement; are all denied to them, or come to them so greatly vitiated, that they rather tend to increase, than to repress, the very evils they were intended to remedy.

The costers invariably say that no persons under the age of fifteen should be allowed by law to vend articles in the streets; the reason they give for this is – that the children under that period of life having fewer wants and requiring less money to live than those who are older, will sell at a less profit than it is fair to expect the articles sold should yield, and thus they tersely conclude, 'they pervents others living, and ruins theirselves'.

There probably is truth in this remark, and I must confess that, for the sake of the children themselves, I should have no objection to see the suggestion acted upon; and yet there immediately rises the plain yet startling question – in such a case, what is to become of the children?

I now cite the histories of street-lads belonging to the several classes above specified, as illustrations of the truth of the statements advanced concerning the children street-sellers generally.

Of Children Sent Out as Street-sellers by Their Parents

[pp. 537–8] Of the boys and girls who are sent out to sell in the streets by parents who are themselves street-traders, I need say but little under this head. I have spoken of them, and given some of their statements in other divisions of this work (see the accounts of the coster boys and girls). When, as is the case with many of the costermongers, and with the Irish fruit-sellers, the parents and children follow the same calling, they form one household, and work, as it were, 'into one another's hands'. The father can buy a larger, and consequently a cheaper quantity, when he can avail himself of a subdivision of labour as inexpensive as that of his own family – whom he must maintain whether employed or unemployed – in order to vend such extra quantity. I have already noticed that in some families (as is common with rude tribes) costermongering seems an hereditary pursuit, and the frequent and constant employment of children in street traffic is one reason why this hereditary pursuit is perpetuated, for street commerce is thus at a very early age made part and parcel of the young coster's existence, and he very probably acquires a distaste for any other occupation, which may entail more of *restraint* and *irksomeness*. It is very rarely that a costermonger apprentices his son to any handicraft business, although a daughter may sometimes be placed in domestic service. The child is usually 'sent out to sell'.

There is another class of children who are 'sent out' as are the children of the costers, and sometimes with the same cheap and readily attained articles – oranges and lemons, nuts, chestnuts, onions, salt (or fresh) herrings, winks, or shrimps, and, more rarely, with water-cresses or cut-flowers. Sometimes the young vendors offer small wares – leather boot-laces, coat-studs, steel pens, or such like. These are often the children, not of street sales-people, but of persons in a measure connected with a street life, or some open-air pursuit; the children of cabmen deprived of their licences, or of the hangers-on of cabmen; of the 'supers' (supernumeraries) of the theatres who have irregular or no employment, or, as they would call it, 'engagement', with the unhappy consequence of irregular or no 'salary': the children, again, of street performers, or Ethiopians, or street-musicians, are 'sent out to sell', as well as those of the poorer class of labourers connected with the river – ballast-heavers, lumpers, &c.; of (Irish) bricklayers' labourers and paviours' assistants; of market-porters and dock-labourers; of coal-heavers out of work, and of the helpers at coal-wharfs, and at the other wharfs; of the Billingsgate 'roughs'; and of the many classes of the labouring, rather than the artisan poor, whose earnings are uncertain, or insufficient, or have failed them altogether.

With such classes as these (and more especially with the Irish), as soon as Pat or Biddy is big enough to carry a basket, and is of sufficiently ripened intellect to understand the relative value of coins, from a farthing to a shilling, he or she *must* do something 'to help', and that something is generally to sell in the streets. One poor woman who made a scanty living in working on corn sacks and bags – her infirmities sometimes preventing her working at all – sent out three children, together or separately, to sell lucifer-matches or small wares. '*They like it,*' she said, '*and always want to be off into the streets*; and when my husband (a labourer) was ill in the hospital, the few pence they brought in was very useful; but now he's well and at work again and we want to send the eldest – she's nine – to school; *but they all* will *go out to sell if they can get hold of any stock.* I would never have sent them at all if I could have helped it, but if they made 6d. a day among the three of them, perhaps it saved their lives when things were at the worst.' If a poor woman, as in this instance, has not been used to street-selling herself, there is always some neighbour to advise her what to purchase for her children's hawking, and instruct her where.

From one little girl I had the following account. She was then selling boot-laces and offered them most perseveringly. She was turned nine, she said, and had sold things in the streets for two years past, but not regularly. The father got his living in the streets by 'playing', she seemed reluctant to talk about his avocation, but I found that he was sometimes a street-musician, or street-performer, and sometimes sung or recited in public houses, and having 'seen better days', had it appears communicated some feeling of dislike for his present pursuits to his daughter, so that I discontinued any allusion to the subject. The mother earned 2s. or 2s. 6d. weekly, in shoe-binding, when she had employment, which was three weeks out of four, and a son of thirteen earned what was sufficient to maintain him as an (occasional) assistant in a wholesale pottery, or rather pot-shop.

'It's in the winter, sir, when things are far worst with us. Father can make very little then – but I don't know what he earns exactly at any time – and though mother has more work then, there's fire and candle to pay for. We were very badly off last winter, and worse, I think, the winter before. Father sometimes came home and had made nothing, and if mother had no work in hand we went to bed to save fire and candle, if it was ever so soon. Father would die afore he would let mother take as much as a loaf from the parish. I was sent out to sell nuts first: "If it's only 1d. you make," mother said, "it's a good piece of bread." I didn't mind being sent out. I knew children that sold things in the streets. Perhaps I liked it better than staying at home without a fire and with nothing to do, and if I went out I saw other children busy. No, I wasn't a bit frightened when I first started, not a bit. Some children – but they was such little things – said: "O, Liz, I wish I was you." I had twelve ha'porths and sold them all. I don't know what it made; 2d. most likely. I didn't crack a single nut myself. I was fond of them then, but I don't care for them now. I could do better if I went into public-houses, but I'm only let go to Mr Smith's, because he knows father, and Mrs Smith and him recommends me and wouldn't let anybody mislest me. Nobody ever offered to. I hear people swear there sometimes, but it's not at me. I sell nuts to children in the streets, and laces to young women. I have sold nuts and oranges to soldiers. They never say anything rude to me, never. I was once in a great crowd, and was getting crushed, and there was a very tall soldier close by me, and he lifted me, basket and all, right up to his shoulder, and carried me clean out of the crowd. He had stripes on his arm. "I shouldn't like you to be in such a trade," says he, "if you was my child." He didn't say why he wouldn't like it. Perhaps because it was beginning to rain. Yes, we are far better off now. Father makes money. I don't go out in bad weather in the summer; in the winter, though, I must. I don't know what I make. I don't know what I shall be when I grow up. I can read a little. I've been to church five or six times in my life. I should go oftener and so would mother, if we had clothes.'

I have no reason to suppose that, in this case, the father was an intemperate man, though some of the parents who thus send their children out *are* intemperate, and, loving to indulge in the idleness to which intemperance inclines them, are forced to live on the labour of their wives and children.

VOLUME TWO

OF THE STREET-JEWS

OF THE TRADES AND LOCALITIES
OF THE STREET-JEWS

[pp. 129–33] The trades which the Jews most affect, I was told by one of themselves, are those in which, as they describe it, 'there's a chance'; that is, they prefer a trade in such commodity as is not subjected to a fixed price, so that there may be abundant scope for speculation, and something like a gambler's chance for profit or loss. In this way, Sir Walter Scott has said, trade has 'all the fascination of gambling, without the moral guilt'; but the absence of moral guilt in connection with such trading is certainly dubious.

The wholesale trades in foreign commodities which are now principally or solely in the hands of the Jews, often as importers and exporters, are, watches and jewels, sponges – fruits, especially green fruits, such as oranges, lemons, grapes, walnuts, cocoa-nuts, &c., and dates among dried fruits – shells, tortoises, parrots and foreign birds, curiosities, ostrich feathers, snuffs, cigars, and pipes; but cigars far more extensively at one time.

The localities in which these wholesale and retail traders reside are mostly at the East-end – indeed the Jews of London, as a congregated body, have been, from the times when their numbers were sufficient to institute a 'settlement' or 'colony', peculiar to themselves, always resident in the eastern quarter of the metropolis.

Of course a wealthy Jew millionaire – merchant, stock-jobber, or stock-broker – resides where he pleases – in a villa near the Marquis of Hertford's in the Regent's-park, a mansion near the Duke of Wellington's in Piccadilly, a house and grounds at Clapham or Stamford-hill; but these are exceptions. The quarters of the Jews are not difficult to describe. The trading-class in the capacity of shopkeepers, warehousemen, or manufacturers, are the thickest in Houndsditch, Aldgate, and the Minories, more especially as regards the 'swag-shops' and the manufacture and sale of wearing apparel. The wholesale dealers in fruit are in Duke's-place and Pudding-lane (Thames-street), but the superior retail Jew fruiterers – some of whose shops are remarkable for the beauty of their fruit – are in Cheapside, Oxford-street, Piccadilly, and most of all in Covent-garden market. The inferior jewellers (some of whom deal with the first shops) are also at the East-end, about Whitechapel, Bevis-marks, and Houndsditch; the wealthier goldsmiths and watchmakers having, like other tradesmen of the class, their shops in the superior thoroughfares. The great congregation of working watchmakers is in Clerkenwell, but in that locality there are only a few Jews. The Hebrew dealers in second-hand garments, and second-hand wares generally, are located about Petticoat-lane, the peculiarities of which place I have lately described. The manufacturers of such things as cigars, pencils, and sealing-wax; the wholesale importers of sponge, bristles and toys, the dealers in quills and in 'looking-glasses', reside in large private-looking houses, when display is not needed for purposes of business, in such parts as Maunsell-street, Great Prescott-street, Great Ailie-street, Leman-street, and other parts of the eastern quarter known as Goodman's-fields. The wholesale dealers in foreign birds and shells, and in the many foreign things known as 'curiosities', reside in East Smithfield, Ratcliffe-highway, High-street (Shadwell), or in some of the parts adjacent to the Thames. In the long range of river-side streets, stretching from the Tower to Poplar and Blackwall, are Jews, who fulfil the many capacities of slop-sellers, &c., called into exercise by the requirements of seafaring people on their return from or commencement of a voyage. A few Jews keep boarding-houses for sailors in Shadwell and Wapping. Of the localities and abodes of the poorest of the Jews I shall speak hereafter.

Concerning the street-trades pursued by the Jews, I believe there is not at present a single one of which they can be said to have a monopoly; nor in any one branch of the street-traffic are there so many of the Jew traders as there were a few years back.

This remarkable change is thus to be accounted for. Strange as the fact may appear, the Jew has been undersold in the streets, and he has been beaten on what might be called his own ground – the buying of old clothes. The Jew boys, and the feebler and elder Jews, had, until some twelve or fifteen years back, almost the monopoly of orange and lemon street-selling, or street-hawking. The costermonger class had possession of the theatre doors and the approaches to the theatres; they had, too, occasionally their barrows full of oranges; but the Jews were the daily, assiduous, and itinerant street-sellers of this most popular of foreign, and perhaps of all, fruits. In their hopes of sale they followed any one a mile if encouraged, even by a few approving glances. The great theatre of this traffic was in the stage-coach yards in such inns as the Bull and Mouth, (St Martin's-le-Grand), the Belle Sauvage (Ludgate-hill), the Saracen's Head (Snow-hill), the Bull (Aldgate), the Swan-with-two-Necks (Lad-lane,

City), the George and Blue Boar (Holborn), the White Horse (Fetter-lane), and other such places. They were seen too, 'with all their eyes about them', as one informant expressed it, outside the inns where the coaches stopped to take up passengers – at the White Horse Cellar in Piccadilly, for instance, and the Angel and the (now defunct) Peacock in Islington. A commercial traveller told me that he could never leave town by any 'mail' or 'stage', without being besieged by a small army of Jew boys, who most pertinaciously offered him oranges, lemons, sponges, combs, pocket-books, pencils, sealing-wax, paper, many-bladed pen-knives, razors, pocket-mirrors, and shaving-boxes – as if a man could not possibly quit the metropolis without requiring a stock of such commodities. In the whole of these trades, unless in some degree in sponges and blacklead-pencils, the Jew is now out-numbered or displaced.

I have before alluded to the underselling of the Jew boy by the Irish boy in the street-orange trade; but the characteristics of the change are so peculiar, that a further notice is necessary. It is curious to observe that the most assiduous, and hitherto the most successful of street-traders, were supplanted, not by a more persevering or more skilful body of street-sellers, but simply by a more *starving* body.

Some few years since poor Irish people, and chiefly those connected with the culture of the land, 'came over' to this country in great numbers, actuated either by vague hopes of 'bettering themselves' by emigration, or working on the railways, or else influenced by the restlessness common to an impoverished people. These men, when unable to obtain employ-ment, without scruple became street-sellers. Not only did the adults resort to street-traffic, generally in its simplest forms, such as hawking fruit, but the children, by whom they were accompanied from Ireland, in great numbers, were put into the trade; and if two or three children earned 2d. a day each, and their parents 5d. or 6d. each, or even 4d., the subsistence of the family was better than they could obtain in the midst of the miseries of the southern and western part of the Sister Isle. An Irish boy of fourteen, having to support himself by street-trade, as was often the case, owing to the death of parents and to divers casualties, would undersell the Jew boys similarly circumstanced.

The Irish boy could live *harder* than the Jew – often in his own country he subsisted on a stolen turnip a day; he could lodge harder – lodge for 1d. a night in any noisome den, or sleep in the open air, which is seldom done by the Jew boy; he could dispense with the use of shoes and stockings – a dispensation at which his rival in trade revolted; he drank only water, or if he took tea or coffee, it was as a meal, and not merely as a beverage;

to crown the whole, the city-bred Jew boy required some evening recreation, the penny or twopenny concert, or a game at draughts or
dominoes; but this the Irish boy, country bred, never thought of, for *his*
sole luxury was a deep sleep, and, being regardless or ignorant of all such
recreations, he worked longer hours, and so sold more oranges, than his
Hebrew competitor. Thus, as the Munster or Connaught lad could live on
less than the young denizen of Petticoat-lane, he could sell at smaller
profit, and did so sell, until gradually the Hebrew youths were displaced
by the Irish in the street orange trade.

It is the same, or the same in a degree, with other street-trades, which
were at one time all but monopolised by the Jew adults. Among these were
the street-sale of spectacles and sponges. The prevalence of slop-work and
slop-wages, and the frequent difficulty of obtaining properly remunerated
employment – the pinch of want, in short – have driven many mechanics
to street-traffic; so that the numbers of street-traffickers have been
augmented, while no small portion of the new comers have adopted the
more knowing street avocations, formerly pursued only by the Jews.

Of the other class of street-traders who have interfered largely with the
old-clothes trade, which, at one time, people seemed to consider a sort of
birthright among the Jews, I have already spoken, when treating of the
dealings of the crockmen in bartering glass and crockery-ware for second-
hand apparel. These traders now obtain as many old clothes as the Jew
clothes men themselves; for, with a great number of 'ladies', the offer of
an ornament of glass or spar, or of a beautiful and fragrant plant, is more
attractive than the offer of a small sum of money, for the purchase of the
left-off garments of the family.

The crockmen are usually strong and in the prime of youth or manhood,
and are capable of carrying heavy burdens of glass or china-wares, for
which the Jews are either incompetent or disinclined.

Some of the Jews which have been thus displaced from the street-traffic
have emigrated to America, with the assistance of their brethren.

The principal street-trades of the Jews are now in sponges, spectacles,
combs, pencils, accordions, cakes, sweetmeats, drugs, and fruits of all
kinds; but, in all these trades, unless perhaps in drugs, they are in a
minority compared with the 'Christian' street-sellers.

There is not among the Jew street-sellers generally anything of the
concubinage or cohabitation common among the costermongers.
Marriage is the rule.

Of the Jew Old-clothes Men

[pp. 133–5] Fifty years ago the appearance of the street-Jews, engaged in the purchase of second-hand clothes, was different to what it is at the present time. The Jew then had far more of the distinctive garb and aspect of a foreigner. He not unfrequently wore the gabardine, which is never seen now in the streets, but some of the long loose frock coats worn by the Jew clothes' buyers resemble it. At that period, too, the Jew's long beard was far more distinctive than it is in this hirsute generation.

In other respects the street-Jew is unchanged. Now, as during the last century, he traverses every street, square, and road, with the monotonous cry, sometimes like a bleat, of 'Clo'! Clo'!' On this head, however, I have previously remarked, when describing the street Jew of a hundred years ago.

In an inquiry into the condition of the old-clothes dealers a year and a half ago, a Jew gave me the following account. He told me, at the commencement of his statement, that he was of opinion that his people were far more speculative than the Gentiles, and therefore the English liked better to deal with them. 'Our people,' he said, 'will be out all day in the wet, and begrudge themselves a bit of anything to eat till they go home, and then, may be, they'll gamble away their crown, just for the love of speculation.' My informant, who could write or speak several languages, and had been 50 years in the business, then said, 'I am no bigot; indeed I do not care where I buy my meat, so long as I can get it. I often go into the Minories and buy some, without looking to how it has been killed, or whether it has a seal on it or not.'

He then gave me some account of the Jewish children, and the number of men in the trade, which I have embodied under the proper heads. The itinerant Jew clothes man, he told me, was generally the son of a former old-clothes man, but some were cigar-makers, or pencil-makers, taking to the clothes business when those trades were slack; but that nineteen out of twenty had been born to it. If the parents of the Jew boy are poor, and the boy a sharp lad, he generally commences business at ten years of age, by selling lemons, or some trifle in the streets, and so, as he expressed it, the boy 'gets a round', or street-connection, by becoming known to the neighbourhoods he visits. If he sees a servant, he will, when selling his lemons, ask if she have any old shoes or old clothes, and offer to be a purchaser. If the clothes should come to more than the Jew boy has in his pocket, he leaves what silver he has as 'an earnest upon them', and then seeks some regular Jew clothes man, who will advance the purchase money. This the old Jew agrees to do upon the understanding that he is to have 'half Rybeck', that is, a moiety of the profit, and then he will accompany the boy to the house, to pass his judgment on the goods, and satisfy himself that the stripling has not made a blind bargain, an error into which he very rarely falls. After this he goes with the lad to Petticoat-lane, and there they share whatever money the clothes may bring over and above what has been paid for them. By such means the Jew boy gets his knowledge of the old-clothes business; and so quick are these lads generally, that in the course of two months they will acquire sufficient experience in connection with the trade to begin dealing on their own account. There are some, he told me, as sharp at 15 as men of 50.

'It is very seldom,' my informant stated, 'very seldom indeed, that a Jew clothes man takes away any of the property of the house he may be called into. I expect there's a good many of 'em,' he continued, for he sometimes spoke of his co-traders, as if they were not of his own class, 'is fond of cheating – that is, they won't mind giving only 2s. for a thing that's worth 5s. They are fond of money, and will do almost anything to get it. Jews are perhaps the most money-loving people in all England. There are certainly some old-clothes men who will buy articles at such a price that they must know them to have been stolen. Their rule, however, is to ask no questions, and to get as cheap an article as possible. A Jew clothes man is seldom or never seen in liquor. They gamble for money, either at their own homes or at public-houses. The favourite games are tossing, dominoes, and cards. I was informed, by one of the people, that he had seen as much as 30l. in silver and gold lying upon the ground when two parties had been playing at throwing three halfpence in the air. On a Saturday, some gamble away the morning and the greater part of the afternoon.' [Saturday, I need hardly say, is the Hebrew Sabbath.] 'They meet in some secret back place, about ten, and begin playing for "one a time" – that is, tossing up three halfpence, and staking 1s. on the result. Other Jews, and a few Christians, will gather round and bet. Sometimes the bets laid by the Jew bystanders are as high as 2l. each; and on more than one occasion the old-clothes men have wagered as much as 50l., but only after great gains at gambling. Some, if they *can*, will cheat, by means of a halfpenny with a head or a tail on both sides, called a "gray". The play lasts till the Sabbath is nearly over, and then they go to business or the theatre. They seldom or never say a word while they are losing, but merely stamp on the ground; it is dangerous, though, to interfere when luck runs against them. The rule is, when a man is losing to let him alone. I have known them play for three hours together and nothing be said all

THE JEW OLD-CLOTHES-MAN.

"Clo', Clo', Clo'."

that time but "head" or "tail". They seldom go to synagogue, and on a Sunday evening have card parties at their own houses. They seldom eat anything on their rounds. The reason is, not because they object to eat meat killed by a Christian, but because they are afraid of losing a "deal", or the chance of buying a lot of old clothes by delay. They are generally too lazy to light their own fires before they start of a morning, and nineteen out of twenty obtain their breakfasts at the coffee-shops about Houndsditch.

'When they return from their day's work they have mostly some stew ready, prepared by their parents or wife. If they are not family men they go to an eating-house. This is sometimes a Jewish house, but if no one is looking they creep into a Christian "cook-shop", not being particular about eating "tryfer" – that is, meat which has been killed by a Christian. Those that are single generally go to a neighbour and agree with him to be boarded on the Sabbath; and for this the charge is generally about 2s. 6d. On a Saturday there's cold fish for breakfast and supper; indeed, a Jew would pawn the shirt off his back sooner than go without fish then; and in holiday-time he will have it, if he has to get it out of the stones. It is not reckoned a holiday unless there's fish.'

'Forty years ago I have made as much as 5l. in a week by the purchase of old clothes in the streets,' said a Jew informant. 'Upon an average then, I could earn weekly about 2l. But now things are different. People are more wide awake. Every one knows the value of an old coat now-a-days. The women know more than the men. The general average, I think, take the good weeks with the bad throughout the year, is about 1l. a week; some weeks we get 2l., and some scarcely nothing.'

I was told by a Jewish professional gentleman that the account of the spirit of gambling prevalent among his people was correct, but the amounts said to be staked, he thought, rare or exaggerated.

The Jew old-clothes men are generally far more cleanly in their habits than the poorer classes of English people. Their hands they always wash before their meals, and this is done whether the party be a strict Jew or 'Meshumet', a convert, or apostate from Judaism. Neither will the Israelite ever use the same knife to cut his meat that he previously used to spread his butter, and he will not even put his meat on a plate that has had butter on it; nor will he use for his soup the spoon that has had melted butter in it. This objection to mix butter with meat is carried so far, that, after partaking of the one, Jews will not eat of the other for the space of two hours. The Jews are generally, when married, most exemplary family men. There are few fonder fathers than they are, and they will starve themselves sooner than their wives and children should want. Whatever their faults may be, they are good fathers, husbands, and sons. Their principal characteristic is their extreme love of money; and, though the strict Jew does not trade himself on the Sabbath, he may not object to employ either one of his tribe, or a Gentile, to do so for him.

The capital required for commencing in the old-clothes line is generally about 1*l*. This the Jew frequently borrows, especially after holiday-time, for then he has generally spent all his earnings, unless he be a provident man. When his stock-money is exhausted, he goes either to a neighbour or to a publican in the vicinity, and borrows 1*l*. on the Monday morning, 'to strike a light with', as he calls it, and agrees to return it on the Friday evening, with 1*s*. interest for the loan. This he always pays back. If he was to sell the coat off his back he would do this, I am told, because to fail in so doing would be to prevent his obtaining any stock-money for the future. With this capital he starts on his rounds about eight in the morning, and I am assured he will frequently begin his work without tasting food, rather than break into the borrowed stock-money. Each man has his particular walk, and never interferes with that of his neighbour; indeed, while upon another's beat he will seldom cry for clothes. Sometimes they go half 'Rybeck' together – that is, they will share the profits of the day's business, and when they agree to do this the one will take one street, and the other another. The lower the neighbourhood the more old clothes are there for sale. At the east end of the town they like the neighbourhoods frequented by sailors, and there they purchase of the girls and the women the sailors' jackets and trowsers. But they buy most of the Petticoat-lane, the Old-Clothes Exchange, and the marine-store dealers; for as the Jew clothes man never travels the streets by night-time, the parties who then have old clothes to dispose of usually sell them to the marine-store or second-hand dealers over-night, and the Jew buys them in the morning. The first thing that he does on his rounds is to seek out these shops, and see what he can pick up there. A very great amount of business is done by the Jew clothes man at the marine-store shops at the west as well as at the east end of London.

At the West-end the itinerant clothes men prefer the mews at the back of gentlemen's houses to all other places, or else the streets where the little tradesmen and small genteel families reside. My informant assured me that he had once bought a Bishop's hat of his lordship's servant for 1*s*. 6*d*. on a Sunday morning.

These traders, as I have elsewhere stated, live at the East-end of the town. The greater number of them reside in Portsoken Ward,

Houndsditch; and their favourite localities in this district are either Cobb's-yard, Roper's-building, or Wentworth-street. They mostly occupy small houses, about 4s. 6d. a week rent, and live with their families. They are generally sober men. It is seldom that a Jew leaves his house and owes his landlord money; and if his goods should be seized the rest of his tribe will go round and collect what is owing.

The rooms occupied by the old-clothes men are far from being so comfortable as those of the English artizans whose earnings are not superior to the gains of these clothes men. Those which I saw had all a littered look; the furniture was old and scant, and the apartment seemed neither shop, parlour, nor bed-room. For domestic and family men, as some of the Jew old-clothes men are, they seem very indifferent to the comforts of a home.

I have spoken of 'Tryfer', or meat killed in the Christian fashion. Now, the meat killed according to the Jewish law is known as 'Coshar', and a strict Jew will eat none other. In one of my letters in the *Morning Chronicle* on the meat markets of London, there appeared the following statement, respecting the Jew butchers in White-chapel-market.

'To a portion of the meat here exposed for sale, may be seen attached the peculiar seal which shows that the animal was killed conformably to the Jewish rites. According to the injunctions of this religion the beast must die from its throat being cut, instead of being knocked on the head. The slaughterer of the cattle for Jewish consumption, moreover, must be a Jew. Two slaughterers are appointed by the Jewish authorities of the synagogue, and they can employ others, who must be likewise Jews, as assistants. The slaughterers I saw were quiet-looking and quiet-mannered men. When the animal is slaughtered and skinned, an examiner (also appointed by the synagogue) carefully inspects the "inside". "If the lights be grown to the ribs," said my informant, who had had many years' experience in this branch of the meat trade, "or if the lungs have any disease, or if there be any disease anywhere, the meat is pronounced unfit for the food of the Jews, and is sent entire to a carcase butcher to be sold to the Christians. This, however, does not happen once in 20 times." To the parts exposed for sale, when the slaughtering has been according to the Jewish law, there is attached a leaden seal, stamped in Hebrew characters with the name of the examining party sealing. In this way, as I ascertained from the slaughterers, are killed weekly from 120 to 140 bullocks, from 400 to 500 sheep and lambs, and about 30 calves. All the parts of the animal thus slaughtered may be and are eaten by the Jews, but three-fourths of the purchase of this meat is confined, as regards the

Jews, to the fore-quarters of the respective animals; the hind-quarters, being the choicer parts, are sent to Newgate or Leadenhall-markets for sale on commission.' The Hebrew butchers consider that the Christian mode of slaughter is a far less painful death to the ox than was the Jewish.

I am informed that of the Jew old-clothes men there are now only from 500 to 600 in London; at one time there might have been 1,000. Their average earnings may be something short of 20s. a week in second-hand clothes alone; but the gains are difficult to estimate.

Of a Jew Street-seller

[p. 136] An elderly man, who, at the time I saw him, was vending spectacles, or bartering them for old clothes, old books, or any second-hand articles, gave me an account of his street-life, but it presented little remarkable beyond the not unusual vicissitudes of the lives of those of his class.

He had been in every street-trade, and had on four occasions travelled all over England, selling quills, sealing-wax, pencils, sponges, braces, cheap or superior jewellery, thermometers, and pictures. He had sold barometers in the mountainous parts of Cumberland, sometimes walking for hours without seeing man or woman. '*I liked it then*,' he said, '*for I was young and strong, and didn't care to sleep twice in the same town*. I was afterwards in the old-clothes line. I buy a few odd hats and light things still, but I'm not able to carry heavy weights, as my breath is getting rather short.' [I find that the Jews generally object to the more laborious kinds of street-traffic.] 'Yes, I've been twice to Ireland, and sold a good many quills in Dublin, for I crossed over from Liverpool. Quills and wax were a great trade with us once; now it's quite different. I've had as much as 60l. of my own, and that more than half-a-dozen times, but all of it went in speculations. Yes, some went in gambling. I had a share in a gaming-booth at the races, for three years. O, I dare say that's more than 20 years back; but we did very little good. There was such fees to pay for the tent on a race-ground, and often such delays between the races in the different towns, and bribes to be given to the town-officers – such as town-sergeants and chief constables, and I hardly know who – and so many expenses altogether, that the profits were mostly swamped. Once at Newcastle races there was a fight among the pitmen, and our tent was in their way, and was demolished almost to bits. A deal of the money was lost or stolen. I don't know how much, but not near so much as my partners wanted to make out. I wasn't on the spot just at the time. I got married after that, and took a shop in the second-hand clothes line in Bristol, but my wife died in child-bed in less than a year, and the shop didn't answer; so I got sick of it, and at last got rid of it. O, I work both the country and London still. I shall take a turn into Kent in a day or two. I suppose I clear between 10s. and 20s. a week in anything, and as I've only myself, I do middling, and am ready for another chance if any likely speculation offers. I lodge with a relation, and sometimes live with his family. No, I never touch any meat but "Coshar". I suppose my meat now costs me 6d. or 7d. a day, but it has cost me ten times that – and 2d. for beer in addition.'

I am informed that there are about 50 adult Jews (besides old-clothes men) in the streets selling fruit, cakes, pencils, spectacles, sponge, accordions, drugs, &c.

Of the Jew-boy Street-sellers

[pp. 136–7] I have ascertained, and from sources where no ignorance on the subject could prevail, that there are now in the streets of London, rather more than 100 Jew-boys engaged principally in fruit and cake-selling in the streets. Very few Jewesses are itinerant street-sellers. Most of the older Jews thus engaged have been street-sellers from their boyhood. The young Jews who ply in street-callings, however, are all men in matters of traffic, almost before they cease, in years, to be children. In addition to the Jew-boy street-sellers above enumerated, there are from 50 to 100, but usually about 50, who are occasional, or 'casual' street-traders, vending for the most part cocoa-nuts and grapes, and confining their sales chiefly to the Sundays.

On the subject of the street-Jew boys, a Hebrew gentleman said to me: 'When we speak of street-Jew boys, it should be understood, that the great majority of them are but little more conversant with or interested in the religion of their fathers, than are the costermonger boys of whom you have written. They are Jews by the accident of their birth, as others in the same way, with equal ignorance of the assumed faith, are Christians.'

I received from a Jew-boy the following account of his trading pursuits and individual aspirations. There was somewhat of a thickness in his utterance, otherwise his speech was but little distinguishable from that of an English street-boy. His physiognomy was decidedly Jewish, but not of the handsomer type. His hair was light-coloured, but clean, and apparently well brushed, without being oiled, or, as I heard a street-boy style it, 'greased'; it was long, and he said his aunt told him it 'wanted cutting sadly'; but he 'liked it that way'; indeed, he kept dashing his curls from his eyes, and back from his temples, as he was conversing, as if he were somewhat vain of doing so. He was dressed in a corduroy suit, old but not ragged, and wore a tolerably clean, very coarse, and altogether button-less shirt, which he said 'was made for one bigger than me, sir.' He had bought it for 9½d. in Petticoat-lane, and accounted it a bargain, as its wear would be durable. He was selling sponges when I saw him, and of the commonest kind, offering a large piece for 3d., which (he admitted) would be rubbed to bits in no time. This sponge, I should mention, is frequently 'dressed' with sulphuric acid, and an eminent surgeon informed me that on his servant attempting to clean his black dress coat with a sponge that he had newly bought in the streets, the colour of the garment, to his horror, changed to a bright purple. The Jew boy said –

'I believe I'm twelve. I've been to school, but it's long since, and my mother was very ill then, and I was forced to go out in the streets to have a chance. I never was kept to school. I can't read; I've forgot all about it. I'd rather now that I could read, but very likely I could soon learn if I could only spare time, but if I stay long in the house I feel sick; it's not healthy. O, no, sir, inside or out it would be all the same to me, just to make a living and keep my health. I can't say how long it is since I began to sell, it's a good long time; one must do something. I could keep myself now, and do sometimes, but my father – I live with him (my mother's dead) is often laid up. Would you like to see him, sir? He knows a deal. No, he can't write, but he can read a little. Can I speak Hebrew? Well, I know what you mean. O, no, I can't. I don't go to synagogue; I haven't time. My father goes, but only sometimes; so he says, and he tells me to look out, for we must both go by-and-by.' [I began to ask him what he knew of Joseph, and others recorded in the Old Testament, but he bristled up, and asked if I wanted to make a Meshumet (a convert) of him?] 'I have sold all sorts of things,' he continued, 'oranges, and lemons, and sponges, and nuts, and sweets. I should like to have a real good ginger-beer fountain of my own; but I must wait, and there's many in the trade. I only go with boys of my own sort. I sell to all sorts of boys, but that's nothing. Very likely they're Christians, but that's nothing to me. I don't know what's the difference between a Jew and Christian, and I don't want to talk about it. The Meshumets are never any good. Anybody will tell you that. Yes, I like music and can sing a bit. I get to a penny and sometimes a two-penny concert. No, I haven't been to Sussex Hall – I know where it is – I shouldn't understand it. You get in for nothing, that's one thing. I've heard of Baron Rothschild. He has more money than I could count in shillings in a year. I don't know about his wanting to get into parliament, or what it means;

but he's sure to do it or anything else, with his money. He's very charitable, I've heard. I don't know whether he's a German Jew, or a Portegee, or what. He's a cut above me, a precious sight. I only wish he was my uncle. I can't say what I should do if I had his money. Perhaps I should go a travelling, and see everything everywhere. I don't know how long the Jews have been in England; always perhaps. Yes, I know there's Jews in other countries. This sponge is Greek sponge, but I don't know where it's grown, only it's in foreign parts. Jerusalem! Yes, I've heard of it. I'm of no tribe that I know of. I buy what I eat about Petticoat-lane. No, I don't like fish, but the stews, and the onions with them is beautiful for two-pence; you may get a pennor'th. The pickles – cowcumbers is best – are stunning. But they're plummiest with a bit of cheese or anything cold – that's my opinion, but you may think different. Pork! Ah! No, I never touched it; I'd as soon eat a cat; so would my father. No, sir, I don't think pork smells nice in a cook-shop, but some Jew boys, as I knows, thinks it does. I don't know why it shouldn't be eaten, only that it's wrong to eat it. No, I never touched a ham-sandwich, but other Jew boys have, and laughed at it, I know.

'I don't know what I make in a week. I think I make as much on one thing as on another. I've sold strawberries, and cherries, and gooseberries, and nuts and walnuts in the season. O, as to what I make, that's nothing to nobody. Sometimes 6d. a day, sometimes 1s.; sometimes a little more, and sometimes nothing. No, I never sells inferior things if I can help it, but if one hasn't stock-money one must do as one can, but it isn't so easy to try it on. There was a boy beaten by a woman not long since for selling a big pottle of strawberries that was rubbish all under the toppers. It was all strawberry leaves, and crushed strawberries, and such like. She wanted to take back from him the two-pence she'd paid for it, and got hold of his pockets and there was a regular fight, but she didn't get a farthing back though she tried her very hardest, 'cause he slipped from her and hooked it. So you see it's dangerous to try it on.' [This last remark was made gravely enough, but the lad told of the feat with such manifest glee, that I'm inclined to believe that he himself was the culprit in question.] 'Yes, it was a Jew-boy it happened to, but other boys in the streets is just the same. Do I like the streets? I can't say I do, there's too little to be made in them. *No, I wouldn't like to go to school, nor to be in a shop, nor be anybody's servant but my own.* O, I don't know what I shall be when I'm grown up. I shall take my chance like others.'

Of the Street Jewesses and Street Jew-girls

[pp. 138–9] I have mentioned that the Jewesses and the young Jew-girls, compared with the adult Jews and Jew-boys, are not street-traders in anything like the proportion which the females were found to bear to the males among the Irish street-folk and the English costermongers. There are, however, a few Jewish females who are itinerant street-sellers as well as stall keepers, in the proportion, perhaps, of one female to seven or eight males. The majority of the street Jew-girls whom I saw on a round were accompanied by boys who were represented to be their brothers, and I have little doubt such was the fact, for these young Jewesses, although often pert and ignorant, are not unchaste. Of this I was assured by a medical gentleman who could speak with sufficient positiveness on the subject.

Fruit is generally sold by these boys and girls together, the lad driving the barrow, and the girl inviting custom and handing the purchases to the buyers. In tending a little stall or a basket at a regular pitch, with such things as cherries or strawberries, the little Jewess differs only from her street-selling sisters in being a brisker trader. The stalls, with a few old knives or scissors, or odds and ends of laces, that are tended by the Jew-girls in the streets in the Jewish quarters (I am told there are not above a dozen of them) are generally near the shops and within sight of their parents or friends. One little Jewess, with whom I had some conversation, had not even heard the name of the Chief Rabbi, the Rev. Dr Adler, and knew nothing of any distinction between German and Portuguese Jews; she had, I am inclined to believe, never heard of either. I am told that the whole, or nearly the whole, of these young female traders reside with parents or friends, and that there is among them far less than the average number of runaways. One Jew told me he thought that the young female members of his tribe did not tramp with the juveniles of the other sex – no, not in the proportion of one to a hundred in comparison, he said with a laugh, with 'young women of the Christian persuasion'. My informant had means of knowing this fact, as although still a young man, he had traversed the greater part of England hawking perfumery, which he had abandoned as a bad trade. A wire-worker, long familiar with tramping and going into the country – a man upon whose word I have every reason to rely – told me that he could not remember a single instance of his having seen a young Jewess 'travelling' with a boy.

There are a few adult Jewesses who are itinerant traders, but very few. I met with one who carried on her arm a not very large basket, filled with glass wares; chiefly salt-cellars, cigar-ash plates, blue glass dessert plates, vinegar-cruets, and such like. The greater part of her wares appeared to be blue, and she carried nothing but glass. She was a good-looking and neatly-dressed woman. She peeped in at each shop-door, and up at the windows of every private house, in the street in which I met her, crying, 'Clo', old clo'!' She bartered her glass for old clothes, or bought the garments, dealing principally in female attire, and almost entirely with women. She declined to say anything about her family or her circumstances, except that she had nothing that way to complain about, but – when I had used some names I had authority to make mention of – she said she would, with pleasure, tell me all about her trade, which she carried on rather than do nothing. 'When I hawk,' she said with an English accent, her face being unmistakeably Jewish, 'I hawk only good glass, and it can hardly be called hawking, as I swop it for more than I sell it. I always ask for the mistress, and if she wants any of my glass we come to a bargain if we can. O, it's ridiculous to see what things some ladies – I suppose they must be called ladies – offer for my glass. Children's green or blue gauze veils, torn or faded, and not worth picking up, because no use whatever; old ribbons, not worth dyeing, and old frocks, not worth washing. People say, "as keen as a Jew", but ladies can't think we're very keen when they offer us such rubbish. I do most at the middle kind of houses, both shops and private. I sometimes give a little money for such a thing as a shawl, or a fur tippet, as well as my glass – but only when I can't help it – to secure a bargain. Sometimes, but not often, I get the old thing and a trifle for my glass. Occasionally I buy outright. I don't do much, there's so many in the line, and I don't go out regularly. I can't say how many women are in my way – very few; O, I do middling. I told you I had no complaints to make. I don't calculate my profits or what I sell. My family do that and I don't trouble myself.'

SCAVENGERS AND CLEANERS

OF THE MUD-LARKS

[pp. 173–6] There is another class who may be termed river-finders,
although their occupation is connected only with the shore; they are
commonly known by the name of 'mud-larks', from being compelled, in
order to obtain the articles they seek, to wade sometimes up to their middle
through the mud left on the shore by the retiring tide. These poor creatures
are certainly about the most deplorable in their appearance of any I have
met with in the course of my inquiries. They may be seen of all ages, from
mere childhood to positive decrepitude, crawling among the barges at the
various wharfs along the river; it cannot be said that they are clad in rags,
for they are scarcely half covered by the tattered indescribable things that
serve them for clothing; their bodies are grimed with the foul soil of the
river, and their torn garments stiffened up like boards with dirt of every
possible description.

Among the mud-larks may be seen many old women, and it is indeed
pitiable to behold them, especially during the winter, bent nearly double
with age and infirmity, paddling and groping among the wet mud for small
pieces of coal, chips of wood, or any sort of refuse washed up by the tide.
These women always have with them an old basket or an old tin kettle,
in which they put whatever they chance to find. It usually takes them a
whole tide to fill this receptacle, but when filled, it is as much as the feeble
old creatures are able to carry home.

The mud-larks generally live in some court or alley in the neighbourhood of the river, and, as the tide recedes, crowds of boys and little girls,
some old men, and many old women, may be observed loitering about the
various stairs, watching eagerly for the opportunity to commence their
labours. When the tide is sufficiently low they scatter themselves along
the shore, separating from each other, and soon disappear among the craft
lying about in every direction. This is the case on both sides of the river,
as high up as there is anything to be found, extending as far as Vauxhall-
bridge, and as low down as Woolwich. The mud-larks themselves,
however, know only those who reside near them, and whom they are
accustomed to meet in their daily pursuits; indeed, with but few
exceptions, these people are dull, and apparently stupid; this is observable
particularly among the boys and girls, who, when engaged in searching

the mud, hold but little converse one with another. The men and women may be passed and repassed, but they notice no one; they never speak, but with a stolid look of wretchedness they plash their way through the mire, their bodies bent down while they peer anxiously about, and occasionally stoop to pick up some paltry treasure that falls in their way.

The mud-larks collect whatever they happen to find, such as coals, bits of old-iron, rope, bones, and copper nails that drop from ships while lying or repairing along shore. Copper nails are the most valuable of all the articles they find, but these they seldom obtain, as they are always driven from the neighbourhood of a ship while being new-sheathed. Sometimes the younger and bolder mud-larks venture on sweeping some empty coal-barge, and one little fellow with whom I spoke, having been lately caught in the act of so doing, had to undergo for the offence seven days' imprisonment in the House of Correction: this, he says, he liked much better than mud-larking, for while he staid there he wore a coat and shoes and stockings, and though he had not over much to eat, he certainly was never afraid of going to bed without anything at all – as he often had to do when at liberty. He thought he would try it on again in the winter, he told me, saying, it would be so comfortable to have clothes and shoes and stockings then, and not be obliged to go into the cold wet mud of a morning.

The coals that the mud-larks find, they sell to the poor people of the neighbourhood at 1*d*. per pot, holding about 14 lbs. The iron and bones and rope and copper nails which they collect, they sell at the rag-shops. They dispose of the iron at 5 lbs. for 1*d*., the bones at 3 lbs. a 1*d*., rope at ½*d*. per lb. wet, and ¾*d*. per lb. dry, and copper nails at the rate of 4*d*. per lb. They occasionally pick up tools, such as saws and hammers; these they dispose of to the seamen for biscuit and meat, and sometimes sell them at the rag-shops for a few halfpence. In this manner they earn from 2½*d*. to 8*d*. per day, but rarely the latter sum; their average gains may be estimated at about 3*d*. per day. The boys, after leaving the river, sometimes scrape their trousers, and frequent the cab-stands, and try to earn a trifle by opening the cab-doors for those who enter them, or by holding gentlemen's horses. Some of them go, in the evening, to a ragged school, in the neighbourhood of which they live; more, as they say, because other boys go there, than from any desire to learn.

At one of the stairs in the neighbourhood of the pool, I collected about a dozen of these unfortunate children; there was not one of them over twelve years of age, and many of them were but six. It would be almost impossible to describe the wretched group, so motley was their appearance, so extraordinary their dress, and so stolid and inexpressive their countenances. Some carried baskets, filled with the produce of their morning's work, and others old tin kettles with iron handles. Some, for want of these articles, had old hats filled with the bones and coals they had picked up; and others, more needy still, had actually taken the caps from their own heads, and filled them with what they had happened to find. The muddy slush was dripping from their clothes and utensils, and forming a puddle in which they stood. There did not appear to be among the whole group as many filthy cotton rags to their backs as, when stitched together, would have been sufficient to form the material of one shirt. There were the remnants of one or two jackets among them, but so begrimed and tattered that it would have been difficult to have determined either the original material or make of the garment. On questioning one, he said his father was a coal-backer; he had been dead eight years; the boy was nine years old. His mother was alive; she went out charing and washing when she could get any such work to do. She had 1s. a day when she could get employment, but that was not often; he remembered once to have had a pair of shoes, but it was a long time since. 'It is very cold in winter,' he said, 'to stand in the mud without shoes,' but he did not mind it in summer. He had been three years mud-larking, and supposed he should remain a mud-lark all his life. What else could he be? for there was nothing else that he knew *how* to do. Some days he earned 1d., and some days 4d.; he never earned 8d. in one day, that would have been a 'jolly lot of money'. He never found a saw or a hammer, he 'only wished' he could, they would be glad to get hold of them at the dolly's. He had been one month at school before he went mud-larking. Some time ago he had gone to the ragged-school; but he no longer went there, for he forgot it. He could neither read nor write, and did not think he could learn if he tried 'ever so much'. He didn't know what religion his father and mother were, nor did know what religion meant. God was God, he said. He had heard he was good, but didn't know what good he was to him. He thought he was a Christian, but he didn't know what a Christian was. He had heard of Jesus Christ once, when he went to a Catholic chapel, but he never heard tell of who or what he was, and didn't 'particular care' about knowing. His father and mother were born in Aberdeen, but he didn't know where Aberdeen was. London was England, and England, he said, was in London, but he couldn't tell in what part. He could not tell where he would go to when he died, and didn't believe any one could tell *that*. Prayers, he told me, were what people said to themselves at night. *He* never said any, and didn't know any; his mother sometimes used to speak to him about them, but he could never learn any. His mother didn't go to church or to

THE MUD-LARK.

chapel, because she had no clothes. All the money he got he gave to his mother, and she bought bread with it, and when they had no money they lived the best way they could.

Such was the amount of intelligence manifested by this unfortunate child.

Another was only seven years old. He stated that his father was a sailor who had been hurt on board ship, and been unable to go to sea for the last two years. He had two brothers and a sister, one of them older than himself; and his elder brother was a mud-lark like himself. The two had been mud-larking more than a year; they went because they saw other boys go, and knew that they got money for the things they found. They were often hungry, and glad to do anything to get something to eat. Their father was not able to earn anything, and their mother could get but little to do. They gave all the money they earned to their mother. They didn't gamble, and play at pitch and toss when they had got some money, but some of the big boys did on the Sunday, when they didn't go a mud-larking. He couldn't tell why they did nothing on a Sunday, 'only they didn't'; though sometimes they looked about to see where the best place would be on the next day. He didn't go to the ragged school; he should like to know how to read a book, though he couldn't tell what good it would do him. He didn't like mud larking, would be glad of some thing else, but didn't know anything else that he could do.

Another of the boys was the son of a dock labourer, – casually employed. He was between seven and eight years of age, and his sister, who was also a mud-lark, formed one of the group. The mother of these two was dead, and there were three children younger than themselves.

The rest of the histories may easily be imagined, for there was a painful uniformity in the stories of all the children: they were either the children of the very poor, who, by their own improvidence or some overwhelming calamity, had been reduced to the extremity of distress, or else they were orphans, and compelled from utter destitution to seek for the means of appeasing their hunger in the mud of the river. That the majority of this class are ignorant, and without even the rudiments of education, and that many of them from time to time are committed to prison for petty thefts, cannot be wondered at. Nor can it even excite our astonishment that, once within the walls of a prison, and finding how much more comfortable it is than their previous condition, they should return to it repeatedly. As for the females growing up under such circumstances, the worst may be anticipated of them; and in proof of this I have found, upon inquiry, that very many of the unfortunate creatures who swell the tide of prostitution in Ratcliff-highway, and other low neighbourhoods in the East of London, have originally been mud-larks; and only remained at that occupation till such time as they were capable of adopting the more easy and more lucrative life of the prostitute.

As to the numbers and earnings of the mud-larks, the following calculations fall short of, rather than exceed, the truth. From Execution Dock to the lower part of Limehouse Hole, there are 14 stairs or landing-places, by which the mud-larks descend to the shore in order to pursue their employment. There are about as many on the opposite side of the water similarly frequented.

At King James' Stairs, in Wapping Wall, which is nearly a central position, from 40 to 50 mud-larks go down daily to the river; the mud-larks 'using' the other stairs are not so numerous. If, therefore, we reckon the number of stairs on both sides of the river at 28, and the average number of mud-larks frequenting them at 10 each, we shall have a total of 280. Each mud-lark, it has been shown, earns on an average 3d. a day, or 1s. 6d. per week; so that the annual earnings of each will be 3l. 18s., or say 4l., a year, and hence the gross earnings of the 280 will amount to rather more than 1,000l. per annum.

But there are, in addition to the mud-larks employed in the neighbourhood of what may be called the pool, many others who work down the river at various places as far as Blackwall, on the one side, and at Deptford, Greenwich, and Woolwich, on the other. These frequent the neighbourhoods of the various 'yards' along shore, where vessels are being built; and whence, at certain times, chips, small pieces of wood, bits of iron, and copper nails, are washed out into the river. There is but little doubt that this portion of the class earn much more than the mud-larks of the pool, seeing that they are especially convenient to the places where the iron vessels are constructed; so that the presumption is, that the number of mud-larks 'at work' on the banks of the Thames (especially if we include those above bridge), and the value of the property extracted by them from the mud of the river, may be fairly estimated at double that which is stated above, or say 550 gaining 2,000l. per annum.

As an illustration of the doctrines I have endeavoured to enforce throughout this publication, I cite the following history of one of the above class. It may serve to teach those who are still sceptical as to the degrading influence of circumstances upon the poor, that many of the humbler classes, if placed in the same easy position as ourselves, would become, perhaps, quite as 'respectable' members of society.

The lad of whom I speak was discovered by me now nearly two years ago 'mud-larking' on the banks of the river near the docks. He was a quick, intelligent little fellow, and had been at the business, he told me, about three years. He had taken to mud-larking, he said, because his clothes were too bad for him to look for anything better. He worked every day, with 20 or 30 boys, who might all be seen at day-break with their trowsers tucked up, groping about, and picking out the pieces of coal from the mud on the banks of the Thames. He went into the river up to his knees, and in searching the mud he often ran pieces of glass and long nails into his feet. When this was the case, he went home and dressed the wounds, but returned to the river-side directly, 'for should the tide come up,' he added, 'without my having found something, why I must starve till next low tide.' In the very cold weather he and his other shoe-less companions used to stand in the hot water that ran down the river side from some of the steam-factories, to warm their frozen feet.

At first he found it difficult to keep his footing in the mud, and he had known many beginners fall in. He came to my house, at my request, the morning after my first meeting with him. It was the depth of winter, and the poor little fellow was nearly destitute of clothing. His trousers were worn away up to his knees, he had no shirt, and his legs and feet (which were bare) were covered with chilblains. On being questioned by me he gave the following account of his life:—

He was fourteen years old. He had two sisters, one fifteen and the other twelve years of age. His father had been dead nine years. The man had been a coal-whipper, and, from getting his work from one of the publican employers in those days, had become a confirmed drunkard. When he married he held a situation in a ware-house, where his wife managed the first year to save 4*l.* 10*s* out of her husband's earnings; but from the day he took to coal-whipping she had never saved one halfpenny, indeed she and her children were often left to starve. The man (whilst in a state of intoxication) had fallen between two barges, and the injuries he received had been so severe that he had lingered in a helpless state for three years before his death. After her husband's decease the poor woman's neighbours subscribed 1*l.* 5*s.* for her; with this sum she opened a green-grocer's shop, and got on very well for five years.

When the boy was nine years old his mother sent him to the Red Lion school at Green-bank, near Old Gravel-lane, Ratcliffe-highway; she paid 1*d.* a week for his learning. He remained there for a year; then the potato-rot came, and his mother lost upon all she bought. About the same time two of her customers died 30*s.* in her debt; this loss, together with the potato-disease, completely ruined her, and the whole family had been in the greatest poverty from that period. Then she was obliged to take all her children from their school, that they might help to keep themselves as best they could. Her eldest girl sold fish in the streets, and the boy went to the river-side to 'pick up' his living. The change, however, was so great that shortly afterwards the little fellow lay ill eighteen weeks with the ague. As soon as the boy recovered his mother and his two sisters were 'taken bad' with a fever. The poor woman went into the 'Great House', and the children were taken to the Fever Hospital. When the mother returned home she was too weak to work, and all she had to depend on was what her boy brought from the river. They had nothing to eat and no money until the little fellow had been down to the shore and picked up some coals, selling them for a trifle. 'And hard enough he had to work for what he got, poor boy,' said his mother to me on a future occasion, sobbing; 'still he never complained, but was quite proud when he brought home enough for us to get a bit of meat with; and when he has sometimes seen me down-hearted, he has clung round my neck, and assured me that one day God would see us cared for if I would put my trust in Him.' As soon as his mother was well enough she sold fruit in the streets, or went out washing when she could get a day's work.

The lad suffered much from the pieces of broken glass in the mud. Some little time before I met with him he had run a copper nail into his foot. This lamed him for three months, and his mother was obliged to carry him on her back every morning to the doctor. As soon, however, as he could 'hobble' (to use his mother's own words) he went back to the river, and often returned (after many hours' hard work in the mud) with only a few pieces of coal, not enough to sell even to get them a bit of bread. One evening, as he was warming his feet in the water that ran from a steam factory, he heard some boys talking about the Ragged School in High-street, Wapping.

'They was saying what they used to learn there,' added the boy. 'They asked me to come along with them for it was great fun. They told me that all the boys used to be laughing and making game of the master. They said they used to put out the gas and chuck the slates all about. They told me, too, that there was a good fire there, so I went to have a warm and see what it was like. When I got there the master was very kind to me. They used to give us tea-parties, and to keep us quiet they used to show us the magic lantern. I soon got to like going there, and went every night for six months. There was about 40 or 50 boys in the school. The most of them was thieves, and they used to go thieving the coals out of barges along shore, and cutting the ropes off ships, and going and selling it at the rag-shops. They used to get ¾d. a lb, for the rope when dry, and ½d. when wet. Some used to steal pudding out of shops and hand it to those outside, and the last boy it was handed to would go off with it. They used to steal bacon and bread sometimes as well. About half of the boys at the school was thieves. Some had work to do at ironmongers, lead-factories, engineers, soap-boilers, and so on, and some had no work to do and was good boys still. After we came out of school at nine o'clock at night, some of the bad boys would go a thieving, perhaps half-a-dozen and from that to eight would go out in a gang together. There was one big boy of the name of C—; he was 18 years old, and is in prison now for stealing bacon; I think he is in the House of Correction. This C— used to go out of school before any of us, and wait outside the door as the other boys came out. Then he would call the boys he wanted for his gangs on one side, and tell them where to go and steal. He used to look out in the daytime for shops where things could be "prigged", and at night he would tell the boys to go to them. He was called the captain of the gangs. He had about three gangs altogether with him, and there were from six to eight boys in each gang. The boys used to bring what they stole to C—, and he used to share it with them. I belonged to one of the gangs. There were six boys altogether in my gang; the biggest lad, that knowed all about the thieving, was the captain of the gang I was in, and C— was captain over him and over all of us.

'There was two brothers of them; you seed them, sir, the night you first met me. The other boys, as was in my gang, was B— B—, and B— L—, and W— B—, and a boy we used to call "Tim"; these, with myself, used to make up one of the gangs, and we all of us used to go a thieving every night after school-hours. When the tide would be right up, and we had nothing to do along shore, we used to go thieving in the daytime as well. It was B— B—, and B— L—, as first put me up to go thieving; they took me with them, one night, up the lane [New Gravel-lane], and I see them take some bread out of a baker's, and they wasn't found out; and, after that, I used to go with them regular. Then I joined C—'s gang; and, after that, C— came and told us that his gang could do better than ourn, and he asked us to join our gang to his'n, and we did so. Sometimes we used to make 3s. and 4s. a day; or about 6d. apiece. While waiting outside the school-doors, before they opened, we used to plan up where we would go thieving after school was over. I was taken up once for thieving coals myself, but I was let go again.'

I was so much struck with the boy's truthfulness of manner, that I asked him, *would* he really lead a different life, if he saw a means of so doing?

He assured me he would, and begged me earnestly to try him. Upon his leaving me, 2s. were given him for his trouble. This small sum (I afterwards learned) kept the family for more than a fortnight. The girl laid it out in sprats (it being then winter-time); these she sold in the streets.

I mentioned the fact to a literary friend, who interested himself in the boy's welfare; and eventually succeeded in procuring him a situation at an eminent printer's. The subjoined letter will show how the lad conducted himself while there.

Whitefriars, April 22, 1850.
Messrs. Bradbury and Evans beg to say that the boy J.C. has conducted himself in a very satisfactory manner since he has been in their employment.

The same literary friend took the girl into his service. She is in a situation still, though not in the same family.

The boy now holds a good situation at one of the daily newspaper offices. So well has he behaved himself, that, a few weeks since, his wages were increased from 6s. to 9s. per week. His mother (owing to the boy's exertions) has now a little shop, and is doing well.

This simple story requires no comments, and is narrated here in the hope that it may teach many to know how often the poor boys reared in the gutter are thieves, merely because society forbids them being honest lads.

OF THE DUSTMEN OF LONDON

[pp. 187–201] Dust and rubbish accumulate in houses from a variety of causes, but principally from the residuum of fires, the white ash and cinders, or small fragments of unconsumed coke, giving rise to by far the greater quantity. Some notion of the vast amount of this refuse annually produced in London may be formed from the fact that the consumption of coal in the metropolis is, according to the official returns, 3,500,000 tons per annum, which is at the rate of a little more than 11 tons per house; the poorer families, it is true, do not burn more than 2 tons in the course of the year, but then many such families reside in the same house, and hence the average will appear in no way excessive. Now the ashes and cinders arising from this enormous consumption of coal would, it is evident, if allowed to lie scattered about in such a place as London, render, ere long, not only the back streets, but even the important thoroughfares, filthy and impassable. Upon the Officers of the various parishes, therefore, has devolved the duty of seeing that the refuse of the fuel consumed throughout London is removed almost as fast as produced; this they do by entering into an agreement for the clearance of the 'dust-bins' of the parishioners as often as required, with some person who possesses all necessary appliances for the purpose – such as horses, carts, baskets, and shovels, together with a plot of waste ground whereon to deposit the refuse. The persons with whom this agreement is made are called 'dust-contractors', and are generally men of considerable wealth.

The collection of 'dust', is now, more properly speaking, the removal of it. The collection of an article implies the voluntary seeking after it, and this the dustmen can hardly be said to do; for though they parade the streets shouting for the dust as they go, they do so rather to fulfil a certain duty they have undertaken to perform than in any expectation of profit to be derived from the sale of the article.

Formerly the custom was otherwise; but then, as will be seen hereafter, the residuum of the London fuel was far more valuable. Not many years ago it was the practice for the various master dust-men to send in their tenders to the vestry, on a certain day appointed for the purpose, offering to pay a considerable sum yearly to the parish authorities for liberty to collect the dust from the several houses. The sum formerly paid to the parish of Shadwell, for instance, though not a very extensive one, amounted to between 400*l*. or 500*l*. per annum; but then there was an immense demand for the article, and the contractors were unable to furnish a sufficient supply from London; ships were frequently freighted with it from other parts, especially from Newcastle and the northern ports, and at that time it formed an article of considerable international commerce – the price being from 15*s*. to 1*l*. per chaldron. Of late years, however, the demand has fallen off greatly, while the supply has been progressively increasing, owing to the extension of the metropolis, so that the Contractors have not only declined paying anything for liberty to collect it, but now stipulate to receive a certain sum for the removal of it. It need hardly be stated that the parishes always employ the man who requires the least money for the performance of what has now become a matter of duty rather than an object of desire. Some idea may be formed of the change which has taken place in this business, from the fact, that the aforesaid parish of Shadwell, which formerly received the sum of 450*l*. per annum for liberty to collect the dust, now pays the Contractor the sum of 240*l*. per annum for its removal.

The Court of Sewers of the City of London, in 1846, through the advice of Mr Cochrane, the president of the National Philanthropic Association, were able to obtain from the contractors the sum of 5,000*l*. for liberty to clear away the dirt from the streets and the dust from the bins and houses in that district. The year following, however, the contractors entered into a combination, and came to a resolution not to bid so high for the privilege; the result was, that they obtained their contracts at an expense of 2,200*l*. By acting on the same principle in the year after, they not only offered no premium whatever for the contract, but the City Commissioners of Sewers were obliged to pay them the sum of 300*l*. for removing the refuse, and at present the amount paid by the City is as much as 4,900*l*.! This is divided among four great contractors, and would, if equally apportioned, give them 1,250*l*. each.

All the metropolitan parishes now pay the contractors various amounts for the removal of the dust, and I am credibly informed that there is a system of underletting and jobbing in the dust contracts extensively carried on. The contractor for a certain parish is often a different person from the master doing the work, who is unknown in the contract. Occasionally the work would appear to be subdivided and underlet a second time.

The parish of St Pancras is split into no less than 21 districts, each district having a separate and independent 'Board', who are generally at war with each other, and make separate contracts for their several divisions. This is also the case in other large parishes, and these and other considerations confirm me in the conclusion that of large and small dust-contractors, job-masters, and middle-men, of one kind or the other, throughout the metropolis, there cannot be less than the number I have stated – 90. With the exception of Bermondsey, there are no parishes who remove their own dust.

It is difficult to arrive at any absolute statement as to the gross amount paid by the different parishes for the removal of the entire dust of the metropolis. From Shadwell the contractor, as we have seen, receives 250*l*.; from the city the four contractors receive as much as 5,000*l*.; but there are many small parishes in London which do not pay above a tithe of the last-mentioned sum. Let us, therefore, assume, that one with another, the several metropolitan parishes pay 200*l*. a year each to the dust contractor. According to the returns before given, there are 176 parishes in London. Hence, the gross amount paid for the removal of the entire dust of the metropolis will be between 30,000*l*. and 40,000*l*. per annum.

The removal of the dust throughout the metropolis, is, therefore, carried on by a number of persons called Contractors, who undertake, as has been stated, for a certain sum, to cart away the refuse from the houses as frequently as the inhabitants desire it. To ascertain the precise numbers of these contractors is a task of much greater difficulty than might at first be conceived.

The London Post Office Directory gives the following number of trades-men connected with the removal of refuse from the houses and streets of the metropolis.

Dustmen	9
Scavengers	10
Nightmen	14
Sweeps	32

But these numbers are obviously incomplete, for even a cursory passenger through London must have noticed a greater number of names upon the various dust carts to be met with in the streets than are here set down.

A dust-contractor, who has been in the business upwards of 20 years, stated that, from his knowledge of the trade, he should suppose that at present there might be about 80 or 90 contractors in the metropolis. Now, according to the returns before given, there are within the limits of the Metropolitan Police District 176 parishes, and comparing this with my informant's statement, that many persons contract for more than one parish (of which, indeed, he himself is an instance), there remains but little reason to doubt the correctness of his supposition – that there are, in all, between 80 or 90 dust-contractors, large and small, connected with the metropolis. Assuming the aggregate number to be 88, there would be one contractor to every two parishes.

These dust-contractors are likewise the contractors for the cleansing of the streets, except where that duty is performed by the Street-Orderlies; they are also the persons who undertake the emptying of the cesspools in their neighbourhood; the latter operation, however, is effected by an arrangement between themselves and the landlords of the premises, and forms no part of their parochial contracts. At the office of the Street Orderlies in Leicester Square, they have knowledge of only 30 contractors connected with the metropolis; but this is evidently defective, and refers to the 'large masters' alone; leaving out of all consideration, as it does, the host of small contractors scattered up and down the metropolis, who are able to employ only two or three carts and six or seven men each; many of such small contractors being merely master sweeps who have managed to 'get on a little in the world', and who are now able to contract, 'in a small way', for the removal of dust, street-sweepings, and night-soil. Moreover, many of even the 'great contractors' being unwilling to venture upon an outlay of capital for carts, horses, &c., when their contract is only for a year, and may pass at the end of that time into the hands of any one who may underbid them – many such, I repeat, are in the habit of underletting a portion of their contract to others possessing the necessary appliances, or of entering into partnership with them. The latter is the case in the parish of Shadwell, where a person having carts and horses shares the profits with the original contractor. The agreement made on such occasions is, of course, a secret, though the practice is by no means uncommon; indeed, there is so much secrecy maintained concerning all matters connected with this business, that the inquiry is beset with every possible difficulty. The gentleman who communicated to me the amount paid by the parish of Shadwell, and who informed me, moreover, that parishes in his neighbourhood paid twice and three times more than Shadwell did, hinted to me the difficulties I should experience at the commencement of my inquiry, and I have certainly found his opinion correct to the letter. I have ascertained that in one yard intimidation was resorted to, and the men were threatened with instant dismissal if they gave me any information but such as was calculated to mislead.

I soon discovered, indeed, that it was impossible to place any reliance on what some of the contractors said; and here I may repeat that the indisputable result of my inquiries has been to meet with far more deception and equivocation from employers generally than from the employed; working men have little or no motive for mis-stating their wages; they know well that the ordinary rates of remuneration for their labour are easily ascertainable from other members of the trade, and seldom or never object to produce accounts of their earnings, whenever they have been in the habit of keeping such things. With employers, however, the case is far different; to seek to ascertain from them the profits of their trade is to meet with evasion and prevarication at every turn; they seem to feel that their gains are dishonestly large, and hence resort to every means to prevent them being made public. That I have met with many honourable exceptions to this rule, I most cheerfully acknowledge; but that the *majority* of tradesmen are neither so frank, communicative, nor truthful, as the men in their employ, the whole of my investigations go to prove. I have already, in the *Morning Chronicle*, recorded the character of my interviews with an eminent Jew slop-tailor, an army clothier, and an enterprising free-trade stay-maker (a gentleman who subscribed his 100 guineas to the League), and I must in candour confess that now, after two years' experience, I have found the industrious poor a thousand-fold more veracious than the trading rich.

With respect to the amount of business done by these contractors, or gross quantity of dust collected by them in the course of the year, it would appear that each employs, on an average, about 20 men, which makes the number of men employed as dustmen through the streets of London amount to 1,800. This, as has been previously stated, is grossly at variance with the number given in the Census of 1841, which computes the dustmen in the metropolis at only 254. But, as I said before, I have long ceased to place confidence in the government returns on such subjects. According to the above estimate of 254, and deducting from this number the 88 master-dustmen, there would be only 166 labouring men to empty the 300,000 dust-bins of London, and as these men always work in couples, it follows that every two dustmen would have to remove the refuse from about 3,600 houses; so that assuming each bin to require emptying once every six weeks they would have to cart away the dust from 2,400 houses every month, or 600 every week, which is at the rate of 100 a day! and as each dust-bin contains about half a load, it would follow that at this rate each cart would have to collect 50 loads of dust daily, whereas 5 loads is the average day's work.

Computing the London dust-contractors at 90, and the inhabited houses at 300,000, it follows that each contractor would have 3,333 houses to remove the refuse from. Now it has been calculated that the ashes and cinders alone from each house average about three loads per annum, so that each contractor would have, in round numbers, 10,000 loads of dust to remove in the course of the year. I find, from inquiries, that every two dustmen carry to the yard about five loads a day, or about 1,500 loads in the course of the year, so that at this rate, there must be between six and seven carts, and twelve and fourteen collectors employed by each master. But this is exclusive of the men employed in the yards. In one yard that I visited there were fourteen people busily employed. Six of these were women, who were occupied in sifting, and they were attended by three men who shovelled the dust into their sieves, and the foreman, who was hard at work loosening and dragging down the dust from the heap, ready for the 'fillers-in'. Besides these there were two carts and four men engaged in conveying the sifted dust to the barges alongside the wharf. At a larger dust-yard, that formerly stood on the banks of the Regent's-canal, I am informed that there were sometimes as many as 127 people at work. It is but a small yard, which has not 30 to 40 labourers connected with it; and the lesser dust-yards have generally from four to eight sifters, and six or seven carts. There are, therefore, employed in a medium-sized yard twelve collectors or cartmen, six sifters, and

THE RUBBISH CARTER.

three fillers-in, besides the foreman or forewoman, making altogether 22 persons; so that, computing the contractors at 90, and
allowing 20 men to be employed by each, there would be 1,800 men
thus occupied in the metropolis, which appears to be very near the
truth.

One who has been all his life connected with the business estimated that
there must be about ten dustmen to each metropolitan parish, large and
small. In Marylebone he believed there were eighteen dust-carts, with two
men to each, out every day; in some small parishes, however, two men
are sufficient. There would be more men employed, he said, but some
masters contracted for two or three parishes, and so 'kept the same men
going', working them hard, and enlarging their regular rounds.
Calculating, then, that ten men are employed to each of the 176 metropolitan parishes, we have 1,760 dustmen in London. The suburban
parishes, my informant told me, were as well 'dustmaned' as any he knew;
for the residents in such parts were more particular about their dust than
in busier places.

It is curious to observe how closely the number of men engaged
in the collection of the 'dust' from the coals burnt in London agrees,
according to the above estimate, with the number of men engaged
in delivering the coals to be burnt. The coal-whippers, who 'discharge the
colliers', are about 1,800, and the coal-porters, who carry the coals
from the barges to the merchants' wagons, are about the same
in number. The amount of residuum from coal after burning cannot,
of course, be equal either in bulk or weight to the original substance;
but considering that the collection of the dust is a much slower operation than the delivery of the coals, the difference is easily accounted
for.

We may arrive, approximately, at the quantity of dust annually
produced in London, in the following manner:

The consumption of coal in London, per annum, is about 3,500,000
tons, exclusive of what is brought to the metropolis per rail. Coals are made
up of the following component parts, viz. (1) the inorganic and fixed
elements; that is to say, the ashes, or the bones, as it were, of the fossil
trees, which cannot be burnt; (2) coke, or the residuary carbon, after being
deprived of the volatile matter; (3) the volatile matter itself given off during
combustion in the form of flame and smoke.

The relative proportions of these materials in the various kinds of coals
are as follows:

	Carbon per cent	Volatile per cent	Ashes, per cent
Cannel or gas coals	40 to 60	60 to 40	10
Newcastle or 'house' coals	57	37	5
Lancashire and Yorkshire coals	50 to 60	35 to 40	4
South Welsh or 'steam' coals	81 to 85	11 to 15	3
Anthracite or 'stone' coals	80 to 95	None	a little

In the metropolis the Newcastle coal is chiefly used, and this, we perceive, yields five per cent. ashes and about 57 per cent. carbon. But a considerable part of the carbon is converted into carbonic acid during combustion; if, therefore, we assume that two-thirds of the carbon are thus consumed, and that the remaining third remains behind in the form of cinder, we shall have about 25 per cent. of 'dust' from every ton of coal. On inquiry of those who have had long experience in this matter, I find that a ton of coal may be fairly said on an average to yield about one-fourth its weight in dust; hence the gross amount of 'dust' annually produced in London would be 900,000 tons, or about three tons per house per annum.

It is impossible to obtain any definite statistics on this part of the subject. Not one in every ten of the contractors keeps any account of the amount that comes into the 'yard'. An intelligent and communicative gentleman whom I consulted on this matter, could give me no information on this subject that was in any way satisfactory. I have, however, endeavoured to check the preceding estimate in the following manner. There are in London upwards of 300,000 inhabited houses, and each house furnishes a certain quota of dust to the general stock. I have ascertained that an average-sized house will produce, in the course of a year, about three cart-loads of dust, while each cart holds about 40 bushels (baskets) – what the dustmen call a chaldron. There are, of course, many houses in the metropolis which furnish three and four times this amount of dust, but against these may be placed the vast preponderance of small and poor houses in London and the suburbs, where there is not one quarter of the quantity produced, owing to the small amount of fuel consumed. Estimating, then, the average annual quantity of dust from each house at three loads, or chaldrons, and the houses at 300,000, it follows that the gross quantity collected throughout the metropolis will be about 900,000 chaldrons per annum.

The next part of the subject is – what becomes of this vast quantity of dust – to what use it is applied.

The dust thus collected is used for two purposes, (1) as a manure for land of a peculiar quality; and (2) for making bricks. The fine portion of the house-dust called 'soil', and separated from the 'brieze', or coarser portion, by sifting, is found to be peculiarly fitted for what is called breaking up a marshy heathy soil at its first cultivation, owing not only to the dry nature of the dust, but to its possessing in an eminent degree a highly separating quality, almost, if not quite, equal to sand. In former years the demand for this finer dust was very great, and barges were continually in the river waiting their turn to be loaded with it for some distant part of the country. At that time the contractors were unable to supply the demand, and easily got 1*l.* per chaldron for as much as they could furnish, and then, as I have stated, many ships were in the habit of bringing cargoes of it from the North, and of realizing a good profit on the transaction. Of late years, however – and particularly, I am told, since the repeal of the corn-laws – this branch of the business has dwindled to nothing. The contractors say that the farmers do not cultivate their land now as they used; it will not pay them, and instead, therefore, of bringing fresh land into tillage, and especially such as requires this sort of manure, they are laying down that which they previously had in cultivation, and turning it into pasture grounds. It is principally on this account, say the contractors, that we cannot sell the dust we collect so well or so readily as formerly. There are, however, some cargoes of the dust still taken, particularly to the lowlands in the neighbourhood of Barking, and such other places in the vicinity of the metropolis as are enabled to realize a greater profit, by growing for the London markets. Nevertheless, the contractors are obliged now to dispose of the dust at 2*s.* 6*d.* per chaldron, and sometimes less.

The finer dust is also used to mix with the clay for making bricks, and barge-loads are continually shipped off for this purpose. The fine ashes are added to the clay in the proportion of one-fifth ashes to four-fifths clay, or 60 chaldrons to 240 cubic yards, which is sufficient to make 100,000 bricks (where much sand is mixed with the clay a smaller proportion of ashes may be used). This quantity requires also the addition of about 15 chaldrons, or, if mild, of about 12 chaldrons of 'brieze', to aid the burning. The ashes are made to mix with the clay by collecting it into a sort of reservoir fitted up for the purpose; water in great quantities is let in upon it, and it is then stirred till it resembles a fine thin paste, in which state the dust easily mingles with every part of it. In this condition it is left till the water either soaks into the earth, or goes off by evaporation, when the bricks are moulded in the usual manner, the dust forming a component part of them.

The ashes, or cindered matter, which are thus dispersed throughout the substance of the clay, become in the process of burning, gradually ignited and consumed. But the 'brieze' (from the French *briser*, to break or crush), that is to say, the coarser portion of the coal-ash, is likewise used in the burning of the bricks. The small spaces left among the lowest courses of the bricks in the kiln, or 'clamp', are filled with 'brieze', and a thick layer of the same material is spread on the top of the kilns, when full. Frequently the 'brieze' is mixed with small coals, and after having been burnt the ashes are collected, and then mixed with the clay to form new bricks. The highest price at present given for 'brieze' is 3s. per ton.

The price of the dust used by the brickmakers has likewise been reduced; this the contractors account for by saying that there are fewer brick-fields than formerly near London, as they have been nearly all built over. They assert, that while the amount of dust and cinders has increased proportionately to the increase of the houses, the demand for the article has decreased in a like ratio; and that, moreover, the greater portion of the bricks now used in London for the new buildings come from other quarters. Such dust, however, as the contractors sell to the brick-makers, they in general undertake, for a certain sum, to cart to the brick-fields, though it often happens that the brick-makers' carts coming into town with their loads of bricks to new buildings, call on their return at the dust-yards, and carry thence a load of dust or cinders back, and so save the price of cartage.

But during the operation of sifting the dust, many things are found which are useless for either manure or brick-making, such as oyster shells, old bricks, old boots and shoes, as old tin kettles, old rags and bones, &c. These are used for various purposes.

The bricks, &c., are sold for sinking beneath foundations, where a thick layer of concrete is spread over them. Many old bricks, too, are used in making new roads, especially where the land is low and marshy. The old tin goes to form the japanned fastenings for the corners of trunks, as well as to other persons, who re-manufacture it into a variety of articles. The old shoes are sold to the London shoemakers, who use them as stuffing between the in-sole and the outer one; but by far the greater quantity is sold to the manufacturers of Prussian blue, that substance being formed out of refuse animal matter. The rags and bones are of course disposed of at the usual places – the marine-store shops.

A dust-heap, therefore, may be briefly said to be composed of the following things, which are severally applied to the following uses:

1. 'Soil', or fine dust, sold to brickmakers for making bricks, and to farmers for manure, especially for clover.

2. 'Brieze', or cinders, sold to brickmakers, for burning bricks.

3. Rags, bones, and old metal, sold to marine-store dealers.

4. Old tin and iron vessels, sold for 'clamps' to trunks, &c., and for making copperas.

5. Old bricks and oyster shells, sold to builders, for sinking foundations, and forming roads.

6. Old boots and shoes, sold to Prussian-blue manufacturers.

7. Money and jewellery, kept, or sold to Jews.

The dust-yards, or places where the dust is collected and sifted, are generally situated in the suburbs, and they may be found all round London, sometimes occupying open spaces adjoining back streets and lanes, and surrounded by the low mean houses of the poor; frequently, however, they cover a large extent of ground in the fields, and there the dust is piled up to a great height in a conical heap, and having much the appearance of a volcanic mountain. The reason why the dust-heaps are confined principally to the suburbs is, that more space is to be found in the out-skirts than in a thickly-peopled and central locality. Moreover, the fear of indictments for nuisance has had considerable influence in the matter, for it was not unusual for the yards in former times, to be located within the boundaries of the city. They are now, however, scattered round London, and always placed as near as possible to the river, or to some canal communicating therewith. In St George's, Shadwell, Ratcliffe, Limehouse, Poplar, and Blackwell, on the north side of the Thames, and in Redriffe, Bermondsey, and Rotherhithe, on the south, they are to be found near the Thames. The object of this is, that by far the greater quantity of the soil or ashes is conveyed in sailing-barges, holding from 70 to 100 tons each, to Feversham, Sittingbourne, and other places in Kent, which are the great brick-making manufactories for London. These barges come up invariably loaded with bricks, and take home in return a cargo of soil. Other dust-yards are situated contiguous to the Regent's and the Surrey canal; and for the same reason as above stated – for the convenience of water carriage. Moreover, adjoining the Limehouse cut, which is a branch of the Lea River, other dust-yards may be found; and again travelling to the opposite end of the metropolis, we discover them not only at Paddington on the banks of the canal, but at Maiden-lane in a similar position. Some time since there was an immense dust-heap in the neighbourhood of Gray's-inn-lane, which sold for 20,000*l*; but that was in the days when 15*s*. and 1*l*. per chaldron could easily be procured for the dust. According to the present rate, not a tithe of that amount could have been realized upon it.

A visit to any of the large metropolitan dust-yards is far from uninteresting. Near the centre of the yard rises the highest heap, composed of what is called the 'soil', or finer portion of the dust used for manure. Around this heap are numerous lesser heaps, consisting of the mixed dust and rubbish carted in and shot down previous to sifting. Among these heaps are many women and old men with sieves made of iron, all busily engaged in separating the 'brieze' from the 'soil'. There is likewise another large heap in some other part of the yard, composed of the cinders or 'brieze' waiting to be shipped off to the brickfields. The whole yard seems alive, some sifting and others shovelling the sifted soil on to the heap, while every now and then the dust-carts return to discharge their loads, and proceed again on their rounds for a fresh supply. Cocks and hens keep up a continual scratching and cackling among the heaps, and numerous pigs seem to find great delight in rooting incessantly about after the garbage and offal collected from the houses and markets.

In a dust-yard lately visited the sifters formed a curious sight; they were almost up to their middle in dust, ranged in a semi-circle in front of that part of the heap which was being 'worked'; each had before her a small mound of soil which had fallen through her sieve and formed a sort of embankment, behind which she stood. The appearance of the entire group at their work was most peculiar. Their coarse dirty cotton gowns were tucked up behind them, their arms were bared above their elbows, their black bonnets crushed and battered like those of fish-women; over their gowns they wore a strong leathern apron, extending from their necks to the extremities of their petticoats, while over this, again, was another leathern apron, shorter, thickly padded, and fastened by a stout string or strap round the waist. In the process of their work they pushed the sieve from them and drew it back again with apparent violence, striking it against the outer leathern apron with such force that it produced each time a hollow sound, like a blow on the tenor drum. All the women present were middle aged, with the exception of one who was very old – 68 years of age she told me – and had been at the business from a girl. She was the daughter of a dustman, the wife, or woman of a dustman, and the mother of several young dustmen – sons and grandsons – all at work at the dust-yards at the east end of the metropolis.

We now come to speak of the labourers engaged in collecting, sifting, or shipping off the dust of the metropolis.

The dustmen, scavengers, and nightmen are, to a certain extent, the

VIEW OF A DUST-YARD.

same people. The contractors generally agree with the various parishes to remove both the dust from the houses and the mud from the streets; the men in their employ are indiscriminately engaged in these two diverse occupations, collecting the dust to-day, and often cleansing the streets on the morrow, and are designated either dustmen or scavengers, according to their particular avocation at the moment. The case is somewhat different, however, with respect to the nightmen. There is no such thing as a contract with the parish for removing the nightsoil. This is done by private agreement with the landlord of the premises whence the soil has to be removed. When a cesspool requires emptying, the occupying tenant communicates with the landlord, who makes an arrangement with a dust-contractor or sweep-nightman for this purpose. This operation is totally distinct from the regular or daily labour of the dust-contractor's men, who receive extra pay for it; sometimes one set go out at night and sometimes another, according either to the selection of the master or the inclination of the men. There are, however, some dustmen who have never been at work as nightmen, and could not be induced to do so, from an invincible antipathy to the employment; still, such instances are few, for the men generally go whenever they can, and occasionally engage in nightwork for employers unconnected with their masters. It is calculated that there are some hundreds of men employed nightly in the removal of the nightsoil of the metropolis during the summer and autumn, and as these men have often to work at dust-collecting or cleansing the streets on the following day, it is evident that the same persons cannot be thus employed every night; accordingly the ordinary practice is for the dustmen to 'take it in turns', thus allowing each set to be employed every third night, and to have two nights' rest in the interim.

The men, therefore, who collect the dust on one day may be cleaning the streets on the next, especially during wet weather, and engaged at night, perhaps, twice during the week, in removing nightsoil; so that it is difficult to arrive at any precise notion as to the number of persons engaged in any one of these branches *per se*.

But these labourers not only work indiscriminately at the collection of dust, the cleansing of the streets, or the removal of nightsoil, but they are employed almost as indiscriminately at the various branches of the dust business; with this qualification, however, that few men apply themselves continuously to any one branch of the business. The labourers employed in a dust-yard may be divided into two classes: those paid by the contractor; and those paid by the foreman or forewoman of the dust-heap, commonly called hill-man or hill-woman. They are as follows:

I. LABOURERS PAID BY THE CONTRACTORS, OR,

1. *Yard foreman*, or superintendent. This duty is often performed by the master, especially in small contracts.

2. *Gangers* or *dust-collectors*. These are called 'fillers' and 'carriers', from the practice of one of the men who go out with the cart filling the basket, and the other carrying it on his shoulder to the vehicle.

3. *Loaders* of carts in the dust-yard for shipment.

4. *Carriers* of cinders to the cinder-heap, or bricks to the brick-heap.

5. *Foreman* or *forewoman* of the heap.

II. LABOURERS PAID BY THE HILL-MAN OR HILL-WOMAN

1. *Sifters*, who are generally women, and mostly the wives or concubines of the dustmen, but sometimes the wives of badly-paid labourers.

2. *Fillers-in*, or shovellers of dust into the sieves of the sifters (one man being allowed to every two or three women).

3. *Carriers off* of bones, rags, metal, and other perquisites to the various heaps; these are mostly children of the dustmen.

A medium-sized dust-yard will employ about twelve collectors, three fillers in, six sifters, and one foreman or forewoman; while a large yard will afford work to about 150 people.

There are four different modes of payment prevalent among the several labourers employed at the metropolitan dust-yards: (1) by the day; (2) by the piece or load; (3) by the lump; (4) by perquisites.

1st. *The foreman of the yard*, where the master does not perform this duty himself, is generally one of the regular dustmen picked out by the master, for this purpose. He is paid the sum of 2s. 6d. per day, or 15s. per week. In large yards there are sometimes two and even three yard-foremen at the same rate of wages. Their duty is merely to superintend the work. They do not labour themselves, and their exemption in this respect is considered, and indeed looked on by themselves, as a sort of premium for good services.

2nd. *The gangers or collectors* are generally paid 8d. per load for every load they bring into the yard. This is, of course, piece work, for the more hours the men work the more loads will they be enabled to bring, and the more pay will they receive. There are some yards where the carters get only 6d. per load, as, for instance, at Paddington. The Paddington men, however, are not considered inferior workmen to the rest of their fellows, but merely to be worse paid. In 1826, or 25 years ago, the carters had 1s. 6d. per load; but at that time the contractors were able to get 1l per chaldron for the soil and 'brieze' or cinders; then it began to fall in value, and according to the decrease in the price of these commodities, so have the wages of the dust-collectors been reduced. It will be at once seen that the reduction in the wages of the dustmen bears no proportion to the reduction in the price of soil and cinders, but it must be borne in mind that whereas the contractors formerly paid large sums for liberty to collect the dust, they now are paid large sums to remove it. This in some measure helps to account for the apparent disproportion, and tends, perhaps, to equalize the matter. The gangers, therefore, have 4d. each, per load when best paid. They consider from four to six loads a good day's work, for where the contract is large, extending over several parishes, they often have to travel a long way for a load. It thus happens that while the men employed by the Whitechapel contractor can, when doing their utmost, manage to bring only four loads a day to the yard, which is situated in a place called the 'ruins' in Lower Shadwell, the men employed by the Shadwell contractor can easily get eight or nine loads in a day. Five loads are about an average day's work, and this gives them 1s. 8½d. per day each, or 10s. per week. In addition to this, the men have their perquisites 'in aid of wages'. The collectors are in the habit of getting beer or money in lieu thereof, at nearly all the houses from which they remove the dust, the public being thus in a manner compelled to make up the rate of wages, which should be paid by the employer, so that what is given to benefit the men really goes to the master, who invariably reduces the wages to the precise amount of the perquisites obtained. This is the main evil of the 'perquisite system of payment' (a system of which the mode of paying waiters may be taken as the special type). As an instance of the injurious effects of this mode of payment in connection with the London dustmen, the collectors are forced, as it were, to extort from the public that portion of their fair earnings of which their master deprives them; hence, how can we wonder that they make it a rule when they receive neither beer nor money from a house to make as great a mess as possible the next time they come, scattering the dust and cinders about in such as manner, that, sooner than have any trouble with them, people mostly give them what they look for? One of the most intelligent men with whom I have spoken, gave me the following account of his perquisites for the last week, viz.: Monday, 5½d.; Tuesday, 6d.; Wednesday, 4½d.; Thursday, 7d.; Friday, 5½d.; and Saturday, 5d. This he received in money, and was independent of beer. He had on the same week drawn rather more than five loads each day, to the yard, which made his gross earnings for the week, wages and perquisites together, to be 14s. 0½d. which he considers to be a fair average of his weekly earnings as connected with dust.

3rd. *The loaders of the carts* for shipment are the same persons as those who collect the dust, but thus employed for the time being. The pay for this work is by the 'piece' also, 2*d.* per chaldron between four persons being the usual rate, or ½*d.* per man. The men so engaged have no perquisites. The barges into which they shoot the soil or 'brieze', as the case may be, hold from 50 to 70 chaldrons, and they consider the loading of one of these barges a good day's work. The average cargo is about 60 chaldrons, which gives them 2*s.* 6*d.* per day, or somewhat more than their average earnings when collecting.

4th. *The carriers of cinders* to the cinder heap. I have mentioned that, ranged round the sifters in the dust-yard, are a number of baskets, into which are put the various things found among the dust, some of these being the property of the master, and others the perquisites of the hill man or woman, as the case may be. The cinders and old bricks are the property of the master, and to remove them to their proper heaps boys are employed by him at 1*s.* per day. These boys are almost universally the children of dustmen and sifters at work in the yard, and thus not only help to increase the earnings of the family, but qualify themselves to become the dustmen of a future day.

5th. *The hill-man or hill-woman.* The hill-man enters into an agreement with the contractor to sift *all* the dust in the yard throughout the year at so much per load and perquisites. The usual sum per load is 6*d.*, nor have I been able to ascertain that any of these people undertake to do it at a less price. Such is the amount paid by the contractor for Whitechapel. The perquisites of the hill-man or hill-woman, are rags, bones, pieces of old metal, old tin or iron vessels, old boots and shoes, and one-half of the money, jewellery, or other valuables that may be found by the sifters.

The hill-man or hill-woman employs the following persons, and pays them at the following rates:

1st. *The sifters* are paid 1*s.* per day when employed, but the employment is not constant. The work cannot be pursued in wet weather, and the services of the sifters are required only when a large heap has accumulated, as they can sift much faster than the dust can be collected. The employment is therefore precarious; the payment has not, for the last 30 years at least, been more than 1*s.* per day, but the perquisites were greater. They formerly were allowed one-half of whatever was found; of late years, however, the hill-man has gradually reduced the perquisites 'first one thing and then another', until the only one they have now remaining is half of whatever money or other valuable article may be found in the process of sifting. These valuables the sifters often pocket, if able to do so unperceived, but if discovered in the attempt, they are immediately discharged.

2nd. *The fillers-in*, or shovellers of dust into the sieves of sifters, are in general any poor fellows who may be straggling about in search of employment. They are sometimes, however, the grown-up boys of dust-men, not yet permanently engaged by the contractor. These are paid 2s. per day for their labour, but they are considered more as casualty men, though it often happens, if 'hands' are wanted, that they are regularly engaged by the contractors, and become regular dustmen for the re-mainder of their lives.

3rd. The little fellows, the children of the dustmen, who follow their mothers to the yard, and help them to pick rags, bones, &c., out of the sieve and put them into the baskets, as soon as they are able to carry a basket between two of them to the separate heaps, are paid 3d. or 4d. per day for this work by the hill-man.

The wages of the dustmen have been increased within the last seven years from 6d. per load to 8d. among the large contractors – the 'small masters', however, still continue to pay 6d. per load. This increase in the rate of remuneration was owing to the men complaining to the commissioners that they were not able to live upon what they earned at 6d.; an enquiry was made into the truth of the men's assertion, and the result was that the commissioners decided upon letting the contracts to such parties only as would undertake to pay a fair price to their workmen. The contractors, accordingly, increased the remuneration of the labourers; since then the principal masters have paid 8d. per load to the collectors. It is right I should add, that I could not hear – though I made special enquiries on the subject – that the wages had been in any one instance reduced since Free-trade has come into operation.

The usual hours of labour vary according to the mode of payment. The 'collectors', or men out with the cart, being paid by the load, work as long as the light lasts; the 'fillers-in' and sifters, on the other hand, being paid by the day, work the ordinary hours, viz., from six to six, with the regular intervals for meals.

The summer is the worst time for all hands, for then the dust decreases in quantity; the collectors, however, make up for the 'slackness' at this period by nightwork, and, being paid by the 'piece' of load at the dust business, are not discharged when their employment is less brisk.

It has been shown that the dustmen who perambulate the streets usually collect five loads in a day; this, at 8*d.* per load, leaves them about 1*s.* 8*d.* each, and so makes their weekly earnings amount to about 10*s.* per week. Moreover, there are the 'perquisites' from the houses whence they remove the dust; and further, the dust-collectors are frequently employed at the night-work, which is always a distinct matter from the dust-collecting, &c., and paid for independent of their regular weekly wages, so that, from all I can gather, the average wages of the men appear to be rather more than 15*s.* Some admitted to me, that in busy times they often earned 25*s.* a week.

Then, again, dustwork, as with the weaving of silk, is a kind of family work. The husband, wife, and children (unfortunately) all work at it. The consequence is, that the earnings of the whole have to be added together in order to arrive at a notion of the aggregate gains.

The following may therefore be taken as a fair average of the earnings of a dustman and his family *when in full employment.* The elder boys when able to earn 1*s.* a day set up for themselves, and do not allow their wages to go into the common purse.

	£	s	d	£	s	d
Man, 5 loads per day, or 30 loads per week, at 4*d.* per load	0	10	0			
Perquisites, or beer money	0	2	9½			
Night-work for 2 nights a week	0	5	0			
				0	17	9½
Woman, or sifter, per week, at 1*s.* per day	0	6	0			
Perquisites, say 3*d.* a day	0	1	6			
				0	7	6
Child, 3*d.* per day, carrying rags, bones, &c.				0	1	6
Total				1	6	9½

These are the earnings, it should be borne in mind, of a family in full employment. Perhaps it may be fairly said that the earnings of the single men are, on an average, 15*s.* a week, and 1*l.* for the family men all the year round.

Now, when we remember that the wages of many agricultural labourers are but 8*s.* a week, and the earnings of many needlewomen not

6*d*. a day, it must be confessed that the remuneration of the dustmen, and even of the dustwomen, is *comparatively* high. This certainly is not due to what Adam Smith, in his chapter on the Difference of Wages, terms the 'disagreeableness of the employment'. 'The wages of labour,' he says, 'vary with the ease or hardship, the cleanliness or dirtiness, the honourableness or dishonourableness, of the employment.' It will be seen – when we come to treat of the nightmen – that the most offensive, and perhaps the least honourable, of all trades, is far from ranking among the best paid, as it should, if the above principle held good. That the disagreeableness of the occupation may in a measure tend to decrease the competition among the labourers, there cannot be the least doubt, but that it will consequently induce, as political economy would have us believe, a larger amount of wages to accrue to each of the labourers, is certainly another of the many assertions of that science which must be pronounced 'not proven'. For the dustmen are paid, if anything, less, and certainly not more, than the usual rate of payment to the London labourers; and if the earnings rank high, as times go, it is because all the members of the family, from the very earliest age, are able to work at the business, and so add to the general gains.

The dustmen are, generally speaking, an hereditary race; when children they are reared in the dust-yard, and are habituated to the work gradually as they grow up, after which, almost as a natural consequence, they follow the business for the remainder of their lives. These may be said to be born-and-bred dustmen. The numbers of the regular men are, however, from time to time recruited from the ranks of the many ill-paid labourers with which London abounds. When hands are wanted for any special occasion an employer has only to go to any of the dock-gates, to find at all times hundreds of starving wretches anxiously watching for the chance of getting something to do, even at the rate of 4*d*. per hour. As the operation of emptying a dust-bin requires only the ability to handle a shovel, which every labouring man can manage, all work-men, however unskilled, can at once engage in the occupation; and it often happens that the men thus casually employed remain at the calling for the remainder of their lives. There are no houses of call whence the men are taken on when wanting work. There are certainly public-houses, which are denominated houses of call, in the neighbourhood of every dust-yard, but these are merely the drinking shops of the men, whither they resort of an evening after the labour of the day is accomplished, and whence they are furnished in the course of the afternoon with beer; but such houses cannot be said to constitute the dustman's 'labour-market', as in the tailoring and other trades, they being never resorted to as hiring-places, but rather used by the men only when hired. If a master have not enough 'hands' he usually inquires among his men, who mostly know some who – owing, perhaps, to the failure of their previous master in getting his usual contract – are only casually employed at other places. Such men are immediately engaged in preference to others; but if these cannot be found, the contractors at once have recourse to the system already stated.

The manner in which the dust is collected is very simple. The 'filler' and the 'carrier' perambulate the streets with a heavily-built high box cart, which is mostly coated with a thick crust of filth, and drawn by a clumsy-looking horse. These men used, before the passing of the late Street Act, to ring a dull-sounding bell so as to give notice to housekeepers of their approach, but now they merely cry, in a hoarse unmusical voice, 'Dust oy-eh!' Two men accompany the cart, which is furnished with a short ladder and two shovels and baskets. These baskets one of the men fills from the dust-bin, and then helps them alternately, as fast as they are filled, upon the shoulder of the other man, who carries them one by one to the cart, which is placed immediately alongside the pavement in front of the house where they are at work. The carrier mounts up the side of the cart by means of the ladder, discharges into it the contents of the basket on his shoulder, and then returns below for the other basket which his mate has filled for him in the interim. This process is pursued till all is cleared away, and repeated at different houses till the cart is fully loaded; then the men make the best of their way to the dust-yard, where they shoot the contents of the cart on to the heap, and again proceed on their regular rounds.

The dustmen, in their appearance, very much resemble the waggoners of the coal-merchants. They generally wear knee-breeches, with ancle boots or gaiters, short dirty smockfrocks or coarse gray jackets, and fantail hats. In one particular, however, they are at first sight distinguishable from the coal-merchants' men, for the latter are invariably black from coal dust, while the dustmen, on the contrary, are gray with ashes.

In their personal appearance the dustmen are mostly tall stalwart fellows; there is nothing sickly-looking about them, and yet a considerable part of their time is passed in the yards and in the midst of effluvia most offensive, and, if we believe 'zymotic theorists', as unhealthy to those unaccustomed to them; nevertheless, the children, who may be said to be reared in the yard and to have inhaled the stench of the dust-heap with their first breath, are healthy and strong. It is said, moreover, that during the plague in London the dustmen were the persons who carted away the

THE LONDON DUSTMAN.

"Dust Hoi! Dust Hoi!"

dead, and it remains a tradition among the class to the present day, that not one of them died of the plague, even during its greatest ravages. In Paris, too, it is well known, that, during the cholera of 1849, the quarter of Belleville, where the night-soil and refuse of the city is deposited, escaped the freest from the pestilence; and in London the dustmen boast that, during both the recent visitations of the cholera, they were altogether exempt from the disease. 'Look at that fellow, sir!' said one of the dust-contractors to me, pointing to his son, who was a stout red-cheeked young man of about twenty. 'Do you see anything ailing about him? Well, he has been in the yard since he was born. There stands my house just at the gate, so you see he hadn't far to travel, and when quite a child he used to play and root away here among the dust all his time. I don't think he ever had a day's illness in his life. The people about the yard are all used to the smell and don't complain about it. It's all stuff and nonsense, all this talk about dust-yards being unhealthy. I've never done anything else all my days and I don't think I look very ill. I shouldn't wonder now but what I'd be set down as being fresh from the sea-side by those very fellows that write all this trash about a matter that they don't know just *that* about'; and he snapped his fingers contemptuously in the air, and, thrusting both hands into his breeches pockets, strutted about, apparently satisfied that he had the best of the argument. He was, in fact, a stout, jolly, red-faced man. Indeed, the dustmen, as a class, appear to be healthy, strong men, and extraordinary instances of longevity are common among them. I heard of one dustman who lived to be 115 years; another, named Wood, died at 100; and the well-known Richard Tyrell died only a short time back at the advanced age of 97. The misfortune is, that we have no large series of facts on this subject, so that the longevity and health of the dustmen might be compared with those of other classes.

In almost all their habits the Dustmen are similar to the Costermongers, with the exception that they seem to want their cunning and natural quickness, and that they have little or no predilection for gaming. Coster-mongers, however, are essentially traders, and all trade is a species of gambling – the risking of a certain sum of money to obtain more; hence spring, perhaps, the gambling propensities of low traders, such as costers, and Jew clothes-men; and hence, too, that natural sharpness which characterizes the same classes. The dustmen, on the contrary, have regular employment and something like regular wages, and therefore rest content with what they can earn in their usual way of business.

Very few of them understand cards, and I could not learn that they ever play at 'pitch and toss'. I remarked, however, a number of parallel lines such as are used for playing 'shove halfpenny', on a deal table in the tap-room frequented by them. The great amusement of their evenings seems to be, to smoke as many pipes of tobacco and drink as many pots of beer as possible.

I believe it will be found that all persons in the habit of driving horses, such as cabmen, 'busmen, stage-coach drivers, &c., are peculiarly partial to intoxicating drinks. The cause of this I leave others to determine, merely observing that there would seem to be two reasons for it: the first is, their frequent stopping at public-houses to water or change their horses, so that the idea of drinking is repeatedly suggested to their minds even if the practice be not *expected* of them; while the second reason is, that being out continually in the wet, they resort to stimulating liquors as a preventive to 'colds' until at length a habit of drinking is formed. Moreover, from the mere fact of passing continually through the air, they are enabled to drink a greater quantity with comparative impunity. Be the cause, however, what it may, the dustmen spend a large proportion of their earnings in drink. There is always some public-house in the neighbourhood of the dust-yard, where they obtain credit from one week to another, and here they may be found every night from the moment their work is done, drinking, and smoking their long pipes – their principal amusement consisting in 'chaffing' each other. This 'chaffing' consists of a species of scurrilous jokes supposed to be given and taken in good part, and the noise and uproar occasioned thereby increases as the night advances, and as the men get heated with liquor. Sometimes the joking ends in a general quarrel; the next morning, however, they are all as good friends as ever, and mutually agree in laying the blame on the 'cussed drink'.

One-half, at least, of the dustmen's earnings, is, I am assured, expended in drink, both man and woman assisting in squandering their money in this way. They usually live in rooms for which they pay from 1s 6d. to 2s. per week rent, three or four dust-men and their wives frequently lodging in the same house. These rooms are cheerless-looking, and almost unfurnished – and are always situate in some low street or lane not far from the dust-yard. The men have rarely any clothes but those in which they work. For their breakfast the dustmen on their rounds mostly go to some cheap coffee-house, where they get a pint or half-pint of coffee, taking their bread with them as a matter of economy. Their midday meal is taken in the public-house, and is almost always bread and cheese and beer, or else a saveloy or a piece of fat pork or bacon, and at night they mostly 'wind up' by deep potations at their favourite house of call.

There are many dustmen now advanced in years born and reared at the

East-end of London, who have never in the whole course of their lives been as far west as Temple-bar, who know nothing whatever of the affairs of the country, and who have never attended a place of worship. As an instance of the extreme ignorance of these people, I may mention that I was furnished by one of the contractors with the address of a dustman whom his master considered to be one of the most intelligent men in his employ. Being desirous of hearing his statement from his own lips I sent for the man, and after some conversation with him was proceeding to note down what he said, when the moment I opened my note-book and took the pencil in my hand, he started up, exclaiming, – 'No, no! I'll have none of that there work – I'm not such a b— fool as you takes me to be – I doesn't understand it, I tells you, and I'll not have it, now that's plain'; – and so saying he ran out of the room, and descended the entire flight of stairs in two jumps. I followed him to explain, but unfortunately the pencil was still in one hand and the book in the other, and immediately I made my appearance at the door he took to his heels, again with three others who seemed to be waiting for him there. One of the most difficult points in my labours is to make such men as these comprehend the object or use of my investigations.

Among 20 men whom I met in one yard, there were only five who could read, and only two out of that five could write, even imperfectly. These two are looked up to by their companions as prodigies of learning and are listened to as oracles, on all occasions, being believed to understand every subject thoroughly. It need hardly be added, however, that their acquirements are of the most meagre character.

The dustmen are very partial to a song, and always prefer one of the doggerel street ballads, with what they call a 'jolly chorus' in which, during their festivities, they all join with stentorian voices. At the conclusion there is usually a loud stamping of feet and rattling of quart pots on the table, expressive of their approbation.

The dustmen never frequent the twopenny hops, but sometimes make up a party for the 'theaytre'. They generally go in a body with their wives, if married, and their 'gals', if single. They are always to be found in the gallery, and greatly enjoy the melodramas performed at the second-class minor theatres, especially if there be plenty of murdering scenes in them. The Garrick, previous to its being burnt, was a favourite resort of the East-end dustmen. Since that period they have patronized the Pavilion and the City of London.

The politics of the dustmen are on a par with their literary attainment – they cannot be said to have any. I cannot say that they are Chartists, for they have no very clear knowledge of what 'the charter' requires. They certainly have a confused notion that it is something against the Government, and that the enactment of it would make them all right; but as to the nature of the benefits which it would confer upon them, or in what manner it would be likely to operate upon their interest, they have not, as a body, the slightest idea. They have a deep-rooted antipathy to the police, the magistrates, and all connected with the administration of justice, looking upon them as their natural enemies. They associate with none but themselves; and in the public-houses where they resort there is a room set apart for the special use of the 'dusties', as they are called, where no others are allowed to intrude, except introduced by one of themselves, or at the special desire of the majority of the party, and on such occasions the stranger is treated with great respect and consideration.

As to the morals of these people, it may easily be supposed that they are not of an over-strict character. One of the contractors said to me, 'I'd just trust one of them as far as I could fling a bull by the tail; *but then,*' he added, with a callousness that proved the laxity of discipline among the men was due more to his neglect of his duty to them than from any special perversity on their parts, '*that's none of my business; they do my work, and that's all I want with them, and all I care about.* You see they're not like other people, they're reared to it. Their fathers before them were dustmen, and when lads they go into the yard as sifters, and when they grow up they take to the shovel, and go out with the carts. They learn all they know in the dust-yards, and you may judge from that what their learning is likely to be. If they find anything among the dust you may be sure that neither you nor I will ever hear anything about it; ignorant as they are, they know a little too much for that. They know, as well as here and there one, where the dolly-shop is; *but, as I said before, that's none of my business. Let every one look out for themselves, as I do, and then they need not care for any one.*' [With such masters professing such principles – though it should be stated that the sentiments expressed on this occasion are but similar to what I hear from the lower class of traders every day – how can it be expected that these poor fellows can be above the level of the mere beasts of burden that they use.] 'As to their women,' continued the master, 'I don't trouble my head about such things. I believe the dustmen are as good to them as other men, and I'm sure their wives would be as good as other women, if they only had the chance of the best. But you see they're all such fellows for drink that they spend most of their money that way, and then starve the poor women, and knock them about at a shocking rate, so that they have the life of dogs, or worse. I don't wonder at anything they do. Yes, they're all married, as far as I know; that is, they live together as man and wife, though they're not very particular, certainly, about the ceremony. The fact is, a regular dustman don't understand much about such matters, and, I believe, don't care much, either.'

From all I could learn on this subject, it would appear that, for one dustman that is married, 20 live with women, but remain constant to them; indeed, both men and women abide faithfully by each other, and for this reason – the woman earns nearly half as much as the man. If the men and women were careful and prudent, they might, I am assured, live well and comfortable; but by far the greater portion of the earnings of both go to the publican, for I am informed, on competent authority, that a dustman will not think of sitting down for a spree without his woman. The children, as soon as they are able to go into the yard, help their mothers in picking out the rags, bones, &c., from the sieve, and in putting them in the basket. They are never sent to school, and as soon as they are sufficiently strong are mostly employed in some capacity or other by the contractor, and in due time become dustmen themselves. Some of the children, in the neighbourhood of the river, are mud-larks and others are bone-grubbers and rag-gatherers, on a small scale; neglected and thrown on their own resources at an early age, without any but the most depraved to guide them, it is no wonder to find that many of them turn thieves. To this state of the case there are, however, some few exceptions.

Some of the dustmen are prudent well-behaved men and have decent homes; many of this class have been agricultural labourers, who by distress, or from some other cause, have found their way to London. This was the case with one whom I talked with: he had been a labourer in Essex, employed by a farmer named Izzod, whom he spoke of as being a kind good man. Mr Izzod had a large farm on the Earl of Mornington's estate, and after he had sunk his capital in the improvement of the land, and was about to reap the fruits of his labour and his money, the farmer was ejected at a moment's notice, beggared and broken-hearted. This occurred near Roydon, in Essex. The labourer, finding it difficult to obtain work in the country, came to London, and, discovering a cousin of his engaged in a dust-yard, got employed through him at the same place, where he remains to the present day. This man was well clothed, he had good strong lace boots, gray worsted stockings, a stout pair of corduroy breeches, a short smockfrock and fantail. He has kept himself aloof, I am told, from the drunkenness and dissipation of the dustmen. He says that many of the new hands that get to dustwork are mechanics or people who have been 'better off', and that these get thinking about what they have been, till to drown their care they take to drinking, and often become, in the course of a year or so, worse than the 'old hands' who have been reared to the business and have 'nothing at all to think about'.

Among the dustmen there is no 'Society' nor 'Benefit Club', specially devoted to the class – no provident institution whence they can obtain 'relief' in the event of sickness or accident. The consequence is that, when ill or injured, they are obliged to obtain letters of admission to some of the hospitals, and there remain till cured. In cases of total incapacity for labour, their invariable refuge is the workhouse; indeed they look forward (whenever they foresee at all) to this asylum as their resting-place in old age, with the greatest equanimity, and talk of it as 'the house' par excellence, or as 'the big house', 'the great house', or 'the old house'. There are, however, scattered about in every part of London numerous benefit clubs made up of working-men of every description, such as Old Friends, Odd Fellows, Foresters, and Birmingham societies, and with some one or other of these the better class of dustmen are connected. The general rule, however, is, that the men engaged in this trade belong to no benefit club whatever, and that in the season of their adversity they are utterly unprovided for, and consequently become burdens to the parishes wherein they happen to reside.

I visited a large dust-yard at the east end of London, for the purpose of getting a statement from one of the men. My informant was, at the time of my visit, shovelling the sifted soil from one of the lesser heaps, and, by a great effort of strength and activity, pitching each shovel-full to the top of a lofty mound, somewhat resembling a pyramid. Opposite to him stood a little woman, stoutly made, and with her arms bare above the elbow; she was his partner in the work, and was pitching shovel-full for shovelfull with him to the summit of the heap. She wore an old soiled cotton gown, open in front, and tucked up behind in the fashion of the last century. She had clouts of old rags tied round her ancles to prevent the dust from getting into her shoes, a sort of coarse towel fastened in front for an apron, and a red handkerchief bound tightly round her head. In this trim she worked away, and not only kept pace with the man, but often threw two shovels for his one, although he was a tall, powerful fellow. She smiled when she saw me noticing her, and seemed to continue her work with greater assiduity. I learned that she was deaf, and spoke so indistinctly that no stranger could understand her. She had also a defect in her sight, which latter circumstance had compelled her to abandon the sifting, as she could not well distinguish the various articles found in the dust-heap. The poor creature had therefore taken to the shovel, and now works with it every day, doing the labour of the strongest men.

From the man above referred to I obtained the following statement: – 'Father vos a dustie; – vos at it all his life, and grandfather afore him for I can't tell how long. Father vos allus a rum 'un; – sich a beggar for lush. Vhy I'm blowed if he vouldn't lush as much as half-a-dozen on 'em can lush now; somehow the dusties hasn't got the stuff in 'em as they used to have. A few year ago the fellers 'u'd think nothink o' lushin avay for five or six days without niver going anigh their home. I niver vos at a school in all my life; I don't know what it's good for. It may be wery well for the likes o' you, but I doesn't know it 'u'd do a dustie any good. You see, ven I'm not out with the cart, I digs here all day; and p'raps I'm up all night, and digs avay agen the next day. Vot does I care for reading, or anythink of that there kind, ven I gets home arter my vork? I tell you vot I likes, though! vhy, I jist likes two or three pipes o' baccer, and a pot or two of good heavy and a song, and then I tumbles in with my Sall, and I'm as happy as here and there von. That there Sall of mine's a stunner – a riglar stunner. There ain't never a voman can sift a heap quickerer nor my Sall. Sometimes she yarns as much as I does; the only thing is, she's sitch a beggar for lush, that there Sall of mine, and then she kicks up sitch jolly rows, you niver see the like in your life. That there's the only fault, as I know on, in Sall; but, barring that, she's a hout-and-houter, and worth a half-a-dozen of t' other sifters – pick 'em out vare you likes. No, we ain't married 'zactly, though it's all one for all that. I sticks to Sall, and Sall sticks to I, and there's an end on 't: – vot is it to any von? I rec'lects a-picking the rags and things out of mother's sieve, when I were a young 'un, and a putting 'em all in the heap jist as it might be there. I vos allus in a dust-yard. I don't think I could do no how in no other place. You see I vouldn't be 'appy like; I only knows how to vork at the dust 'cause I'm used to it, and so vos father afore me, and I'll stick to it as long as I can. I yarns about half-a-bull [2s. 6d.] a day, take one day with another. Sall sometimes yarns as much, and ven I goes out at night I yarns a bob or two more, and so I gits along pretty tidy; sometimes yarnin more and sometimes yarnin less. I niver vos sick as I knows on; I've been queerish of a morning a good many times, but I doesn't call that sickness; it's only the lush and nothink more. The smells nothink at all, ven you gits used to it. Lor' bless you! You'd think nothink on it in a veek's time, – no, no more nor I do. There's twenty on us vorks here – riglar. I don't think there's von on 'em 'cept Scratchey Jack can read, but he can do it stunning; he's out vith the cart now, but he's the chap as can patter to you as long as he likes.'

Concerning the capital and income of the London dust business, the following estimate may be given as to the amount of property invested in and accruing to the trade.

It has been computed that there are 90 contractors, large and small; of these upwards of two-thirds, or about 35, may be said to be in a considerable way of business, possessing many carts and horses, as well as employing a large body of people; some yards have as many as 150 hands connected with them. The remaining 55 masters are composed of 'small men', some of whom are known as 'running dustmen', that is to say, persons who collect the dust without any sanction from the parish; but the number belonging to this class has considerably diminished since the great deterioration in the price of 'brieze'. Assuming, then, that the great and little master dustmen employ on an average between six and seven carts each, we have the following statement as to the capital of the London dust trade:

600	Carts, at 20*l*. each	£12,000
600	Horses, at 25*l*. each	15,000
600	Sets of harness, at 2*l*. per set	1,200
600	Ladders, at 5*s*. each	150
1,200	Baskets, at 2*s*. each	120
1,200	Shovels, at 2*s*. each	120
	Being a total capital of	£28,590

If, therefore, we assert that the capital of this trade is between 25,000*l*. and 30,000*l*. in value, we shall not be far wrong either way.

Of the annual income of the same trade, it is almost impossible to arrive at any positive results; but, in the absence of all authentic information on the subject, we may make the subjoined conjecture:

Sum paid to contractors for the removal of dust from the 176 metropolitan parishes, at 200*l*. each parish	£35,200
Sum obtained for 900,000 loads of dust, at 2*s*. 6*d*. per load	112,500
	£147,700

Thus it would appear that the total income of the dust trade may be taken at between 145,000*l.* and 150,000*l.* per annum.

Against this we have to set the yearly out-goings of the business, which may be roughly estimated as follows:

Wages of 1,800 labourers, at 10*s.* a week each (including sifters and carriers)	£46,800
Keep of 600 horses, at 10*s.* a week each	15,600
Wear and tear of stock in trade	4,000
Rent for 90 yards, at 100*l.* a year each (large and small)	9,000
	£75,400

The above estimates give us the following aggregate results:

Total yearly incomings of the London dust trade	£147,700
Total yearly out-goings	75,400
Total yearly profit	£72,300

Hence it would appear that the profits of the dust-contractors are very nearly at the rate of 100*l.* per cent. on their expenditure. I do not think I have over estimated the incomings, or under estimated the out-goings; at least I have striven to avoid doing so, in order that no injustice might be done to the members of the trade.

This aggregate profit, when divided among the 90 contractors, will make the clear gains of each master dustman amount to about 800*l.* per annum: of course some derive considerably more than this amount, and some considerably less.

OF THE GENERAL CHARACTERISTICS OF THE WORKING CHIMNEY-SWEEPERS

[pp. 409–14]   There are many reasons why the chimney-sweepers have ever been a distinct and peculiar class. They have long been looked down upon as the lowest order of workers, and treated with contumely by those who were but little better than themselves. The peculiar nature of their work giving them not only a filthy appearance, but an offensive smell, of itself, in a manner, prohibited them from associating with other working men; and the natural effect of such proscription has been to compel them to herd together apart from others, and to acquire habits and peculiarities of their own widely differing from the characteristics of the rest of the labouring classes.

Sweepers, however, have not from this cause generally been an hereditary race – that is, they have not become sweepers from father to son for many generations. Their numbers were, in the days of the climbing boys, in most instances increased by parish apprentices, the parishes usually adopting that mode as the cheapest and easiest of freeing themselves from a part of the burden of juvenile pauperism. The climbing boys, but more especially the unfortunate parish apprentices, were almost always cruelly used, starved, beaten, and over-worked by their masters, and treated as outcasts by all with whom they came in contact: there can be no wonder, then, that, driven in this manner from all other society, they gladly availed themselves of the companionship of their fellow-sufferers; quickly inbibed all their habits and peculiarities; and, perhaps, ended by becoming themselves the most tyrannical masters to those who might happen to be placed under their charge.

Notwithstanding the disrepute in which sweepers have ever been held, there are many classes of workers beneath them in intelligence. All the tribe of finders and collectors (with the exception of the dredgermen, who are an observant race, and the sewer-hunters, who, from the danger of their employment, are compelled to exercise their intellects) are far inferior to them in this respect; and they are clever fellows compared to many of the dustmen and scavagers. The great mass of the agricultural labourers are known to be almost as ignorant as the beasts they drive; but the sweepers, from whatever cause it may arise, are known, in many instances, to be shrewd, intelligent, and active.

But there is much room for improvement among the operative chimney-sweepers. Speaking of the men generally, I am assured that there is scarcely one out of ten who can either read or write. One man in Chelsea informed me that some ladies, in connection with the Rev. Mr Cadman's church, made an attempt to instruct the sweepers of the neighbourhood in reading and writing; but the master sweepers grew jealous, and became afraid lest their men should get too knowing for them. When the time came, therefore, for the men to prepare for the school, the masters always managed to find out some job which prevented them from attending at the appointed time, and the consequence was that the benevolent designs of the ladies were frustrated.

ONE OF THE FEW REMAINING CLIMBING SWEEPS.

The sweepers, as a class, in almost all their habits, bear a strong resemblance to the costermongers. The habit of going about in search of their employment has, of itself, implanted in many of them the wandering propensity peculiar to street people. Many of the better-class costermongers have risen into coal-shed men and greengrocers, and become settled in life; in like manner the better-class sweepers have risen to be masters and, becoming settled in a locality, have gradually obtained the trade of the neighbourhood; then, as their circumstances improved, they have been able to get horses and carts, and become nightmen; and there are many of them at this moment men of wealth, comparatively speaking. The great body of them, however, retain in all their force their original characteristics; the masters themselves, although shrewd and sensible men, often betray their want of education, and are in no way particular as to their expressions, their language being made up, in a great measure, of the terms peculiar to the costermongers, especially the denominations of the various sorts of money. I met with some sweepers, however, whose language was that in ordinary use, and their manners not vulgar. I might specify one, who, although a workhouse orphan and apprentice, a harshly-treated climbing-boy, is now prospering as a sweeper and nightman, is a regular attendant at all meetings to promote the good of the poor, and a zealous ragged-school teacher, and teetotaller.

When such men are met with, perhaps the class cannot be looked upon as utterly cast away, although the need of reformation in the habits of the working sweepers is extreme, and especially in respect of drinking, gambling, and dirt. The journeymen (who have often a good deal of leisure) and the single-handed men are – in the great majority of cases at least – addicted to drinking, beer being their favourite beverage, either because it is the cheapest or that they fancy it the most suitable for washing away the sooty particles which find their way to their throats. These men gamble also, but with this proviso – they seldom play for money; but when they meet in their usual houses of resort – two famous ones are in Back C— lane and S— street, Whitechapel – they spend their time and what money they may have in tossing for beer, till they are either drunk or penniless. Such men present the appearance of having just come out of a chimney. There seems never to have been any attempt made by them to wash the soot off their faces. I am informed that there is scarcely one of them who has a second shirt or any change of clothes, and that they wear their garments night and day till they literally rot, and drop in fragments from their backs. Those who are not employed as journeymen by the masters are frequently whole days without food, especially in

THE SWEEPS' HOME.

summer, when the work is slack; and it usually happens that those who are what is called 'knocking about on their own account' seldom or never have a farthing in their pockets in the morning, and may, perhaps, have to travel till evening before they get a threepenny or sixpenny chimney to sweep. When night comes, and they meet their companions, the tossing and drinking again commences; they again get drunk; roll home to wherever it may be, to go through the same routine on the morrow; and this is the usual tenour of their lives, whether earning 5s. or 20s. a week.

The chimney-sweepers generally are fond of drink; indeed their calling, like that of dustmen, is one of those which naturally lead to it. The men declare they are ordered to drink gin and smoke as much as they can, in order to rid the stomach of the soot they may have swallowed during their work.

Washing among chimney-sweepers seems to be much more frequent than it was. In the evidence before Parliament it was stated that some of the climbing-boys were washed once in six months, some once a week, some once in two or three months. I do not find it anywhere stated that any of these children were never washed at all; but from the tenour of the evidence it may be reasonably concluded that such was the case.

A master sweeper, who was in the habit of bathing at the Marylebone baths once and sometimes twice a week, assured me that, although many now eat and drink and sleep sooty, washing is more common among his class than when he himself was a climbing-boy. He used then to be stripped, and compelled to step into a tub, and into water sometimes too hot and sometimes too cold, while his mistress, to use his own word, *scoured* him. Judging from what he had seen and heard, my informant was satisfied that, from 30 to 40 years ago, climbing-boys, with a very few exceptions, were but seldom washed; and then it was looked upon by them as a most disagreeable operation, often, indeed, as a species of punishment. Some of the climbing-boys used to be taken by their masters to bathe in the Serpentine many years ago; but one boy was unfortunately drowned, so that the children could hardly be coerced to go into the water afterwards.

The washing among the chimney-sweepers of the present day, when there are scarcely any climbing-boys, is so much an individual matter that it is not possible to speak with any great degree of certainty on the subject, but that it increases may be concluded from the fact that the number of sweeps who resort to the public baths increases.

The first public baths and washhouses opened in London were in the 'north-west district', and situated in George-street, Euston-square, near

the Hampstead-road. This establishment was founded by voluntary
contribution in 1846, and is now self-supporting.

There are three more public baths: one in Goulston-street, Whitechapel
(on the same principle as that first established); another in St Martin's,
near the National Gallery, which are parochial; and the last in
Marylebone, near the Yorkshire Stingo tavern, New-road, also parochial.
The charge for a cold bath, each being secluded from the others, is 1d.,
with the use of a towel; a warm bath is 2d. in the third class. The following
is the return of the number of bathers at the north-west district baths, the
establishment most frequented:

	1847	1848	1849	1850
Bathers	110,940	111,788	96,726	86,597
Washers, Dryers, Ironers, &c.	39,418	61,690	65,934	73,023
Individuals Washed for	137,672	246,760	263,736	292,092

I endeavoured to ascertain the proportion of sweepers, with other
working men, who availed themselves of these baths; but there are unfortunately no data for instituting a comparison as to the relative cleanliness of the several trades. When the baths were first opened an
endeavour was made to obtain such a return; but it was found to be distasteful to the bathers, and so was discontinued. We find, then, that in
four years there have been 406,051 bathers. The following gives the
proportion between the sexes, a portion of 1846 being included:

Bathers – Males	417,424
– Females	47,114
– Total bathers	464,538

The falling off in the number of bathers at this establishment is, I am
told, attributable to the opening of new baths, the people, of course,
resorting to the nearest.

I have given the return of washers, &c, as I endeavoured to ascertain
the proportion of washing by the chimney-sweeper's wives; but there is
no specification of the trades of the persons using this branch of the
establishment any more than there is of those frequenting the baths, and
for the same reason as prevented its being done among the bathers. One
of the attendants at these washhouses told me that he had no doubt the

sweepers' wives did wash there, for he had more than once seen a sweeper waiting to carry home the clothes his wife had cleansed. As no questions concerning their situation in life are asked of the poor women who resort to these very excellent institutions (for such they appear to be on a cursory glance) of course no data can be supplied. This is to be somewhat regretted; but a regard to the feelings, and in some respects to the small prejudices, of the industrious poor is to be commended rather than otherwise, and the managers of these baths certainly seem to have manifested such a regard.

I am informed, however, by the secretary of the north-west district institution, that in some weeks of the summer 80 chimney-sweepers bathed there; always having, he believed, warm baths, which are more effective in removing soot or dirt from the skin than cold. Summer, it must be remembered, is the sweep's 'brisk' season. In a winter week as few as 25 or 20 have bathed, but the weekly average of sweeper-bathers, the year through, is about 50; and the number of sweeper-bathers, he thought, had increased since the opening of the baths about 10 per cent. yearly. As in 1850 the average number of bathers of all classes did not exceed 1646 per week, the proportion of sweepers, 50, is high. The number of female bathers is about one-ninth, so that the males would be about 1480; and the 50 sweepers a week constitute about a thirtieth part of the whole of the third-class bathers. The number of sweep-bathers was known because a sweep is known by his appearance.

I was told by the secretary that the sweepers, the majority bathing on Saturday nights, usually carried a bundle to the bath; this contained their 'clean things'. After bathing they assumed their 'Sunday clothes'; and from the change in their appearance between ingress and egress, they were hardly recognisable as the same individuals.

In the other baths, where also there is no specification of the bathers, I am told, that of sweepers bathing the number (on computation) is 30 at Marylebone, 25 at Goulston-street, and 15 (at the least) at St Martin's, as a weekly average. In all, 120 sweepers bathe weekly, or about a seventh of the entire working body. The increase at the three baths last mentioned, in sweepers bathing, is from 5 to 10 per cent.

Among the lower-class sweepers there are but few who wash themselves even once throughout the year. They eat, drink, and sleep in the same state of filth and dirt as when engaged in their daily avocation. Others, however, among the better class are more cleanly in their habits, and wash themselves every night.

CROSSING-SWEEPERS

[pp. 527–8]   That portion of the London street-folk who earn a scanty living by sweeping crossings constitute a large class of the Metropolitan poor. We can scarcely walk along a street of any extent, or pass through a square of the least pretensions to 'gentility', without meeting one or more of these private scavengers. Crossing-sweeping seems to be one of those occupations which are resorted to as an excuse for begging; and, indeed, as many expressed it to me, 'it was the last chance left of obtaining an honest crust'.

The advantages of crossing-sweeping as a means of livelihood seem to be:

1st, the smallness of the capital required in order to commence the business:

2ndly, the excuse the apparent occupation it affords for soliciting gratuities without being considered in the light of a street-beggar;

And 3rdly, the benefits arising from being constantly seen in the same place, and thus exciting the sympathy of the neighbouring householders, till small weekly allowances or 'pensions' are obtained.

The first curious point in connexion with this subject is what constitutes the *property*, so to speak, in a crossing, or the *right* to sweep a pathway across a certain thoroughfare. A nobleman, who has been one of her Majesty's Ministers, whilst conversing with me on the subject of crossing-sweepers, expressed to me the curiosity he felt on the subject, saying that he had noticed some of the sweepers in the same place for years. 'What were the rights of property,' he asked, 'in such cases, and what constituted the title that such a man had to a particular crossing? Why did not the stronger sweeper supplant the weaker? Could a man bequeath a crossing to a son, or present it to a friend? How did he first obtain the spot?'

The answer is, that crossing-sweepers are, in a measure, under the protection of the police. If the accommodation afforded by a well-swept pathway is evident, the policeman on that district will protect the original sweeper of the crossing from the intrusion of a rival. I have, indeed, met with instances of men who, before taking to a crossing, have asked for and obtained permission of the police; and one sweeper, who gave me his statement, had even solicited the authority of the inhabitants before he applied to the inspector at the station-house.

If a crossing have been vacant for some time, another sweeper may take to it; but should the original proprietor again make his appearance, the officer on duty will generally re-establish him. One man to whom I spoke, had fixed himself on a crossing which for years another sweeper had kept clean on the Sunday morning only. A dispute ensued; the one claimant pleading his long Sabbath possession, and the other his continuous everyday service. The quarrel was referred to the police, who decided that he who was oftener on the ground was the rightful owner; and the option was given to the former possessor, that if he would sweep there every day the crossing should be his.

I believe there is only one crossing in London which is in the gift of a householder, and this proprietorship originated in a tradesman having, at his own expense, caused a paved footway to be laid down over the Macadamized road in front of his shop, so that his customers might run less chance of dirtying their boots when they crossed over to give their orders.

Some bankers, however, keep a crossing-sweeper, not only to sweep a clean path for the 'clients' visiting their house, but to open and shut the doors of the carriages calling at the house.

Concerning the *causes which lead or drive* people to this occupation, they are various. People take to crossing-sweeping either on account of their bodily afflictions, depriving them of the power of performing ruder work, or because the occupation is the last resource left open to them of earning a living, and they considered even the scanty subsistence it yields preferable to that of the workhouse. The greater proportion of crossing-sweepers are those who, from some bodily infirmity or injury, are prevented from a more laborious mode of obtaining their living. Among the bodily infirmities the chief are old age, asthma, and rheumatism; and the injuries mostly consist of loss of limbs. Many of the rheumatic sweepers have been brick-layers' labourers.

The classification of crossing-sweepers is not very complex. They may be divided into the *casual* and the *regular*.

By the casual I mean such as pursue the occupation only on certain days in the week, as, for instance, those who make their appearance on the Sunday morning, as well as the boys who, broom in hand, travel about the streets, sweeping before the foot-passengers or stopping an hour at one place, and then, if not fortunate, moving on to another.

The regular crossing-sweepers are those who have taken up their posts at the corners of streets or squares; and I have met with some who have kept to the same spot for more than forty years.

The crossing-sweepers in the squares may be reckoned among the most fortunate of the class. With them the crossing is a kind of stand, where any one requiring their services knows they may be found. These sweepers are often employed by the butlers and servants in the neighbouring mansions for running errands, posting letters, and occasionally helping in the packing-up and removal of furniture or boxes when the family goes out of town. I have met with other sweepers who, from being known for years to the inhabitants, have at last got to be regularly employed at some of the houses to clean knives, boots, windows, &c.

It is not at all an unfrequent circumstance, however, for a sweeper to be in receipt of a weekly sum from some of the inhabitants in the district. The crossing itself is in these cases but of little value for chance customers, for were it not for the regular charity of the householders, it would be deserted. Broken victuals and old clothes also form part of a sweeper's means of living; nor are the clothes always old ones, for one or two of this class have for years been in the habit of having new suits presented to them by the neighbours at Christmas.

The irregular sweepers mostly consist of boys and girls who have formed themselves into a kind of company, and come to an agreement to work together on the same crossings. The principal resort of these is about Trafalgar-square, where they have seized upon some three or four crossings, which they visit from time to time in the course of the day.

One of these gangs I found had appointed its king and captain, though the titles were more honorary than privileged. They had framed their own laws repecting each one's right to the money he took, and the obedience to these laws was enforced by the strength of the little fraternity.

One or two girls whom I questioned, told me that they mixed up ballad-singing or lace-selling with crossing-sweeping, taking to the broom only when the streets were wet and muddy. These children are usually sent out by their parents, and have to carry home at night their earnings. A few of them are orphans with a lodging-house for a home.

Taken as a class, crossing-sweepers are among the most honest of the London poor. They all tell you that, without a good character and 'the respect of the neighbourhood', there is not a living to be got out of the broom. Indeed, those whom I found best-to-do in the world were those who had been longest at their posts.

Among them are many who have been servants until sickness or accident deprived them of their situations, and nearly all of them have had their minds so subdued by affliction, that they have been tamed so as to be incapable of mischief.

The *earnings*, or rather '*takings*', of crossing-sweepers are difficult to estimate – generally speaking – that is, to strike the average for the entire class. An erroneous idea prevails that crossing-sweeping is a lucrative employment. All whom I have spoken with agree in saying, that some thirty years back it was a good living; but they bewail piteously the spirit of the present generation. I have met with some who, in former days, took their 3*l.* weekly; and there are but few I have spoken to who would not, at one period, have considered fifteen shillings a bad week's work. But now 'the takings' are very much reduced. The man who was known to this class as having been the most prosperous of all – for from one nobleman alone he received an allowance of seven shillings and sixpence weekly – assured me that twelve shillings a week was the average of his present gains, taking the year round; whilst the majority of the sweepers agree that a shilling is a good day's earnings.

A shilling a day is the very limit of the average incomes of the London sweepers, and this is rather an over than an under calculation; for, although a few of the more fortunate, who are to be found in the squares or main thoroughfares or opposite the public buildings, may earn their twelve or fifteen shillings a week, yet there are hundreds who are daily to be found in the by-streets of the metropolis who assert that eightpence a day is their average taking; and, indeed, in proof of their poverty, they refer you to the workhouse authorities, who allow them certain quartern-loaves weekly. The old stories of delicate suppers and stockings full of money have in the present day no foundation of truth.

The black crossing-sweeper, who bequeathed 500*l.* to Miss Waithman, would almost seem to be the last of the class whose earnings were above his positive necessities.

Lastly, concerning the *numbers* belonging to this large class, we may add that it is difficult to reckon up the number of crossing-sweepers in London. There are few squares without a couple of these pathway scavengers; and in the more respectable squares, such as Cavendish or Portman, every corner has been seized upon. Again, in the principal thoroughfares, nearly every street has its crossing and attendant.

The Maimed Irish Crossing-sweeper

[pp. 559–60] He stands at the corner of — street, where the yellow omnibuses stop, and refers to himself every now and then as the 'poor lame man'. He has no especial mode of addressing the passers-by, except that of hobbling a step or two towards them and sweeping away an imaginary accumulation of mud. He has lost one leg (from the knee) by a fall from a scaffold, while working as a bricklayer's labourer in Wales, some six years ago; and speaks bitterly of the hard time he had of it when he first

THE CROSSING-SWEEPER THAT HAS BEEN A MAID-SERVANT.

came to London, and hobbled about selling matches. He says he is thirty-six, but looks more than fifty; and his face has the ghastly expression of death. He wears the ordinary close cloth street-cap and corduroy trousers. Even during the warm weather he wears an upper coat – a rough thick garment, fit for the Arctic regions. It was very difficult to make him understand my object in getting information from him: he thought that he had nothing to tell, and laid great stress upon the fact of his never keeping 'count' of anything.

He accounted for his miserably small income by stating that he was an invalid – 'now and thin continually'. He said –

'I can't say how long I have been on this crossin'; I think about five year. When I came on it there had been no one here before. No one interferes with me at all, at all. I niver hard of a crossin' bein' sould; but I don't know any other sweepers. I makes no fraydom with no one, and I always keeps my own mind.

'I dunno how much I earn a-day – p'rhaps I may git a shilling, and p'rhaps sixpence. I didn't git much yesterday (Sunday) – only sixpence. I was not out on Saturday; I was ill in bed, and I was at home on Friday. Indeed, I did not get much on Thursday, only tuppence ha'penny. The largest day? I dunno. Why, about a shilling. Well, sure, I might git as much as two shillings, if I got a shillin' from a lady. Some gintlemen are good – such a gintleman as you, now, might give me a shilling.

'Well, as to weather, I likes half dry and half wit; of course I wish for the bad wither. Every one must be glad of what brings good to him; and, there's one thing, I can't make the wither – I can't make a fine day nor a wit one. I don't think anybody would interfere with me; certainly, if I was a blaggya'rd I should not be left here; no, nor if I was a thief; but if any other man was to come on to my crossing, I can't say whether the police *would* interfere to protect me – p'rhaps they might.

'What is it I say to shabby people? Well, by J—, they're all shabby, I think. I don't see any difference; but what can I do? I can't insult thim, and I was niver insulted mysilf, since here I've been, nor, for the matter of that, ever had an angry worrud spoken to me.

'Well, sure, I dunno who's the most liberal; if I got a fourpinny bit from a moll I'd take it. Some of the ladies are very liberal; a good lady will give a sixpence. I never hard of sweepin' the mud back again; and as for the boys annoying me, I has no coleaguein' with boys, and they wouldn't be allowed to interfere with me – the police wouldn't allow it.

'After I came from Wales, where I was on one leg, selling matches, then it was I took to sweep the crossin'. A poor divil must put up with anything, good or bad. Well, I was a laborin' man, a bricklayer's labourer, and I've been away from Ireland these sixteen year. When I came from Ireland I went to Wales. I was there a long time; and the way I broke my leg was, I fell off a scaffold. I am not married; a lame man wouldn't get any woman to have him in London at all, at all. I don't know what age I am. I am not fifty, nor forty; I think about thirty-six. No, by J——, it's not mysilf that iver knew a well-off crossin'-sweeper. I don't dale in them at all.

'I got a dale of friends in London assist me (but only now and thin). If I depinded on the few ha'pence I get, I wouldn't live on 'em; what money I get here wouldn't buy a pound of mate; and I wouldn't live, only for my frinds. You see, sir, I can't be out always. I am laid up nows and thins continually. Oh, it's a poor trade to big on the crossin' from morning till night, and not get sixpence. I couldn't do with it, I know.

'Yes, sir, I smoke; it's a comfort, it is. I like any kind I'd get to smoke. I'd like the best if I got it.

'I am a Roman Catholic, and I go to St Patrick's, in St Giles's; a many people from my neighbourhood go there. I go every Sunday, and to Confession just once a year – that saves me.

'By the Lord's mercy! I don't get broken victuals, nor broken mate, not as much as you might put on the tip of a forruk; they'd chuck it out in the dust-bin before they'd give it to me. I suppose they're all alike.

'The divil an odd job I iver got, master, nor knives to clane. If I got their knives to clane, p'rhaps I might clane them.

'My brooms cost threepence ha'penny; they are very good. I wear them down to a stump, and they last three weeks, this fine wither. I niver got any ould clothes – not but I want a coat very bad, sir.

'I come from Dublin; my father and mother died there of cholera; and when they died, I come to England, and that was the cause of my coming.

'By my oath it didn't stand me in more than eighteenpence that I took here last week.

'I live in — lane, St Giles's Church, on the second landing, and I pay eightpence a week. I haven't a room to mysilf, for there's a family lives in it wid me.

'When I goes home I just smokes a pipe, and goes to bid, that's all.'

Boy Crossing-sweepers and Tumblers

[pp. 560–64]   A remarkably intelligent lad, who, on being spoken to, at once consented to give all the information in his power, told me the following story of his life.

It will be seen from this boy's account, and the one or two following, that a kind of partnership exists among some of these young sweepers. They have associated themselves together, appropriated several crossings to their use, and appointed a captain over them. They have their forms of trial, and 'jury-house' for the settlement of disputes; laws have been framed, which govern their commercial proceedings, and a kind of language adopted by the society for its better protection from its arch-enemy, the policeman.

I found the lad who first gave me an insight into the proceedings of the associated crossing-sweepers crouched on the stone steps of a door in Adelaide-street, Strand; and when I spoke to him he was preparing to settle down in a corner and go to sleep – his legs and body being curled round almost as closely as those of a cat on a hearth.

The moment he heard my voice he was upon his feet, asking me to 'give a halfpenny to poor little Jack'.

He was a good-looking lad, with a pair of large mild eyes, which he took good care to turn up with an expression of supplication as he moaned for his halfpenny.

A cap, or more properly a stuff bag, covered a crop of hair which had matted itself into the form of so many paint-brushes, while his face, from its roundness of feature and the complexion of dirt, had an almost Indian look about it; the colour of his hands, too, was such that you could imagine he had been shelling walnuts.

He ran before me, treading cautiously with his naked feet, until I reached a convenient spot to take down his statement, which was as follows:

'I've got no mother or father; mother has been dead for two years, and father's been gone more than that – more nigh five years – he died at Ipswich, in Suffolk. He was a perfumer by trade, and used to make hair-dye, and scent, and pomatum, and all kinds of scents. He didn't keep a shop himself, but he used to serve them as did; he didn't hawk his goods about, neether, but had regular customers, what used to send him a letter, and then he'd take them what they wanted. Yes, he used to serve some good shops: there was H—'s, of London Bridge, what's a large chemist's. He used to make a good deal of money, but he lost it betting; and so his brother, my uncle, did all his. He used to go up to High Park, and then go round by the Hospital, and then turn up a yard, where all the men are who play for money [Tattersall's]; and there he'd lose his money, or sometimes win – but that wasn't often. I remember he used to come home tipsy, and say he'd lost on this or that horse, naming wot one he'd laid on; and then mother would coax him to bed, and afterwards sit down and begin to cry.

'I was not with father when he died (but I was when he was dying), for I was sent up along with eldest sister to London with a letter to uncle, who was head servant at a doctor's. In this letter, mother asked uncle to pay back some money wot he owed, and wot father lent him, and she asked him if he'd like to come down and see father before he died. I recollect I went back again to mother by the Orwell steamer. I was well dressed then, and had good clothes on, and I was given to the care of the captain – Mr King his name was. But when I got back to Ipswich, father was dead.

'Mother took on dreadful; she was ill for three months afterwards, confined to her bed. She hardly eat anything: only beef-tea – I think they call it – and eggs. All the while she kept on crying.

'Mother kept a servant; yes, sir, we always had a servant, as long as I can recollect; and she and the woman as was there – Anna they called her, an old lady – used to take care of me and sister. Sister was fourteen years old (she's married to a young man now, and they're gone to America; she went from a place in the East India Docks, and I saw her off). I used, when I was with mother, to go to school in the morning, and go at nine and come home at twelve to dinner, then go again at two and leave off at half-past four,– that is, if I behaved myself and did all my lessons right; for if I did not I was kept back till I *did* them so. Mother used to pay one shilling a-week, and extra for the copy-books and things. I can read and write – oh, yes, I mean read and write well – read anything, even old English; and I write pretty fair – though I don't get much reading now, unless it's a penny paper – I've got one in my pocket now – it's the *London Journal* – there's a tale in it now about two brothers, and one of them steals the child away and puts another in his place, and then he gets found out, and all that, and he's just been falling off a bridge now.

'After mother got better, she sold all the furniture and goods and came up to London; – poor mother! She let a man of the name of Hayes have the greater part, and he left Ipswich soon after, and never gave mother the money. We came up to London, and mother took two rooms in Westminster, and I and sister lived along with her. She used to make hair-nets, and sister helped her, and used to take 'em to the hair-dressers to sell. She made these nets for two or three years, though she was suffering with a bad breast; – she died of that – poor thing! – for she had what doctors calls cancer – perhaps you've heard of 'em, sir – and they had to cut all round here (making motions with his hands from the shoulder to the bosom). Sister saw it, though I didn't.

'Ah! she was a very good, kind mother, and very fond of both of us; though father wasn't, for he'd always have a noise with mother when he come home, only he was seldom with us when he was making his goods.

'After mother died, sister still kept on making nets, and I lived with her for some time, until she told me she couldn't afford to keep me no longer, though she seemed to have a pretty good lot to do; but she would never let me go with her to the shops, though I could crochet, which she'd learned me, and used to run and get her all her silks and things what she wanted. But she was keeping company with a young man, and one day they went out, and came back and said they'd been and got married. It was him as got rid of me.

'He was kind to me for the first two or three months, while he was keeping her company; but before he was married he got a little cross, and after he was married he begun to get more cross, and used to send me to play in the streets, and tell me not to come home again till night. One day he hit me, and I said I wouldn't be hit about by him, and then at tea that night sister gave me three shillings, and told me I must go and get my own living. So I bought a box and brushes (they cost me just the money) and went cleaning boots, and I done pretty well with them, till my box was stole from me by a boy where I was lodging. He's in prison now – got six calendar for picking pockets.

'Sister kept all my clothes. When I asked her for 'em, she said they was disposed of along with all mother's goods; but she gave me some shirts and stockings, and such-like, and I had very good clothes, only they was all worn out. I saw sister after I left her, many times. I asked her many times to take me back, but she used to say, "It was not her likes, but her husband's, or she'd have had me back;" and I think it was true, for until he came she was a kind-hearted girl; but he said he'd enough to do to look after his own living; he was a fancy-baker by trade.

'I was fifteen the 24th of last May, sir, and I've been sweeping crossings now near upon two years. There's a party of six of us, and we have the crossings from St Martin's Church as far as Pall Mall. I always go along with them as lodges in the same place as I do. In the daytime, if it's dry, we do anythink what we can – open cabs, or anythink; but if it's wet, we separate, and I and another gets a crossing – those who gets on it first, keeps it, – and we stand on each side and take our chance.

'We do it in this way: if I was to see two gentlemen coming, I should cry out, "Two toffs!" and then they are mine; and whether they give me anythink or not they are mine, and my mate is bound not to follow them; for if he did he would get a hiding from the whole lot of us. If we both cry out together, then we share. If it's a lady and gentleman, then we cries, "A toff and a doll!" Sometimes we are caught out in this way. Perhaps it is a lady and gentleman and a child; and if I was to see them, and only say, "A toff and a doll," and leave out the child, then my mate can add the child; and as he is right and I wrong, then it's his party.

'If there's a policeman close at hand we mustn't ask for money; but we are always on the look-out for the policeman, and if we see one, then we calls out "Phillup!" for that's our signal. One of the policemen at St Martin's Church – Bandy, we calls him – knows what Phillup means, for he's up to us; so we had to change the word. (At the request of the young crossing-sweeper the present signal is omitted.)

'Yesterday on the crossing I got threepence halfpenny, but when it's dry like to-day I do nothink, for I haven't got a penny yet. We never carries no pockets, for if the policemen find us we generally pass the money to our mates, for if money's found on us we have fourteen days in prison.

'If I was to reckon all the year round, that is, one day with another, I think we make fourpence every day, and if we were to stick to it we should make more, for on a very muddy day we do better. One day, the best I ever had, from nine o'clock in the morning till seven o'clock at night, I made seven shillings and sixpence, and got not one bit of silver money among it. Every shilling I got I went and left a shop near where my crossing is, for fear I might get into any harm. The shop's kept by a woman we deals with for what we wants – tea and butter, or sugar, or brooms – anythink we wants. Saturday night week I made two-and-sixpence; that's what I took altogether up to six o'clock.

'When we see the rain we say together, "Oh! there's a jolly good rain! we'll have a good day to-morrow." If a shower comes on, and we are at our room, which we general are about three o'clock, to get somethink to eat – besides, we general go there to see how much each other's taken in the day – why, out we run with our brooms.

'We're always sure to make money if there's mud – that's to say, if we look for our money, and ask; of course, if we stand still we don't. Now, there's Lord Fitzhardinge, he's a good gentleman, what lives in Spring-gardens, in a large house. He's got a lot of servants and carriages. Every time he crosses the Charing-cross crossing he always gives the girl half a sovereign.' (This statement was taken in June 1856.) 'He doesn't cross often, because, hang it, he's got such a lot of carriages, but when he's on foot he always does. If they asks him he doesn't give nothink, but if they touches their caps he does. The housekeeper at his house is very kind to us. We run errands for her, and when she wants any of her own letters

taken to the post then she calls, and if we are on the crossing we takes
them for her. She's a very nice lady, and gives us broken victuals. I've got
a share in that crossing – there are three of us, and when he gives the half
sovereign he always gives it to the girl, and those that are in it shares it.
She would do us out of it if she could, but we all takes good care of that,
for we are all cheats.

'At night-time we tumbles – that is, if the policeman ain't nigh. We goes
general to Waterloo-place when the Opera's on. We sends on one of us
ahead, as a looker-out, to look for the policeman, and then we follows. It's
no good tumbling to gentlemen *going* to the Opera; it's when they're
coming back they gives us money. When they've got a young lady on their
arm they laugh at us tumbling; some will give us a penny, others threepence, sometimes a sixpence or a shilling, and sometimes a halfpenny. We
either do the cat'un-wheel, or else we keep before the gentleman and lady,
turning head-over-heels, putting our broom on the ground and then
turning over it.

'I work a good deal fetching cabs after the Opera is over; we general open
the doors of those that draw up at the side of the pavement for people to
get into as have walked a little down the Haymarket looking for a cab. We
gets a month in prison if we touch the others by the columns. I once had
half a sovereign give me by a gentleman; it was raining awful, and I run
all about for a cab, and at last I got one. The gentleman knew it was half
a sovereign, because he said – "Here, my little man, here's half a sovereign
for your trouble." He had three ladies with him, beautiful ones, with
nothink on their heads, and only capes on their bare shoulders; and he
had white kids on, and his regular Opera togs, too. I liked him very much,
and as he was going to give me somethink the ladies says – "Oh, give him
somethink extra!" It was pouring with rain, and they couldn't get a cab;
they were all engaged, but I jumped on the box of one as was driving along
the line. Last Saturday Opera night I made fifteen pence by the gentlemen
coming from the Opera.

'After the Opera we go into the Haymarket, where all the women are
who walk the streets all night. They don't give us no money, but they tell
the gentlemen to. Sometimes, when they are talking to the gentlemen,
they say, "Go away, you young rascal!" and if they are saucy, then we
say to them, "We're not talking to you, my doxy, we're talking to the
gentleman" – but that's only if they're rude, for if they speak civil we
always goes. They knows what "doxy" means. What is it? Why that they
are no better than us! If we are on the crossing, and we says to them as
they go by, "Good luck to you!" they always give us somethink either that

night or the next. There are two with bloomer bonnets, who always give us somethink if we says "Good luck". Sometimes a gentleman will tell us to go and get them a young lady, and then we goes, and they general gives us sixpence for that. If the gents is dressed finely we gets them a handsome girl; if they're dressed middling, then we gets them a middling-dressed one; but we usual prefers giving a turn to girls that have been kind to us, and they are sure to give us somethink the next night. If we don't find any girls walking, we knows where to get them in the houses in the streets round about.

'We always meet at St Martin's steps – the "jury house", we calls 'em – at three o'clock in the morning, that's always our hour. We reckons up what we've taken, but we don't divide. Sometimes, if we owe anythink where we lodge, the women of the house will be waiting on the steps for us: then, if we've got it, we pay them; if we haven't, why it can't be helped, and it goes on. We gets into debt, because sometimes the women where we live gets lushy; then we don't give them anythink, because they'd forget it, so we spends it ourselves. We can't lodge at what's called model lodging-houses, as our hours don't suit them folks. We pays threepence a-night for lodging. Food, if we get plenty of money, we buys for ourselves. We buys a pound of bread, that's two-pence farthing – best seconds, and a farthing's worth of dripping – that's enough for a pound of bread – and we gets a ha'porth of tea and a ha'porth of sugar; or if we're hard up, we gets only a penn'orth of bread. We make our own tea at home; they lends us a kittle, tea-pot, and cups and saucers, and all that.

'Once or twice a-week we gets meat. We all club together, and go into Newgate Market and gets some pieces cheap, and biles them at home. We tosses up who shall have the biggest bit, and we divide the broth, a cupful in each basin, until it's lasted out. If any of us has been unlucky we each gives the unlucky one one or two halfpence. Some of us is obliged at times to sleep out all night; and sometimes, if any of us gets nothink, then the others gives him a penny or two, and *he* does the same for us when *we* are out of luck.

'Besides, there's our clothes: I'm paying for a pair of boots now. I paid a shilling off Saturday night.

'When we gets home at half-past three in the morning, whoever cries out "first wash" has it. First of all we washes our feet, and we all uses the same water. Then we washes our faces and hands, and necks, and whoever fetches the fresh water up has first wash; and if the second don't like to go and get fresh, why he uses the dirty. Whenever we come in the landlady makes us wash our feet. Very often the stones cuts our feet and makes them bleed; then we bind a bit of rag round them. We like to put on boots and shoes in the day-time, but at night-time we can't, because it stops the tumbling.

'On the Sunday we all have a clean shirt put on before we go out, and then we go and tumble after the omnibuses. Sometimes we do very well on a fine Sunday, when there's plenty of people out on the roofs of the busses. We never do anythink on a wet day, but only when it's been raining and then dried up. I have run after a Cremorne bus, when they've thrown us money, as far as from Charing-cross right up to Piccadilly, but if they don't throw us nothink we don't run very far. I should think we gets at that work, taking one Sunday with another, eightpence all the year round.

'When there's snow on the ground we puts our money together, and goes and buys an old shovel, and then, about seven o'clock in the morning, we goes to the shops and asks them if we shall scrape the snow away. We general gets twopence every house, but some gives sixpence, for it's very hard to clean the snow away, particularly when it's been on the ground some time. It's awful cold, and gives us chilblains on our feet; but we don't mind it when we're working, for we soon gets hot then.

'Before winter comes, we general save up our money and buys a pair of shoes. Sometimes we makes a very big snowball and rolls it up to the hotels, and then the gentlemen laughs and throws us money; or else we pelt each other with snowballs, and then they scrambles money between us. We always go to Morley's Hotel, at Charing-cross. The police in winter times is kinder to us than in summer, and they only laughs at us – p'rhaps it is because there is not so many of us about then – only them as is obligated to find a living for themselves; for many of the boys has fathers and mothers as sends them out in summer, but keeps them at home in winter when it's piercing cold.

'I have been to the station-house, because the police always takes us up if we are out at night; but we're only locked up till morning, – that is, if we behaves ourselves when we're taken before the gentleman. Mr Hall, at Bow-street, only says, "Poor boy, let him go." But it's only when we've done nothink but stop out that he says that. He's a kind old gentleman; but mind, it's only when you have been before him two or three times he says so, because if it's a many times, he'll send you for fourteen days.

'But we don't mind the police much at night-time, because we jumps over the walls round the place at Trafalgar-square, and they don't like to follow us at that game, and only stands looking at you over the parrypit. There was one tried to jump the wall, but he split his trousers all to bits, and now they're afraid. That was Old Bandy as bust his breeches; and we all hate him, as well as another we calls Black Diamond, what's general along with the Red Liners, as we calls the Mendicity officers, who goes about in disguise as gentlemen, to take up poor boys caught begging.

'When we are talking together we always talk in a kind of slang. Each policeman we gives a regular name – there's "Bull's Head", "Bandy Shanks", and "Old Cherry Legs", and "Dot-and-carry-one", they all knows their names as well as us. We never talks of crossings, but "fakes". We don't make no slang of our own, but uses the regular one.

'A broom doesn't last us more than a week in wet weather, and they costs us twopence halfpenny each; but in dry weather they are good for a fortnight.'

Young Mike's Statement

[pp. 564–5]   The next lad I examined was called Mike. He was a short, stout-set youth, with a face like an old man's, for the features were hard and defined, and the hollows had got filled up with dirt till his countenance was brown as an old wood carving. I have seldom seen so dirty a face, for the boy had been in a perspiration, and then wiped his cheeks with his muddy hands, until they were marbled, like the covering to a copy-book.

The old lady of the house in which the boy lived seemed to be hurt by the unwashed appearance of her lodger. 'You ought to be ashamed of yourself – and that's God's truth – not to go and sluice yourself afore spaking to the jintlemin,' she cried, looking alternately at me and the lad, as if asking me to witness her indignation.

Mike wore no shoes, but his feet were as black as if cased in gloves with short fingers. His coat had been a man's, and the tails reached to his ankles; one of the sleeves was wanting, and a dirty rag had been wound round the arm in its stead. His hair spread about like a tuft of grass where a rabbit has been squatting.

He said, 'I haven't got neither no father nor no mother – never had, sir; for father's been dead these two year, and mother getting on for eight. They was both Irish people, please sir, and father was a bricklayer. When father was at work in the country, mother used to get work carrying loads at Covent-garden Market. I lived with father till he died, and that was from a complaint in his chest. After that I lived along with my big brother, what's 'listed in the Marines now. He used to sweep a crossing in Camden-town, opposite the Southampting Harms, near the toll gate.

'He did pretty well up there sometimes, such as on Christmas-day, where he has took as much as six shillings sometimes, and never less than one and sixpence. All the gentlements knowed him thereabouts, and one or two used to give him a shilling a week regular.

'It was he as first of all put me up to sweep a crossing, and I used to take my stand at St Martin's Church.

'I didn't see anybody working there, so I planted myself on it. After a time some other boys come up. They come up and wanted to turn me off, and began hitting me with their brooms, – they hit me regular hard with the old stumps; there was five or six of them; so I couldn't defend myself, but told the policeman, and he turned them all away except me, because he saw me on first, sir. Now we are all friends, and work together, and all that we earns ourself we has.

'On a good day, when it's poured o' rain and then leave off sudden, and made it nice and muddy, I've took as much as ninepence; but it's too dry now, and we don't do more than fourpence.

'At night, I go along with the others tumbling. I does the cat'en-wheel [probably a contraction of Catherine-wheel]; I throws myself over sideways on my hands with my legs in the air. I can't do it more than four times running, because it makes the blood to the head, and then all the things seems to turn round. Sometimes a chap will give me a lick with a stick just as I'm going over – sometimes a reg'lar good hard whack; but it ain't often, and we general gets a halfpenny or a penny by it.

'The boys as runs after the busses was the first to do these here cat'en-wheels. I know the boy as was the very first to do it. His name is Gander, so we calls him the Goose.

'There's about nine or ten of us in our gang, and as is reg'lar; we lodges at different places, and we has our reg'lar hours for meeting, but we all comes and goes when we likes, only we keeps together, so as not to let any others come on the crossings but ourselves.

'If another boy tries to come on we cries out, "Here's a Rooshian", and then if he won't go away, we all sets on him and gives him a drubbing; and if he still comes down the next day, we pays him out twice as much, and harder.

'There's never been one down there yet as can lick us all together.

'If we sees one of our pals being pitched into by other boys, we goes up and helps him. Gander's the leader of our gang, 'cause he can tumble back'ards (no, that ain't the cat'en-wheel, that's tumbling); so he gets more tin give him, and that's why we makes him cap'an.

'After twelve at night we goes to the Regent's Circus, and we tumbles there to the gentlemen and ladies. The most I ever got was sixpence at a time. The French ladies never give us nothink, but they all says, "Chit, chit, chit," like hissing at us, for they can't understand us, and we're as bad off with them.

'If it's a wet night we leaves off work about twelve o'clock, and don't bother with the Haymarket.

'The first as gets to the crossing does the sweeping away of the mud. Then they has in return all the halfpence they can take. When it's been wet every day, a broom gets down to stump in about four days. We either burns the old brooms, or, if we can, we sells 'em for a ha'penny to some other boy, if he's flat enough to buy 'em.'

Gander – the 'Captain' of the Boy Crossing-sweepers

[pp. 565–7] Gander, the captain of the gang of boy crossing-sweepers, was a big lad of sixteen, with a face devoid of all expression, until he laughed, when the cheeks, mouth, and forehead instantly became crumpled up with a wonderful quantity of lines and dimples. His hair was cut short, and stood up in all directions, like the bristles of a hearth-broom, and was a light dust tint, matching with the hue of his complexion, which also, from an absence of washing, had turned to a decided drab, or what house-painters term a stone-colour.

He spoke with a lisp, occasioned by the loss of two of his large front teeth, which allowed the tongue as he talked to appear through the opening in a round nob like a raspberry.

The boy's clothing was in a shocking condition. He had no coat, and his blue-striped shirt was as dirty as a French-polisher's rags, and so tattered, that the shoulder was completely bare, while the sleeve hung down over the hand like a big bag.

From the fish-scales on the sleeves of his coat, it had evidently once belonged to some coster in the herring line. The nap was all worn off, so that the lines of the web were showing like a coarse carpet; and instead of buttons, string had been passed through holes pierced at the side.

Of course he had no shoes on, and his black trousers, which, with the grease on them, were gradually assuming a tarpaulin look, were fastened over one shoulder by means of a brace and bits of string.

During his statement, he illustrated his account of the tumbling backwards – the 'caten-wheeling' – with different specimens of the art, throwing himself about on the floor with an ease and almost grace, and taking up so small a space of the ground for the performance, that his limbs seemed to bend as though his bones were flexible like cane.

'To tell you the blessed truth, I can't say the last shilling I handled.'

'Don't you go a-believing on him,' whispered another lad in my ear, whilst Gander's head was turned: 'he took thirteenpence last night, he did.'

It was perfectly impossible to obtain from this lad any account of his average earnings. The other boys in the gang told me that he made more than any of them. But Gander, who is a thorough street-beggar, and speaks with a peculiar whine, and who, directly you look at him, puts on an expression of deep distress, seemed to have made up his mind, that if he made himself out to be in great want I should most likely relieve him – so he would not budge an inch from his twopence a-day, declaring it to be the maximum of his daily earnings.

'Ah,' he continued, with a persecuted tone of voice, 'if I had only got a little money, I'd be a bright youth! The first chance as I get of earning a few halfpence, I'll buy myself a coat, and be off to the country, and I'll lay something I'd soon be a gentleman then, and come home with a couple of pounds in my pocket, instead of never having ne'er a farthing, as now.'

One of the other lads here exclaimed, 'Don't go on like that there, Goose; you're making us out all liars to the gentleman.'

The old woman also interfered. She lost all patience with Gander, and reproached him for making a false return of his income. She tried to shame him into truthfulness, by saying –

'Look at my Johnny – my grandson, sir, he's not a quarther the Goose's size, and yet he'll bring me home his shilling, or perhaps eighteenpence or two shillings – for shame on you, Gander! Now, did you make six shillings last week? – now, speak God's truth!'

'What! six shillings?' cried the Goose – 'six shillings!' and he began to look up at the ceiling, and shake his hands. 'Why, I never heard of sich a sum. I did once *see* a half-crown; but I don't know as I ever touched e'er a one.'

'Thin,' added the old woman, indignantly, 'it's because you're idle, Gander, and you don't study when you're on the crossing; but lets the gintlefolk go by without ever a word. That's what it is, sir.'

The Goose seemed to feel the truth of this reproach, for he said with a sigh, 'I knows I am fickle-minded.'

He then continued his statement, –

'I can't tell how many brooms I use; for as fast as I gets one, it is took from me. God help me! They watch me put it away, and then up they comes and takes it. What kinds of brooms is the best? Why, as far as I am concerned, I would sooner have a stump on a dry day – it's lighter and handier to carry; but on a wet day, give me a new un.

'I'm sixteen, your honour, and my name's George Gandea, and the boys calls me "the Goose" in consequence; for it's a nickname they gives me, though my name ain't spelt with a *har* at the end, but with a *h'ay*, so that I ain't Gand*er* after all, but Gand*ea*, which is a sell for 'em.

'God knows what I am – whether I'm h'Irish or h'*I*talian, or what; but I was christened here in London, and that's all about it.

'Father was a bookbinder. I'm sixteen now, and father turned me away when I was nine year old, for mother had been dead before that. I was told my right name by my brother-in-law, who had my register. He's a sweep, sir, by trade, and I wanted to know about my real name when I was going down to the *Waterloo* – that's a ship as I wanted to get aboard as a cabin-boy.

'I remember the first night I slept out after father got rid of me. I slept on a gentleman's door-step, in the winter, on the 15th January. I packed my shirt and coat, which was a pretty good one, right over my ears, and then scrunched myself into a door-way, and the policeman passed by four or five times without seeing on me.

'I had a mother-in-law at the time; but father used to drink, or else I should never have been as I am; and he came home one night, and says he, "Go out and get me a few ha'pence for breakfast," and I said I had never been in the streets in my life, and couldn't; and, says he, "Go out, and never let me see you no more," and I took him to his word, and have never been near him since.

'Father lived in Barbican at that time, and after leaving him, I used to go to the Royal Exchange, and there I met a boy of the name of Michael, and he first learnt me to beg, and made me run after people, saying, "Poor boy, sir – please give us a ha'penny to get a mossel of bread." But as fast as I got anythink, he used to take it away, and knock me about shameful; so I left him, and then I picked up with a chap as taught me tumbling. I soon larnt how to do it, and then I used to go tumbling after busses. That was my notion all along, and I hadn't picked up the way of doing it half an hour before I was after that game.

'I took to crossings about eight year ago, and the very fust person as I asked, I had a fourpenny-piece give to me. I said to him, "Poor little Jack, yer honour," and, fust of all, says he, "I haven't got no coppers," and then he turns back and give me a fourpenny-bit. I thought I was made for life when I got that.

'I wasn't working in a gang then, but all by myself, and I used to do

275

well, making about a shilling or ninepence a-day. I lodged in Church-lane at that time.

'It was at the time of the Shibition year [1851] as these gangs come up. There was lots of boys that came out sweeping, and that's how they picked up the tumbling off me, seeing me do it up in the Park, going along to the Shibition.

'The crossing at St Martin's Church was mine fust of all; and when the other lads come to it I didn't take no heed of 'em – only for that I'd have been a bright boy by now, but they carnied me over like; for when I tried to turn 'em off they'd say, in a carnying way, "Oh, let us stay on," so I never took no heed of 'em.

'There was about thirteen of 'em in my gang at that time.

'They made me cap'an over the lot – I suppose because they thought I was the best tumbler of 'em. They obeyed me a little. If I told 'em not to go to any gentleman, they wouldn't, and leave him to me. There was only one feller as used to give me a share of his money, and that was for larning him to tumble – he'd give a penny or twopence, just as he yearnt a little or a lot. I taught 'em all to tumble, and we used to do it near the crossing, and at night along the streets.

'We used to be sometimes together of a day, some a-running after one gentleman, and some after another; but we seldom kept together more than three or four at a time.

'I was the fust to introduce tumbling backwards, and I'm proud of it – yes, sir, I'm proud of it. There's another little chap as I'm larning to do it; but he ain't got strength enough in his arms like. ("Ah!" exclaimed a lad in the room, "he *is* a one to tumble, is Johnny – go along the streets like anythink.")

'He is the King of the Tumblers,' continued Gander – 'King, and I'm Cap'an.'

The old grandmother here joined in. 'He was taught by a furreign gintleman, sir, whose wife rode at a circus. He used to come here twice a-day and give him lessons in this here very room, sir. That's how he got it, sir.'

'Ah,' added another lad, in an admiring tone, 'see him and the Goose have a race! Away they goes, but Jacky will leave him a mile behind.'

The history then continued: 'People liked the tumbling backards and forards, and it got a good bit of money at fust, but they is getting tired with it, and I'm growing too hold, I fancy. It hurt me awful at fust. I tried it fust under a railway arch of the Blackwall Railway; and when I goes backards, I thought it'd cut my head open. It hurts me if I've got a thin cap on.

'The man as taught me tumbling has gone on the stage. Fust he went about with swords, fencing, in public-houses, and then he got engaged. Me and him once tumbled all round the circus at the Rotunda one night wot was a benefit, and got one-and-eightpence a-piece, and all for only five hours and a half – from six to half-past eleven, and we acting and tumbling, and all that. We had plenty of beer, too. We was wery much applauded when we did it.

'I was the fust boy as ever did ornamental work in the mud of my crossings. I used to be at the crossing at the corner of Regent-suckus; and that's the wery place where I fust did it. The wery fust thing as I did was a hanker (anchor) – a regular one, with turn-up sides and a rope down the centre, and all. I sweeped it away clean in the mud in the shape of the drawing I'd seen. It paid well, for I took one-and-ninepence on it. The next thing I tried was writing "God save the Queen"; and that, too, paid capital, for I think I got two bob. After that I tried We Har (V. R.) and a star, and that was a sweep too. I never did no flowers, but I've done imitations of laurels, and put them all round the crossing, and very pretty it looked, too, at night. I'd buy a farthing candle and stick it over it, and make it nice and comfortable, so that the people could look at it easy. Whenever I see a carriage coming I used to douse the glim and run away with it, but the wheels would regularly spile the drawings, and then we'd have all the trouble to put it to rights again, and that we used to do with our hands.

'I fust learnt drawing in the mud from a man in Adelaide-street, Strand; he kept a crossing, but he only used to draw 'em close to the kerb-stone. He used to keep some soft mud there, and when a carriage come up to the Lowther Arcade, after he'd opened the door and let the lady out, he would set to work, and by the time she come back he'd have some flowers, or a We Har, or whatever he liked, done in the mud, and underneath he'd write, "Please to remember honnest hindustry."

'I used to stand by and see him do it, until I'd learnt, and when I knowed, I went off and did it at my crossing.

'I was the fust to light up at night though, and now I wish I'd never done it, for it was that which got me turned off my crossing, and a capital one it was. I thought the gentlemen coming from the play would like it, for it looked very pretty. The policeman said I was destructing (obstructing) the thoroughfare, and making too much row there, for the people used to stop in the crossing to look, it were so pretty. He took me in charge three times on one night, cause I wouldn't go away; but he let me go again, till at last I thought he would lock me up for the night, so I hooked it.

'It was after this as I went to St Martin's Church, and I haven't done half as well there. Last night I took three-ha'pence; but I was larking, or I might have had more.'

As a proof of the very small expense which is required for the toilette of a crossing-sweeper, I may mention, that within a few minutes after Master Gander had finished his statement, he was in possession of a coat, for which he had paid the sum of fivepence.

When he brought it into the room, all the boys and the women crowded round to see the purchase.

'It's a very good un,' said the Goose. 'It only wants just taking up here and there; and this cuff putting to rights.' And as he spoke he pointed to tears large enough for a head to be thrust through.

'I've seen that coat before, sum'ares,' said one of the women; 'where did you get it?'

'At the chandly-shop,' answered the Goose.

The 'King' of the Tumbling-boy Crossing-sweepers

[pp. 567–9] The young sweeper who had been styled by his companions the 'King' was a pretty-looking boy, only tall enough to rest his chin comfortably on the mantel-piece as he talked to me, and with a pair of grey eyes that were as bright and clear as drops of sea-water. He was clad in a style in no way agreeing with his royal title; for he had on a kind of dirt-coloured shooting-coat of tweed, which was fraying into a kind of cobweb at the edges and elbows. His trousers too, were rather faulty, for there was a pink-wrinkled dot of flesh at one of the knees; while their length was too great for his majesty's short legs, so that they had to be rolled up at the end like a washer-woman's sleeves.

His royal highness was of a restless disposition, and, whilst talking, lifted up, one after another, the different ornaments on the mantel-piece, frowning and looking at them side-ways, as he pondered over the replies he should make to my questions.

When I arrived at the grandmother's apartment the 'king' was absent, his majesty having been sent with a pitcher to fetch some spring-water.

The 'king' also was kind enough to favour me with samples of his wondrous tumbling powers. He could bend his little legs round till they curved like the long German sausages we see in the ham-and-beef shops; and when he turned head over heels, he curled up his tiny body as closely as a wood-louse, and then rolled along, wabbling like an egg.

'The boys call me Johnny,' he said; 'and I'm getting on for eleven, and

I goes along with the Goose and Harry, a-sweeping at St Martin's Church, and about there. I used, too, to go to the crossing where the statute is, sir, at the bottom of the Haymarket. I went along with the others; sometimes there were three or four of us, or sometimes one, sir. I never used to sweep unless it was wet. I don't go out not before twelve or one in the day; it ain't no use going before that; and beside, I couldn't get up before that, I'm too sleepy. I don't stop out so late as the other boys; they sometimes stop all night, but I don't like that. The Goose was out all night along with Martin; they went all along up Piccirilly, and there they climbed over the Park railings and went a birding all by themselves, and then they went to sleep for an hour on the grass – so they says. I likes better to come home to my bed. It kills me for the next day when I do stop out all night. The Goose is always out all night; he likes it.

'Neither father nor mother's alive, sir, but I lives along with grand-mother and aunt, as owns this room, and I always gives them all I gets.

'Sometimes I makes a shilling, sometimes sixpence, and sometimes less. I can never take nothink of a day, only of a night, because I can't tumble of a day, and I can of a night.

'The Gander taught me tumbling, and he was the first as did it along the crossings. I can tumble quite as well as the Goose; I can turn a caten-wheel, and he can't, and I can go further on forards than him, but I can't tumble backards as he can. I can't do a handspring, though. Why, a handspring's pitching yourself forards on both hands, turning over in front, and lighting on your feet; that's very difficult, and very few can do it. There's one little chap, but he's very clever, and can tie himself up in a knot a'most. I'm best at caten-wheels; I can do 'em twelve or fourteen times running – keep on at it. It just *does* tire you, that's all. When I gets up I feels quite giddy. I can tumble about forty times over head and heels. I does the most of that, and I thinks it's the most difficult, but I can't say which gentlemen likes best. You see they are anigh sick of the head-and-heels tumbling, and then werry few of the boys can do caten-wheels on the crossings – only two or three besides me.

'When I see anybody coming, I says, "Please, sir, give me a halfpenny," and touches my hair, and then I throws a caten-wheel, and has a look at 'em, and if I sees they are laughing, then I goes on and throws more of 'em. Perhaps one in ten will give a chap something. Some of 'em will give you a threepenny-bit or p'rhaps sixpence, and others only give you a kick. Well, sir, I should say they likes tumbling over head and heels; if you can keep it up twenty times then they begins laughing, but if you only does it once, some of 'em will say, "Oh, I could do that myself," and then they don't give nothink.

'I know they calls me the King of Tumblers, and I think I can tumble the best of them; none of them is so good as me, only the Goose at tumbling backards.

'We don't crab one another when we are sweeping; if we was to crab one another, we'd get to fighting and giving slaps of the jaw to one another. So when we sees anybody coming, we cries, "My gentleman and lady coming here"; "My lady"; "My two gentlemens"; and if any other chap gets the money, then we says, "I named them, now I'll have halves." And if he won't give it, then we'll smug his broom or his cap. I'm the littlest chap among our lot, but if a fellow like the Goose was to take my naming then I'd smug somethink. I shouldn't mind his licking me, I'd smug his money and get his halfpence or somethink. If a chap as can't tumble sees a sporting gent coming and names him, he says to one of us tumblers, "Now, then, who'll give us halves?" and then we goes and tumbles and shares. The sporting gentlemens likes tumbling; they kicks up more row laughing than a dozen others.

'Sometimes at night we goes down to Covent Garden, to where Hevans's is, but not till all the plays is over, cause Hevans's don't shut afore two or three. When the people comes out we gets tumbling afore them. Some of the drunken gentlemens is shocking spiteful, and runs after a chap and gives us a cut with the cane; some of the others will give us money, and some will buy our broom off us for sixpence. Me and Jemmy sold the two of our brooms for a shilling to two drunken gentlemens, and they began kicking up a row, and going before other gentlemens and pretending to sweep, and taking off their hats begging, like a mocking of us. They danced about with the brooms, flourishing 'em in the air, and knocking off people's hats; and at last they got into a cab, and chucked the brooms away. The drunken gentlemens is always either jolly or spiteful.

'But I goes only to the Haymarket, and about Pall Mall, now. I used to be going up to Hevans's every night, but I can't take my money up there now. I stands at the top of the Haymarket by Windmill-street, and when I sees a lady and gentleman coming out of the Argyle, then I begs of them as they comes across. I says – "Can't you give me a ha'penny, sir, poor little Jack? I'll stand on my nose for a penny" – and then they laughs at that.

'Goose can stand on his nose as well as me; we puts the face flat down on the ground, instead of standing on our heads. There's Duckey Dunnovan, and the Stuttering Baboon, too, and two others as well, as can do it; but the Stuttering Baboon's getting too big and fat to do it well; he's a very awkward tumbler. It don't hurt, only at larning; cos you bears more on your hands than your nose.

'Sometimes they says – "Well, let us see you do it," and then p'raps they'll search in their pockets, and say – "O, I haven't got any coppers:" so then we'll force 'em, and p'raps they'll pull out their purse and gives us a little bit of silver.

'Ah, we works hard for what we gets, and then there's the policeman birching us. Some of 'em is so spiteful, they takes up their belt what they uses round the waist to keep their coat tight, and 'll hit us with the buckle; but we generally gives 'em the lucky dodge and gets out of their way.

'One night, two gentlemen, officers they was, was standing in the Haymarket, and a drunken man passed by. There was snow on the ground, and we'd been begging of 'em, and says one of them – "I'll give you a shilling if you'll knock than drunken man over." We was three of us; so we set on him, and soon had him down. After he got up he went and told the policemen, but we all cut round different ways and got off, and then met again. We didn't get the shilling, though, cos a boy crabbed us. He went up to the gentleman, and says he – "Give it me, sir, I'm the boy;" and then we says – "No, sir, it's us." So, says the officer – "I sharn't give it to none of you," and puts it back again in his pockets. We broke a broom over the boy as crabbed us, and then we cut down Waterloo-place, and afterwards we come up to the Haymarket again, and there we met the officers again. I did a caten-wheel, and then says I – "Then won't you give me un now?" and they says – "Go and sweep some mud on that woman." So I went and did it, and then they takes me in a pastry-shop at the corner, and they tells me to tumble on the tables in the shop. I nearly broke one of 'em, they were so delicate. They gived me a fourpenny meat-pie and two penny sponge-cakes, which I puts in my pocket, cos there was another sharing with me. The lady of the shop kept on screaming – "Go and fetch me a police – take the dirty boy out," cos I was standing on the tables in my muddy-feet, and the officers was a bursting their sides with laughing; and says they, "No, he sharn't stir."

'I was frightened, cos if the police had come they'd been safe and sure to have took me. They made me tumble from the door to the end of the shop, and back again, and then I turned 'em a caten-wheel, and was near knocking down all the things as was on the counter.

'They didn't give me no money, only pies; but I got a shilling another time for tumbling to some French ladies and gentlemen in a pastry-cook's shop under the Colonnade. I often goes into a shop like that; I've done it a good many times.

'There was a gentleman once as belonged to a "suckus", [circus] as wanted to take me with him abroad, and teach me tumbling. He had a little mustache, and used to belong to Drury-lane play-house, riding on horses. I went to his place, and stopped there some time. He taught me to put my leg round my neck, and I was just getting along nicely with the splits (going down on the ground with both legs extended), when I left him. They (the splits) used to hurt worst of all; very bad for the thighs. I used, too, to hang with my leg round his neck. When I did anythink he liked, he used to be clapping me on the back. He wasn't so very stunning well off, for he never had what I calls a good dinner – grandmother used to have a better dinner than he, – perhaps only a bit of scrag of mutton between three of us. I don't like meat nor butter, but I likes dripping, and they never had none there. The wife used to drink – ay, very much, on the sly. She used when he was out to send me round with a bottle and sixpence to get a quartern of gin for her, and she'd take it with three or four oysters. Grandmother didn't like the notion of my going away, so she went down one day, and says she – "I wants my child;" and the wife says – "That's according to the master's likings;" and then grandmother says – "What, not my own child?" And then grandmother began talking, and at last, when the master come home, he says to me – "Which will you do, stop here, or go home with your grandmother?" So I come along with her.

'I've been sweeping the crossings getting on for two years. Before that I used to go caten-wheeling after the busses. I don't like the sweeping, and I don't think there's e'er a one of us wot likes it. In the winter we has to be out in the cold, and then in summer we have to sleep out all night, or go asleep on the church-steps, reg'lar tired out.

'One of us'll say at night – "Oh, I'm sleepy now, who's game for a doss? I'm for a doss" – and when we go eight or ten of us into a doorway of the church, where they keep the dead in a kind of airy-like underneath, and there we go to sleep. The most of the boys has got no homes. Perhaps they've got the price of a lodging, but they're hungry, and they eats the money, and then they must lay out. There's some of 'em will stop out in the wet for perhaps the sake of a halfpenny, and get themselves sopping wet. I think all our chaps would like to get out of the work if they could; I'm sure Goose would, and so would I.

'All the boys call me the King, because I tumbles so well, and some calls me "Pluck", and some "Judy". I'm called "Pluck", cause I'm so plucked a going at the gentlemen! Tommy Dunnovan – "Tipperty Tight" – we calls

THE BOY CROSSING-SWEEPERS.

him, cos his trousers is so tight he can hardly move in them sometimes,
– he was the first as called me "Judy". Dunnovan once swallowed a pill
for a shilling. A gentleman in the Haymarket says – "If you'll swallow this
here pill I'll give you a shilling;" and Jimmy says, "All right, sir;" and he
puts it in his mouth, and went to the water-pails near the cab-stand and
swallowed it.

'All the chaps in our gang likes me, and we all likes one another. We
always shows what we gets given to us to eat.

'Sometimes we gets one another up wild, and then that fetches up a
fight, but that isn't often. When two of us fights, the others stands round
and sees fair play. There was a fight last night between "Broke his Bones"
– as we calls Antony Hones – and Neddy Hall – the "Sparrow", or
"Spider", we calls him – something about the root of a pineapple, as we
was aiming with at one another, and that called up a fight. We all stood
round and saw them at it, but neither of 'em licked, for they gived in for
to-day, and they're to finish it to-night. We makes 'em fight fair. We all
of us likes to see a fight, but not to fight ourselves. Hones is sure to beat,
as Spider is as thin as a wafer, and all bones. I can lick the Spider, though
he's twice my size.'

The Street Where the Boy Sweepers Lodged

[pp. 569–70]   I was anxious to see the room in which the gang of boy
crossing-sweepers lived, so that I might judge of their peculiar style of
house-keeping, and form some notion of their principles of domestic
economy.

I asked young Harry and 'the Goose' to conduct me to their lodgings,
and they at once consented, 'the Goose' prefacing his compliance with the
remark, that 'it wern't such as genilmen had been accustomed to, but then
I must take 'em as they was.'

The boys led me in the direction of Drury-lane; and before entering one
of the narrow streets which branch off like the side-bones of a fish's spine
from that long thoroughfare, they thought fit to caution me that I was not
to be frightened, as nobody would touch me, for all was very civil.

The locality consisted of one of those narrow streets which, were it not
for the paved cart-way in the centre would be called a court. Seated on
the pavement at each side of the entrance was a costerwoman with her
basket before her, and her legs tucked up mysteriously under her gown
into a round ball, so that her figure resembled in shape the plaster tumblers
sold by the Italians. These women remained as inanimate as if they had

been carved images, and it was only when a passenger went by that they gave signs of life, by calling out in a low voice, like talking to themselves, 'Two for three haarpence – her-rens' – 'Fine hinguns.'

The street itself is like the description given of thoroughfares in the East. Opposite neighbours could not exactly shake hands out of window, but they could talk together very comfortably; and, indeed, as I passed along, I observed several women with their arms folded up like a cat's paws on the sill, and chatting with their friends over the way.

Nearly all the inhabitants were costermongers, and, indeed, the narrow cartway seemed to have been made just wide enough for a truck to wheel down it. A beershop and a general store, together with a couple of sweeps – whose residences were distinguished by a broom over the door – formed the only exceptions to the street-selling class of inhabitants.

As I entered the place, it gave me the notion that it belonged to a distinct coster colony, and formed one large hawkers' home; for everybody seemed to be doing just as he liked, and I was stared at as if considered an intruder. Women were seated on the pavement, knitting, and repairing their linen; the doorways were filled up with bonnetless girls, who wore their shawls over their head, as the Spanish women do their mantillas; and the youths in corduroy and brass buttons, who were chatting with them, leant against the walls as they smoked their pipes, and blocked up the pavement, as if they were the proprietors of the place. Little children formed a convenient bench out of the kerb-stone; and a party of four men were seated on the footway, playing with cards which had turned to the colour of brown paper from long usage, and marking the points with chalk upon the flags.

The parlour-windows of the houses had all of them wooden shutters, as thick and clumsy-looking as a kitchen flap-table, the paint of which had turned to the dull dirt-colour of an old slate. Some of these shutters were evidently never used as a security for the dwelling, but served only as tables on which to chalk the accounts of the day's sales.

Before most of the doors were costermongers trucks – some standing ready to be wheeled off, and others stained and muddy with the day's work. A few of the costers were dressing up their barrows, arranging the sieves of waxy-looking potatoes – and others taking the stiff herrings, browned like a meerschaum with the smoke they had been dried in, from the barrels beside them, and spacing them out in pennyworths on their trays.

You might guess what each costermonger had taken out that day by the heap of refuse swept into the street before the doors. One house had a blue mound of mussel-shells in front of it – another, a pile of the outside leaves of broccoli and cabbages, turning yellow and slimy with bruises and moisture.

Hanging up beside some of the doors were bundles of old strawberry pottles, stained red with the fruit. Over the trap-doors to the cellars were piles of market-gardeners' sieves, ruddled like a sheep's back with big red letters. In fact, everything that met the eye seemed to be in some way connected with the coster's trade.

From the windows poles stretched out, on which blankets, petticoats, and linen were drying; and so numerous were they, that they reminded me of the flags hung out at a Paris fête. Some of the sheets had patches as big as trap-doors let into their centres; and the blankets were – many of them – as full of holes as a pigeon-house.

As I entered the court, a 'row' was going on; and from a first-floor window a lady, whose hair sadly wanted brushing, was haranguing a crowd beneath, throwing her arms about like a drowning man, and in her excitement thrusting her body half out of her temporary rostrum as energetically as I have seen Punch lean over his theatre.

'The willin dragged her,' she shouted, 'by the hair of her head, at least three yards into the court – the willin! and then he kicked her, and the blood was on his boot.'

It was a sweep who had been behaving in this cowardly manner; but still he had his defenders in the women around him. One with very shiny hair, and an Indian kerchief round her neck, answered the lady in the window, by calling her a 'd—d old cat'; whilst the sweep's wife rushed about, clapping her hands together as quickly as if she was applauding at a theatre, and styled somebody or other 'an old wagabones as she wouldn't dirty her hands to fight with'.

This 'row' had the effect of drawing all the lodgers to the windows – their heads popping out as suddenly as dogs from their kennels in a fancier's yard.

The Boy Sweepers' Room

[pp. 570–71] The room where the boys lodged was scarcely bigger than a coach-house; and so low was the ceiling, that a fly-paper suspended from a clothes-line was on a level with my head, and had to be carefully avoided when I moved about.

One corner of the apartment was completely filled up by a big four-post bedstead, which fitted into a kind of recess as perfectly as if it had been built to order.

286

The old woman who kept this lodging had endeavoured to give it a homely look of comfort, by hanging little black-framed pictures, scarcely bigger than pocket-books, on the walls. Most of these were sacred subjects, with large yellow glories round the heads; though between the drawing representing the bleeding heart of Christ, and the Saviour bearing the Cross, was an illustration of a red-waistcoated sailor smoking his pipe. The Adoration of the Shepherds, again, was matched on the other side of the fireplace by a portrait of Daniel O'Connell.

A chest of drawers was covered over with a green baize cloth, on which books, shelves, and clean glasses were tidily set out.

Where so many persons (for there were about eight of them, including the landlady, her daughter, and grandson) could all sleep, puzzled me extremely.

The landlady wore a frilled nightcap, which fitted so closely to the skull, that it was evident she had lost her hair. One of her eyes was slowly recovering from a blow, which, to use her own words, 'a blackgeyard gave her'. Her lip, too, had suffered in the encounter, for it was swollen and cut.

'I've a nice flock-bid for the boys,' she said, when I inquired into the accommodation of her lodging-house, 'where three of them can slape aisy and comfortable.'

'It's a large bed, sir,' said one of the boys, 'and a warm covering over us; and you see it's better then a regular lodging-house; for, if you want a knife or a cup, you don't have to leave something on it till it's returned.'

The old woman spoke up for her lodgers, telling me that they were good boys, and very honest; 'for,' she added, 'they pays me rig'lar ivery night, which is threepence.'

The only youth as to whose morals she seemed to be at all doubtful was 'the Goose', 'for he kept late hours, and sometimes came home without a penny in his pocket'.

The Girl Crossing-sweeper Sent Out by her Father

[pp. 571–2] A little girl, who worked by herself at her own crossing, gave me some curious information on the subject.

This child had a peculiarly flat face, with a button of a nose, while her mouth was scarcely larger than a button-hole. When she spoke, there was not the slightest expression visible in her features; indeed, one might have fancied she wore a mask and was talking behind it; but her eyes were shining the while as brightly as those of a person in a fever, and kept moving about, restless with her timidity. The green frock she wore was fastened close to the neck, and was turning into a kind of mouldy tint; she also wore a black stuff apron, stained with big patches of gruel, 'from feeding baby at home', as she said. Her hair was tidily dressed, being drawn tightly back from the forehead, like the buy-a-broom girls; and as she stood with her hands thrust up her sleeves, she curtseyed each time before answering, bobbing down like a float, as though the floor under her had suddenly given way.

'I'm twelve years old, please sir, and my name is Margaret R—, and I sweep a crossing in new Oxford-street, by Dunn's-passage, just facing Moses and Sons', sir; by the Catholic school, sir. Mother's been dead these two years, sir, and father's a working cutler, sir; and I lives with him, but he don't get much to do, and so I'm obligated to help him, doing what I can, sir. Since mother's been dead, I've had to mind my little brother and sister, so that I haven't been to school; but when I goes a crossing-sweeping I takes them along with me, and they sits on the steps close by, sir. If it's wet I has to stop at home and take care of them, for father depends upon me for looking after them. Sister's three and a-half year old, and brother's five year, so he's just beginning to help me, sir. I hope he'll get something better than a crossing when he grows up.

'First of all I used to go singing songs in the streets, sir. It was when father had no work, so he stopped at home and looked after the children. I used to sing the "Red, White, and Blue", and "Mother, is the Battle over?" and "The Gipsy Girl", and sometimes I'd get fourpence or fivepence, and sometimes I'd have a chance of making ninepence, sir. Sometimes, though, I'd take a shilling of a Saturday night in the markets.

'At last the songs grew so stale people wouldn't listen to them, and, as I carn't read, I couldn't learn any more, sir. My big brother and father used to learn me some, but I never could get enough out of them for the streets; besides, father was out of work still, and we couldn't get money enough to buy ballads with, and it's no good singing without having them to sell. We live over there, sir, (pointing to a window on the other side of the narrow street).

'The notion come into my head all of itself to sweep crossings, sir. As I used to go up Regent-street I used to see men and women, and girls and boys, sweeping, and the people giving them money, so I thought I'd do the same thing. That's how it come about. Just now the weather is so dry, I don't go to my crossing, but goes out singing. I've learnt some new songs, such as "The Queen of the Navy for ever", and "The Widow's Last Prayer", which is about the wars. I only go sweeping in wet weather, because then's the best time. When I am there, there's some ladies and gentlemen as gives to me regular. I knows them by sight; and there's a beer-shop where they give me some bread and cheese whenever I go.

'I generally takes about sixpence, or sevenpence, or eightpence on the crossing, from about nine o'clock in the morning till four in the evening, when I come home. I don't stop out at nights because father won't let me, and I'm got to be home to see to baby.

'My broom costs me twopence ha'penny, and in wet wether it lasts a week, but in dry weather we seldom uses it.

'When I sees the busses and carriages coming I stands on the side, for I'm afeard of being runned over. In winter I goes out and cleans ladies' doors, general about Lincoln's-inn, for the housekeepers. I gets twopence a door, but it takes a long time when the ice is hardened, so that I carn't do only about two or three.

'I carn't tell whether I shall always stop at sweeping, but I've no clothes, and so I carn't get a situation; for, though I'm small and young, yet I could do housework, such as cleaning.

'No, sir, there's no gang on my crossing – I'm all alone. If another girl or a boy was to come and take it when I'm not there, I should stop on it as well as him or her, and go shares with 'em.'

Girl Crossing-sweeper

[pp. 572–3] I was told that a little girl formed one of the association of young sweepers, and at my request one of the boys went to fetch her.

She was a clean-washed little thing, with a pretty, expressive countenance, and each time she was asked a question she frowned, like a baby in its sleep, while thinking of the answer. In her ears she wore instead of rings loops of string, 'which the doctor had put there because her sight was wrong'. A cotton velvet bonnet, scarcely larger than the sun-shades worn at the sea-side, hung on her shoulders, leaving exposed her head, with the hair as rough as tow. Her green stuff gown was hanging in tatters, with long three-cornered rents as large as penny kites, showing the grey lining underneath; and her mantle was separated into so many pieces, that it was only held together by the braiding at the edge.

As she conversed with me, she played with the strings of her bonnet, rolling them up as if curling them, on her singularly small and also singularly dirty fingers.

'I'll be fourteen, sir, a fortnight before next Christmas. I was born in Liquorpond-street, Gray's Inn-lane. Father come over from Ireland, and was a bricklayer. He had pains in his limbs and wasn't strong enough, so he give it over. He's dead now – been dead a long time, sir. I was a littler girl then than I am now, for I wasn't above eleven at that time. I lived with mother after father died. She used to sell things in the streets – yes, sir, she was a coster. About a twelvemonth after father's death, mother was taken bad with the cholera, and died. I then went along with both grandmother and grandfather, who was a porter in Newgate Market; I stopped there until I got a place as servant of all-work. I was only turned, just turned, eleven then. I worked along with a French lady and gentleman in Hatton Garden, who used to give me a shilling a week and my tea. I used to go home to grandmother's to dinner every day. I hadn't to do any work only just to clean the room and nuss the child. It was a nice little thing. I couldn't understand what the French people used to say, but there was a boy working there, and he used to explain to me what they meant.

'I left them because they was going to a place called Italy – perhaps you may have heerd tell of it, sir. Well, I suppose they must have been Italians, but we calls everybody, whose talk we don't understand, French. I went back to grandmother's, but, after grandfather died, she couldn't keep me, and so I went out begging – she sent me. I carried lucifer-matches and stay-laces fust. I used to carry about a dozen laces, and perhaps I'd sell six out of them. I suppose I used to make about sixpence a day, and I used to take it home to grandmother, who kept and fed me.

'At last, finding I didn't get much at begging, I thought I'd go crossing-sweeping. I saw other children doing it. I says to myself, "I'll go and buy a broom", and I spoke to another little girl, who was sweeping up Holborn, who told me what I was to do. "But," says she, "don't come and cut up me."

'I went fust to Holborn, near to home, at the end of Red Lion-street. Then I was frightened of the cabs and carriages, but I'd get there early, about eight o'clock, and sweep the crossing clean, and I'd stand at the side on the pavement, and speak to the gentlemen and ladies before they crossed.

'There was a couple of boys, sweepers at the same crossing before I went there. I went to them and asked if I might come and sweep there too, and they said Yes, if I would give them some of the halfpence I got. These was boys about as old as I was, and they said, if I earned sixpence, I was to give them twopence a-piece; but they never give me nothink of theirs. I never took more than sixpence, and out of that I had to give fourpence, so that I did not do so well as with the laces.

'The crossings made my hands sore with the sweeping, and, as I got so little, I thought I'd try somewhere else. Then I got right down to the Fountings in Trafalgar-square, by the crossing at the statey on 'orseback.

There were a good many boys and girls on that crossing at the time – five of them; so I went along with them. When I fust went they said, "Here's another fresh 'un." They come up to me and says, "Are you going to sweep here?" and I says, "Yes;" and they says, "You mustn't come here, there's too many;" and I says, "They're different ones every day" – for they're not regular there, but shift about, sometimes one lot of boys and girls, and the next day another. They didn't say another word to me, and so I stopped.

'It's a capital crossing, but there's so many of us, it spiles it. I seldom gets more than sevenpence a day, which I always takes home to grandmother.

'I've been on that crossing about three months. They always calls me Ellen, my regular name, and behaves very well to me. If I see anybody coming, I call them out as the boys does, and then they are mine.

'There's a boy and myself, and another strange girl, works on our side of the statey, and another lot of boys and girls on the other.

'I like Saturdays the best day of the week, because that's the time as gentlemen as has been at work has their money, and then they are more generous. I gets more then, perhaps ninepence, but not quite a shilling, on the Saturday.

'I've had a threepenny-bit give to me, but never sixpence. It was a gentleman, and I should know him again. Ladies gives me less than gentlemen. I foller 'em, saying, "If you please, sir, give a poor girl a halfpenny;" but if the police are looking, I stop still.

'I never goes out on Sunday, but stops at home with grandmother. I don't stop out at nights like the boys, but I gets home by ten at latest.'

VOLUME THREE

OUR STREET FOLK

STREET ENTERTAINMENT

Punch

[pp. 51-5] The performer of Punch that I saw was a short, dark, pleasant-looking man, dressed in a very greasy and very shiny green shooting-jacket. This was fastened together by one button in front, all the other button-holes having been burst through. Protruding from his bosom, a corner of the pandean pipes was just visible, and as he told me the story of his adventures, he kept playing with the band of his very limp and very rusty old beaver hat. He had formerly been a gentleman's servant, and was especially civil in his manners. He came to me with his hair tidily brushed for the occasion, but apologised for his appearance on entering the room. He was very communicative, and took great delight in talking like Punch, with his call in his mouth, while some young children were in the room, and who, hearing the well-known sound of Punch's voice, looked all about for the figure. Not seeing the show, they fancied the man had the figure in his pocket, and that the sounds came from it. The change from Punch's voice to the man's natural tone was managed without an effort, and instantaneously. It had a very peculiar effect.

'I am the proprietor of a Punch's show', he said. 'I goes about with it myself, and performs inside the frame behind the green baize. I have a pardner what plays the music – the pipes and drum; him as you see'd with me. I have been five-and-twenty year now at the business. I wish I'd never seen it, though it's *been* a money-making business – indeed, the best of all the street hexhibitions I may say. I am fifty years old. I took to it for money gains – that was what I done it for. I formerly lived in service – was a footman in a gentleman's family. When I first took to it, I could make two and three pounds a day – I could so. You see, the way in which I took first to the business was this here – there was a party used to come and "cheer" for us at my master's house, and her son having a hexhibition of his own, and being in want of a pardner, axed me if so be I'd go out, which was a thing that I degraded at the time. He gave me information as to what the money-taking was, and it seemed to me that good, that it would pay me better nor service. I had twenty pounds a-year in my place, and my

295

board and lodging, and two suits of clothes, but the young man told me as how I could make one pound a day at the Punch-and-Judy business, after a little practice. I took a deal of persuasion, though, before I'd join him – it was beneath my dignity to fall from a footman to a showman. But, you see, the French gennelman as I lived with (he were a merchant in the city, and had fourteen clerks working for him) went back to his own country to reside, and left me with a written kerrackter; but that was no use to me: though I'd fine recommendations at the back of it, no one would look at it; so I was five months out of employment, knocking about – living first on my wages and then on my clothes, till all was gone but the few rags on my back. So I began to think that the Punch-and-Judy business was better than starving after all. Yes, I should think anything was better than that, though it's a business that, after you've once took to, you never can get out of – people fancies you know too much, and won't have nothing to say to you. If I got a situation at a tradesman's, why the boys would be sure to recognise me behind the counter, and begin a shouting into the shop (they *must* shout, you know): "Oh, there's Punch and Judy – there's Punch a-sarving out the customers!" Ah, it's a great annoyance being a public kerrackter, I can assure you, sir; go where you will, it's "Punchy, Punchy!" As for the boys, they'll never leave me alone till I die, I know; and I suppose in my old age I shall have to take to the parish broom. All our forefathers died in the workhouse. I don't know a Punch's showman that hasn't. One of my pardners was buried by the workhouse; and even old Pike, the most noted showman as ever was, died in the workhouse – Pike and Porsini. Porsini was the first original street Punch, and Pike was his apprentice; their names is handed down to posterity among the noblemen and footmen of the land. They both died in the workhouse, and, in course, I shall do the same. Something else *might* turn up, to be sure. We can't say what this luck of the world is. I'm obliged to strive very hard – very hard indeed, sir, now, to get a living; and then not to get it after all – at times, compelled to go short, often.

'Punch, you know, sir, is a dramatic performance in two hacts. It's a play, you may say. I don't think it can be called a tragedy hexactly; a drama is what we names it. There is a tragic parts, and comic and sentimental parts, too. Some families where I performs will have it most sentimental – in the original style; them families is generally sentimental theirselves. Others is all for the comic, and then I has to kick up all the games I can. To the sentimental folk I am obliged to perform werry steady and werry slow, and leave out all comic words and business. They won't have no ghost, no coffin, and no devil; and that's what I call spiling the performance entirely. It's the march of hintellect wot's a doing all this – it is, sir. But I was a going to tell you about my first jining the business. Well, you see, after a good deal of persuading, and being drew to it, I may say, I consented to go out with the young man as I were a-speaking about. He was to give me twelve shillings a week and my keep, for two years certain, till I could get my own show things together, and for that I was to carry the show, and go round and *collect*. Collecting, you know, sounds better than begging; the pronounciation's better like. Sometimes the people says, when they sees us a coming round, "Oh, here they comes a-begging" – but it can't be begging, you know, when you're a hexerting yourselves. I couldn't play the drum and pipes, so the young man used to do that himself, to call the people together before he got into the show. I used to stand outside, and patter to the figures. The first time that ever I went out with Punch was in the beginning of August, 1825. I did all I could to avoid being seen. My dignity was hurt at being hobligated to take to the streets for a living. At fust I fought shy, and used to feel queer somehow, you don't know how like, whenever the people used to look at me. I remember werry well the first street as ever I performed in. It was off Gray's Inn, one of them quiet, genteel streets, and when the mob began to gather round I felt all-overish, and I turned my head to the frame instead of the people. We hadn't had no rehearsals aforehand, and I did the patter quite permiscuous. There was not much talk, to be sure, required then; and what little there was, consisted merely in calling out the names of the figures as they came up, and these my master prompted me with from inside the frame. But little as there was for me to do, I know I never could have done it, if it hadn't been for the spirits – the false spirits, you see (a little drop of gin), as my master guv me in the morning. The first time as ever I made my appearance in public, I collected as much as eight shillings, and my master said, after the performance was over, "You'll do!" You see I was partly in livery, and looked a little bit decent like. After this was over, I kept on going out with my master for two years, as I had agreed, and at the end of that time I had saved enough to start a show of my own. I bought the show of old Porsini, the man as first brought Punch into the streets of England. To be sure, there was a woman over here with it before then. Her name was – I can't think of it just now, but she never performed in the streets, so we consider Porsini as our real forefather. It isn't much more nor seventy years since Porsini (he was a werry old man when he died, and blind) showed the hexhibition in the streets of London. I've heerd tell that old Porsini used to take very often as much as ten pounds a-day, and he used to sit down to his fowls and wine, and the very best of everything, like the first gennelman in the land; indeed, he made enough money at the business to be quite tip-top gennelman, that he did. But he never took care of a halfpenny he got. He was that independent, that if he was wanted to perform, sir, he'd come at his time, not your'n. At last, he reduced himself to want, and died in St Giles's workhouse. Ah, poor fellow! he oughtn't to have been allowed to die where he did, after amusing the public for so many years. Every one in London knowed him. Lords, dukes, princes, squires, and wagabonds – all used to stop to laugh at his performance, and a funny clever old fellow he was. He was past performing when I bought my show of him, and werry poor. He was living in the Coal-yard, Drury-lane, and had scarcely a bit of food to eat. He had spent all he had got in drink, and in treating friends – aye, any one, no matter who. He didn't study the world, nor himself neither. As fast as the money came it went, and when it was gone, why, he'd go to work and get more. His show was a very inferior one, though it were the fust – nothing at all like them about now – nothing near as good. If you only had four sticks then, it was quite enough to make plenty of money out of, so long as it was Punch. I gave him thirty-five shillings for the stand, figures and all. I bought it cheap, you see, for it was thrown on one side, and was of no use to any one but such as myself. There was twelve figures and the other happaratus, such as the gallows, ladder, horse, bell, and stuffed dog. The characters was Punch, Judy, Child, Beadle, Scaramouche, Nobody, Jack Ketch, the Grand Senoor, the Doctor, the Devil (there was no Ghost used then), Merry Andrew, and the Blind Man. These last two kerrackters are quite done with now. The heads of the kerrackters was all carved in wood, and dressed in the proper costume of the country. There was at that time, and is now a real carver for the Punch business. He was dear, but werry good and hexcellent. His Punch's head was the best as I ever seed. The nose and chin used to meet quite close together. A set of new figures, dressed and all, would come to about fifteen pounds. Each head costs five shillings for the bare carving alone, and every figure that we has takes at least a yard of cloth to dress him, besides ornaments and things that comes werry expensive. A good show at the present time will cost three pounds odd for the stand alone – that's including baize, the frontispiece, the back scene, the cottage, and the letter cloth, or what is called the drop-scene at the theatres. In the old ancient style, the back scene used to pull up and change into a gaol scene, but that's all altered now.

'We've got more upon the comic business now, and tries to do more with Toby than with the prison scene. The prison is what we calls the sentimental style. Formerly Toby was only a stuffed figure. It was Pike who first hit upon hintroducing a live dog, and a great hit it were – it made a grand alteration in the hexhibition, for now the performance is called Punch and Toby *as well*. There is one Punch about the streets at present that tries it on with three dogs, but that ain't much of a go – too much of a good thing I calls it. Punch, as I said before, is a drama in two hacts. We don't drop the scene at the end of the first – the drum and pipes strikes up instead. The first act we consider to end with Punch being taken to prison for the murder of his wife and child. The great difficulty in performing Punch consists in the speaking, which is done by a call, or whistle in the mouth, such as this here.' (He then produced the call from his waistcoat pocket. It was a small flat instrument, made of two curved pieces of metal about the size of a knee-buckle, bound together with black thread. Between these was a plate of some substance (apparently silk), which he said was a secret. The call, he told me, was tuned to a musical instrument, and took a considerable time to learn. He afterwards took from his pocket two of the small metallic plates unbound. He said the composition they were made of was also one of the 'secrets of the purfession'. They were not tin, nor zinc, because 'both of them metals were poisons in the mouth, and hinjurious to the constitution.') 'These calls,' he continued, 'we often sell to gennelmen for a sovereign a-piece, and for that we give 'em a receipt how to use them. They ain't whistles, but calls, or unknown tongues, as we sometimes names 'em, because with them in the mouth we can pronounce each word as plain as any parson. We have two or three kinds – one for out-of-doors, one for in-doors, one for speaking and for singing, and another for selling. I've sold many a one to gennelmen going along, so I generally keeps a hextra one with me. Porsini brought the calls into this country with him from Italy, and we who are now in the purfession have all learnt how to make and use them, either from him or those as he had taught 'em to. I larnt the use of mine from Porsini himself. My master whom I went out with at first would never teach me, and was werry partickler in keeping it all secret from me. Porsini taught me the call at the time I bought his show of him. I was six months in perfecting myself in the use of it. I kept practising away night and morning with it, until I got it quite perfect. It was no use trying at home, 'cause it sounds

PUNCH'S SHOWMEN.

quite different in the hopen hair. Often when I've made 'em at home, I'm obliged to take the calls to pieces after trying 'em out in the streets, they've been made upon too weak a scale. When I was practising, I used to go into the parks, and fields, and out-of-the-way places, so as to get to know how to use it in the hopen hair. Now I'm reckoned one of the best speakers in the whole purfession. When I made my first appearance as a regular performer of Punch on my own account, I did feel uncommon narvous, to be sure: though I know'd the people couldn't see me behind the baize, still I felt as if all the eyes of the country were upon me. It was as much as hever I could do to get the words out, and keep the figures from shaking. When I struck up the first song, my voice trembled so as I thought I never should be able to get to the hend of the first hact. I soon, however, got over that there, and at present I'd play before the whole bench of bishops as cool as a cowcumber. We always have a pardner now to play the drum and pipes, and collect the money. This, however, is only a recent dodge. In older times we used to go about with a trumpet – that was Porsini's ancient style; but now that's stopped. Only her majesty's mails may blow trumpets in the streets at present. The fust person who went out with me was my wife. She used to stand outside, and keep the boys from peeping through the baize, whilst I was performing behind it; and she used to collect the money afterwards as well. I carried the show and trumpet, and she the box. She's been dead these five years now. Take one week with another, all through the year, I should say I made then five pounds regular. I *have* taken as much as two pounds ten shillings in one day in the streets; and I used to think it a bad day's business at that time if I took only one pound. You can see Punch has been good work – a money-making business – and beat all mechanics right out. If I could take as much as I did when I first began, what must my forefathers have done when the business was five times as good as ever it were in my time? Why, I leaves you to judge what old Porsini and Pike must have made. Twenty years ago I have often and often got seven shillings and eight shillings for one hexhibition in the streets: two shillings and three shillings I used to think low to get at one collection; and many times I'd perform eight or ten times in a day. We didn't care much about work then, for we could get money fast enough; but now I often show twenty times in the day, and get scarcely a bare living at it arter all. That shows the times, you know, sir – what things was and is now. Arter performing in the streets of a day we usd to attend private parties in the hevening, and get sometimes as much as two pounds for the hexhibition. This used to be at the juvenile parties of the nobility; and the performance lasted about an hour and a half. For a short performance of half-an-hour at a gennelman's house we never had less than one pound. A performance outside the house was two shillings and sixpence; but we often got as much as ten shillings for it. I have performed afore almost all the nobility. Lord — was particular partial to us, and one of our greatest patronizers. At the time of the Police Bill I met him at Cheltenham on my travels, and he told me as he had saved Punch's neck once more; and it's through him principally that we are allowed to exhibit in the streets. Punch is exempt from the Police Act. If you read the hact throughout, you won't find Punch mentioned in it. But all I've been telling you is about the business as it was. What it *is*, is a werry different consarn. A good day for us now seldom gets beyond five shillings, and that's between myself and my pardner, who plays the drum and pipes. Often we are out all day, and get a mere nuffing. Many days we have been out and taken nuffing at all – that's werry common when we dwells upon horders. By dwelling on horders, I means looking out for gennelmen what want us to play in front of their houses. When we strike up in the hopen street we take upon a haverage only threepence a show. In course we *may* do more, but that's about the sum, take one street performance with another. Them kind of performances is what we calls "short showing". We gets the halfpence and hooks it. A "long pitch" is the name we gives to performances that lasts about half an hour or more. Them long pitches we confine solely to street corners in public thoroughfares; and then we take about a shilling upon a haverage, and more if it's to be got – we never turns away nuffing. "Boys, look up your fardens," says the outside man; "it ain't half over yet, we'll show it all through." The short shows we do only in private by-streets, and of them we can get through about twenty in the day; that's as much as we can tackle – ten in the morning, and ten in the afternoon. Of the long pitches we can only do eight in the day. We start on our rounds at nine in the morning, and remain out till dark at night. We gets a snack at the publics on our road. The best hours for Punch are in the morning from nine till ten, because then the children are at home. Arter that, you know, they goes out with the maids for a walk. From twelve till three is good again, and then from six till nine; that's because the children are mostly at home at them hours. We make much more by horders for performance houtside the gennelmen's houses, than we do by performing in public in the hopen streets. Monday is the best day for street business; Friday is no day at all, because then the poor people has spent all their money. If we was to pitch on a Friday, we shouldn't take a halfpenny in the streets, so we in general on that day goes round for horders. Wednesday, Thursday, and Friday is the best days for us with horders at gennelmen's houses. We do much better in the spring than at any other time in the year, excepting holiday time, at Midsummer and Christmas. That's what we call Punch's season. We do most at hevening parties in the holiday time, and if there's a pin to choose between them, I should say Christmas holidays was the best. For attending hevening parties now we generally get one pound and our refreshments – as much more as they like to give us. But the business gets slacker and slacker every season. Where I went to ten parties twenty years ago, I don't go to two now. People isn't getting tired of our performances, but stingier – that's it. Everybody looks at their money now afore they parts with it, and gennelfolks haggles and cheapens us down to shillings and sixpences, as if they was guineas in the holden time. Our business is werry much like hackney-coach work; we do best in vet vether. It looks like rain this evening, and I'm uncommon glad on it, to be sure. You see, the vet keeps the children in-doors all day, and then they wants something to quiet 'em a bit; and the mothers and fathers, to pacify the dears, gives us a horder to perform. It mustn't rain cats and dogs – that's as bad as no rain at all. What we likes is a regular good, steady Scotch mist, for then we takes double what we takes on other days. In summer we does little or nothing; the children are out all day enjoying themselves in the parks. The best pitch of all in London is Leicester-square; there's all sorts of classes, you see, passing there. Then comes Regent-street (the corner of Burlington-street is uncommon good, and there's a good publican there besides). Bond-street ain't no good now. Oxford-street, up by Old Cavendish-street, or Oxford-market, or Wells-street, are all favourite pitches for Punch. We don't do much in the City. People has their heads all full of business there, and them as is greedy arter the money ain't no friend of Punch's. Tottenham-court-road, the New-road, and all the henvirons of London, is pretty good. Hampstead, tho', ain't no good; they've got too poor there. I'd sooner not go out at all than to Hampstead. Belgrave-square, and all about that part, is uncommon good; but where there's many chapels Punch won't do at all. I did once, though, strike up hopposition to a street preacher wot was a holding forth in the New-road, and did uncommon well. All his flock, as he called 'em, left him, and come over to look at me. Punch and preaching is two different creeds – hopposition parties, I may say. We in generally walks from twelve to twenty mile every day, and carries the show, which weighs a good half-hundred, at the least. Arter great exertion, our woice werry often fails us; for speaking all day through the "call" is werry trying, 'specially when we are chirruping up so as to bring the children to the vinders. The boys is the greatest nuisances we has to contend with. Wherever we goes we are sure of plenty of boys for a hindrance; but they've got no money, bother 'em! and they'll follow us for miles, so that we're often compelled to go miles to awoid 'em. Many parts is swarming with boys, such as Vitechapel. Spitalfields that's the worst place for boys I ever come a-near; they're like flies in summer there, only much more thicker. I never shows my face within miles of them parts. Chelsea, again, has an uncommon lot of boys; and wherever we know the children swarm, there's the spots we makes a point of awoiding. Why, the boys is such a hobstruction to our performance, that often we are obliged to drop the curtain for 'em. They'll throw one another's caps into the frame while I'm inside on it, and do what we will, we can't keep 'em from poking their fingers through the baize and making holes to peep through. Then they *will* keep tapping the drum; but the worst of all is, the most of 'em ain't got a farthing to bless themselves with, and they *will* shove into the best place. Soldiers, again, we don't like, they've got no money – no, not even so much as pockets, sir. Nusses ain't no good. Even if the mothers of the dear little children has given 'em a penny to spend, why the nusses takes it from 'em, and keeps it for ribbins. Sometimes we can coax a penny out of the children, but the nusses knows too much to be gammoned by us. Indeed, servants in generally don't do the thing what's right to us – some is good to us, but the most of 'em will have poundage out of what we gets. About sixpence out of every half-crown is what the footman takes from us. We in generally goes into the country in the summer time for two or three months. Watering-places is werry good in July and August. Punch mostly goes down to the sea-side with the quality. Brighton, though, ain't no account; the Pavilion's done up with, and therefore Punch had discontinued his visits. We don't put up at the trampers' houses on our travels, but in generally inns is where we stays; because we considers ourselves to be above the other showmen and mendicants. At one lodging-house as I stopped at once in Warwick, there was as many as fifty staying there what got their living by street performances – the greater part were Italian boys and girls. There are altogether as many as sixteen Punch-and-Judy frames in England. Eight of these is at work in London, and the other eight in the country; and to each of these frames there are two men. We are all acquainted with one another; are all sociable together, and know where each other is, and what they are a-doing on. When one comes home, another goes out; that's the way we proceed through life. It wouldn't do for two to go to the same place. If two of us happens to meet at one town, we jine, and shift pardners, and share the money. One goes one way, and one another, and we meet at night, and reckon up over a sociable pint or a glass. We shift pardners so as each may know how much the other has taken. It's the common practice for the man what performs Punch to share with the one wot plays the drum and pipes – each has half wot is collected; but if the pardner can't play the drum and pipes, and only carries the frame, and collects, then his share is but a third of what is taken till he learns how to perform himself. The street performers of London lives mostly in little rooms of their own; they has generally wives, and one or two children, who are brought up to the business. Some lives about the Westminster-road, and St George's East. A great many are in Lock's-fields – they are all the old school that way. Then some, or rather the principal part of the showmen, are to be found about Lisson-grove. In the neighbourhood there is a house of call, where they all assembles in the evening. There are a very few in Brick-lane, Spital-fields, now; that is mostly deserted by showmen. The West-end is the great resort of all; for it's there the money lays, and there the showmen abound. We all know one another, and can tell in what part of the country the others are. We have intelligence by letters from all parts. There's a Punch I knows on now is either in the Isle of Man, or on his way to it.'

The Street Conjurer

[pp. 117–20] 'I call myself a wizard as well; but that's only the polite term for conjurer; in fact, I should think that wizard meant an astrologer, and more of a fortune-teller. I was fifteen years of age when I first began my professional life; indeed I opened with Gentleman Cooke at the Rotunda, in Blackfriars'-road, and there I did Jeremiah Stitchem to his Billy Button.

'My father held a very excellent situation in the Customs, and lived at his ease, in very affluent circumstances. His library alone was worth two hundred pounds. I was only ten years of age when my father died. He was a very gay man, and spent his income to the last penny. He was a very gay man, very gay. After my mother was left a widow, the library was swept off for a year's rent. I was too young to understand its value, and my mother was in too much grief to pay attention to her affairs. Another six-months' rent sold up the furniture. We took a small apartment close in the neighbourhood. My mother had no means, and we were left to shift for ourselves. I was a good boy, and determined to get something to do. The first day I went out I got a situation at four shillings a week, to mind the boots outside a boot-maker's shop in Newington Causeway. The very first week I was there I was discharged, for I fell asleep on my stool at the door, and a boy stole a pair of boots. From there I went to a baker's, and had to carry out the bread, and for four years I got different employments, as errand boy or anything.

'For many years the mall opposite Bedlam was filled with nothing else but shows and show-people. All the caravans and swing-boats, and what not, used to assemble there till the next fair was on. They didn't perform there, it was only their resting-place. My mother was living close by, and every opportunity I had I used to associate with the boys belonging to the shows, and then I'd see them practising their tumbling and tricks. I was so fond of this that I got practising with these boys. I'd go and paint my face as clown, and although dressed in my ordinary clothes I'd go and tumble with the rest of the lads, until I could do it as well as they could. I did it for devilment, that's what I call it, and that it was which first made me think of being a professional.

'From there I heard of a situation to sell oranges, biscuits, and ginger-beer, at the Surrey Theatre. It was under Elliston's management. I sold the porter up in the gallery, and I had three-halfpence out of every shilling, and I could make one shilling and sixpence a-night; but the way I used to do it at that time was this: I went to fetch the beer, and then I'd get half-a-gallon of table-beer and mix it with the porter; and I tell you, I've made such a thing as fifteen shillings of a boxing-night. I alone could sell five gallons of a night; but then their pints at that time was tin measures, and little more than half-a-pint: besides, I'd froth it up. It was threepence a pint, and a wonderful profit it must have been. From there I got behind the scenes as supernumerary, at the time Nelson Lee was manager of the supers.

'At this time the Rotunda in the Blackfriars'-road was an hotel kept by a Mr Ford. Mr Cook rented certain portions of the building, and went to a wonderful expense building a Circus there. The history of the Rotunda is that at one time it was a museum, and the lecture-hall is there to the present day. It's a beautiful building, and the pillars are said to be very valuable, and made of rice. It's all let to one party, a Frenchman, but he keeps the lecture-hall closed. When Cook took the Rotunda I asked him for an engagement, and he complied. I was mad for acting. I met with great success as Jeremiah Stitchem; and the first week he gave me one pound. Cook didn't make a good thing of it. Nobody could get their money, and the circus was closed. Then a Mr Edwards took it. He was an optician, and opened it as a penny exhibition, with a magic lantern and a conjurer. Now comes how I became a conjurer. I couldn't tear myself away from the Rotunda. I went there and hovered about the door day and night. I wanted to get a situation there. He knew me when I was in the circus, and he asked me what I was a-doing of. I said, "Nothing, sir." Then he offered to give me one of the door-keeper's places, from ten in the morning till eleven at night, for three shillings a day, and I took it. One day the conjurer that was there didn't come, but they opened the doors just the same, and there was an immense quantity of people waiting there. They couldn't do nothing without the conjurer. He always left his apparatus there of a night, in a bag. Well, this Edwards, knowing that I could do a few tricks, he came up to me and asks whether I knew where the wizard lived. I didn't, and Edwards says, "What am I to do? I shall have to return this money: I shall go mad." I said I could do a few tricks; and he says, "Well, go and do it." The people was making a row, stamping and calling out, "Now then, is this here wizard coming!" When I went in, I give great satisfaction. I went and did all the tricks, just as the other had done it. At that time it was the custom to say after each performance, "Ladies and gentlemen, allow me to inform you that I get no salary here, and only have to rely upon your generosity for a collection." When the plate went round I got one shilling and sixpence. "Hulloa!" I said to myself, "is this the situation?" Then I sold some penny books, explaining how the tricks was done, and I got sixpence more. That was two shillings. I had four shillings a day besides, and they would have sometimes twenty houses a day, and I have seen thirty. The houses were not always very good. Sometimes we'd perform to seven or to twenty. It all told up. It was at night we did the principal work – crowded upwards of two hundred there. We weren't in the Circus, but in the Rotunda. I'd make fifteen shillings a night then. I got a permanent engagement then. I made too much money. I went and bought a pack of cards and card-boxes, and a pea-caddy for passing peas from a handkerchief to a vase, and linking-rings, and some tape. That, with tying knots in a silk handkerchief, concluded the whole of my performances. In fact, it was all I knew. My talking helped me immensely, for I could patter well to them, and the other wizard couldn't.

'I left the Rotunda in consequence of the party having other novelties. He had Ambrosini, who done the sticks and string balls; but I was there three or four years, and that's a long time to be at one place. Then I joined a street-performer. He used to do the fire-proof business, such as eating the link, and the burning tow, and so on. Then I manufactured a portable

table: it folded up, and I could carry it under my arm. It was as large as an ordinary dressing-table. We went in equal shares. I was dressed with ballet shirt, and braces, with spangled tights and fleshings. We pulled our coats off when we begun to perform. All the tricks we carried in a bag.

'The first pitch we made was near Bond-street. He began with his part of the performance whilst I was dressing up the table. It was covered with black velvet with fringe, and the apparatus ranged on it. After him I began my performance, and he went round for the nobbings. I did card tricks, such as the sautez-le-coup with the little finger. It's dividing the pack in half, and then bringing the bottom half to the top; and then, if there's a doubt, you can convey the top card to the bottom again; or if there's any doubt, you can bring the pack to its original position. It was Lord de Roos' trick. He won heaps of money at it. He had pricked cards. You see, if you prick a card at the corner, card-players skin their finger at the end, so as to make it sensitive, and they can tell a pricked card in a moment. Besides sautez-le-coup, I used to do innumerable others, such as telling a named card by throwing a pack in the air and catching the card on a sword point. Then there was telling people's thoughts by the cards. All card tricks are feats of great dexterity and quickness of hand. I never used a false pack of cards. There are some made for amateurs, but professionals never use trick cards. The greatest art is what is termed forcing, that is, making a party take the card you wish him to; and let him try ever so well, he will have it, though he's not conscious of it. Another feat of dexterity is slipping the card, that is, slipping it from top, bottom, or centre, or placing one or two cards from the top. If you're playing a game at all-fours and you know the ace of clubs is at the bottom, you can slip it one from the top, so that you know your partner opposite has it. These are the only two principal things in card tricks, and if you can do them dexterously you can do a great part of a wizard's art. Sautez-le-coup is the principal thing, and it's done by placing the middle finger in the centre of the pack, and then with the right hand working the change. I can do it with one hand.

'We did well with pitching in the streets. We'd take ten shillings of a morning, and then go out in the afternoon again and take perhaps fifteen shillings of nobbings. The footmen were our best customers in the morning, for they had leisure then. We usually went to the squares and such parts at the West-end. This was twenty years ago, and it isn't anything like so good now, in consequence of my partner dying of consumption; brought on, I think, by fire eating, for he was a very steady young fellow and not at all given to drink. I was for two years in the streets with the fire-eating, and we made I should say such a thing as fifty shillings

STREET CONJURER PERFORMING.

a week each. Then you must remember, we could have made more if we had liked; for some mornings, if we had had a good day before, we wouldn't go out if it was raining, or we had been up late. I next got a situation, and went to a wax works to do conjuring. It was a penny exhibition in the New Cut, Lambeth. I had four shillings a day and nobbings – a collection, and what with selling my books, it came to ten shillings a day, for we had never less than ten and often twenty performances a day. They had the first dissecting figure there – a Samson – and they took off the cranium and showed the brains, and also the stomach, and showed the intestines. It was the first ever shown in this country, and the maker of it had (so they say) a pension of one hundred pounds a year for having composed it. He was an Italian.

'We were burnt down at Birmingham, and I lost all my rattle-traps. However, the inhabitants made up a subscription which amply repaid me for my loss, and I then came to London, hearing that the Epsom races was on at the time, which I wouldn't have missed Epsom races, not at that time, not for any amount of money, for it was always good to one as three pounds, and I have had as much as seven pounds from one carriage alone. It was Lord Chesterfield's, and each gentleman in it gave us a sov. I went down with three acrobats to Epsom, but they were dealing unfair with me, and there was something that I didn't like going on; so I quarrelled with them and joined with another conjurer, and it was on this very occasion we got the seven pounds from one carriage. We both varied in our entertainments; because, when I had done my performance, he made a collection; and when he had done I got the nobbings. We went to Lord Chesterfield's carriage on the hill, and there I did the sovereign trick. "My Lord, will you oblige me with the temporary loan of a sovereign?" "Yes, old fellow: what are you going to do with it?" I then did passing the sovereign, he having marked it first; and then, though he held it tightly, I changed it for a farthing. I did this for Lord Waterford and Lord Walde-grave, and the whole of them in the carriage. I always said, "Now, my Lord, are you sure you hold it?" "Yes, old fellow." "Now, my Lord, if I was to take the sovereign away from you without you knowing it, wouldn't you say I was perfectly welcome to it?" He'd say, "Yes, old fellow; go on." Then, when he opened the handkerchief he had a farthing, and all of them made me a present of the sovereign I had performed with.

'Then we went to the Grand Stand, and then after our performance they'd throw us halfpence from above. We had our table nicely fitted up. We wouldn't take halfpence. We would collect up the coppers, perhaps five or six shillings worth, and then we'd throw the great handful among the boys. "A bit of silver, your honours, if you please"; then sixpence would come, and then a shilling, and in ten minutes we would have a sovereign. We must have earned our six pounds each that Epsom Day; but then our expenses were heavy, for we paid three shillings a night for our lodging alone.

'It was about this time that I took to busking. I never went into tap-rooms, only into parlours; because one parlour would be as good as a dozen tap-rooms, and two good parlours a night I was quite satisfied with. My general method was this: If I saw a good company in the parlour, I could tell in a moment whether they were likely to suit me. If they were conversing on politics it was no good, you might as well attempt to fly. I have many a time gone into a parlour, and called for my half-quartern of gin and little drop of cold water, and then, when I began my per-formances, it has been "No, no! we don't want anything of that kind," and there has been my half-hour thrown away. The company I like best are jolly-looking men, who are sitting silently smoking, or reading the paper. I always got the privilege of performing by behaving with civility to my patrons. Some conjurers, when the company ain't agreeable, will say, "But I will perform"; and then comes a quarrel, and the room is in future forbid to that man. But I, if they objected, always said, "Very well, gentlemen, I'm much obliged to you all the same: perhaps another time. Bad to-night, better next night." Then when I came again some would say, "I didn't give you anything the other night, did I? Well, here's a fourpenny bit," and so on.

'When I went into a parlour I usually performed with a big dice, three inches square. I used to go and call for a small drop of gin and water, and put this dice on the seat beside me, as a bit of a draw. Directly I put it down everybody was looking at it. Then I'd get into conversation with the party next to me, and he'd be sure to say, "What the deuce is that?" I'd tell him it was a musical box, and he'd be safe to say, "Well, I should like to hear it, very much." Then I'd offer to perform, if agreeable, to the company; often the party would offer to name it to the company, and he'd call to the other side of the room, (for they all know each other in these parlours) "I say, Mr So-and-so, have you any objection to this gentleman showing us a little amusement?" and they are all of them safe to say, "Not in the least. I'm perfectly agreeable if others are so;" and then I'd begin. I'd pull out my cards and card-boxes, and the bonus genius or the wooden doll, and then I'd spread a nice clean cloth (which I always carried with me) on the table, and then I'd go to work. I worked the dice by placing it on the top of a hat, and with a penknife pretending to make an incision in the crown to let the solid block pass through. It is done by having a tin covering to the solid dice, and the art consists in getting the solid block into the hat without being seen. That's the whole of the trick. I begin by striking the block to show it is solid. Then I place two hats one on the other, brim to brim. Then I slip the solid dice into the under hat, and place the tin covering on the crown of the upper one. Then I ask for a knife, and pretend to cut the hat-crown the size of the tin-can on the top, making a noise by dragging my nail along the hat, which closely resembles cutting with a knife. I've often heard people say, "None of that!" thinking I was cutting their hat. Then I say, "Now, gentlemen, if I can pass this dice through the crown into the hat beneath, you'll say it's a very clever deception," because all conjurers acknowledge that they deceive; indeed, I always say when I perform in parlours, "If you can detect me in my deceptions I shall be very much obliged to you by naming it, for it will make me more careful; but if you can't, the more credit to me." Then I place another tin-box over the imitation dice; it fits closely. I say, "Presto – quick – begone!" and clap my hands three times, and then lift up the tin-cases, which are both coloured black inside, and tumble the wooden dice out of the under hat. You see, the whole art consists in passing the solid block unseen into the hat.

'The old method of giving the order for the things to pass was this: "Albri kira mumma tousha cocus co shiver de freek from the margin under the crippling hook," and that's a language.'

The Street Fire-king, or Salamander

[pp. 123–7] This person came to me recommended by one of my street acquaintances as the 'pluckiest fire-eater going', and that as he was a little 'down at heel', he should be happy for a consideration to give me any information I might require in the 'Salamander line'.

He was a tall, gaunt man, with an absent-looking face, and so pale that his dark eyes looked positively wild.

I could not help thinking, as I looked at his bony form, that fire was not the most nutritious food in the world, until the poor fellow explained to me that he had not broken his fast for two days.

He gave the following account of himself:

'My father was a barber – a three-ha'penny one – and doing a good business, in Southwark. I used to assist him, lathering up the chins and shaving 'em – torturing, I called it. I was a very good light hand. You see, you tell a good shaver by the way he holds the razor, and the play from the wrist. All our customers were tradesmen and workmen, but father would never shave either coalheavers or fishermen, because they always threw down a penny, and said there was plenty of penny barbers, and they wouldn't give no more. The old man always stuck up for his price to the day of his death. There was a person set up close to him for a penny, and that injured us awful. I was educated at St George's National and Parochial School, and I was a national lad, and wore my own clothes; but the parochials wore the uniform of blue bob-tailed coats, and a badge on the left side. When they wanted to make an appearance in the gallery of the church on charity-sermon days, they used to make all the nationals dress like the parochials, so as to swell the numbers up. I was too fond of entertainments to stick to learning, and I used to step it. Kennington-common was my principal place. I used, too, to go to the outside of the Queen's-bench and pick up the racket-balls as they were chucked over, and then sell them for three-ha'pence each. I got promoted from the outside to the inside; for, from being always about, they took me at threepence a day, and gave me a bag of whitening to whiten the racket-balls. When I used to hop the wag from school I went there, which was three times a week, which was the reg'lar racket-days. I used to spend my threepence in damaged fruit – have a pen'orth of damaged grapes or plums – or have a ha'porth of wafers from the confectioner's. Ah, I've eat thousands and thousands of ha'porths. It's a kind of a paste, but they stick like wafers – my father's stuck a letter many a time with 'em. They goes at the bottom of the russetfees cake – ah, ratafees is the word.

'I got so unruly, and didn't attend to school, so I was turned out, and then I went to help father and assist upon the customers. I was confined so in the shop, that I only stopped there three months, and then I run away. Then I had no home to go to, but I found a empty cart, situated in Red-cross-street, near the Borough-market, and there I slept for five nights. Then Greenwich fair came on. I went round the fair, and got assisting a artist as was a likeness-cutter, and had a booth, making black profiles. I assisted this man in building his booth, and he took a great fancy to me, and kept me as one of his own. He was a shoemaker as well, and did that when fair was over. I used to fetch his bristles and leather, and nuss the child. He lived near the Kent-road; and one day as I was going out for the leather, I fell upon mother, and she solaced me, and took me home; and then she rigged me out, and kept me, till I run away again; and that was when Greenwich fair came on again, for I wanted to go back then. At the fair I got to be doorsman and grease-pot boy inside a exhibition, to let the people out and keep the lamps. I got a shilling a day for my attendance during fair time, and I travelled with them parties for five months. That was Peterson's, the travelling comedian, or what we call a "mumming concern". When we got to Bexley, I thought I should like to see a piece called "Tricks and Trials", then being performed at the Surrey Theatre, so I cut away and come up to London again. There I got employment at a japanner, boiling up the stuff. I made a little bit of an appearance, and then I went home. I had learnt three or four comic songs, and I used to go singing at consart-rooms. I was a reg'lar professional. I went a busking at the free consart-rooms, and then go round with the cap. I principally sing "The Four-and-nine", or "The Dark Arches", or "The Ship's Carpenter", and "The Goose Club".

'It was at one of these free consart-rooms that I first saw a chap fire-eating. You see, at a free consart-room the professionals ain't paid, no more do the audience to come in, but the performers are allowed to go round with a cap for their remuneration. They are the same as the cock-and-hen clubs. This fire-eater was of the name of West, and I know'd him afore, and he used to ask me to prepare the things for him. His performance was, he had a link a-light in his hand, and he used to take pieces off with a fork and eat it. Then he would get a plate with some sulphur, light it, place it under his nose, and inhale the fumes that rose from it; and then he used to eat it with a fork whilst alight. After that he'd get a small portion of gunpowder, put it in the palm of his hand, and get a fusee to answer for a quick-match, to explode the powder, and that concluded the performance – only three tricks. I was stunned the first time I see him do it; but when I come to prepare the things for him, I got enlightened into the business. When his back was turned, I used to sniff at the sulphur on the sly. I found it rather hard, for the fumes used to get up your head, and reg'lar confuse you, and lose your memory. I kept on the singing at consarts, but I practised the fire-eating at home. I tried it for the matter of two months, before I found the art of it. It used to make me very thick in my voice; and if I began it before breakfast it used to make you feel ill: but I generally began it after meals. I tried the link and sulphur till I got perfect in these two. It blistered my mouth swallowing the fire, but I never burnt myself seriously at it.

'After I learnt those, I got travelling again with a man that swallowed a poker, of the name of Yates. One of his tricks was with tow. He'd get some, and then get a fryingpan, and he'd put the tow in the fire-pan, and he'd get some ground rosin and brimstone together and put them on top of the tow in the pan. Then, when he'd set light to it, he used to bring it on the outside of the show and eat it with a knife and fork, while I held the pan. I learnt how to do the trick; this was when he had done with it, and I'd take it away. Then I used to eat the portion that was left in the pan, till I became the master of that feat.

'When I left Yates I practised again at home until I was perfect, and then I went about doing the performance myself. The first place that I attempted was at the Fox and Cock, Gray's-inn-lane, and I was engaged there at three shillings a night, and with collections of what people used to throw to me I'd come away with about seven shillings and sixpence. I was very successful indeed, and I stopped there for about seven months, doing the fire-business; and I got another job at the same place, for one of the potmen turned dishonest, and the master gave me eight shillings a-week to do his work as well. I have continued ever since going to different concert-rooms, and giving my performances. My general demand for a night's engagement is four shillings and six pen'orth of refreshment. When I perform I usually have a decanter of ale and two glasses upon the table, and after every trick I sit down whilst an overture is being done and wash my mouth out, for it gets very hot. You're obliged to pause a little, for after tasting one thing, if the palate doesn't recover, you can't tell when the smoke is coming.

'I wore a regular dress, a kind of scale-armour costume, with a red lion on the breast. I do up my moustache with cork, and rouge a bit. My tights is brown, with black enamel jack-boots. On my head I wears a king's coronet and a ringlet wig, bracelets on my wrists, and a red twill petticoat under the armour dress, where it opens on the limps.

'For my performances I begin with eating the lighted link, an ordinary one as purchased at oil-shops. There's no trick in it, only confidence. It won't burn you in the inside, but if the pitch falls on the outside, of course it will hurt you. If you hold your breath the moment the lighted piece is put in your mouth, the flame goes out on the instant. Then we squench the flame with spittle. As we takes a bit of link in the mouth, we tucks it on one side of the cheek, as a monkey do with nuts in his pouch. After I have eaten sufficient fire I take hold of the link, and extinguish the lot by putting the burning end in my mouth. Sometimes, when I makes a slip, and don't put it in careful, it makes your moustache fiz up. I must also mind how I opens my mouth, 'cos the tar sticks to the lip wherever it touches, and pains sadly. This sore on my hand is caused by the melted pitch dropping on my fingers, and the sores is liable to be bad for a week or eight days. I don't spit out my bits of link; I always swallow them. I never did spit 'em out, for they are very wholesome, and keeps you from having any sickness. Whilst I'm getting the next trick ready I chews them up and eats them. It tastes rather roughish, but not nasty when you're accustomed to it. It's only like having a mouthful of dust, and very wholesome.

'My next trick is with a piece of tow with a piece of tape rolled up in the interior. I begin to eat a portion of this tow – plain, not alight – till I find a fitting opportunity to place the tape in the mouth. Then I pause for a time, and in the meantime I'm doing a little pantomime business – just like love business, serious – till I get the end of this tape between my teeth, and then I draws it out, supposed to be manufactured in the pit of the stomach. After that – which always goes immensely – I eat some more tow, and inside this tow there is what I call the fire-ball – that is, a lighted fusee bound round with tow and placed in the centre of the tow I'm eating – which I introduce at a fitting opportunity. Then I blows out with my breath, and that sends out smoke and fire. That there is a very hard trick, for it's according how this here fire-ball bustes. Sometimes it bustes on the side, and then it burns all the inside of the mouth, and the next morning you can take out pretty well the inside of your mouth with your finger; but if it bustes near the teeth, then it's all right, for there's vent for it. I also makes the smoke and flame – that is, sparks – come down my nose, the same as coming out of a blacksmith's chimney. It makes the eyes water, and there's a tingling; but it don't burn or make you giddy.

'My next trick is with the brimstone. I have a plate of lighted sulphur, and first inhale the fumes, and then devour it with a fork and swallow it. As a costermonger said when he saw me do it, "I say, old boy, your game ain't all brandy." There's a kind of a acid, nasty, sour taste in this feat, and at first it used to make me feel sick; but now I'm used to it, and it don't. When I puts it in my mouth it clings just like sealing-wax, and forms a kind of a dead ash. Of a morning, if I haven't got my breakfast by a certain time, there's a kind of a retching in my stomach, and that's the only inconvenience I feel from swallowing the sulphur for that there feat.

'The next is, with two sticks of sealing-wax and the same plate. They are lit by the gas and dropped on one another till they are bodily alight. Then I borrow either a ring of the company, or a pencil-case, or a seal. I set the sealing-wax alight with a fork, and I press the impression of whatever article I can get with the tongue, and the seal is passed round to the company. Then I finish eating the burning wax. I always spits that out after, when no one's looking. The sealing-wax is all right if you get it into the interior of the mouth, but if it is stringy, and it falls, you can't get it off, without it takes away skin and all. It has a very pleasant taste, and I always prefer the red, as its flavour is the best. Hold your breath and

it goes out, but still the heat remains, and you can't get along with that
so fast as the sulphur. I often burn myself, especially when I'm bothered
in my entertainment; such as any person talking about me close by, then
I listen to 'em perhaps, and I'm liable to burn myself. I haven't been able
to perform for three weeks after some of my burnings. I never let any of
the audience know anything of it, but smother up the pain, and go on with
my other tricks.

'The other trick is a feat which I make known to the public as one of
Ramo Samee's, which he used to perform in public-houses and tap-rooms,
and made a deal of money out of. With the same plate and a piece of dry
tow placed in it, I have a pepper-box, with ground rosing and sulphur
together. I light the tow, and with a knife and fork I set down to it and
eat it, and exclaim, 'This is my light supper.' There isn't no holding the
breath so much in this trick as in the others, but you must get it into the
mouth any how. It's like eating a hot beef-steak when you are ravenous.
The rosin is apt to drop on the flesh and cause a long blister. You see, we
have to eat it with the head up, full-faced; and really, without it's seen,
nobody would believe what I do.

'There's another feat, of exploding the gunpower. There's two ways of
exploding it. This is my way of doing it, though I only does it for my own
benefits and on grand occasions, for it's very dangerous indeed to the
frame, for it's sure to destroy the hair of the head; or if anything smothers
it, it's liable to shatter a thumb or a limb.

'I have a man to wait on me for this trick, and he unloops my dress and
takes it off, leaving the bare back and arms. Then I gets a quarter of a
pound of powder, and I has an ounce put on the back part of the neck,
in the hollow, and I holds out each arm with an orange in the palm of
each hand, with a train along the arms, leading up to the neck. Then I
turns my back to the audience, and my man fires the gunpowder, and it
blew up in a minute, and ran down the train and blew up that in my
hands. I've been pretty lucky with this trick, for it's only been when the
powder's got under my bracelets, and then it hurts me. I'm obliged to hold
the hand up, for if it hangs down it hurts awful. It looks like a scurvy, and
as the new skin forms, the old one falls off.

'That's the whole of my general performance for concert business, when
I go busking at free concerts or outside of shows (I generally gets a crown
a day at fairs). I never do the gunpowder, but only the tow and the link.

'I have been engaged at the Flora Gardens, and at St Helena Gardens,
Rotherhithe, and then I was Signor Salamander, the great fire-king from
the East-end theatres. At the Eel-pie-house, Peckham, I did the "terrific

flight through the air", coming down a wire surrounded by fire-works. I was called Herr Alma, the flying fiend. There was four scaffold-poles placed at the top of the house to form a tower, just large enough for me to lie down on my belly, for the swivels on the rope to be screwed into the cradle round my body. A wire is the best, but they had a rope. On this cradle were places for the fireworks to be put in it. I had a helmet of fire on my head, and the three spark cases (they are made with steel-filings, and throw out sparks) made of Prince of Wales feathers. I had a sceptre in my hand of two serpents, and in their open mouths they put fire-balls, and they looked as if they was spitting fiery venom. I had wings, too, formed from the ankle to the waist. They was netting, and spangled, and well sized to throw off the fire. I only did this two nights, and I had ten shillings each performance. It's a momentary feeling coming down, a kind of suffocation like, so that you must hold your breath. I had two men to cast me off. There was a gong first of all, knocked to attract the attention, and then I made my appearance. First, a painted pigeon, made of lead, is sent down the wire as a pilot. It has moveable wings. Then all the fire-works are lighted up, and I come down right through the thickest of 'em. There's a trap-door set in the scene at the end, and two men is there to look after it. As soon as I have passed it, the men shut it, and I dart up against a feather-bed. The speed I come down at regularly jams me up against it, but you see I throw away this sceptre and save myself with my hands a little. I feel fagged for want of breath. It seems like a sudden fright, you know. I sit down for a few minutes, and then I'm all right.

'I'm never afraid of fire. There was a turner's place that took fire, and I saved that house from being burned. He was a friend of mine, the turner was, and when I was there, the wife thought she heard the children crying, and asked me to go up and see what it was. As I went up I could smell fire worse and worse, and when I got in the room it was full of smoke, and all the carpet, and bed-hangings, and curtains smouldering. I opened the window, and the fire burst out, so I ups with the carpet and throw'd it out of window, together with the blazing chairs, and I rolled the linen and drapery up and throw'd them out. I was as near suffocated as possible. I went and felt the bed, and there was two children near dead from the smoke; I brought them down, and a medical man was called, and he brought them round.

'I don't reckon no more than two other fire-kings in London beside myself. I only know of two, and I should be sure to hear of 'em if there were more. But they can only do three of the tricks, and I've got novelties enough to act for a fortnight, with fresh performances every evening.

There's a party in Drury-lane is willing to back me for five, fifteen, or twenty pounds, against anybody that will come and answer to it, to perform with any other man for cleanness and cleverness, and to show more variety of performance.

'I'm always at fire-eating. That's how I entirely get my living, and I perform five nights out of the six. Thursday night is the only night, as I may say, I'm idle. Thursday night everybody's fagged, that's the saying – Got no money. Friday, there's many large firms pays their men on, especially in Bermondsey.

'I'm out of an engagement now, and I don't make more than eleven shillings a week, because I'm busking; but when I'm in an engagement my money stands me about thirty-five shillings a week, putting down the value of the drink as well – that is, what's allowed for refreshment. Summer is the worst time for me, 'cos people goes to the gardens. In the winter season I'm always engaged three months out of the six. You might say, if you counts the overplus at one time, and minus at other time, that I makes a pound a week. I know what it is to go to the treasury on a Saturday, and get my thirty shillings, and I know what it is to have the landlord come with his "Hallo! hallo! here's three weeks due, and another week running on."

'I was very hard up at one time – when I was living in Friar-street – and I used to frequent a house kept by a betting-man, near the St George's Surrey Riding-school. A man I knew used to supply this betting-man with rats. I was at this public-house one night when this rat-man comes up to me, and says he, "Hallo! my pippin; here, I want you: I want to make a match. Will you kill thirty rats against my dog?" So I said, "Let me see the dog first;" and I looked at his mouth, and he was an old dog; so I says, "No, I won't go in for thirty; but I don't mind trying at twenty." He wanted to make it twenty-four, but I wouldn't. They put the twenty in the rat-pit and the dog went in first and killed his, and he took a quarter of an hour and two minutes. Then a fresh lot were put in the pit, and I began; my hands were tied behind me. They always make an allowance for a man, so the pit was made closer, for you see a man can't turn round like a dog; I had half the space of the dog. The rats lay in a cluster, and then I picked them off where I wanted 'em and bit 'em between the shoulders. It was when they came to one or two that I had the work, for they cut about. The last one made me remember him, for he gave me a bite, of which I've got the scar now. It festered, and I was obliged to have it cut out. I took Dutch drops for it, and poulticed it by day, and I was bad for three weeks. They made a subscription in the room of fifteen shillings for killing these rats. I won the match, and beat the dog by four minutes. The wager was five shillings, which I had. I was at the time so hard up, I'd do anything for some money; though, as far as that's concerned, I'd go into a pit now, if anybody would make it worth my while.'

Street Clown

[pp. 129–31]   He was a melancholy-looking man, with the sunken eyes and other characteristics of semi-starvation, whilst his face was scored with lines and wrinkles, telling of paint and premature age.

I saw him performing in the streets with a school of acrobats soon after I had been questioning him, and the readiness and business-like way with which he resumed his professional buffoonery was not a little remarkable. His story was more pathetic than comic, and proved that the life of a street clown is, perhaps, the most wretched of all existence. Jest as he may in the street, his life is literally no joke at home.

'I have been a clown for sixteen years,' he said, 'having lived totally by it for that time. I was left motherless at two years of age, and my father died when I was nine. He was a carman, and his master took me as a stable boy, and I stayed with him until he failed in business. I was then left destitute again, and got employed as a supernumerary at Astley's, at one shilling a night. I was a "super" some time, and got an insight into theatrical life. I got acquainted, too, with singing people, and could sing a good song, and came out at last on my own account in the streets, in the Jim Crow line. My necessities forced me into a public line, which I am far from liking. I'd pull trucks at one shilling a day, rather than get twelve shillings a week at my business. I've tried to get out of the line. I've got a friend to advertise for me for any situation as groom. I've tried to get into the police, and I've tried other things, but somehow there seems an impossibility to get quit of the street business. Many times I have to play the clown, and indulge in all kinds of buffoonery, with a terrible heavy heart. I have travelled very much, too, but I never did over-well in the profession. At races I may have made ten shillings for two or three days, but that was only occasional; and what is ten shillings to keep a wife and family on, for a month maybe? I have three children, one now only eight weeks old. You can't imagine, sir, what a curse the street business often becomes, with its insults and starvations. The day before my wife was confined, I jumped and labour'd doing Jim Crow for twelve hours – in the wet, too – and earned one shilling and threepence; with this I returned to a home without a bit of coal, and with only half a quartern loaf in it.

I know it was one shilling and threepence; for I keep a sort of log of my earnings and my expenses; you'll see on it what I've earn'd as clown, or the funnyman, with a party of acrobats, since the beginning of this year.'

He showed me this log, as he called it, which was kept in small figures, on paper folded up as economically as possible. His latest weekly earnings were, 12s. 6d., 1s. 10d., 7s. 7d., 2s. 5d., 3s 11¼d., 7s. 7½d., 7s. 9½d., 6s. 4½d., 10s. 10½d., 9s. 7d., 6s. 1½d., 15s 6½d., 6s. 5d., 4s. 2d., 12s. 10¼d., 15s. 5½d., 14s. 4d. Against this was set off what the poor man had to expend for his dinner, &c., when out playing the clown, as he was away from home and could not dine with his family. The ciphers intimate the weeks when there was no such expense, or in other words, those which had been passed without dinner. 0, 0, 0, 0, 2s. 2½d., 3s. 9½d., 4s. 2d., 4s. 5d., 5s. 8¼d., 5s. 11¼d., 4s. 10½d., 2s. 8¼d., 3s. 7¾d., 3s. 4¼d., 6s. 5¼d., 4s. 6¼d., 4s 3d. This account shows an average of 8s. 6½d. a-week as the gross gain, whilst, if the expenses be deducted, not quite six shillings remain as the average weekly sum to be taken home to wife and family.

'I dare say,' continued the man, 'that no persons think more of their dignity than such as are in my way of life. I would rather starve than ask for parochial relief. Many a time I have gone to my labour without breaking my fast, and played clown until I could raise dinner. I have to make jokes as clown, and could fill a volume with all I knows.'

He told me several of his jests; they were all of the most venerable kind, as for instance: 'A horse has ten legs: he has two fore legs and two hind ones. Two fores are eight, and two others are ten.' The other jokes were equally puerile, as, 'Why is the City of Rome,' (he would have it Rome), 'like a candle wick? Because it's in the midst of Greece.' 'Old and young are both of one age: your son at twenty is young, and your horse at twenty is old: and so old and young are the same.' 'The dress,' he continued, 'that I wear in the streets consists of red striped cotton stockings, with full trunks, dotted red and black. The body, which is dotted like the trunks, fits tight like a woman's gown, and has full sleeves and frills. The wig or scalp is made of horse-hair, which is sown on to a white cap, and is in the shape of a cock's comb. My face is painted with dry white lead. I grease my skin first and then dab the white paint on (flake-white is too dear for us street clowns); after that I colour my cheeks and mouth with vermilion. I never dress at home; we all dress at public-houses. In the street where I lodge, only a very few know what I do for a living. I and my wife both strive to keep the business a secret from our neighbours. My wife does a little washing when able, and often works eight hours for sixpence. I go out at eight in the morning and return at dark. My children hardly know what I do. They see my dresses lying about, but that is all. My eldest is a girl of thirteen. She has seen me dressed at Stepney fair, where she brought me my tea (I live near there); she laughs when she sees me in my clown's dress, and wants to stay with me: but I would rather see her lay dead before me (and I had two dead in my place at one time, last Whitsun Monday was a twelvemonth) than she should ever belong to my profession.'

I could see the tears start from the man's eyes as he said this.

'Frequently when I am playing the fool in the streets, I feel very sad at heart. I can't help thinking of the bare cupboards at home; but what's that to the world? I've often and often been at home all day when it has been wet, with no food at all, either to give my children or take myself, and have gone out at night to the public-houses to sing a comic song or play the funnyman for a meal – you may imagine with what feelings for the part – and when I've come home I've call'd my children up from their beds to share the loaf I had brought back with me. I know three or more clowns as miserable and bad off as myself. The way in which our profession is ruined is by the stragglers or outsiders, who are often men who are good tradesmen. They take to the clown's business only at holiday or fair time, when there is a little money to be picked up at it, and after that they go back to their own trades; so that, you see, we, who are obliged to continue at it the year through, are deprived of even the little bit of luck we should otherwise have. I know only of another regular street clown in London besides myself. Some schools of acrobats, to be sure, will have a comic character of some kind or other, to keep the pitch up; that is, to amuse the people while the money is being collected: but these, in general, are not regular clowns. They are mostly dressed and got up for the occasion. They certainly don't do anything else but the street comic business, but they are not pantomimists by profession. The street clowns generally go out with dancers and tumblers. There are some street clowns to be seen with the Jacks-in-the-greens; but they are mostly sweeps, who have hired their dress for the two or three days, as the case may be. I think there are three regular clowns in the metropolis, and one of these is not a professional: he never smelt the sawdust, I know, sir. The most that I have known have been shoemakers before taking to the business. When I go out as a street clown, the first thing I do is a comic medley dance; and then after that I crack a few jokes, and that is the whole of my entertainment. The first part of the medley dance is called "the good St Anthony" (I was the first that ever danced the polka in the streets); then I do a waltz, and wind up with a hornpipe. After that I go through a little burlesque business. I fan myself, and one of the school asks me whether I am out of breath? I answer, "No, the breath is out of me." The leading questions for the jokes are all regularly prepared beforehand. The old jokes always go best with our audiences. The older they are, the better for the streets. I know, indeed, of nothing new in the joking way; but even if there was, and it was in anyway deep, it would not do for the public thoroughfares. I have read a great deal of "Punch", but the jokes are nearly all too high there; indeed, I can't say I think very much of them myself. The principal way in which I've got up my jokes is through associating with other clowns. We don't make our jokes ourselves; in fact, I never knew one clown who did. I must own that the street clowns like a little drop of spirits, and occasionally a good deal. They are in a measure obligated to it. I can't fancy a clown being funny on small beer; and I never in all my life knew one who was a teetotaller. I think such a person would be a curious character, indeed. Most of the street clowns die in the workhouses. In their old age they are generally very wretched and poverty-stricken. I can't say what I think will be the end of me. I daren't think of it, sir.'

A few minutes afterwards I saw this man dressed as Jim Crow, with his face blackened, dancing and singing in the streets as if he was the lightest-hearted fellow in all London.

Blind Irish Piper

[pp. 172–3] Of the Irish Pipers, a well-dressed, middle-aged man, of good appearance, wearing large green spectacles, led by a young girl, his daughter, gave me the following account:

'I was eleven years old when I lost my sight from cold, and I was brought up to the musical profession, and practised it several years in Ireland, of which country I am a native. I was a man of private property, – small property – and only played occasionally at the gentle-people's places; and then more as a guest – yes, more indeed than professionally. In 1838 I married, and began to give concerts regularly; I was the performer, and played only on the union pipes at my concerts. I'm acknowledged to be the best performer in the world, even by my own craft – excuse what seems self-praise. The union pipes are the old Irish pipes improved. In former times there was no chromatic scale; now we have eight keys to the chanter, which produce the chromatic scale as on the flute, and so the pipes are improved in the melody, and more particularly in the harmony. We have had fine performers of old. I may mention Caroll O'Daly, who flourished in the 15th century, and was the composer of the air that the

Scotch want to steal from us, "Robin Adair", which is "Alleen ma ruen", or "Ellen, my dear". My concerts in Ireland answered very well indeed, but the famine reduced me so much that I was fain to get to England with my family, wife and four children; and in this visit I have been disappointed, completely so. Now I'm reduced to play in the streets, and make very little by it. I may average 15s. in the week in summer, and not half that in winter. There are many of my countrymen now in England playing the pipes, but I don't know one respectable enough to associate with; so I keep to myself, and so I cannot tell how many there are.'

The English Street Bands

[pp. 173–4] Concerning these, a respectable man gave me the following details:

'I was brought up to the musical profession, and have been a street-performer 22 years, and I'm now only 26. I sang and played the guitar in the streets with my mother when I was four years old. We were greatly patronised by the nobility at that time. It was a good business when I was a child. A younger brother and I would go out into the street for a few hours of an evening, from five to eight, and make 7s. or 8s. the two of us. Ours was, and is, the highest class of street music. For the last ten years I have been a member of a street band. Our band is now four in number. I have been in bands of eight, and in some composed of as many as 25; but a small band answers best for regularity. With eight in the band it's not easy to get 3s. apiece on a fine day, and play all day, too. I consider that there are 1,000 musicians now performing in the streets of London; and as very few play singly, 1,000 performers, not reckoning persons who play with niggers or such-like, will give not quite 250 street bands. Four in number is a fair average for a street band; but I think the greater number of bands have more than four in them. All the better sort of these bands play at concerts, balls, parties, processions, and water excursions, as well as in the streets. The class of men in the street bands is, very generally, those who can't read music, but play by ear; and their being unable to read music prevents their obtaining employment in theatres, or places where a musical education is necessary; and yet numbers of street musicians (playing by ear) are better instrumentalists than many educated musicians in the theatres. I only know a few who have left other businesses to become musicians. The great majority – 19/20ths of us, I should say – have been brought regularly up to be street-performers. Children now are taught very early, and seldom leave the profession for any other business. Every year the street musicians increase. The better sort are, I think, prudent men, and struggle hard for a decent living. All the street-performers of wind instruments are short-lived. Wind performers drink more, too, than the others. They must have their mouths wet, and they need some stimulant or restorative after blowing an hour in the streets. There are now twice as many wind as stringed instruments played in the streets; fifteen or sixteen years ago there used to be more stringed instruments. Within that time new wind instruments have been used in the streets. Cornopeans, or cornet-à-pistons, came into vogue about fourteen years ago; opheicleides about ten years ago (I'm speaking of the streets); and saxhorns about two years since. The cornopean has now quite superseded the bugle. The worst part of the street-performers, in point of character, are those who play before or in public-houses. They drink a great deal, but I never heard of them being charged with dishonesty. In fact, I believe there's no honester set of men breathing than street musicians. The better class of musicians are nearly all married men, and they generally dislike to teach their wives music; indeed, in my band, and in similar bands, we wouldn't employ a man who was teaching his wife music, that she might play in the streets, and so be exposed to every insult and every temptation, if she's young and pretty. Many of the musicians' wives have to work very hard with their needles for the slop-shops, and earn very little in such employ; 3s. a week is reckoned good earnings, but it all helps. The German bands injure our trade much. They'll play for half what we ask. They are very mean, feed dirtily, and the best band of them, whom I met at Dover, I know slept three in a bed in a common lodging-house, one of the very lowest. They now block us out of all the country places to which we used to go in the summer. The German bands have now possession of the whole coast of Kent and Sussex, and wherever there are watering-places. I don't know anything about their morals, excepting that they don't drink. An English street-performer in a good and respectable band will now average 25s. a week the year through. Fifteen years ago he could have made 3l. a week. Inferior performers make from 12s. to 15s. a week. I consider Regent-street and such places our best pitches. Our principal patrons in the parties' line are tradesmen and professional men, such as attorneys: 10s. a night is our regular charge.'

The German Street Bands

[p. 174]   Next come the German Bands. I had the following statement from a young flaxen-haired and fresh-coloured German, who spoke English very fairly:

'I am German, and have been six year in zis country. I was nearly fourteen when I come. I come from Oberfeld, eighteen miles from Hanover. I come because I would like to see how it was here. I heard zat London was a good place for foreign music. London is as goot a place as I expect to find him. There was other six come over with me, boys and men. We come to Hull, and play in ze country about half a year; we do middling. And zen we come to London. I didn't make money at first when I come, I had much to learn; but ze band, oh! it did well. We was seven. I play ze clarionet, and so did two others; two play French horns, one ze trambone, and one ze saxhorn. Sometime we make 7s. or 8s. apiece in a day now, but the business is not so goot. I reckon 6s. a day is goot now. We never play at fairs, nor for caravans. We play at private parties or public ball-rooms, and are paid so much a dance – sixpence a dance for ze seven of us. If zare is many dances, it is goot; if not, it is bad. We play sheaper zan ze English, and we don't spent so much. Ze English players insult us, but we don't care about that. Zey abuse us for playing sheap. I don't know what zair terms for dances are. I have saved money in zis country, but very little of it. I want to save enough to take me back to Hanover. We all live togeder, ze seven of us. We have three rooms to sleep in, and one to eat in. We are all single men, but one; and his wife, a German woman, lives wis us, and cooks for us. She and her husband have a bedroom to themselves. Anysing does for us to eat. We all join in housekeeping and lodging, and pay alike. Our lodging costs 2s. a week each, our board costs us about 15s. a week each; sometime rather less. But zat include beer; and ze London beer is very goot, and sometime we drink a goot deal of it. We drink very little gin, but we live very well, and have goot meals every day. We play in ze streets, and I zink most place are alike to us. Ladies and gentlemen are our best friends; ze working people give us very little. We play opera tunes chiefly. We don't associate with any Englishmen. Zare are three public-houses kept by Germans, where we Germans meet. Sugar-bakers, and other trades are of ze number. There are now five German brass-bands, with thirty-seven performers in zem, reckoning our own, in London. Our band lives near Whitechapel. I sink zare is one or two more German bands in ze country. I sink my countrymen, some of them, ave money; but I have not saved much yet.'

Of the Bagpipe Players

[p. 174] A well-looking young man, dressed in full Highland costume, with modest manners and of slow speech, as if translating his words from the Gaelic before he uttered them, gave me these details:

'I am a native of Inverness, and a Grant. My father was a soldier, and a player in the 42nd. In my youth I was shepherd in the hills, until my father was unable to support me any longer. He had 9d. a day pension for seventeen years' service, and had been thrice wounded. He taught me and my brither the pipes; he was too poor to have us taught any trade; so we started on our own accounts. We travelled up to London, had only our pipes to depend upon. We came in full Highland dress. The tartan is cheap there, and we mak it up oursels. My dress as I sit here, without my pipes, would cost about 4l. in London. Our mithers spin the tartan in Inverness-shire, and the dress comes to maybe 30s., and is better than the London. My pipes cost me three guineas new. It's between five and six years since I first came to London, and I was twenty-four last November. When I started, I thought of making a fortune in London; there was such great talk of it in Inverness-shire, as a fine place with plenty of money; but when I came I found the difference. I was rather a novelty at first, and did pretty well. I could make 1l. a week then, but now I can't make 2s. a day, not even in summer. There are so many Irishmen going about London, and dressed as Scotch Highlanders, that I really think I could do better as a piper even in Scotland. A Scotch family will sometimes give me a shilling or two when they find out I am a Scotchman. Chelsea is my best place, where there are many Scotchmen. There are now only five real Scotch Highlanders playing the bagpipes in the streets of London, and seven or eight Irishmen that I know of. The Irishmen do better than I do, because they have more face. We have our own rooms. I pay 4s. a week for an empty room, and have my ain furniture. We are all married men, and have no connexion with any other street musicians. "Tullochgorum", "Money-musk", "The Campbells are comin'", and "Lord Macdonald's Reel", are among the performances best liked in London. I'm very seldom insulted in the streets, and then mostly by being called an Irishman, which I don't like; but I pass it off just as well as I can.'

Scotch Piper and Dancing-girl

[pp. 174–8] 'I was full corporal in the 93rd Southern Highlanders, and I can get the best of characters from my commanding officers. If I couldn't get a good character I wouldn't be orderly to the colonel; and wherever he and the lady went, I was sure to be with them. Although I used to wear the colonel's livery, yet I had the full corporal's stripes on my coat. I was first orderly to Colonel Sparkes of the 93rd. He belonged to Dublin, and he was the best colonel that ever belonged to a regiment. After he died I was orderly to Colonel Aynsley. This shows I must have been a good man, and have a good character. Colonel Aynsley was a good friend to me, and he always gave me my clothes, like his other private servants. The orderly's post is a good one, and much sought after, for it exempts you from regimental duty. Colonel Aynsley was a severe man on duty, but he was a good colonel after all. If he wasn't to be a severe man he wouldn't be able to discharge the post he had to discharge. Off duty he was as kind as anybody could be. There was no man he hated more than a dirty soldier. He wouldn't muddle a man for being drunk, not a quarter so much as for dirty clothing. I was reckoned the cleanest soldier in the regiment; for if I was out in a shower of rain, I'd polish up my brass and pipeclay my belt, to make it look clean again. Besides, I was very supple and active, and many's the time Colonel Aynsley has sent me on a message, and I have been there and back, and when I've met him he's scolded me for not having gone, for I was back so quick he thought I hadn't started.

'Whilst I was in the regiment I was attacked with blindness; brought on, I think by cold. There was a deserter, that the policemen took up and brought to our barracks at Weedon, where the 93rd was stationed in 1852. It was very wet weather, and he was brought in without a stitch on him, in a pair of breeches and a miserable shirt – that's all. He was away two years, but he was always much liked. No deserters ever escape. We made a kit up for this man in less than twenty minutes. One gave him a kilt, another a coat, and I gave him the shoes off my feet, and then went to the regiment stores and got me another pair. Soldiers always help one another; it's their duty to such a poor, miserable wretch as he was.

'This deserter was tried by court-martial, and he got thirty-one days in prison, and hard labour. He'd have had three months, only he gave himself up. He was so weak with lying out, that the doctor wouldn't let him be flogged. He'd have had sixty lashes if he'd been strong. Ah! sixty is nothing. I've seen one hundred and fifty given. When this man was marched off to Warwick gaol I commanded the escort, and it was a very severe day's rain that day, for it kept on from six in the morning till twelve at night. It was a twenty-one miles' march; and we started at six in the morning, and arrived at Warwick by four in the afternoon. The prisoner was made to march the distance in the same clothes as when he gave himself up.

He had only a shirt and waistcoat on his back, and that got so wet, I took off my greatcoat and gave it to him to wear to warm him. They wouldn't let him have the kit of clothes made up for him by the regiment till he came out of prison. From giving him my greatcoat I caught a severe cold. I stood up by a public-house fire and dried my coat and kilt, and the cold flew to the small of my back. After we had delivered our prisoner at Warwick we walked on to Coventry – that's ten miles more. We did thirty-one miles that day in the rain. After we got back to barracks I was clapped in hospital. I was there twenty-one days. The doctor told me I shouldn't leave it for twenty-eight days, but I left it in twenty-one, for I didn't like to be in that same place. My eyes got very blood-shot, and I lost the sight of them. I was very much afraid that I'd never see a sight with my eyes, and I was most miserable. I used to be, too, all of a tremble with a shiver of cold. I only stopped in the regiment for thirty-one days after I came out of hospital, and then I had my discharge. I could just see a little. It was my own fault that I had my discharge, for I thought I could do better to cure myself by going to the country doctors. The men subscribed for me all the extra money of their pay – that's about 4d. each man – and it made me up 10l. When I told Colonel Aynsley of this, says he, "Upon my word, M'Gregor, I'm as proud of it as if I had 20,000l." He gave me a sovereign out of his own pocket. Besides that, I had as many kilts given me as have lasted me up to this time. My boy is wearing the last of 'em now.

'At Oxford I went to a doctor, and he did me a deal of good; for now I can read a book, if the thread of it isn't too small. I can read the Prayer-book, or Bible, or newspaper, just for four hours, and then I go dim.

'I've served in India, and I was at the battles of Punjaub, 1848, and Moultan, 1849. Sir Colin Campbell commanded us at both, and says he, "Now, my brave 93rd, none of your nonsense here, for it must be death and glory here to-day;" and then Serjeant Cameron says, "The men are all right, Sir Colin, but they're afraid you won't be in the midst of them;" and says he, "Not in the midst of them! I'll be here in ten minutes." Sir Colin will go in anywhere; he's as brave an officer as any in the service. He's the first into the fight and the last out of it.

'Although I had served ten years, and been in two battles, yet I was not entitled to a pension. You must serve twenty-one years to be entitled to 1s. 0½d. I left the 93rd in 1852, and since that time I've been wandering about the different parts of England and Scotland, playing on the bagpipes. I take my daughter Maria about with me, and she dances whilst I play to her. I leave my wife and family in town. I've been in London three weeks this last time I visited it. I've been here plenty of times before. I've done duty in Hyde-Park before the 46th came here.

'I left the army just two years before the war broke out, and I'd rather than twenty thousand pounds I'd been in my health to have gone to the Crimea, for I'd have had more glory after that war than ever any England was in. Directly I found the 93rd was going out, I went twice to try and get back to my old regiment; but the doctor inspected me, and said I wouldn't be fit for service again. I was too old at the time, and my health wasn't good, although I could stand the cold far better than many hundreds of them that were out there, for I never wear no drawers, only my kilt, and that very thin, for it's near worn. Nothing at all gives me cold but the rain.

'The last time I was in London was in May. My daughter dances the Highland fling and the sword-dance called "Killim Callam". That's the right Highland air to the dance – with two swords laid across each other. I was a good hand at it before I got stiff. I've done it before all the regiment. We'd take two swords from the officers and lay them down when they've been newly ground. I've gone within the eighth of an inch of them, and never cut my shoe. Can you cut your shoes? aye, and your toes, too, if you're not lithe. My brother was the best dancer in the army: so the Duke of Argyle and his lady said. At one of the prize meetings at Blair Athol, one Tom Duff, who is as good a dancer as from this to where he is, says he, "There's ne'er a man of the Macgregor clan can dance against me to-day!" and I, knowing my brother Tom – he was killed at Inkermann in the 93rd – was coming, says I, "Don't be sure of that, Tom Duff, for there's one come every inch of the road here to-day to try it with you." He began, and he took an inch off his shoes, and my brother never cut himself at all; and he won the prize.

'My little girl dances that dance. She does it pretty, but I'd be rather doubtful about letting her come near the swords, for fear she'd be cutting herself, though I know she could do it at a pinch, for she can be dancing across two baccy-pipes without breaking them. When I'm in the streets, she always does it with two baccy-pipes. She can dance reels, too, such as the Highland fling and the reel Hoolow. They're the most celebrated.

'Whenever I go about the country I leave my wife and family in London, and go off with my girl. I send them up money every week, according to what I earn. Every farthing that I can spare I always send up. I always, when I'm travelling, make the first part of my journey down to Hull in Yorkshire. On my road I always stop at garrison towns, and they always behave very well to me. If they've a penny they'll give it to me, either English, Scotch, or Irish regiments; or I'd as soon meet the 23rd Welsh

Fusiliers as any, for they've all been out with me on service. At Hull there is a large garrison, and I always reckon on getting 3s. or 4s. from the barracks. When I'm travelling, it generally comes to 15s. a week, and out of that I manage to send the wife 10s. and live on 5s. myself. I have to walk all the way, for I wouldn't sit on a rail or a cart for fear I should lose the little villages off the road. I can do better in many of them than I can in many of the large towns. I tell them I am an old soldier. I don't go to the cottages, but to the gentlemen's houses. Many of the gentlemen have been in the army, and then they soon tell whether I have been in service. Some have asked me the stations I have been at, and who commanded us; and then they'll say, "This man is true enough, and every word of it is truth."

'I've been in Balmoral many a dozen of times. Many a time I've passed by it when it was an old ruin, and fit for nothing but the ravens and the owls. Balmoral is the fourth oldest place in Scotland. It was built before any parts of Christianity came into the country at all. I've an old book that gives an account of all the old buildings entirely, and a very old book it is. Edinbro' Castle is the oldest building, and then Stirling Castle, and then Perth Castle, and then Balmoral. I've been there twice since the Queen was there. If I'd see any of the old officers that I knew at Balmoral, I'd play then, and they might give me something. I went there more for curiosity, and I went to see the Queen come out. She was always very fond of the 93rd. They'd fight for her in any place, for there isn't a man discharged after this war but they're provided for.

'I do pretty well in London, taking my 4s. a day, but out of that I must pay 1s. 9d. a week lodging-money, for I can't go into apartments, for if I did it would be but poorly furnished, for I've no beds, or furniture, or linen.

'I can live in Scotland much cheaper then here. I can give the children a good breakfast of oatmeal-porridge every morning, and that will in seven weeks make them as fat as seven years of tea and coffee will do here. Besides, in Scotland, I can buy a very pretty little stand-up bedstead for 2s., which here would come to 4s. I'm thinking of sending my family down to Scotland, and sending them the money I earn in London. They'll have to walk to Hull and then take the boat. They can get to Aberdeen from there. We shall have to work the money on the road.

'When I go out working with the little girl, I get out about nine in the summer and ten in the winter. I can't work much more than four hours a day on the pipes, for the blowing knocks me up and leaves me very weak. No, it don't hurt my chest, but I'll be just quite weak. That's from my bad health. I've never had a day's health ever since I left the regiment. I have pains in my back and stitches in the side. My girl can't dance without my playing, so that when I give over she must give over too. I sometimes go out with two of my daughters. Lizzy don't dance, only Maria. I never ax anybody for money. Anybody that don't like to give we never ax them.

'I can't eat meat, for it won't rest on my stomach, and there's nothing I take that goes so well with me as soup. I live principally on bread, for coffee or tea won't do for me at all. If I could get a bit of meat that I like, such as a small fowl, or the like of that, it would do with me very well; but either bacon or beef, or the like of that, is too strong for me. I'm obliged to be very careful entirely with what I eat, for I'm sick. A lady gave me a bottle of good old foreign port about three months ago, and I thought it did me more good than all the meat in the world.

'When I'm in London I make about 4s. a day, and when I'm in the country about 15s. a week. My old lady couldn't live when I travel if it wasn't for my boy, who goes out and gets about 1s. a day. Lord Panmure is very good to him, and gives him something whenever he meets him. I wouldn't get such good health if I stopped in London. Now there's Barnet, only eleven miles from St Giles's, and yet I can get better health in London than I can there, on account of it's being on rising ground and fresh air coming into it every minute.

'I never be a bit bad with the cold. It never makes me bad. I've been in Canada with the 93rd in the winter. In the year '43 was a very fearful winter indeed, and we were there, and the men didn't seem to suffer anything from the cold, but were just as well as in any other climate or in England. They wore the kilt and the same dress as in summer. Some of them wore the tartan trowsers when they were not on duty or parade, but the most of them didn't – not one in a dozen, for they looked upon it as like a woman. There's nothing so good for the cold as cold water. The men used to bathe their knees and legs in the cold water, and it would make them ache for the time, but a minute or two afterwards they were all right and sweating. I've many a time gone into the water up to my neck in the coldest days of the year, and then when I came out and dried myself, and put on my clothes, I'd be sweating afterwards. There can't be a better thing for keeping away the rheumatism. It's a fine thing for rheumatism and aches to rub the part with cold frosty water or snow. It makes it leave him and knocks the pains out of his limbs. Now, in London, when my hands are so cold I can't play on my pipes, I go to a pump and wash them in the frosty water, and then dry them and rub them together, and then they're as warm as ever. The more a man leans to the fire the worse he is after. It was leaning to a fire that gave me my illness.

'The chanter of the pipes I play on has been in my family very near 450 years. It's the oldest in Scotland, and is a heir-loom in our family, and they wouldn't part with it for any money. Many's a time the Museum in Edinburgh has wanted me to give it to them, but I won't give it to any one till I find myself near death, and then I'll obligate them to keep it. Most likely my youngest son will have it, for he's as steady as a man. You see, the holes for the fingers is worn as big round as sixpences, and they're quite sharp at the edges. The ivory at the end is the same original piece as when the pipe was made. It's breaking and splitting with age, and so is the stick. I'll have my name and the age of the stick engraved on the sole of the ivory, and then, if my boy seems neglectful of the chanter, I'll give it to the Museum of Edinburgh. I'll have German silver rings put round the stick, to keep it together, and then, with nice waxed thread bound round it, it will last for centuries yet.

'This chanter was made by old William McDonnall, who's been dead these many hundred years. He was one of the best pipe-makers that's in all Scotland. There's a brother of mine has a set of drones made by him, and he wouldn't give them for any sit of money. Everybody in Scotland knows William McDonnall. Ask any lad, and he'll tell you who was the best pipe-maker that ever lived in Scotland – aye, and ever will live. There's many a farmer in Scotland would give 30l. for a set of pipes by old William McDonnall, sooner than they'd give 30s. for a set of pipes made now. This chanter has been in our family ever since McDonnall made it. It's been handed down from father to son from that day to this. They always give it to the eldest. William McDonnall lived to be 143 years old, and this is the last chanter he made. A gentleman in London, who makes chanters, once gave me a new one, merely for letting him take a model of my old one, with the size of the bore and the place for the holes. You tell a good chanter by the tone, and some is as sweet as a piano. My old chanter has got rather too sharp by old age, and it's lost its tone; for when a stick gets too sharp a sound, it's never no good. This chanter was played by my family in the battles of Wallace and Bruce, and at the battle of Bannockburn, and every place whenever any of the Macgregor clan fought. These are the traditions given from family to family. I heard it from my father, and now I tell my lads, and they know it as well as I do myself. My great grandfather played on this stick when Charley Stuart, the Pretender, came over to Scotland from France, and he played on it before the Prince himself, at Stirling and the Island of Skye, and at Preston Pans and Culloden. It was at Preston Pans that the clans were first formed, and could be told by their tartans – the Macgregors, and the Stuart, and the Macbeths, and the Camerons, and all of them. I had three brothers older than me, but I've got this chanter, for I begged it of them. It's getting too old to play on, and I'll have a copper box made for it, and just carry it at my side, if God is good to me, and gives me health to live three weeks.

'About my best friends in London are the French people – they are the best I can meet, they come next to the Highlanders. When I meet a Highlander he will, if he's only just a labouring man, give me a few coppers. A Highlander will never close his eye upon me. It's the Lowlander that is the worse to me. They never takes no notice of me when I'm passing: they'll smile and cast an eye as I pass by. Many a time I'll say to them when they pass, "Well, old chap, you don't like the half-naked men, I know you don't!" and many will say, "No, I don't!" I never play the pipes when I go through the Lowlands – I'd as soon play poison to them. They never give anything. It's the Lowlanders that get the Scotch a bad name for being miserable, and keeping their money, and using a small provision. They're a disgrace to their country.

'The Highlander spends his money as free as a duke. If a man in the 93rd had a shilling in his pocket, it was gone before he could turn it twice. All the Lowlanders would like to be Highlanders if they could, and they learn Gaelic, and then marry Highland lassies, so as to become Highlanders. They have some clever regiments composed out of the Lowlanders, but they have only three regiments and the Highlanders have seven; yet there's nearly three to one more inhabitants in the Lowlands. It's a strange thing, they'd sooner take an Irishman into a Highland regiment than a Lowlander. They owe them such a spleen, they don't like them. Bruce was a Lowlander, and he betrayed Wallace; and the Duke of Buccleuch, who was a Lowlander, betrayed Stuart.

'I never go playing at public-houses, for I don't like such places. I am not a drinker, for as much whisky as will fill a teaspoon will lay me up for a day. If I take anything, it's a sup of porter. I went once into a public-house, and there was a woman drinking in it, and she was drunk. It was the landlord told me to come inside. She told me to leave the house, and I said the master told me to come: then she took up one of these pewter pots and hit me in the forehead. It was very sore for three weeks afterwards, and made a hole. I wouldn't prosecute her.

'My little boy that goes about is fourteen years old, and he's as straight and well-formed as if he was made of wax-work. He's the one that shall have the chanter, if anybody does; but I'm rather doubtful about it, for he's not steady enough, and I think I'll leave it to a museum.

'If I had a good set of pipes, there's not many going about the streets could play better; but my pipes are not in good order. I've got three tunes for one that the Queen's piper plays; and I can play in a far superior style, for he plays in the military style. McKay the former piper to her majesty, he was reckoned as good a player as there is in Scotland. I knew him very well, and many and many a time I've played with him. He was took bad in the head and obliged to go back to Scotland. He is in the Isle of Skye now. I belong to Peterhead. If I had a good set of pipes I wouldn't be much afraid of playing with any of the pipers.

'In the country towns I would sometimes be called into Highland gentlemen's houses, to play to them, but never in London.

'I make all my reeds myself to put in the stick. I make them of Spanish cane. It's the outer glazed bark of it. The nearer you go to the shiny part, the harder the reed is, and the longer it lasts. In Scotland they use the Spanish cane. I have seen a man, at one time, who made a reed out of a piece of white thorn, and it sounded as well as ever a reed I saw sound; but I never see a man who could make them, only one.'

STATEMENT OF A PHOTOGRAPHIC MAN

[pp. 216–20] 'I've been on and off at photographic-portrait taking since its commencement – that is to say, since they were taken cheap – two years this summer. I lodged in a room in Lambeth, and I used to take them in the back-yard – a kind of garden; I used to take a blanket off the bed, and used to tack it on a clothes-horse, and my mate used to hold it, if the wind was high, whilst I took the portrait.

'The reason why I took to photographing was, that I thought I should like it better than what I was at. I was out busking and drag-pitching with a banjo then. Busking is going into public-houses and playing, and singing, and dancing; and drag-pitching is going out in the day down the little courts – tidy places, little terraces, no thoroughfares, we call drags. I'm a very determined chap, and when I take a hidea into my head I always do it somehow or other. I didn't know any thing about photographs then, not a mite, but I saved up my money; sometimes a 1s.; if I had a good day, 1s. 6d.; and my wife she went to work at day boot-binding, and at night dancing at a exhibition, or such-like (she's a tolerable good dancer – a penny exhibition or a parade dancer at fairs; that is, outside a show); sometimes she is Mademoiselle, or Madame, or what it may be. I got a loan of 3l. (and had to pay 4l. 3s. for it), and with what I'd saved, I managed to get together 5l. 5s., and I went to Gilbert Flemming's, in

Oxford-street, and bought a complete apparatus for taking pictures; 6½ by 4¾, for 5*l*. 5*s*. Then I took it home and opened the next day to take portraits for what we could get – 1*s*. and over. I never knew anything about taking portraits then, though they showed me when I bought the apparatus (but that was as good as nothing, for it takes months to learn). But I had cards ready printed to put in the window before I bought the apparatus. The very next day I had the camera, I had a customer before I had even tried it, so I tried it on him, and I gave him a black picture (for I didn't know how to make the portrait, and it was all black when I took the glass out), and told him that it would come out bright as it dried, and he went away quite delighted. I took the first Sunday after we had opened 1*l*. 5*s*. 6*d*., and everybody was quite pleased with their spotted and black pictures, for we still told them they would come out as they dried. But the next week they brought them back to be changed, and I could do them better, and they had middling pictures – for I picked it up very quick.

'I had one fellow for a half-guinea portrait, and he was from Woolwich, and I made him come three times, like a lamb, and he stood pipes and 'bacca, and it was a thundering bad one after all. He was delighted, and he swears now it's the best he ever had took, for it don't fade, but will stop black to the end of the world; though he remarks that I deceived him in one thing, for it don't come out bright.

'You see, when first photography come up I had my eye on it, for I could see it would turn me in something some time. I went and worked as a regular labourer, carrying pails and so on, so as to try and learn something about chemistry; for I always had a hankling after science. Me and Jim was out at Stratford, pitching with the banjo, and I saw some men coming out of a chemical works, and we went to "nob" them (that's get some halfpence out of them). Jim was tambo beating, and we was both black, and they called us lazy beggars, and said we ought to work as they did. So we told them we couldn't get work, we had no characters. As we went home I and Jim got talking, and he says, "What a fine thing if we could get into the berth, for you'd soon learn about them portraits if you get among the chemicals;" so I agreed to go and try for the situation, and told him that if I got the berth I'd "nanti panka his nabs snide;" that means, I wouldn't turn him up, or act nasty to him, but would share money the same as if we were pitching again. That slang is mummers' slang, used by strolling professionals.

'I stopped there for near twelve months, on and off. I had 10*s*. at first, but I got up to 16*s*.; and if I'd stopped I've no doubt I should have been foreman of one of the departments, for I got at last to almost the management of the oxalic acid. They used to make sulphate of iron – ferri sulp is the word for it – and carbonate of iron, too, and I used to be like the red man of Agar then, all over red, and a'most thought of cutting that to go for a soldier, for I shouldn't have wanted a uniform. Then I got to charging the retorts to make carbonate of ammonia, and from that I went to oxalic acid.

'At night me and Jim used to go out with the banjo and tamborine, and we could manage to make up our shares to from 18s. to a guinea a week each; that is, sharing my wages and all; for when we chum together we always panka each other bona (that is, share). We always made our ponta (that is, a pound) a week, for we could average our duey bionk peroon a darkey,' or two shillings each, in the night.

'That's how I got an idea of chemicals, and when I went to photography many of the very things I used to manufacture was the very same as we used to take portraits, such as the hyposulphate of soda, and the nitrate of silver, and the sulphate of iron.

'One of the reasons why I couldn't take portraits was, that when I bought my camera at Flemming's he took a portrait of me with it to show me how to use it, and as it was a dull afternoon he took 90 seconds to produce the picture. So, you see, when I went to work I thought I ought to let my pictures go the same time; and hang me if I didn't, whether the sun was shining or not. I let my plate stop 90 seconds, and of course they used to come out overdone and quite white, and as the evening grew darker they came better. When I got a good one I was surprised, and that picture went miles to be shown about. Then I formed an idea that I had made a miscalculation as to my time, and by referring to the sixpenny book of instructions I saw my mistake, and by the Sunday – that was five days after – I was very much improved, and by a month I could take a very tidy picture.

'I was getting on so well I got some of my portraits, when they was good ones, put in a chandler's shop; and to be sure I got first-rate specimens. I used to go to the different shilling portrait galleries and have a likeness of myself or friends done, to exhibit in my own window. That's the way I got my samples to begin with, and I believe it's done all over London.

'I kept at this all the winter, and all the time I suppose I earned 30s. a week. When summer come again I took a place with a garden in the Old Kent-road, and there I done middling, but I lost the majority of my business by not opening on a Sunday, for it was a religious neighbourhood, and I could have earned my 5l. a week comfortable, for as it was I cleared my 2l. regular. Then I had a regular tent built up out of clothes-horses. I stopped there till I had an offer of a good situation, and I accepted of it, at 2*l.* a week.

'My new place was in Whitechapel, and we lowered the price from a shilling to sixpence. We did well there, that is the governor did, you know, for I've taken on the average from 60 to 100 a day, varying in price from sixpence to half-a-guinea, and the majority was shilling ones. The greatest quantity I ever took was 146 in one day, and 124 was taken away as they was done. The governor used to take 20*l.* a week, and of that 8*l.* clear profit, after paying me 2*l.*, the men at the door 24*s.*, a man and woman 29*s.*, and rent 2*l.* My governor had, to my knowledge, 11 other shops, and I don't know all of his establishments; I managed my concern for him, and he never come near us sometimes for a month.

'I left on my own accord after four months, and I joined two others on equal shares, and opened a place of my own in Southwark. Unfortunately, I begun too late in the season, or I should have done well there; but at first we realised about 2*l.* a week each, and up to last week we have shared our 25*s.* a head.

'Sunday is the best day for shilling portraits; in fact, the majority is shilling ones, because then, you see, people have got their wages, and don't mind spending. Nobody knows about men's ways better than we do. Sunday and Monday is the Derby-day like, and then after that they are about cracked up and done. The largest amount I've taken at Southwark on a Sunday is 80 – over 4*l.* worth, but then in the week-days it's different; Sunday's 15*s.* we think that very tidy, some days only 3*s.* or 4*s.*

'You see we are obliged to resort to all sort of dodges to make sixpenny portraits pay. It's a very neat little picture our sixpenny ones is; with a little brass rim round them, and a neat metal inside, and a front glass; so how can that pay if you do the legitimate business? The glass will cost you 2*d.* a dozen – this small size – and you give two with every picture; then the chemicals will cost quite a halfpenny, and varnish, and frame, and fittings, about 2*d.* We reckon 3*d.* out of each portrait. And then you see there's house-rent and a man at the door, and boy at the table, and the operator, all to pay their wages out of this 6*d.*; so you may guess where the profit is.

'One of our dodges is what we term "An American Air-Preserver"; which is nothing more than a card – old benefit tickets, or, if we are hard up, even brown paper, or anythink – soap wrappings, just varnished on one side. Between our private residence and our shop, no piece of card or old paper escapes us. Supposing a party come in, and says "I should like a portrait;" then I inquire which they'll have, a shilling or a sixpenny one.

If they prefer a sixpenny one, I then make them one up, and I show them one of the air-preservers, – which we keep ready made up – and I tell them that they are all chemicalized, and come from America, and that without them their picture will fade. I also tell them that I make nothing out of them, for that they are only 2d. and cost all the money; and that makes 'em buy one directly. They always bite at them; and we've actually had people come to us to have our preservers put upon other persons' portraits, saying they've been everywhere for them and can't get them. I charge 3d. if it's not one of our pictures. I'm the original inventor of the "Patent American Air-Preserver". We first called them the "London Air-Preservers"; but they didn't go so well as since they've been the Americans.

'Another dodge is, I always take the portrait on a shilling size; and after they are done, I show them what they can have for a shilling – the full size, with the knees; and table and a vase on it – and let them understand that for sixpence they have all the back-ground and legs cut off; so as many take the shilling portraits as sixpenny ones.

'Talking of them preservers, it is astonishing how they go. We've actually had photographers themselves come to us to buy our "American Air-Preservers". We tells them it's a secret, and we manufacture them ourselves. People won't use their eyes. Why, I've actually cut up an old band-box afore the people's eyes, and varnished it and dried it on the hob before their eyes, and yet they still fancy they come from America! Why, we picks up the old paper from the shop-sweeping, and they make first-rate "Patent American Air-Preservers". Actually, when we've been short, I've torn off a bit of old sugar-paper, and stuck it on without any varnish at all, and the party has gone away quite happy and contented. But you must remember it is really a useful thing, for it does do good and do preserve the picture.

'Another of our dodges – and it is a splendid dodge, though it wants a nerve to do it – is the brightening solution, which is nothing more than aqua distilled, or pure water. When we take a portrait, Jim, my mate, who stops in the room, hollows to me, "Is it bona?" That is – Is it good? If it is, I say, "Say" That is – Yes. If not, I say "Nanti." If it is a good one he takes care to publicly expose that one, that all may see it, as a recommendation to others. If I say "Nanti," then Jim takes it and finishes it up, drying it and putting it up in its frame. Then he wraps it up in a large piece of paper, so that it will take sometime to unroll it, at the same time crying out "Take sixpence from this lady, if you please." Sometimes she says, "O let me see it first;" but he always answers, "Money first, if you please ma'am; pay for it first, and then you can do what you like with it. Here, take sixpence from this lady." When she sees it, if it is a black one, she'll say, "Why this ain't like me; there's no picture at all." Then Jim says, "It will become better as it dries, and come to your natural complexion." If she still grumbles, he tells her that if she likes to have it passed through the brightening solution, it will come out lighter in an hour or two. They in general have it brightened; and then, before their face, we dip it into some water. We then dry it off and replace it in the frame, wrap it up carefully, and tell them not to expose it to the air, but put it in their bosom, and in an hour or two it will be all right. This is only done when the portrait come out black, as it doesn't pay to take two for sixpence. Sometimes they brings them back the next day, and says, "It's not dried out as you told us;" and then we take another portrait, and charge them 3*d*. more.

'We also do what we call the "bathing" – another dodge. Now to-day a party came in during a shower of rain, when it was so dark it was impossible to take a portrait; or they will come in, sometimes, just as we are shutting up, and when the gas is lighted, to have their portraits taken; then we do this. We never turn business away, and yet it's impossible to take a portrait; so we ask them to sit down, and then we go through the whole process of taking a portrait, only we don't put any plate in the camera. We always make 'em sit a long time, to make 'em think it's all right – I've had them for two and a half minutes, till their eyes run down with water. We then tell them that we've taken the portrait, but that we shall have to keep it all night in the chemical bath to bring it out, because the weather's so bad. We always take the money as a deposit, and give them a written paper as an order for the picture. If in the morning they come themselves we get them to sit again, and then we do really take a portrait of them; but if they send anybody, we either say that the bath was too strong and eat the picture out, or that it was too weak and didn't bring it out; or else I blow up Jim, and pretend he has upset the bath and broke the picture. We have had as many as ten pictures to bathe in one afternoon.

'If the eyes in a portrait are not seen, and they complain, we take a pin and dot them; and that brings the eye out, and they like it. If the hair, too, is not visible we takes the pin again, and soon puts in a beautiful head of hair. It requires a deal of nerve to do it; but if they still grumble I say, "It's a beautiful picture, and worth half-a-crown, at the least;" and in the end they generally go off contented and happy.

'When we are not busy, we always fill up the time taking specimens for the window. Anybody who'll sit we take him; or we do one another, and the young woman in the shop who colours. Specimens are very useful things to us, for this reason – if anybody comes in a hurry, and won't give us time to do the picture, then, as we can't afford to let her go, we sit her and goes through all the business, and I says to Jim, "Get one from the window," and then he takes the first specimen that comes to hand. Then we fold it up in paper, and don't allow her to see it until she pays for it, and tell her not to expose it to the air for three days, and that if then she doesn't approve of it and will call again we will take her another. Of course they in general comes back. We have made some queer mistakes doing this. One day a young lady came in, and wouldn't wait, so Jim takes a specimen from the window, and, as luck would have it, it was the prtrait of a widow in her cap. She insisted upon opening, and then she said, "This isn't me; it's got a widow's cap, and I was never married in all my life!" Jim answers, "Oh, miss! why it's a beautiful picture, and a correct like-ness" – and so it was, and no lies, but it wasn't of her – Jim talked to her, and says he, "Why this ain't a cap, it's the shadow of the hair" – for she had ringlets – and she positively took it away believing that such was the case; and even promised to send us customers, which she did.

'There was another lady that came in a hurry, and would stop if we were not more than a minute; so Jim ups with a specimen, without looking at it, and it was the picture of a woman and her child. We went through the business of focussing the camera, and then gave her the portrait and took the 6d. When she saw it she cries out, "Bless me! there's a child: I haven't ne'er a child!" Jim looked at her, and then at the picture, as if comparing, and says he, "It is certainly a wonderful likeness, miss, and one of the best we ever took. It's the way you sat; and what has occasioned it was a child passing through the yard.' She said she supposed it must be so, and took the portrait away highly delighted.

'Once a sailor came in, and as he was in haste, I shoved on to him the picture of a carpenter, who was to call in the afternoon for his portrait. The jacket was dark, but there was a white waistcoat; still I persuaded him that it was his blue Guernsey which had come up very light, and he was so pleased that he gave us 9d. instead of 6d. The fact is, people don't know their own faces. Half of 'em have never looked in a glass half a dozen times in their life, and directly they see a pair of eyes and a nose, they fancy they are their own.

'The only time we were done was with an old woman. We had only one specimen left, and that was a sailor man, very dark – one of our black pictures. But she put on her spectacles, and she looked at it up and down, and says, "Eh?" I said, "Did you speak, ma'am?" and she cries, "Why, this is a man! here's the whiskers." I left, and Jim tried to humbug her, for I was bursting with laughing. Jim said, "It's you ma'am; and a very excellent likeness, I assure you." But she kept on saying, "Nonsense, I ain't a man," and wouldn't have it. Jim wanted her to leave a deposit, and come next day, but she never called. It was a little too strong.

'There was an old woman come in once and wanted to be taken with a favourite hen in her lap. It was a very bad picture, and so black there was nothing but the outline of her face and a white speck for the beak of the bird. When she saw it, she asked where the bird was? So Jim took a pin and scratched in an eye, and said, "There it is, ma'am – that's her eye, it's coming out," and then he made a line for the comb on the head, and she kept saying, "Wonderful!" and was quite delighted.

'The only bad money we have taken was from a Methodist clergyman, who came in for a 1s. 6d. portrait. He gave us a bad sixpence.

'For colouring we charge 3d. more. If the portraits are bad or dark we tell them, that if they have them coloured the likeness will be perfect. We flesh the face, scratch the eye in, and blue the coat and colour the tablecloth. Sometimes the girl who does it puts in such a lot of flesh paint, that you can scarcely distinguish a feature of the person. If they grumble, we tell them it will be all right when the picture's dry. If it's a good picture, the colour looks very nice, but in the black ones we are obliged to stick it on at a tremendous rate, to make it show.

'Jim stands at the door, and he keeps on saying, "A correct portrait, framed and glazed, for sixpence, beautifully enamelled." Then, when they are listening, he shows the specimen in his hands, and adds, "If not approved of, no charge made."

'One morning, when we had been doing "quisby", that is, stopping idle, we hit upon another dodge. Some friends dropped in to see me, and as I left to accompany them to a tavern close by, I cried to Jim, "Take that public-house opposite." He brought the camera and stand to the door, and a mob soon collected. He kept saying, "Stand back, gentlemen, stand back! I am about to take the public-house in front by this wonderful process." Then he went over to the house, and asked the landlord, and asked some gentlemen drinking there to step into the road whilst he took the house with them facing it. Then he went to a policeman and asked him to stop the carts from passing, and he actually did. By this way he got up a tremendous mob. He then put in the slide, pulled off the cap of the camera, and focussed the house, and pretended to take the picture, though he had no prepared glass, nor nothing. When he had done, he called out,

"Portraits taken in one minute. We are now taking portraits for 6*d.* only. Time of sitting, two seconds only. Step inside and have your'n taken immediately." There was a regular rush, and I had to be fetched, and we took 6*s.* worth right off.

'People seem to think the camera will do anything. We actually persuade them that it will mesmerise them. After their portrait is taken, we ask them if they would like to be mesmerised by the camera, and the charge is only 2*d.* We then focus the camera, and tell them to look firm at the tube; and they stop there for two or three minutes staring, till their eyes begin to water, and then they complain of a dizziness in the head, and give it up, saying they "can't stand it". I always tell them the operation was beginning, and they were just going off, only they didn't stay long enough. They always remark, "Well, it certainly is a wonderful machine, and a most curious invention." Once a coalheaver came in to be mesmerised, but he got into a rage after five or six minutes, and said, "Strike me dead, ain't you keeping me a while!" He wouldn't stop still, so Jim told him his sensitive nerves was too powerful, and sent him off cursing and swearing because he couldn't be mesmerised. We don't have many of these mesmerism customers, not more than four in these five months; but it's a curious circumstance, proving what fools people is. Jim says he only introduces these games when business is dull, to keep my spirits up – and they certainly are most laughable.

'I also profess to remove warts, which I do by touching them with nitric acid. My price is a penny a wart, or a shilling for the job; for some of the hands is pretty well smothered with them. You see, we never turn money away, for it's hard work to make a living at sixpenny portraits. My wart patients seldom come twice, for they screams out ten thousand blue murders when the acid bites them.

'Another of my callings is to dye the hair. You see I have a good many refuse baths, which is mostly nitrate of silver, the same as all hair-dyes is composed of. I dyes the whiskers and moustache for 1*s.* The worst of it is, that nitrate of silver also blacks the skin wherever it touches. One fellow with carroty hair came in one day to have his whiskers died, and I went clumsily to work and let the stuff trickle down his chin and on his cheeks, as well as making the flesh at the roots as black as a hat. He came the next day to have it taken off, and I made him pay 3*d.* more, and then removed it with cyanide, which certainly did clean him, but made him smart awfully.

'I have been told that there are near upon 250 houses in London now getting a livelihood taking sixpenny portraits. There's ninety of 'em I'm personally acquainted with, and one man I know has ten different shops of his own. There's eight in the Whitechapel-road alone, from Butcher-row to the Mile-end turnpike. Bless you, yes! they all make a good living at it. Why, I could go to-morrow, and they would be glad to employ me at 2*l.* a week – indeed they have told me so.

'If we had begun earlier this summer, we could, only with our little affair, have made from 8*l.* to 10*l.* a week, and about one-third of that is expenses. You see, I operate myself, and that cuts out 2*l.* a week.'

TOYS

The Doll's-eye Maker

[pp. 241–3] A curious part of the street toy business is the sale of dolls, and especially that odd branch of it, doll's-eye making. There are only two persons following this business in London, and by the most intelligent of these I was furnished with the following curious information –

'I make all kinds of eyes,' the eye-manufacturer said, 'both dolls' and human eyes; birds' eyes are mostly manufactured in Birmingham, and as you say, sir, bulls' eyes at the confectioner's. Of dolls' eyes there are two sorts, the common and the natural, as we call it. The common are simply small hollow glass spheres, made of white enamel, and coloured either black or blue, for only two colours of these are made. The bettermost dolls' eyes, or the natural ones, are made in a superior manner, but after a similar fashion to the commoner sort. The price of the common black and blue dolls' eyes is five shillings for twelve dozen pair. We make very few of the bettermost kind, or natural eyes for dolls, for the price of those is about fourpence a pair, but they are only for the very best dolls. Average it throughout the year, a journeyman doll's-eye maker earns about thirty shillings a week. The common dolls' eyes were twelve shillings the twelve dozen pairs twenty-five years ago, but now they are only five shillings. The decrease of the price is owing to competition, for though there are only two of us in the trade in London, still the other party is always pushing his eyes and underselling our'n. Immediately the demand ceases at all, he goes round the trade with his eyes in a box, and offers them at a lower figure than in the regular season, and so the prices have been falling every year. There is a brisk and a slack season in our business, as well as in most others. After the Christmas holidays up to March we have generally little to do, but from that time eyes begin to look up a bit, and the business remains pretty good till the end of October. Where we make one pair of eyes for home consumption, we make ten for exportation; a great many eyes go abroad. Yes, I suppose we should be soon over-populated with dolls if a great number of them were not to emigrate every year. The annual increase of dolls goes on at an alarming rate. As you say, sir, the yearly rate of mortality must be very high, to be sure, but still it's nothing to the rate at which they are brought into the world. They can't make wax dolls in America, sir, so we ship off a great many there. The reason why they can't produce dolls in America is owing to the climate. The wax won't set in very hot weather, and it cracks in extreme cold. I knew a party who went out to the United States to start as doll-maker. He took several gross of my eyes with him, but he couldn't succeed. The eyes that we make for Spanish America are all black. A blue-eyed doll wouldn't sell at all there. Here, however, nothing but blue eyes goes down; that's because it's the colour of the Queen's eyes, and she sets the fashion in our eyes as in other things. We make the same kind of eyes for the gutta-percha dolls as for the wax. It is true, the gutta-percha complexion isn't particularly clear; nevertheless, the eyes I make for the washable faces are all of the natural tint, and if the gutta-percha dolls look rather bilious, why I ain't a going to make my eyes look bilious to match.

'I also make human eyes. These are two cases; in the one I have black and hazel, and in the other blue and grey.' [Here the man took the lids off a couple of boxes, about as big as binnacles, that stood on the table: they each contained 190 different eyes, and so like nature, that the effect produced upon a person unaccustomed to the sight was most peculiar, and far from pleasant. The whole of the 380 optics all seemed to be staring directly at the spectator, and occasioned a feeling somewhat similar to the bewilderment one experiences on suddenly becoming an object of general notice; as if the eyes, indeed, of a whole lecture-room were crammed into a few square inches, and all turned full upon you. The eyes of the whole world, as we say, literally appeared to be fixed upon one, and it was almost impossible at first to look at them without instinctively averting the head. The hundred eyes of Argus were positively insignificant in comparison to the 380 belonging to the human eye-maker.] 'Here you see are the ladies' eyes,' he continued, taking one from the blue-eye tray. 'You see there's more sparkle and brilliance about them than the gentlemen's. Here's two different ladies' eyes; they belong to fine-looking young women, both of them. When a lady or gentleman comes to us for an eye, we are obliged to have a sitting just like a portrait-painter. We take no sketch, but study the tints of the perfect eye. There are a number of eyes come over from France, but these are generally what we call misfits; they are sold cheap, and seldom match the other eye. Again, from not fitting tight over the ball like those that are made expressly for the person, they seldom move "consentaneously", as it is termed, with the natural eye, and have therefore a very unpleasant and fixed stare, worse almost than the defective eye itself. Now, the eyes we make move so freely, and have such a natural appearance, that I can assure you a gentleman who had one of his from me passed nine doctors without the deception being detected.

'There is a lady customer of mine who has been married three years to her husband, and I believe he doesn't know that she has a false eye to this day.

'The generality of persons whom we serve take out their eyes when they go to bed, and sleep with them either under their pillow, or else in a tumbler of water on the toilet-table at their side. Most married ladies, however, never take their eyes out at all.

'Some people wear out a false eye in half the time of others. This doesn't arise from the greater use of them, or rolling them about, but from the increased secretion of the tears, which act on the false eye like acid on metal, and so corrodes and roughens the surface. This roughness produces inflammation, and then a new eye becomes necessary. The Scotch lose a great many eyes, why I cannot say; and the men in this country lose more eyes, nearly two to one. We generally make only one eye, but I did once make two false eyes for a widow lady. She lost one first, and we repaired the loss so well, that on her losing the other eye she got us to make her a second.

'False eyes are a great charity to servants. If they lose an eye no one will engage them. In Paris there is a charitable institution for the supply of false eyes to the poor; and I really think, if there was a similar establishment in this country for furnishing artificial eyes to those whose bread depends on their looks, like servants, it would do a great deal of good. We always supplies eyes to such people at half-price. My usual price is 2l. 2s. for one of my best eyes. That eye is a couple of guineas, and as fine an eye as you would wish to see in any young woman's head.

'I suppose we make from 300 to 400 false eyes every year. The great art in making a false eye is in polishing the edges quite smooth. Of dolls' eyes we make about 6,000 dozen pairs of the common ones every year. I take it that there are near upon 24,000 dozen, or more than a quarter of a million, pairs of all sorts of dolls' eyes made annually in London.'

LONDON OMNIBUS DRIVERS AND CONDUCTORS

[pp. 346–8]   The subject of omnibus conveyance is one to the importance of which the aspect of every thoroughfare in London bears witness. Yet the dweller in the Strand, or even in a greater thoroughfare, Cheapside, can only form a partial notion of the magnitude of this mode of transit, for he has but a partial view of it; he sees, as it were, only one of its details.

The routes of the several omnibuses are manifold. Widely apart as are their starting-points, it will be seen how their courses tend to common centres, and how generally what may be called the great trunk-lines of the streets are resorted to.

The principal routes lie north and south, east and west, through the central parts of London, to and from the extreme suburbs. The majority of them commence running at eight in the morning, and continue till twelve at night, succeeding each other during the busy part of the day every five minutes. Most of them have two charges – 3d. for part of the distance, and 6d. for the whole distance.

The omnibuses proceeding on the northern and southern routes are principally the following:

The Atlases run from the Eyre Arms, St John's Wood, by way of Baker-street, Oxford-street, Regent-street, Charing-cross, Westminster-bridge and road, and past the Elephant and Castle, by the Walworth-road, to Camberwell-gate. Some turn off from the Elephant (as all the omnibus people call it) and go down the New Kent-road to the Dover railway-station; while others run the same route, but to and from the Nightingale, Lisson-grove, instead of the Eyre Arms. The Waterloos journey from the York and Albany, Regent's-park, by way of Albany-street, Portland-road, Regent-street, and so over Waterloo-bridge, by the Waterloo, London, and Walworth-roads, to Camberwell-gate. The Waterloo Association have also a branch to Holloway, *via* the Camden Villas. There are likewise others which run from the terminus of the South-Western Railway in the Waterloo-road, *via* Stamford-street, to the railway termini on the Surrey side of London-bridge, and thence to that of the Eastern Counties in Shoreditch.

The Hungerford-markets pursue the route from Camden Town along Tottenham Court-road, &c. to Hungerford; and many run from this spot to Paddington.

The Kentish Town run from the Eastern Counties station, and from Whitechapel to Kentish Town, by way of Tottenham Court-road, &c.

347

The Hampsteads observe the like course to Camden Town, and then run straight on to Hampstead.

The King's-crosses run from Kennington-gate by the Blackfriar's-road and bridge, Fleet-street, Chancery-lane, Gray's-inn-lane, and the New-road, to Euston-square, while some go on to Camden Town.

The Great Northerns, the latest route started, travel from the railway terminus, Maiden-lane, King's-cross, to the Bank and the railway-stations, both in the city and across the Thames; also to Paddington, and some to Kennington.

The Favourites' route is from Westminster Abbey, along the Strand, Chancery-lane, Gray's-inn-lane, and Coldbath-fields, to the Angel, Islington, and thence to Holloway; while some of them run down Fleet-street, and so past the General Post-office, and thence by the City-road to the Angel and to Holloway. The Favourites also run from Holloway to the Bank.

The Islington and Kennington line is from Barnsbury-park, by the Post-office and Blackfriars-bridge, to Kennington-gate.

The Camberwells go from Gracechurch-street, over London-bridge, to Camberwell, while a very few start from the west end of the town, and some two or three from Fleet-street; the former crossing Westminster and the latter Blackfriars-bridge, while some Nelsons run from Oxford-street to Camberwell or to Brixton.

The Brixtons and Claphams go, some from the Regent-circus, Oxford-street, by way of Regent-street, over Westminster-bridge; and some from Gracechurch-street, over London-bridge, to Brixton or Clapham, as the case may be.

The Paragons observe the same route, and some of these conveyances go over Blackfriar's-bridge to Brixton.

The Carshaltons follow the track of the Mitchams, Tootings, and Claphams, and go over London-bridge to the Bank.

The Paddingtons go from the Royal Oak, Westbourne-Green, and from the Pine-applegate by way of Oxford-street and Holborn to the Bank, the London-bridge, Eastern Counties, or Blackwall railway termini; while some reach the same destination by the route of the New-road, City-road, and Finsbury. These routes are also pursued by the vehicles lettered 'New-road Conveyance Association', and 'London Conveyance Company'; while some of the vehicles belonging to the same proprietors run to Notting-hill, and some have branches to St John's Wood and elsewhere.

The Wellingtons and Marlboroughs pursue the same track as the Paddingtons, but some of them diverge to St John's Wood.

The Kensall-greens go from the Regent-circus, Oxford-street, to the Cemetery.

The course of the Bayswaters is from Bayswater *via* Oxford-street, Regent-street, and the Strand to the Bank.

The Bayswaters and Kensingtons run from the Bank *via* Finsbury, and then by the City-road and New-road, down Portland-road, and by Oxford-street and Piccadilly to Bayswater and Kensington.

The Hammersmith and Kensingtons convey their passengers from Hammersmith, by way of Kensington, Knightsbridge, Piccadilly, &c. to the Bank.

The Richmond and Hampton Courts, from St Paul's-churchyard to the two places indicated.

The Putneys and Bromptons run from Putney-bridge *via* Brompton, &c. to the Bank and the London-bridge railway station.

The Chelseas proceed from the Man in the Moon to the Bank, Mile-end-road, and City railway stations.

The Chelsea and Islingtons observe the route from Sloane-square to the Angel, Islington, travelling along Piccadilly, Regent-street, Portland-road, and the New-road.

The Royal Blues go from Pimlico *via* Grosvenor-gate, Piccadilly, the Strand, &c. to the Blackwall railway station.

The direction of the Pimlicos is through Westminster, Whitehall, Strand, &c. to Whitechapel.

The Marquess of Westminsters follow the route from the Vauxhall-bridge *via* Millbank, Westminster Abbey, the Strand, &c. to the Bank.

The Deptfords go from Gracechurch-street, and over London-bridge, and some from Charing-cross, over Westminster-bridge, to Deptford.

The route of the Nelsons is from Charing-cross, over Westminster-bridge, and by the New and Old Kent-roads to Deptford, Greenwich, and Woolwich; some go from Gracechurch-street, over London-bridge.

The Shoreditches pursue the direction of Chelsea, Piccadilly, the Strand, &c. to Shoreditch, their starting-place being Battersea-bridge.

The Hackneys and Claptons run from Oxford-street, to Clapton-square.

Barber's run from the Bank, and some from Oxford-street, to Clapton.

The Blackwalls run some from Sloane-street to the Docks, and the Bow and Stratfords from different parts of the West-end to their respective destinations.

I have enumerated these several conveyances from the information of persons connected with the trade, using the terms they used, which better distinguish the respective routes than the names lettered on the carriages, which would but puzzle the reader, the principal appellation giving no intimation of the destination of the omnibus.

The routes above specified are pursued by a series of vehicles belonging to one company or to one firm, or one individual, the number of their vehicles varying from twelve to fifty. One omnibus, however, continues to run from the Bank to Finchley, and one from the Angel to Hampton Court.

The total number of omnibuses traversing the streets of London is about 3,000, paying duty including mileage, averaging 9*l*. per month each, or 324,000*l*. per annum. The number of conductors and drivers is about 7,000 (including a thousand 'odd men', – a term that will be explained hereafter), paying annually 5s. each for their licenses, or 1,750*l*. collectively. The receipts of each vehicle vary from 2*l*. to 4*l*. per day. Estimating the whole 3,000 at 3*l*., it follows that the entire sum expended annually in omnibus hire by the people of London amounts to no less than 3,285,000*l*., which is more than 30s. a-head for every man, woman, and child, in the metropolis. The average journey as regards length of each omnibus is six miles, and that distance is in some cases travelled twelve times a day by each omnibus, or, as it is called, 'six there and six back'. Some perform the journey only ten times a day (each omnibus), and some, but a minority, a less number of times. Now taking the average as between forty-five and fifty miles a day, travelled by each omnibus, and that I am assured on the best authority is within the mark, while sixty miles a day might exceed it, and computing the omnibuses running daily at 3,000, we find 'a travel', as it was worded to me, upwards of 140,000 miles a day, or a yearly travel of more than 50,000,000 of miles: an extent that almost defies a parallel among any distances popularly familiar. And that this estimate in no way exceeds the truth is proved by the sum annually paid to the Excise for 'mileage', which, as before stated, amounts on an average to 9*l*. each 'bus', per month, or, collectively, to 324,000*l*. per annum, and this as 1½d. per mile (the rate of duty charged) gives 51,840,000 miles as the distance travelled by the entire number of omnibuses every year.

On each of its journeys experienced persons have assured me an omnibus carries on the average fifteen persons. Nearly all are licensed to carry twenty-two (thirteen inside and nine out), and that number perhaps is sometimes exceeded, while fifteen is a fair computation; for as every omnibus has now the two fares, 3d. and 6d., or, as the busmen call them, 'long uns and short uns', there are two sets of passengers, and the number of fifteen through the whole distance on each journey of the omnibus is, as I have said, a fair computation: for sometimes the vehicle is almost empty, as a set-off to its being crammed at other times. This computation shows the daily 'travel', reckoning ten journeys a day, of 450,000 passengers. Thus we might be led to believe that about one-fourth the entire population of the metropolis and its suburbs, men, women, and children, the inmates of hospitals, gaols, and workhouses, paupers, peers, and their families all included, were daily travelling in omnibuses. But it must be borne in mind, that as most omnibus travellers use that convenient mode of conveyance at least twice a day, we may compute the number of individuals at 225,000, or, allowing three journeys as an average daily travel, at 150,000. Calculating the payment of each passenger at $4\frac{1}{2}d.$, and so allowing for the set-off of the 'short uns' to the 'long uns', we have a daily receipt for omnibus fares of 8,439*l.*, a weekly receipt of 58,073*l.*, and a yearly receipt of 2,903,650*l.*; which it will be seen is several thousands less than the former estimate: so that it may be safely assured, that at least three millions of money is annually expended on omnibus fares in London.

The extent of individual travel performed by some of the omnibus drivers is enormous. One man told me that he had driven his 'bus' seventy-two miles (twelve stages of six miles) every day for six years, with the exception of twelve miles less every second Sunday, so that this man had driven in six years 179,568 miles.

Origin of Omnibuses

[pp. 349–50] This vast extent of omnibus transit has been the growth of twenty years, as it was not until the 4th July, 1829, that Mr Shillibeer, now the proprietor of the patent mourning coaches, started the first omnibus. Some works of authority as books of reference, have represented that Mr Shillibeer's first omnibus ran from Charing-cross to Greenwich, and that the charge for outside and inside places was the same. Such was not the case; the first omnibus, or rather, the first pair of those vehicles (for Mr Shillibeer started two), ran from the Bank to the Yorkshire Stingo. Neither could the charge out and in be the same, as there were no outside passengers. Mr Shillibeer was a naval officer, and in his youth stepped from a midshipman's duties into the business of a coach-builder, he learning that business from the late Mr Hatchett, of Long Acre. Mr Shillibeer then established himself in Paris as a builder of English carriages, a demand for which had sprung up after the peace, when the current of English travel was directed strongly to France. In this speculation Mr Shillibeer was eminently successful. He built carriages for Prince Polignac, and others of the most influential men under the dynasty of the elder branch of the Bourbons, and had a bazaar for the sale of his vehicles. He was thus occupied in Paris in 1819, when M. Lafitte first started the omnibuses which are now so common and so well managed in the French capital. Lafitte was the banker (afterwards the minister) of Louis Philippe, and the most active man in establishing the Messageries Royales. Five or six years after the omnibuses had been successfully introduced into Paris, Mr Shillibeer was employed by M. Lafitte to build two in a superior style. In executing this order, Mr Shillibeer thought that so comfortable and economical a mode of conveyance might be advantageously introduced in London. He accordingly disposed of his Parisian establishment, and came to London, and started his omnibus as I have narrated. In order that the introduction might have every chance of success, and have the full prestige of respectability, Mr Shillibeer brought over with him from Paris two youths, both the sons of British naval officers; and these young gentlemen were for a few weeks his 'conductors'. They were smartly dressed in 'blue cloth and togs', to use the words of my informant, after the fashion of Lafitte's conductors, each dress costing 5l. Their addressing any foreign passenger in French, and the French style of the affair, gave rise to an opinion that Mr Shillibeer was a Frenchman, and that the English were indebted to a foreigner for the improvement of their vehicular transit, whereas Mr Shillibeer had served in the British navy, and was born in Tottenham-court-road. His speculation was particularly and at once successful. His two vehicles carried each twenty-two, and were filled every journey. The form was that of the present omnibus, but larger and roomier, as the twenty-two were all accommodated inside, nobody being outside but the driver. Three horses yoked abreast were used to draw these carriages.

There were for many days, until the novelty wore off, crowds assembled to see the omnibuses start, and many ladies and gentlemen took their places in them to the Yorkshire Stingo, in order that they might have the pleasure of riding back again. The fare was one shilling for the whole and sixpence for half the distance, and each omnibus made twelve journeys to and fro every day. Thus Mr Shillibeer established a diversity of fares, regulated by distance; a regulation which was afterwards in a great measure abandoned by omnibus proprietors, and then re-established on our present threepenny and sixpenny payments, the 'long uns' and the 'short uns'. Mr Shillibeer's receipts were 100l. a-week. At first he provided a few books, chiefly magazines, for the perusal of his customers; but this peripatetic library was discontinued, for the customers (I give the words of my informant) 'boned the books'. When the young-gentlemen conductors retired from their posts, they were succeeded by persons hired by Mr Shillibeer, and liberally paid, who were attired in a sort of velvet livery. Many weeks had not elapsed before Mr Shillibeer found a falling off in his receipts, although he ascertained that there was no falling off in the public support of his omnibuses. He obtained information, however, that the persons in his employ robbed him of at least 20*l.* a week, retaining that sum out of the receipts of the two omnibuses, and that they had boasted of their cleverness and their lucrative situations at a champagne supper at the Yorkshire Stingo. This necessitated a change, which Mr Shillibeer effected, in his men, but without prosecuting the offenders, and still it seemed that defalcations continued. That they continued was soon shown, and in 'a striking manner', as I was told. As an experiment, Mr Shillibeer expended 300*l.* in the construction of a machine fitted to the steps of an omnibus which should record the number of passengers as they trod on a plate in entering and leaving the vehicle, arranged on a similar principle to the tell-tales in use on our toll-bridges. The inventor, Mr —, now of Woolwich, himself worked the omnibus containing it for a fortnight, and it supplied a correct index of the number of passengers: but at the fortnight's end, one evening after dark, the inventor was hustled aside while waiting at the Yorkshire Stingo, and in a minute or two the machine was smashed by some unknown men with sledge-hammers. Mr Shillibeer then had recourse to the use of such clocks as were used in the French omnibuses as a check. It was publicly notified that it was the business of the conductor to move the hand of the clock a given distance when a pasenger entered the vehicle, but this plan did not succeed. It is common in France for a passenger to inform the proprietor of any neglect on the part of his servant, but Mr Shillibeer never received any such intimation in London.

In the meantime Mr Shillibeer's success continued, for he insured punctuality and civility; and the cheapness, cleanliness, and smartness of his omnibuses, were in most advantageous contrast with the high charges, dirt, dinginess, and rudeness of the drivers of many of the 'short stages'. The short-stage proprietors were loud in their railings against what they were pleased to describe as a French innovation. In the course of from six to nine months Mr Shillibeer had twelve omnibuses at work. The new omnibuses ran from the Bank to Paddington, both by the route of Holborn and Oxford-street, as well as by Finsbury and the New-road. Mr Shillibeer feels convinced, that had he started fifty omnibuses instead of two in the first instance, a fortune might have been realised. In 1831–2, his omnibuses became general in the great street thoroughfares; and as the short stages were run off the road, the proprietors started omnibuses in opposition to Mr Shillibeer. The first omnibuses, however, started after Mr Shillibeer's were not in opposition. They were the Caledonians, and were the property of Mr Shillibeer's brother-in-law. The third started, which were two-horse vehicles, were foolishly enough called 'Les Dames Blanches'; but as the name gave rise to much low wit in *équivoques* it was abandoned. The original omnibuses were called 'Shillibeers' on the panels, from the name of their originator; and the name is still prevalent on those conveyances in New York, which affords us another proof that not in his own country is a benefactor honoured, until perhaps his death makes honour as little worth as an epitaph.

The opposition omnibuses, however, continued to increase as more and more short stages were abandoned; and one oppositionist called his omnibuses 'Shillibeers', so that the real and the sham Shillibeers were known in the streets. The opposition became fiercer. The 'busses', as they came to be called in a year or two, crossed each other and raced or drove their poles recklessly into the back of one another; and accidents and squabbles and loitering grew so frequent, and the time of the police magistrates was so much occupied with 'omnibus business', that in 1832 the matter was mentioned in Parliament as a nuisance requiring a remedy, and in 1833 a Bill was brought in by the Government and passed for the 'Regulation of Omnibuses (as well as other conveyances) in and near the metropolis'. Two sessions after, Mr Alderman Wood brought in a bill for the better regulation of omnibuses, which was also passed, and one of the provisions of the bill was that the drivers and conductors of omnibuses should be licensed. The office of Registrar of Licenses was promised by a noble lord in office to Mr Shillibeer (as I am informed on good authority), but the appointment was given to the present Commissioner of the City Police, and the office next to the principal was offered to Mr Shillibeer, which that gentleman declined to accept. The reason assigned for not appointing him to the registrarship was that he was connected with omnibuses. At the beginning of 1834, Mr Shillibeer abandoned his metropolitan trade, and began running omnibuses from London to Greenwich and Woolwich, employing 20 carriages and 120 horses; but the increase of steamers and the opening of the Greenwich Railway in 1835 affected his trade so materially, that Mr Shillibeer fell into arrear with his payments to the Stamp Office, and seizures of his property and reseizures after money was paid, entailed such heavy expenses, and such a hindrance to Mr Shillibeer's business, that his failure ensued.

Omnibus Proprietors

[pp. 352–4] The 'labourers' immediately connected with the trade in omnibuses are the proprietors, drivers, conductors, and time-keepers. Those less immediately but still in connexion with the trade are the 'odd men' and the horsekeepers.

The earlier history of omnibus proprietors presents but a series of struggles and ruinous lawsuits, one proprietor with another, until many were ruined; and then several opposed companies or individuals coalesced or agreed; and these proprietaries now present a united, and, I believe, a prosperous body. They possess in reality a monopoly in omnibus convey-ance; but I am assured it would not be easy under any other plan to serve the public better. All the proprietors of omnibuses may be said to be in union, as they act systematically and by arrangement, one proprietary with another. Their profits are, of course, apportioned, like those of other joint-stock companies, according to the number of shares held by individual members. On each route one member of the proprietary is appointed ('directed') by his co-proprietors. The directory may be classed as the 'executive department' of the body. The director can displace a driver on a week's notice: but by some directors, who pride themselves on dealing summarily, it seems that the week's notice is now and then dispensed with. The conductor he can displace at a day's notice. The 'odd men' sometimes supply the places of the officials so discharged until a meeting of the proprietary, held monthly for the most part, when new officers are appointed; there being always an abundance of applicants, who send or carry in testimonials of their fitness from persons known to the proprietors, or known to reside on the line of the route. The director may indeed appoint either driver or conductor at his discretion, if he see good reason to do so. The driver, however, is generally appointed and paid by the proprietor, while the conductor is more particularly the servant of the association. The proprietaries have so far a monopoly of the road, that they allow no new omnibuses to be started upon it. If a speculator should be bold enough to start new conveyances, the pre-existing proprietaries put a greater number of conveyances on the route, so that none are well filled; and one of the old proprietaries' vehicles immediately precedes the omnibus of the speculator, and another immediately follows it; and thus three vehicles are on the ground, which may yield only customers for one:

hence, as the whole number on the route has been largely increased, not one omnibus is well filled, and the speculator must in all probability be ruined, while the associated proprietors suffer but a temporary loss. So well is this now understood, that no one seems to think of embarking his money in the omnibus trade unless he 'buys his times', that is to say, unless he arranges by purchase; and a 'new man' will often pay 400*l*. or 500*l*. for his 'times', to have the privilege of running his vehicles on a given route, and at given periods: in other words, for the privilege of becoming a recognised proprietor.

The proprietors pay their servants fairly, as a general rule; while, as a universal rule, they rigidly exact sobriety, punctuality, and cleanliness. Their great difficulty, all of them concur in stating, is to ensure honesty. Every proprietor insists upon the excessive difficulty of trusting men with uncounted money, if the men feel there is no efficient check to ensure to their employers a knowledge of the exact amount of their daily receipts. Several plans have been resorted to in order to obtain the desired check. Mr Shillibeer's I have already given. One plan now in practice is to engage a well-dressed woman, sometimes accompanied by a child, and she travels by the omnibus; and immediately on leaving it, fills up a paper for the proprietor, showing the number of insides and outs, of short and long fares. This method, however, does not ensure a thorough accuracy. It is difficult for a woman, who must take such a place in the vehicle as she can get, to ascertain the precise number of outsides and their respective fares. So difficult, that I am assured such a person has returned a *smaller* number than was actually conveyed. One gentleman who was formerly an omnibus proprietor, told me he employed a 'ladylike', and, as he believed, trusty woman, as a 'check'; but by some means the conductors found out the calling of the 'ladylike' woman, treated her, and she made very favourable returns for the conductors. Another lady was observed by a conductor, who bears an excellent character, and who mentioned the circumstances to me, to carry a small bag, from which, whenever a passenger got out, she drew, not very deftly it would seem, a bean, and placed it in one glove, as ladies carry their sixpences for the fare, or a pea, and placed it in the other. This process, the conductor felt assured, was 'a check'; that the beans indicated the 'long uns', and the peas the 'short uns': so, when the unhappy woman desired to be put down at the bottom of Cheapside on a wintry evening, he contrived to land her in the very thickest of the mud, handing her out with great politeness. I may here observe, before I enter upon the subject, that the men who have maintained a character for integrity regard the checks with great bitterness, as they naturally feel more annoyed at being suspected than men who may be dishonestly inclined. Another conductor once found a memorandum-book in his omnibus, in which were regularly entered the 'longs' and 'shorts'.

One proprietor told me he had once employed religious men as conductors; 'but,' said he, 'they grew into thieves. A Methodist parson engaged one of his sons to me – it's a good while ago – and was quite indignant that I ever made any question about the young man's honesty, as he was strictly and religiously brought up; but he turned out one of the worst of the whole batch of them.' One check resorted to, as a conductor informed me, was found out by them. A lady entered the omnibus carrying a brown-paper parcel, loosely tied, and making a tear on the edge of the paper for every 'short' passenger, and a deeper tear for every 'long'. This difficulty in finding a check where an indefinite amount of money passes through a man's hands – and I am by no means disposed to undervalue the difficulty – has led to a summary course of procedure, not unattended by serious evils. It appears that men are now discharged suddenly, at a moment's notice, and with no reason assigned. If a reason be demanded, the answer is, 'You are not wanted any longer.' Probably, the discharge is on account of the man's honesty being suspected. But whether the suspicion be well founded or unfounded, the consequences are equally serious to the individual discharged; for it is a rule observed by the proprietors not to employ any man discharged from another line. He will not be employed, I am assured, if he can produce a good character; and even if the ''bus he worked' had been discontinued as no longer required on that route. New men, who are considered unconnected with all versed in omnibus tricks, are appointed; and this course, it was intimated to me very strongly, was agreeable to the proprietors for two reasons – as widely extending their patronage, and as always placing at their command a large body of unemployed men, whose services can at any time be called into requisition at reduced wages, should 'slop-drivers' be desirable. It is next to impossible, I was further assured, for a man discharged from an omnibus to obtain other employ. If the director goes so far as to admit that he has nothing to allege against the man's character, he will yet give no reason for his discharge; and an inquirer naturally imputes the with-holding of a reason to the mercy of the director.

357

Omnibus Drivers

[pp. 354–5] The driver is paid by the week. His remuneration is 34s. a week on most of the lines. On others he receives 21s. and his box – that is, the allowance of a fare each journey for a seat outside, if a seat be so occupied. In fine weather this box plan is more remunerative to the driver than the fixed payment of 34s.; but in wet weather he may receive nothing from the box. The average then the year through is only 34s. a week; or, perhaps, rather more, as on some days in sultry weather the driver may make 6s., 'if the 'bus do twelve journeys', from his box.

The omnibus drivers have been butchers, farmers, horsebreakers, cheesemongers, old stage-coachmen, broken-down gentlemen, turf-men, gentlemen's servants, grooms, and a very small sprinkling of mechanics. Nearly all can read and write, the exception being described to me as a singularity; but there are such exceptions, and all must have produced good characters before their appointment. The majority of them are married men with families; their residences being in all parts, and on both sides of the Thames. I did not hear of any of the wives of coachmen in regular employ working for the slop-tailors. 'We can keep our wives too respectable for that,' one of them said, in answer to my inquiry. Their children, too, are generally sent to school; frequently to the national schools. Their work is exceedingly hard, their lives being almost literally spent on the coach-box. The most of them must enter 'the yard' at a quarter to eight in the morning, and must see that the horses and carriages are in a proper condition for work; and at half-past eight they start on their long day's labour. They perform (I speak of the most frequented lines), twelve journeys during the day, and are so engaged until a quarter-past eleven at night. Some are on their box till past midnight. During these hours of labour they have twelve 'stops'; half of ten and half of fifteen minutes' duration. They generally breakfast at home, or at a coffee-shop, if unmarried men, before they start; and dine at the inn, where the omnibus almost invariably stops, at one or other of its destinations. If the driver be distant from his home at his dinner hour, or be unmarried, he arranges to dine at the public-house; if near, his wife, or one of his children, brings him his dinner in a covered basin, some of them being provided with hot-water plates to keep the contents properly warm, and that is usually eaten at the public-house, with a pint of beer for the accompanying beverage. The relish with which a man who has been employed several hours in the open air enjoys his dinner can easily be understood. But if his dinner is brought to him on one of his shorter trips, he often hears the cry before he has completed his meal, 'Time's up!' and he carries the remains of his repast to be consumed at his next resting place. His tea, if brought to him by his family, he often drinks within the omnibus, if there be an opportunity. Some carry their dinners with them, and eat them cold. All these men live 'well'; that is, they have sufficient dinners of animal food every day, with beer. They are strong and healthy men, for their calling requires both strength and health. Each driver, (as well as the time-keeper and conductor), is licensed, at a yearly cost to him of 5s. From a driver I had the following statement:

'I have been a driver fourteen years. I was brought up as a builder, but had friends that was using horses, and I sometimes assisted them in driving and grooming when I was out of work. I got to like that sort of work, and thought it would be better than my own business if I could get to be connected with a 'bus; and I had friends, and first got employed as a time-keeper; but I've been a driver for fourteen years. I'm now paid by the week, and not by the box. It's a fair payment, but we must live well. It's hard work is mine; for I never have any rest but a few minutes, except every other Sunday, and then only two hours; that's the time of a journey there and back. If I was to ask leave to go to church, and then go to work again, I know what answer there would be – "You can go to church as often as you like, and we can get a man who doesn't want to go there." The cattle I drive are equal to gentlemen's carriage-horses. One I've driven five years, and I believe she was worked five years before I drove her. It's very hard work for the horses, but I don't know that they are over-worked in 'busses. The starting after stopping is the hardest work for them; it's such a terrible strain. I've felt for the poor things on a wet night, with a 'bus full of big people. I think that it's a pity that anybody uses a bearing rein. There's not many uses it now. It bears up a horse's head, and he can only go on pulling, pulling up a hill, one way. Take off his bearing rein, and he'll relieve the strain on him by bearing down his head, and flinging his weight on the collar to help him pull. If a man had to carry a weight up a hill on his back, how would he like to have his head tied back? Perhaps you may have noticed Mr —'s horses pull the 'bus up Holborn Hill. They're tightly borne up; but then they are very fine animals, fat and fine: there's no such cattle, perhaps, in a London 'bus – least-ways there's none better – and they're borne up for show. Now, a jib-horse won't go in a bearing rein, and will without it. I've seen that myself; so what can be the use of it? It's just teasing the poor things for a sort of fashion. I must keep exact time at every place where a time-keeper's stationed. Not a minute's excused – there's a fine for the least delay. I can't say that it's often levied; but still we are liable to it. If I've been blocked, I must make up for the block by galloping; and if I'm seen to gallop, and anybody tells our people, I'm called over the coals. I must drive as quick with a thunder-rain pelting in my face, and the roads in a muddle, and the horses starting – I can't call it shying, I have 'em too well in hand – at every flash, just as quick as if it was a fine hard road, and fine weather. It's not easy to drive a 'bus; but I can drive, and must drive, to an inch: yes, sir, to half an inch. I know if I can get my horses' heads through a space, I can get my splinter-bar through. I drive by my pole, making it my centre. If I keep it fair in the centre, a carriage must follow, unless it's slippery weather, and then there's no calculating. I saw the first 'bus start in 1829. I heard the first 'bus called a Punch-and-Judy carriage, 'cause you could see the people inside without a frame. The shape was about the same as it is now, but bigger and heavier. A 'bus changes horses four or five times a day, according to the distance. There's no cruelty to the horses, not a bit, it wouldn't be allowed. I fancy that 'busses now pay the proprietors well. The duty was $2\frac{1}{2}d$. a mile, and now it's $1\frac{1}{2}d$. Some companies save twelve guineas a week by the doing away of toll-gates. The 'stablishing the threepennies – the short uns – has put money in their pockets. I'm an unmarried man. A 'bus driver never has time to look out for a wife. Every horse in our stables has one day's rest in every four; but it's no rest for the driver.'

Omnibus Conductors

[pp. 355–6]   The conductor, who is vulgarly known as the 'cad', stands on a small projection at the end of the omnibus; and it is his office to admit and set down every passenger, and to receive the amount of fare, for which amount he is, of course, responsible to his employers. He is paid 4s. a day, which he is allowed to stop out of the monies he receives. He fills up a waybill each journey, with the number of passengers. I find that nearly all classes have given a quota of their number to the list of conductors. Among them are grocers, drapers, shopmen, barmen, printers, tailors, shoe-makers, clerks, joiners, saddlers, coach-builders, porters, town-travellers, carriers, and fish-mongers. Unlike the drivers, the majority of the conductors are unmarried men; but, perhaps, only a mere majority. As a matter of necessity, every conductor must be able to read and write. They are discharged more frequently than the drivers; but they require good characters before their appointment. From one of them, a very intelligent man, I had the following statement:

'I am 35 or 36, and have been a conductor for six years. Before that I was a lawyer's clerk, and then a picture-dealer; but didn't get on, though I maintained a good character. I'm a conductor now, but wouldn't be long behind a 'bus if it wasn't from necessity. It's hard to get anything else to do that you can keep a wife and family on, for people won't have you from off a 'bus. The worst part of my business is its uncertainty, I may be discharged any day, and not know for what. If I did, and I was accused unjustly, I might bring my action; but it's merely, "You're not wanted." I think I've done better as a conductor in hot weather, or fine weather, than in wet; though I've got a good journey when it's come on showery, as people was starting for or starting from the City. I had one master, who, when his 'bus came in full in the wet, used to say, "This is prime. Them's God Almighty's customers; he sent them." I've heard him say so many a time. We get far more ladies and children, too, on a fine day; they go more a-shopping then, and of an evening they go more to public places. I pay over my money every night. It runs from 40s. to 4l. 4s., or a little more on extraordinary occasions. I have taken more money since the short uns were established. One day before that I took only 18s. There's three riders and more now, where there was two formerly at the higher rate. I never get to a public place, whether it's a chapel or a play-house, unless, indeed, I get a holiday, and that is once in two years. I've asked for a day's holiday and been refused. I was told I might take a week's holiday, if I liked, or as long as I lived. I'm quite ignorant of what's passing in the world, my time's so taken up. We only know what's going on from hearing people talk in the 'bus. I never care to read the paper now, though I used to like it. If I have two minutes to spare, I'd rather take a nap than anything else. We know no more politics than the backwoodsmen of America, because we haven't time to care about it. I've fallen asleep on my step as the 'bus was going on, and almost fallen off. I have often to put up with insolence from vulgar fellows, who think it fun to chaff a cad, as they call it. There's no help for it. Our masters won't listen to complaints: if we are not satisfied we can go. Conductors are a sober set of men. We must be sober. It takes every farthing of our wages to live well enough, and keep a wife and family. I never knew but one teetotaller on the road. He's gone off it now, and he looked as if he was going off altogether. The other day a teetotaller on the 'bus saw me take a drink of beer, and he began to talk to me about its being wrong; but I drove him mad with argument, and the passengers took part with me. I live one and a half mile off the place I start from. In summer I sometimes breakfast before I start. In winter, I never see my three children, only as they're in bed; and I never hear their voices, if they don't wake up early. If they cry at night it don't disturb me; I sleep so heavy after fifteen hours' work out in the air. My wife doesn't do anything but mind the family, and that's plenty to do with young children. My business is so uncertain. Why, I knew a conductor who found he had paid 6*d*. short – he had left it in a corner of his pocket; and he handed it over next morning, and was discharged for that – he was reckoned a fool. They say the sharper the man the better the 'busman. There's a great deal in understanding the business, in keeping a sharp look-out for people's hailing, and in working the time properly. If the conductor's slow the driver can't get along; and if the driver isn't up to the mark the conductor's bothered. I've always kept time except once, and that was in such a fog, that I had to walk by the horses' heads with a link, and could hardly see my hand that held the link; and after all I lost my 'bus, but it was all safe and right in the end. We're licensed now in Scotland-yard. They're far civiller there than in Lancaster-place. I hope, too, they'll be more particular in granting licenses. They used to grant them day after day, and I believe made no inquiry. It'll be better now. I've never been fined: if I had I should have to pay it out of my own pocket. If you plead guilty it's 5*s*. If not, and it's very hard to prove that you did display your badge properly if the City policeman – there's always one on the look-out for us – swears you didn't, and summons you for that: or, if you plead not guilty, because you weren't guilty, you may pay 1*l*. I don't know of the checks now; but I know there are such people. A man was discharged the other day because he was accused of having returned three out of thirteen short. He offered to make oath he was correct; but it was of no use – he went.'

Omnibus Timekeepers

[pp. 356–7] Another class employed in the omnibus trade are the time-keepers. On some routes there are five of these men, on others four. The timekeeper's duty is to start the omnibus at the exact moment appoin-ted by the proprietors, and to report any delay or irregularity in the arrival of the vehicle. His hours are the same as those of the drivers and conductors, but as he is stationary his work is not so fatiguing. His remuneration is generally 21*s*. a week, but on some stations more. He must never leave the spot. A timekeeper on Kennington Common has 28*s*. a week. He is employed 16 hours daily, and has a box to shelter him from the weather when it is foul. He has to keep time for forty 'busses. The men who may be seen in the great thorough-fares noting every omnibus that passes, are not timekeepers; they are employed by Government, so that no omnibus may run on the line without paying the duty.

A timekeeper made the following statement to me:

'I was a grocer's assistant, but was out of place and had a friend who got me a timekeeper's office. I have 21s. a week. Mine's not hard work, but it's very tiring. You hardly ever have a moment to call your own. If we only had our Sundays, like other working-men, it would be a grand relief. It would be very easy to get an odd man to work every other Sunday, but masters care nothing about Sundays. Some 'busses do stop running from 11 to 1, but plenty keep running. Sometimes I am so tired of a night that I dare hardly sit down, for fear I should fall asleep and lose my own time, and that would be to lose my place. I think timekeepers continue longer in their places than the others. We have nothing to do with money-taking. I'm a single man, and get all my meals at the — Inn. I dress my own dinners in the tap-room. I have my tea brought to me from a coffee-shop. I can't be said to have any home – just a bed to sleep in, as I'm never ten minutes awake in the house where I lodge.'

The 'odd men' are, as their name imports, the men who are employed occasionally, or, as they term it, 'get odd jobs'. These form a considerable portion of the unemployed. If a driver be ill, or absent to attend a summons, or on any temporary occasion, the odd man is called upon to do the work. For this the odd man receives 10d. a journey, to and fro. One of them gave me the following account: 'I was brought up to a stable life, and had to shift for myself when I was 17, as my parents died then. It's nine years ago. For two or three years, till this few months, I drove a 'bus. I was discharged with a week's notice, and don't know for what – it's no use asking for a reason: I wasn't wanted. I've been put to shifts since then, and almost everything's pledged that could be pledged. I had a decent stock of clothes, but they're all at my uncle's. Last week I earned 3s. 4d., the week before 1s. 8d., but this week I shall do better, say 5s. I have to pay 1s. 6d. a week for my garret. I'm a single man, and have nothing but a bed left in it now. I did live in a better place. If I didn't get a bite and sup now and then with some of my old mates I think I couldn't live at all. Mine's a wretched life, and a very bad trade.'

CHARACTER OF CABDRIVERS

[pp. 361–3] Among the present cabdrivers are to be found, as I learned from trustworthy persons, quondam greengrocers, costermongers, jewellers, clerks, broken-down gentlemen, especially turf gentlemen, carpenters, joiners, saddlers, coach-builders, grooms, stable-helpers, footmen, shopkeepers, pickpockets, swell-mobsmen, housebreakers, inn-keepers, musicians, musical-instrument makers, ostlers, some good scholars, a good number of broken-down pawnbrokers, several ex-policemen, draper's assistants, barmen, scene-shifters, one baronet, and as my informant expressed it, 'such an uncommon sight of folks that it would be uncommon hard to say what they was'. Of the truthfulness of the list of callings said to have contributed to swell the numbers of the cabmen there can be no doubt, but I am not so sure of 'the baronet'. I was told his name, but I met with no one who could positively say that he knew Sir V— C— as a cabdriver. This baronet seems a tradition among them. Others tell me that the party alluded to is merely nicknamed the Baron, owing to his being a person of good birth, and having had a college education. The 'flashiest' cabman, as he is termed, is the son of a fashion-able master-tailor. He is known among cabdrivers as the 'Numpareil', and drives one of the Hansom cabs. I am informed on excellent authority, a tenth, or, to speak beyond the possibility of cavil, a twelfth of the whole number of cabdrivers are 'fancy men'. These fellows are known in the cab trade by a very gross appellation. They are the men who live with women of the town, and are supported, wholly or partially, on the wages of the women's prostitution.

These are the fellows who, for the most part, are ready to pay the highest price for the hire of their cabs. One swell-mobsman, I was told, had risen from 'signing' for cabs to become a cab proprietor, but was now a prisoner in France for picking pockets.

The worse class of cabmen which, as I have before said, are but a twelfth of the whole, live in Granby Street, St Andrew's Place, and similar localities of the Waterloo Road; in Union Street, Pearl Row, &c., of the Borough Road; in Princes Street, and others, of the London Road; in some unpaved streets that stretch from the New Kent Road to Lock's Fields; in the worst parts of Westminster, in the vicinity of Drury Lane, Whitechapel, and of Lisson Grove, and wherever low depravity flourishes. 'To get on a cab,' I was told, and that is the regular phrase, 'is the ambition of more loose fellows than for anything else, as it's reckoned both an idle life and an exciting one.' Whetstone Park is full of cabmen, but not wholly of the fancy-man class. The better sort of cabmen usually reside in the neighbourhood of the cab-proprietors' yards, which are in all directions. Some of the best of these men are, or rather have been mechanics, and have left a sedentary employment, which affected their health, for the open air of the cab business. Others of the best description have been connected with country inns, but the majority of them are London men.

They are most of them married, and bringing up families decently on earnings of from 15s. to 25s. a week. Some few of their wives work with their needles for the tailors.

Some of the cab-yards are situated in what were old inn-yards, or the stable-yards attached to great houses, when great houses flourished in parts of the town that are now accounted vulgar. One of those I saw in a very curious place. I was informed that the yard was once Oliver Cromwell's stable-yard; it is now a receptacle for cabs. There are now two long ranges of wooden erections, black with age, each carriage-house opening with large folding-doors, fastened in front with padlocks, bolts, and hasps. In the old carriage-houses are the modern cabs, and mixed with them are superannuated cabs, and the disjointed or worn-out bodies and wheels of cabs. Above one range of the buildings, the red-tiled roofs of which project a yard and more beyond the exterior, are apartments occupied by the stable-keepers and others. Nasturtiums with their light green leaves and bright orange flowers were trained along light trellis-work in front of the windows, and presented a striking contrast to the dinginess around.

Of the cabdrivers there are several classes, according to the time at which they are employed. These are known in the trade by the names of the 'long-day men', 'the morning-men', the 'long-night men', and the 'short-night men', and 'the bucks'. The long-day man is the driver who is supposed to be driving his cab the whole day. He usually fetches his cab out between 9 and 10 in the morning, and returns at 4 or 5, or even 7 or 8, the next morning; indeed it is no matter at what hour he comes in so long as he brings the money that he signs for; the long-day men are mostly employed for the contractors, though some of the respectable masters work their cabs with long-day men, but then they leave the yard between 8 and 9 and are expected to return between 12 and 1. These drivers when working for the contractors sign for 16s. a day in the season, as before stated, and 12s. out of the season; and when employed by the respectable masters, they are expected to bring home 14s. or 9s., according to the season of the year. The long-day men are the parties who mostly employ the 'bucks', or unlicensed drivers. They are mostly out with their cabs from 16 to 20 hours, so that their work becomes more than they can constantly endure, and they are consequently glad to avail themselves of the services of a buck for some hours at the end of the day, or rather night. The morning man generally goes out about 7 in the morning and returns to the yard at 6 in the evening. Those who contract sign to bring home from 10s. to 11s. per day in the season, and 7s. for the rest of the

CAB DRIVER.

year, while those working for the better class of masters are expected to give the proprietor 8s. a day, and 5s. or 6s. according to the time of the year. The morning man has only one horse found him, whereas the long-day man has two, and returns to the yard to change horses between three and six in the afternoon. The long-night man goes out at 6 in the evening and returns at 10 in the morning. He signs when working for contractors for 7s. or 8s. per night, at the best time of the year, and 5s. or 6s. at the bad. The rent required by the good masters differs scarcely from these sums. He has only one horse found him. The short-night man fetches his cab out at 6 in the evening and returns at 6 in the morning, bringing with him 6s. in the season and 4s. or 5s. out of it. The contractors employ scarcely any short-night men, while the better masters have but few long-day or long-night men working for them. It is only such persons as the Westminster masters who like the horses or the men to be out so many hours together, and they, as my informant said, 'don't care what becomes of either, so long as the day's money is brought to them'. The bucks are unlicensed cabdrivers, who are employed by those who have a license to take charge of the cab while the regular drivers are at their meals or enjoying themselves. These bucks are generally cabmen who have been deprived of their license through bad conduct, and who now pick up a living by 'rubbing up' (that is, polishing the brass of the cabs) on the rank, and 'giving out buck' as it is called amongst the men. They usually loiter about the watering-houses (the public-houses) of the cab-stands, and pass most of their time in the tap-rooms. They are mostly of intemperate habits, being generally 'confirmed sots'. Very few of them are married men. They have been fancy-men in their prime, but, to use the words of one of the craft, 'got turned up'. They seldom sleep in a bed. Some few have a bedroom in some obscure part of the town, but the most of them loll about and doze in the tap-rooms by day, and sleep in the cabs by night. When the watering-houses close they resort to the night coffee-shops, and pass the time there till they are wanted as bucks. When they take a job for a man they have no regular agreement with the driver, but the rule is that they shall do the best they can. If they take 2s. they give the driver one and keep the other for themselves. If 1s. 6d. they usually keep only 6d. The Westminster men have generally got their regular bucks, and these mostly take to the cab with the second horse and do all the night-work. At three or four in the morning they meet the driver at some appointed stand or watering-place. Burleigh Street in the Strand, or Palace Yard, are the favourite places of rendezvous of the Westminster men, and then they hand over to the long-day man 'the stuff' as they call it. The regular driver has no check upon these men, but unless they do well they never employ them again. For 'rubbing up' the cabs on the stand these bucks generally get 6d. in the season, and for this they are expected to dish-clout the whole of the panels, clean the glasses, and polish the harness and brasses, the cabdriver having to do these things himself or having to pay for it. Some of the bucks in the season will make from 2s. to 2s. 6d. a day by rubbing up alone, and it is difficult to say what they make by driving. They are the most extortionate of all cabdrivers. For a shilling fare they will generally demand 2s. and for a 3s. fare they will get 5s. or 6s., according to the character of the party driven. Having no licenses, they do not care what they charge. If the number of the cab is taken, and the regular driver of it summoned, the party overcharged is unable to swear that the regular driver was the individual who defrauded him, and so the case is dismissed. It is supposed that the bucks make quite as much money as the drivers, for they are not at all particular as to how they get their money, The great majority, indeed 99 out of 100, have been in prison, and many more than once, and they consequently do not care about revisiting gaol. It is calculated that there are at least 800 or 1,000 bucks, hanging about the London cab-stands, and these are mostly regular thieves. If they catch any person asleep or drunk in a cab, they are sure to have a dive into his pockets; nor are they particular if the party belong to their own class, for I am assured that they steal from one another while dozing in the cabs or tap-rooms. Very few of the respectable masters work their cabs at night, except those who do so merely because they have not stable-room for the whole of their horses and vehicles at the same time. Some of the cabdrivers are the owners of the vehicles they drive. It is supposed that out of the 5,000 drivers in London, at least 2,000, or very nearly half, are small masters, and they are amongst the most respectable men of the ranks. Of the other half of the cabdrivers about 1,500 are long-day men, and about 150 long-night men (there are only a few yards, and they are principally at Islington, that employ long-night men). Of the morning-men and the short-night men there are, as near as I can learn, about 500 belonging to each class, in addition to the small masters.

CHARACTERISTICS OF THE VARIOUS CLASSES OF VAGRANTS

[pp. 381–7]   I now come to the characteristics of vagrant life, as seen in the casual wards of the metropolitan unions. The subject is one of the most important with which I have yet had to deal, and the facts I have collected are sufficiently startling to give the public an idea of the great social bearings of the question; for the young vagrant is the budding criminal.

Previously to entering upon my inquiry into this subject, I consulted with a gentleman who had long paid considerable attention to the question, and who was, moreover, in a position peculiarly fitted for gaining the greatest experience, and arriving at the correctest notions upon the matter. I consulted, I say, with the gentleman referred to, as to the Poor-law officers, from whom I should be likely to obtain the best information; and I was referred by him to Mr Knapp, the master of the Wandsworth and Clapham Union, as one of the most intelligent and best-informed upon the subject of vagrancy. I found that gentleman all that he had been represented to me as being, and obtained from him the following statement, which, as an analysis of the vagrant character, and a description of the habits and propensities of the young vagabond, has, perhaps, never been surpassed.

He had filled the office of master of the Wandsworth and Clapham Union for three years, and immediately before that he was the relieving officer for the same union for upwards of two years. He was guardian of Clapham parish for four years previously to his being elected relieving officer. He was a member of the first board of guardians that was formed under the new Poor-law Act, and he has long given much attention to the habits of the vagrants that have come under his notice or care. He told me that he considered a casual ward necessary in every union, because there is always a migratory population, consisting of labourers seeking employment in other localities, and destitute women travelling to their husbands or friends. He thinks a casual ward is necessary for the shelter and relief of such parties, since the law will not permit them to beg. These, however, are by far the smaller proportion of those who demand admittance into the casual ward. Formerly, they were not five per cent of the total number of casuals. The remainder consisted of youths, prostitutes, Irish families, and a few professional beggars. The youths formed more than one-half of the entire number, and their ages were from twelve to twenty. The largest number were seventeen years old – indeed, he adds, just that age when youth becomes disengaged from parental control. These lads had generally run away, either from their parents or masters, and many had been reared to a life of vagrancy. They were mostly shrewd and acute youths; some had been very well educated. Ignorance, to use the gentleman's own words, is certainly not the prevailing characteristic of the class; indeed, with a few exceptions, he would say it is the reverse. These lads are mostly distinguished by their aversion to continuous labour of any kind. He never knew them to work – they are, indeed, essentially the idle and the vagabond. Their great inclination is to be on the move, and wandering from place to place; and they appear, he says, to receive a great deal of pleasure from the assembly and conversation of the casual ward. They are physically stout, healthy lads, and certainly not emaciated or sickly. They belong especially to the able-bodied class, being, as he says, full of health and mischief. When in London, they live in the day-time by holding horses, and carrying parcels from the steam-piers and railway termini. Some loiter about the markets in the hope of a job, and others may be seen in the streets picking up bones and rags, or along the water-side searching for pieces of old metal, or anything that may be sold at the marine-store shops. They have nearly all been in prison more than once, and several a greater number of times than they are years old. They are the most dishonest of all thieves, having not the least respect for the property of even the members of their own class. He tells me he has frequently known them to rob one another. They are very stubborn and self-willed. They have often broken every window in the oakum-room, rather than do the required work. They are a most difficult class to govern, and are especially restive under the least restraint; they can ill brook control, and they find great delight in thwarting the authorities of the workhouse. They are particularly fond of amusements of all kinds. My informant has often heard them discuss the merits of the different actors at the minor theatres and saloons. Sometimes they will elect a chairman, and get up a regular debate, and make speeches from one end of the ward to the other. Many of them will make very clever comic orations; others delight in singing comic songs, especially those upon the workhouse and gaols. He never knew them love reading. They mostly pass under fictitious names. Some will give the name of 'John Russell', or 'Robert Peel', or 'Richard Cobden'. They often come down to the casual wards in large bodies of twenty or thirty, with sticks hidden down the legs of their trousers, and with these they rob and beat those who do not belong to their own gang. The gang will often consist of a hundred lads, all under twenty, one-fourth of whom regularly come together in a body; and in the casual ward they generally arrange where to meet again on the following night. In the winter of 1846, the guardians of Wandsworth and Clapham, sympathising with their ragged and wretched appearance, and desirous of affording them the means of obtaining an honest livelihood, gave my informant instructions to offer an asylum to any who might choose to remain in the workhouse. Under this arrangement, about fifty were admitted. The majority were under seventeen years of age. Some of them remained a few days – others a few weeks – none stopped longer than three months; and the generality of them decamped over the wall, taking with them the clothes of the union. The confinement, restraint, and order of the workhouse were especially irksome to them. This is the character of the true vagrant, for whom my informant considers no provision what-soever should be made at the unions, believing as he does that most of them have settlements in or around London. The casual wards, he tells me, he knows to have been a great encouragement to the increase of these characters. Several of the lads that have come under his care had sought shelter and concealment in the casual wards, after having absconded from their parents. In one instance, the father and mother of a lad had un-availingly sought their son in every direction: he discovered that the youth had ran away, and he sent him home in the custody of one of the inmates; but when the boy got to within two or three doors of his father's residence, he turned round and scampered off. The mother afterwards came to the union in a state of frantic grief, and said that he had disappeared two years before. My informant believes that the boy has never been heard of his parents since. Others he has restored to their parents, and some of the young vagrants who have died in the union have, on their death-beds, disclosed the names and particulars of their families, who have been always of a highly respectable character. To these he has sent, and on their visits to their children scenes of indescribable grief and anguish have taken place. He tells me he is convinced that it is the low lodging-houses and the casual wards of the unions that offer a ready means for youths absconding from their homes, immediately on the least disagreement or restraint. In most of the cases that he has investigated, he has found that the boys have left home after some rebuke or quarrel with their parents. On restoring one boy to his father, the latter said that, though the lad was not ten years old, he had been in almost every workhouse in London; and the father bitterly complained of the casual wards for offering shelter to a youth of such tender years. But my informant is convinced that, even if the casual wards throughout the country were entirely closed – the low lodging-houses being allowed to remain in their present condition – the evil would not be remedied, if at all abated. A boy after running away from home, generally seeks shelter in one of the cheap lodging-houses, and there he makes acquaintance with the most depraved of both sexes. The boys at the house become his regular companions, and he is soon a confirmed vagrant and thief like the rest. The youths of the vagrant class are particularly distinguished for their libidinous propensities. They frequently come to the gate with a young prostitute, and with her they go off in the morning. With this girl, they will tramp through the whole of the country. They are not remarkable for a love of drink – indeed, my informant never saw a regular vagrant in a state of intoxication, nor has he known them to exhibit any craving for liquor. He has had many drunkards under his charge, but the vagrant is totally distinct, having propensities not less vicious, but of a very different kind. He considers the young tramps to be generally a class of lads possessing the keenest intellect, and of a highly enterprising character. They seem to have no sense of danger, and to be especially delighted with such acts as involve any peril. They are likewise characterised by their exceeding love of mischief. The property destroyed in the union of which my informant is the master has been of considerable value, consisting of windows broken, sash-frames demolished, beds and bedding torn to pieces, and rags burnt. They will frequently come down in large gangs, on purpose to destroy the property in the union. They generally are of a most restless and volatile disposition. They have great quickness of perception, but little power of continuous attention or perseverance. They have a keen sense of the ridiculous, and are not devoid of deep feeling. He has often known them to be dissolved to tears on his remonstrating with them on the course they were following – and then they promise amendment; but in a few days, and sometimes hours, they would forget all, and return to their old habits. In the summer they make regular tours through the country, visiting all places that they have not seen, so that there is scarcely one that is not acquainted with every part within 100 miles of London, and many with all England. They are perfectly organised, so that any regulation affecting their comforts or interests becomes known among the whole body in a remarkably short space of time. As an instance, he informs me that on putting out a notice that no able-bodied man or youth would be received in the casual ward after a certain day, there was not a single application made by any such party, the regular vagrants having doubtless informed each other that it was useless seeking admission at this union. In the winter the young vagrants come to London, and find shelter in the asylums for the houseless poor. At this season of the year, the number of vagrants in the casual wards would generally be diminished one half. The juvenile vagrants constitute one of the main sources from which the criminals of the country are continually recruited and augmented. Being repeatedly committed to prison for disorderly conduct and misdemeanour, the gaol soon loses all terrors for them; and, indeed, they will frequently destroy their own clothes, or the property of the union, in order to be sent there. Hence they soon become practised and dexterous thieves, and my informant has detected several burglaries by the property found upon them. The number of this class is stated, in the Poor-law Report on Vagrancy, to have been, in 1848, no less than 16,086, and they form one of the most restless, discontented, vicious, and dangerous elements of society. At the period of any social commotion, they are sure to be drawn towards the scene of excitement in a vast concourse. During the Chartist agitation, in the June quarter of the year 1848, the number of male casuals admitted into the Wandsworth and Clapham Union rose from 2,501 to 3,968, while the females (their companions) increased from 579 to 1,388.

Of the other classes of persons admitted into the casual wards, the Irish generally form a large proportion. At the time when juvenile vagrancy prevailed to an alarming extent, the Irish hardly dared to show themselves in the casual wards, for the lads would beat them and plunder them of whatever they might have – either the produce of their begging, or the ragged kit they carried with them. Often my informant has had to quell violent disturbances in the night among these characters. The Irish tramp generally makes his appearance with a large family, and frequently with three or four generations together – grandfather, grandmother, father, and mother, and children – all coming at the same time. In the year ending June, 1848, the Irish vagrants increased to so great an extent that, of the entire number of casuals relieved, more than one-third in the first three quarters, and more than two-thirds in the last quarter, were from the sister island. Of the Irish vagrants, the worst class – that is the poorest and most abject – came over to this country by way of Newport, in Wales. The expense of the passage to that port was only 2s. 6d.; whereas the cost of the voyage to Liverpool and London was considerably more, and consequently the class brought over by that way were less destitute. The Irish vagrants were far more orderly than the English. Out of the vast number received into the casual ward of this union during the distress in Ireland, it is remarkable that not one ever committed an act of insubordination. They were generally very grateful for the relief afforded, and appeared to subsist entirely by begging. Some of them were not particularly fond of work, but they were invariably honest, says my informant – at least so far as his knowledge went. They were exceedingly filthy in their habits, and many diseased.

These constitute the two large and principal classes of vagrants. The remainder generally consist of persons temporarily destitute, whereas the others are habitually so. The temporarily destitute are chiefly railway and agricultural labourers, and a few mechanics travelling in search of employment. These are easily distinguishable from the regular vagrant; indeed, a glance is sufficient to the practised eye. They are the better class of casuals, and those for whom the wards are expressly designed, but they only form a very small proportion of the vagrants applying for shelter. In the height of vagrancy, they formed not one per cent of the entire number admitted. Indeed, such was the state of the casual wards, that the destitute mechanics and labourers preferred walking through the night to availing themselves of the accommodation. Lately, the artisans and labourers have increased greatly in proportion, owing to the system adopted for the exclusion of the habitual vagrant, and the consequent decline of their number. The working man travelling in search of employment is now generally admitted into what are called the receiving wards of the work-house, instead of the tramp-room, and he is usually exceedingly grateful for the accommodation. My informant tells me that persons of this class seldom return to the workhouse after one night's shelter, and this is a conclusive proof that the regular working-man seldom passes into an habitual beggar. They are an entirely distinct class, having different habits, and, indeed, different features, and I am assured that they are strictly honest. During the whole experience of my informant, he never knew one who applied for a night's shelter commit one act of dishonesty, and he has seen them in the last stage of destitution. Occasionally they have sold the shirt and waistcoat off their backs before they applied for admittance into the workhouse, while some of them have been so weak from long starvation, that they could scarcely reach the gate. Such persons are always allowed to remain several days to recruit their strength. It is for such as these that my informant considers the casual wards indispensable to every well-conducted union – whereas it is his opinion that the habitual vagrant, as contradistinguished from the casual vagrant or wayfaring poor, should be placed under the management of the police, at the charge of the union.

Let me, however, first run over, as briefly as possible, the several classes of vagrants falling under the notice of the parish authorities. The different kinds of vagrants or tramps to be found in the casual wards of the unions throughout the country, may be described as follows: 'The more important class, from its increasing numbers,' says Mr Boase, in the Poor-law Report upon Vagrancy, 'is that of the regular young English vagabond, generally the native of a large town. He is either a runaway apprentice, or he has been driven from home by the cruelty of his parents, or allowed by them to go wild in the streets: in some cases he is an orphan, and has lost his father and mother in early life. Having no ties to bind him, he travels about

374

the country, being sure of a meal, and a roof to shelter him at night. The youths of this class are principally of from fifteen to twenty-five years of age. They often travel in parties of two or three – frequently in large bodies, with young women, as abandoned as themselves, in company.'

Approaching these in character are the young countrymen who have absconded – perhaps for some petty poaching offence – and to whom the facility for leading an idle vagabond life has proved too great a temptation.

The next class of vagrants is the sturdy English mendicant. He, though not a constant occupant of the tramp-ward in the workhouse, frequently makes his appearance there to partake of the shelter, when he has spent his last shilling in dissipation.

Besides these, there are a few calling themselves agricultural labourers, who are really such, and who are to be readily distinguished. There are also a few mechanics – chiefly tailors, shoemakers, and masons, who are occasionally destitute. The amount of those really destitute, however, is very small in proportion to the numbers relieved.

Of the age and sex of tramps, the general proportion seems to be four-fifths male and one-fifth female.

Of the female English tramps, little can be said, but that they are in great part prostitutes of the lowest class. The proportion of really destitute women in the tramp-wards (generally widows with young children) is greater than that of men – probably from the ability to brave the cold night wind being less in the female, and the love of the children getting the shelter, above dread of vile association. Girls of thirteen or fourteen years old, who run away from masters or factory employment, often find shelter in the tramp-ward.

The Irish, who, till very recently, formed the majority of the applicants for casual relief, remain to be described. These can scarcely be classified in any other way than as those who come to England to labour, and those who come to beg. The former class, however, yield readily to their disposition to idleness – the difficulties of providing supper, breakfast, and lodging for themselves being removed by the workhouse. This class are physically superior to the mass of Irish vagrants. It appears that for very many years considerable numbers of these have annually come to England in the spring to work at hay-harvest, remaining for corn-harvest and hop-picking, and then have carried home their earnings in the autumn, seldom resorting to begging. Since the failure of the potato crop greater numbers have come to England, and the tramp-ward has been their principal refuge, and an inducement to many to remain in the country. A great many harvest men land at Newport and the Welsh ports;

VAGRANTS IN THE CASUAL WARD OF WORKHOUSE.

but by far the greater proportion of the Irish in Wales are, or were, women with small children, old men apparently feeble, pregnant women, and boys about ten years old. They are brought over by coal-vessels as a return cargo (living ballast) at very low fares, (2s. 6d. is the highest sum), huddled together like pigs, and communicating disease and vermin on their passage.

Harriet Huxtable, the manager of the tramp-house at Newport, says: 'There is hardly an Irish family that came over and applied to me, but we have found a member or two of it ill, some in a shocking filthy state. They don't live long, diseased as they are. They are very remarkable; they will eat salt by basins' full, and drink a great quantity of water after. I have frequently known those who could not have been hungry, eat cabbage-leaves and other refuse from the ash-heap. I really believe they would eat almost anything.'

'A remarkable fact is, that all the Irish whom I met on my route between Wales and London,' says Mr Boase, 'said they came from Cork county. Mr John, the relieving officer at Cardiff, on his examination, says, "that not 1 out of every 100 of the Irish come from any other county than Cork."'

In the township of Warrington, the number of tramps relieved between the 25th of March, 1847, and the 25th of March, 1848, was:

Irish	12,038
English	4,701
Scotch	427
Natives of other places	156
Making a total of	17,322

Of the original occupations or trades of the vagrants applying for relief at the different unions throughout the country, there are no returns. As, however, a considerable portion of these were attracted to London on the opening of the Metropolitan Asylums for the Houseless Poor, we may, by consulting the Society's yearly Reports, where an account of the callings of those receiving shelter in such establishments is always given, be enabled to arrive at some rough estimate as to the state of destitution and vagrancy existing among the several classes of labourers and artisans for several years.

The following table, being an average drawn from the returns for

seventeen years of the occupation of the persons admitted into the
Asylums for the Houseless Poor, which I have been at considerable trouble
in forming, exhibits the only available information upon this subject,
synoptically arranged:

Umbrella-makers	415	Musicians	730
Sailmakers	455	Leatherdressers and curriers	802
Carvers and gilders	500	Coachmakers	989
Gunsmiths	554	Engravers	1,133
Trunkmakers	569	Shipwrights	1,358
Chairmakers	586	Artists	1,374
Fishmongers	643	Drapers	2,047
Tanners	643	Milliners and dressmakers	10,390

Of the disease and fever which mark the course of the vagrants where-soever they go, I have before spoken. The 'tramp-fever', as the most dangerous infection of the casual wards is significantly termed, is of a typhoid character, and seems to be communicated particularly to those who wash the clothes of the parties suffering from it. This was likewise one of the characteristics of cholera. That the habitual vagrants should be the means of spreading a pestilence over the country in their wanderings will not be wondered at, when we find it stated in the Poor-law Report on Vagrancy, that 'in very few workhouses do means exist of drying the clothes of these paupers when they come in wet, and it often happens that a considerable number are, of necessity, placed together wet, filthy, infested with vermin, and diseased, in a small, unventilated space'. 'The majority of tramps, again,' we are told, 'have a great aversion to being washed and cleaned. A regular tramper cannot bear it; but a distressed man would be thankful for it.'

The cost incurred for the cure of the vagrant sick in 1848, was considerably more than the expense of the food dispensed to them. Out of 13,406 vagrants relieved at the Wandsworth and Clapham Union in 1848, there were 322 diseased, or ill with the fever.

The number of vagrants relieved throughout England and Wales in the same year was 1,647,975; and supposing that the sickness among these prevailed to the same extent as it did among the casuals at Wandsworth (according to the Vagrancy Report, it appears to have been much more severe in many places), there would have been as many as 40,812 sick in the several unions throughout the country in 1848. The cost of relieving the 332 sick at Wandsworth was 300*l.*; at the same rate, the expense of the 40,812 sick throughout the country unions would amount to 36,878*l.* According to the above proportion, the number of sick relieved in the metropolitan unions would have been 7,678, and the cost for their relief would amount to 6,931*l.*

Of the tide of crime which, like that of pestilence, accompanies the stream of vagrants, there are equally strong and conclusive proofs. 'The most prominent body of delinquents in the rural districts,' says the Report of the Constabulary Commissioners, 'are vagrants, and these vagrants appear to consist of two classes: first, the habitual depredators, house-breakers, horse-stealers, and common thieves; secondly, of vagrants, properly so called, who seek alms as mendicants. Besides those classes who travel from fair to fair, and from town to town, in quest of dishonest gains, there are numerous classes who make incursions from the provincial towns upon the adjacent rural districts.'

'The classes of depredators who perambulate the country (says the same Report) are the vagrants, properly so called. Upwards of 18,000 commitments per annum of persons for the offence of vagrancy mark the extent of the body from which they are taken.

'It will be seen that vagrancy, or the habit of wandering abroad, under colour either of distress, or of some ostensible, though illegal occupation, having claims on the sympathies of the uninformed, constitutes one great source of delinquency, and especially of juvenile delinquency. The returns show that the vagrant classes pervade every part of the country, rendering property insecure, propagating pernicious habits, and afflicting the minds of the sensitive with false pictures of suffering, and levying upon them an offensive impost for the relief of that destitution for which a heavy tax is legally levied in the shape of poor's rates.

'Mr Thomas Narrill, a sergeant of the Bristol police, was asked – "What proportion of the vagrants do you think are thieves, that make it a point to take anything for which they find a convenient opportunity?" "We have found it so invariably." "Have you ever seen the children who go about as vagrants turn afterwards from vagrancy to common thieving – thieving wholly or chiefly?" "We have found it several times." "Therefore the suppression of vagrancy or mendicity would be to that extent the suppression of juvenile delinquency?" "Yes, of course."'

Mr J. Perry, another witness, states: 'I believe vagrancy to be the first step towards the committal of felony, and I am supported in that belief by the number of juvenile vagrants who are brought before the magistrates as thieves.'

An officer, appointed specially to take measures against vagrancy in Manchester, was asked, 'Does your experience enable you to state that the large proportion of vagrants are thieves too, whenever they come in the way of thieving?' 'Yes, and I should call the larger proportion there thieves.' 'Then, from what you have observed of them, would you say that the suppression of vagrancy would go a great way to the suppression of a great quantity of depredation?' 'I am sure of it.'

The same valuable Report furnishes us with a table of the numbers and character of the known depredators and suspected persons frequenting five of the principal towns; from which it appears that in these towns alone there are 28,706 persons of known bad character. According to the average proportion of these to the population, there will be in the other large towns nearly 32,000 persons of a similar character, and upwards of 69,000 of such persons dispersed throughout the rest of the country. Adding these together, we shall have as many as 130,000 persons of known bad character living in England and Wales, without the walls of the prisons. To form an accurate notion of the total number of the criminal population, we must add to the above amount the number of persons resident within the walls of the prisons. These, according to the last census, are 19,888, which, added to the 130,000 above enumerated, gives within a fraction of 150,000 individuals for the entire criminal population of the country.

In order to arrive at an estimate of the number of known depredators, or suspected persons, continually tramping through the country, we must deduct from the number of persons of bad character without the walls of the prisons, such as are not of migratory habits; and it will be seen on reference to the table above given, that a large proportion of the classes there specified have usually some fixed residence (those with an asterisk set before them may be said to be non-migratory). As many as 10,000 individuals out of the 20,000 and odd above given certainly do not belong to the tramping tribe; and we may safely say that there must be as many as 35,000 more in the country, who, though of known bad character, are not tramps like the rest. Hence, in order to ascertain the number of depredators and suspected persons belonging to the tramping or vagrant class, we must deduct 10,000 + 35,000 from 85,000, which gives us 40,000 for the number of known bad characters continually traversing the country.

This sum, though arrived at in a very different manner from the estimate given in my last letter, agrees very nearly with the amount there stated. We may therefore, I think, without fear of erring greatly upon the matter, assert that our criminal population, within and without the walls of the prisons, consists of 150,000 individuals, of whom nearly one-third belong to the vagrant class; while, of those without the prison walls, upwards of one half are persons who are continually tramping through the country.

The number of commitments for vagrancy throughout the country is stated, in the Constabulary Report, at upwards of 18,000 per annum. This amount, large as it is, will not surprise when we learn from Mr Pigott's Report on Vagrancy to the Poor-law Commissioners, that 'it is becoming a system with the vagrants to pass away the cold months by fortnightly halts in different gaols. As soon as their fourteen days have expired they make their way to some other union-house, and commit the same depredation there, in order to be sent to gaol again.'

'There are some characters,' say the officers of the Derby Union, in the same Report, 'who come on purpose to be committed, avowedly. These have generally itch, venereal disease, and lice, all together. Then there are some who tear their clothes for the purpose of being committed.'

Statements of Vagrants

[pp. 388–96] The first vagrant was one who had the thorough look of a 'professional'. He was literally a mass of rags and filth. He was, indeed, exactly what in the Act of Henry VIII is denominated a 'valiant beggar'. He stood near upon six feet high, was not more than twenty-five, and had altogether the frame and constitution of a stalwart labouring man. His clothes, which were of fustian and corduroy, tied close to his body with pieces of string, were black and shiny with filth, which looked more like pitch than grease. He had no shirt, as was plain from the fact that, where his clothes were torn, his bare skin was seen. The ragged sleeves of his fustian jacket were tied like the other parts of his dress, close to his wrists, with string. This was clearly to keep the bleak air from his body. His cap was an old, brimless 'wide-awake', and when on his head gave the man a most unprepossessing appearance. His story was as follows:

'I am a carpet-weaver by trade. I served my time to it. My father was a clerk in a shoe-thread manufactory at —. He got 35s. a week, and his house, coals, and candles found him. He lived very comfortably; indeed, I was very happy. Before I left home, I knew none of the cares of the world that I have known since I left him. My father and mother are living still. He is still as well off as when I was at home. I know this, because I have heard from him twice, and seen him once. He won't do anything to assist me. I have transgressed so many times, that he won't take me in hand any more. I will tell you the truth, you may depend upon it; yes, indeed, I would, even if it were to injure myself. He has tried me many times, but now he has given me up. At the age of twenty-one he told me to go from home and seek a living for myself. He said he had given me a home ever since I was a child, but now I had come to manhood I was able to provide for myself. He gave me a good education, and I might have been a better scholar at the present time, had I not neglected my studies. He put me to a day-school in the town when I was eight years old, and I continued there till I was between twelve and thirteen. I learnt reading, writing, and ciphering. I was taught the catechism, the history of England, geography, and drawing. My father was a very harsh man when he was put out of his way. He was a very violent temper when he was vexed, but kind to us all when he was pleased. I have five brothers and six sisters. He never beat me more than twice, to my remembrance. The first time he thrashed me with a cane, and the last with a horsewhip. I had stopped out late at night. I was then just rising sixteen, and had left school. I am sure those thrashings did me no good, but made me rather worse than before. I was a self-willed lad, and determined, if I couldn't get my will in one way, I would have it another. After the last thrashing he told me he would give me some trade, and after that he would set me off and get rid of me. Then I was bound apprentice as a carpet-weaver for three years. My master was a very kind one. I runned away once. The cause of my going off was a quarrel with one of the workmen that was put over me. He was very harsh, and I scarce could do anything to please him; so I made up my mind to leave. The first place I went when I bolted was to Crewkerne, in Somersetshire. There I asked for employment at carpet-weaving. I got some, and remained there three days, when my father found out where I was, and sent my brother and a special constable after me. They took me from the shop where I was at work, and brought me back to —, and would have sent me to prison had I not promised to behave myself, and serve my time out as I ought. I went to work again; and when the expiration of my apprenticeship occurred, my father said to me, "Sam, you have a trade at your fingers' ends: you are able to provide for yourself." So then I left home. I was twenty-one years of age. He gave me money, 3*l*. 10*s*., to take me into Wales, where I told him I should go. I was up for going about through the country. I made my father believe I was going into Wales to get work; but all I wanted was, to go and see the place. After I had runned away once from my apprenticeship, I found it very hard to stop at home. I couldn't bring myself to work somehow. While I sat at the work, I thought I should like to be away in the country: work seemed a burden to me. I found it very difficult to stick to anything for a long time; so I made up my mind, when my time was out, that I'd be off roving, and see a little of life. I went by the packet from Bristol to Newport. After being there three weeks, I had spent all the money that I had brought from home. I spent it in drinking – most of it, and idling about. After that I was obliged to sell my clothes, &c. The first thing I sold was my watch; I got 2*l*. 5*s*. for that. Then I was obliged to part with my suit of clothes. For these I got 1*l*. 5*s*. With this I started from Newport to go farther up over the hills. I liked this kind of life much better than working, while the money lasted. I was in the public-house three parts of my time out of four. I was a great slave to drink. I began to like drink when I was ' tween thirteen and fourteen. At that time my uncle was keeping a public-house, and I used to go there, backwards and forward, more or less every week. Whenever I went to see my uncle he gave me some beer. I very soon got to like it so much, that, while an apprentice, I would spend all I could get in liquor. This was the cause of my quarrels with my father, and when I went away to Newport I did so to be my own master, and drink as much as I pleased, without anybody saying anything to me about it. I got up to Nant-y-glô, and there I sought for work at the iron-foundry, but I could not get it. I stopped at this place three weeks, still drinking. The last day of the three weeks I sold the boots off my feet to get food, for all my money and clothes were now gone. I was sorry then that I had ever left my father's house; but, alas! I found it too late. I didn't write home to tell them how I was off; my stubborn temper would not allow me. I then started off barefoot, begging my way from Nant-y-glô to Monmouth. I told the people that I was a carpet-weaver by trade, who could not get any employment, and that I was obliged to travel the country against my own wish. I didn't say a word about the drink – that would never have done. I only took 2½*d*. on the road, 19 miles long; and I'm sure I must have asked assistance from more than a hundred people. They said, some of them, that they had "nout" for me; and others did give me a bit of "bara caws", or "bara minny" (that is, bread and cheese, or bread and butter). Money is very scarce among the Welsh, and what they have they are very fond of. They don't mind giving food; if you wanted a bagful you might have it there of the working people. I inquired for a night's lodging at the union in Monmouth. That was the first time I ever asked for shelter in a workhouse in my life. I was admitted into the tramp-room. Oh, I felt then that I would much rather be in prison than in such a place, though I never knew what the inside of a prison was – no, not then. I thought of the kindness of my father and mother. I would have been better, but I knew that, as I had been carrying on, I never could expect shelter under my father's roof any more; I knew he would not have taken me in had I gone back, or I would have returned. Oh, I was off from home, and I didn't much trouble my head about it after a few minutes; I plucked up my spirits and soon forgot where I was. I made no male friends in the union; I was savage that I had so hard a bed to lie upon; it was nothing more than the bare boards, and a rug to cover me. I knew very well it wasn't my bed, but still I thought I ought to have a better. I merely felt annoyed at its being so bad a place, and didn't think much about the rights of it. In the morning I was turned out, and after I had left I picked up with a young woman, who had slept in the union over-night. I said I was going on the road across country to Birmingham, and I axed her to go with me. I had never seen her before. She consented, and we went along together, begging our way. We passed as man and wife, and I was a carpet-weaver out of employment. We slept in unions and lodging-houses by the way. In the lodging-houses we lived together as man and wife, and in the unions we were separated. I never stole anything during all this time. After I got to Birmingham I made my way to Wolverhampton. My reason for going to Wolverhampton was, that there was a good many weavers there, and I thought I should make a good bit of money by begging of them. Oh, yes, I have found that I could always get more money out of my own trade than any other people. I did so well at Wolverhampton, begging, that I stopped there three weeks. I never troubled my head whether I was doing right or wrong by asking my brother-weavers for a portion of their hard earnings to keep me in idleness. Many a time I have given part of my wages to others myself. I can't say that I would have given it to them if I had known they wouldn't work like me. I wouldn't have worked sometimes if I could have got it. I can't tell why, but somehow it was painful to me to stick long at anything. To tell the truth, I loved a roving, idle life. I would much rather have been on the road than at my home. I drank away all I got, and feared and cared for nothing. When I got drunk over-night, it would have been impossible for me to have gone to work in the morning, even if I could have got it. The drink seemed to take all the work out of me. This oftentimes led me to think of what my father used to tell me, that "the bird that can sing and won't sing ought to be made to sing". During my stay in Wolverhampton I lived at a tramper's house, and there I fell in with two men well acquainted with the town, and they asked me to join them in breaking open a shop. No, sir, no, I didn't give a thought whether I was doing right or wrong at it. I didn't think my father would ever know anything at all about it, so I didn't care. I like my mother best, much the best. She had always been a kind, good soul to me, often kept me from my father's blows, and helped me to things unknown to my father. But when I was away on the road I gave no heed to her. I didn't think of either father or mother till after I was taken into custody for that same job. Well, I agreed to go with the other two; they were old hands at the business – regular housebreakers. We went away between twelve and one at night. It was pitch dark. My two pals broke into the back part of the house, and I stopped outside to keep watch. After watching for about a quarter of an hour, a policeman came up to me and asked what I was stopping there for. I told him I was waiting for a man that was in a public-house at the corner. This led him to suspect me, it being so late at night. He went to the public-house to see whether it was open, and found it shut, and then came back to me. As he was returning he saw my two comrades coming through the back window (that was the way they had got in). He took us all three in custody; some of the passers-by assisted him in seizing us. The other two had six months' imprisonment each, and I, being a stranger, had only fourteen days. When I was sent to prison, I thought of my mother. I would have written to her, but couldn't get leave. Being the first time I ever was nailed, I was very downhearted at it. I didn't say I'd give it up. While I was locked up, I thought I'd go to work again, and be a sober man, when I got out. These thoughts used to come over me when I was "on the stepper", that is, on the wheel. But I concealed all them thoughts in my breast. I said nothing to no one. My mother was the only one that I ever thought upon. When I got out of prison, all these thoughts went away from me, and I went again at my old tricks. From Wolverhampton I went to Manchester, and from Manchester I came to London, begging and stealing wherever I had a chance. This is not my first year in London. I tell you the truth, because I am known here; and if I tell you a lie, you'll say "You spoke an untruth in one thing, and you'll do so in another." The first time I was in London, I was put in prison fourteen days for begging, and after I had a month at Westminster Bridewell, for begging and abusing the policeman. Sometimes I'd think I'd rather go anywhere, and do anything, than continue as I was; but then I had no clothes, no friends, no house, no home, no means of doing better. I had made myself what I was. I had made my father and mother turn their backs upon me, and what could I do, but go on? I was as bad off then as I am now, and I couldn't have got work then if I would. I should have spent all I got in drink then, I know. I wrote home twice. I told my mother I was hard up; had neither a shoe to my foot, a coat to my back, nor a roof over my head. I had no answer to my first letter, because it fell into the hands of my brother, and he tore it up, fearing that my mother might see it. To the second letter that I sent home my mother sent me an answer herself. She sent me a sovereign. She told me that my father was the same as when I first left home, and it was no use my coming back. She sent me the money, bidding me get some clothes and seek for work. I didn't do as she bade. I spent the money – most part in drink. I didn't give any heed whether it was wrong or right. Soon got, soon gone; and I know they could have sent me much more than that if they had pleased. It was last June twelvemonth when I first came to London, and I stopped till the 10th of last March. I lost the young woman when I was put in prison in Manchester. She never came to see me in quod. She cared nothing for me. She only kept company with me to have some one on the road along with her; and I didn't care for her, not I. One half of my time last winter I stopped at the "Strawyards", that is, the asylums for the houseless poor here and at Glasshouse. When I could get money I had a lodging. After March I started off through Somersetshire. I went to my father's house then. I didn't go in. I saw my father at the door, and he wouldn't let me in. I was a little better dressed than I am now. He said he had enough children at home without me, and gave me 10s. to go. He could not have been kind to me, or else he would not have turned me from his roof. My mother came out to the garden in front of the house, after my father had gone to his work, and spoke to me. She wished me to reform my character. I could not make any rash promises then. I had but very little to say to her. I felt myself at that same time, for the very first time in my life, that I was doing wrong. I thought, if I could hurt my mother so, it must be wrong to go on as I did. I had never had such thoughts before. My father's harsh words always drove such thoughts out of my head; but when I saw my mother's tears, it was more than I could stand. I was wanting to get away as fast as I could from the house. After that I stopped knocking about the country, sleeping in unions, up to November. Then I came to London again, and remained up to this time. Since I have been in town I have sought for work at the floor-cloth and carpet manufactory in the Borough, and they wouldn't even look at me in my present state. I am heartily tired of my life now altogether, and would like to get out of it if I could. I hope at least I have given up my love of drink, and I am sure, if I could once again lay my hand on some work, I should be quite a reformed character. Well, I am altogether tired of carrying on like this. I haven't made 6d. a day ever since I have been in London this time. I go tramping it across the country just to pass the time, and see a little of new places. When the summer comes I want to be off. I am sure I have seen enough of this country now, and I should like to have a look at some foreign land. Old England has nothing new in it now for me. I think a beggar's life is the worst kind of life that a man can lead. A beggar is no more thought upon than a dog in the street, and there are too many at the trade. I wasn't brought up to a bad life. You can see that by little things – by my handwriting; and, indeed, I should like to have a chance at something else. I have had the feelings of a vagabond for full ten years. I know, and now I am sure, I'm getting a different man. I begin to have thoughts and ideas I never had before. Once I never feared nor cared for anything, and I wouldn't have altered if I could; but now I'm tired out, and if I haven't a chance of going right, why I must go wrong.'

The next was a short, thick-set man, with a frequent grin on his countenance, which was rather expressive of humour. He wore a very dirty smock-frock, dirtier trousers, shirt, and neckerchief, and broken shoes. He answered readily, and as if he enjoyed his story.

'I never was at school, and was brought up as a farm labourer at Devizes,' he said, 'where my parents were labourers. I worked that way three or four years, and then ran away. My master wouldn't give me money enough – only 3s. 6d. a week, – and my parents were very harsh; so I ran away, rather than be licked for ever. I'd heard people say, "Go to Bath," and I went there; and I was only about eleven then. I'm now twenty-three. I tried to get work on the railway there, and I did. I next got into prison for stealing three shovels. I was hard-up, having lost my work, and so I stole them. I was ten weeks in prison. I came out worse than I went in, for I mixed with the old hands, and they put me up to a few capers. When I got out I thought I could live as well that way as by hard work; so I took to the country. I began to beg. At first I took "No" for an answer, when I asked for "Charity to a poor boy"; but I found that wouldn't do, so I learned to stick to them. I was forced, or I must have starved, and that wouldn't do at all. I did middling; plenty to eat, and sometimes a drop to drink, but not often. I was forced to be merry, because it's no good being down-hearted. I begged for two years – that is, steal and beg together: I couldn't starve. I did best in country villages in Somersetshire; there's always odds and ends to be picked up there. I got into scrapes now and then. Once, in Devonshire, me and another slept at a farm-house, and in the morning we went egg-hunting. I must have stowed three dozen of eggs about me, when a dog barked, and we were alarmed and ran away, and in getting over a gate I fell, and there I lay among the smashed eggs. I can't help laughing at it still: but I got away. I was too sharp for them. I have been twenty or thirty times in prison. I have been in for stealing bread, and a side of bacon, and cheese, and shovels, and other things; generally provisions. I generally learn something new in prison. I shall do no good while I stop in England. It's not possible a man like me can get work, so I'm forced to go on this way.

Sometimes I haven't a bit to eat all day. At night I may pick up something. An uncle of mine once told me he would like to see me transported, or come to the gallows. I told him I had no fear about the gallows; I should never come to that end: but if I were transported I should be better off than I am now. I can't starve, and I won't; and I can't 'list, I'm too short. I came to London the other day, but could do no good. The London hands are quite a different set to us. We seldom do business together. My way's simple. If I see a thing, and I'm hungry, I take it if I can, in London or anywhere. I once had a turn with two Londoners, and we got two coats and two pair of trousers; but the police got them back again. I was only locked up one night for it. The country's the best place to get away with anything, because there's not so many policemen. There's lots live as I live, because there's no work. I can do a country policeman, generally. I've had sprees at the country lodging-houses – larking, and drinking, and carrying on, and playing cards and dominoes all night for a farthing a game; sometimes fighting about it. I can play at dominoes, but I don't know the cards. They try to cheat one another. Honour among thieves! why there's no such thing; they take from one another. Sometimes we dance all night – Christmas time, and such times. Young women dance with us, and sometimes old women. We're all merry; some's lying on the floor drunk; some's jumping about, smoking; some's dancing; and so we enjoy ourselves. That's the best part of the life. We are seldom stopped in our merrymakings in the country. It's no good the policemen coming among us; give them beer, and you may knock the house down. We have good meat sometimes; sometimes very rough. Some are very particular about their cookery, as nice as anybody is. They must have their pickles, and their peppers, and their fish-sauces (I've had them myself), to their dishes. Chops, in the country, has the call; or ham and eggs – that's relished. Some's very particular about their drink, too; won't touch bad beer; same way with the gin. It's chiefly gin (I'm talking about the country), very little rum; no brandy: but sometimes, after a good day's work, a drop of wine. We help one another when we are sick, where we're knowed. Some's very good that way. Some lodging-house keepers get rid of anybody that's sick, by taking them to the relieving-officer at once.'

A really fine-looking lad of eighteen gave me the following statement. He wore a sort of frock-coat, very thin, buttoned about him, old cloth trousers, and bad shoes. His shirt was tolerably good and clean, and altogether he had a tidy look and an air of quickness, but not of cunning:

'My father,' he said, 'was a bricklayer in Shoreditch parish, and my mother took in washing. They did pretty well; but they're dead and buried two years and a half ago. I used to work in brick-fields at Ball's-pond, living with my parents, and taking home every farthing I earned. I earned 18s. a week, working from five in the morning until sunset. They had only me. I can read and write middling; when my parents died, I had to look out for myself. I was off work, attending to my father and mother when they were sick. They died within about three weeks of each other, and I lost my work, and I had to part with my clothes, before that I tried to work in brick-fields, and couldn't get it, and work grew slack. When my parents died I was thirteen; and I sometimes got to sleep in the unions; but that was stopped, and then I took to the lodging-houses, and there I met with lads who were enjoying themselves at push-halfpenny and cards; and they were thieves, and they tempted me to join them, and I did for once – but only once. I then went begging about the streets and thieving, as I knew the others do. I used to pick pockets. I worked for myself, because I thought that would be best. I had no fence at all – no pals at first, nor anything. I worked by myself for a time. I sold the handkerchiefs I got to Jews in the streets, chiefly in Field-lane, for 1s. 6d., but I have got as much as 3s. 6d. for your real fancy ones. One of these buyers wanted to cheat me out of 6d., so I would have no more dealings with him. The others paid me. The "Kingsmen" they call the best handkerchiefs – those that have the pretty-looking flowers on them. Some are only worth 4d. or 5d., some's not worth taking. Those I gave away to strangers, boys like myself, or wore them myself, round my neck. I only threw one away, but it was all rags, though he looked quite like a gentleman that had it. Lord-mayor's day and such times is the best for us. Last Lord-mayor's day I got four handkerchiefs, and I made 11s. There was a 6d. tied up in the corner of one handkerchief; another was pinned to the pocket, but I got it out, and after that another chap had him, and cut his pocket clean away, but there was nothing in it. I generally picked my men – regular swells, or good-humoured looking men. I've often followed them a mile. I once got a purse with 3s. 6d. in it from a lady when the Coal Exchange was opened. I made 8s. 6d. that day – the purse and handkerchiefs. That's the only lady I ever robbed. I was in the crowd when Manning and his wife were hanged. I wanted to see if they died game, as I heard them talk so much about them at our house. I was there all night. I did four good handkerchiefs and a rotten one not worth picking up. I saw them hung. I was right under the drop. I was a bit startled when they brought him up and put the rope round his neck and the cap on, and then they brought her out. All said he was hung innocently; it was she that should have been hung by herself. They both dropped together, and I felt faintified, but I soon felt all right again. The police drove us away as soon as it was over, so that I couldn't do any more business; besides, I was knocked down in the crowd and jumped upon, and I won't go to see another hung in a hurry. He didn't deserve it, but she did, every inch of her. I can't say I thought, while I was seeing the execution, that the life I was leading would ever bring me to the gallows. After I'd worked by myself a bit, I got to live in a house where lads like me, big and little, were accommodated. We paid 3*d*. a night. It was always full; there was twenty or twenty-one of us. We enjoyed ourselves middling. I was happy enough: we drank sometimes, chiefly beer, and sometimes a drop of gin. One would say, "I've done so much," and another, "I've done so much;" and stand a drop. The best I ever heard done was 2*l*. for two coats from a tailor's, near Bow-church, Cheapside. That was by one of my pals. We used to share our money with those who did nothing for a day, and they shared with us when we rested. There never was any blabbing. We wouldn't do one another out of a farthing. Of a night some one would now and then read hymns, out of books they sold about the streets – I'm sure they were hymns; or else we'd read stories about Jack Sheppard and Dick Turpin, and all through that set. They were large thick books, borrowed from the library. They told how they used to break open the houses, and get out of Newgate, and how Dick got away to York. We used to think Jack and them very fine fellows. I wished I could be like Jack (I did then), about the blankets in his escape, and that old house in West-street – it is a ruin still. We played cards and dominoes sometimes at our house, and at pushing a halfpenny over the table along five lines. We struck the halfpenny from the edge of the table, and according to what line it settled on was the game – like as they play at the Glasshouse – that's the "model lodging-house" they calls it. Cribbage was always played at cards. I can only play cribbage. We have played for a shilling a game, but oftener a penny. It was always fair play. That was the way we passed the time when we were not out. We used to keep quiet, or the police would have been down upon us. They knew of the place. They took one boy there. I wondered what they wanted. They catched him at the very door. We lived pretty well; anything we liked to get, when we'd money: we cooked it ourselves. The master of the house was always on the look-out to keep out those who had no business there. No girls were admitted. The master of the house had nothing to do with what we got. I don't know of any other such house in London; I don't think there are any. The master would sometimes drink with us – a larking like. He used us pretty kindly at times. I have been three times in prison, three months each time; the Compter, Brixton and Maidstone. I went down to Maidstone fair, and was caught by a London policeman down there. He was dressed as a bricklayer. Prison always made me worse, and as I had nothing given me when I came out, I had to look out again. I generally got hold of something before I had been an hour out of prison. I'm now heartily sick of this life. I wish I'd been transported with some others from Maidstone, where I was tried.'

A cotton-spinner (who had subsequently been a soldier), whose appearance was utterly abject, was the next person questioned. He was tall, and had been florid-looking (judging by his present complexion). His coat – very old and worn, and once black – would not button, and would have hardly held together if buttoned. He was out at elbows, and some parts of the collar were pinned together. His waistcoat was of a match with his coat, and his trousers were rags. He had some shirt, as was evident by his waistcoat, held together by one button. A very dirty handkerchief was tied carelessly round his neck. He was tall and erect, and told his adventures with heartiness.

'I am thirty-eight,' he said, 'and have been a cotton-spinner, working at Chorlton-upon-Medlock. I can neither read nor write. When I was a young man, twenty years ago, I could earn 2l. 10s., clear money, every week, after paying two piecers and a scavenger. Each piecer had 7s. 6d. a week – they are girls; the scavenger – a boy to clean the wheels of the cotton-spinning machine – had 2s. 6d. I was master of them wheels in the factory. This state of things continued until about the year 1837. I lived well and enjoyed myself, being a hearty man, noways a drunkard, working every day from half-past five in the morning till half-past seven at night – long hours, that time, master. I didn't care about money as long as I was decent and respectable. I had a turn for sporting at the wakes down there. In 1837, the "self-actors" (machines with steam power) had come into common use. One girl can mind three pairs – that used to be three men's work – getting 15s. for the work which gave three men 7l. 10s. Out of one factory 400 hands were flung in one week, men and women together. We had a meeting of the union, but nothing could be done, and we were told to go and mind the three pairs, as the girls did, for 15s. a week. We wouldn't do that. Some went for soldiers, some to sea, some to Stopport (Stockport), to get work in factories where the "self-actors" wern't agait. The masters there wouldn't have them – at least, some of them. Manchester was full of them; but one gentleman in Hulme still won't have them, for he says he won't turn the men out of bread. I 'listed for a soldier in the 48th. I liked a soldier's life very well until I got flogged – 100 lashes for selling my kit (for a spree), and 150 for striking a corporal, who called me an English robber. He was an Irishman. I was

confined five days in the hospital after each punishment. It was terrible.
It was like a bunch of razors cutting at your back. Your flesh was dragged
off by the cats. Flogging was then very common in the regiment. I was
flogged in 1840. To this day I feel a pain in the chest from the triangles.
I was discharged from the army about two years ago, when the reduction
took place. I was only flogged the times I've told you. I had no pension
and no friends. I was discharged in Dublin. I turned to, and looked for
work. I couldn't get any, and made my way for Manchester. I stole myself
aboard of a steamer, and hid myself till she got out to sea, on her way from
Dublin to Liverpool. When the captain found me there, he gave me a kick
and some bread, and told me to work, so I worked for my passage twenty-
four hours. He put me ashore at Liverpool. I slept in the union that night
– nothing to eat and nothing to cover me – no fire; it was winter. I walked
to Manchester, but could get nothing to do there, though I was twelve
months knocking about. It wants a friend and a character to get work.
I slept in unions in Manchester, and had oatmeal porridge for breakfast,
work at grinding logwood in the mill, from six to twelve, and then turn
out. That was the way I lived chiefly; but I got a job sometimes in driving
cattle, and 3d. for it, – or 2d. for carrying baskets in the vegetable markets;
and went to Shoedale Union at night. I would get a pint of coffee and half-
a-pound of bread, and half-a-pound of bread in the morning, and no work.
I took to travelling up to London, half-hungered on the road – that was
last winter – eating turnips out of this field, and carrots out of that, and
sleeping under hedges and haystacks. I slept under one haystack, and
pulled out the hay to cover me, and the snow lay on it a foot deep in the
morning. I slept for all that, but wasn't I froze when I woke? An old farmer
came up with his cart and pitchfork to load hay. He said: "Poor fellow!
have you been here all night?" I answered, "Yes." He gave me some coffee
and bread, and one shilling. That was the only good friend I met with on
the road. I got fourteen days of it for asking a gentleman for a penny; that
was in Stafford. I got to London after that, sleeping in unions sometimes,
and begging a bite here and there. Sometimes I had to walk all night. I
was once forty-eight hours without a bite, until I got hold at last of a Swede
turnip, and so at last I got to London. Here I've tried up and down
everywhere for work as a labouring man, or in a foundry. I tried London
Docks, and Blackwall, and every place; but no job. At one foundry, the
boiler-makers made a collection of 4s. for me. I've walked the streets for
three nights together. Here, in this fine London, I was refused a night's
lodging in Shoreditch and in Gray's-inn-lane. A policeman, the fourth
night, at twelve o'clock, procured me a lodging, and gave me 2d. I couldn't

drag on any longer. I was taken to a doctor's in the city. I fell in the street from hunger and tiredness. The doctor ordered me brandy and water, 2s. 6d., and a quartern loaf, and some coffee, sugar, and butter. He said, what I ailed was hunger. I made that run out as long as I could, but I was then as bad off as ever. It's hard to hunger for nights together. I was once in "Steel" (Coldbath-fields) for begging. I was in Tothill-fields for going into a chandler's shop, asking for a quartern loaf and half a pound of cheese, and walking out with it. I got a month for that. I have been in Brixton for taking a loaf out of a baker's basket, all through hunger. Better a prison than to starve. I was well treated because I behaved well in prison. I have slept in coaches when I had a chance. One night on a dunghill, covering the stable straw about me to keep myself warm. This place is a relief. I shave the poor people and cut their hair, on a Sunday. I was handy at that when I was a soldier. I have shaved in public-houses for halfpennies. Some landlords kicks me out. Now, in the days, I may pick up a penny or two that way, and get here of a night. I met two Manchester men in Hyde Park on Saturday, skating. They asked me what I was. I said, "A beggar." They gave me 2s. 6d., and I spent part of it for warm coffee and other things. They knew all about Manchester, and knew I was a Manchester man by my talk.'

The statement I then took was that of a female vagrant – a young girl with eyes and hair of remarkable blackness. Her complexion was of the deepest brunette, her cheeks were full of colour, and her lips very thick. This was accounted for. She told me that her father was a mulatto from Philadelphia. She was short, and dressed in a torn old cotton gown, the pattern of which was hardly discernible from wear. A kind of of half-shawl, patched and mended in several places, and of very thin woollen texture, was pinned around her neck; her arms, which, with her hands, were full and large, were bare. She wore very old broken boots and ragged stockings. Her demeanour was modest.

'I am now eighteen,' she stated. 'My father was a coloured man. He came over here as a sailor, I have heard, but I never saw him; for my mother, who was a white woman, was not married to him, but met him at Oxford; and she married afterwards a box-maker, a white man, and has two other children. They are living, I believe, but I don't know where they are. I have heard my mother say that my father – that's my own father – had become a missionary, and had been sent out to America from England as a missionary, by Mr —. I believe that was fifteen years ago. I don't know who Mr — was, but he was a gentleman, I've heard my mother say. She told me, too, that my father was a good scholar, and that he could speak seven different languages, and was a very religious man. He was sent out to Boston, but I never heard whether he was to stay or not, and I don't know what he was to missionary about. He behaved very well to my mother, I have heard her say, until she took up with the other man (the box-maker), and then he left her, and gave her up, and came to London. It was at Oxford that they all three were then; and when my father got away, or came away to London, my mother followed him (she told me so, but she didn't like to talk about it), as she was then in the family way. She didn't find him; but my father heard of her, and left some money with Mr — for her, and she got into Poland-street workhouse through Mr — I've heard. While there, she received 1s. 6d. a week, but my father never came to see her or me. At one time, my father used to live by teaching languages. He had been in Spain, and France, and Morocco. I've heard, at any rate, that he could speak the Moors' language, but I know nothing more. All this is what I've heard from my mother and my grandmother – that's my mother's mother. My grandfather and grandmother are dead. He was a sawyer. I have a great grandmother living in Oxford, now ninety-two, supported by her parish. I lived with my grandmother at Oxford, who took me out of pity, as my mother never cared about me, when I was four months old. I remained with her until I was ten, and then my mother came from Reading, where she was living, and took me away with her. I lived with her and my stepfather, but they were badly off. He couldn't get much to do at his trade as a box-maker, and he drank a great deal. I was with them about nine months, when I ran away. He beat me so; he never liked me. I couldn't bear it. I went to Pangbourne, but there I was stopped by a man my stepfather had sent – at least I suppose so – and I was forced to walk back to Reading – ten miles, perhaps. My father applied to the overseer for support for me, and the overseer was rather harsh, and my father struck him, and for that he was sent to prison for three months. My mother and her children then got into the workhouse, but not until after my stepfather had been some time in prison. Before that she had an allowance, which was stopped; I don't know how much. I was in the workhouse twenty-one days. I wasn't badly treated. My mother sweared my parish, and I was removed to St James's, Poland-street, London. I was there three weeks, and then I was sent to New Brentford – it was called the Juvenile Establishment – and I went to school. There was about 150 boys and girls; the boys were sent to Norwood when they were fifteen. Some of the girls were eighteen, kept there until they could get a place. I don't know whether they all belonged to St James's, or to different parishes, or how. I stayed there about two years. I was very well treated, sufficient to eat; but we worked hard at scrubbing, cleaning, and making shirts. We made all the boys' clothes as well, jackets and trousers, and all. I was then apprenticed a maid-of-all-work, in Duke-street, Grosvenor-square, for three years. I was there two years and a half, when my master failed in business, and had to part with me. They had no servant but me. My mistress was sometimes kind, pretty well. I had to work very hard. She sometimes beat me if I stopped long on my errands. My master beat me once for bringing things wrong from a grocer's. I made a mistake. Once my mistress knocked me down-stairs for being long on an errand to Pimlico, and I'm sure I couldn't help it, and my eye was cut. It was three weeks before I could see well. [There is a slight mark under the girl's eye still.] They beat me with their fists. After I left my master, I tried hard to get a place; I'm sure I did, but I really couldn't; so to live, I got watercresses to sell up and down Oxford-street. I stayed at lodging-houses. I tried that two or three months, but couldn't live. My mother had been "through the country", and I knew other people that had, through meeting them at the lodging-houses. I first went to Croydon, begging my way. I slept in the workhouse. After that I went to Brighton, begging my way, but couldn't get much, not enough to pay my lodgings. I was constantly insulted, both in the lodging-houses and in the streets. I sung in the streets at Brighton, and got enough to pay my lodgings, and a little for food. I was there a week, and then I went to the Mendicity, and they gave me piece of bread (morning and night) and a night's lodging. I then went to Lewes and other places, begging, and got into prison at Tunbridge Wells for fourteen days, for begging. I only used to say I was a poor girl out of place, could they relieve me? I told no lies. I didn't pick my oakum one day, it was such hard stuff: three and a half pounds of it to do from nine to half-past three: so I was put into solitary for three days and three nights, having half a pound of bread and a pint of cold water morning and night; nothing else, and no bed to sleep on. I'm sure I tell you the truth. Some had irons on their hands if they were obstropolous. That's about two months ago. I'm sorry to say that during this time I couldn't be virtuous. I know very well what it means, for I can read and write, but no girl can be so circumstanced as I was. I seldom got money for being wicked; I hated being wicked, but I was tricked and cheated. I am truly sorry for it, but what could a poor girl do? I begged my way from London to Hastings, and got here on Saturday last, and having no money, came here. I heard of this asylum from a girl in Whitechapel, who had been here. I met her in a lodging-house, where I called to rest in the daytime. They let us rest sometimes in lodging-houses in the daytime. I never was in any prison but Tunbridge

Wells, and in Gravesend lock-up for being out after twelve at night, when I had no money to get a lodging. I was there one Saturday night, and got out on Sunday morning, but had nothing given me to eat – I was in by myself. It's a bad place – just straw to sleep on, and very cold. I told you I could read and write. I learnt that partly at Oxford, and finished my learning at the Juvenile Establishment at Brentford. There I was taught, reading, writing, sums, marking, sewing, and scrubbing. Once I could say all the multiplication table, but I've forgot most of it. I know how to make lace, too, because I was taught by a cousin in Oxford, another grandchild of my grandmother's. I can make it with knitting-needles. I could make cushion-lace with pins, but I'm afraid I've forgot how now. I should like, if I could to get into service again, here or abroad. I have heard of Australia, where I have a cousin. I am sure I could and would conduct myself well in service, I have suffered so much out of it. I am sure of it. I never stole anything in my life, and have told all I have done wrong.'

Statement of a Returned Convict

[pp. 396–8] I shall now give the statement of a man who was selected at random from amongst a number such as himself, congregated in one of the most respectable lodging-houses. He proved, on examination, to be a returned convict, and one who had gone through the severest bodily and mental agony. He had lived in the bush, and been tried for his life. He was an elderly-looking man, whose hair was just turning grey, and in whose appearance there was nothing remarkable, except that his cheek-bones were unusually high and that his face presented that collected and composed expression which is common to men exposed to habitual watchfulness from constant danger. He gave me the following statement. His dress was bad, but differed in nothing from that of a long-distressed mechanic. He said:

'I am now 43 [he looked much older], and had respectable parents, and a respectable education. I am a native of London. When I was young I was fond of a roving life, but cared nothing about drink. I liked to see "life", as it was called, and was fond of the company of women. Money was no object in those days; it was like picking up dirt in the streets. I ran away from home. My parents were very kind to me; indeed, I think I was used too well, I was petted so, when I was between 12 and 13. I got acquainted with some boys at Bartlemy-fair a little before that, and saw them spending lots of money and throwing at cock-shies, and such-like; and one of them said, "Why don't you come out like us?" So afterwards I ran away and joined them. I was not kept shorter of money than other boys like me, but I couldn't settle. I couldn't fix my mind to any regular business but a waterman's, and my friends wouldn't hear of that. There was nine boys of us among the lot that I joined, but we didn't all work together. All of 'em came to be sent to Van Dieman's Land as transports except one, and he was sent to Sydney. While we were in London it was a merry life, with change of scene, for we travelled about. We were successful in nearly all our plans for several months. I worked in Fleet Street, and could make 3*l.* a week at handkerchiefs alone, sometimes falling across a pocket-book. The best handkerchiefs then brought 4*s.* in Field-lane. Our chief enjoyments were at the "Free and Easy", where all the thieves and young women went, and sang and danced. I had a young woman for a partner then; she went out to Van Dieman's Land. She went on the lift in London (shopping and stealing from the counter). She was clever at it. I carried on in this way for about 15 months, when I was grabbed for an attempt on a gentleman's pocket by St Paul's Cathedral, on a grand charity procession day. I had two months in the Old Horse (Bridewell). I never thought of my parents at this time – I wouldn't. I was two years and a half at this same trade. One week was very like another – successes and escapes, and free-and-easies, and games of all sorts, made up the life. At the end of the two years and a half I got into the way of forged Bank-of-England notes. A man I knew in the course of business, said, "I would cut that game of 'smatter-hauling', (stealing handkerchiefs), and do a little soft," (pass bad notes). So I did, and was very successful at first. I had a mate. He afterwards went out to Sydney, too, for 14 years. I went stylishly dressed as a gentleman, with a watch in my pocket, to pass my notes. I passed a good many in drapers' shops, also at tailors' shops. I never tried jewellers, they're reckoned too good judges. The notes were all finnies, (5*l.* notes), and a good imitation. I made more money at this game, but lived as before, and had my partner still. I was fond of her; she was a nice girl, and I never found that she wronged me in any way. I thought at four months' end of retiring into the country with gambling-tables, as the risk was becoming considerable. They hung them for it in them days, but that never daunted me the least in life. I saw Cashman hung for that gunsmith's shop on Snow-hill, and I saw Fauntleroy hung, and a good many others, but it gave me no uneasiness and no fear. The gallows had no terror for people in my way of life. I started into the country with another man and his wife – his lawful wife – for I had a few words with my own young woman, or I shouldn't have left her behind me, or, indeed, have started at all. We carried gambling on in different parts of the country for six months. We made most at the E. O. tables – not those played with a ball, they weren't in vogue then, but throwing dice for prizes marked on a table. The highest prize was ten guineas, but the dice were so made that no prize could be thrown; the numbers were not regular as in good dice, and they were loaded as well. If anybody asked to see them, we had good dice ready to show. All sorts played with us. London men and all were taken in. We made most at the races. My mate and his wife told me that at the last Newmarket meeting we attended, 65l. was made, but they rowed in the same boat. I know they got a deal more. The 65l. was shared in three equal portions, but I had to maintain the horse and cart out of my own share. We used to go out into the roads (highway robbery) between races, and if we met an "old bloke" (man) we "propped him" (knocked him down), and robbed him. We did good stakes that way, and were never found out. We lived as well as any gentleman in the land. Our E. O. table was in a tilted cart. I stayed with this man and his wife two months. She was good-looking, so as to attract people. I thought they didn't use me altogether right, so at Braintree I gave another man in the same way of business 25l. for his kit – horse, harness, tilted-cart, and table. I gave him two good 5l. notes and three bad ones, for I worked that way still, not throwing much of a chance away. I came to London for a hawker's stock, braces and such-like, to sell on the road, just to take the down off (remove suspicion). In the meantime, the man that I bought the horse, &c., of, had been nailed passing a bad note, and he stated who he got it from, and I was traced. He was in a terrible rage to find himself done, particularly as he used to do the same to other people himself. He got acquitted for that there note after he had me "pinched" (arrested). I got "fullied" (fully committed). I was tried at the "Start" (Old Bailey), and pleaded guilty to the minor offence (that of utterance, not knowing the note to be forged), or I should have been hanged for it then. It was a favourable sessions when I was tried. Thirty-six were cast for death, and only one was "topped' (hanged), the very one that expected to be "turned up" (acquitted) for highway robbery. I was sentenced to 14 years' transportation. I was ten weeks in the Bellerophon hulk at Sheerness, and was then taken to Hobart Town, Van Dieman's Land, in the Sir Godfrey Webster. At Hobart Town sixty of us were picked out to go to Launceston. There (at Launceston) we lay for four days in an old church, guarded by constables; and then the settlers came there from all parts, and picked their men out. I got a very bad master. He put me to harvest work that I had never even seen done before, and I had the care of pigs as wild as wild boars. After that I was sent to Launceston with two letters from my master to the superintendent, and the other servants thought I had luck to get away from Red Barks to Launceston, which was 16 miles off. I then worked in a Government potato-field; in the Government charcoal-works for about 11 months; and then was in the Marine department, going by water from Launceston to George Town, taking Government officers down in gigs, provisions in boats, and such-like. There was a crew of six (convicts) in the gigs, and four in the watering-boats. All the time I consider I was very hardly treated. I hadn't clothes half the time, being allowed only two slop-suits in a year, and no bed to lie on when we had to stay out all night with the boats by the river Tamar. With 12 years' service at this my time was up, but I had incurred several punishments before it was up. The first was 25 lashes, because a bag of flour had been burst, and I picked up a capfull. The flogging is dreadfully severe, a soldier's is nothing to it. I once had 50 lashes, for taking a hat in a joke when I was tipsy; and a soldier had 300 the same morning. I was flogged as a convict, and he as a soldier; and when we were both at the same hospital after the flogging, and saw each other's backs, the other convicts said to me, "D— it, you've got it this time;" and the soldier said, when he saw my back, "You've got it twice as bad I have." "No," said the doctor, "ten times as bad – he's been flogged; but you, in comparison, have only had a child's whipping." The cats the convicts were then flogged with were each six feet long, made out of the log-line of a ship of 500 tons burden; nine over-end knots were in each tail, and nine tails whipped at each end with wax-end. With this we had half-minute lashes; a quick lashing would have been certain death. One convict who had 75 lashes was taken from the triangles to the watch-house in Launceston, and was asked if he would have some tea, – he was found to be dead. The military surgeon kept on saying in the case, "Go on, do your duty." I was mustered there, as was every hand belonging to the Government, and saw it, and heard the doctor. When I was first flogged, there was inquiry among my fellow-convicts, as to "How did D— (meaning me) stand it – did he sing?" The answer was, "He was a pebble;" that is, I never once said, "Oh!" or gave out any expression of the pain I suffered. I took my flogging like a stone. If I had sung, some of the convicts would have given me some lush with a locust in it (laudanum hocussing), and when I was asleep would have given me a crack on the head that would have laid me straight. That first flogging made me ripe. I said to myself, "I can take it like a bullock." I could have taken the flogger's life at the time, I felt such revenge. Flogging always gives that feeling; I know it does, from what I've heard others say who had been flogged like myself. In all I had 875 lashes at my different punishments. I used to boast of it at last. I would say, "I don't care, I can take it till they see my backbone." After a flogging, I've rubbed my back against a wall, just to show my bravery like, and squeezed the congealed blood out of it. Once I would not let them dress my back after a flogging, and I had 25 additional for that. At last I bolted to Hobart Town, 120 miles off. There I was taken before Mr H——, the magistrate, himself a convict formerly, I believe from the Irish Rebellion; but he was a good man to a prisoner. He ordered me 50, and sent me back to Launceston. At Launceston I was "fullied" by a bench of magistrates, and had 100. Seven years before my time was up I took to the bush. I could stand it no longer, of course not. In the bush I met men with whom, if I had been seen associating, I should have been hanged on any slight charge, such as Brittan was and his pals.'

I am not at liberty to continue this man's statement at present: it would be a breach of the trust reposed in me. Suffice it, he was in after days tried for his life. Altogether it was a most extraordinary statement; and, from confirmations I received, was altogether truthful. He declared that he was so sick of the life he was now leading, that he would, as a probation, work on any kind of land anywhere for nothing, just to get out of it. He pronounced the lodging-houses the grand encouragements and concealments of crime, though he might be speaking against himself, he said, as he had always hidden safely there during the hottest search. A policeman once walked through the ward in search of him, and he was in bed. He knew the policeman well, and was as well known to the officer, but he was not recognised. He attributed his escape to the thick, bad atmosphere of the place giving his features a different look, and to his having shaved off his whiskers, and pulled his nightcap over his head. The officer, too, seemed half-sick, he said.

It ought also to be added, that this man stated that the severity of the Governments in this penal colony was so extreme, that men thought little of giving others a knock on the head with an axe, to get hanged out of the way. Under the discipline of Captain Macconochie, however, who introduced better order with a kindlier system, there wasn't a man but what would have laid down his life for him.

*Lives of the Boy Inmates of the Casual Wards
of the London Workhouses*

[pp. 398–402] An intelligent-looking boy, of sixteen years of age, whose dress was a series of ragged coats, three in number – as if one was to obviate the deficiency of another, since one would not button, and another was almost sleeveless – gave me the following statement. He had long and rather fair hair, and spoke quietly. He said:

'I'm a native of Wisbeach, in Cambridgeshire, and am sixteen. My father was a shoe-maker, and my mother died when I was five years old, and my father married again. I was sent to school, and can read and write well. My father and step-mother were kind enough to me. I was apprenticed to a tailor three years ago, but I wasn't long with him; I runned away. I think it was three months I was with him when I first runned away. It was in August – I got as far as Boston in Lincolnshire, and was away a fortnight. I had 4s. 6d. of my own money when I started, and that lasted two or three days. I stopped in lodging-houses until my money was gone, and then I slept anywhere – under the hedges, or anywhere. I didn't see so much of life then, but I've seen plenty of it since. I had to beg my way back from Boston, but was very awkward at first. I lived on turnips mainly. My reason for running off was because my master ill-used me so; he beat me, and kept me from my meals, and made me sit up working late at nights for a punishment: but it was more to his good than to punish me. I hated to be confined to a tailor's shopboard, but I would rather do that sort of work now than hunger about like this. But you see, sir, God punishes you when you don't think of it. When I went back my father was glad to see me, and he wouldn't have me go back again to my master, and my indentures were cancelled. I stayed at home seven months, doing odd jobs, in driving sheep, or any country work, but I always wanted to be off to sea. I liked the thoughts of going to sea far better than tailoring. I determined to go to sea if I could. When a dog's determined to have a bone, it's not easy to hinder him. I didn't read stories about the sea then, not even "Robinson Crusoe" – indeed I haven't read that still, but I know very well there is such a book. My father had no books but religious books; they were all of a religious turn, and what people might think dull, but they never made me dull. I read Wesley's and Watts's hymns, and religious magazines of different connexions. I had a natural inclination for the sea, and would like to get to it now. I've read a good deal about it since – Clark's "Lives of Pirates", "Tales of Shipwrecks", and other things in penny numbers (Clark's I got out of a library though). I was what people called a deep boy for a book; and am still. Whenever I had a penny, after I got a bellyful of victuals, it went for a book, but I haven't bought many lately. I did buy one yesterday – the "Family Herald" – one I often read when I can get it. There's good reading in it; it elevates your mind – anybody that has a mind for studying. It has good tales in it. I never read "Jack

Sheppard" – that is, I haven't read the big book that's written about him; but I've often heard the boys and men talk about it at the lodging-houses and other places. When they haven't their bellies and money to think about they sometimes talk about books; but for such books as them – that's as "Jack" – I haven't a partiality. I've read "Windsor Castle", and "The Tower" – they're by the same man. I liked "Windsor Castle", and all about Henry VIII and Herne the hunter. It's a book that's connected with history, and that's a good thing in it. I like adventurous tales. I know very little about theatres, as I was never in one.

'Well, after that seven months – I was kindly treated all the time – I runned away again to get to sea; and hearing so much talk about this big London, I comed to it. I couldn't settle down to anything but the sea. I often watched the ships at Wisbeach. I had no particular motive, but a sort of pleasure in it. I was aboard some ships, too; just looking about, as lads will. I started without a farthing, but I couldn't help it. I felt I must come. I forgot all I suffered before – at least, the impression had died off my mind. I came up by the unions when they would take me in. When I started, I didn't know where to sleep any more than the dead; I learned it from other travellers on the road. It was two winters ago, and very cold weather. Sometimes I slept in barns, and I begged my way as well as I could. I never stole anything then or since, except turnips; but I've been often tempted. At last I got to London, and was by myself. I travelled sometimes with others as I came up, but not as mates – not as friends. I came to London for one purpose just by myself. I was a week in London before I knew where I was. I didn't know where to go. I slept on door-steps, or anywhere. I used often to stand on London-bridge, but I didn't know where to go to get to sea, or anything of that kind. I was sadly hungered, regularly starved; and I saw so many policemen, I durstn't beg – and I dare not now, in London. I got crusts, but I can hardly tell how I lived. One night I was sleeping under a railway-arch, somewhere about Bishopsgate-street, and a police-man came and asked me what I was up to? I told him I had no place to go to, so he said I must go along with him. In the morning he took me and four or five others to a house in a big street. I don't know where; and a man – a magistrate, I suppose he was – heard what the policeman had to say, and he said there was always a lot of lads there about the arches, young thieves, that gave him a great deal of trouble, and I was one associated with them. I declare I didn't know any of the other boys, nor any boys in London – not a soul; and I was under the arch by myself, and only that night. I never saw the policeman himself before that, as I know of. I got fourteen days of it, and they took me in an omnibus, but I don't know to what prison. I was committed for being a rogue and something else. I didn't very well hear what other things I was, but "rogue" I know was one. They were very strict in prison, and I wasn't allowed to speak. I was put to oakum some days, and others on a wheel. That's the only time I was ever in prison, and I hope it will always be the only time. Something may turn up – there's nobody knows. When I was turned out I hadn't a farthing given to me. And so I was again in the streets, without knowing a creature, and without a farthing in my pocket, and nothing to get one with but my tongue. I set off that day for the country. I didn't try to get a ship, because I didn't know where to go to ask, and I had got ragged, and they wouldn't hear me out if I asked any people about the bridges. I took the first road that offered, and got to Greenwich. I couldn't still think of going back home. I would if I had had clothes, but they were rags, and I had no shoes but a pair of old slippers. I was sometimes sorry I left home, but then I began to get used to travelling, and to beg a bit in the villages. I had no regular mate to travel with, and no sweethearts. I slept in the unions whenever I could get in – that's in the country. I didn't never sleep in the London workhouses till afterwards. In some country places there were as many as forty in the casual wards, men, women, and children; in some, only two or three. There used to be part boys, like myself, but far more bigger than I was; they were generally from eighteen to twenty-three: London chaps, chiefly, I believe. They were a regularly jolly set. They used to sing and dance a part of the nights and mornings in the wards, and I got to sing and dance with them. We were all in a mess; there was no better or no worse among us. We used to sing comic and sentimental songs, both. I used to sing "Tom Elliott", that's a sea song, for I hankered about the sea, and "I'm Afloat". I hardly know any but sea-songs. Many used to sing indecent songs; they're impudent blackguards. They used to sell these songs among the others, but I never sold any of them, and I never had any, though I know some, from hearing them often. We told stories sometimes; romantic tales, some; others blackguard kind of tales, about bad women; and others about thieving and roguery; not so much about what they'd done themselves, as about some big thief that was very clever at stealing, and could trick anybody. Not stories such as Dick Turpin or Jack Sheppard, or things that's in history, but inventions. I used to say when I was telling a story – for I've told one story that I invented till I learnt it –

[I give this story to show what are the objects of admiration with these vagrants.]

'"You see, mates, there was once upon a time, and a very good time

404

it was, a young man, and he runned away, and got along with a gang of thieves, and he went to a gentleman's house, and got in, because one of his mates sweethearted the servant, and got her away, and she left the door open." ['But don't,' he expostulated, 'take it all down that way; it's foolishness. I'm ashamed of it – it's just what we say to amuse ourselves.'] "And the door being left open, the young man got in and robbed the house of a lot of money, 1000l., and he took it to their gang at the cave. Next day there was a reward out to find the robber. Nobody found him. So the gentleman put out two men and a horse in a field, and the men were hidden in the field, and the gentleman put out a notice that anybody that could catch the horse should have him for his cleverness, and a reward as well; for he thought the man that got the 1000l. was sure to try to catch that there horse, because he was so bold and clever, and then the two men hid would nab him. This here Jack (that's the young man) was watching, and he saw the two men, and he went and caught two live hares. Then he hid himself behind a hedge, and let one hare go, and one man said to the other, "There goes a hare," and they both run after it, not thinking Jack's there. And while they were running he let go the t'other one, and they said, "There's another hare," and they ran different ways, and so Jack went and got the horse, and took it to the man that offered the reward, and got the reward; it was 100l.; and the gentleman said "D—n it, Jack's done me this time." The gentleman then wanted to serve out the parson, and he said to Jack, "I'll give you another 100l. if you'll do something to the parson as bad as you've done to me." Jack said, "Well, I will;" and Jack went to the church and lighted up the lamps, and rang the bells, and the parson he got up to see what was up. Jack was standing in one of the pews like an angel, when the parson got to the church. Jack said, "Go and put your plate in a bag; I'm an angel come to take you up to heaven." And the parson did so, and it was as much as he could drag to church from his house in a bag; for he was very rich. And when he got to the church Jack put the parson in one bag, and the money stayed in the other; and he tied them both together, and put them across his horse, and took them up hills and through water to the gentleman's, and then he took the parson out of the bag, and the parson was wringing wet. Jack fetched the gentleman, and the gentleman gave the parson a horsewhipping, and the parson cut away, and Jack got all the parson's money and the second 100l., and gave it all to the poor. And the parson brought an action against the gentleman for horsewhipping him, and they both were ruined. That's the end of it." That's the sort of story that's liked best, sir. Sometimes there was fighting in the casual-wards. Sometimes I was in it, I was like the rest. We jawed each other often, calling names and coming to fight at last. At Romsey a lot of young fellows broke all the windows they could get at, because they were too late to be admitted. They broke them from the outside. We couldn't get at them from inside. I've carried on begging, and going from union to union to sleep, until now. Once I got work in Northampton with a drover. I kept working when he'd a job, from August last to the week before Christmas. I always tried to get a ship in a seaport, but couldn't. I've been to Portsmouth, Plymouth, Bristol, Southampton, Ipswich, Liverpool, Brighton, Dover, Shoreham, Hastings, and all through Lincolnshire, Nottinghamshire, Cambridgeshire, and Suffolk – not in Norfolk – they won't let you go there. I don't know why. All this time I used to meet boys like myself, but mostly bigger and older; plenty of them could read and write, some were gentlemen's sons, they said. Some had their young women with them that they'd taken up with, but I never was much with them. I often wished I was at home again, and do now, but I can't think of going back in these rags; and I don't know if my father's dead or alive [his voice trembled], but I'd like to be there and have it over. I can't face meeting them in these rags, and I've seldom had better, I make so little money. I'm unhappy at times, but I get over it better than I used, as I get accustomed to this life. I never heard anything about home since I left. I have applied at the Marine Society here, but it's no use. If I could only get to sea, I'd be happy; and I'd be happy if I could get home, and would, but for the reasons I've told you.'

The next was a boy with a quiet look, rather better drressed than most of the vagrant boys, and far more clean in his dress. He made the following statement:

'I am now seventeen. My father was a cotton-spinner in Manchester, but has been dead ten years; and soon after that my mother went into the workhouse, leaving me with an aunt; and I had work in a cotton factory. As young as I was, I earned 2s. 2d. a week at first. I can read well, and can write a little. I worked at the factory two years, and was then earning 7s. a week. I then ran away, for I had always a roving mind; but I should have stayed if my master hadn't knocked me about so. I thought I should make my fortune in London – I'd heard it was such a grand place. I had read in novels and romances – halfpenny and penny books – about such things, but I've met with nothing of the kind. I started without money, and begged my way from Manchester to London, saying I was going up to look for work. I wanted to see the place more than anything else. I suffered very much on the road, having to be out all night often; and the nights were cold, though it was summer. When I got to London all my hopes were blighted. I could get no further. I never tried for work in London, for I believe there are no cotton factories in it; besides, I wanted to see life. I begged, and slept in the unions. I got acquainted with plenty of boys like myself. We met at the casual wards, both in London and the country. I have now been five years at this life. We were merry enough in the wards, we boys, singing and telling stories. Songs such as "Paul Jones" was liked, while some sung very blackguard songs; but I never got hold of such songs, though I have sold lots of songs in Essex. Some told long stories, very interesting; some were not fit to be heard; but they made one laugh sometimes. I've read "Jack Sheppard" through, in three volumes; and I used to tell stories out of that sometimes. We all told in our turns. We generally began – "Once upon a time, and a very good time it was, though it was neither in your time, nor my time, nor nobody else's time." The best man in the story is always called Jack.'

At my request, this youth told me a long story, and told it very readily, as if by rote. I give it for its peculiarity, as it is extravagant enough, without humour.

'A farmer hired Jack, and instructed him over-night. Jack was to do what he was required, or lose his head. "Now, Jack," said the farmer [I give the conclusion in the boy's words,], "what's my name?" "Master, to be sure," says Jack. "No," said he, "you must call me Tom Per Cent." He showed his bed next, and asked, "What's this, Jack?" "Why, the bed," said Jack. "No, you must call that He's of Degree." And so he bid Jack call his leather breeches "forty cracks"; the cat "white-faced Simeon"; the fire "hot coleman"; the pump the "resurrection"; and the haystack the "little cock-a-mountain". Jack was to remember these names or lose his head. At night the cat got under the grate, and burned herself, and hot cinder struck her fur, and she ran under the haystack and set it on fire. Jack ran up-stairs to his master, and said:

'Tom Per Cent, arise out of he's of degree,
Put on your forty cracks, come down and see:
For the little white-faced Simeon
Has run away with hot coleman
Under the little cock-a-mountain,
And without the aid of the resurrection
We shall be damned and burnt to death.'

So Jack remembered his lesson, and saved his head. That's the end. Blackguard stories were often told about women. There was plenty told, too, about Dick Turpin, Sixteen-string Jack, Oxford Blue, and such as them; as well as about Jack Sheppard; about Bamfylde Moore Carew, too, and his disguises. We very often had fighting and quarrelling among ourselves. Once, at Birmingham, we smashed all the windows, and did all the damage we could. I can't tell exactly why it was done, but we must all take part in it, or we should be marked. I believe some did it to get into prison, they were so badly off. They piled up the rugs; there was no straw; and some put their clothes on the rugs, and then the heap was set fire to. There was no fire, and no light, but somebody had a box of lucifers. We were all nearly suffocated before the people of the place could get to us. Seventeen of us had a month a-piece for it: I was one. The rugs were dirty and filthy, and not fit for any Christian to sleep under, and so I took part in the burning, as I thought it would cause something better. I've known wild Irishmen get into the wards with knives and sticks hidden about their persons, to be ready for a fight. I met two young men in Essex who had been well off – very well, – but they liked a tramper's life. Each had his young woman with him, living as man and wife. They often change their young women; but I never did travel with one, or keep company with any more than twelve hours or so. There used to be great numbers of girls in the casual wards in London. Any young man travelling the country could get a mate among them, and can get mates – partners they're often called – still. Some of them are very pretty indeed; but among them are some horrid ugly – the most are ugly; bad expressions and coarse faces, and lame, and disgusting to the eye. It was disgusting, too, to hear them in their own company; that is, among such as themselves; – beggars, you know. Almost every word was an oath, and every blackguard word was said plain out. I think the pretty ones were worst. Very few have children. I knew two who had. One was seventeen, and her child was nine months old; the other was twenty-one, and her child was eighteen months. They were very good to their children. I've heard of some having children, and saying they couldn't guess at the fathers of them, but I never met with any such myself. I didn't often hear them quarrel – I mean the young men and young women that went out as partners – in the lodging-houses. Some boys of fifteen have their young women as partners, but with young boys older women are generally partners – women about twenty. They always pass as man and wife. All beggar-girls are bad, I believe. I never heard but of one that was considered virtuous, and she was always reading a prayer-book and a testament in her lodging-house. The last time I saw her was at Cambridge. She is about thirty, and has traces of beauty left. The boys used to laugh at her, and say, "Oh! how virtuous and righteous we are! but you get your living by it." I never knew her to get anything by it. I don't see how she could, for she said nothing about her being righteous when she was begging about, I believe. If it wasn't for the casual wards, I couldn't get about. If two partners goes to the same union, they have to be parted at night, and join again the morning. Some of the young women are very dirty, but some's as clean. A few, I think, can read and write. Some boasts of their wickedness, and others tell them in derision it's wrong to do that, and then a quarrel rages in the lodging-house. I liked a roving life, at first, being my own master. I was fond of going to plays, and such-like, when I got money; but now I'm getting tired of it, and wish for something else. I have tried for work at cotton factories in Lancashire and Yorkshire, but never could get any. I've been all over the country. I'm sure I could settle now. I couldn't have done that two years ago, the roving spirit was so strong upon me, and the company I kept got a strong hold on me. Two winters back, there was a regular gang of us boys in London. After sleeping at a union, we would fix where to meet at night to get into another union to sleep. There were thirty of us that way, all boys; besides forty young men, and thirty young women. Sometimes we walked the streets all night. We didn't rob, at least I never saw any robbing. We had pleasure in chaffing the policemen, and some of us got taken up. I always escaped. We got broken up in time, – some's dead, some's gone to sea, some into the country, some home, and some lagged. Among them were many lads very expert in reading, writing, and arithmetic. One young man – he was only twenty-five – could speak several languages: he had been to sea. He was then begging, though a strong young man. I suppose he liked that life: some soon got tired of it. I often have suffered from cold and hunger. I never made more than 3d. a day in money, take the year round, by begging; some make more than 6d.: but then, I've had meat and bread given besides. I say nothing when I beg, but that I am a poor boy out of work and starving. I never stole anything in my life. I've often been asked to do so by my mates. I never would. The young women steal the most. I know, least, I did know, two that kept young men, their partners, going about the country with them, chiefly by their stealing. Some do so by their prostitution. Those that go as partners are all prostitutes. There is a great deal of sickness among the young men and women, but I never was ill these last seven years. Fevers, colds, and venereal diseases, are very common.'

The last statement I took was that of a boy of thirteen. I can hardly say that he was clothed at all. He had no shirt, and no waistcoat; all his neck and a great part of his chest being bare. A ragged cloth jacket hung about him, and was tied, so as to keep it together, with bits of tape. What he had wrapped round for trousers did not cover one of his legs, while one of his thighs was bare. He wore two old shoes; one tied to his foot with an old ribbon, the other a woman's old boot. He had an old cloth cap. His features were distorted somewhat, through being swollen with the cold. 'I was born,' he said, 'at a place called Hadley, in Kent. My father died when I was three days old, I've heard my mother say. He was married to her, I believe, but I don't know what he was. She had only me. My mother went about begging, sometimes taking me with her; at other times she left me at the lodging-house in Hadley. She went in the country, round about Tunbridge and there, begging. Sometimes she had a day's work. We had plenty to eat then, but I haven't had much lately. My mother died at Hadley a year ago. I didn't know how she was buried. She was ill a long time, and I was out begging; for she sent me out to beg for myself a good while before that, and when I got back to the lodging-house they told me she was dead. I had sixpence in my pocket, but I couldn't help crying to think I'd lost my mother. I cry about it still. I didn't wait to see her buried, but I started on my own account. I met two navvies in Bromley, and they paid my first night's lodging; and there was a man passing, going to London with potatoes, and the navvies gave the man a pot of beer to take me up to London in the van, and they went that way with me. I came to London to beg, thinking I could get more there than anywhere else, hearing that London was such a good place. I begged; but sometimes wouldn't get a farthing in a day; often walking about the streets all night. I have been begging about all the time till now. I am very weak – starving to death. I never stole anything: I always kept my hands to myself. A boy wanted me to go with him to pick a gentleman's pocket. We was mates for two days, and then he asked me to go picking pockets; but I wouldn't. I know it's wrong, though I can neither read nor write. The boy asked me to do it to get into prison, as that would be better than the streets. He picked pockets to get into prison. He was starving about the streets like me. I never slept in a bed since I've been in London: I am sure I haven't: I generally slept under the dry arches in West-street, where they're building houses – I mean the arches for the cellars. I begged chiefly from the Jews about Petticoat-lane, for they all give away bread that their children leave – pieces of crust, and such-like. I would do anything to be out of this misery.'

Increase and Decrease of Number of Applicants
to Casual Wards of London Workhouses

[pp. 402–6] The vagrant applying for shelter is admitted at all times of the day and night. He applies at the gate, he has his name entered in the vagrant book, and he is then supplied with six ounces of bread and one ounce of cheese. As the admission generally takes place in the evening, no work is required of them until the following morning. At one time every vagrant was searched and bathed, but in the cold season of the year the bathing is discontinued; neither are they searched unless there are grounds for suspecting that they have property secreted upon them. The males are conducted to the ward allotted to them, and the females to their ward. These wards consist each of a large chamber, in which are arranged two large guard-beds, or inclined boards, similar to those used in soldiers' guard-rooms; between these there is a passage from one end of the chamber to the other. The boards are strewn with straw, so that, on entering the place in the daytime, it has the appearance of a well-kept stable. All persons are supplied with two, and in the cold season with three, rugs to cover them. These rugs are daily placed in a fumigating oven, so as to decompose all infectious matter. Formerly beds were supplied in place of the straw, but the habitual vagrants used to amuse themselves with cutting up the mattresses, and strewing the flock all over the place; the blankets and rugs they tore into shreds, and wound them round their legs, under their trousers. The windows of the casual ward are protected on the inside with a strong guard, similar to those seen in the neighbourhood of racket-grounds. No lights are allowed in the casual ward, so that they are expected to retire to rest immediately on their entrance, and this they invariably are glad to do. In the morning they are let out at eight in the winter, and seven in the summer. And then another six ounces of bread and one ounce of cheese is given to them, and they are discharged. In return for this, three hours' labour at the hand corn-mill was formerly exacted; but now the numbers are so few, and the out-door paupers so numerous, and so different from the class of vagrants, that the latter are allowed to go on their road immediately the doors of the casual ward are opened. The labour formerly exacted was not in any way remunerative. In the three hours that they were at work, it is supposed that the value of each man's labour could not be expressed in any coin of the realm. The work was demanded as a test of destitution and industry, and not as a matter of compensation. If the vagrants were very young, they were put to oakum-picking instead of the hand-mill. The women were very rarely

employed at any time, because there was no suitable place in the
union for them to pick oakum, and the master was unwilling to allow
them, on account of their bad and immoral characters, as well as
their filthy habits, to communicate with the other inmates. The female
vagrants generally consist of prostitutes of the lowest and most miserable kind. They are mostly young girls, who have sunk into a state of dirt,
disease, and almost nudity. There are few of them above twenty years of
age, and they appear to have commenced their career of vice frequently
as early as ten or twelve years old. They mostly are found in the company
of mere boys.

The above descriptions apply rather to the state of the vagrants some
two or three years back, than to things as they exist at present. In the year
1837, a correspondence took place between the Commissioners of Police
and the Commissioners of the Poor-law, in which the latter declare that
'if a person state that he has no food, and that he is destitute, or otherwise
express or signify that he is in danger of perishing unless relief be given
to him, then any officer charged with the administration of relief is bound,
unless he have presented to him some reasonable evidence to rebut such
statement, to give relief to such destitute person in the mode prescribed
by law.' The Poor-law Commissioners further declare in the same document, that they will feel it their duty to make the officers responsible in
their situations for any serious neglect to give prompt and adequate relief
in any case of real destitution and emergency. The consequence of this
declaration was, that Poor-law officers appeared to feel themselves bound
to admit all vagrants upon their mere statements of destitution, whereas
before that time parties were admitted into the casual wards either by
tickets from the ratepayers, or else according to the discretion of the
master. Whether or not the masters imagined that they were compelled
to admit every applicant from that period my informant cannot say, but
it is certain that after the date of that letter vagrancy began to increase
throughout the country; at first gradually, but after a few years with a
most enormous rapidity; so that in 1848, it appeared from the Poor-law
Report on vagrancy (presented to both Houses of Parliament in that year)
that the number of vagrants had increased to upwards of 16,000. The rate
of increase for the three years previous to that period is exhibited in the
following table:

*Summary of the number of Vagrants in Unions and Places under Local Acts,
in England and Wales, at different periods, as appears from the Returns which
follow:*

Average number relieved in one night in 603 Unions, &c., in the
    week ending 20th December, 1845   1,791
Average number relieved in one night in 603 Unions, &c., in the
    week ending 19th December, 1846   2,224
Average number relieved in one night in 596 Unions, &c., in the
    week ending 18th December, 1847   4,508
Total number relieved, whether in or out of the workhouse in
    626 Unions, &c., on the 25th March, 1848   16,086

Matters had reached this crisis, when the late Mr C. Buller, President
of the Poor-law Board, issued, in August 1848, a minute, in which – after
stating that the Board had received representations from every part of
England and Wales respecting the continual and rapid increase of
vagrancy – he gives the following instructions to the officers employed in
the administration of the Poor-law:

'With respect to the applicants that will thus come before him, the
relieving officer will have to exercise his judgement as to the truth of their
assertions of destitution, and to ascertain by searching them whether they
possess any means of supplying their own necessities. He will not be likely
to err in judging from their appearance whether they are suffering from
want of food. He will take care that women and children, the old and
infirm, and those who, without absolutely serious disease, present an
enfeebled or sickly appearance, are supplied with necessary food and
shelter. As a general rule, he would be right in refusing relief to able-bodied
and healthy men; though in inclement weather he might afford them
shelter, if really destitute of the means of procuring it for themselves. His
duties would necessarily make him acquainted with the persons of the
habitual vagrants; and to these it would be his duty to refuse relief, except
in case of evident and urgent necessity.

'It was found necessary by the late Poor-law Commissioners at one time
to remind the various unions and their officers of the responsibility which
would be incurred by refusing relief where it was required. The present
state of things renders it necessary that this Board should now impress on
them the grievous mischiefs that must arise, and the responsibilities that
may be incurred, by a too ready distribution of relief to tramps and
vagrants not entitled to it. Boards of guardians and their officers may, in
their attempts to restore a more wise and just system, be subjected to some
obloquy from prejudices that confound poverty with profligacy. They will,
however, be supported by the consciousness of discharging their duty to
those whose funds they have to administer, as well as to the deserving
poor, and of resisting the extension of a most pernicious and formidable

abuse. They may confidently reckon on the support of public opinion, which the present state of things has aroused and enlightened; and those who are responsible to the Poor-law Board may feel assured that, while no instance of neglect or hardship to the poor will be tolerated, they may look to the Board for a candid construction of their acts and motives, and for a hearty and steadfast support of those who shall exert themselves to guard from the grasp of imposture that fund which should be sacred to the necessities of the poor.'

Thus authorised and instructed to exercise their own discretion, rather than trust to the mere statements of the vagrants themselves, the officers immediately proceeded to act upon the suggestions given in the minute above quoted, and the consequence was, that the number of vagrants diminished more rapidly even than they had increased throughout the country. In the case of one union alone – the Wandsworth and Clapham – the following returns will show both how vagrancy was fostered under the one system, and how it has declined under the other:

The number of vagrants admitted into the casual ward of Wandsworth and Clapham was,

	In 1846	6,759
	1847	11,322
	1848	14,675
	1849	3,900

In the quarter ending June 1848, previously to the issuing of the minute, the number admitted was 7,325, whereas, in the quarter ending December, after the minute had been issued, the number fell to 1,035.

The cost of relief for casuals at the same union in the year 1848 was 94l. 2s. 9½d.; in 1849 it was 24l. 10s. 1½d.

The decrease throughout all London has been equally striking. From the returns of the Poor-law Commissioners, as subjoined, I find that the total number of vagrants relieved in the metropolitan unions in 1847–48 was no less than 310,058, whereas, in the year 1848–49, it had decreased to the extent of 166,000 and odd, the number relieved for that year being only 143,064.

During the great prevalence of vagrancy, the cost of the sick was far greater than the expense of relief. In the quarter ending June 1848, no less than 322 casuals were under medical treatment, either in the workhouse of the Wandsworth and Clapham union or at the London Fever Hospital. The whole cost of curing the casual sick in 1848 was near upon 300l., whereas, during 1849 it is computed not to have exceeded 30l.

Another curious fact, illustrative of the effect of an alteration in the administration of the law respecting vagrancy, is to be found in the proportion of vagrants committed for acts of insubordination in the work-houses. In the year 1846, when those who broke the law were committed to Brixton, where the diet was better than that allowed at the workhouse – the cocoa and soup given at the treadmill being especial objects of attraction, and indeed the allowance of food being considerably higher there – the vagrants generally broke the windows, or tore their clothes, or burnt their beds, or refused to work, in order to be committed to the treadmill; and this got to such a height in that year, that no less than 467 persons were charged and convicted with disorderly conduct in the work-house. In the year following, however, an alteration was made in the diet of prisoners sentenced to not more than fourteen days, and the prison of Kingston, of which they had a greater terror, was substituted for that of Brixton, and then the number of committals decreased from 467 to 57; while in 1848, when the number of vagrants was more than double what it had been in 1846, the committals again fell to 37; and in 1849, out of 3,900 admissions, there were only 10 committed for insubordination.

Of the character of the vagrants frequenting the unions in the centre of the metropolis, and the system pursued there, one description will serve as a type of the whole.

At the Holborn workhouse (St Andrew's) there are two casual wards, established just after the passing of the Poor-law Amendment Act in 1834. The men's ward will contain 40, and the women's 20. The wards are underground, but dry, clean, and comfortable. When there was a 'severe pressure from without', as a porter described it to me, as many as 106 men and women have been received on one night, but some were disposed in other parts of the workhouse away from the casual wards.

'Two years and a half ago, "a glut of Irish"' (I give the words of my informant) 'came over and besieged the doors incessantly; and when above a hundred were admitted, as many were remaining outside, and when locked out they lay in the streets stretched along by the almshouse close to the workhouse in Gray's-inn-lane.' I again give the statement (which afterwards was verified) *verbatim*: 'They lay in camps,' he said, 'in their old cloaks, some having brought blankets and rugs with them for the purpose of sleeping out; pots, and kettles, and vessels for cooking when they camp; for in many parts of Ireland they do nothing – I've heard from people that have been there – but wander about; and these visitors to the workhouse behaved just like gipsies, combing their hair and dressing themselves. The girls' heads, some of them, looked as if they were full of caraway seeds – vermin, sir – shocking! I had to sit up all night; and the young women from Ireland – fine-looking young women; some of them finer-looking women than the English, well made and well formed, but uncultivated – seemed happy enough in the casual wards, singing songs all night long, but not too loud. Some would sit up all night washing their clothes, coming to me for water. They had a cup of tea, if they were poorly. They made themselves at home, the children did, as soon as they got inside; they ran about like kittens used to a place. The young women were often full of joke; but I never heard an indecent word from any of them, nor an oath, and I have no doubt, not in the least, that they were chaste and modest. Fine young women, too, sir. I have said, "Pity young women like you should be carrying on this way" (for I felt for them), and they would say, "What can we do? It's better than starving in Ireland, this workhouse is." I used to ask them how they got over, and they often told me their passages were paid, chiefly to Bristol, Liverpool, and Newport, in Monmouthshire. They told me that was done to get rid of them. They told me that they didn't know by whom; but some said, they believed the landlord paid the captain. Some declared they knew it, and that it was done just to get rid of them. Others told me the captain would bring them over for any trifle they had; for he would say, "I shall have to take you back again, and I can charge my price then." The men were uncultivated fellows compared to the younger women. We have had old men with children who could speak English, and the old man and his wife could not speak a word of it. When asked the age of their children (the children were the interpreters), they would open the young creatures' mouths and count their teeth, just as horse-dealers do, and then they would tell the children in Irish what to answer, and the children would answer in English. The old people could never tell their own age. The man would give his name, but his wife would give her maiden name. I would say to an elderly man, "Give me your name." "Dennis Murphy, your honour." Then to his wife, "And your name?" "The widdy Mooney, your honour." "But you're married?" "Sure, then, yes, by Father —." This is the case with them still. Last night we took in a family, and I asked the mother – there was only a woman and three children – her name. "The widdy Callaghan, indeed, then, sir." "But your Christian name?" "The widdy" (widow) was the only answer. It's shocking, sir, what ignorance is, and what their sufferings is. My heart used to ache for the poor creatures, and yet they seemed happy. Habit's a great thing – second nature, even when people's shook. The Irishmen behaved well among themselves; but the English cadgers were jealous of the Irish, and chaffed them, as spoiling their trade – that's what the cadging fellows did. The Irish were quiet, poor things, but they were provoked to quarrel, and many a time I've had to turn the English rips out. The Irish were always very thankful for what they had, if it was only a morsel; the English cadger is never satisfied. I don't mean the decent beat-out man, but the regular cadger, that won't work, and isn't a good beggar, and won't starve, so they steal. Once, now and then, there was some suspicion about the Irish admitted, that they had money, but that was never but in those that had families. It was taken from them, and given back in the morning. They wouldn't have been admitted again if they had any amount. It was a kindness to take their money, or the English rascals would have robbed them. I'm an Englishman, but I speak the truth of my own countrymen, as I do of the Irish. The English we had in the casual wards were generally a bad cadging set, as saucy as could be, particularly men that I knew, from their accent, came from Nottinghamshire. I'd tell one directly. I've heard them, of a night, brag of their dodges – how they'd done through the day – and the best places to get money. They would talk of gentlemen in London. I've often heard them say, —, in Piccadilly, was good; but they seldom mentioned names, only described the houses, especially club-houses in St James's-street. They would tell just where it was in the street, and how many windows there was in it, and the best time to go, and "you're sure of grub," they'd say. Then they'd tell of gentlemen's seats in the country – sure cards. They seldom give names, and, I believe, don't know them, but described the houses and the gentlemen. Some were good for bread and money, some for bread and ale. As to the decent people, we had but few, and I used to be sorry for them when they had to mix with the cadgers; but when the cadgers saw a stranger, they used their slang. I was up to it. I've heard it many a night when I sat up, and they thought I was asleep. I wasn't to be had like the likes o' them. The poor mechanic would sit like a lost man – scared, sir. There might be one deserving character to thirty cadgers. We have had gipsies in the casual wards; but they're not admitted a second time, they steal so. We haven't one Scotch person in a month, or a Welshman, or perhaps two Welshmen, in a month, among the casuals. They come from all counties in England. I've been told by inmates of "the casual", that they had got 2s. 6d. from the relieving officers, particularly in Essex and Suffolk – different unions – to start them to London when the "straw-yards" (the asylums for the houseless) were opened; but there's a many very decent people. How they suffer before they come to that! you can't fancy how much; and so there should be straw-yards in a Christian land – we'll call it a Christian land, sir. There's far more good people in the straw-yards than the casuals; the dodgers is less frequent there, considering the numbers. It's shocking to think a decent mechanic's houseless. When he's beat out, he's like a bird out of a cage; he doesn't know where to go, or how to get a bit – but don't the cadgers! The expense of relieving the people in the casual ward was twopence per head, and the numbers admitted for the last twelve months averaged only twelve nightly.'

ASYLUM FOR THE HOUSELESS POOR

[pp. 417–22]   The only refuge for the houseless now open which is really a home for the homeless, is that in Playhouse-yard, Cripplegate. The doors open into a narrow by-street, and the neighbourhood needs no other announcement that the establishment is open for the reception of the houseless, than the assembly of a crowd of ragged shivering people, certain to be seen on the night of opening, as if they knew by instinct where they might be housed under a warm and comfortable roof. The crowd gathers in Playhouse-yard, and many among them look sad and weary enough. Many of the women carry infants at the breast, and have children by their sides holding by their gowns. The cries of these, and the wrangling of the hungry crowds for their places, is indeed disheartening to hear. The only sounds of merriment come from the errand-boys, as they call themselves, whom even starvation cannot make sorrowful for two hours together. The little struggle that there usually is among the applicants is not for a rush when the doors are opened, but for what they call the 'front rank'. They are made to stand clear of the footpath; and when five o'clock – the hour of admission – comes, an officer of the Refuge steps out, and quietly, by a motion of his hand, or a touch on the shoulder, sends in about 150 men and boys, and about 50 women and girls. He knows the great majority of those who have tickets which entitle them to one or two nights' further lodging (the tickets are generally for three nights), and these are commonly in the foremost rank. The number thus admitted show themselves more or less at home. Some are quiet and abashed; but some proceed briskly, and in a business-like way, to the first process, to wash themselves. This is done in two large vessels, in what may be called the hall or vestibule of the building. A man keeps pumping fresh water into the vessels as fast as that used is drained off, and soap and clean towels are supplied when thought necessary; the clean towels, which are long, and attached to rollers, soon becoming, in truth, exceedingly dirty. I noticed some little contention – whether to show an anxiety to conform to the rules of the Refuge, or to hurry through a disagreeable but inevitable task, or really for the comfort of ablution, I will not pretend to determine – but there was some little contention for the first turn among the young men at the washing. To look down upon them from the main staircase, as I did, was to survey a very motley scene. There they were – the shirtless, the shoeless, the coatless, the unshaven, the uncouth, ay, and the decent and respectable. There were men from every part of the United Kingdom, with a coloured man or two, a few seamen, navigators, agricultural labourers, and artizans. There were no foreigners on the nights that I was there; and in the returns of those admitted there will not be found one Jew. It is possible that Jews may be entered under the heads of 'Germans' or 'Poles' – I mean, foreign Jews; but on my visits I did not see so much as any near approach to the Hebrew physiognomy. To attempt to give an account of anything like a prevailing garb among these men is impossible, unless I described it as rags. As they were washing, or waiting for a wash, there was some stir, and a loud buzz of talk, in which 'the brogue' strongly predominated. There was some little fun, too, as there must be where a crowd of many youths is assembled. One in a ragged, coarse, striped shirt, exclaimed as he shoved along, 'By your leave gentlemen!' with a significant emphasis of his 'gentlemen'. Another man said to his neighbour, 'The bread's fine, Joe; but the sleep, isn't that plummy?' Some few, I say, seemed merry enough, but that is easily accounted for. Their present object was attained, and your real professional vagabond is always happy by that – for a forgetfulness of the past, or an indifference to it, and a recklessness as to the future, are the primary elements of a vagrant's enjoyment. Those who had tickets were of course subjected to no further examination, unless by the surgeon subsequently; but all the new candidates for admission – and the officers kept admitting fresh batches as they were instructed – were not passed before a rigid examination, when a ticket for three nights was given to each fresh applicant. On the right hand, as you enter the building, is the office. The assistant-superintendant sits before a large ledger, in which he enters every name and description. His questions to every fresh candidate are: 'Your name?' 'How old are you?' 'What trade?' 'How do you live (if no trade)?' 'Where did you sleep last night?' 'To what parish do you belong?' In order to answer these questions, each fresh applicant for admission stands before the door of the office, a portion of the upper division of the door being thrown open. Whilst I was present, there was among a portion of the male applicants but little hesitation in answering the inquiries glibly and promptly. Others answered reluctantly. The answers of some of the boys, especially the Irish boys, were curious. 'Where did you sleep last night?' 'Well, then, sir, I sleep walking about the streets all night, and very cowld it was, sir.' Another lad was asked, after he had stated his name and age, how he lived? 'I beg, or do anything,' he answered. 'What's your parish?' 'Ireland.' (Several pronounced their parish to be the 'county Corruk'.) 'Have you a father here?' 'He died before we left Ireland.' 'How did you get here, then?' 'I came with my mother.' 'Well, and where's she?' 'She died after we came to England.' So the child had the streets for a stepmother.

Some of the women were as glib and systematic in their answers as the men and boys. Others were much abashed. Among the glib-tongued women, there seemed no shamefacedness. Some of the women admitted here, however, have acquitted themselves well when provided (through charitable institutions) with situations. The absence of shame which I have remarked upon is the more notable, because these women were questioned by men, with other men standing by. Some of the women were good-looking; and when asked how old they were, they answered at once, and, judging by their appearance, never understated their years. Many I should have pronounced younger than they stated. Vanity, even with silliness and prettiness, does not seem to exist in their utter destitution.

All the regular processes having been observed (and the women have a place for their ablutions after the same fashion as the men), the applicants admitted enter their several wards. The women's ward is at the top of the building. It supplies accommodation, or berths, for 95 women in an apartment 35 yards in length and 6 in width. At one corner of this long chamber, a few steps lead down to what is called 'the nursery', which has 30 berths. Most of these berths may be described as double, and are large enough to accommodate a mother and her children. The children, when I saw them, were gambolling about in some of the berths as merry as children elsewhere, or perhaps merrier, for they were experiencing the unwonted luxuries of warmth and food. The matron can supply these women and their children with gruel at her discretion; and it appeared to be freely given. Some who had children seemed to be the best of all there in point of physiognomy. They had not, generally, the stolid, stupid, indifferent, or shameless look of many of the other women; it was as though the motherly feeling had somewhat humanized them. Some of the better sort of women spoke so low as to be hardly audible. Among them were, indeed, many decent-looking females.

The men's wards are the Chapel Ward (for the better sort of persons), containing 90 berths, one line being ranged 2 berths deep; the Lower Ward, containing 120 berths; the Boys' Ward, containing 60 berths; and the Straw Loft, 40. There is a walk alongside the berths in each ward.

What is called the Boys' Ward is not confined to boys: it used to be so, but they were found so noisy that they could no longer be allowed a separate apartment. They are now scattered through the several wards with the men, the officers arranging them, and varying the arrangements as they consider best. Before there can be any retirement to rest, each man, woman, and child must be examined by a surgeon. Whilst I was present, a young assistant conducted the investigation in a careful, yet kindly and gentlemanly manner. Indeed, I was much struck with the sympathy and gentleness he displayed; and it was evident from the respect of the people, that kindness and consideration are the very qualities to impress and control the class he has to deal with. All afflicted with cutaneous disorders (and there were but five men so afflicted) were lodged apart from the others. Bronchitis and rheumatism are the prevalent disorders, occasioned by their exposure to the weather, and their frequent insufficiency of food. Ninety per cent of them, I was told by Mr Gay, the intelligent surgeon of the establishment, might have coughs at some periods, but of that they thought nothing. Women advanced in pregnancy, and men with any serious (especially any infectious) ailment, are not permitted to sleep in the Refuge; but the institution, if they have been admitted, finds them lodgings elsewhere.

Each person admitted receives in the evening half-a-pound of the best bread. Every child has the same allowance. If a woman be admitted with four children, she receives two half-pounds of bread – a half-pound for every one, no matter if one be at the breast, as is not unfrequently the case. The same quantity of bread is given in the mornings. In the night that I was present 430 were admitted, and consequently (including the evening and morning allowances), 430 lbs. of bread were disposed of. On Sundays, when Divine Service is celebrated by a clergyman of the Church of England, three half-pounds of bread and three ounces of cheese are distributed to each inmate, children and babies included. I witnessed a number of young men eating the bread administered to them. They took it with a keen appetite; nothing was heard among them but the champing of the teeth, as they chewed large mouthfuls of the food.

The berths, both in the men's and women's wards, are on the ground, and divided one from another only by a wooden partition about a foot high; a similar partition is at the head and feet; so that in all the wards it looks as if there were a series of coffins arranged in long catacombs. This burial-like aspect is the more striking when the inmates are all asleep, as they were, with the rarest exceptions, when I walked round at ten o'clock at night. Each sleeper has for covering a large basil (dressed sheep-skin), such as cobblers use for aprons. As they lie in long rows, in the most profound repose, with these dark brown wrappers about them, they present the uniform look and arrangement of a long line of mummies. Each bed in the coffin, or trough-like division, is made of waterproof cloth, stuffed with hay, made so as to be easily cleaned. It is soft and pleasant to the touch. Formerly the beds were plain straw, but the present plan has been in use for seven years. In this Refuge only three men have died since it was established, thirty years ago. One fell dead at the sink-stone while washing himself; the other two were found dead in their berths during the prevalence of the cholera.

Every part of the building was scrupulously clean. On the first night of the opening, the matron selects from the women who have sought an asylum there, three, who are engaged for the season to do the household work. This is done during the day when the inmates are absent. All must leave by eight in the morning, the doors being open for their departure at five, in case any wish to quit early – as some do for the chance of a job at Covent-garden, Farringdon, or any of the early markets. The three women-helpers receive 7s. a week each, the half of that sum being paid them in money every Saturday, and the other half being retained and given to each of them, in a round sum, at the closing of the Refuge. The premises in which this accommodation to the houseless is now supplied were formerly a hat manufactory on a large scale; but the lath and plaster of the ceilings, and the partitions, have been removed, so that what was a suite of apartments on one floor is now a long ward. The rafters of the ceilings are minutely whitewashed, as are the upright beams used in the construction of the several rooms before the place was applied to its present charitable end. Those now are in the nature of pillars, and add to the catacomb-like aspect that I have spoken of. In different parts of each ward are very large grates, in which bright fires are kept glowing and crackling; and as these are lighted some time before the hour of opening, the place has a warmth and cosiness which must be very grateful to those who have encountered the cold air all the day, and perhaps all the night before.

In order to arrive at a correct estimate as to the number of the really poor and houseless who availed themselves of the establishment (to afford nightly shelter to whom the refuge was originally instituted by the bene-volent founder, Mr Hick, the City mace-bearer) I consulted with the superintendent as to the class of persons he found most generally seeking refuge there. These were – among the men – mostly labourers out of work – agricultural, railway, and dock; discharged artisans, chiefly carpenters and painters; sailors, either cast away or without their registry tickets; broken-down tradesmen, clerks, shopmen, and errand-boys, who either through illness or misfortune had been deprived of their situations; and, above all, Irish immigrants, who had been starved out of their own country. These he considered the really deserving portion of the inmates for whom the institution was designed. Among the females, the better and largest class of poor were needlewomen, servants, charwomen, garden-women, sellers of laces in the street, and occasionally a beggar-woman. Under his guidance I selected such as appeared the most meritorious among the classes he had enumerated, and now subjoin the statements of a portion of the number.

The first of the houseless that I saw was a railway navigator. He was a fine, stoutly-built fellow, with a fresh-coloured open countenance, and flaxen hair – indeed, altogether a splendid specimen of the Saxon labourer. He was habited in a short blue smockfrock, yellow in parts with clay, and he wore the heavy high lace-up boots, so characteristic of the tribe. These were burst, and almost soleless with long wear.

The poor fellow told the old story of the labourer compelled to squander the earnings at the public-house of his master:

'I have been a navvy for about eighteen years. The first work that I done was on the Manchester and Liverpool. I was a lad then. I used to grease the railway waggons, and got about 1s. 6d. a day. There we had a tommy-shop, and we had to go there to get our bit of victuals, and they used to charge us an extra price. The next place I had after that was on the London and Brummagem. There I went as horse-driver, and had 2s. 6d. a day. Things was dear then, and at the tommy-shop they was much dearer; for there was tommy-shops on every line then; and indeed every contractor and sub-contractor had his shop that he forced his men to deal at, or else he wouldn't have them in his employ. At the tommy-shop we was charged half as much again as we should have had to pay elsewhere; and it's the same now, wherever these tommy-shops is. What the contractors, you see, can't make out of the company, they fleeces out of the men. Well, sir, I worked on that line through all the different contracts till it was finished: sometimes I was digging, sometimes shovelling. I was mostly at work at open cuttings. All this time I was getting from 2s. 6d. to 3s. and 3s. 6d. a day; that was the top price; and if I'd had the ready-money to lay out myself, I could have done pretty well, and maybe have put a penny or two by against a rainy day: but the tommy-shop and the lodging-house took it all out of us. You see, the tommy-shop found us in beer, and they would let us drink away all our earnings there if we pleased, and when pay-time came we should have nothing to take. If we didn't eat and drink at the tommy-shop we should have no work. Of an evening, we went to the tommy-shop after the drink, and they'd keep drawing beer for us there as long as we'd have anything coming to us next pay-day (we were paid every fortnight, and sometimes every month), and when we had drunk away all that would be coming to us, why they'd turn us out. The contractor, who keeps these tommy-shops, is generally a gentleman, a man of great property, who takes some four, five, or seven lengths to do. Well, with such goings on, in course there wasn't no chance in the world for us to save a halfpenny. We had a sick fund among ourselves, but our masters never cared nothing about us further than what they could get out of us at their tommy-shops. They were never satisfied if a man didn't spend all his money with them; if we had a penny to take at the month's end, they didn't like it; and now the half of us has to walk about and starve, or beg, or go to the union. After I left the Brummagem line, I went on to the Great Western. I went to work at Maidenhead. There it was on the same system, and on the same rules – the poor man being fleeced and made drunk by his master. Sometimes the contractor would lot the work out to some sub-contractor, and he, after the men had worked for a month, would run away, and we should never see the colour of his money. After the Great Western, I went into Lancashire, on the Manchester and Oldham branch. I started there to work at nights, and there I worked a month for the contractors, when they went bankrupt, and we never received a farthing but what we had got out of the tommy-shop. Well, I came away from there, and got on to the London and Brighton, and I worked all up and down that, saving the tunnels; and it was the same there – the tommy-shop and imposition was wherever we went. Well, from there I went on to the London and Dover. It was monthly payments on that. There, too, I worked for a month, when the sub-contractor runned away with all the men's money – 900l., sir, it were calculated. After that another party took it, and it was the same all the way up and down – the tommy-shop and beer as much as we liked, on credit. Then I went on to the London and Cambridge, and there it was the same story over and over again. Just about this time, railway work began to get slack, and then farmers' work was slack too; and you see that made things worse for the navvies, for all came to look for employment on the railroads. This is about seven years ago. After that some more fresh lines started throughout Lancashire and Yorkshire, and trade being bad in them parts, all the weavers applied for work on the railways, and the regular navvies had a hard time of it then. But we managed to get on somehow – kept lingering

VOLUME THREE

on – till about three years agone, when trade got a little bit better. That
was about the time when things was very dear, and our wages was rose
to 3s. 6d. a day.: they'd been only 2s. 6d. and 3s. before that; and we did
much better when our pay was increased, because we had the ready-
money then, and there was no tommy-shops that summer, for the company wouldn't have them on that line. At the end of that year the work
was all stopped, on account of the Chartist rising, and then there was
hundreds of men walking about begging their bread from door to door,
with nothing to do. After this, (that's two years ago, the back end of this
year,) I went to work on the London and York. Here we had only 2s. 9d.
a day. and we had only four days' work in the week to do besides; and
then there was a tommy-shop, where we were forced to get our victuals
and drink: so you see we were very bad off then. I stopped on this line (for
work was very scarce, and I thought myself lucky to have any) till last
spring. Then all the work on it stopped, and I dare say 2,000 men were
thrown out of employ in one day. They were all starving, the heap of them,
or next door to it. I went away from there over to the Brummagem and
Beechley branch line. But there I found things almost as bad as what I left
before. Big, strong, able-bodied men were working for 1s. 8d. a day, and
from that to 2s.: that was the top price; for wages had come down, you
see, about one-half, and little or no work to do at that price; and tommy-
shop and beer, sir, as before, out of the little we did get. The great cause
of our wages being cut down was through the work being so slack in the
country; everybody was flocking to them parts for employment, and the
contractors, seeing a quantity of men walking backwards and forwards,
dropped the wages: if one man wouldn't work at the price, there was
hundreds ready to do it. Besides, provisions was very cheap, and the
contractors knew we could live on less, and do their work quite as well.
Whenever provisions goes down our wages does, too; but when they goes
up, the contractors is very slow in rising them. You see, when they find
so many men walking about without work, the masters have got the
chance of the poor man. Three year agone this last winter – I think it was
'46 – provisions was high and wages was good; and in the summer of the
very same year, food got cheap again, and our wages dropped from 3s.
6d. to 3s. and 2s. 9d. The fall in our wages took place immediately the food
got cheaper. The contractors said, as we could live for less, we must do
the work for less. I left the Brummagem and Beechley line, about two
months before the Christmas before last, and then I came to Copenhagen-
fields, on the London and York – the London end, sir; and there I was till
last March, when we were all paid off, about 600 on us; and I went back

to Barnet, and there I worked till the last seven weeks, and had 2s. 9d.
a day for what, four years ago, I had 3s. 6d. for; and I could only have
three or four days' work in the week then. Whilst I was there, I hurted
my leg, and was laid up a month. I lived all that time on charity; on what
the chaps would come and give me. One would give a shilling, another
sixpence, another a shilling, just as they could spare it; and poorly they
could do that, God knows! I couldn't declare on to the sick fund, because
I hadn't no bones broken. Well, when I come to look for work, and that's
three weeks agone, when I could get about again, the work was all
stopped, and I couldn't get none to do. Then I come to London, and I've
looked all about for a job, and I can't find nothing to do. I went to a lodging-
house in the Borough, and I sold all my things – shovel and grafting-tool
and all, to have a meal of food. When all my things was gone, I didn't know
where to go. One of my mates told me of this Refuge, and I have been here
two nights. All that I have had to eat since then is the bread night and
morning they gives us here. This will be the last night I shall have to stop
here, and after that I don't know what I shall do. There's no railway work
– that is, there's none to speak of, seeing the thousands of men that's
walking about with nothing to do, and not knowing where to lay their
heads. If I could get any interest, I should like to go away as an emigrant.
I shouldn't like to be sent out of my native country as a rogue and a
vagabone; but I'm tired of stopping here and if I can't get away, why I must
go home and go to the parish, and it's hard for a young man that's willing
and able like me to work, and be forced to want because he can't get it.
I know there is thousands – thousands, sir, like I am – I know there is,
in the very same condition as I am at this moment: yes, I know there is.'
[This he said with a very great feeling and emphasis.] 'We are all starving.
We are all willing to work, but it ain't to be had. This country is getting
very bad for labour; it's so overrun with Irish that the Englishman hasn't
a chance in his own land to live. Ever since I was nine years old I've got
my own living, but now I'm dead beat, though I'm only twenty-eight next
August.'

The next man to whom I spoke was tall and hale-looking, except that
his features were pinched, and his eyes had a dull lack-lustre look,
common to men suffering from cold and hunger. His dress was a coarse
jacket, fustian trousers, and coarse, hard-worn shoes. He spoke without
any very provincial accent.

'I am now forty-eight, and have been a farm-labourer all my life. I am
a single man. When I was a boy of twelve, I was put to dig, or see after
the birds, or break clods, or anything, on a farm at Croland, in Lancashire.

I had very little school before that, and can neither read nor write. I was then living with my parents, poor people, who worked on the land whenever they could get a day's work. We had to live very hard, but at hay and harvest times we had meat, and lived better. I had 3s. a week as a boy. When I grew up to fourteen I left home. I thought my father didn't use me well: perhaps it was my own fault. I might have been a bad boy; but he was severe when he did begin with me, though he was generally quiet. When his passion was up, there was no bearing it. Anyhow, I started into the world at fourteen to do the best I could for myself – to make my fortune if I could. Since then, I have had work in all sorts of counties; Midland counties, principally. When a boy, I got employment readily enough at bird-scaring, or hay-making; but I soon grew up, and took a man's place very early, and I could then do any kind of farmer's work, except ploughing or seeding. They have men on purpose for that. Farm work was far better in my younger days than it is now. For a week, when hired by the day, I never get more than 15s., regular work. For taken work (by the job), I have made as much as 42s. in a week; that is, in reaping and mowing, when I could drop on such jobs in a difficult season, when the weather was uncertain. I talk of good times. The last good job I had was three years ago, come next summer. Now I should be glad to get 9s. a week, constant work: anything but what I'm doing now. As I went about from place to place, working for farmers, I generally lodged at the shepherds' houses, or at some labourer's. I never was in a lodging-house when I was in work, only when money runs low one must have shelter. At some lodging-houses I've had a good feather-bed; others of them are bad enough: the best, I think, are in Norfolk. I have saved a bit of money several times – indeed, year after year, until the last three or four years; but what I saved in the summer, went in the winter. In some summers, I could save nothing. It's how the season comes. I never cared for drink. I've done middling till these last two seasons. My health was good, to be sure; but when a man's in health his appetite is good also; and when I'm at regular work I don't eat half so much as when I'm knocking about idle, and get hold of a meal. I often have to make up for three or four days then. The last job I had was six weeks before Christmas, at Boston, in Lincolnshire. I couldn't make 1s. 6d. a day on account of the weather. I had 13s., however, to start with, and I went on the road, not standing for a straight road, but going where I heard there was a chance of a job, up or down anywhere, here or there, but there was always the same answer, "Nobody wanted – no work for their own constant men." I was so beat out as soon as my money was done – and it lasted ten days – that I parted with my things one by one. First my waist-coat, then my stockings (three pair of them), then three shirts. I got 2s. 4d. for three shirts, and 6d. a pair for my stockings. My clothes were done, and I parted with my pocket-knife for 2d., and with my 'bacco-box for 1½d. After I left Boston, I got into Leicestershire, and was at Cambridge, and Wisbeach, and Lynn, and Norwich; and I heard of a job among brickmakers at Low Easthrop, in Suffolk, but it was no go. The weather was against it, too. It was when the snow set in. And then I thought I would come to London, as God in his goodness might send me something to do. I never meant anything slinking. I'm only happy when I'm at work, but here I am destitute. Some days as I walked up I had nothing to eat. At others I got half-pennies or pennies from men like myself that I saw at work. I've given shillings away that way myself at times. Sometimes I had to take to the road, but I'm a very poor beggar. When I got to London I was a stranger, and lodged here the first night – that's a week ago. A policeman sent me here. I've tried every day to get work – labouring-work for builders, or about manure-carts, or anything like that, as there's no farming in London, but got none; so but for this place I had starved. When this place is closed I must tramp into the country. There are very many farm-labourers now going from farm to farm, and town to town, to seek work, more than ever I saw before. I don't know that the regular farm-workmen come so much to London. As I travelled up from Suffolk I lay rough often enough. I got into stables, or any places. Such places as this save many a man's life. It's saved mine, for I might have been found dead in the street, as I didn't know where to go.'

This man appeared to me to be a very decent character.

[pp. 427–9] There is a world of wisdom to be learnt at the Asylum for the Houseless Poor. Those who wish to be taught in this, the severest school of all, should pay a visit to Playhouse-yard, and see the homeless crowds gathered about the Asylum, waiting for the first opening of the doors, with their bare feet, blue and ulcerous with the cold, resting for hours on the ice and snow in the streets, and the bleak stinging wind blowing through their rags. To hear the cries of the hungry, shivering children, and the wrangling of the greedy men, scrambling for a bed and a pound of dry bread, is a thing to haunt one for life. There are 400 and odd creatures utterly destitute – mothers with infants at their breasts – fathers with boys holding by their side – the friendless – the penniless – the shirtless, shoeless, breadless, homeless; in a word, the very poorest of this the very richest city in the world.

The Asylum for the Houseless is the confluence of the many tides of poverty that, at this period of the year, flow towards the metropolis. It should be remembered that there are certain callings, which yield a subsistence to those who pursue them only at particular seasons. Brick-makers, agricultural labourers, garden-women, and many such vocations, are labours that admit of being performed only in the summer, when, indeed, the labourer has the fewest wants to satisfy. The privations of such classes, then, come at a period when even the elements conspire to make their destitution more terrible. Hence, restless with want, they wander in hordes across the land, making, in vain hope, for London, as the great emporium of wealth – the market of the world. But London is as overstocked with hands as every other nook and corner of the country. And then the poor creatures, far away from home and friends, find at last to their cost, that the very privations they were flying from pursue them here with a tenfold severity. I do not pretend to say that all found within the walls of these asylums are such as I have described; many, I know, trade upon the sympathy of those who would ease the sufferings of the destitute labourers, and they make their appearance in the metropolis at this especial season. Winter is the beggar's harvest. That there are hundreds of professional vagabonds drawn to London at such a time, I am well aware; but with them come the unemployed workmen. We must not, therefore, confound one with the other, nor let our indignation at the vagabond who will not work, check our commiseration for the labourer or artisan who cannot get work to do.

A homeless painter gave me the following statement. His appearance presented nothing remarkable. It was merely that of the poor artisan. There was nothing dirty or squalid about him:

'I was brought up a painter,' he said, 'and I am now 27. I served my apprenticeship in Yorkshire, and stayed two years after my term was out with the same master. I then worked in Liverpool, earning but little through illness, and working on and off as my health permitted. I got married in Liverpool, and went with my wife to Londonderry, in Ireland, of which place she was a native. There she died of the cholera in 1847. I was very ill with diarrhoea myself. We lived with her friends, but I got work, though wages are very low there. I never earned more than 2s. 6d. a day there. I have earned 5s. 6d. a day in Liverpool, but in Londonderry provisions are very cheap – the best meat at 4d. a pound. It was an advantage to me being an Englishman. English workmen seem to be preferred in Ireland, so far as I can tell, and I have worked in Belfast and Coleraine, and a short time in Dublin, as well as in Londonderry. I came back to Liverpool early in 1848, and got work, but was again greatly distressed through sickness. I then had to travel the country again, getting a little employment at Hemel Hempstead, and St Alban's, and other places about, for I aimed at London, and at last I got to London. That was in November, 1848. When in the country I was forced to part with my clothes. I had a beautiful suit of black among them. I very seldom got even a trifle from the painters in the country towns; sometimes 2d. or 3d. from a master. In London I could get no work, and my shirts and my flannel-shirts went to keep me. I stayed about a month, and having nothing left, was obliged to start for the country. I got a job at Luton, and at a few other places. Wages are very low. I was always a temperate man. Many a time I have never tasted drink for a week together, and this when I had money in my pocket, for I had 30l. when I got married. I have, too, the character of being a good workman. I returned to London again three weeks back, but could find no work. I had again to part with any odd things I had. The last I parted with was my stopping-knife and diamond, for I can work as a glazier and plumber; country painters often can – I mean those appren-ticed in the country. I have no clothes but what I have on. For the last ten days, I declare solemnly, I have had nothing but what I picked up in the streets. I picked up crusts that I saw in the streets, put out on the steps by the mistresses of the houses for the poor like myself. I got so weak and ill that I had to go to King's College Hospital, and they gave me medicine which did me good. I often had to walk the streets all night. I was so perished I could hardly move my limbs. I never asked charity, I can't; but I could have eaten anything. I longed for the fried fish I saw; yes, I was ravenous for that, and such-like, though I couldn't have touched it when I had money, and was middling well off. Things are so different in the country that I couldn't fancy such meat. I was brought to that pitch, I had the greatest mind to steal something to get into prison, where, at any rate, I said to myself, I shall have some food and shelter. I didn't – I thought better of it. I hoped something might turn up next day; besides, it might have got into the papers, and my friends might have seen it, and I should have felt I disgraced them, or that they would think so, because they couldn't know my temptations and my sufferings. When out all night, I used to get shelter, if I could, about Hungerford Market, among the straw. The cold made me almost dead with sleep; and when obliged to move, I couldn't walk at first, I could only crawl along. One night I had a penny given me, all I had gotten in five bitter nights in the streets. For that penny I got half a pint of coffee; it made me sick, my stomach was so weak. On Tuesday I asked a policeman if he couldn't recommend me to some workhouse, and he told me to come here, and I was admitted, and was very thankful to get under shelter.'

[pp. 433–7] Of the class of distressed tradesmen seeking shelter at this asylum, the two following may be taken as fair types. One was a bankrupt linendraper, and appeared in a most destitute state. When he spoke of his children, his eyes flooded with tears:

'I have been in business in the linendrapery line – that's five years ago. I had about 600l. worth of stock at first starting, and used to take about 65l. every week. My establishment was in a country village in Essex. I went on medium well for the first two or three years, but the alteration of the poor-laws and the reduction of the agricultural labourers' wages destroyed my business. My customers were almost all among the working classes. I had dealings with a few farmers, of whom I took butter, and cheese, and eggs, in exchange for my goods. When the poor-laws were altered, the out-door relief was stopped, and the paupers compelled to go inside the house. Before that, a good part of the money given to the poor used to be expended at my shop. The overseers used to have tickets for flannels, blankets, and shirtings, and other goods; with these they used to send the paupers to my house. I used to take full 8l. or 10l. a week in this manner; so that when the poor-laws were altered, and the previous system discontinued, I suffered materially. Besides, the wages of the agricultural labourers being lowered, left them less money to lay out with me. On a market-day they were my chief customers. I would trust them one week under the other, and give them credit for 7s. or 10s., if they wanted it. After their wages came down, they hadn't the means of laying out a sixpence with me; and where I had been taking 65l. a week, my receipts dwindled to 30l. I had been in the habit of keeping two shopmen before, but after the reduction I was obliged to come down to one. Then the competition of the large houses in other towns was more than I could stand against. Having a larger capital, they could buy cheaper, and afford to take a less profit, and so of course they could sell much cheaper than I could. Then, to try and keep pace with my neighbours, I endeavoured to extend my capital by means of accommodation bills, but the interest I had to pay on these was so large, and my profits so little, that it soon became impossible for me to meet the claims upon me. I was made a bankrupt. My debts at the time were 300l. This is about six years ago. After that I took a public-house. Some property was left me. I came into about 1,000l.; part of this went to my creditors, and I superseded my bankruptcy. With the rest I determined upon starting in the publican line. I kept at this for about ten months, but I could do nothing with it. There was no custom to the house. I had been deceived into taking it. By the time I got out of it all my money was gone. After that I got a job as a referee at the time of the railway mania, and when that was over, I got appointed as a policeman on the Eastern Union line. There I remained two years and upwards, but then they began reducing their establishment, both in men and in wages. I was among the men who were turned off. Since that time, which is now two years this Christmas, I have had no constant employment. Occasionally I have got a little law-writing to do; sometimes I have got a job as under-waiter at a tavern. After I left the waiter's place, I got to be very badly off. I had a decent suit of clothes to my back up to that time, but then I became so reduced, I was obliged to go and live in a low lodging-house in Whitechapel. I was enabled to get along somehow; I know many friends, and they gave me a little money now and then. But at last I had exhausted these. I could get nothing to do of any kind. I have been to Shoreditch station to try to pick up a few pence at carrying parcels, but there were so many there that I could not get a crust that way. I was obliged to pawn garment after garment to pay for my food and lodging; and when they were all gone, I was wholly destitute. I couldn't even raise two-pence for a night's lodging, so I came here and asked for a ticket. My wife is dead. I have three children; but I would rather you would not say anything about them, if you please.'

I assured the man that his name should not be printed, and he then consented to his children being mentioned.

'The age of my eldest child is fourteen, and my youngest nine. They do not know of the destitution of their father. They are staying with one of my relations, who has supported them since my failure. I wouldn't have them know of my state on any account. None of my family are aware of my misery. My eldest child is a girl, and it would break her heart to know where I am, and see the state of distress I am in. My boy, I think, would never get over it. He is eleven years old. I have tried to get work at carrying placard-boards about, but I can't. My clothes are now too bad for me to do anything else. I write a good hand, and would do anything, I don't care what, to earn a few pence. I can get a good character from every place I have been in.'

The other tradesman's story was as follows:

'I am now thirty-three, and am acquainted with the grocery trade, both as master and assistant. I served a five-years' apprenticeship in a town in Berkshire. The very late hours and the constant confinement made me feel my apprenticeship a state of slavery. The other apprentices used to say they felt it so likewise. During my apprenticeship I consider that I never learnt my trade properly. I knew as much at the year's end as at the five years' end. My father gave my master fifty pounds premium; the same premium, or more, was paid with the others. One, the son of a gentleman at — , paid as much as eighty pounds. My master made an excellent thing of his apprentices. Nearly all the grocers in the part of Berkshire I'm acquainted with do the same. My master was a severe man to us, in respect of keeping us in the house, and making us attend the Methodist Chapel twice, and sometimes thrice, every Sunday. We had prayers night and morning. I attribute my misfortunes to this apprenticeship, because there was a great discrepancy between profession and practice in the house; so there could be no respect in the young men for their employer, and they grew careless. He carried on his business in a way to inspire anything else than respect. On the cheesemongery side we were always blamed if we didn't keep the scale well wetted, so as to make it heavier on one side than the other – I mean the side of the scale where the butter was put – that was filled or partly filled with water, under pretence of preventing the butter sticking, and so the customer was wronged half an ounce in every purchase. With regard to the bacon, which, on account of competition, we had to sell cheap – at no profit sometimes – he used to say to us, "You must make the ounces pay;" that is, we were expected to add two or more ounces, calculating on what the customer would put up with, to every six odd ounces in the weight of a piece. For instance, if a hock of bacon weighed six pounds seven ounces, at $4\frac{1}{2}d$. per pound, we were to charge 2s. 3d. for the six pounds, and (if possible) adding two ounces to the seven which was the actual weight, charge each ounce a halfpenny, so getting 2s. $7\frac{1}{2}d$. instead of 2s. 5d. This is a common practice in all the cheap shops I am acquainted with. With his sugars and teas, inferior sorts were mixed. In grinding pepper, a quantity of rice was used, it all being ground together. Mustard was adulterated by the manufacturers, if the price given showed that the adulterated stuff was wanted. The lowest priced coffee was always half chiccory, the second quality one-third chiccory; the best was one pound of chiccory to three pounds of coffee, or one-fourth. We had it either in chiccory-nibs, which is the root of the endive cultivated in Yorkshire, Prussia, &c., or else a spurious chiccory powdered, twopence per pound cheaper, the principal ingredient being parsnips and carrots cut in small pieces, and roasted like chiccory. A quart of water is the allowance to every twenty-eight pounds of tobacco. We had to keep pulling it, so as to keep it loose, for if left to lie long it would mould, and get a very unpleasant smell. In weighing sugar, some was always spilt loose in the

scale opposite the weight, which remains in the scale, so that every pound
or so is a quarter of an ounce short. This is the practice only in cutting
shops. Often enough, after we have been doing all these rogueries, we were
called into prayers. In my next situation, with an honourable tradesman
in Yorkshire, I found I had to learn my business over again, so as to carry
it on fairly. In two or three years I went into business in the town where
I was apprenticed; but I had been subjected to such close confinement, and
so many unnecessary restrictions, without any opportunity of improving
by reading, that when I was my own master, and in possession of money,
and on the first taste of freedom, I squandered my money foolishly and
extravagantly, and that brought me into difficulties. I was 150*l*. deficient
to meet my liabilities, and my friends advanced that sum, I undertaking
to be more attentive to business. After that, a man started as a grocer in
the same street, in the "cutting" line, and I had to compete with him, and
he sold his sugar a halfpenny a pound less than it cost, and I was obliged
to do the same. The preparing of the sugar for the market-day is a country
grocer's week's work, and all at a loss. That's the ruin of many a grocer.
My profits dwindled year by year, though I stuck very close to business;
and in eighteen months I gave it up. By that time other "cutting" shops
were opened – none have done any good. I was about 100*l*. bad, which
my friends arranged to pay by instalments. After that I hawked tea. I did
no good in that. The system is to leave it at the working men's houses,
giving a week's credit, the customers often taking more. Nothing can be
honestly made in that trade. The Scotchmen in the trade are the only men
that can do any good in it. The charge is six shillings for what's four
shillings in a good shop. About nine months ago my wife – I had been
married seven years – was obliged to go and live with her sister, a
dressmaker, as I was too poor to keep her or myself either. I then came
to London, to try for employment of any kind. I answered advertisements,
and there were always forty or fifty young men after the same situation.
I never got one, except for a short time at Brentford. I had also a few days'
work at bill delivery – that is, grocers' circulars. I was at last so reduced
that I couldn't pay for my lodgings. Nobody can describe the misery I felt
as I have walked the streets all night, falling asleep as I went along, and
then roused myself up half-frozen, my limbs aching, and my whole body
trembling. Sometimes, if I could find a penny, I might sit up in a coffee-
shop in Russell-street, Covent-garden, till five in the morning, when I had
to roam the streets all day long. Two days I was without food, and
determined to commit some felony to save me from starvation, when, to
my great joy – for God knows what it saved me from, as I was utterly

careless what my fate would be – I was told of this refuge by a poor man who had been there, who found me walking about the Piazzas in Covent-garden as a place of shelter. I applied, and was admitted. I don't know how I can get a place without clothes. I have one child with my wife, and she supports him and herself very indifferently by dressmaking.'

A soldier's wife, speaking with a strong Scotch accent, made the following statement. She had altogether a decent appearance, but her features – and there were the remains of prettiness in her look – were sadly pinched. Her manners were quiet, and her voice low and agreeable. She looked like one who had 'seen better days', as the poor of the better sort not unfrequently say in their destitution, clinging to the recollection of past comforts. She wore a very clean checked cotton shawl, and a straw bonnet tolerably entire. The remainder of her dress was covered by her shawl, which was folded closely about her, over a dark cotton gown.

'I was born twenty miles from Inverness, (she said), and have been a servant since I was eleven. I always lived in good places – the best of places. I never was in inferior places. I have lived as cook, housemaid, or servant-of-all-work, in Inverness, Elgin, and Tain, always maintaining a good character. I thank God for that. In all my distress I've done nothing wrong, but I didn't know what distress was when in service. I continued in service until I married; but I was not able to save much money, because I had to do all I could for my mother, who was a very poor widow, for I lost my father when I was two years old. Wages are very low in Scotland to what they are in England. In the year 1847 I lived in the service of the barrack-master of Fort George, twelve miles below Inverness. There I became acquainted with my present husband, a soldier, and I was married to him in March, 1847, in the chapel at Fort George. I continued two months in service after my marriage. My mistress wouldn't let me away she was very kind to me; so was my master: they all were. I have a written character from my mistress.' [This, at my request, she produced.] 'Two months after, the regiment left Fort George for Leith, and there I lived with my husband in barracks. It is not so bad for married persons in the artillery as in the line (we were in the artillery), in barracks. In our barrack rooms no single men were allowed to sleep where the married people were accommodated. But there were three or four married families in our room. I lived two years in barracks with my husband, in different barracks. I was very comfortable. I didn't know what it was to want anything I ought to have. My husband was a kind, sober man.' [This she said very feelingly.] 'His regiment was ordered abroad, to Nova Scotia. I had no family. Only six soldiers' wives are allowed to go out with each company, and there were seventeen married men in the company to which my husband belonged. It's determined by lot. An officer holds the tickets in his cap, and the men draw them. None of the wives are present. It would be too hard a thing for them to see. My husband drew a blank.' She continued:

'It was a sad scene when they embarked at Woolwich last March. All the wives were there, all crying and sobbing, you may depend upon that; and the children, too, and some of the men; but I couldn't look much at them, and I don't like to see men cry. My husband was sadly distressed. I hoped to get out there and join him, not knowing the passage was so long and expensive. I had a little money then, but that's gone, and I'm brought to misery. It would have cost me 6l. at that time to get out, and I couldn't manage that, so I stayed in London, getting a day's work at washing when I could, making a very poor living of it; and I was at last forced to part with all my good clothes after my money went; and my husband, God bless him! always gave me his money to do what I thought best with it. I used to earn a little in barracks with my needle, too. I was taken ill with cholera at the latter end of August. Dear, dear, what I suffered! And when I was getting better I had a second attack, and that was the way my bit of money all went. I was then quite destitute; but I care nothing for that, and would care nothing for anything if I could get out to my husband. I should be happy then. I should never be so happy since I was born before. It's now a month since I was entirely out of halfpence. I can't beg; it would disgrace me and my husband, and I'd die in the streets first. Last Saturday I hadn't a farthing. I hadn't a thing to part with. I had a bed by the night, at 3d. a night, not a regular lodging-house; but the mistress wouldn't trust me no longer, as I owed her 2s. 6d., and for that she holds clothes worth far more than that. I heard of this Asylum, and got admitted, or I must have spent the night in the street – there was nothing else for me; but, thank God! I've been spared that. On Christmas day I had a letter from my husband.'

This she produced. It contained the following passage:

'I am glad this letter only costs you a penny, as your purse must be getting very low, but there is a good time coming, and i trust in God it will not be long, my deir wife. i hope you will have got a good place before this raches you. I am dowing all in my power to help you. i trust in good in 3 months more, if you Help me, between us we make it out.'

She concluded:

'I wouldn't like him to know how badly I am off. He knows I would do nothing wrong. He wouldn't suspect me; he never would. He knows me too well. I have no clothes but what are detained for 2s. 6d., and what

I have on. I have on just this shawl and an old cotton gown, but it's not broke, and my under-clothing. All my wish is to get out to my husband. I care for nothing else in this world.'

Next comes the tale of a young girl who worked at velvet embossing. She was comely, and modestly spoken. By her attire it would have been difficult to have told that she was so utterly destitute as I afterwards discovered. She was scrupulously neat and clean in her dress; indeed it was evident, even from her appearance, that she belonged to a better class than the ordinary inmates of the Asylum. As she sat alone in the long, un-occupied wards, she sighed heavily, and her eyes were fixed continually on the ground. Her voice was very sorrowful. Her narrative was as follows:

'I have been out of work for a very long while, for full three months now, and all the summer I was only on and off. I mostly had my work given out to me. It was in pieces of 100 yards, and sometimes less, and I was paid so much for the dozen yards. I generally had $3\frac{1}{2}d$., and sometimes $1\frac{1}{2}d$., according to what it was; $3\frac{1}{2}d$. was the highest price that I had. I could, if I rose at five in the morning, and sat up till twelve, earn between $1s$. and $1s$. $3d$. in a day. I had to cut the velvet after it had been embossed. I could, if a diamond pattern, do five dozen yards in a day, and if a leaf pattern, I could only do three dozen and a half. I couldn't get enough of it to do, even at these prices. Sometimes I was two days in the week without work, and sometimes I had work for only one day in the week. They wanted, too, to reduce the $1\frac{1}{2}d$. diamond work to $1d$. the dozen yards; and so they would have done, only the work got so slack that we had to leave it altogether. That is now seven weeks ago. Before that, I did get a little to do, though it was very little, and since then I have called almost every week at the warehouse, but they have put me off, telling me to come in a fortnight or a week's time. I never kept acquaintance with any of the other young women working at the warehouse, but I dare say about twenty-five were thrown out of work at the same time as I was. Sometimes I made $6s$. a week, and sometimes only $3s$., and for the last fortnight I got $1s$. $6d$. a week, and out of that I had my own candles to find, and $1s$. $6d$. a week to pay for my lodgings. After I lost my work, I made away with what little clothes I had, and now I have got nothing but what I stand upright in.' [The tears were pouring down the cheeks of the poor girl; she was many minutes afterwards before she could answer my questions, from sobbing.] 'I can't help crying,' she said, 'when I think how destitute I am. Oh, yes, indeed [she cried through her sobs,], I have been a good girl in all my trials. I might have been better off if I had chosen to take to that life. I need not have been here if I had chosen to part with my character.

I don't know what my father was. I believe he was a clerk in one of the foreign confectionery houses. He deserted my mother two months before I was born. I don't know whether he is dead or not, for I never set eyes on him. If he is alive, he is very well off. I know this from my aunt, who was told by one of his fellow-clerks that he had married a woman of property and gone abroad. He was disappointed with my mother. He expected to have had a good bit of money with her; but after she married him, her father wouldn't notice her. My mother died when I was a week old, so I do not recollect either of my parents. When my aunt, who was his own sister, wrote to him about myself, my brother and sister, he sent word back that the children might go to the workhouse. But my aunt took pity on us, and brought us all up. She had a little property of her own. She gave us a decent education, as far as lay in her power. My brother she put to sea. My father's brother was a captain, and he took my brother with him. The first voyage he went (he was fourteen), a part of the rigging fell on him and the first mate, and they were both killed on the spot. My sister went as lady's-maid to Lady —, and went abroad with her, now eighteen months ago, and I have never heard of her since. The aunt who brought me up is dead now. She was carried off two years and three months ago. If she had lived I should never have wanted a friend. I remained with her up to the time of her death, and was very happy before that time. After that I found it very hard for a poor lone girl like me to get an honest living. I have been struggling on ever since, parting with my clothes, and often going for two days without food. I lived upon the remainder of my clothes for some little time after I was thrown entirely out of work; but at last I got a fortnight in debt at my lodgings, and they made me leave; that's a week and three days ago now. Then I had nowhere but the streets to lay my head. I walked about for three days and nights without rest. I went into a chapel. I went there to sit down and pray; but I was too tired to offer up any prayers, for I fell asleep. I had been two nights and three days in the streets before this, and all I had during that time was a penny loaf, and that I was obliged to beg for. On the day that I was walking about, it thawed in the morning, and froze very hard at night. My shoes were very bad, and let in water; and as the night came on, my stockings froze to my feet. Even now I am suffering from the cold of those nights. It is as much as I can do to bend my limbs at present. I have been in the Asylum a week, and to-night is my last night here. I have nowhere to go, and what will become of me the Lord God only knows.' [Again she burst out crying most piteously.] 'My things are not fit to go into any respectable workroom, and they won't take me into a lodging either,

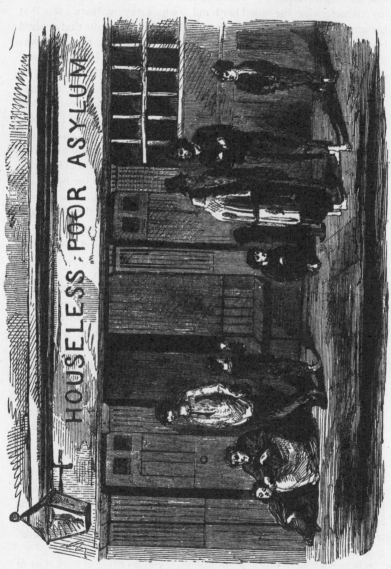

ASYLUM FOR THE HOUSELESS POOR, CRIPPLEGATE.

unless I've got clothes. I would rather make away with myself than lose my character.' [As she raised her hand to wipe away her tears, I saw that her arms were bare; and on her moving the old black mantle that covered her shoulders, I observed that her gown was so ragged that the body was almost gone from it, and it had no sleeves.] 'I shouldn't have kept this,' she said, 'If I could have made away with it.' She said that she had no friend in the world to help her, but that she would like much to emigrate.

I afterwards inquired at the house at which this poor creature had lodged, as to whether she had always conducted herself with propriety while living there. To be candid, I could hardly believe that any person could turn a young friendless girl into the streets because she owed two weeks' rent; though the girl appeared too simple and truthful to fabricate such a statement. On inquiry, I found her story true from the beginning to the end. The landlady, an Irishwoman, acknowledged that the girl was in her debt but 3s.; that she had lodged with her for several months, and always paid her regularly when she had money; but she couldn't afford, she said, to keep people for nothing. The girl had been a good, well-behaved, modest girl with her.

[p. 438]   The Asylum for the Houseless Poor of London is opened only when the thermometer reaches freezing-point, and offers nothing but dry bread and warm shelter to such as avail themselves of its charity.

To this place swarm, as the bitter winter's night comes on, some half-thousand penniless and homeless wanderers. The poverty-stricken from every quarter of the globe are found within its wards; from the haggard American seaman to the lank Polish refugee, the pale German 'out-wanderer', the tearful black sea-cook, the shivering Lascar crossing-sweeper, the helpless Chinese beggar, and the half-torpid Italian organ-boy. It is, indeed, a ragged congress of nations – a convocation of squalor and misery – of destitution, degradation, and suffering, from all the corners of the earth.

Nearly every shade and grade of misery, misfortune, vice, and even guilt, are to be found in the place; for characters are not demanded previous to admission, want being the sole qualification required of the applicants. The Asylum for the Houseless is at once the beggar's hotel, the tramp's town-house, the outcast's haven of refuge – the last dwelling, indeed, on the road to ruin.

It is impossible to mistake the Asylum if you go there at dark, just as the lamp in the wire cage over the entrance-door is being lighted. This is the hour for opening; and ranged along the kerb is a kind of ragged regiment, drawn up four deep, and stretching far up and down the narrow lane, until the crowd is like a hedge to the roadway. Nowhere in the world can a similar sight be witnessed.

It is a terrible thing, indeed, to look down upon that squalid crowd from one of the upper windows of the institution. There they stand shivering in the snow, with their thin, cobwebby garments hanging in tatters about them. Many are without shirts; with their bare skin showing through the rents and gaps of their clothes, like the hide of a dog with the mange. Some have their greasy coats and trousers tied round their wrists and ankles with string, to prevent the piercing wind from blowing up them. A few are without shoes; and these keep one foot only to the ground, while the bare flesh that has had to tramp through the snow is blue and livid-looking as half cooked meat. It is a sullenly silent crowd, without any of the riot and rude frolic which generally ensue upon any gathering in the London streets; for the only sounds heard are the squealing of the beggar infants, or the wrangling of the vagrant boys for the front ranks, together with a continued succession of hoarse coughs, that seem to answer each other like the bleating of a flock of sheep.

To each person is given half-a-pound of the best bread on coming in at night, and a like quantity on going out in the morning; and children, even if they be at the breast, have the same, which goes to swell the mother's allowance. A clerk enters in a thick ledger the name, age, trade, and place of birth of the applicants, as well as where they slept the night before.

As the eye glances down the column of the register, indicating where each applicant has passed the previous night, it is startled to find how often the clerk has had to write down, 'in the streets'; so that 'ditto', 'ditto', continually repeated under the same head, sounded as an ideal chorus of terrible want in the mind's ear.

[pp. 438–9] Around the fierce stove, in the centre of the ward, there is generally gathered a group of the houseless wanderers, the crimson rays tinting the cluster of haggard faces with a bright lurid light that colours the skin as red as wine. One and all are stretching forth their hands, as if to let the delicious heat soak into their half-numbed limbs. They seem positively greedy of the warmth, drawing up their sleeves and trousers so that their naked legs and arms may present a larger surface to the fire.

Not a laugh nor sound is heard, but the men stand still, munching their bread, their teeth champing like horses in a manger. One poor wretch, at the time of my visit, had been allowed to sit on a form inside the railings round the stove, for he had the ague; and there he crouched, with his legs near as a roasting-joint to the burning coals, as if he were trying to thaw his very marrow.

Then how fearful it is to hear the continued coughing of the wretched inmates! It seems to pass round the room from one to another, now sharp and hoarse as a bark, then deep and hollow as a lowing, or – with the old – feeble and trembling as a bleat.

In an hour after the opening the men have quitted the warm fire and crept one after another to their berths, where they lie rolled round in their leathers – the rows of tightly-bound figures, brown and stiff as mummies, suggesting the idea of some large catacomb.

The stillness is broken only by the snoring of the sounder sleepers and the coughing of the more restless.

It is a marvellously pathetic scene. Here is a herd of the most wretched and friendless people in the world, lying down close to the earth as sheep; here are some two centuries of outcasts, whose days are an unvarying round of suffering, enjoying the only moments when they are free from pain and care – life being to them but one long painful operation as it were, and sleep the chloroform which, for the time being, renders them insensible.

The sight sets the mind speculating on the beggars' and the outcasts' dreams. The ship's company, starving at the North Pole, dreamt, every man of them, each night, of feasting; and are those who compose this miserable, frozen-out beggar crew, now regaling themselves, in their sleep, with visions of imaginary banquets? – are they smacking their mental lips over ideal beef and pudding? Is that poor wretch yonder, whose rheumatic limbs rack him each step he takes – is *he* tripping over green fields with an elastic and joyous bound, that in his waking moments he can never know again? Do that man's restlessness and heavy moaning come from nightmare terrors of policemen and treadwheels? – and which among those runaway boys is fancying that he is back home again, with his mother and sisters weeping on his neck?

The next moment the thoughts shift, and the heart is overcome with a sense of the vast heap of social refuse – the mere human street-sweepings – the great living mixen – that is destined, as soon as the spring returns, to be strewn far and near over the land, and serve as manure to the future crime-crops of the country.

Then come the self-congratulations and the self-questionings! and as a man, sound in health and limb, walking through a hospital, thanks God that he has been spared the bodily ailments, the mere sight of which sickens him, so in this refuge for the starving and the homeless, the first instinct of the well-to-do visitor is to breathe a thanksgiving (like the Pharisee in the parable) that 'he is not as one of these'.

But the vain conceit has scarcely risen to the tongue before the better nature whispers in the mind's ear, 'By what special virtue of your own are you different from them? How comes it that you are well clothed and well fed, whilst so many go naked and hungry?' And if you in your arrogance, ignoring all the accidents that have helped to build up your worldly prosperity, assert that you have been the 'architect of your own fortune', who, let us ask, gave you the genius or energy for the work?

Then get down from your moral stilts, and confess it honestly to yourself, that you are what you are by that inscrutable grace which decreed your birthplace to be a mansion or a cottage rather than a 'padding-ken', or which granted you brains and strength, instead of sending you into the world, like many of these, a cripple or an idiot.

It is hard for smug-faced respectability to acknowledge these dirt-caked, erring wretches as brothers, and yet, if from those to whom little is given little is expected, surely, after the atonement of their long suffering, they will make as good angels as the best of us.

VOLUME FOUR

THOSE THAT WILL NOT WORK

INTRODUCTION

by Henry Mayhew

[pp. 1–11] I enter upon this part of my subject with a deep sense of the misery, the vice, the ignorance, and the want that encompass us on every side – I enter upon it after much grave attention to the subject, observing closely, reflecting patiently, and generalizing cautiously upon the phenomena and causes of the vice and crime of this city – I enter upon it after a thoughtful study of the habits and character of the 'outcast' class generally – I enter upon it, moreover, not only as forming an integral and most important part of the task I have imposed upon myself, but from a wish to divest the public mind of certain 'idols' of the platform and conventicle – 'idols' peculiar to our own time, and unknown to the great Father of the inductive philosophy – and 'idols', too, that appear to me greatly to obstruct a proper understanding of the subject. Further, I am led to believe that I can contribute some new facts concerning the physics and economy of vice and crime generally, that will not only make the solution of the social problem more easy to us, but, setting more plainly before us some of its latent causes, make us look with more pity and less anger on those who want the fortitude to resist their influence; and induce us, or at least the more earnest among us, to apply ourselves steadfastly to the removal or alleviation of those social evils that appear to create so large a proportion of the vice and crime that we seek by punishment to prevent.

Such are the *ultimate* objects of my present labours: the result of them is given to the world with an earnest desire to better the condition of the wretched social outcasts of whom I have now to treat, and to contribute, if possible, my mite of good towards the common weal.

But though such be my ultimate object, let me here confess that my immediate aim is the elimination of the truth; without this, of course, all other principles must be sheer sentimentality – sentiments being, to my mind, opinions engendered by the feelings rather than the judgment. The attainment of the truth, then, will be my primary aim; but by the truth, I wish it to be understood, I mean something *more* than the bare facts.

Facts, according to my ideas, are merely the elements of truths, and not the truths themselves; of all matters there are none so utterly useless by themselves as your mere matters of fact. A fact, so long as it remains an isolated fact, is a dull, dead, uninformed thing; no object nor event by itself can possibly give us any knowledge, we must compare it with some other, even to distinguish it; and it is the distinctive quality thus developed that constitutes the essence of a thing – that is to say, the point by which we cognize and recognise it when again presented to us. A fact must be assimilated with, or discriminated from, some other fact or facts, in order to be raised to the dignity of a truth, and made to convey the least knowledge to the mind. To say, for instance, that in the year 1850 there were 26,813 criminal offenders in England and Wales, is merely to oppress the brain with the record of a fact that, *per se*, is so much mental lumber. This is the very mummery of statistics; of what rational good can such information by itself be to any person? who can tell whether the number of offenders in that year be large or small, unless they compare it with the number of some other year, or in some other country? but to do this will require another fact, and even then this second fact can give us but little real knowledge. It may teach us, perhaps, that the past year was more or less criminal than some other year, or that the people of this country, in that year, were more or less disposed to the infraction of the laws than some other people abroad; still, what will all this avail us? If the year which we select to contrast criminally with that of 1850 be not itself compared with other years, how are we to know whether the number of criminals appertaining to it be above or below the average? or, in other words, how can the one be made a measure of the other?

To give the least mental value to facts, therefore, we must generalize them, that is to say, we must contemplate them in connection with other facts, and so discover their agreements and differences, their antecedents, concomitants, and consequences. It is true we may frame erroneous and defective theories in so doing; we may believe things which are similar in appearance to be similar in their powers and properties also; we may distinguish between things having no real difference; we may mistake concomitant events for consequences; we may generalize with too few particulars, and hastily infer that to be common to all which is but the special attribute of a limited number; nevertheless, if theory may occasionally teach us wrongly, facts without theory or generalization cannot possibly teach us at all. What the process of digestion is to food, that of generalizing is to fact; for as it is by the assimilation of the substances we eat with the elements of our bodies that our limbs are enlarged and our whole frames strengthened, so is it by associating perception with perception in our brains that our intellect becomes at once expanded and invigorated. Contrary to the vulgar notion, theory, that is to say, theory in its true Baconian sense, is not opposed to fact, but consists rather of a *large* collection of facts; it is not true of this or that thing alone, but of *all* things belonging to the same class – in a word, it consists not of *one* fact but an *infinity*. The theory of gravitation, for instance, expresses not only what occurs when a stone falls to the earth, but when every other body does the same thing; it expresses, moreover, what takes place in the revolution of the moon round our planet, and in the revolution of our planet and of all the other planets round our sun, and of all other suns round the centre of the universe; in fine, it is true not of one thing merely, but of every material object in the entire range of creation.

There are, of course, two methods of dealing philosophically with every subject – deductively and inductively. We may either proceed from principles to facts, or recede from facts to principles. The one explains, the other investigates; the former applies known general rules to the comprehension of particular phenomena, and the latter classifies the particular phenomena, so that we may ultimately come to comprehend their unknown general rules. The deductive method is the mode of *using* knowledge, and the inductive method the mode of *acquiring* it.

In a subject like the crime and vice of the metropolis, and the country in general, of which so little is known – of which there are so many facts, but so little comprehension – it is evident that we must seek by induction, that is to say, by a careful classification of the known phenomena, to render the matter more intelligible; in fine, we must, in order to arrive at a *comprehensive* knowledge of its antecedents, consequences, and concomitants, contemplate as large a number of facts as possible in as many different relations as the statistical records of the country will admit of our doing.

With this brief preamble I will proceed to treat generally of the class that will not work, and then particularly of that portion of them termed prostitutes. But, first, who are those that *will* work, and who those that *will not* work? This is the primary point to be evolved.

OF THE WORKERS AND NON-WORKERS

The essential quality of an animal is that it seeks its own living, whereas a vegetable has its living brought to it. An animal cannot stick its feet in the ground and suck up the inorganic elements of its body from the soil, nor drink in the organic elements from the atmosphere. The leaves of plants are not only their lungs but their stomachs. As *they* breathe they acquire food and strength, but as animals breathe *they* gradually waste away. The carbon which is *secreted* by the process of respiration in the vegetable is excreted by the very same process in the animal. Hence a fresh supply of *carbonaceous* matter must be sought after and obtained at frequent intervals, in order to repair the continual waste of animal life.

But in the act of seeking for substances fitted to replace that which is lost in respiration, nerves must be excited and muscles moved; and recent discoveries have shown that such excitation and motion are attended with decomposition of the organs in which they occur. Muscular action gives rise to the destruction of muscular tissue, nervous action to a change in the nervous matter; and this destruction and decomposition necessarily involve a fresh supply of *nitrogenous* matter, in order that the loss may be repaired.

Now a tree, being inactive, has little or no waste. All the food that it obtains goes to the invigoration of its frame; not one atom is destroyed in seeking more: but the essential condition of animal life is muscular action; the essential condition of muscular action is the destruction of muscular tissue; and the essential condition of the destruction of muscular tissue is a supply of food fitted for the reformation of it, or – *death*. It is impossible for an animal – like a vegetable – to stand still and not destroy. If the limbs are not moving, the heart is beating, the lungs playing, the bosom heaving. Hence an animal, in order to continue its existence, must obtain its subsistence either by its own exertions or by those of others – in a word, it must be *autobious* or *allobious*.

The procuration of sustenance, then, is the necessary condition of animal life, and constitutes the sole apparent reason for the addition of the locomotive apparatus to the vegetative functions of sentient nature; but the faculties of comparison and volition have been further added to the animal nature of Man, in order to enable him, among other things, the better to gratify his wants – to give him such a mastery over the elements of material nature, that he may force the external world the more readily to contribute to his support. Hence the derangement of either one of those functions must degrade the human being – as regards his means of sustenance – to the level of the brute. If his intellect be impaired, and the faculty of perceiving 'the fitness of things' be consequently lost to him – or, this being sound, if the power of moving his muscles in compliance with his will be deficient – then the individual becomes no longer capable, like his fellows, of continuing his existence by his own exertions.

Hence, in every state, we have two extensive causes of allobiism, or living by the labour of others; the one intellectual, as in the case of lunatics and idiots, and the other physical, as in the case of the infirm, the crippled, and the maimed – the old and the young.

But a third, and a more extensive class, still remains to be particularized. The members of every community may be divided into the *energetic* and the *an-ergetic*; that is to say, into the hardworking and the non-working, the industrious and the indolent classes; the distinguishing characteristic of the *anergetic* being the extreme irksomeness of all labour to them, and their consequent indisposition to work for their subsistence. Now, in the circumstances above enumerated, we have three capital causes why, in every State, a certain portion of the community must derive their subsistence from the exertions of the rest; the first proceeds from some *physical* defect, as in the case of the old and the young, the super-annuated and the sub-annuated, the crippled and the maimed; the second from some *intellectual* defect, as in the case of lunatics and idiots; and the third from some *moral* defect, as in the case of the indolent, the vagrant, the professional mendicant, and the criminal. In all civilized countries, there will necessarily be a greater or less number of human parasites living on the sustenance of their fellows. The industrious must labour to support the lazy, and the sane to keep the insane, and the able-bodied to maintain the infirm.

Still, to complete the social fabric, another class requires to be specified. As yet, regard has been paid only to those who must needs labour for their living, or who, in default of so doing, must prey on the proceeds of the industry of their more active or more stalwart brethren. There is, however, in all civilized society, a farther portion of the people distinct from either of those above mentioned, who, being already provided – no matter how – with a sufficient stock of sustenance, or what will exchange for such, have no occasion to toil for an additional supply.

Hence all society would appear to arrange itself into four different classes:

    I. Those that will work
    II. Those that cannot work
    III. Those that will not work
    IV. Those that need not work

Under one or other section of this quadruple division, every member, not only of our community, but of every other civilized State, must necessarily be included; the rich, the poor, the industrious, the idle, the honest, the dishonest, the virtuous, and the vicious – each and all must be comprised therein.

Let me now proceed specially to treat of each of these classes – to distribute under one or other of these four categories the diverse modes of living peculiar to the members of our own community, and so to enunciate, for the first time, the natural history, as it were, of the industry and idleness of Great Britain in the nineteenth century.

It is no easy matter, however, to classify the different kinds of labour scientifically. To arrange the several varieties of work into 'orders', and to group the manifold species of arts under a few comprehensive genera – so that the mind may grasp the whole at one effort – is a task of a most perplexing character. Moreover, the first attempt to bring any number of diverse phenomena within the rules of logical division is not only a matter of considerable difficulty, but one, unfortunately, that is generally unsuccessful. It is impossible, however, to proceed with the present inquiry without making some attempt at systematic arrangement; for of all scientific processes, the classification of the various phenomena, in connection with a given subject, is perhaps the most important; indeed, if we consider that the function of cognition is essentially *discriminative*, it is evident, that without distinguishing between one object and another, there can be no knowledge, nor, indeed, any perception. Even as the seizing of a particular difference causes the mind to *apprehend* the special character of an object, so does the discovery of the agreements and differences among the several phenomena of a subject enable the understanding to *comprehend* it. What the generalization of events is to the ascertainment of natural laws, the generalization of things is to the discovery of natural systems. But classification is no less dangerous than it is important to science; for in precisely the same proportion as a correct grouping of objects into genera and species, orders and varieties, expands and assists our understanding, so does any erroneous arrangement cripple and retard all true knowledge. The reduction of all external substances into four elements by the ancients – earth, air, fire, and water – perhaps did more to obstruct the progress of chemical science than even a prohibition of the study could have effected.

But the branches of industry are so multifarious, the divisions of labour so minute and manifold, that it seems at first almost impossible to reduce them to any system. Moreover, the crude generalizations expressed in the names of the several arts, render the subject still more perplexing.

Some kinds of workmen, for example, are called after the *articles they make* – as saddlers, hatters, boot-makers, dress-makers, breeches-makers, stay-makers, lace-makers, button-makers, glovers, cabinet-makers, artificial-flower-makers, ship-builders, organ-builders, boat-builders, nailers, pin-makers, basket-makers, pump-makers, clock and watch makers, wheel-wrights, ship-wrights, and so forth.

Some operatives, on the other hand, take their names not from what they make, but from the *kind of work they perform*. Hence we have carvers, joiners, bricklayers, weavers, knitters, engravers, embroiderers, tanners, curriers, bleachers, thatchers, lime-burners, glass-blowers, seamstresses, assayers, refiners, embossers, chasers, painters, paper-hangers, printers, book-binders, cab-drivers, fishermen, graziers, and so on.

Other artizans, again, are styled after the *materials upon which they work*, such as tinmen, jewellers, lapidaries, goldsmiths, braziers, plumbers, pewterers, glaziers, &c. &c.

And lastly, a few operatives are named after the *tools they use*; thus we have ploughmen, sawyers, and needlewomen.

But these divisions, it is evident, are as unscientific as they are arbitrary; nor would it be possible, by adopting such a classification, to arrive at any practical result.

Now, I *had* hoped to have derived some little assistance in my attempt to reduce the several varieties of work to system from the arrangement of the products of industry and art at 'the Great Exhibition'. I knew, however, that the point of classification had proved the great stumbling block to the French Industrial Exhibitions. In the Exposition of the Arts and Manufactures of France in 1806, for instance, M. Costaz adopted a topographical arrangement, according to the departments of the kingdom whence the specimens were sent. In 1819, again, finding the previous arrangement conveyed little or no knowledge, depending, as it did, on the mere local association of the places of manufacture, the same philosopher attempted to classify all arts into a sort of natural system, but the separate divisions amounted to thirty-nine, and were found to be confused and inconvenient. In 1827 M. Payon adopted a classification into five great divisions, arranging the arts according as they are chemical, mechanical, physical, economical, or 'miscellaneous' in their nature. It was found, however, in practice, that two, or even three, of these characteristics often belonged to the same manufacture. In 1834 M. Dupin proposed a classification that was found to work better than any which preceded it. He viewed man as a locomotive animal, a clothed animal, a domiciled animal, &c., and thus tracing him through his various daily wants and employments, he arrived at a classification in which all arts are placed under nine headings, according as they contribute to the alimentary, sanitary,

453

vestiary, domiciliar, locomotive, sensitive, intellectual, preparative, or social tendencies of man. In 1844 and 1849 attempts were made towards an eclectic combination of two or three of the above-mentioned systems, but it does not appear that the latter arrangements presented any marked advantages.

Now, with all the experience of the French nation to guide us, I naturally expected that especial attention would be directed towards the point of classification with us, and that a technological system would be propounded, which would be found at least an improvement on the bungling systems of the French. It must be confessed, however, that no nation could possibly have stultified itself so egregiously as we have done in this respect. Never was there anything half so puerile as the classification of the works of industry in our own Exhibition!

But this comes of the patronage of Princes; for we are told that at one of the earliest meetings at Buckingham Palace his Royal Highness *propounded* the system of classification according to which the works of industry *were to be* arranged. The published minutes of the meeting on the 30th of June, 1849, inform us –

'His Royal Highness communicated his views regarding the formation of a Great Collection of Works of Industry and Art in London in 1851, for the purposes of exhibition, and of competition and encouragement. His Royal Highness considered that such a collection and exhibition should consist of the following divisions:

Raw Materials
Machinery and Mechanical Inventions
Manufactures
Sculpture and Plastic Art generally.'

Now, were it possible for monarchs to do with natural laws as with social ones, namely, to blow a trumpet and declaring '*le roi le veut,*' to have their will pass into one of the statutes of creation, it might be advantageous to science that Princes should seek to lay down orders of arrangement and propound systems of classification. But seeing that Science is as pure a republic as Letters, and that there are no 'Highnesses' in philosophy – for if there be any aristocracy at all in such matters, it is at least an aristocracy of intellect – it is rather an injury than a benefit that those who are high in authority should interfere in these affairs at all; since, from the very circumstances of their position it is utterly impossible for them to arrive at anything more than the merest surface knowledge on such subjects. The influence, too, that their mere 'authority' has over men's minds is directly opposed to the perception of truth, preventing that free and independent exercise of the intellect from which alone all discovery and knowledge can proceed.

Judging the quadruple arrangement of the Great Exhibition by the laws of logical division, we find that the three classes – Raw Materials, Machinery, and Manufactures – which refer more particularly to the Works of Industry, are neither distinct nor do they include the whole. What is a raw material, and what a manufacture? It is from the difficulty of distinguishing between these two conditions that leather is placed under Manufactures, and steel under Raw Materials – though surely steel is iron *plus* carbon, and leather skin *plus* tannin; so that, technologically considered, there is no difference between them. If by the term raw material is meant some natural product in its crude state, then it is evident that 'Geological maps, plans, and sections; prussiate of potash, and other mixed chemical manufactures; sulphuric, muriatic, nitric, and other acids; medicinal tinctures, cod liver oil, dried fruits, fermented liquors and spirits, preserved meats, portable soups, glue, and the alloys' cannot possibly rank as *raw* materials, though one and all of these articles are to be found so 'classified' at the Great Exhibition; but if the meaning of a 'raw material' be extended to any product which constitutes the substance to be operated upon in an industrial art, then the answer is that leather, which is the material of shoes and harness, is no more a manufacture than steel, which is placed among the raw materials, because forming the constituent substance of cutlery and tools. So interlinked are the various arts and manufactures, that what is the product of one process of industry is the material of another – thus, yarn is the product of spinning, and the material of weaving, and in the same manner the cloth, which is the product of weaving, becomes the material of tailoring.

But a still greater blunder than the non-distinction between products and materials lies in the confounding of *processes* with *products*. In an Industrial Exhibition to reserve no special place for the processes of industry is very much like the play of Hamlet with the part of Hamlet omitted; and yet it is evident that, in the quadruple arrangement before mentioned, those most important industrial operations which consist merely in arriving at the same result by simpler means – as, for instance, the hot blast in metallurgical operations – can find no distinct expression. The consequence is that methods of work are arranged under the same head as the work itself; and the 'Executive' have been obliged to group under the first subdivision of *Raw Materials* the following inconsistent jumble: Salt deposits; ventilation; safety lamps and other methods of lighting; methods of lowering and raising miners, and draining; methods of roasting, smelting, or otherwise reducing ores; while under the second subdivision of Raw Materials chemical and pharmaceutical *processes* and *products* are indiscriminately confounded.

Another most important defect is the omission of all mention of those industrial processes which have *no special or distinct products of their own,* but which are rather engaged *in adding to the beauty or durability of others*: as, for instance, the bleaching of some textile fabrics, the embroidering of others, the dyeing and printing of others; the binding of books; the cutting of glass; the painting of china, &c. From the want of an express division for this large portion of our industrial arts, there is a jumbling and a bungling throughout the whole arrangement. Under the head of *manufactures* are grouped printing and bookbinding, the 'dyeing of woollen, cotton, and linen goods', 'embroidery, fancy, and industrial work', the cutting and engraving of glass; and, lastly, the art of 'decoration generally', including 'ornamental, coloured decoration', and the 'imitations of woods, marbles, &c.' – though surely these are one and all *additions* to manufactures rather than *manufactures* themselves. Indeed, a more extraordinary and unscientific hotch-potch than the entire arrangement has never been submitted to public criticism and public ridicule.

Amid all this confusion and perplexity, then, how are we to proceed? Why, we must direct our attention to some more judicious and more experienced guide. In such matters, at least, as the Exposition of the Science of Labour, it is clear that we must 'put not our trust in princes'.

That Prince Albert has conferred a great boon on the country in the establishment of the Great Exhibition (for it is due not only to his patronage but to his own personal exertions), no unprejudiced mind can for a moment doubt; and that he has, ever since his first coming among us, filled a most delicate office in the State in a highly decorous and commendable manner, avoiding all political partizanship, and being ever ready to give the influence of his patronage, and, indeed, co-operation, to anything that appeared to promise an amelioration of the condition of the working classes of this country, I am most glad to have it in my power to bear witness; but that, *because of this*, we should pin our faith to a 'hasty generalization' propounded by him, would be to render ourselves at once silly and servile.

If, with the view of obtaining some more precise information concerning the several branches of industry, we turn our attention to the Government analysis of the different modes of employment among the people, we shall find that for all purposes of a scientific or definite character the Occupation Abstract of the Census of this country is comparatively useless. Previous to 1841, the sole attempt made at generalization was the division of the entire industrial community into three orders, viz.:

I. *Those employed in agriculture*
   1. Agricultural Occupiers
     a. Employing Labourers
     b. Not employing Labourers
   2. Agricultural Labourers
II *Those employed in manufacturers*
   1. Employed in manufactures
   2. Employed in making Manufacturing Machinery
III. *All other classes*
   1. Employed in Retail Trade or in Handicraft, as Masters or Workmen
   2. Capitalists, Bankers, Professional and other educated men
   3. Labourers employed in labour not Agricultural – as Miners, Quarriers, Fishermen, Porters, &c.
   4. Male Servants
   5. Other Males, 20 years of age

The defects of this arrangement must be self-evident to all who have paid the least attention to economical science. It offends against both the laws of logical division, the parts being neither distinct nor equal to the whole. In the first place, what is a manufacturer? and how is such an one to be distinguished from one employed in handicraft? How do the workers in metal, as the 'tin manufacturers', 'lead manufacturers', 'iron manufacturers' – who are one and all classed under the head of manufacturers – differ, in an economical point of view, from the workers in wood, as the carpenters and joiners, the cabinet-makers, ship-builders, &c., who are all classed under the head of handicraftsmen? Again, according to the census of 1831, a brewer is placed among those employed in retail trade or in handicrafts, while a vinegar maker is ranked with the manufacturers. According to Mr Babbage, *manufacturing* differs from mere *making* simply in the quantity produced – he being a manufacturer who makes a great number of the same articles; manufacturing is thus simply production in a large way, in connection with the several handicrafts. Dr Ure, however, appears to consider such articles manufactures as are produced by means of machinery, citing the word which originally signified production by hand (being the Latin equivalent for the Saxon *handicraft*) as an instance of those singular verbal corruptions by which terms come to stand for the very opposite to their literal meaning. But with all deference to the Doctor, for whose judgment I have the highest respect, Mr Babbage's definition of a manufacturer, viz., as a producer on a large scale, appears to me the more correct; for it is in this sense that we speak of manufacturing chemists, boot and shoe manufacturers, ginger-beer manufacturers, and the like.

The Occupation Abstract of the Census of 1841, though far more comprehensive than the one preceeding it, is equally unsatisfactory and unphilosophical. In this document the several members of Society are thus classified:

    I. *Persons engaged in commerce, trade, and manufacture*
    II. *Agriculture*
    III. *Labour, not agricultural*
    IV. *Army and navy merchant seamen, fishermen, and watermen*
    V. *Professions and other pursuits requiring education*
    VI. *Government, Civil Service, and municipal and parochial officers*
    VII. *Domestic servants*
    VIII. *Persons of independent means*
    IX. *Almspeople, pensioners, paupers, lunatics, and prisoners*
    X. *Remainder of population, including women and children*

Here it will be seen that the defects arising from drawing distinctions where no real differences exist, are avoided, those engaged in handicrafts being included under the same head as those engaged in manufacture; but the equally grave error of confounding or grouping together occupations which are essentially diverse, is allowed to continue. Accordingly, the first division is made to include those who are engaged in trade and commerce as well as manufacture, though surely – the one belongs strictly to the distributing, and the other to the producing class – occupations which are not only essentially distinct, but of which it is absolutely necessary for a right understanding of the state of the country that we know the proportion that the one bears to the other. Again, the employers in both cases are confounded with the employed, so that, though the capitalists who supply the materials, and pay the wages for the several kinds of work are a distinct body of people from those who *do* the work, and a body, moreover, that it is of the highest possible importance, in an economical point of view, that we should be able to estimate numerically – no attempt is made to discriminate the one from the other. Now these three classes, distributors, employers, and operatives, which in the Government returns of the people are jumbled together in one heterogeneous crowd, as if the distinctions between Capital, Labour, and Distribution had never been propounded, are precisely those concerning which the social inquirer desires the most minute information.

The Irish census is differently arranged from that of Great Britain. There the several classes are grouped under the following heads:

    I. *Ministering to food*
      1. As producers
      2. As preparers
      3. As distributors
   II. *Ministering to clothing*
      1. As manufacturers of materials
      2. As handicraftsmen and dealers
  III. *Ministering to lodging, furniture, machinery, &c.*
  IV. *Ministering to health*
   V. *Ministering to charity*
  VI. *Ministering to justice*
 VII. *Ministering to education*
VIII. *Ministering to religion*
  IX. *Various arts and employments, not included in the foregoing*
   X. *Residue of population*, not having specified occupations, and including unemployed persons and women.

This, however, is no improvement upon the English classification. There is the same want of discrimination, and the same disregard of the great 'economical' divisions of society.

Moreover, to show the extreme fallacy of such a classification, it is only necessary to make the following extract from the Report of the Commissioners for Great Britain:

'We would willingly have given a classification of the occupations of the inhabitants of Great Britain into the various wants to which they respectively minister, but, in attempting this, we were stopped by the various anomalies and uncertainties to which such a classification seemed necessarily to lead, from the fact that many persons supply more than one want, though they can only be classed under one head. Thus to give but a single instance – *the farmer and grazier may be deemed to minister quite as much to clothing by the fleece and hides as he does to food by the flesh of his sheep and cattle.*'

He, therefore, who would seek to elaborate the natural history of the industry of the people of England, must direct his attention to some social philosopher, who has given the subject more consideration than either princes or Government officials can possibly be expected to devote to it.

Among the whole body of economists, Mr Stuart Mill appears to be the only man who has taken a comprehensive and enlightened view of the several functions of society. Following in the footsteps of M. Say, the French social philosopher, he first points out concerning the products of industry, that labour is not creative of objects but of utilities, and then proceeds to say:

'Now the utilities produced by labour are of three kinds; they are –

'First, utilities *fixed and embodied in outward objects*; by labour employed in investing external *material* things with properties which render them serviceable to human beings. This is the common case, and requires no illustration.

'Secondly, utilities *fixed and embodied in human beings*; the labour being in this case employed in conferring on human beings qualities which render them serviceable to themselves and others. To this class belongs the labour of all concerned in education; not only schoolmasters, tutors, and professors, but governments, so far as they aim successfully at the improvement of the people; moralists and clergymen, as far as productive of benefit; the labour of physicians, as far as instrumental in preserving life and physical or mental efficiency; of the teachers of bodily exercises, and of the various trades, sciences, and arts, together with the labour of the learners in acquiring them, and all labour bestowed by any persons, throughout life, in improving the knowledge or cultivating the bodily and mental faculties of themselves or others.

'Thirdly, and lastly, utilities *not fixed or embodied in any object*, but consisting in a mere *service rendered*, a pleasure given, an inconvenience or pain averted, during a longer or a shorter time, but without leaving a *permanent* acquisition in the improved qualities of any person or thing; the labour here being employed in producing an utility *directly*, not (as in the two former cases) in *fitting some other* thing to afford an utility. Such, for example, is the labour of the musical performer, the actor, the public declaimer or reciter, and the showman.

'Some good may, no doubt, be produced beyond the moment, upon the feeling and disposition, or general state of enjoyment of the spectators; or instead of good there may be harm, but neither the one nor the other is the effect intended, is the result for which the exhibitor works and the spectator pays, but the immediate pleasure. Such, again, is the labour of the army and navy; they, at the best, prevent a country from being conquered, or from being injured or insulted, which is a service, but in all other respects leave the country neither improved nor deteriorated. Such, too, is the labour of the legislator, the judge, the officer of justice, and all other agents of Government, in their ordinary functions, apart from any influence they may exert on the improvement of the national mind. The service which they render is to maintain peace and security; these compose the utility which they produce. It may appear to some that carriers, and merchants or dealers, should be placed in this same class, since their labour does not add any properties to objects, but I reply that it does, it adds the property of being in the place where they are wanted, instead of being in some other place, which is a very useful property, and the utility it confers is embodied in the things themselves, which now actually are in the place where they are required for use, and in consequence of that increased utility could be sold at an increased price proportioned to the labour expended in conferring it. This labour, therefore, does not belong to the third class, but to the first.'

To the latter part of the above classification, I regret to say I cannot assent. Surely the property of being in the place where they are wanted, which carriers and distributors are said to confer on external objects, cannot be said to be fixed – if, indeed, it be strictly *embodied* in the objects, since the very act of distribution consists in the alteration of this local relation, and transferring such objects to the possession of another. Is not the utility which the weaver fixes and embodies in a yard of cotton, a very different utility from that effected by the linendraper in handing the same yard of cotton over the counter in exchange for so much money? and in this particular act, it would be difficult to perceive what is fixed and embodied, seeing that it consists essentially in an exchange of commodities.

Mr Mill's mistake appears to consist in not discerning that there is another class of labour besides that employed in producing utilities *directly*, and that occupied in *fitting other things* to afford utilities: viz., that which is engaged in *assisting* those who are so occupied in fitting things to be useful. This class consists of such as are engaged in aiding the producers of permanent material utilities either *before* or during production, and such as are engaged in aiding them *after* production. Under the first division are comprised capitalists, or those who supply the materials and tools for the work, superintendents and managers, or those who direct the work, and labourers, or those who perform some minor office connected with the work, as in turning the large wheel for a turner, in carrying the bricks to a bricklayer, and the like; while in the second division, or those who are engaged in assisting producers *after* production, are included carriers, or those who remove the produce to the market, and dealers and shopmen, or those who obtain purchasers for it. Now it is evident that the function of all these classes is merely *auxiliary* to the labour of the producers, consisting principally of so many modes of economizing their time and labour. Whether the gains of some of these auxiliary classes are as disproportionately large, as the others are disproportionately small, this is not the place to inquire. My present duty is merely to record the fact of the existence of such classes, and to assign them their proper place in the social fabric, as at present constituted.

Now, from the above it will appear, that there are four distinct classes of workers:

I. *Enrichers*, or those who are employed in producing utilities fixed and embodied in material things, that is to say, in producing exchangeable commodities or riches.

II. *Auxiliaries*, or those who are employed in aiding the production of exchangeable commodities.

III. *Benefactors*, or those who are employed in producing utilities fixed and embodied in human beings, that is to say, in conferring upon them some permanent good.

IV. *Servitors*, or those who are employed in rendering some service, that is to say, in conferring some temporary good upon another.

Class 1 is engaged in investing *material* objects with qualities which render them serviceable to others.

Class 2 is engaged in aiding the operations of Class 1.

Class 3 is engaged in conferring on *human beings* qualities which render them serviceable to themselves or others.

Class 4 is engaged in giving a pleasure, averting a pain (during a longer or shorter period), or preventing an inconvenience, by performing some office for others that they would find irksome to do for themselves.

Hence it appears that the operations of the first and third of the above classes, or the *Enrichers* and *Benefactors* of Society, tend to leave some *permanent acquisition* in the improved qualities of either persons or things, – whereas the operations of the second and fourth classes, or the *Auxiliaries* and *Servitors*, are limited merely to promoting either the labours or the pleasures of the other members of the community.

Such, then, are the several classes of Workers; and here it should be stated that, I apply the title Worker to all those who do *anything* for their living, who perform any act whatsoever that is considered worthy of being paid for by others, without regard to the question whether such labourers tend to add to or decrease the aggregate wealth of the community. I consider all persons doing or giving something for the comforts they obtain, as self-supporting individuals. Whether that something be really an equivalent for the emoluments they receive, it is not my vocation here to inquire. Suffice it some real or imaginary benefit is conferred upon society, or a particular individual, and what is thought a fair and proper reward is given in return for it. Hence I look upon soldiers, sailors, Government and parochial officers, capitalists, clergymen, lawyers, wives, &c., &c., as self-supporting – a certain amount of labour, or a certain desirable commodity, being given by each and all in exchange for other commodities, which are considered less desirable to the individuals parting with them, and more desirable to those receiving them.

Nevertheless, it must be confessed that, economically speaking, the most important and directly valuable of all classes are those whom I have here denominated *Enrichers*. These consist not only of Producers, but of the Collectors and Extractors of Wealth, concerning whom a few words are necessary.

There are three modes of obtaining the materials of our wealth – (1) by collecting, (2) by extracting, and (3) by producing them. The industrial processes concerned in the collection of the materials of wealth are of the rudest and most primitive kind – being pursued principally by such tribes as depend for their food, and raiment, and shelter, on the spontaneous productions of nature. The usual modes by which the collection is made is by gathering the vegetable produce (which is the simplest and most direct form of all industry), and when the produce is of an animal nature, by hunting, shooting, or fishing, according as the animal sought after inhabits the land, the air, or the water. In a more advanced state of society, where the erection of places of shelter has come to constitute one of the acts of life, the felling of trees will also form one of the modes by which the materials making up the wealth of the nation are collected. In Great Britain there appears to be fewer people connected with the mere *collection* of wealth than with any other general industrial process. The fishermen are not above 25,000, and the wood-cutters and woodmen not 5,000; so that even with gamekeepers, and others engaged in the taking of game, we may safely say that there are about 30,000 out of 18,000,000, or only one-six hundredth of the entire population, engaged in this mode of industry – a fact which strongly indicates the artificial character of our society.

The *production* of the materials of wealth, which indicates a far higher state of civilization and which consists in the several agricultural and farming processes for increasing the natural stock of animal and vegetable food, employs upwards of one million; while those who are engaged in the *extraction* of our treasures from the earth, either by mining or quarrying, both of which processes – depending, as they do, upon a knowledge of some of the subtler natural powers – could only have been brought into operation in a highly advanced stage of the human intellect, number about a quarter of a million. Altogether, there appear to be about one million and a half of individuals engaged in the industrial processes connected with the collection, extraction, and production of the materials of wealth; those who are employed in operating upon these materials, in the fashioning of them into manufactures, making them up into commodities, as well as those engaged in the distribution of them – that is to say, the transport and sale of them when so fashioned or made up – appear to amount to another two millions and a half, so that the industrial classes of Great Britain, taken altogether, may be said to amount to four millions. For the more perfect comprehension, however, of the several classes of society, let me subjoin a table in round numbers, calculated from the census of 1841, and including among the first items both the employers as well as employed:

Engaged in Trade and Manufacture	3,000,000	
Agriculture	1,500,000	
Mining, Quarrying, and Transit	750,000	
Total Employers and Employed		5,250,000
Domestic Servants		1,000,000
Independent persons		500,000
Educated pursuits (including Professions and Fine Arts)		200,000
Government Officers (including Army, Navy, Civil Service, and Parish Officers)		200,000
Alms-people (including Paupers, Prisoners, and Lunatics)		200,000
		7,350,000
Residue of Population (including 3,500,000 wives and 7,500,000 children)		11,000,000
		18,350,000

Now, of the 5,250,000 individuals engaged in Agriculture, Mining, Transit, Manufacture and Trade, it would appear that about one million and a quarter may be considered as employers; and, consequently, that the remaining four millions may be said to represent the numerical strength of the operatives of England and Scotland. Of these about one million, or a quarter of the whole, may be said to be engaged in producing the materials of wealth; and about a quarter of a million, or one-sixteenth of the entire number, in extracting from the soil the substances upon which many of the manufacturers have to operate.

The artizans, or those who are engaged in the several handicrafts or manufactures operating upon the various materials of wealth thus obtained, are distinct from the workmen above-mentioned, belonging to what are called skilled labourers, whereas those who are employed in the collection, extraction, or growing of wealth, belong to the unskilled class.

An artisan is an *educated* handicraftsman, following a calling that requires an apprenticeship of greater or less duration in order to arrive at perfection in it; whereas a labourer's occupation needs no education whatever. Many years must be spent in practising before a man can acquire sufficient manual dexterity to make a pair of boots or a coat; dock labour or porter's work, however, needs neither teaching nor learning, for any man can carry a load or turn a wheel. The artisan, therefore, is literally a handicraftsman – one who by practice has acquired manual dexterity enough to perform a particular class of work, which is consequently called 'skilled'. The natural classification of artisans, or skilled labourers, appears to be according to the materials upon which they work, for this circumstance seems to constitute the peculiar quality of the art more than the tool used – indeed, it appears to be the principal cause of the modification of the implements in different handicrafts. The tools used to fashion, as well as the instruments and substances used to join the several materials operated upon in the manufactures and handicrafts, differ according as those materials are of different kinds. We do not, for instance, attempt to saw cloth into shape nor to cut bricks with shears; neither do we solder the soles to the upper leathers of our boots, nor nail together the seams of our shirts. And even in those crafts where the means of uniting the materials are similar, the artisan working upon one kind of substance is generally incapable of operating upon another. The tailor who stitches woollen materials together would make but a poor hand at sewing leather. The two substances are joined by the same means, but in a different manner, and with different instruments. So the turner, who has been accustomed to turn wood, is unable to fashion metals by the same method.

The most natural mode of grouping the artisans into classes would appear to be according as they pursue some *mechanical* or *chemical* occupation. The former are literally mechanics or handicraftsmen – the latter chemical manufacturers. The handicraftsmen consist of (1) The workers in silk, wool, cotton, flax, and hemp – as weavers, spinners, knitters, carpet-makers, lace-makers, rope-makers, canvas-weavers, &c. (2) The workers in skin, gut, and feathers – as tanners, curriers, furriers, feather dressers, &c. (3) The makers up of silken, woollen, cotton, linen, hempen, and leathern materials – as tailors, milliners, shirt-makers, sail-makers, hatters, glove-makers, saddlers, and the like. (4) The workers in wood, as the carpenters, the cabinet-makers, &c. (5) The workers in cane, osier, reed, rush, and straw – as basket-makers, straw-plait manufacturers, thatchers, and the like. (6) The workers in brick and stones – as bricklayers, masons, &c. (7) The workers in glass and earthenware – as potters, glass-blowers, glass-cutters, bottle-makers, glaziers, &c. (8) The workers in metals – as braziers, tinmen, plumbers, goldsmiths, pewterers, coppersmiths, iron-founders, blacksmiths, whitesmiths, anchorsmiths, locksmiths, &c. (9) The workers in paper – as the paper-makers, cardboard-makers. (10) The chemical manufacturers – as powder-makers, white-lead-makers, alkali and acid manufacturers, lucifer-match-makers, blacking-makers, ink-makers, soap-boilers, tallow-chandlers, &c. (11) The workers at the superlative or extrinsic arts – that is to say, those which have no manufactur of their own, but which are engaged in adding to the utility or beauty of others – as printing, bookbinding, painting, and decorating, gilding, burnishing, &c.

The circumstances which govern the classification of *trades* are totally different from those regulating the division of work. In trade the convenience of the purchaser is mainly studied, the sale of such articles being associated as are usually required together. Hence the master coachmaker is frequently a harness manufacturer as well, for the purchaser of the one commodity generally stands in need of the other. The painter and house-decorator not only follows the trade of the glazier, but of the plumber, too; because these arts are one and all connected with the 'doing up' of houses. For the same reason the builder combines the business of the plasterer with that of the bricklayer, and not unfrequently that of the carpenter and joiner in addition. In all of these businesses, however, a distinct set of workmen are required, according as the materials operated upon are different.

We are now in a position to proceed with the arrangement of the several members of society into different classes, according to the principles of classification which have been here laid down. The difficulties of the task, however, should be continually borne in mind; for where so many have failed it cannot be expected that perfection can be arrived at by any one individual; and, slight as the labour of such a task may at the first glance appear to some, still the system here propounded has been the work and study of many months.

THE AGENCIES AT PRESENT IN OPERATION WITHIN THE METROPOLIS FOR THE SUPPRESSION OF VICE AND CRIME

By the Rev. William Tuckniss, B.A.

[pp. xxi–xxiv] On of the oldest and most privileged institutions within the metropolis, for bringing the influences of religion to bear upon the dense masses of our population is the *London City Mission*. It was founded in 1835, and its growth has steadily progressed up to the present date. The object of the mission is to 'extend the knowledge of the Gospel, among the inhabitants of London and its vicinity (especially the poor), without any reference to denominational distinctions, or the peculiarities of Church government. To effect this object, missionaries of approved character and qualifications are employed, whose duty it is to visit from house to house in the respective districts assigned to them, to read the Scriptures, engage in religious conversation, and urge those who are living in the neglect of religion to observe the Sabbath and attend public worship. They are also required to see that all persons possess the Scriptures, to distribute approved religious tracts, and to aid in obtaining Scriptural education for the children of the poor. By the approval of the committee they also hold meetings for reading and expounding the Scriptures and prayer, and adopt such other means as are deemed necessary for the accomplishment of the mission.'

The London City Mission maintains a staff of 389 missionaries, who are employed in the various London and suburban districts; and thus the entire city is more or less compassed by this effective machinery, and brought under the saving influences of the Gospel. The very silent and unobtrusive character of the work thus effected, precludes anything like an accurate estimate of results, or a showy parade of success.

It works secretly, quietly, and savingly, in districts too vast to admit of pastoral supervision, and in neighbourhoods too outwardly unattractive and unpropitious, to win the attention of any who are not animated with a devoted love of souls. The influence which is thus exerted in a social and religious point of view is inestimable, and the benefits conferred by this mission, are of an order that would be best understood and appreciated by the community, if they were for a time to be suddenly withdrawn.

In addition to the regular visitation of the poor, the missionaries are employed in conducting religious services in some of the 'worst spots that can be found in the metropolis, and the audiences have been, in such cases, ordinarily the most vicious and debased classes of the population'.

Six missionaries are appointed, whose exclusive duty it is to visit the various public-houses and coffee-shops in London, and to converse with the *habitués* on subjects of vital importance. There are also three missionaries to the London cabmen, a class greatly needing their religious offices, and by their occupation almost excluded from any social or elevating influences.

The following summary of missionary work, and its results for 1861, is sufficiently encouraging, as pointing in some instances, at least, to a sensible diminution of crime, and as being suggestive of a vast amount of good effected by this pervasive evangelistic machinery.

Number of Missionaries employed	381
Visits paid	1,815,332
Of which to the sick and dying	237,599
Scriptures distributed	11,458
Religious Tracts given away	2,721,730
Books lent	54,000
In-door Meetings and Bible Classes held	41,777
Gross attendance at ditto	1,467,006
Out-door Services held	4,489
Gross attendance at ditto	465,070
Readings of Scripture in visitation	584,166
Communicants	1,535
Families induced to commence family prayer	681
Drunkards reclaimed	1,230
Unmarried couples induced to marry	361
Fallen females rescued or reclaimed	681
Shops closed on the Sabbath	212
Children sent to school	10,158
Adults who died having been visited by the Missionary *only*	1,796

The income of the London City Mission, during the past year, amounted to 35,018*l*. 6*s*. 10*d*.; 5,763*l*. 15*s*. 7*d*. having been contributed by country associations.

Next to the London City Mission, the *Church of England Scripture Readers'*

Society is one of the most extensive and important channels for disseminating a religious influence among the masses by means of a parochial lay agency.

It is the special duty of the Scripture readers to visit from house to house; to read the Scriptures to all with whom they come in contact; to grapple with vice and crime *where they abound*; and to shrink from no effort to arrest their career.

'To overtake and overlook the growing multitudes which crowd our large and densely-peopled parishes,' was a work universally admitted to be beyond the present limits of clerical effort; and this *desideratum* has been supplied, at least to some extent, by the appointment of a lay agency, acting under the direction and control of the parochial clergy. By this means 'cases are brought to light and doors opened to the pastoral visit, which were either closed against it or not discovered before; and an amount of information concerning the religious condition of the parish is obtained, such as the minister, single-handed, or with the aid of a curate, never had before.' The following results, which are reported as having attended the labours of a single Scripture reader, during a period of fourteen years, will serve as an illustration of the nature of those services rendered by this instrumentality:

Visits paid to the poor	23,986
Infants and adults baptized on his recommendation	3,510
Children and adults persuaded to attend school	2,411
Persons led to attend church for the first time	307
Persons confirmed during visitation	429
Communicants obtained by ditto	269
Persons living in sin induced to marry	48

One hundred and twenty-five grants are now made by the Society for the maintenance of Scripture readers in eighty-seven parishes and districts in the metropolis, embracing a population of upwards of a million.

The Society's income for the past year amounted to 9,850*l.* 2*s.* 10*d.*

Second only in importance to personal evangelistic effort is the influence of a *Religious Press*. Public opinion being often fluctuating, and its general estimates of morality being, to a considerable extent, formed by the current literature of the age, it is essential that this mighty and controlling power should be exerted on the side of religion and virtue.

Works of a high moral tone, inculcating correct principles and instilling lessons of practical piety, conduce, therefore, in the highest degree, to a wholesome state of society, and to the preservation of public morals.

The two great emporiums of religious literature, most directly concerned in producing these results, are the *Religious Tract Society* and the *Society for the Promotion of Christian Knowledge*. The latter has already been referred to, as one of the main channels for the diffusion of the Scriptures.

None of the works issued by the *Religious Tract Society* can compete in point of interest or usefulness with those widely-circulated and deservedly-popular serials the Leisure Hour, the Sunday at Home, and the Cottager, a periodical lately published, and admirably adapted for the homes of the working classes.

The publications issued by the Society during the past year amounted to 41,883,921; half of which number were English tracts and handbills; 537,729 were foreign tracts; and 13,194,155 fall under the head of periodicals.

The entire number of both English and foreign publications issued by the Society, since its foundation in 1799, amount to 912,000,000.

Grants of books and tracts are annually made by the Society for schools and village libraries, prisons, workhouses, and hospitals, for the use of soldiers, sailors, emigrants, and for circulation at fairs and races, by city missionaries and colporteurs.

The total number of such grants during the past year amounted to 5,762,241; and were of the value of £6,116 14s. 4d.

The entire receipts of the Society from all sources for the past year amounted to £103,127 16s. 11d.; the benevolent contributions being £9,642 9s. 2d.

Other channels for the supply and extension of religious literature are the *Weekly Tract Society*, the *English Monthly Tract Society*, and the *Book Society*, which latter aims especially at promoting religious knowledge among the poor.

As a supplemental agency for the collection and dissemination of a wholesome literature, the *Pure Literature Society*, established 1854, is deserving of especial commendatory notice.

The following is a list of the periodicals recommended by the Society; and the circulation of which it seeks to facilitate:

For Adults: Leisure Hour, British Workman, Good Words, Old Jonathan, Youth's Magazine, Appeal, Bible-Class Magazine, Christian Treasury, Churchman's Penny Magazine, Evening Hour, Family Treasury, Family Paper, Friendly Visitor, Mother's Friend, Servant's Magazine, Sunday at Home, The Cottager, Tract Magazine.

For Children: Young England, Band of Hope Review, Child's Own Magazine, Child's Companion, Child's Paper, Children's Friend, Children's

Paper, Our Children's Magazine, Sabbath School Messenger, Sunday Scholar's Companion.

Upwards of 140,000 periodicals are sent out annually by the Society in monthly parcels.

The Society's income during the past year amounted to £2,783 12s. 2d.

PROSTITUTION IN LONDON*

by Bracebridge Hemyng

[pp. 210–12] The liberty of the subject is very jealously guarded in England, and so tenacious are the people of their rights and privileges that the legislature has not dared to infringe them, even for what by many would be considered a just and meritorious purpose. Neither are the magistracy or the police allowed to enter improper or disorderly houses, unless to suppress disturbances that would require their presence in the most respectable mansion in the land, if the aforesaid disturbances were committed within their precincts. Until very lately the police had not the power of arresting those traders, who earned an infamous livelihood by selling immoral books and obscene prints. It is to the late Lord Chancellor Campbell that we owe this salutary reform, under whose meritorious exertions the disgraceful trade of Holywell Street and kindred districts has received a blow from which it will never again rally.

If the neighbours choose to complain before a magistrate of a disorderly house, and are willing to undertake the labour, annoyance, and expense of a criminal indictment, it is probable that their exertions may in time have the desired effect; but there is no summary conviction, as in some continental cities whose condition we have studied in another portion of this work.

To show how difficult it is to give from any data at present before the public anything like a correct estimate of the number of prostitutes in London, we may mention (extracting from the work of Dr Ryan) that while the Bishop of Exeter asserted the number of prostitutes in London to be 80,000, the City Police stated to Dr Ryan that it did not exceed 7,000 to 8,000. About the year 1793 Mr Colquhoun, a police magistrate, concluded, after tedious investigations, that there were 50,000 prostitutes in

*We rely for certain facts, statistics, &c., upon Reports of the Society for the Suppression of Vice; information furnished by the Metropolitan Police; Reports of the Society for the Prevention of Juvenile Prostitution; Returns of the Registrar-General; Ryan, Duchatelet, M. les Docteurs G. Richelot, Léon Faucher, Talbot, Acton, &c., &c.; and figures, information, facts, &c., supplied from various quarters: and lastly, on our own researches and investigations.

this metropolis. At that period the population was one million, and as it is now more than double we may form some idea of the extensive ramifications of this insidious vice.

In the year 1802, when immorality had spread more or less all over Europe, owing to the demoralizing effects of the French Revolution, a society was formed, called 'The Society for the Suppression of Vice', of which its secretary, Mr Wilberforce, thus speaks:

'The particular objects to which the attention of this Society is directed are as follow, viz. –

'1. The prevention of the profanation of the Lord's day.
'2. Blasphemous publications.
'3. Obscene books, prints, etc.
'4. Disorderly houses.
'5. Fortunetellers.'

When speaking of the third division a report of the Society says –

'In consequence of the renewed intercourse with the Continent, incidental to the restoration of peace, there has been a great influx into the country of the most obscene articles of every description, as may be inferred from the exhibition of indecent snuff-boxes in the shop windows of tobacconists. These circumstances having tended to a revival of this trade the Society have had occasion within the last twelve months to resort to five prosecutions, which have greatly tended to the removal of that indecent display by which the public eye has of late been too much offended.'

Before the dissolution of the Bristol Society for the Suppression of Vice, its secretary, Mr Birtle, wrote (1808) to London the following letter:

'Sir, – The Bristol Society for the Suppression of Vice being about to dissolve, and the agents before employed having moved very heavily, I took my horse and rode to Stapleton prison to inquire into the facts contained in your letter. Inclosed are some of the drawings which I purchased in what they call their market, without the least privacy on their part or mine. They wished to intrude on me a variety of devices in bone and wood of the most obscene kind, particularly those representing a crime 'inter Christianos non nominandum', which they termed the new fashion. I purchased a few, but they are too bulky for a letter. This market is held before the door of the turnkey every day between the hours of ten and twelve.'

At the present day the police wage an internecine war with these people, who generally go about from fair to fair to sell indecent images, mostly imported from France; but this traffic is very much on the decline, if it is not altogether extinguished.

The reports of the Society for the Suppression of Vice are highly interesting, and may be obtained gratis on application at the Society's chambers.

Another Society was instituted in May 1835, called 'The London Society for the Protection of Young Females, and Prevention of Juvenile Prostitution'. We extract a few passages from its opening address.

'The committee cannot avoid referring to the present dreadfully immoral state of the British metropolis. No one can pass through the streets of London without being struck with the awfully depraved condition of a certain class of the youth of both sexes at this period (1835). Nor is it too much to say that in London crime has arrived at a frightful magnitude; nay, it is asserted that nowhere does it exist to such an extent as in this highly-favoured city. Schools for the instruction of youth in every species of theft and immorality are here established *****. It has been proved that 400 individuals procure a livelihood by trepanning females from eleven to fifteen years of age for the purposes of prostitution. Every art is practised, every scheme is devised, to effect this object, and when an innocent child appears in the streets without a protector, she is insidiously watched by one of those merciless wretches and decoyed under some plausible pretext to an abode of infamy and degradation. No sooner is the unsuspecting helpless one within their grasp than, by a preconcerted measure, she becomes a victim to their inhuman designs. She is stripped of the apparel with which parental care or friendly solicitude had clothed her, and then, decked with the gaudy trappings of her shame, she is compelled to walk the streets, and in her turn, while producing to her master or mistress the wages of her prostitution, becomes the ensnarer of the youth of the other sex. After this it is useless to attempt to return to the path of virtue or honour, for she is then watched with the greatest vigilance, and should she attempt to escape from the clutches of her seducer she is threatened with instant punishment, and often barbarously treated. Thus situated she becomes reckless, and careless of her future course. It rarely occurs that one so young escapes contamination; and it is a fact that numbers of these youthful victims imbibe disease within a week or two of their seduction. They are then sent to one of the hospitals under a fictitious name by their keepers, or unfeelingly turned into the streets to perish; and it is not an uncommon circumstance that within the short space of a few weeks the bloom of health, of beauty, and of innocence gives place to the sallow hue of disease, of despair, and of death.

*

In 1857, according to the best authorities, there were 8,600 prostitutes known to the police, but this is far from being even an approximate return of the number of loose women in the metropolis. It scarcely does more than record the circulating harlotry of the Haymarket and Regent Street. Their actual numerical strength is very difficult to compute, for there is an amount of oscillatory prostitution it is easy to imagine, but impossible to substantiate. One of the peculiarities of this class is their remarkable freedom from disease. They are in the generality of cases notorious for their mental and physical elasticity. Syphilis is rarely fatal. It is an entirely distinct race that suffer from the ravages of the insidious diseases that the licence given to the passions and promiscuous intercourse engender. Young girls, innocent and inexperienced, whose devotion has not yet bereft them of their innate modesty and sense of shame, will allow their systems to be so shocked, and their constitutions so impaired, before the aid of the surgeon is sought for, that when he does arrive his assistance is almost useless.

We have before stated the assumed number of prostitutes in London to be about 80,000, and large as this total may appear, it is not improbable that it is below the reality rather than above it. One thing is certain – if it be an exaggerated statement – that the real number is swollen every succeeding year, for prostitution is an inevitable attendant upon extended civilization and increased population.

We divide prostitutes into three classes. First, those women who are kept by men of independent means; secondly, those women who live in apartments, and maintain themselves by the produce of their vagrant amours; and thirdly, those who dwell in brothels.

The state of the first of these is the nearest approximation to the holy state of marriage, and finds numerous defenders and supporters. These have their suburban villas, their carriages, horses, and sometimes a box at the opera. Their equipages are to be seen in the park, and occasionally through the influence of their aristocratic friends they succeed in obtaining vouchers for the most exclusive patrician balls.

Houses in which prostitutes lodge are those in which one or two prostitutes occupy private apartments; in most cases with the connivance of the proprietor. These generally resort to night-houses, where they have a greater chance of meeting with customers than they would have were they to perambulate the streets.

Brothels are houses where speculators board, dress, and feed women, living upon the farm of their persons. Under this head we must include introducing houses, where the women do not reside, but merely use the house as a place of resort in the daytime. Married women, imitating the custom of Messalina, whom Juvenal so vividly describes in his Satires, not uncommonly make use of these places. A Frenchwoman in the habit of frequenting a notorious house in James Street, Haymarket, said that she came to town four or five times in the week for the purpose of obtaining money by the prostitution of her body. She loved her husband, but he was unable to find any respectable employment, and were she not to supply him with the necessary funds for their household expenditure they would sink into a state of destitution, and anything, she added, with simplicity, was better than that. Of course her husband connived at what she did. He came to fetch her home every evening about ten o'clock. She had no children. She didn't wish to have any.

[pp. 221–2]   The depravity of manners amongst boys and girls begins so very early, that they think it rather a distinction than otherwise to be unprincipled. Many a shoeblack, in his uniform and leathern apron, who cleans your boots for a penny at the corners of the streets, has his sweetheart. Their connection begins probably at the low lodging-houses they are in the habit of frequenting, or, if they have a home, at the penny gaffs and low cheap places of amusement, where the seed of so much evil is sown. The precocity of the youth of both sexes in London is perfectly astounding. The drinking, the smoking, the blasphemy, indecency, and immorality that does not even call up a blush is incredible, and charity schools and the spread of education do not seem to have done much to abate this scourge. Another very fruitful source of early demoralization is to be looked for in the quantities of penny and halfpenny romances that are sold in town and country. One of the worst of the most recent ones is denominated, 'Charley Wag, or the New Jack Shepherd, a history of the most successful thief in London'. To say that these are not incentives to lust, theft, and crime of every description is to cherish a fallacy. Why should not the police, by act of Parliament, be empowered to take cognizance of this shameful misuse of the art of printing? Surely some clauses could be added to Lord Campbell's Act, or a new bill might be introduced that would meet the exigencies of the case, without much difficulty.

[pp. 227–30]   Whitechapel has always been looked upon as a suspicious, unhealthy locality. To begin, its population is a strange amalgamation of Jews, English, French, Germans, and other antagonistic elements that must clash and jar, but not to such an extent as has been surmised and reported. Whitechapel has its theatres, its music-halls, the cheap rates of admission to which serve to absorb numbers of the inhabitants, and by innocently amusing them soften their manners and keep them out of mischief and harm's way.

The Earl of Effingham, a theatre in Whitechapel Road, has been lately done up and restored, and holds three thousand people. It has no boxes; they would not be patronized if they were in existence. Whitechapel does not go to the play in kid-gloves and white ties. The stage of the Effingham is roomy and excellent, the trapwork very extensive, for Whitechapel rejoices much in pyrotechnic displays, blue demons, red demons, and vanishing Satans that disappear in a cloud of smoke through an invisible hole in the floor. Great is the applause when gauzy nymphs rise like so many Aphrodites from the sea, and sit down on apparent sunbeams midway between the stage and the theatrical heaven.

The Pavilion is another theatre in the Whitechapel Road, and perhaps ranks higher than the Effingham. The Pavilion may stand comparison, with infinite credit to itself and its architect, with more than one West-end theatre. People at the West-end who never in their dreams travel farther east than the dividend and transfer department of the Bank of England in Threadneedle Street, have a vague idea that East-end theatres strongly resemble the dilapidated and decayed Soho in Dean Street, filled with a rough, noisy set of drunken thieves and prostitutes. It is time that these ideas should be exploded. Prostitutes and thieves of course do find their way into theatres and other places of amusement, but perhaps if you were to rake up all the bad characters in the neighbourhood they would not suffice to fill the pit and gallery of the Pavilion.

On approaching the play-house, you observe prostitutes standing out-side in little gangs and knots of three or four, and you will also see them inside, but for the most part they are accompanied by their men. Sergeant Prior of the H division, for whose services I am indebted to the courtesy of Superintendent White, assured me that when sailors landed in the docks, and drew their wages, they picked up some women to whom they considered themselves married pro tem., and to whom they gave the money they had made by their last voyage. They live with the women until the money is gone, (and the women generally treat the sailors honour-ably). They go to sea again, make some more, come home, and repeat the same thing over again. There are perhaps twelve or fifteen public-houses licensed for music in St George's Street and Ratcliff Highway: most of them a few years ago were thronged, now they can scarcely pay their expenses; and it is anticipated that next year many of them will be obliged to close.

This is easily accounted for. Many sailors go further east to the K division, which includes Wapping, Bluegate, &c.; but the chief cause, the *fons et origo* of the declension is simply the institution of sailors' savings banks. There is no longer the money to be spent that there used to be. When a sailor comes on shore, he will probably go to the nearest sailors' home, and place his money in the bank. Drawing out again a pound or so, with which he may enjoy himself for a day or two, he will then have the rest of his money transmitted to his friends in the country, to whom he will himself go as soon as he has had his fling in town; so that the money that used formerly to be expended in one centre is spread over the entire country, *ergo* and very naturally the public-house keepers feel the change acutely. To show how the neighbourhood has improved of late years, I will mention that six or eight years ago the Eastern Music Hall was frequented by such ruffians that the proprietor told me he was only too glad when twelve o'clock came, that he might shut the place up, and turn out his turbulent customers, whose chief delight was to disfigure and ruin each other's physiognomy.

Mr Wilton has since then rebuilt his concert-room, and erected a gallery that he sets apart for sailors and their women. The body of the hall is filled usually by tradesmen, keepers of tally-shops, &c., &c.

And before we go further a word about tally-shops. Take the New Road, Whitechapel, which is full of them. They present a respectable appearance, are little two-storied houses, clean, neat, and the owners are reputed to have the Queen's taxes ready when the collectors call for them. The principle of the tally business is this: A man wants a coat, or a woman wants a shawl, a dress, or some other article of feminine wearing apparel. Being somewhat known in the neighbourhood, as working at some trade or other, the applicant is able to go to the tally-shop, certain of the success of his or her application.

She obtains the dress she wishes for, and agrees to pay so much a week until the whole debt is cleared off. For instance, the dress costs three pounds, a sum she can never hope to possess in its entirety. Well, five shillings a week for three months will complete the sum charged; and the woman by this system of accommodation is as much benefited as the tallyman.

The British Queen, a concert-room in the Commercial Road, is a respect-able, well-conducted house, frequented by low prostitutes, as may be expected, but orderly in the extreme, and what more can be wished for? The sergeant remarked to me, if these places of harmless amusement were not licensed and kept open, much evil would be sown and disseminated throughout the neighbourhood, for it may be depended something worse and ten times lower would be substituted. People of all classes must have recreation. Sailors who come on shore after a long cruise *will* have it; and, added the sergeant, we give it them in a way that does no harm to themselves or anybody else. Rows and disturbances seldom occur, although, of course, they may be expected now and then. The dancing-rooms close at twelve – indeed their frequenters adjourn to other places generally before that hour, and very few publics are open at one. I heard that there had been three fights at the Prussian Eagle, in Ship Alley, Wellclose Square, on the evening I visited the locality; but when I arrived I saw no symptoms of the reported pugnacity of the people assembled, and this was the only rumour of war that reached my ears.

Ship Alley is full of foreign lodging-houses. You see written on a blind an inscription that denotes the nationality of the keeper and the character of the establishment; for instance *Hollandsche lodgement*, is sufficient to show a Dutchman that his own language is spoken, and that he may have a bed if he chooses.

That there are desperate characters in the district was sufficiently evidenced by what I saw when at the station-house. Two women, both well-known prostitutes, were confined in the cells, one of whom had been there before no less than *fourteen times*, and had only a few hours before been brought up charged with nearly murdering a man with a poker. Her face was bad, heavy, and repulsive; her forehead, as well as I could distinguish by the scanty light thrown into the place by the bullseye of the policeman, was low; her nose was short and what is called pudgy, having the nostrils dilated; and she abused the police for disturbing her when she wished to go to sleep, a thing, from what I saw, I imagined rather difficult to accomplish, as she had nothing to recline upon but a hard sort of locker attached to the wall, and running all along one side and at the bottom of the cell.

The other woman, whose name was O'Brien, was much better looking than her companion in crime; her hand was bandaged up, and she appeared faint from loss of blood. The policeman lifted her head up, and asked her if she would like anything to eat. She replied she could drink some tea, which was ordered for her. She had met a man in a public-house in the afternoon, who was occupied in eating some bread and cheese. In order to get into conversation with him, she asked him to give her some, and on his refusing she made a snatch at it, and caught hold of the knife he was using with her right hand, inflicting a severe wound: notwith-standing the pain of the wound, which only served to infuriate her, she flew at the man with a stick and beat him severely over the head, endangering his life; for which offence she was taken by the police to the station-house and locked up.

There are very few English girls who can be properly termed sailors' women; most of them are either German or Irish. I saw numbers of German, tall brazen-faced women, dressed in gaudy colours, dancing and pirouetting in a fantastic manner in a dancing-room in Ratcliff Highway.

It may be as well to give a description of one of the dancing-rooms frequented by sailors and their women.

Passing through the bar of the public-house you ascend a flight of stairs and find yourself in a long room well lighted by gas. There are benches placed along the walls for the accommodation of the dancers, and you will not fail to observe the orchestra, which is well worthy of attention. It consists, in the majority of cases, of four musicians, bearded shaggy-looking foreigners, probably Germans, including a fiddle, a cornet, and two fifes or flutes. The orchestra is usually penned up in a corner of the room, and placed upon a dais or raised desk, to get upon which you ascend two steps; the front is boarded up with deal, only leaving a small door at one end to admit the performers, for whose convenience either a bench is erected or chairs supplied. There is a little ledge to place the music on, which is as often as not embellished with pewter pots. The music itself is striking in the extreme, and at all events exhilarating in the highest degree. The shrill notes of the fifes, and the braying of the trumpet in very quick time, rouses the excitement of the dancers, until they whirl round in the waltz with the greatest velocity.

I was much struck by the way in which the various dances were executed. In the first place, the utmost decorum prevailed, nor did I notice the slightest tendency to indecency. Polkas and waltzes seemed to be the favourites, and the steps were marvellously well done, considering the position and education of the company. In many cases there was an exhibition of grace and natural ease that no one would have supposed possible; but this was observable more amongst foreigners than English. The generality of the women had not the slightest idea of dancing. There was very little beauty abroad that night, at least in the neighbourhood of Ratcliff Highway. It might have been hiding under a bushel, but it was not patent to a casual observer. Yet I must acknowledge there was something prepossessing about the countenances of the women, which is more than could be said of the men. It might have been a compound of resignation, indifference, and recklessness, through all of which phases of her career a prostitute must go; nor is she thoroughly inured to her vocation until they have been experienced, and are in a manner mingled together. There was a certain innate delicacy about those women, too, highly commendable to its possessors. It was not the artificial refinement

481

of the West-end, nothing of the sort, but genuine womanly feeling. They did not look as if they had come there for pleasure exactly, they appeared too business-like for that; but they did seem as if they would like, and intended, to unite the two, business and pleasure, and enjoy themselves as much as the circumstances would allow. They do not dress in the dancing-room, they attire themselves at home, and walk through the streets in their ball costume, without their bonnets, but as they do not live far off this is not thought much of. I remarked several women unattached sitting by themselves, in one place as many as half-a-dozen.

The faces of the sailors were vacant, stupid, and beery. I could not help thinking one man I saw at the Prussian Eagle a perfect Caliban in his way. There was an expression of owlish cunning about his heavy-looking features that, uniting with the drunken leer sitting on his huge mouth, made him look but a 'very indifferent monster'.

I noticed a sprinkling of coloured men and a few thorough negroes scattered about here and there.

The sergeant chanced to be in search of a woman named Harrington, who had committed a felony, and in the execution of his duty he was obliged to search some notorious brothels that he thought might harbour the delinquent.

We entered a house in Frederick Street (which is full of brothels, almost every house being used for an immoral purpose). But the object of our search was not there, and we proceeded to Brunswick Street, more generally known in the neighbourhood and to the police as 'Tiger Bay'; the inhabitants and frequenters of which place are very often obliged to enter an involuntary appearance in the Thames police court. Tiger Bay, like Frederick Street, is full of brothels and thieves' lodging houses. We entered No. 6, accompanied by two policemen in uniform, who happened to be on duty at the entrance to the place, as they wished to apprehend a criminal whom they had reason to believe would resort for shelter, after the night's debauch, to one of the dens in the Bay. We failed to find the man the police wanted, but on descending to the kitchen, we discovered a woman sitting on a chair, evidently waiting up for some one.

'That woman,' said the sergeant, 'is one of the lowest class we have; she is not only a common prostitute herself, and a companion of ruffians and thieves, but the servant of prostitutes and low characters as debased as herself, with the exception of their being waited upon by her.'

We afterwards searched two houses on the opposite side of the way. The rooms occupied by the women and their sailors were larger and more roomy than I expected to find them. The beds were what are called 'fourposters', and in some instances were surrounded with faded, dirty-looking, chintz curtains. There was the usual amount of cheap crockery on the mantel-pieces, which were surmounted with a small looking-glass in a rosewood or gilt frame. When the magic word 'Police' was uttered, the door flew open, as the door of the robbers' cave swung back on its hinges when Ali Baba exclaimed 'Sesame'. A few seconds were allowed for the person who opened the door to retire to the couch, and then our visual circuit of the chamber took place. The sailors did not evince any signs of hostility at our somewhat unwarrantable intrusion, and we in every case made our exit peacefully, but without finding the felonious woman we were in search of; which might cause sceptical people to regard her as slightly apocryphal, but in reality such was not the case, and in all probability by this time justice has claimed her own.

A glance at the interior of the Horse and Leaping Bar concluded our nocturnal wanderings. This public-house is one of the latest in the district, and holds out accommodation for man and beast till the small hours multiply themselves considerably.

[pp. 230-32]   Shadwell, Spitalfields, and contiguous districts are infested with nests of brothels as well as Whitechapel. To attract sailors, women and music must be provided for their amusement. In High Street, Shadwell, there are many of these houses, one of the most notorious of which is called The White Swan, or, more commonly, Paddy's Goose; the owner of which is reported to make money in more ways than one. Brothel-keeping is a favourite mode of investing money in this neighbourhood. Some few years ago a man called James was prosecuted for having altogether thirty brothels; and although he was convicted, the nuisance was by no means in the slightest degree abated, as the informer, by name Brooks, has them all himself at the present time.

There are two other well-known houses in High Street, Shadwell – The Three Crowns, and The Grapes, the latter not being licensed for dancing.

Paddy's Goose is perhaps the most popular house in the parish. It is also very well thought of in high quarters. During the Crimean war, the landlord, when the Government wanted sailors to man the fleet, went among the shipping in the river, and enlisted numbers of men. His system of recruiting was very successful. He went about in a small steamer with a band of music and flags, streamers and colours flying. All this rendered him popular with the Admiralty authorities, and made his house extensively known to the sailors, and those connected with them.

Inspector Price, under whose supervision the low lodging-houses in that part of London are placed, most obligingly took me over one of the lowest lodging-houses, and one of the best, forming a strange contrast, and both presenting an admirable example of the capital working of the most excellent Act that regulates them. We went into a large room, with a huge fire blazing cheerily at the furthest extremity, around which were grouped some ten or twelve people, others were scattered over various parts of the room. The attitudes of most were listless; none seemed to be reading; one was cooking his supper; a few amused themselves by criticising us, and canvassing as to the motives of our visit, and our appearance altogether. The inspector was well known to the keeper of the place, who treated him with the utmost civility and respect. The greatest cleanliness prevailed everywhere. Any one was admitted to this house who could command the moderate sum of threepence. I was informed those who frequented it were, for the most part, prostitutes and thieves. That is thieves and their associates. No questions were asked of those who paid their money and claimed a night's lodging in return. The establishment contained forty beds. There were two floors. The first was divided into little boxes by means of deal boards, and set apart for married people, or those who represented themselves to be so. Of course, as the sum paid for the night's lodging was so small, the lodgers could not expect clean sheets, which were only supplied once a week. The sheets were indeed generally black, or very dirty. How could it be otherwise? The men were often in a filthy state, and quite unaccustomed to anything like cleanliness, from which they were as far as from godliness. The floors and the surroundings were clean, and highly creditable to the management upstairs; the beds were not crowded together, but spread over the surface in rows, being a certain distance from one another. Many of them were already occupied, although it was not eleven o'clock, and the house is generally full before morning. The ventilation was very complete, and worthy of attention. There were several ventilators on each side of the room, but not in the roof – all were placed in the side.

The next house we entered was more aristocratic in appearance. You entered through some glass doors, and going along a small passage found yourself in a large apartment, long and narrow, resembling a coffee-room. The price of admission was precisely the same, but the frequenters were chiefly working men, sometimes men from the docks, respectable mechanics, &c. No suspicious characters were admitted by the proprietor on any pretence, and he by this means kept his house select. Several men were seated in the compartments reading newspapers, of which there appeared to be an abundance. The accommodation was very good, and everything reflected great credit upon the police, who seem to have the most unlimited jurisdiction, and complete control over the low people and places in the East-end of London.

Bluegate fields is nothing more or less than a den of thieves, prostitutes, and ruffians of the lowest description. Yet the police penetrate unarmed without the slightest trepidation. There I witnessed sights that the most morbid novelist has described, but which have been too horrible for those who have never been on the spot to believe. We entered a house in Victoria Place, running out of Bluegate, that had no street-door, and penetrating a small passage found ourselves in a kitchen, where the landlady was sitting over a miserable coke fire; near her there was a girl, haggard and woe-begone. We put the usual question, Is there any one upstairs? And on being told that the rooms were occupied, we ascended to the first floor, which was divided into four small rooms. The house was only a two-storied one. The woman of the place informed me, she paid five shillings a-week rent, and charged the prostitutes who lodged with her four shillings a-week for the miserable apartments she had to offer for their accommodation; but as the shipping in the river was very slack just now, times were hard with her.

The house was a wretched tumble-down hovel, and the poor woman complained bitterly that her landlord would make no repairs. The first room we entered contained a Lascar, who had come over in some vessel, and his woman. There was a sickly smell in the chamber, that I discovered proceeded from the opium he had been smoking. There was not a chair to be seen; nothing but a table, upon which were placed a few odds-and-ends. The Lascar was lying on a palliasse placed upon the floor (there was no bedstead), apparently stupefied from the effects of the opium he had been taking. A couple of old tattered blankets sufficed to cover him. By his bedside sat his woman, who was half idiotically endeavouring to derive some stupefaction from the ashes he had left in his pipe. Her face was grimy and unwashed, and her hands so black and filthy that mustard-and-cress might have been sown successfully upon them. As she was huddled up with her back against the wall she appeared an animated bundle of rags. She was apparently a powerfully made woman, and although her face was wrinkled and careworn, she did not look exactly decrepit, but more like one thoroughly broken down in spirit than in body. In all probability she was diseased; and the disease communicated by the Malays, Lascars, and Orientals generally, is said to be the most frightful form of lues to be met with in Europe. It goes by the name of Dry—, and is much dreaded by all the women in the neighbourhood of the docks.

Leaving this wretched couple, who were too much overcome with the fumes of opium to answer any questions, we went into another room, which should more correctly be called a hole. There was not an atom of furniture in it, nor a bed, and yet it contained a woman. This woman was lying on the floor, with not even a bundle of straw beneath her, wrapped up in what appeared to be a shawl, but which might have been taken for the dress of a scarecrow feloniously abstracted from a corn-field, without any very great stretch of the imagination. She started up as we kicked open the door that was loose on its hinges, and did not shut properly, creaking strangely on its rusty hinges as it swung sullenly back. Her face was shrivelled and famine-stricken, her eyes bloodshot and glaring, her features disfigured slightly with disease, and her hair dishevelled, tangled, and matted. More like a beast in his lair than a human being in her home was this woman. We spoke to her, and from her replies concluded she was an Irishwoman. She said she was charged nothing for the place she slept in. She cleaned out the water-closets in the daytime, and for these services she was given a lodging gratis.

[pp. 234–6] Those women who, for the sake of distinguishing them from the professionals, I must call amateurs, are generally spoken of as 'Dolly-mops'. Now many servant-maids, nurse-maids who go with children into the Parks, shop girls and milliners who may be met with at the various 'dancing academies', so called, are 'Dollymops'. We must separate these latter again from the 'Demoiselle de Comptoir', who is just as much in point of fact a 'Dollymop', because she prostitutes herself for her own pleasure, a few trifling presents or a little money now and then, and not altogether to maintain herself. But she will not go to casinos, or any similar places to pick up men; she makes their acquaintance in a clandestine manner: either she is accosted in the street early in the evening as she is returning from her place of business to her lodgings, or she carries on a flirtation behind the counter, which, as a matter of course, ends in an assignation.

Soldiers are notorious for hunting up these women, especially nurse-maids and those that in the execution of their duty walk in the Parks, when they may easily be accosted. Nurse-maids feel flattered by the attention that is lavished upon them, and are always ready to succumb to the 'scarlet fever'. A red coat is all powerful with this class, who prefer a soldier to a servant, or any other description of man they come in contact with.

This also answers the soldier's purpose equally well. He cannot afford to employ professional women to gratify his passions, and if he were to do so, he must make the acquaintance of a very low set of women, who in all probability will communicate some infectious disease to him. He feels he is never safe, and he is only too glad to seize the opportunity of forming an intimacy with a woman who will appreciate him for his own sake, cost him nothing but the trouble of taking her about occasionally, and who, whatever else she may do, will never by any chance infect. I heard that some of the privates in the Blues and the brigade of Guards often formed very reprehensible connections with women of property, tradesmen's wives, and even ladies, who supplied them with money, and behaved with the greatest generosity to them, only stipulating for the preservation of secrecy in their intrigues. Of course numbers of women throng the localities which contain the Knightsbridge, Albany Street, St George's, Portman, and Wellington Barracks in Birdcage Walk. They may have come up from the provinces; some women have been known to follow a particular regiment from place to place, all over the country, and have only left it when it has been under orders for foreign service.

A woman whom I met with near the Knightsbridge barracks, in one of the beer-houses there, told me she had been a soldiers' woman all her life.

'When I was sixteen,' she said, 'I went wrong. I'm up'ards of thirty now. I've been fourteen or fifteen years at it. It's one of those things you can't well leave off when you've once took to it. I was born in Chatham. We had a small baker's shop there, and I served the customers and minded the shop. There's lots of soldiers at Chatham, as you know, and they used to look in at the window in passing, and nod and laugh whenever they could catch my eye. I liked to be noticed by the soldiers. At last one young fellow, a recruit, who had not long joined I think, for he told me he hadn't been long at the depot, came in and talked to me. Well, this went on, and things fell out as they always do with girls who go about with men, more especially soldiers, and when the regiment went to Ireland, he gave me a little money that helped me to follow it; and I went about from place to place, time after time, always sticking to the same regiment. My first man got tired of me in a year or two, but that didn't matter. I took up with a sergeant then, which was a cut above a private, and helped me on wonderful. When we were at Dover, there was a militia permanently embodied artillery regiment quartered with us on the western heights, and I got talking to some of the officers, who liked me a bit. I was a — sight prettier then than I am now, you may take your dying oath, and they noticed me uncommon; and although I didn't altogether cut my old friends, I carried on with these fellows all the time we were there, and made a lot of money, and bought better dresses and some jewellery, that altered me wonderful. One officer offered to keep me if I liked to come and live with him. He said he would take a house for me in the town, and keep a pony carriage if I would consent; but although I saw it would make me rise in the world, I refused. I was fond of my old associates, and did not like the society of gentlemen; so, when the regiment left Dover, I went with them, and I remained with them till I was five-and-twenty. We were then stationed in London, and I one day saw a private in the Blues with one of my friends, and for the first time in my life I fell in love. He spoke to me, and I immediately accepted his proposals, left my old friends, and went to live in a new locality, among strangers; and I've been amongst the Blues ever since, going from one to the other, never keeping to one long, and not particler as long as I get the needful. I don't get much – very little, hardly enough to live upon. I've done a little needlework in the day-time. I don't now, although I do some washing and mangling now and then to help it out. I don't pay much for my bed-room, only six bob a week, and dear at that. It ain't much of a place. Some of the girls about here live in houses. I don't; I never could abear it. You ain't your own master, and I always liked my freedom. I'm not comfortable exactly; it's a brutal sort of life this. It isn't the sin of it, though, that worries me. I don't dare think of that much, but I do think how happy I might have been if I'd always lived at Chatham, and married as other women do, and had a nice home and children; that's what I want, and when I think of all that, I do cut up. It's enough to drive a woman wild to think that she's given up all chance of it. I feel I'm not respected either. If I have a row with any fellow, he's always the first to taunt me with being what he and his friends have made me. I don't feel it so much now. I used to at first. One dovetails into all that sort of thing in time, and the edge of your feelings, as I may say, wears off by degrees. That's what it is. And then the drink is very pleasant to us, and keeps up our spirits; for what could a woman in my position do without spirits, without being able to talk and blackguard and give every fellow she meets as good as he brings?'

It is easy to understand, the state of mind of this woman, who had a craving after what she knew she never could possess, but which the maternal instinct planted within her forced her to wish for. This is one of the melancholy aspects of prostitution. It leads to nothing – marriage of course excepted; the prostitute has no future. Her life, saving the excitement of the moment, is a blank. Her hopes are all blighted, and if she has a vestige of religion left in her, which is generally the case, she must shudder occasionally at what she has merited by her easy compliance when the voice of the tempter sounded so sweetly.

The happy prostitute, and there is such a thing, is either the thoroughly hardened, clever infidel, who knows how to command men and use them for her own purposes; who is in the best set both of men and women; who frequents the night-houses in London, and who in the end seldom fails to marry well; or the quiet woman who is kept by the man she loves, and who she feels is fond of her; who has had a provision made for her to guard her against want, and the caprice of her paramour.

The sensitive, sentimental, weak-minded, impulsive, affectionate girl, will go from bad to worse, and die on a dunghill or in a workhouse. A woman who was well known to cohabit with soldiers, of a masculine appearance but good features, and having a good-natured expression, was pointed out to me as the most violent woman in the neighbourhood. When she was in a passion she would demolish everything that came in her way, regardless of the mischief she was doing. She was standing in the bar of a public-house close to the barracks talking to some soldiers, when I had an opportunity of speaking to her. I did not allow it to pass without taking advantage of it. I told her I had heard she was very passionate and violent.

'Passionate!' she replied; 'I believe yer. I knocked my father down and wellnigh killed him with a flat-iron before I wor twelve year old. I was a beauty then, an I aint improved much since I've been on my own hook. I've had lots of rows with these 'ere sodgers, and they'd have slaughter'd me long afore now if I had not pretty near cooked their goose. It's a good bit of it self-defence with me now-a-days, I can tell yer. Why, look here; look at my arm where I was run through with a bayonet once three or four years ago.'

She bared her arm and exhibited the scar of what appeared to have once been a serious wound.

'You wants to know if them rowses is common. Well, they is, and it's no good one saying they aint, and the sodgers is such — cowards they think nothing of sticking a woman when they'se riled and drunk, or they'll wop us with their belts. I was hurt awful onst by a blow from a belt; it hit me on the back part of the head, and I was laid up weeks in St George's Hospital with a bad fever. The sodger who done it was quodded, but only for a drag,* and he swore to God as how he'd do for me the next time as he comed across me. We had words sure enough, but I split his skull with a pewter, and that shut him up for a time. You see this public; well, I've smashed up this place before now; I've jumped over the bar, because they

*Imprisoned for three months.

wouldn't serve me without paying for it when I was hard up, and I've smashed all the tumblers and glass, and set the cocks agoing, and fought like a brick when they tried to turn me out, and it took two peelers to do it; and then I lamed one of the bobbies for life by hitting him on the shin with a bit of iron – a crow or summet, I forget what it was. How did I come to live this sort of life? Get along with your questions. If you give me any of your cheek, I'll — soon serve you the same.'

It may easily be supposed I was glad to leave this termagant, who was popular with the soldiers, although they were afraid of her when she was in a passion. There is not much to be said about soldiers' women. They are simply low and cheap, often diseased, and as a class do infinite harm to the health of the service.

[pp. 255–6] I met a woman in Fleet Street, who told me that she came into the streets now and then to get money not to subsist upon, but to supply her with funds to meet the debts her extravagance caused her to contract. But I will put her narrative into a consecutive form.

'Ever since I was twelve,' she said, 'I have worked in a printing office where a celebrated London morning journal is put in type and goes to press. I get enough money to live upon comfortably; but then I am extravagant, and spend a great deal of money in eating and drinking, more than you would imagine. My appetite is very delicate, and my constitution not at all strong. I long for certain things like a woman in the family way, and I must have them by hook or by crook. The fact is the close confinement and the night air upset me and disorder my digestion. I have the most expensive things sometimes, and when I can, I live in a sumptuous manner, comparatively speaking. I am attached to a man in our office, to whom I shall be married some day. He does not suspect me, but on the contrary believes me to be true to him, and you do not suppose that I ever take the trouble to undeceive him. I am nineteen now, and have carried on with my 'typo' for nearly three years now. I sometimes go to the Haymarket, either early in the evening, or early in the morning, when I can get away from the printing; and sometimes I do a little in the day-time. This is not a frequent practice of mine; I only do it when I want money to pay anything. I am out now with the avowed intention of picking up a man, or making an appointment with some one for to-morrow or some time during the week. I always dress well, at least you mayn't think so, but I am always neat, and respectable, and clean, if the things I have on ain't worth the sight of money that some women's things cost them. I have good feet too, and as I find they attract attention, I always parade them.

And I've hooked many a man by showing my ankle on a wet day. I shan't think anything of all this when I'm married. I believe my young man would marry me just as soon if he found out I went with others as he would now. I carry on with him now, and he likes me very much. I ain't of any particular family; to tell the truth, I was put in the workhouse when I was young, and they apprenticed me. I never knew my father or my mother, although "my father was, as I've heard say, a well-known swell of capers gay, who cut his last fling with great applause", or, if you must know, I heard that he was hung for killing a man who opposed him when committing a burglary. In other words, he was "a macing-cove what robs", and I'm his daughter, worse luck, I used to think at first, but what was the good of being wretched about it? I couldn't get over for some time, because I was envious, like a little fool, of other people, but I reasoned, and at last I did recover myself, and was rather glad that my position freed me from certain restrictions. I had no mother whose heart I shou'd break by my conduct, or no father who could threaten me with bringing his grey hairs with sorrow to the grave. I had a pretty good example to follow set before me, and I didn't scruple to argue that I was not to be blamed for what I did. Birth is the result of accident. It is the merest chance in the world whether you're born a countess or a washerwoman. I'm neither one nor t'other; I'm only a mot who does a little typographing by way of variety. Those who have had good nursing, and all that, and the advantages of a sound education, who have a position to lose, prospects to blight, and relations to dishonour, may be blamed for going on the loose, but I'll be hanged if I think that priest or moralist is to come down on me with the sledge-hammer of their denunciation. You look rather surprised at my talking so well. I know I talk well, but you must remember what a lot has passed through my hands for the last seven years, and what a lot of copy I've set up. There is very little I don't know, I can tell you. It's what old Robert Owen would call the spread of education.'

I had to talk some time to this girl before she was so communicative; but it must be allowed my assiduity was amply repaid. The common sense she displayed was extraordinary for one in her position; but, as she said, she certainly had had superior opportunities, of which she had made the most. And her arguments, though based upon fallacy, were exceedingly clever and well put. So much for the spread of education amongst the masses. Who knows to what it will lead?

THIEVES

by John Binny

FELONIES ON THE RIVER THAMES

[pp. 366] There are a great number of robberies of various descriptions committed on the Thames by different parties. These depredations differ in value, from the little ragged mudlarks stealing a piece of rope or a few handfuls of coals from a barge, to the lighterman carrying off bales of silk several hundred pounds in value. When we look to the long lines of shipping along each side of the river, and the crowds of barges and steamers that daily ply along its bosom, and the dense shipping in its docks, laden with untold wealth, we are surprised at the comparatively small aggregate amount of these felonies.

The Mudlarks

[pp. 366-7] They generally consist of boys and girls, varying in age from eight to fourteen or fifteen; with some persons of more advanced years. For the most part they are ragged, and in a very filthy state, and are a peculiar class, confined to the river. The parents of many of them are coalwhippers – Irish cockneys – employed getting coals out of the ships, and their mothers frequently sell fruit in the street. Their practice is to get between the barges, and one of them lifting the other up will knock lumps of coal into the mud, which they pick up afterwards; or if a barge is laden with iron, one will get into it and throw iron out to the other, and watch an opportunity to carry away the plunder in bags to the nearest marine-storeshop.

They sell the coals among the lowest class of people for a few halfpence. The police make numerous detections of these offences. Some of the mudlarks receive a short term of imprisonment, from three weeks to a month, and others two months with three years in a reformatory. Some of them are old women of the lowest grade, from fifty to sixty, who occasionally wade in the mud up to the knees. One of them may be seen beside the Thames Police-office, Wapping, picking up coals in the bed of the river, who appears to be about sixty-five years of age. She is a robust woman, dressed in an old cotton gown, with an old straw bonnet tied round with a handkerchief, and wanders about without shoes and stockings. This person has never been in custody. She may often be seen walking through the streets in the neighbourhood with a bag of coals on her head.

In the neighbourhood of Blackfriars Bridge clusters of mudlarks of various ages may be seen from ten to fifty years, young girls and old women, as well as boys.

They are mostly at work along the coal wharves where the barges are lying a-ground, such as at Shadwell and Wapping, along Bankside, Borough; above Waterloo Bridge, and from the Temple down to St Paul's Wharf. Some of them pay visits to the City Gasworks, and steal coke and coal from their barges, where the police have made many detections.

As soon as the tide is out they make their appearance, and remain till it comes in. Many of them commence their career with stealing rope or coals from the barges, then proceed to take copper from the vessels, and afterwards go down into the cabins and commit piracy.

These mudlarks are generally strong and healthy, though their clothes are in rags. Their fathers are robust men. By going too often to the public-house they keep their families in destitution, and the mothers of the poor children are glad to get a few pence in whatever way they can.

RECEIVERS OF STOLEN PROPERTY

[p. 373] When we look to the number of common thieves prowling over the metropolis – the thousands living daily on beggary, prostitution, and crime – we naturally expect to find extensive machineries for the receiving of stolen property. These receivers are to be found in different grades of society, from the keeper of the miserable low lodging-houses and dolly shops in Petticoat Lane, Rosemary Lane, and Spitalfields, in the East-end, and Dudley Street and Drury Lane in the West-end of the metropolis, to the pawnbroker in Cheapside, the Strand, and Fleet Street, and the opulent Jews of Houndsditch and its vicinity, whose coffers are said to be overflowing with gold.

Dolly Shops

[pp. 373–4] As we walk along Dudley Street, near the Seven Dials – the Petticoat Lane of the West-end – a curious scene presents itself to our notice. There we do not find a colony of Jews, as in the East-end, but a colony of Irish shopkeepers, with a few cockneys and Jews intermingled among them. Dudley Street is a noted mart for old clothes, consisting principally of male and female apparel, and second-hand boots and shoes.

We pass by several shops without sign boards – which by the way is a characteristic of this strange by-street – where boots and shoes, in general sadly worn, are exposed on shelves under the window, or carefully ranged in rows on the pavement before the shop. We find a middle-aged or elderly Irishman with his leathern apron, or a young Irish girl brushing shoes at the door, in Irish accent inviting customers to enter their shop.

We also observe old clothes stores, where male apparel is suspended on wooden rods before the door, and trousers, vests, and coats of different descriptions, piled on chairs in front of the shop, or exposed in the dirty unwashed windows, while the shopmen loiter before the door, hailing the customers as they pass by.

Alongside of these we see what is more strictly called dolly or leaving shops – the fertile hot-beds of crime. The dolly shop is often termed an unlicensed pawn-shop. Around the doorway, in some cases of ordinary size, in others more spacious, we see a great assortment of articles, chiefly of female dress, suspended on the wall – petticoats, skirts, stays, gowns, shawls, and bonnets of all patterns and sizes, the gowns being mostly of dirty cotton, spotted and striped; also children's petticoats of different kinds, shirt-fronts, collars, handkerchiefs, and neckerchiefs exposed in the window. As we look into these suspicious-looking shops we see large piles of female apparel, with articles of men's dress headed around the walls, or deposited in bundles and paper packages on shelves around the shop, with strings of clothes hung across the apartment to dry, or offered for sale. We find in some of the back-rooms, stores of shabby old clothes, and one or more women of various ages loitering about.

In the evening these dolly shops are dimly lighted, and look still more gloomy and forbidding than during the day.

Many of these people buy other articles besides clothes. They are in the habit of receiving articles left with them, and charge 2d. or 3d. a shilling on the articles, if redeemed in a week. If not redeemed for a week, or other specified time, they sell the articles, and dispose of them, having given the party a miserably small sum, perhaps only a sixth or eighth part of their value. These shops are frequented by common thieves, and by poor dissipated creatures living in the dark slums and alleys in the vicinity, or residing in low lodging-houses. The persons who keep them often conceal the articles deposited with them from the knowledge of the police, and get punished as receivers of stolen property. Numbers of such cases occur over the metropolis in low neighbourhoods. For this reason the keepers of these shops are often compelled to remove to other localities.

The articles they receive, such as old male and female wearing apparel, are also resold by keepers of low coffee-houses and lodging-houses, and are occasionally bought by chandlers, low hairdressers, and others.

They also receive workmen's tools of an inferior quality, and cheap articles of household furniture, books, &c., from poor dissipated people, beggars, and thieves; many of which would be rejected by the licensed pawnbrokers.

They are frequently visited by the wives and daughters of the poorest labouring people, and others, who deposit wearing apparel, or bed-linen, with them for a small piece of money when they are in want of food, or when they wish to get some intoxicating liquor, in which many of them indulge too freely. They are also haunted by the lowest prostitutes on like errands. The keepers of dolly shops give more indulgence to their regular customers than they do to strangers. They charge a less sum from them, and keep their articles longer before disposing of them.

It frequently occurs that these low traders are very unscrupulous, and sell the property deposited with them, when they can make a small piece of money thereby.

There is a pretty extensive traffic carried on in the numerous dolly-shops scattered over the metropolis, as we may find from the extensive stores heaped up in their apartments, in many cases in such dense piles as almost to exclude the light of day, and from the groups of wretched creatures who frequent them – particularly in the evenings.

The principal trade in old clothes is in the East-end of the metropolis – in Rosemary Lane, Petticoat Lane, and the dark by-streets and alleys in the neighbourhood, but chiefly at the Old Clothes Exchange, where huge bales are sold in small quantities to crowds of traders, and sent off to various parts of Scotland, England, and Ireland, and exported abroad. The average weekly trade has been estimated at about 1,500*l*.

Pawnbrokers, &c.

[p. 374] A great amount of valuable stolen property passes into the hands of pawnbrokers and private receivers. The pawnbrokers often give only a third or fourth of the value of the article deposited with them, which lies secure in heir hands for twelve months.

A good many of them deal honestly in their way, and are termed respectable dealers; but some of them deal in an illegal manner, and are punished as receivers. Many of those who are reputed as the most respectable pawnbrokers, receive stolen plate, jewellery, watches, &c.

When *plate* is stolen, it is sometimes carried away on the night of the robbery in a cab, or other conveyance, to the house of the burglars. Some thieves take it to a low beershop, where they lodge for the night; others to coffee-shops; others to persons living in private houses, pretending possibly to be bootmakers, watchmakers, copper-plate printers, tailors, marine store-dealers, &c. Such parties are private receivers well-known to the burglars. The doors of their houses are opened at any time of the night.

Burglars frequently let them know previously when they are going to work, and what they expect to get, and the crucible or silver pot is kept ready on a slow fire to receive the silver plate, sometimes marked with the crest of the owner. Within a quarter of an hour a large quantity is melted down. The burglar does not stay to see the plate melted, but makes his bargain, gets his money, and goes away.

These private receivers have generally an ounce and a quarter for their ounce of silver, and the thief is obliged to submit, after he has gone into the house. The former are understood in many cases to keep quantities of silver on hand before they sell it to some of the refiners, or other dealers, who give them a higher price for it, generally 4s. 10d. per ounce. The burglar himself obtains only from 3s. 6d. to 4s. an ounce.

NARRATIVE OF A RETURNED CONVICT

[pp. 376–7] We give the following brief autobiography of a person who has recently returned from one of our penal settlements, having been transported for life. In character he is very different from the generality of our London thieves, having hot African blood in his veins and being a man of passionate, unbridled character. He was formerly a daring highway robber. He was introduced to us accidentally in Drury-lane, by a Bow-street police officer, who occasionally acts as a detective. On this occasion the latter displayed very little tact and discretion, which made it exceedingly difficult for us to get from him even the following brief tale:

'I was born in a tent at Southampton, on the skirts of a forest, among the gipsies, my father and mother being of that stock of people. We had generally about seven or eight tents in our encampment, and were frequently in the forest between Surrey and Southampton. The chief of our gang, termed the gipsey king, had great influence among us. He was then a very old, silver-headed man, and had a great number of children. I learned when a boy to play the violin, and was tolerably expert at it. I went to the public-houses and other dwellings in the neighbourhood, with three or four other gipsey boys, who played the triangle and drum, as some of the Italian minstrels do. We went during the day and often in the evening. At other times we had amusement beside the tents, jumping, running, and single-stick, and begged from the people passing by in the vehicles or on foot.

'During the day some of the men of our tribe went about the district, and looked out over the fields for horses which would suit them, and came during the night and stole them away. They never carried away horses from the stables. They generally got their booty along the by-roads, and took them to the fairs in the neighbourhood and sold them, usually for about 10*l*. or 12*l*. The horses they stole were generally light and nimble, such as might be useful to themselves. They disfigured them by putting a false mark on them, and by clipping their mane and tail. When a horse is in good order they keep it for a time till it becomes more thin and lank, to make it look older. They let the horse generally go loose on the side of a road at a distance from their encampment, till they have an opportunity to sell it; and it is generally placed alongside one or two other horses, so that it is not so much observed. The same person who steals it frequently takes it to the fair to be sold.

'The gipsies are not so much addicted to stealing from farms as is generally supposed. They are assisted in gaining a livelihood by their wives and other women going over the district telling fortunes. Some of them take to hawking for a livelihood. This is done by boys and girls, as well as old men and women. They sell baskets, brushes, brooms, and other articles.

'I spent my early years wandering among the gipsies till I was thirteen years of age, and was generally employed going about the country with my violin, along with some of my brothers.

'My father died when I was about six years of age. A lady in Southampton, of the Methodist connexion, took an interest in my brothers and me, and we settled there with our mother, and afterwards learned coach-making. I lived with my mother in Southampton for five or six years. My brothers were well-behaved, industrious boys, but I was wild and disobedient.

'The first depredation I committed was when thirteen years old. I robbed my mother of a box of old-fashioned coins and other articles, and went to Canterbury, where I got into company with prostitutes and thieves. The little money I had was soon spent.

'After this I broke the window of a pawnbroker's shop as a cart was

497

passing by, put my hand through the broken pane of glass, and carried off a bowl of gold and silver coins, and ran off with them and made my way to Chatham.

'Some time after this I was, one day at noon, in the highway between Chatham and Woolwich, when I saw a carriage come up. The postillion was driving the horses smartly along. A gentleman and lady were inside, and the butler and a female servant were on the seat behind. I leaped on the back of the conveyance as it was driving past, and took away the portmanteau with the butler's clothes, and carried it off to the adjoining woods. I sold them to a Jew at Southampton for 3*l*. or 4*l*.

'Shortly after I came up to London, and became acquainted with a gang of young thieves in Ratcliffe Highway. I lived in a coffee-house there for about eighteen months. The boys gained their livelihood picking gentlemen's pockets, at which I soon became expert. After this I joined a gang of men, and picked ladies' pockets, and resided for some time at Whitechapel.

'Several years after I engaged with some other men in highway robbery. I recollect on one occasion we learned that a person was in the habit of going to one of the City banks once a week for a large sum of money – possibly to pay his workmen. He was generally in the habit of calling at other places in town on business, and carried the money with him in a blue serge bag. We followed him from the bank to several places where he made calls, until he came to a quiet by-street, near London bridge. It was a dark wintry night, and very stormy. I rushed upon him and garotted him, while one of my companions plundered him of his bag. He was a stout old man, dressed like a farmer. I was then about twenty-two years of age.

'At this time I went to music and dancing saloons, and played on my violin.

'Soon after I went to a fair at Maidstone with several thieves, all young men like myself. One of us saw a farmer in the market, a robust middle-aged man, take out his purse with a large sum of money. We followed him from the market. I went a little in advance of my companions for a distance of sixteen miles, till we came to a lonely cross turning surrounded with woods. The night happened to be dark. I went up to him and seized him by the leg, and pulled him violently off his horse, and my companions came up to assist me. While he lay on the ground we rifled his pockets of a purse containing about 500*l*. and some silver money. He did not make very much resistance and we did not injure him. We came back to London and shared the booty among us.

'About the time of the great gathering of the Chartists on Kennington

Common, in 1848, I broke into a pawnbroker's shop in the metropolis, and stole jewellery to the amount of 2,000*l*., consisting of watches, rings, &c., and also carried off some money. I sold the jewels to a Jewish receiver for about 500*l*. I was arrested some time after, and tried for this offence, and sentenced to transportation for life.

'I returned from one of the penal settlements about a year ago, and have since led an honest life.'

BEGGARS AND SWINDLERS

by Andrew Halliday

PETTY TRADING BEGGARS

[pp. 438–40]   This is perhaps the most numerous class of beggars in London. Their trading in such articles as lucifers, boot-laces, cabbage-nets, tapes, cottons, shirt-buttons, and the like, is in most cases a mere 'blind' to evade the law applying to mendicants and vagrants. There are very few of the street vendors of such petty articles as lucifers and shirt-buttons who can make a living from the profits of their trade. Indeed they do not calculate upon doing so. The box of matches, or the little deal box of cottons, is used simply as a passport to the resorts of the charitable. The police are obliged to respect the trader, though they know very well that under the disguise of the itinerant merchant there lurks a beggar.

Beggars of this class use their trade to excite compassion and obtain a gift rather than to effect a sale. A poor half-clad wretch stands by the kerb exposing for sale a single box of matches, the price being 'only a half-penny'. A charitable person passes by and drops a halfpenny or a penny into the poor man's hand, and disdains to take the matches. In this way a single box will be sufficient for a whole evening's trading, unless some person should insist upon an actual 'transaction', when the beggar is obliged to procure another box at the nearest oilman's. There are very few articles upon which an actual profit is made by legitimate sale. Porcelain shirt-buttons, a favourite commodity of the petty trading beggars, would not yield the price of a single meal unless the seller could dispose of at least twenty dozen in a day. Cottons, stay-laces, and the like, can now be obtained so cheaply at the shops, that no one thinks of buying these articles in the streets unless it be in a charitable mood. Almost the only commodities in which a legitimate trade is carried on by the petty traders of the streets are flowers, songs, knives, combs, braces, purses, port-monnaies. The sellers of knives, combs, &c., are to a certain extent legitimate traders, and do not calculate upon charity. They are cheats, perhaps, but not beggars. The vendors of flowers and songs, though they really make an effort to sell their goods, and often realize a tolerable profit, are nevertheless beggars, and trust to increase their earnings by obtaining money without giving an equivalent. A great many children are sent out by their parents to sell flowers during the summer and autumn. They find their best market in the bars of public-houses, and especially those frequented by prostitutes. If none else give prostitutes a good character, the very poor do. 'I don't know what we should do but for them,' said an old beggar-woman to me one day. 'They are good-hearted souls – always kind to the poor. I hope God will forgive them.' I have had many examples of this sympathy for misfortune and poverty on the part of the fallen women of the streets. A fellow feeling no doubt makes them wondrous kind. They know what it is to be cast off, and spurned, and despised; they know, too, what it is to starve, and, like the beggars, they are subject to the stern 'move on' of the policeman.

The relations which subsist between the prostitutes and the beggars reveal some curious traits. Beggars will enter a public-house because they see some women at the bar who will assist their suit. They offer their little wares to some gentlemen at the bar, and the women will say, 'Give the poor devil something', or 'buy bouquets for us', or if the commodity should be laces or buttons, they say, 'Don't take the poor old woman's things; give her the money.' And the gentlemen, just to show off, and appear liberal, do as they are told. Possibly, but for the pleading of their gay companions, they would have answered the appeal with a curse and gruff command to begone. I once saw an old woman kiss a bedizened prostitute's hand, in real gratitude for a service of this kind. I don't know that I ever witnessed anything more touching in my life. The woman, who a few minutes before had been flaunting about the bar in the reckless manner peculiar to her class, was quite moved by the old beggar's act, and I saw a tear mount in her eye and slowly trickle down her painted cheek, making a white channel through the rouge as it fell. But in a moment she dashed it away, and the next was flaunting and singing as before. Prostitutes are afraid to remain long under the influence of good thoughts. They recall their days of innocence, and overpower them with an intolerable sadness – a sadness which springs of remorse. The gay women assume airs of patronage towards the beggars, and as such are looked up to; but a beggar-woman, however poor, and however miserable, if she is conscious of being virtuous, is always sensible of her superiority in that respect. She is thankful for the kindness of the 'gay lady', and extols her goodness of heart; but she pities while she admires, and mutters as a last word, 'May God forgive her.' Thus does one touch of nature make all the world akin, and thus does virtue survive all the buffets of evil fortune to raise even a beggar to the level of the most worthy, and be a treasure dearer and brighter than all the pleasures of the world.

The sellers of flowers and songs are chiefly boys and young girls. They buy their flowers in Covent Garden, when the refuse of the market is cleared out, and make them up into small bouquets, which they sell for a penny. When the flower season is over they sell songs – those familiar productions of Ryle, Catnach and company, which, it is said, the great Lord Macaulay was wont to collect and treasure up as collateral evidences of history. Some of the boys who pursue this traffic are masters of all the trades that appertain to begging. I have traced one boy, by the identifying mark of a most villainous squint, through a career of ten years. When I first saw him he was a mere child of about four years of age. His mother sent him with a ragged little girl (his sister) into public-house bars to beg. Their diminutive size attracted attention and excited charity. By-and-by, possibly in consequence of the interference of the police, they carried pennyworths of flowers with them, at other times matches, and at others halfpenny sheets of songs. After this the boy and the girl appeared dressed in sailor's costume (both as boys) and sung duets. I remember that one of the duets, which had a spoken part, was not very decent; the poor children evidently did not understand what they said; but the thoughtless people at the bar laughed and gave them money. By-and-by the boy became too big for this kind of work, and I next met him selling fuzees. After the lapse of about a year he started in the shoe-black line. His station was at the end of Endell Street, near the baths; but as he did not belong to one of the regularly organized brigades, he was hunted about by the police, and could not make a living. On the death of the crossing-sweeper at the corner he succeeded to that functionary's broom, and in his new capacity was regarded by the police as a useful member of society. The last time I saw him he was in possession of a costermonger's barrow selling mackerel. He had grown a big strong fellow, but I had no difficulty in identifying the little squinting child, who begged, and sold flowers and songs in public-house bars, with the strong loud-lunged vendor of mackerel. I suppose this young beggar may be said to have pursued an honourable career, and raised himself in the world. Many who have such an introduction to life finish their course in a penal settlement.

There are not a few who assume the appearance of petty traders for the purpose of committing thefts, such as picking a gentleman's pocket when he is intoxicated, and slinking into parlours to steal bagatelle balls. Police spies occasionally disguise themselves as petty traders. There is a well-known man who goes about with a bag of nuts, betting that he will tell within two how many you take up in your hand. This man is said to be a police spy. I have not been able to ascertain whether this is true or not; but I am satisfied that the man does not get his living by his nut trick. In the day-time he appears without his nuts, dressed in a suit of black, and looking certainly not unlike a policeman in mufti.

Among the petty trading beggars there are a good many idiots and half-witted creatures, who obtain a living – and a very good one too – by dancing in a grotesque and idiotic manner on the pavement to amuse children. Some of them are not such idiots as they appear, but assume a half-witted appearance to give oddness to their performance, and excite compassion for their misfortune. The street boys are the avengers of this imposition upon society.

The idiot performer has a sad life of it when the boys gather about him. They pull his clothes, knock off his hat, and pelt him with lime and mud. But this persecution sometimes redounds to his advantage; for when the grown-up folks see him treated thus, they pity him the more. These beggars always take care to carry something to offer for sale. Halfpenny songs are most commonly the merchandise.

The little half-witted Italian man who used to go about grinding an organ that 'had no inside to it', as the boys said, was a beggar of this class, and I really think he traded on his constant persecution by the *gamins*. Music, of course, he made none, for there was only one string left in his battered organ; but he always acted so as to convey the idea that the boys had destroyed his instrument. He would turn away at the handle in a desperate way, as if he were determined to spare no effort to please his patrons; but nothing ever came of it but a feeble tink-a-tink at long intervals. If his organ could at any time have been spoiled, certainly the boys might have done it; for their great delight was to put stones in it, and batter in its deal back with sticks. I am informed that this man had a good deal more of the rogue than of the fool in his composition. A gentleman offered to have his organ repaired for him; but he declined; and at length when the one remaining string gave way he would only have that one mended. It was his 'dodge' to grind the air, and appear to be unconscious that he was not discoursing most eloquent music.

Tract-selling in the streets is a line peculiar to the Hindoos. I find that the tracts are given to them by religious people, and that they are bought by religious people, who are not unfrequently the very same persons who provided the tracts. Very few petty trading beggars take to tract-selling from their own inspiration; for in good sooth it does not pay, except when conducted on the principle I have just indicated. Some find it convenient to exhibit tracts simply to evade the law applying to beggars and vagrants; but they do not use them if they can procure a more popular article. In these remarks it is very far from my intention to speak of 'religious people' with any disrespect. I merely use the expression 'religious people' to denote those who employ themselves actively and constantly in disseminating religious publications among the people. Their motives and their efforts are most praiseworthy, and my only regret is that their labours are not rewarded by a larger measure of success.

An Author's Wife

[pp. 440–41]   In the course of my inquiry into the habits, condition, and mode of life of the petty trading beggars of London, I met with a young woman who alleged that the publications she sold were the production of her husband. I encountered her at the bar of a tavern, where I was occupied in looking out for 'specimens' of the class of beggars, which I am now describing. She entered the bar modestly and with seeming diffidence. She had some printed sheets in her hand. I asked her what they were. She handed me a sheet. It was entitled the *Pretty Girls of London*. It was only a portion of the work, and on the last page was printed 'to be continued'. 'Do you bring this out in numbers?' I asked. 'Yes, sir,' she replied, 'it is written by my husband, and he is continuing it from time to time.' 'Are you then his publisher?' I inquired. 'Yes, sir, my husband is ill a-bed, and I am obliged to go out and sell his work for him.' I looked through the sheet, and I saw that it was not a very decent work. 'Have you ever read this?' I enquired. 'Oh yes, sir, and I think it's very clever; don't you think so, sir?' It certainly was written with some little ability, and I said so; but I objected to its morality. Upon which she replied, 'But it's what takes, sir.' She sold several copies while I was present, at twopence each; but one or two gave her fourpence and sixpence. As she was leaving I made further inquiries about her husband. She said he was an author by profession, and had seen better days. He was very ill, and unable to work. I asked her to give me his address as I might be of some assistance to him. This request seemed to perplex her; and at length she said, she was afraid her husband would not like to see me; he was very proud. I have since ascertained that this author's pretty little wife is a dangerous impostor. She lives, or did live at the time I met her, at the back of Clare Market, with a man (not her husband) who was well known to the police as a notorious begging-letter writer. He was not the author of anything but those artful appeals, with forged signatures, of which I have previously given specimens under the heading of 'Screevers'. I was also assured by an officer that the pretended author's wife had on one occasion been concerned in decoying a young man to a low lodging near Lincoln's Inn Fields, where the unsuspecting youth was robbed and maltreated.

DISTRESSED OPERATIVE BEGGARS

[pp. 446–7] All beggars are ingenious enough to make capital of public events. They read the newspapers, judge the bent of popular sympathy, and decide on the 'lay' to be adopted. The 'Times' informs its readers that two or three hundred English navigators have been suddenly turned adrift in France. The native labourers object to the employment of aliens, and our stalwart countrymen have been subjected to insult as well as privation. The beggar's course is taken; he goes to Petticoat Lane, purchases a white smock frock, a purple or red plush waistcoat profusely ornamented with wooden buttons, a coloured cotton neckerchief, and a red nightcap. If procurable 'in the Lane', he also buys a pair of coarse-ribbed grey worsted-stockings, and boots whose enormous weight is increased by several pounds of iron nails in their thick soles; even then he is not perfect, he seeks a rag and bottle and old iron shop – your genuine artist-beggar never asks for what is new, he prefers the worn, the used, the ragged and the rusty – and bargains for a spade. The proprietor of the shop knows perfectly well that his customer requires an article for show, not service, and they part with a mutual grin, and the next day every street swarms with groups of distressed navigators. Popular feeling is on their side, and halfpence shower round them. Meanwhile the poor fellows for whom all this generous indignation is evoked are waiting in crowds at a French port till the British Consul pass them over to their native soil as paupers.

The same tactics are pursued with manufactures. Beggars read the list of patents, and watch the effect of every fresh discovery in mechanics on the operatives of Lancashire and Yorkshire. A new machine is patented. So many hands are thrown out of work. So many beggars, who have never seen Lancashire, except when on the tramp, are heard in London. A strike takes place at several mills, pretended 'hands' next day parade the streets. Even the variability of our climate is pressed into the 'cadging' service; a frost locks up the rivers, and hardens the earth, rusty spades and gardening tools are in demand, and the indefatigable beggar takes the pavement in another 'fancy dress'. Every social shipwreck is watched and turned to account by these systematic land-wreckers, who have reduced false signals to a regular code, and beg by rule and line and chart and compass.

Starved-out manufacturers parade in gangs of four and five, or with squalid wives and a few children. They wear paper-caps and white aprons with 'bibs' to them, or a sort of cross-barred pinafore, called in the manufacturing districts a 'chequer-brat'. Sometimes they make a 'pitch', that is, stand face to face, turning their backs upon a heartless world, and sing. The well-known ditty of

> We are all the way from Manches-ter
> And we've got no work to do!

set to the tune of, 'Oh let us be joyful', was first introduced by this class of beggars. Or they will carry tapes, stay-laces, and papers of buttons, and throw imploring looks from side to side, and beg by implication. Or they will cock their chins up in the air, so as to display the unpleasantly prominent apples in their bony throats, and drone a psalm. When they go out 'on the blob', they make a long oration, not in the Lancashire or Yorkshire dialects, but in a cockney voice, of a strong Whitechapel flavour. The substance of the speech varies but slightly from the 'patter' of the hand-loom weaver; indeed, the Nottingham 'driz' or lace-man, the hand on strike, the distressed weaver, and the 'operative' beggar, generally bear so strong a resemblance to each other, that they not only look like but sometimes positively *are* one and the same person.

Unemployed agriculturists and frozen-out gardeners are seen during a frost in gangs of from six to twenty. Two gangs generally 'work' together, that is, while one gang begs at one end of a street, a second gang begs at the other. Their mode of procedure, their 'programme', is very simple. Upon the spades which they carry is chalked 'Frozen-out!' or 'Starving!' and they enhance the effect of this 'slum or fakement', by shouting out sturdily 'frozen out', 'We're all frozen-out!' The gardeners differ from the agriculturists or 'navvies' in their costume. They affect aprons and old straw hats, their manner is less demonstrative, and their tones less rusty and unmelodious. The 'navvies' roar; the gardeners squeak. The navvies' petition is made loud and lustily, as by men used to work in clay and rock; the gardeners' voice is meek and mild, as of a gentle nature trained to tend on fruits and flowers. The young bulky, sinewy beggar plays navvy; the shrivelled, gravelly, pottering, elderly cadger performs gardener.

There can be no doubt that in times of hardship many honest labourers are forced into the streets to beg. A poor hardworking man, whose children cry to him for food, can feel no scruple in soliciting charity – against such the writer of these pages would urge nothing; all credit to the motive that compels them unwillingly to ask alms; all honour to the feeling that prompts the listener to give. It is not the purpose of the author of this work to write down every mendicant an impostor, or every alms-giver a fool; on the contrary, he knows how much real distress, and how much real benevolence exist, and he would but step between the open hand of true charity, and the itching palm of the professional beggar, who stands between the misery that asks and the philanthropy that would relieve.

The winter of 1860–61 was a fine harvest for the 'frozen out' impostors, some few of whom, happily, reaped the reward of their deserts in the police-courts. Three strong hearty men were brought up at one office; they said that they were starving, and they came from Horselydown; when searched six shillings and elevenpence were found upon them; they re-iterated that they were starving and were out of work, on which the sitting magistrate kindly provided them with both food and employment, by sentencing them to seven days' hard labour.

The 'profits' of the frozen-out gardener and agriculturist are very large, and generally quadruples the sum earned by honest labour. In the February of 1861, four of these 'distressed navvies' went into a public-house to divide the 'swag' they had procured by one day's shouting. Each had a handkerchief filled with bread and meat and cheese. They called for pots of porter and drank heartily, and when the reckoning was paid and the spoils equally divided, the share of each man was seven shillings.

The credulity of the public upon one point has often surprised me. A man comes out into the streets to say that he is starving, a few halfpence are thrown to him. If really hungry he would make for the nearest baker's shop; but no, he picks up the coppers, pockets them, and proclaims again that he is starving, though he has the means of obtaining food in his fingers. Not that this obvious anachronism stops the current of bene-volence or the chink of coin upon the stones – the fainting, famished fellow walks leisurely up the street, and still bellows out in notes of thunder, 'I am starving!' If one of my readers will try when faint and exhausted to produce the same tone in the open air, he will realize the impossibility of shouting and starving simultaneously.

Hand-loom Weavers and Others
Deprived of Their Living by Machinery

[pp. 447–8] As has been before stated, the regular beggar seizes on the latest pretext for a plausible tale of woe. Improvements in mechanics, and consequent cheapness to the many, are usually the causes of loss to the few. The sufferings of this minority is immediately turned to account by veteran cadgers, who rush to their wardrobes of well-chosen rags, attire themselves in appropriate costume, and ply their calling with the last grievance out. When unprovided with 'patter', they seek the literati of their class, and buy a speech; this they partly commit to memory, and trust to their own ingenuity to improvise any little touches that may prove effective. Many 'screevers, slum-scribblers, and fakement-dodgers' eke out a living by this sort of authorship. Real operatives seldom stir from their own locality. The sympathy of their fellows, their natural habits, and the occasional relief afforded by the parish bind them to their homes, and the 'distressed weaver' is generally a spurious metropolitan production. The following is a copy of one of their prepared orations:

My kind Christian Friends,

We are poor working-men from — which cannot obtain bread by our labour, owing to the new alterations and inventions which the master-manufacturers have introduced, which spares them the cost of employing hands, and does the work by machinery instead. Yes, kind friends, machinery and steam-engines now does the work, which formerly was done by our hands and work and labour. Our masters have turned us off, and we are without bread and knowing no other trade but that which we was born and bred to, we are compelled to ask your kind assistance, for which, be sure of it, we shall be ever grateful. As we have said, masters now employs machinery and steam-engines instead of men, forgetting that steam-engines have no families of wives or children, and consequently are not called on to provide for them. We are without bread to put into our mouths, also our wives and children are the same. Foreign competition has drove our masters to this step, and we working-men are the sufferers thereby. Kind friends, drop your compassion on us: the smallest trifle will be thankfully received, and God will bless you for the relief you give to us. May you never know what it is to be as we are now, drove from our work, and forced to come out into the streets to beg your charity from door to door. Have pity on us, for our situation is most wretched. Our wives and families are starving, our children cry to us for bread, and we have none to give them. Oh, my friends, look down on us with compassion. We are poor working-men, weavers from — which cannot obtain bread by our labour owing to the new inventions in machinery, which, &c. &c. &c.

In concluding this section of our work, I would commend to the notice of my readers the following observations on almsgiving:

The poor will never cease from the land. There always will be exceptional excesses and outbreaks of distress that no plan could have provided against, and there always will be those who stand with open palm to receive, in the face of heaven, our tribute of gratitude for our own happier lot. Yet there is a duty of the head as well as of the heart, and we are bound as much to use our reason as to minister of our abundance. The same heaven that has rewarded our labours, and filled our garners or our coffers, or at least, given us favour in the sight of merchants and bankers, has given us also brains, and consequently a charge to employ them. So we are bound to sift appeals, and consider how best to direct our benevolence. Whoever thinks that charity consists in mere giving, and that he has only to put his hand in his pocket, or draw a check in favour of somebody who is very much in want of money, and looks very grateful for favours to be received, will find himself taught better, if not in the school of adversity, at least by many a hard lesson of kindness thrown away, or perhaps very brutishly repaid. As animals have their habits, so there is a large class of mankind whose single cleverness is that of representing themselves as justly and naturally dependent on the assistance of others, who look paupers from their birth, who seek givers and forsake those who have given as naturally as a tree sends its roots into new soil and deserts the exhausted. It is the office of reason – reason improved by experience – to teach us not to waste our own interest and our resources on beings that will be content to live on our bounty, and will never return a moral profit to our charitable industry. The great opportunities or the mighty powers that heaven may have given us, it never meant to be lavished on mere human animals who eat, drink and sleep, and whose only instinct is to find out a new caterer when the old one is exhausted.

READ MORE IN PENGUIN

In every corner of the world, on every subject under the sun, Penguin represents quality and variety – the very best in publishing today.

For complete information about books available from Penguin – including Puffins, Penguin Classics and Arkana – and how to order them, write to us at the appropriate address below. Please note that for copyright reasons the selection of books varies from country to country.

In the United Kingdom: Please write to *Dept. EP, Penguin Books Ltd, Bath Road, Harmondsworth, West Drayton, Middlesex UB7 0DA*

In the United States: Please write to *Consumer Sales, Penguin Putnam Inc., P.O. Box 12289 Dept. B, Newark, New Jersey 07101-5289.* VISA and MasterCard holders call 1-800-788-6262 to order Penguin titles

In Canada: Please write to *Penguin Books Canada Ltd, 10 Alcorn Avenue, Suite 300, Toronto, Ontario M4V 3B2*

In Australia: Please write to *Penguin Books Australia Ltd, P.O. Box 257, Ringwood, Victoria 3134*

In New Zealand: Please write to *Penguin Books (NZ) Ltd, Private Bag 102902, North Shore Mail Centre, Auckland 10*

In India: Please write to *Penguin Books India Pvt Ltd, 11 Community Centre, Panchsheel Park, New Delhi 110017*

In the Netherlands: Please write to *Penguin Books Netherlands bv, Postbus 3507, NL-1001 AH Amsterdam*

In Germany: Please write to *Penguin Books Deutschland GmbH, Metzlerstrasse 26, 60594 Frankfurt am Main*

In Spain: Please write to *Penguin Books S. A., Bravo Murillo 19, 1° B, 28015 Madrid*

In Italy: Please write to *Penguin Italia s.r.l., Via Benedetto Croce 2, 20094 Corsico, Milano*

In France: Please write to *Penguin France, Le Carré Wilson, 62 rue Benjamin Baillaud, 31500 Toulouse*

In Japan: Please write to *Penguin Books Japan Ltd, Kaneko Building, 2-3-25 Koraku, Bunkyo-Ku, Tokyo 112*

In South Africa: Please write to *Penguin Books South Africa (Pty) Ltd, Private Bag X14, Parkview, 2122 Johannesburg*